CRIMINAL
EVIDENCE

For NBB

CRIMINAL EVIDENCE

Matthew Lippman

University of Illinois at Chicago

Los Angeles | London | New Delhi
Singapore | Washington DC | Boston

Los Angeles | London | New Delhi
Singapore | Washington DC | Boston

FOR INFORMATION:

SAGE Publications, Inc.
2455 Teller Road
Thousand Oaks, California 91320
E-mail: order@sagepub.com

SAGE Publications Ltd.
1 Oliver's Yard
55 City Road
London EC1Y 1SP
United Kingdom

SAGE Publications India Pvt. Ltd.
B 1/I 1 Mohan Cooperative Industrial Area
Mathura Road, New Delhi 110 044
India

SAGE Publications Asia-Pacific Pte. Ltd.
3 Church Street
#10-04 Samsung Hub
Singapore 049483

Acquisitions Editor: Jerry Westby
Digital Content Editor: Nick Pachelli
Editorial Assistant: Laura Kirkhuff
Production Editor: Tracy Buyan
Copy Editor: Melinda Masson
Typesetter: C&M Digitals (P) Ltd.
Proofreader: Sarah J. Duffy
Indexer: Wendy Allex
Cover Designer: Leonardo March
Marketing Manager: Terra Schultz

Printed in the United States of America

Library of Congress Cataloging-in-Publication Data

Lippman, Matthew Ross, author.
Criminal evidence / Matthew Lippman.

pages cm
Includes references and index.

ISBN 978-1-4833-5955-7 (pbk.: alk. paper) 1. Evidence, Criminal—United States. I. Title.

KF9660.L57 2015
345.73'06—dc23   2015005162

This book is printed on acid-free paper.

Certified Chain of Custody
SUSTAINABLE FORESTRY INITIATIVE
Promoting Sustainable Forestry
www.sfiprogram.org
SFI-01268
SFI label applies to text stock

18 19 10 9 8 7 6 5 4 3

■■ BRIEF CONTENTS

PREFACE   xiii

Chapter 1. Introduction   1

Chapter 2. The Criminal Justice Process   27

Chapter 3. Types of Evidence   57

Chapter 4. Direct and Circumstantial Evidence   81

Chapter 5. Witnesses   103

Chapter 6. The Opinion Rule and Expert Testimony   138

Chapter 7. Crime Scene Evidence and Experiments   153

Chapter 8. Documentary Evidence, Models, Maps, and Diagrams   172

Chapter 9. Hearsay   189

Chapter 10. Privileges   224

Chapter 11. The Exclusionary Rule   244

Chapter 12. Searches and Seizures and Privacy   268

Chapter 13. Stop and Frisk   289

Chapter 14. Probable Cause and Arrests   316

Chapter 15. Searches and Seizures of Property   341

Chapter 16. Interrogations and Confessions   375

Chapter 17. Eyewitness Identifications   412

GLOSSARY   437

INDEX   445

ABOUT THE AUTHOR   475

■ ■ DETAILED CONTENTS

PREFACE xiii

Introduction xiii

Chapter Organization xiii

Organization of the Text xiii

Acknowledgments xiv

Chapter 1. Introduction 1

Burden of Proof 2

The Judge and the Jury 3

The Development of the Law of Evidence 4

The United States Constitution 6

The United States Supreme Court 7

Federal District Courts and Courts of Appeal 10

State Constitutions and State Courts 10

State Judicial Systems 13

Precedent 13

The Development of Due Process 15

The Fourteenth Amendment 15

    The Due Process Clause 16

Fundamental Fairness 17

Total Incorporation 20

Selective Incorporation 20

Rules of Evidence 21

    Federal Rules of Evidence 22

    Uniform Rules of Evidence 23

    State Rules of Evidence 23

Do We Need Rules of Evidence? 23

Chapter Summary 24

Chapter Review Questions 25

Legal Terminology 25

Chapter 2. The Criminal Justice Process 27

Introduction 28

The Criminal Complaint 28

First Appearance 30

Preliminary Hearing 30

Grand Jury 31

Arraignment 31

Suppression Hearings and Pretrial Motions 32

Discovery 33

Plea Bargaining 34

Jury Selection 36

The Trial 39

    Opening Statements 39

    Prosecution's Case-in-Chief 40

    The Contemporaneous Objection Rule 40

    Cross-Examination 41

    Defense's Case-in-Chief 41

    Prosecution's Rebuttal and Defendant's Surrebuttal 42

    Closing Arguments 42

    Jury Instructions 43

    Jury Deliberations 44

    Jury Unanimity 44

    Verdict 45

The Judicial Sentencing Process 45

Sentencing Guidelines and the Role of the Jury in Sentencing 46

Criminal Appeals 48

Habeas Corpus 50

Chapter Summary 53

Chapter Review Questions 55

Legal Terminology 56

Chapter 3. Types of Evidence 57

Introduction 58

Relevance 59

Competence 61

Exclusion of Relevant Evidence Based on Prejudice and Other Concerns 62

    Prejudicial, Misleading, and Confusing Evidence 63

    Other Grounds for Excluding Evidence Under Rule 403 65

Direct and Circumstantial Evidence 66

Testimonial and Real Evidence 68

Substitutes for Evidence 71

Stipulations 71

Judicial Notice 72

    Adjudicative Facts 72

    Indisputable Facts 72

    Common Knowledge 72

    Matters Capable of Accurate Determination 73

    Personal Knowledge of the Judge 73

    Procedure 73

Presumptions 74

    Conclusive and Rebuttable Presumptions 74

    Presumptions and Social Policy 75

Presumptions and Criminal Law 75
    Mandatory Presumptions and Criminal Law 75
    Rebuttable Presumptions and Criminal Law 76
Case Analysis 78
Chapter Summary 79
Chapter Review Questions 80
Legal Terminology 80

Chapter 4. Direct and Circumstantial Evidence 81

Introduction 82
Jury Decision-Making 83
Circumstantial Evidence of Ability to Commit the Crime 83
    Specialized Skill 83
    Means to Commit the Crime 83
    Physical Capacity 84
    Mental Capacity 84
Circumstantial Evidence of an Inference of Consciousness of Guilt and of Guilt 85
    Flight 85
    Concealing Evidence 85
    Offers to Plead Guilty 86
    Possession of Stolen Property 86
    Sudden Wealth 86
Circumstantial Evidence That an Individual Is the Victim of Rape 87
Character Evidence 87
    Character and Public Policy 87
    Character as an Essential Element of a Crime 89
    Victim's Character in a Criminal Case 89
    Victim's Character in a Homicide Case 90
    Character and Habit 91
Other Acts Evidence 93
Other Acts Evidence and Circumstantial Evidence of Identity 93
    Modus Operandi 93
Other Acts Evidence and Circumstantial Evidence of Intent 94
    Intent 94
    Knowledge 94
    Motive 94
    Threats 95
    Opportunity 95
    Act Not Performed Inadvertently, Accidentally, Involuntarily, or Without Guilty Knowledge 96
    Prior False Claims 96
    Plan 96
    Preparation 97

Case Analysis 100
Chapter Summary 101
Chapter Review Questions 102
Legal Terminology 102

Chapter 5. Witnesses 103

Introduction 104
    Oath or Affirmation 105
    Personal Knowledge 106
    Mental Capacity 107
    Narration 108
Competency Hearings 108
Hypnosis 109
Child Testimony 109
Judges as Witnesses 113
Jurors as Witnesses 114
Spousal Competence 116
Religion 117
    Criminal Convictions 118
Mental Incapacity 118
Impeachment 119
Bias 120
Prior Felony Convictions 120
    Felony Convictions to Impeach Nonparty Witnesses 121
    Felony Convictions to Impeach Defendant-Witnesses 121
Crimes Involving a Dishonest Act or False Statement 122
    Time Limits 122
    Pardons, Annulments, and Certificates of Rehabilitation 123
    Juvenile Adjudications 123
    Appeals 123
Character for Truthfulness 124
Uncharged Crimes and Immoral Acts 125
Prior Inconsistent Statements 127
Specific Contradiction 128
Physical and Psychological Incapacity 129
Rehabilitation 129
Corroboration 130
Recorded Recollection 131
    Present Recollection Refreshed 131
    Past Recollection Recorded 132
Case Analysis 134
Chapter Summary 136
Chapter Review Questions 137
Legal Terminology 137

Chapter 6. The Opinion Rule and Expert Testimony   138

Introduction	139
Unavailable Witnesses	139
Opinion Rule	140
Lay Witnesses	140
Expert Testimony	142
Qualifying an Expert Witness	144
Testimony on Ultimate Issues	145
Scope of Expert Testimony	146
Court-Appointed Experts	149
Case Analysis	150
Chapter Summary	152
Chapter Review Questions	152
Legal Terminology	152

Chapter 7. Crime Scene Evidence and Experiments   153

Introduction	154
Crime Scene Evidence	155
Chain of Custody	156
Scientific Evidence	157
Laying the Foundation for Scientific Evidence	158
Right to Defense Experts	158
Judicially Accepted Scientific Tests	159
Fingerprints	159
Blood Alcohol	160
Blood Typing	161
DNA	161
Analysis of Controlled Substances	163
Ballistics	164
Other Judicially Recognized Tests	164
Tests Not Accepted by the Courts	165
Polygraph	165
Experiments	166
Case Analysis	167
Chapter Summary	170
Chapter Review Questions	171
Legal Terminology	171

Chapter 8. Documentary Evidence, Models, Maps, and Diagrams   172

Introduction	172
Authentication of Documents	173
Methods of Authenticating Documents	175
Self-Authenticating Documents	177
Government Documents	177
Visual Images	178
Authentication of Photographs and Videos	178
Authentication of Medical Images	179
Authentication of Objects	179
Authentication of Voice Communication	179
The Best Evidence Rule	180
Application of the Best Evidence Rule	182
Models, Maps, Diagrams, and Charts	183
In-Court Exhibitions	184
Case Analysis	184
Chapter Summary	187
Chapter Review Questions	188
Legal Terminology	188

Chapter 9. Hearsay   189

Introduction	190
The Development of the Rule Against Hearsay	191
The Definition of Hearsay	191
The Reasons for the Hearsay Rule	192
Hearsay Objections	193
The Sixth Amendment and Hearsay	193
Exceptions to the Hearsay Rule	195
Admission and Confessions	195
Admissions by a Party	196
Adoptive Admissions	196
Authorized Admissions	197
Admissions by an Agent	197
Admissions by a Co-Conspirator	197
Prior Statements	199
Prior Inconsistent Statements	199
Prior Consistent Statements	200
Identifications	200
Hearsay Exceptions When Declarant Is Not Required to Be Available	201
Present Sense Impression	201
Excited Utterance	203
Then-Existing Mental, Emotional, or Physical Condition	204
Medical Treatment-Diagnosis	206
Business Records	207
Absence of Business Records	208
Public Records	209
Vital Statistics	211

Unavailability of Declarant 211

Former Testimony 212

Statement Under Belief of Impending Death 214

Declaration Against Interest 216

Statement of Personal or Family History 217

Statement Offered Against a Party That Wrongfully Caused the Declarant's Unavailability 218

Residual Exception 219

Hearsay Within Hearsay 220

Case Analysis 220

Chapter Summary 221

Chapter Review Questions 222

Legal Terminology 222

Chapter 10. Privileges 224

Introduction 225

Attorney-Client Privilege 226

Holder of the Privilege 227

Scope of the Privilege 227

Exceptions 228

Clergy-Penitent Privilege 230

Holder of the Privilege 231

Definition of Clergy 231

Scope of the Privilege 231

Confidentiality 231

Exceptions 231

Waiver 232

Physician-Patient Privilege 232

Psychotherapist-Patient Privilege 233

Husband-Wife Privilege 234

Marital Communication Privilege 234

Marital Testimony Privilege 235

Government Privileges 236

Executive Privilege 236

State Secrets Privilege 236

Official Information Privilege 237

Confidential Informant's Privilege 237

Grand Jury Confidentiality 238

News Media Privilege 238

Case Analysis 240

Chapter Summary 242

Chapter Review Questions 242

Legal Terminology 243

Chapter 11. The Exclusionary Rule 244

Introduction 245

The Exclusionary Rule 246

The Exclusionary Rule and Federal Courts 246

The Exclusionary Rule and State Courts 246

The Extension of the Exclusionary Rule to State Courts 248

Debating the Exclusionary Rule 248

The Justification for the Exclusionary Rule 248

Arguments Against the Exclusionary Rule 249

Alternative Remedies to the Exclusionary Rule 250

Invoking the Exclusionary Rule 250

Standing 251

Exceptions to the Exclusionary Rule 253

Collateral Proceedings 253

Attenuation 254

Good Faith Exception 256

Independent Source 260

Inevitable Discovery Rule 261

Impeachment 262

Case Analysis 264

Chapter Summary 266

Chapter Review Questions 267

Legal Terminology 267

Chapter 12. Searches and Seizures and Privacy 268

Introduction 269

The Historical Background of the Fourth Amendment 270

Searches 271

Expectation of Privacy 271

Informants and Electronic Eavesdropping 273

Plain View 274

Expectation of Privacy 274

Open Fields 275

Curtilage and Aerial Surveillance 276

Technology and Searches and Seizures 277

Public Places and Private Businesses 279

Abandoned Property 280

Seizures of Persons 282

Case Analysis 285

Chapter Summary 286

Chapter Review Questions   287
Legal Terminology   288

Chapter 13. Stop and Frisk   289

Introduction   290
Reasonable Suspicion   291
    The Balancing Test   291
    Reasonable Suspicion and Terry v. Ohio   292
    The Reasonable Suspicion Determination   292
    Facts Constituting Reasonable Suspicion 293
Informants and Hearsay   295
Drug Courier Profiles   298
Race and Reasonable Suspicion   299
The Scope and Duration of *Terry* Stops   302
    Movement   303
    Length of Detention   303
    Intrusiveness   304
Stop-and-Identify Statutes   306
    Automobiles and Terry *Stops*   307
Frisks   309
    The Terry *Standard*   309
    Terry *Searches of Passengers
in Automobiles*   310
    Terry *Searches of Automobiles*   310
    Terry *Searches for Illegal Narcotics*   311
Case Analysis   312
Chapter Summary   313
Chapter Review Questions   315
Legal Terminology   315

Chapter 14. Probable Cause and Arrests   316

Introduction   317
Arrests   317
Probable Cause   318
    Direct Observations   319
    Hearsay   320
    The Aguilar-Spinelli *Test*   321
    Totality of the Circumstances   322
Reasonableness and Arrests   324
Probable Cause, Warrants, and the Courts   324
Arrests and Warrants   325
    Arrests in the Home   326
    Exigent Circumstances   327

    Deadly Force and Arrests   330
    Non-Deadly Force   331
    Misdemeanor Arrests and Citations 334
Case Analysis   336
Chapter Summary   338
Chapter Review Questions   339
Legal Terminology   340

Chapter 15. Searches and Seizures of Property   341

Introduction   342
Search Warrants   343
    Knock and Announce   343
Warrantless Searches   349
    Searches Incident to an Arrest   349
    *Searches Incident to an Arrest and the
Contemporaneous Requirement*   351
    *Searches of the Area of Immediate
Control and Automobiles*   352
    *Misdemeanors and Searches Incident
to an Arrest*   353
    *Pretext Arrests and Searches Incident
to an Arrest*   354
Consent Searches   356
    The Scope of a Consent Search   359
    Withdrawal of Consent   360
    Third-Party Consent   361
Probable Cause Searches of Motor Vehicles   364
    *Probable Cause Searches of Containers in
Automobiles*   365
Other Warrantless Searches   366
    Inventories   367
    Administrative Inspections   368
    Special-Needs Searches   369
Case Analysis   370
Chapter Summary   373
Chapter Review Questions   374
Legal Terminology   374

Chapter 16. Interrogations and Confessions   375

Introduction   376
    Interrogations   376
    *Three Constitutional Limitations on Police
Interrogations*   377

Due Process	378
The Voluntariness Test	378
Voluntariness	378
The Due Process Test Today	379
The Right Against Self-Incrimination	380
Miranda v. Arizona	383
Miranda *and the Constitution*	385
Custodial Interrogation	386
The Public Safety Exception	390
The Miranda *Warnings*	391
Invoking the Miranda *Rights*	393
Waiver	394
Waiver: Question First and Warn Later	397
Waiver Following Invocation of the Miranda *Rights*	399
Interrogation	403
Sixth Amendment Right to Counsel: Police Interrogations	404
Case Analysis	406
Chapter Summary	408
Chapter Review Questions	410
Legal Terminology	411

Chapter 17. Eyewitness Identifications — **412**
Introduction	413
The Psychology of Identifications	415
Perception	415
Memory	416
Identifications	416
The Sixth Amendment and Eyewitness Identifications	416
The Sixth Amendment and Critical Stages of Criminal Prosecution	417
The Threat of Suggestive Lineups	417
The Role of the Defense Attorney	418
Tainted Lineups and Courtroom Identifications	418
The Sixth Amendment and Prearraignment Identifications	419
The Sixth Amendment and Photographic Displays	421
The Due Process Test	422
Suggestiveness, Reliability, and the Totality of the Circumstances	422
The Due Process Test and Suggestiveness	424
The Requirement of Police Involvement	429
Case Analysis	432
Chapter Summary	433
Chapter Review Questions	434
Legal Terminology	435

GLOSSARY	**437**
INDEX	**445**
ABOUT THE AUTHOR	**475**

■ ■ PREFACE

■ INTRODUCTION

This text is an introduction to the law of criminal evidence and to the criminal investigative process. Evidence is a class that is central to the study of criminal justice. Students learn to understand the process of gathering material for trial and the challenge of establishing a defendant's guilt or innocence at trial. The study of the investigative and trial process also gives students an appreciation of the rights and values underlying the American system of justice. Learning about evidence makes a more general contribution to students' education by helping them to improve their ability to think logically and to apply general principles to facts along with a capacity to evaluate the strengths and weaknesses of arguments and types of proof.

Evidence has obvious relevance to students hoping to pursue a career in criminal justice, forensic science, the law, or social work. My goal in writing the text was to enhance student learning by writing an accessible, interesting, and interactive text that provides comprehensive coverage of evidence and criminal investigation.

■ CHAPTER ORGANIZATION

Chapters begin with a **chapter outline**, a **Test Your Knowledge** feature, and an **introduction**. Most chapters include an **opening vignette**. The text also includes an interactive **You Decide** feature, which asks students to apply the concepts and rules of evidence covered in the chapter to factual scenarios drawn from appellate decisions. Most chapters also include **legal equations** that summarize the rules of evidence and criminal investigation. The chapters on criminal evidence and procedure also include **Criminal Evidence in the News** and **Criminal Evidence and Public Policy** features. A number of chapters also include a **Case Analysis**. The chapters conclude with a **chapter summary**, **chapter review questions**, and **legal terminology**.

■ ORGANIZATION OF THE TEXT

The text covers the structure of the legal system, the criminal justice process, and essential aspects of the law of evidence. The book devotes particular attention to a comprehensive review of criminal investigation with a focus on the exclusionary rule, searches and seizures, interrogations, and lineups.

The structure of the legal system. Chapter One discusses the federal and state judicial systems, the U.S. Constitution, and the basis of the rules of evidence.

The criminal justice process. Chapter Two outlines the criminal justice process from arrest through sentencing.

Types of evidence. Chapter Three discusses relevance, competence, direct and circumstantial evidence, stipulations, judicial notice, and presumptions.

Direct and circumstantial evidence. Chapter Four covers circumstantial evidence, character evidence, and "other acts" evidence.

Witnesses. Chapter Five focuses on competency, impeachment, corroboration, and memory failures. Chapter Six discusses the opinion rule and expert testimony.

Crime scene evidence and experiments. Chapter Seven discusses chain of custody, scientific evidence, scientific tests, and experiments.

Documentary evidence, models, maps, and diagrams. Chapter Eight addresses authentication, the best evidence rule, models, maps, diagrams, charts, and in-court exhibitions.

Hearsay. Chapter Nine covers hearsay.

Privileges. Chapter Ten discusses testimonial privileges.

The exclusionary rule. Chapter Eleven covers the exclusionary rule.

Searches and seizures. Chapter Twelve discusses the Fourth Amendment and the legal tests for searches and seizures, Chapter Thirteen covers stop and frisk, Chapter Fourteen discusses arrests, and Chapter Fifteen focuses on searches of property.

Interrogations, lineups, and identifications. The final two chapters introduce two other methods of gathering evidence. Chapter Sixteen covers interrogations, and Chapter Seventeen discusses lineups and eyewitness identifications.

■ ACKNOWLEDGMENTS

I profited from the comments and suggestions of outstanding reviewers, all of whom made important and thoughtful contributions to the text.

Joseph D. Anderson, Santa Rosa Junior College

Valerie Brown, Georgia Piedmont Technical College

John M. Claffey, Western New England College

Janet A. Heuer, Bemidji State University

Barry R. Langford, Columbia College

Eric Metchik, Salem State University

Giancarlo Panagia, Westminster College

Stacy K. Parker, Muskingum University

Harold W. Peterson, San Jose State University

Karen S. Price, Stephen F. Austin State University

Jo Ann M. Short, Northern Virginia Community College

James Stewart, Calhoun Community College

The people at SAGE are among the most skilled professionals an author is likely to encounter. An author is fortunate to publish with SAGE, a company that is committed to quality books. Publisher Jerry Westby provided intelligent suggestions, encouragement, and expert direction and in my opinion is unmatched in the field. Denise Simon and Editorial Assistant Laura Kirkhuff were invaluable in shaping the book. Production Editor Tracy Buyan expertly organized a myriad of details associated with the publication of the manuscript. Nick Pachelli created an excellent study site. I would also like to thank the expert professionals at SAGE in production and design who contributed their talents, particularly Marketing Manager Terra Schultz. The text was immensely improved by the meticulous copyediting of Melinda Masson. Brooke Monea worked on the study site.

At the University of Illinois at Chicago, I must mention colleagues Greg Matoesian, John Hagedorn, Lisa Frohmann, Beth Richie, the late Gordon Misner, Laurie Schaffner, Dagmar Lorenz, Dennis Judd, Bill McCarty, Evan McKenzie, Dennis Rosenbaum, the late Gene Scaramella, Dick Simpson, Nancy Cirillo, Natasha Barnes, and Dean Bette Bottoms. A great debt of gratitude, of course, is owed to my students, who constantly provide new and creative insights.

I am fortunate to have loyal friends who provided inspiration and encouragement. These include my dear friends, Wayne Kerstetter, Deborah Allen-Baber, Agata Fijalkowski, Sharon Savinski, Mindie Lazarus-Black, Kris Clark, the late Leanne Lobravico, Sean McConville, Sheldon Rosing, Bryan Burke, Maeve Burke, Bill Lane, Ken Janda, Annamaria Pastore, Kerry Petersen, Jess Maghan, Oneida Meranto, Robin Wagner, Jennifer Woodard, Tom Morante, Marrianne Splitter, and the late Paul Rice. I also must thank the late Ralph Semsker and Isadora Semsker and their entire family. Dr. Mary Hallberg has continued to be an important source of support throughout the writing of the text, and the late Lidia Janus remains my true north and inspiration.

I have two members of my family living in Chicago. My sister, Dr. Jessica Lippman, and niece, Professor Amelia Barrett, remain a source of encouragement and generous assistance. Finally, the book is dedicated to my parents, Mr. and Mrs. S. G. Lippman, who provided me with a love of learning. My late father, S. G. Lippman, practiced law for seventy years in the service of the most vulnerable members of society. He believed that law was the highest calling and never turned away a person in need. Law, for him, was a passionate calling to pursue justice and an endless source of discussion, debate, and fascination.

SAGE was founded in 1965 by Sara Miller McCune to support the dissemination of usable knowledge by publishing innovative and high-quality research and teaching content. Today, we publish more than 750 journals, including those of more than 300 learned societies, more than 800 new books per year, and a growing range of library products including archives, data, case studies, reports, conference highlights, and video. SAGE remains majority-owned by our founder, and after Sara's lifetime will become owned by a charitable trust that secures our continued independence.

Los Angeles | London | Washington DC | New Delhi | Singapore | Boston

CHAPTER OUTLINE

Burden of Proof
The Judge and the Jury
The Development of the Law of Evidence
The United States Constitution
The United States Supreme Court
Federal District Courts and Courts of Appeal
State Constitutions and State Courts
State Judicial Systems
Precedent
The Development of Due Process

The Fourteenth Amendment
Fundamental Fairness
Total Incorporation
Selective Incorporation
Rules of Evidence
Do We Need Rules of Evidence?
Chapter Summary
Chapter Review Questions
Legal Terminology

TEST YOUR KNOWLEDGE

1. Do you know the definition of evidence?

2. Can you distinguish between burden of production, burden of persuasion, and burden of proof and the relationship between burden of proof and guilt beyond a reasonable doubt?

3. Are you able to explain the different roles of the judge and jury at trial in terms of the determination of the law and the determination of the facts?

4. Can you describe the origin of trial by jury in England?

5. Are you able to explain the development and significance of judicial review?

6. Can you explain the relationship between the U.S. Supreme Court, federal courts of appeal, and federal district courts?

7. Are you able to describe the structure of state court systems?

8. Do you know why courts rely on precedent?

9. Can you explain the debate over the Fourteenth Amendment and the incorporation of the Bill of Rights?

10. Are you able to describe the relationship between the Federal Rules of Evidence and state rules of evidence? Why do we need rules of evidence?

We rely on evidence each and every day. An instructor who claims to be a good teacher may cite as evidence his or her class evaluations. On the other hand, there often is disagreement on what constitutes reliable evidence. Other instructors may contend that class observations from other instructors or the academic improvement of students in the class are the best measures of quality teaching. Yet another instructor may argue that all of these factors should be required.

Evidence in the legal sense of course has a specific meaning, which will make more sense to you as you read the text. Section 140 of the California Evidence Code defines evidence as "testimony, writings, material objects, or other things presented to the senses that are offered to prove the existence or nonexistence of a fact." This definition makes clear that along with the testimony of witnesses a number of items, objects, and documents may constitute evidence in a trial. The definition also suggests that what is considered evidence in a specific case depends on the facts involved. A knife would not be evidence in a murder prosecution involving a killing by a firearm.

The police gather evidence, which they bring to the prosecutor. The prosecutor decides whether to pursue the prosecution, and in the event the case goes to trial the jury will evaluate the evidence presented by the prosecutor and the evidence presented by the defense attorney and reach a verdict.

Legal evidence refers to the information and items formally introduced by the prosecutor and by the defense during trial. An item that is ruled "inadmissible" at trial does not constitute evidence.

We already have seen that evidence encompasses a large number of items that may prove or disprove a fact. Witnesses swear an oath to be truthful and testify about what they observed or heard. Witnesses also testify about the genuineness of physical objects introduced at trial. A witness, for example, may establish that the firearm introduced at trial is the same gun that was used in the commission of the crime.

A wide variety of documents introduced through the testimony of a witness also may constitute evidence. These may be written notes, contracts, deeds, promissory notes, diaries, or electronic files and e-mails. Documents also may include ransom notes, counterfeit money, and even graffiti.

Evidence also may include videos or sound recordings. In some instances, copies of trial records and of criminal convictions may be introduced as evidence at trial.

Various forensic and scientific tests constitute yet another type of evidence. Crime laboratories conduct tests on evidence, the results of which are presented at trial. These tests include DNA, blood tests, fingerprints, and ballistic tests on weapons. A developing area of evidence involves scale models and computer-generated simulations of crime scenes and bullet trajectories.

In *Mapp v. Ohio* (1961), the U.S. Supreme Court extended the exclusionary rule to the states, which meant that evidence that is collected in an unconstitutional fashion is excluded from evidence. This has made it important for the police to follow constitutionally required standards under the Fourth Amendment prohibition on unreasonable searches and seizures in gathering evidence. Confessions obtained in violation of the Fifth Amendment right against self-incrimination as articulated in *Miranda v. Arizona* (1966) also are inadmissible in evidence.

■ BURDEN OF PROOF

The prosecution has the **burden of proof** to establish a defendant's **guilt beyond a reasonable doubt**. This means that there is no "reasonable doubt" in the mind of a reasonable person that the defendant is guilty. The shorthand phrase is that the defendant must be proved guilty beyond a moral certainty. Another way to think about reasonable doubt that judges frequently use in their jury instructions is that you would not hesitate to rely and act on it in making the most important decisions in your lives.

The defendant is presumed not guilty. The prosecution in most cases has the **burden of production**, the burden of presenting evidence ("moving forward"), and the **burden of persuasion** or the obligation to persuade the jury of the defendant's guilt beyond a reasonable doubt. The defendant has no obligation to present a defense, and unless the prosecution presents evidence that establishes the defendant's guilt beyond a reasonable doubt, the defendant will not be found not guilty.

A crime has various elements. For example, first-degree murder requires a premeditated intent concurrent with (at the same time as) an act that causes the death of another individual. The prosecutor must establish each element **beyond a reasonable doubt**. State and federal judicial systems typically adopt pattern jury instructions that judges read to the jurors instructing them on the elements of the crime. Both defense attorneys and prosecutors typically are provided the opportunity to review the instructions and propose modifications. An error in the jury instructions that results in an incorrect application of the law by the jury is grounds for reversal of a guilty verdict on appeal.

Defendants possess a Fifth Amendment right against self-incrimination and are not required to take the stand to testify and to subject themselves to cross-examination. The judge instructs the jury that they may not draw a negative inference that the defendant is guilty because he or she did not testify. The defense attorney in conjunction with the defendant has to make a strategic decision whether it is advisable for the defendant to take the stand. Most defense attorneys believe that jurors expect a defendant to testify. On the other hand, the prosecution may have a weak case, and a good strategy may be to focus attention on the weaknesses in the prosecution's case and to rely on cross-examination of prosecution witnesses. For example, the attorney may highlight that a prosecution witness was not in a position to accurately identify the perpetrator of the crime or that the witness failed to select the defendant in a lineup. The defendant also may be an inarticulate or unimpressive witness or may have skeletons in his or her closet that the prosecutor can use to impeach (attack) his or her credibility.

The defense may mount a legal defense through various witnesses. Alibi witnesses may be used to establish that the defendant was not at the crime scene or was present and did not participate in the crime or that his or her appearance on the day of the crime did not fit the description of the offender.

The defense attorney also relies on what are termed affirmative offenses. These include self-defense, necessity, duress, intoxication, and legal insanity. The defendant typically has the burden of production, and then the burden of persuasion shifts to the prosecution to rebut the defense beyond a reasonable doubt. In other instances, the defendant may have the burden of production and of persuasion by a lower standard than beyond a reasonable doubt.

■ THE JUDGE AND THE JURY

The judge is the *law giver*, and the jury is the *fact finder*. In a case heard without a jury, the judge is both the trier of the law and the fact finder. The law giver is responsible for the law that will be applied in the prosecution; the fact finder is required to apply the law to what he or she determines are the facts of the case.

An equally important role for the judge is to rule on what evidence will be introduced at trial. Some of these decisions involve a fairly straightforward application of the law of evidence. A member of the clergy in general does not have to testify about statements made to him or her by the defendants.

There are some evidentiary rulings in which there is no clear right or wrong answer and that thus require the exercise of *judicial discretion*. This means that the judge is required to make a decision based on his or her evaluation of the competing considerations.

Other situations, such as whether a prosecutor's closing argument to the jury was inflammatory and potentially prejudiced the jury against the defendant, also call for an exercise of judicial discretion and are less clear cut.

A judge's rulings can shape the outcome of a trial by deciding to admit or to exclude evidence. A judge often is asked to decide if the value of evidence is outweighed by the risk of prejudice against a defendant. What if the victim in the case before the judge is an African American, and a decade ago the defendant who shot the victim and is charged with first-degree murder was a member of a white supremacist motorcycle club? There always is a question whether it is prejudicial to admit photos of the body of a crime victim to demonstrate the cold and cruel character of the killing or whether the value of the photos is outweighed by the risk of prejudice.

The judge also is the "traffic cop" in the courtroom. In addition to making rulings on evidence, he or she is responsible for ensuring that the lawyer's questions are asked in the appropriate form and that the witness's answers are responsive to the question. A well-known example of a restriction on a lawyer's question is the general prohibition on asking a witness a leading question on direct examination. The basis of this rule is that a leading question suggests an answer rather than allowing the witness to testify. An example of a leading question by a lawyer is a question in which the lawyer asks the witness whether "you would agree that you had too much to drink that night" or to "tell us about your inability to think clearly." The judge of course also needs to remain aware that there are situations in which a leading question is permissible on direct examination and that a leading question is permissible on cross-examination. A lawyer also may not "badger" or "abuse" a witness. In addition, judges also are to make certain that a witness answers rather than avoids answering a lawyer's question to ensure that all the facts are presented to the jury. Judges in an extreme case may hold a lawyer in contempt of court who defies the judge and refuses to follow the judge's ruling.

The jury as the trier of fact is asked to make difficult decisions. Jurors often have to decide which of two conflicting stories to believe or to trust. They also have to avoid being influenced by emotion and personal biases and are required to reach a conclusion based on the facts that are presented in the courtroom.

The next section discusses the historical origins of the American system of criminal justice and law of evidence.

■ THE DEVELOPMENT OF THE LAW OF EVIDENCE

Every society has developed forms of settling disputes. In settling disagreements, a system of determining the facts is required. The famous evidence scholar John Henry Wigmore identified sixteen predominantly ancient legal systems: Egyptian, Mesopotamian, Chinese, Indian, Hebrew, Greek, Maritime, Roman, Celtic, Germanic, Church, Japanese, Mohammedan, Slavic, Romanesque, and Anglican. These legal systems had tremendous variation. In some of these systems, innocence and guilt were based on the decision of professional judges, and in others, decisions were made by laypersons. Legal systems differed in whether they allowed lawyers to participate in the proceeding or individuals to represent themselves. Evidence in some instances was based on the testimony of witnesses although in other legal systems the outcome of the trial was based on whether a defendant was willing to take a religious oath attesting to his or her innocence.

Today there are two principal legal systems, the Anglo-American common law system and the civil law system derived from Roman law, which is the predominant legal system in most of the world. Islamic law and socialist law also have significant influence in the world.

The origins of the law in the United States can be traced to England. The earliest form of dispute settlement was in the British Isles.

Despite the decline of the Roman Empire, the digests or books that recorded Roman law spread throughout Europe and formed the basis of the modern continental European system of civil law. The tribes of Great Britain, despite being occupied by Rome for almost four centuries, maintained their own customary forms of law and dispute resolution and resisted adopting Roman law. The British gradually developed a unique legal system that formed the basis of the British common law that later was transported to America by English colonists.

The determination of guilt or innocence was based on the **ordeals**. Appeals were made to God to reveal whether the accused was responsible. A defendant who plunged his or her hand into hot water without injury was adjudged innocent. Individuals who sank when thrown into the water were innocent; individuals who floated were guilty. Another form of the ordeals was trial by combat in which the accused and the victim or the victim's representative engaged in combat. The vestiges of the system lasted until 1215 when the Lateran Council prohibited clergy from taking part in the ordeals.

The crucial event in English legal history is the Norman Conquest of 1066 over the Saxons. William the Conqueror created a system of royal courts. The Court of Common Pleas was a traveling court that resolved disputes between ordinary individuals revolving around land, trespass, debt, and personal property. The judges would follow local customs in deciding cases. These decisions gradually were compiled into a system of law common to the English people and formed the basis of the common law that was shared by the English people. The judges' decisions formed the precedent (*stare decisis*) that was to be followed by other judges.

An individual wishing to file a legal action had to obtain a writ or a license to bring a case to court. The writ (or "form of action") had to meet highly technical and involved language. An individual who failed to follow the required form could not proceed ("where there is no writ, there is no right"). The defendant then was required to follow an exact formula in response. The system then proceeded with each individual trading highly technical complaints and responses.

A judge and an individual filing a complaint had to be well versed in the law to participate in this system of common law pleading, and there clearly was a need for some formal system of legal training. The solution was the Inns of Court. These started out as residence halls and working rooms in London for judges, lawyers, and students and were located near the king's courts. In 1292, King Edward I assigned judges responsibility for legal education, and the judges responded by creating an apprentice program at the Inns of Court.

The origin of the criminal jury is uncertain. As noted, in 1066, William the Conqueror defeated King Harald's army in the Norman Conquest of England. The Norman kings would summon a "body of neighbors" to offer sworn testimony on who owned various pieces of property, and this information was used to impose taxes. A group of neighbors also was asked to investigate criminal activity. A presenting jury of twelve "lawful men" was charged (a "presenting jury") with informing the king's judges of individuals in local jurisdiction who had committed a crime and should be brought to trial (Green 1985: 7).

In 1215, following the Church's prohibition on trial by ordeal, the king's judges responded by creating an alternative mode of determining a defendant's guilt or innocence. Twelve individuals acquainted with the defendant or with the events surrounding the criminal accusation were ordered to appear and to swear an oath attesting to the defendant's guilt or innocence. The interesting point is that this is very different from the modern notion that jurors are to be impartial and to have formed no opinion regarding a case. Reliance on sworn oaths may have continued to be used to determine guilt or innocence in some areas of England as late as the fifteenth century.

In the fourteenth and fifteenth centuries, the determination of a defendant's guilt or innocence at trial began to be based on the testimony of witnesses. The petit jury (small jury) was created to evaluate the evidence that was presented during a trial, and jurors no longer were expected to rely on their own knowledge of the facts. The jurors' judgments were to reflect the conscience of the community, and jurors were to be selected from the community in which the crime had been committed. In those instances in which jurors were unable to be fair, the trial was to be moved to a different location.

A defendant was authorized to waive a jury trial and, instead, to submit to "strong and continuing pain," typically involving being crushed to death. Individuals at times accepted this harsh alternative because a conviction at trial resulted in the forfeiture of all possessions, which deprived offspring of an inheritance. This harsh alternative was not entirely abandoned until 1772 when it was declared that an individual who waived a jury trial was presumed guilty. A hundred years later, this rule was slightly modified, and a refusal of a jury trial was considered to be equivalent to a plea of guilt.

Trials were not elaborate affairs. The judge would question witnesses, and the jury would meet and return a verdict. Judges exercised stringent controls over the jury and punished jurors who returned the "wrong verdict." In 1554, heavy fines were imposed on eight of the twelve jurors who acquitted Sir Nicholas Throckmorton of high treason for conspiring and plotting the death of Queen Mary.

The trial of Quakers William Penn and William Mead in 1670 was a historical turning point in the development of the jury. Penn addressed a group of Quaker worshippers outside of the Friends Meeting House on Gracechurch Street in London. Penn was held to be in violation of the Conventicle Act, which prohibited worship that did not conform to the requirements of the Anglican Church. Penn and Mead were charged with what in modern terms may be considered unlawful assembly and disturbance of the peace. Penn proclaimed that praising God and assembling to worship God was a lawful act. When asked by the judge whether he pled guilty, Penn responded that the question was not "whether I am guilty of this Indictment but whether the Indictment is legal" (Abramson 2000: 70–71). As he was removed from the courtroom, Penn appealed to the jury to refuse to cooperate with the prosecution, which was "devoid of all law" (Green 1985: 224).

The jury adjourned for ninety minutes and when they returned acquitted Mead and could not agree on whether to convict or to acquit Penn. The judge ordered the jurors to continue to deliberate, and when they returned to the courtroom, they once again acquitted Mead and refused to convict Penn and proclaimed that his only "crime" was speaking on Gracechurch Street. The court ordered the jury to continue its deliberations, and they once again returned with not-guilty verdicts. The judge ordered the entire jury incarcerated, and the next morning the jury once again refused to convict the defendants. The same scenario was repeated for a fourth time, and the jury once again stood firm and returned a verdict of not guilty for both Penn and Mead (Abrahamson 1994: 70–71). Historian Thomas Green writes that the jury by "assessing the law themselves had rebuffed the tyranny of the judiciary and vindicated their own true historical and moral purpose" (Green 1985: 225–226).

This did not end the matter. A number of jurors were fined for refusing to follow the law. Juror Edward Bushel refused to pay his fine, and he was imprisoned. Bushel and three other jurors filed a suit in the Court of Common Pleas and claimed that Bushel's imprisonment as well as the fine imposed on the three jurors was unlawful. Chief Justice John Vaughan upheld Bushel's claim and held that jurors rather than judges are the finders of fact and that jurors may not be fined or imprisoned because officials disagree with their verdict.

As late as 1800, English law provided for the death penalty for 230 offenses, many of which resulted in only minimal social harm. Juries responded by regularly acquitting defendants to avoid the death penalty. Juries, for example, excused thefts by their neighbors who were known to be of decent character and background who may have acted out of momentary weakness. The death penalty for theft tended to be reserved for highway robbers who killed during the course of the crime (Green 1985: 28–54).

The English jury was transported to the American colonies and to other British colonies, and today fifty-two countries employ some form of jury decision-making. In the early colonial period, American juries followed the independent pattern established by the English jury.

The common law tradition embodies a strong concern with individual rights and liberties. The Magna Carta of 1215, known as the "Great Charter," was a significant step in the development of the common law. This document was drafted by English barons to limit the power of King John. The charter established the foundation for certain rights that we take for granted today including the right to trial by jury, the right against self-incrimination, and limitations on criminal punishment.

A second important event in the development of civil rights and liberties was the Glorious Revolution of 1689, which resulted in the installation of King William III and Mary II and led to the adoption of the Bill of Rights. William and Mary agreed to accept the Bill of Rights and announced that the monarchy would be subject to the laws of parliament and would not impose taxes without parliamentary approval. The Bill of Rights established a number of rights to protect individuals against the Crown including the election of parliament, the prohibition on cruel and unusual punishment, and the right to petition the government for the redress of grievances. These principles proved important when the common law spread to the British colonies in North America.

William Blackstone's *Commentaries on the Laws of England* written between 1765 and 1769 stands as one of the most significant documents in the spread of the common law to America and Canada. Blackstone's four-volume work compiled the common law on individual rights, torts, legal procedure, property, and criminal law. It is said that only the Bible had a greater impact on the thinking of the Founding Fathers. The vocabulary of "inalienable rights" and the claim of "no taxation without representation" both derived from Blackstone's commentaries and profoundly influenced the drafting of the Declaration of Independence and the U.S. Constitution.

The common law is the predominant legal system in Great Britain, Wales, and Ireland and Northern Ireland; in Canada (except Quebec); in New Zealand and Australia; and in most of England's other former colonies. In reality, there is no pure common law system. In the United States from the early days of the founding of the Republic, there was a distrust of lawyers and a resistance to relying on judge-made law, which was viewed as undemocratic. State legislatures and the U.S. Congress reacted by embodying common law rules in written legislative statutes. American judges continue to use common law precedents and principles in interpreting the statutes passed by the legislative branch. In other countries, the common law tradition has been combined with other influences. South Africa, for instance, combines English common law with Roman-Dutch law, and India combines the common law with Hindu law.

The law of evidence is the product of a number of sources. These are outlined in the next few sections. The United States Constitution and the accompanying Bill of Rights establish a number of principles that are important in the law of evidence and in ensuring fair trials. These provisions will be discussed later in the text.

■ THE UNITED STATES CONSTITUTION

In 1787, representatives from twelve of the original thirteen states met in Philadelphia and drafted a Constitution. The Continental Congress was formed by the Articles of Confederation, which created a weak central government lacking the power to raise revenues, establish a common foreign policy, raise an army, and impose uniform policies. The framers of the Constitution experienced the tyranny of British colonial rule and were reluctant to give too much power to the newly established government. The colonialists under British rule were subjected to warrantless searches, detentions without trial, the quartering of soldiers in homes, and criminal prosecutions for criticizing the government.

The convention succeeded in creating the United States Constitution. The Constitution is the supreme law of the land and created a "representative democracy" in which the people govern through their elective representatives. The powers of the federal government are delegated by the states, which retain those powers not delegated to the central government ("federalism"). The document created the powers of the presidency, Congress, and the judiciary (separation of powers) and the relations between the various branches of government. Each branch of government has authority to check the powers of other branches, which ensures that no branch of government will become all-powerful and a threat to individual liberty ("checks and balances").

The Constitution is intentionally difficult to amend. This prevents a government from coming to power and changing the rules of the game by passing a law that, for instance, states that you do not have a right to an attorney or a right to a jury trial in a prosecution for serious criminal offenses.

The Constitution in Article I, Section 9 includes several provisions that protect individuals in the criminal justice system. These include the right to seek a writ of *habeas corpus*, which ensures that an individual cannot be held in detention without cause. The document also prohibits bills of attainder, which is a legislative punishment imposed on an individual without trial, and ex post facto laws, which declare a legal act criminal after the fact. Article III, Section 2 provides that all crimes shall be tried before a jury and that such trials shall be held in the state where the crime has been committed.

The American colonists' concern with individual rights is indicated by the fact that the Constitution was accepted by several state legislatures on the condition that a Bill of Rights would be incorporated into the document. The first ten amendments comprising the Bill of Rights were added to the Constitution in 1791. The first eight amendments include fifteen provisions relevant to the law of evidence and criminal procedure. Most of the provisions originally only applied to the federal government. The last half of the twentieth century witnessed the nationalization or "constitutionalization" of the law of criminal procedure. The U.S. Supreme Court has held that most of the provisions of the Bill of Rights of the U.S. Constitution are incorporated into the Fourteenth Amendment applicable to the states. This has meant that both federal and state governments are required to provide the same basic rights to criminal defendants. The result is that defendants generally enjoy the same protections in both federal and state criminal justice systems. (See Table 1.1.)

■ THE UNITED STATES SUPREME COURT

Article VI of the U.S. Constitution, the **Supremacy Clause**, specifically states that the Constitution and the laws passed by Congress are the supreme law of the land and trump any state laws or court decisions that address the same issue. Article VI reads as follows:

> This constitution, and the laws of the United States which shall be made in pursuance thereof . . . shall be the supreme Law of the Land; and the judges in every state shall be bound thereby, anything in the constitution or laws of any state to the contrary notwithstanding.

The U.S. Constitution is the supreme law of the land, and federal and state laws must conform to the constitutional standard. Alexander Hamilton in the *Federalist Papers* observed that the Constitution is the "standard . . . for the laws" and that where there is a conflict, the laws "ought to give place to the constitution." The constitutional requirements, however, are not always clear from the text of the document. The Sixth Amendment's provision for "assistance in all criminal prosecutions," for instance, does not tell us whether the federal government and the states must appoint lawyers to represent the indigent and poor during police lineups and does not tell us whether a lawyer must be provided free of charge to defendants undertaking an appeal following a conviction.

In 1803, in *Marbury v. Madison*, the U.S. Supreme Court claimed the authority of **judicial review**, the right to define the meaning of the Constitution and to throw out federal, state, and local laws as unconstitutional that do not conform to the Constitution. *Marbury* is a complicated case to disentangle, and at this point, you merely should appreciate that the lasting significance of this famous case is Justice John Marshall's proclamation that "an act that is repugnant to the Constitution is void" and that "[i]t is emphatically the province and duty of the judicial department to say what the law is" (*Marbury v. Madison*, 5 U.S. [1 Cranch] 137 [1803]).

In two later cases, *Martin v. Hunter's Lessee* and *Cohens v. Virginia*, the Supreme Court explicitly asserted the authority to review whether state laws and court decisions are consistent with the Constitution (*Martin v. Hunter's Lessee*, 14 U.S. [1 Wheat.] 304 [1816]); *Cohens v. Virginia*, 19 U.S. [6 Wheat.] 264 [1821]). In 1958, the Supreme Court affirmed this authority in the famous civil rights case of *Cooper v. Aaron*. In *Cooper*, the Supreme Court ordered Arkansas to desegregate the Little Rock school system and reminded local officials that the Constitution is the supreme law of the land and that *Marbury v. Madison* "declared the basic principle that the federal judiciary is supreme in the exposition of the law of the Constitution, and that principle has ever since been respected by this Court and the Country as a permanent and indispensable feature of our constitutional system. . . . Every state legislator and executive and judicial officer is solemnly committed by oath . . . to support this Constitution" (*Cooper v. Aaron*, 358 U.S. 1, 18 [1958]).

Table 1.1 ■ Criminal Procedure Provisions in the Bill of Rights

Fourth Amendment

Unreasonable searches and seizures

Warrants

The right of the people to be secure in their persons, houses, papers, and effects, against unreasonable searches and seizures, shall not be violated, and no Warrants shall issue, but upon probable cause, supported by Oath or affirmation, and particularly describing the place to be searched, and the persons or things to be seized.

Fifth Amendment

Indictment by grand jury

Prohibition against double jeopardy

Right against self-incrimination

Due process of law

No person shall be held to answer for a capital, or otherwise infamous crime, unless on a presentment or indictment of a Grand Jury, except in cases arising in the land or naval forces, or in the Militia, when in actual service in time of War or public danger; nor shall any person be subject for the same offence to be twice put in jeopardy of life or limb; nor shall be compelled in any criminal case to be a witness against himself, or be deprived of life, liberty, or property, without due process of law; nor shall private property be taken for public use, without just compensation.

Sixth Amendment

Speedy and public trial

Impartial jury

Informed charge

Confrontation with witnesses

Obtaining witnesses

Assistance of a lawyer

In all criminal prosecutions, the accused shall enjoy the right to a speedy and public trial, by an impartial jury of the State and district wherein the crime shall have been committed, which district shall have been previously ascertained by law, and to be informed of the nature and cause of the accusation; to be confronted with the witness against him; to have compulsory process for obtaining witnesses in his favor, and to have the Assistance of Counsel for his defence.

Eighth Amendment

Excessive bail

Excessive fines

Cruel and unusual punishment

Excessive bail shall not be required, nor excessive fines imposed, nor cruel and unusual punishments inflicted.

As the chief interpreter of the meaning of the Constitution, the Supreme Court's judgments bind all state and federal judges, the president, Congress, state officials, and every official in the criminal justice system. Justice Robert Jackson observed that "we are not final because we are infallible, but we are infallible . . . because we are final" (*Brown v. Allen*, 344 U.S. 443, 540 [1953]). The Supreme Court cannot review every state and federal criminal case that raises a constitutional question. The Court takes a limited number of cases each term and tends to address those issues in which there is a disagreement among federal appellate courts over the constitutionality of a specific practice or where an issue is particularly important. This results in the vast number of criminal procedure cases being decided by lower federal and state courts. In many instances, these courts merely follow Supreme Court precedent. In other cases, we may find that there is no controlling Supreme Court judgment on an issue and that, in order to determine the law, we must look to various federal circuit court decisions and state supreme court judgments. In this instance, each court establishes the law for its own jurisdiction until the Supreme Court rules on the issue.

On several occasions, the Supreme Court has relied on what it terms its **supervisory authority** over the administration of justice in the federal courts to impose standards that are not required by the U.S. Constitution. This is based on the Supreme Court's authority to maintain "civilized standards of procedure and evidence" in the practice of the federal courts. In *McNabb*, the Supreme Court held that federal agents had blatantly disregarded the requirements of a congressional statute. The Court invoked its supervisory authority and held that although federal agents had not violated the Constitution, permitting the trial court to consider the resulting confession would make the judiciary "accomplices in willful disobedience of the law" (*McNabb v. United States*, 318 U.S. 332 [1943]).

The Supreme Court consists of a chief justice and eight associate justices. The Court reviews a relatively limited number of cases. In an active year, the Supreme Court may rule on 150 of the 7,000 cases it is asked to consider. These cases generally tend to focus on issues in which different federal circuit courts of appeals have made different decisions or on significant issues that demand attention. There are two primary ways for a case to reach the Supreme Court.

- *Original jurisdiction.* The Court has **original jurisdiction** over disputes between the federal government and a state, between states, and in cases involving foreign ministers or ambassadors. Conflicts between states have arisen in cases of boundary disputes in which states disagree over which state has a right to water or to natural resources. These types of cases are extremely rare.
- *Writ of certiorari.* The Court may take an appeal from the decision of a court of appeals. The Supreme Court also will review state supreme court decisions that are decided on the basis of the U.S. Constitution. Four judges must vote to grant **certiorari** for a lower court decision to be reviewed by the Supreme Court. This is termed the **rule of four**.

The U.S. Supreme Court requires the lawyers for the opposing sides of a case to submit a **brief** or a written argument. The Court also conducts oral arguments, in which the lawyers present their points of view and are questioned by the justices. The party appealing a lower court judgment is termed the **appellant,** and the second name in the title of a case typically is the party against whom the appeal is filed, or the **appellee.**

Individuals who have been convicted and incarcerated and have exhausted their state appeals may file a constitutional challenge or **collateral attack** against their conviction. The first name in the title of the case on collateral attack is the name of the inmate bringing the case, or the **petitioner**, while the second name, or **respondent,** typically is that of the warden or individual in charge of the prison in which the petitioner is incarcerated. These *habeas corpus* actions typically originate in federal district courts and are appealed to the federal court of appeals and to the U.S. Supreme Court. In a collateral attack, an inmate bringing the action files a petition for habeas corpus review, requesting a court to issue an order requiring the state to demonstrate that the petitioner is lawfully incarcerated. The ability of a petitioner to compel the state to demonstrate that he or she has been lawfully detained is one of the most important safeguards for individual liberty and is guaranteed in Article I, Section 9, Clause 2 of the U.S. Constitution.

Five of the nine Supreme Court justices are required to agree if they are to issue a **majority opinion**. This is a decision that will constitute a legal precedent. A justice may agree with the majority and want to write a **concurring opinion** that expresses his or her own view. A justice, for example, may agree with the majority decision but base his or her decision on a different reason. In some cases, four justices may agree and, along with various concurring opinions from other justices, constitute a majority. In this instance, there is a **plurality opinion,** and no single majority opinion. A justice who disagrees with the majority may draft a **dissenting opinion** that may be joined by other justices who also disagree with the majority decision. In some instances, a justice may disagree with some aspects of a majority decision while concurring with other parts of the decision. There are examples of dissenting opinions that many years later attract a majority of the justices and come to be recognized as the "law of the land." A fifth type of decision is termed a **per curiam** decision. This is an opinion of the entire court without any single judge being identified as the author.

Supreme Court justices and other federal judges are appointed by the U.S. president with the approval of the U.S. Senate, and they have lifetime appointments so long as they maintain "good behavior." The thinking is that this protects judges from political influence and pressure. There is a question whether Supreme Court justices should have limited tenure, rather than a lifetime appointment, to ensure that there is a turnover on the Court. The notion that an unelected judge should hold a powerful court appointment for many years strikes some commentators as inconsistent with democratic principles.

■ FEDERAL DISTRICT COURTS AND COURTS OF APPEAL

Article III, Section 1 of the U.S. Constitution provides that the judicial power of the United States shall be vested in one Supreme Court and in such "inferior Courts as the Congress may establish." The federal judicial system is based on a pyramid. At the lowest level are ninety-four district courts. These are federal trial courts of general jurisdiction that hear every type of case. District courts are the workhorses of the federal system and are the venue for prosecutions of federal crimes. A single judge presides over the trial. There is at least one judicial district in each state. In larger states with multiple districts, the district courts are divided into geographic divisions (e.g., Eastern District and Western District). There also are judicial districts in the District of Columbia, in the Commonwealth of Puerto Rico, and for the territories of the Virgin Islands, Guam, and the Northern Mariana Islands. Appeals to district courts may be taken from the U.S. Tax Court and from various federal agencies, such as the Federal Communications Commission. One or more U.S. magistrate judges are assigned to each district court. A magistrate judge is authorized to issue search warrants, conduct preliminary hearings, and rule on pretrial motions submitted by lawyers. Magistrates also may conduct trials for misdemeanors (crimes carrying criminal penalties of less than a year in prison) with the approval of the defendant. (See Figure 1.1.)

The ninety-four district courts, in turn, are organized into eleven regional circuits and the District of Columbia. Appeals may be taken from district courts to the court of appeals in each circuit. The eleven regional circuit courts of appeals have jurisdiction over district courts in a geographical region. The United States Court of Appeals for the Fifth Circuit, for example, covers Texas, Mississippi, and Louisiana. The United States Court of Appeals for the Tenth Circuit encompasses Colorado, Kansas, New Mexico, Oklahoma, Utah, and Wyoming. The United States Court of Appeals for the District of Columbia hears appeals from cases involving federal agencies. A thirteenth federal circuit court of appeals has jurisdiction over the Federal Circuit in Washington, D.C., and has nationwide jurisdiction over patent and copyright cases and other specialized appeals involving federal law. (See Figure 1.2.)

Circuit courts of appeals sit in three-judge panels. In certain important cases, all of the judges in the circuit will sit **en banc.** The decisions of a court of appeals are binding on district courts within the court's circuit. In the event that an appeal is not taken from a district court decision, the district court decision will be final. The number of judges in each circuit varies depending on the size of the circuit. The Ninth Circuit, which includes California, has twenty-eight judges, while the First Circuit in New England has six. Courts of appeals tend to have differing levels of respect and influence within the legal community based on the reputation of the judges on the circuit. One measure of the importance of a circuit is the frequency with which the circuit court's decisions are affirmed by the U.S. Supreme Court. You should also be aware that there are a number of specialized federal courts with jurisdiction that is limited to narrow questions. Two special courts are the U.S. Court of Federal Claims, which considers suits against the government, and the U.S. Court of International Trade, which sits in New York and decides international trade disputes and tariff claims. There are also a number of other "non–Article III" courts. These are courts that the framers of the Constitution did not provide for in Article III of the U.S. Constitution and that have been created by Congress. These courts include the U.S. Tax Court, bankruptcy courts, the U.S. Court of Appeals for the Armed Forces and U.S. Court of Appeals for Veterans Claims, and the courts of administrative law judges who decide the cases of individuals who appeal an administrative agency's denial of benefits (e.g., a claim for social security benefits).

■ STATE CONSTITUTIONS AND STATE COURTS

Each of the fifty states has a constitution, and virtually all of these constitutions contain a "declaration of rights." In most cases, the provisions are the same as the criminal procedure provisions in the Bill of Rights to the U.S. Constitution. In

Figure 1.1 ■ Federal Court Hierarchy

Supreme Court

- Highest court in the federal system

- Nine justices, meeting in Washington, D.C.

- Appeals jurisdiction through *certiorari* process

- Limited original jurisdiction over some cases

Courts of Appeal

- Intermediate level in the federal system

- 12 regional circuit courts, including D.C. circuit

- No original jurisdiction; strictly appellate

District Courts

- Lowest level in the federal system

- 94 judicial districts in 50 states and territories

- No appellate jurisdiction

- Original jurisdiction over most cases

Source: Administrative Office of the U.S. Courts; Supreme Court Photo: © 2009 Jupiterimages Corporation; Court of Appeals Photo, © iStock photo.com/David Lewis; District Courts Photo: Public domain.

Figure 1.2 ■ Map of Federal Court of Appeals

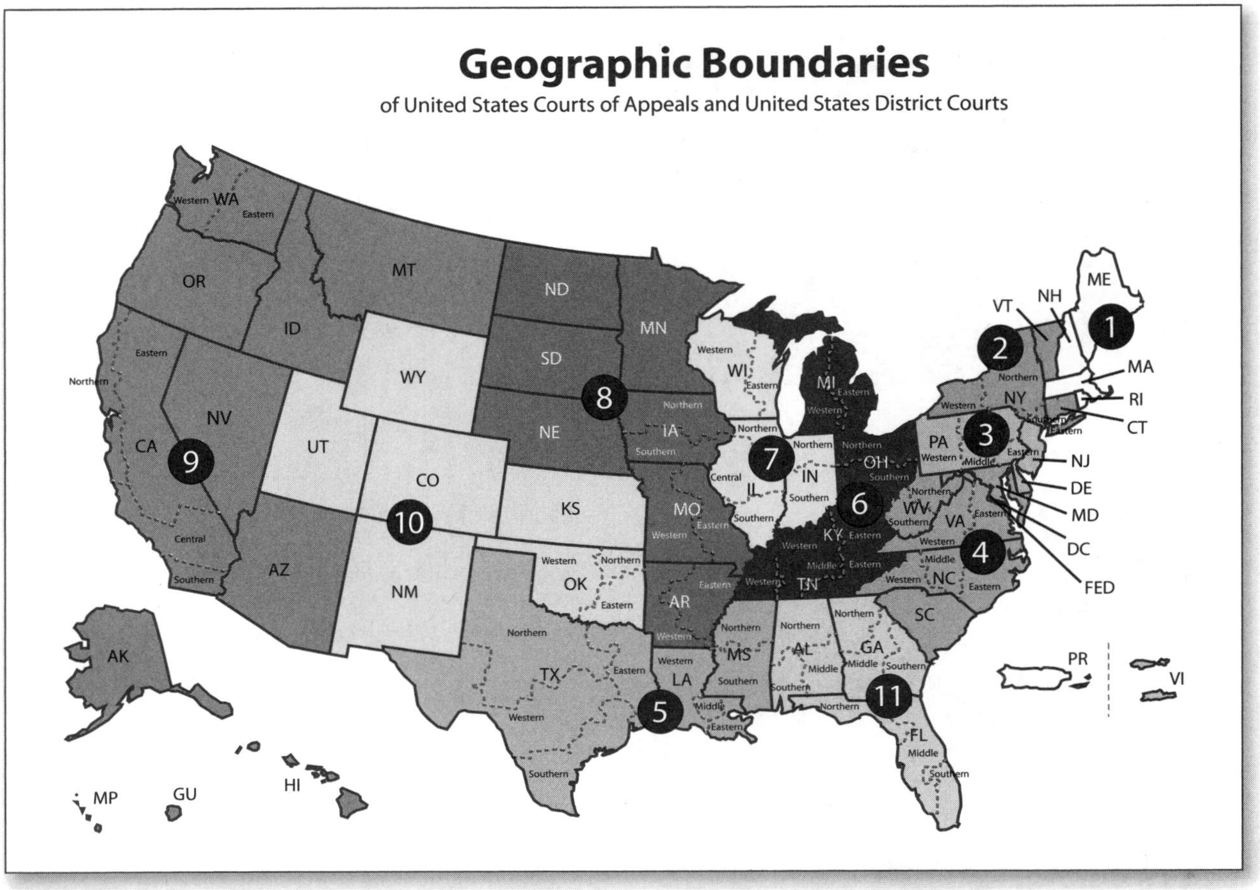

Geographic Boundaries
of United States Courts of Appeals and United States District Courts

Source: Curtis D. Edmonds, J.D. The Center for Assistive Technology and Environmental Access, Georgia Institute of Technology, College of Architecture, http://www.catea.gatech.edu/grade/legal/circuits.html. Printed with permission of the College of Architecture, Georgia Institute of Technology.

some instances, state constitutions have provided for additional rights or have clarified the meaning of particular rights. Alaska, Florida, and Illinois, along with other states, recognize the rights of crime victims to confer with prosecutors and to attend trials. In another example, New York makes it explicit that the freedom from unreasonable searches and seizures includes the freedom from the unreasonable interception of telephonic and telegraphic communications.

The interpretation of state constitutions is a matter for state courts. The decisions of state supreme courts are binding on all lower state courts. The rule is that a state provision may not provide a defendant with less protection than the corresponding federal provision. A state, however, may provide a defendant with more protection. In 1977, Supreme Court Justice William Brennan called on state supreme courts to provide defendants with more rights than what he viewed as the increasingly conservative and "law and order"–oriented U.S. Supreme Court. In a 1989 study, Justice Robert Utter of the Washington Supreme Court found 450 published state court opinions that interpreted state constitutions as "going beyond federal constitutional guarantees." Most of these decisions were handed down in Alaska, California, Florida, and Massachusetts. In reaction to this trend, California, Florida, and several other states have amended their constitutions to instruct state court judges that their constitutions' criminal procedure provisions shall be interpreted in "conformity" with the decisions of the U.S. Supreme Court and are not to provide greater protections to individuals.

As you read the text, you will see that in some instances, state courts continue to engage in what has been called the *new judicial federalism*. The important point to keep in mind is that defendants possess the same rights under both the constitutions of the fifty states and the Bill of Rights to the U.S. Constitution (see the discussion of due process below). The next section discusses federal and state laws as a source of the law of criminal procedure.

■ STATE JUDICIAL SYSTEMS

There is significant variation among the states in the structure of their state court systems. Most follow the general structure outlined below. See Figure 1.3 for an example.

Prosecutions are first initiated or originate in **courts of original jurisdiction**. There are two types of courts in which a criminal prosecution may originate. First, there are trial **courts of limited jurisdiction**. These local courts are commonly called municipal courts, police courts, or magistrate's courts. The courts prosecute misdemeanors and in some instances specified felonies. Judges in municipal courts also hear traffic offenses, set bail, and conduct preliminary hearings in felony cases. In most instances, judges preside over criminal cases in these courts without a jury. A case in which a judge sits without a jury is termed a **bench trial**. Most jurisdictions also have specialized courts of limited jurisdiction to hear particular types of cases. These include juvenile courts, traffic courts, family or domestic courts, small claims courts, and courts that hear offenses against local ordinances.

Trial **courts of general jurisdiction** hear more serious criminal and civil cases. In some states, courts of general jurisdiction have jurisdiction over criminal appeals from courts of limited jurisdiction. This typically entails a **trial de novo**, which means that a completely new trial is conducted that may involve the same witnesses, evidence, and legal arguments that formed the basis of the first trial. These courts of general jurisdiction commonly are referred to as circuit courts, district courts, or courts of common pleas and have jurisdiction over cases that arise in a specific county or region of the state. New York curiously names its court of general jurisdiction the supreme court.

Appeals from courts of general jurisdiction are taken in forty of the fifty states to **intermediate appellate courts**. An appeal as a matter of right may be filed to an intermediate court, which typically sits in panels of two or three judges. The court usually decides the case based on the transcript or written record of the trial from the lower court. The appeals court does not hear witnesses or consider new evidence.

The supreme court is the court of last resort in a state system and has the final word on the meaning of local ordinances, state statutes, and the state constitution. (Note that New York is different and refers to its court of last resort as the Court of Appeals.) A *discretionary appeal* may be available from an intermediate court. This means that the supreme court is not required to review the decision of a lower court and will do so at its discretion. In those states that do not have intermediate appellate courts, appeals may be directly taken from trial courts to the state supreme court. State supreme courts function in a similar fashion to the U.S. Supreme Court and hear every type of case. The U.S. Supreme Court has no authority to tell a state supreme court how to interpret the meaning of its state constitution.

State court judges are selected using a variety of procedures. Some states elect judges in a partisan election in which judges run under the label of a political party, while other states hold nonpartisan elections in which judges are not identified as belonging to a political party. In other states, judges are elected by the state legislature. A fourth approach is appointment by the governor with the consent of the legislature. The so-called Missouri Plan provides for appointment by the governor, and following a judge's initial period of judicial service, the electorate is asked whether to retain or to reject the judge's continuation in office. A minority of states provide for the lifetime appointment of judges. Most states limit the length of the judge's term in office. In many states, different procedures are used for different courts. There is a continuing debate over whether judges should be elected or appointed based on merit and qualifications.

■ PRECEDENT

We have seen that courts follow *stare decisis*, which means that once a court has established a legal principle, this rule constitutes a precedent that will be followed by courts in future cases that involve the same legal issue. The advantage of precedent is that courts do not have to reinvent the wheel each time that they confront an issue and,

Figure 1.3 ■ California State Court System

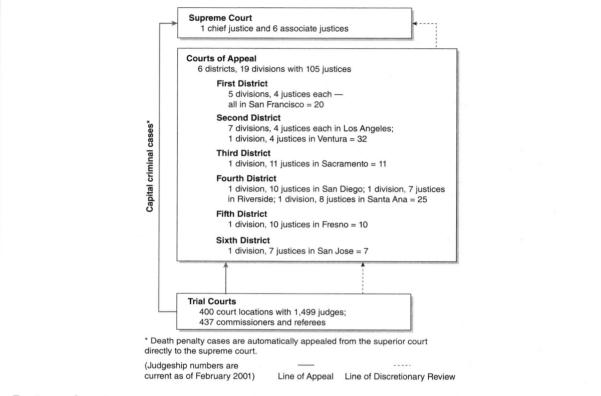

Supreme Court
1 chief justice and 6 associate justices

Courts of Appeal
6 districts, 19 divisions with 105 justices

First District
5 divisions, 4 justices each —
all in San Francisco = 20

Second District
7 divisions, 4 justices each in Los Angeles;
1 division, 4 justices in Ventura = 32

Third District
1 division, 11 justices in Sacramento = 11

Fourth District
1 division, 10 justices in San Diego; 1 division, 7 justices
in Riverside; 1 division, 8 justices in Santa Ana = 25

Fifth District
1 division, 10 justices in Fresno = 10

Sixth District
1 division, 7 justices in San Jose = 7

Capital criminal cases*

Trial Courts
400 court locations with 1,499 judges;
437 commissioners and referees

* Death penalty cases are automatically appealed from the superior court directly to the supreme court.

(Judgeship numbers are current as of February 2001) Line of Appeal   Line of Discretionary Review

Two types of courts
California has two types of courts: 58 trial courts, one in each county, and appellate courts. Trial courts are the superior courts; appellate courts are the six districts of the Courts of Appeal and the California Supreme Court. In the trial courts, a judge and sometimes a jury hear witnesses' testimony and other evidence and decide cases by applying the relevant law to the relevant facts. In the appellate courts, people who are not satisfied with a trial court decision appeal cases to judges. The California courts serve nearly 34 million people.

Trial courts. In June 1998, California voters approved Proposition 220, a constitutional amendment that permitted the judges in each county to merge their superior and municipal courts into a "unified," or single, superior court. As of February 2001, all of California's 58 counties have voted to unify their trial courts.

Superior courts now have trial jurisdiction over all criminal cases including felonies, misdemeanors, and traffic matters. They also have jurisdiction over all civil cases, including family law, probate, juvenile, and general civil matters. Nearly 8.8 million cases were filed in the trial courts at some 400 court locations throughout the state during 1998–1999. Appeals in limited civil cases (where $25,000 or less is at issue) and misdemeanors are heard by the appellate division of the superior court. When a small claims case is appealed, a superior court judge decides the case.

Appellate courts
Supreme Court: The state's highest court, the supreme court, may grant review of cases decided by the courts of appeal. Certain other cases, such as death penalty appeals and disciplinary cases involving judges and attorneys, are appealed directly to this court. At least four of the seven justices must agree on decisions of the court. The court's decisions are binding on all other state courts.

Courts of Appeals: Panels of three justices hear appeals from superior courts, except in death penalty cases, which are appealed automatically to the supreme court. The courts of appeal determine whether a trial court committed legal error in handling the cases that are presented on appeal.

Source: Superior Court of California, County of Glenn (2009). Structure of California Court System, http://www.genncourt.ca.gov/general_info/teachers/structure.html.

instead, are able to rely on the opinion of other judges. A judgment that is based on precedent and the existing law also takes on credibility and is likely to be respected and followed. Precedent is merely the method that all of us rely on when undertaking a new challenge: we ask how other people went about doing the same task.

Courts have different degrees of authority in terms of precedent. As noted, U.S. Supreme Court decisions constitute precedent for all other courts in interpreting the U.S. Constitution and federal laws. Circuit courts of appeals, U.S. district courts, and state courts are bound by Supreme Court precedent. Circuit courts of appeals and state supreme courts establish binding precedents within their territorial jurisdictions. In other words, a state supreme court decision constitutes precedent for all courts within the state.

What if there is no precedent? A case that presents an issue that a court has never previously decided is termed a case of *first impression*. In these instances, a court will look to see how other courts have decided the issue. These other court decisions do not constitute precedent, but they are viewed as **persuasive authority**, or cases to be considered in reaching a decision. For example, a federal court of appeals will look to see how other courts of appeals have decided an issue and will view these decisions as persuasive authority rather than as **binding authority**.

A decision of the supreme court of California has binding authority on all lower courts in California. The decision of a lower-level California court that fails to follow precedent likely will be appealed and reversed by the supreme court of California. The decisions of the supreme court of California do not have binding authority on courts outside of California, but they may be consulted as persuasive authority. Courts are viewed as carrying different degrees of status within the legal world in regard to their persuasive authority. For example, the Second Circuit Court of Federal Appeals in New York is viewed as particularly knowledgeable on financial matters, because the judges are experienced in deciding cases involving Wall Street, banking, and finance.

Courts are reluctant to overturn precedents, although this does occur on rare occasions. A court may avoid a precedent by distinguishing the facts of the case that it is deciding from the facts involved in the case that constitutes a precedent.

■ THE DEVELOPMENT OF DUE PROCESS

The last half of the twentieth century witnessed the *nationalization* or what law professors refer to as the **constitutionalization of the Bill of Rights**. This involved interpreting the Fourteenth Amendment **Due Process Clause** to extend most of the protections of the Bill of Rights to the states. There now is a single standard of criminal procedure that all levels of government must satisfy. You may be prosecuted in Indiana, in Iowa, or in the federal system, and your rights are fundamentally the same. This *constitutionalization* or development of a single standard that applies to the federal government as well as to the states marked a true revolution in the law.

The question of the nationalization of criminal procedure remains a topic of lively debate and disagreement. The development of consistent procedures is intended to ensure uniform and fair treatment for individuals wherever they live and whatever their backgrounds. On the other hand, there is strong argument that the states should be left free to experiment and to develop their own criminal procedures. The procedures that may be appropriate for federal agents investigating fraud, environmental crime, or corporate abuse are far removed from the daily demands confronting a police officer on the beat in a major city or officers in a small department with a tight budget. Supreme Court judges sitting in Washington, D.C., with little or no experience in local government or in law enforcement may be ill equipped to be telling the police in Detroit or Los Angeles how to conduct an interrogation or lineup, and the court's well-intentioned decisions may result in "handcuffing" the police and in frustrating police investigations. Observers of the Supreme Court predict that in the next few years, we are likely to see a renewed debate among the Supreme Court justices over whether each state should be required to follow uniform procedures or whether states should be provided with greater flexibility in their criminal procedures. The Supreme Court, for instance, might hold that the Fifth Amendment does not require states to tape interrogations and that the states may decide for themselves whether to adopt this practice. We now turn our attention to the process of incorporating the Bill of Rights into the Due Process Clause of the Fourteenth Amendment.

■ THE FOURTEENTH AMENDMENT

In 1833, the U.S. Supreme Court in *Barron v. Mayor & City Council of Baltimore* ruled that the Bill of Rights limited the federal government and did not apply to state and local governments. Justice John Marshall wrote that the "constitution was ordained and established by the people of the United States for themselves for their own government, and not for the government of the individual states." He observed that if the framers had intended for the Bill of Rights to apply to the states, "they would have declared this purpose in plain and intelligible language" (*Barron v. Mayor & City Council of Baltimore*, 32 U.S. [7 Pet.] 243, 247, 250 [1833]).

Professor Erwin Chemerinsky observed that if the Bill of Rights applies only to the federal government, the state and local governments "then are free to infringe even the most precious liberties" and to "violate basic constitutional rights" (Chemerinsky 2002: 472). On the other hand, the *Barron* decision represents the widespread belief in the nineteenth century that the federal government should not intrude into the affairs of state governments and that the citizens of each state should be left free to determine what rights and liberties they wish to preserve and to protect. Criminal justice, in particular, was viewed as a local matter.

This system of states' rights did not fully survive the Civil War. Slavery in the states of the former Confederacy would no longer be tolerated, and former African American slaves were to enjoy the full rights of citizenship. The **Fourteenth Amendment** was added to the Constitution in 1868 in order to guarantee equal treatment and opportunity for African Americans. The amendment reads as follows:

> All persons born or naturalized in the United States, and subject to the jurisdiction thereof, are citizens of the United States and of the state wherein they reside. No state shall make or enforce any law which shall abridge the privileges and immunities of citizens of the United States nor shall any state deprive any person of life, liberty, or property without due process of law; nor deny to any person within its jurisdiction the equal protection of the laws.

The first sentence recognized that African Americans are citizens of the United States and of the state in which they reside. The purpose was to reverse the Supreme Court's 1857 decision *Scott v. Sandford*, which held that African American slaves were not eligible to become U.S. citizens (*Dred Scott v. Sandford*, 60 U.S. [19 How.] 393 [1857]). Several judges argued that the debates in Congress over the Fourteenth Amendment indicated that the amendment's prohibition on a state's passing a law that abridges "the privileges and immunities of citizens of the United States" was shorthand that was intended to extend the protections of the federal Bill of Rights to the states. What good was citizenship unless African Americans were protected against the violation of their rights by both federal and state governments? This theory, however, was rejected by the Supreme Court in the *Slaughter-House Cases*. Justice Samuel Freeman Miller held that the Privileges or Immunities Clause was not intended to extend the Bill of Rights to state citizens. Extending the Bill of Rights to the states would establish the Supreme Court as "a perpetual censor upon all legislation of the States, on the civil rights of their own citizens, with authority to nullify such as it did not approve as consistent with those rights. . . . We are convinced that no such results were intended" (*Slaughter-House Cases*, 83 U.S. [16 Wall.] 36 [1873]). Individuals now looked to the Due Process Clause of the Fourteenth Amendment to secure their rights against state governments.

The twentieth century witnessed continued efforts by defendants to extend the protection of the Bill of Rights to the states. Professor Lawrence Friedman, in his book *Crime and Punishment in American History*, notes that with the dawn of the mid-twentieth century, there was an increasing call for fairer procedures in state courts. Lawyers now argued that the Due Process Clause of the Fourteenth Amendment, which applied to the states, included various provisions of the Bill of Rights to the U.S. Constitution. The Supreme Court employed one of three approaches to this argument (Friedman 1993: 295–323).

- *Fundamental fairness.* The Supreme Court decides on a case-by-case basis whether rights are fundamental to the concept of ordered liberty and therefore apply to the states.
- *Total incorporation and total incorporation plus.* The entire Bill of Rights applies to the states. Total incorporation plus includes additional rights not in the Bill of Rights along with the entire Bill of Rights.
- *Selective incorporation.* Particular rights in the Bill of Rights apply to the states. Selective incorporation plus includes additional rights not in the Bill of Rights along with the particular rights in the Bill of Rights.

The Due Process Clause

There are strong arguments that the individuals who drafted the Bill of Rights intended that the Due Process Clause incorporate the Bill of Rights and extend these protections to state governments. Judges favoring the **total**

incorporation approach argue that these rights were viewed as fundamental by the drafters of the U.S. Constitution and clearly were intended to be guaranteed to African American citizens by the congressional sponsors of the Fourteenth Amendment.

A second approach contends that the Due Process Clause left states free to conduct criminal trials so long as the procedures are consistent with **fundamental fairness**. This leaves states with the flexibility to prosecute individuals without being bound to apply the same procedures as the federal government. There is no indication according to individuals favoring this *freestanding due process* approach that the Fourteenth Amendment incorporates the Bill of Rights. After all, the drafters of the Fourteenth Amendment could have expressly stated that the Amendment incorporates the Bill of Rights if this is what they intended. The Fourteenth Amendment employs broad language like "due process of law" to provide flexibility to state governments and to allow the states to adjust their procedures to meet changing conditions. Proponents of fundamental fairness point out that the Fifth Amendment also contains the language that "[n]o person shall be denied life, liberty, or property without due process of law," and if this language were meant to incorporate the entire Bill of Rights, it would have been unnecessary to include the Bill of Rights in the Constitution. On the other hand, critics of fundamental fairness point out that the drafters of the Fourteenth Amendment could have used the term *fundamental fairness* rather than *due process* if this was their intent.

Other judges favored **selective incorporation**. They argue that only those provisions of the Bill of Rights that are essential to liberty are incorporated into the Fourteenth Amendment. States are otherwise free to structure their criminal procedures. A small number of judges advocated **selective incorporation plus** and contended that there are rights that are not part of the Bill of Rights that also applied to the states. The challenge confronting the selective incorporation approach is to identify what parts of the Bill of Rights are essential.

Keep these points in mind as you read about the Supreme Court's gradual incorporation of the Bill of Rights into the Due Process Clause of the Fourteenth Amendment.

■ FUNDAMENTAL FAIRNESS

The Supreme Court developed the fundamental fairness test in a series of cases between 1884 and 1908. Lawyers and their clients were continually disappointed over the next forty years by the Supreme Court's reluctance to recognize that the rights protected by the Bill of Rights were protected by the Fourteenth Amendment.

The fundamental fairness test was first established by the U.S. Supreme Court in 1884 in *Hurtado v. California*. Jose Hurtado had been charged with homicide based on an **information** (i.e., a document signed by a prosecutor charging an individual with a crime) filed by a prosecutor, and subsequently, he was convicted and sentenced to death. Hurtado claimed that the prosecutor had denied Hurtado's due process rights by disregarding the Fifth Amendment's requirement of indictment (called a "presentment" in England) before a grand jury for a "capital or otherwise infamous crime." The Supreme Court rejected Hurtado's claim and held that the ancient institution of the grand jury was not essential to the preservation of "liberty and justice." States were free to design their own criminal procedures "within the limits of those fundamental principles of liberty and justice which lie at the base of all our civil and political institutions, and the greatest security for which resides in the right of the people to make their own laws, and alter them at their pleasure."

The Supreme Court stressed that the information filed by the prosecutor in California was subject to review in a hearing conducted by a magistrate. At any rate, whether a defendant is brought to trial as a result of an information filed by a prosecutor or an indictment issued by a grand jury is not fundamental to a fair prosecution because the defendant's guilt ultimately is determined by the evidence presented at a criminal trial. The important point is that although the Supreme Court rejected Hurtado's claim, the Court opened the door for defense lawyers to argue in the future that their clients had been denied a right that was a "fundamental principle of liberty and justice" that was embodied in the Fourteenth Amendment (*Hurtado v. California*, 110 U.S. 516, 535 [1884]).

Twining v. New Jersey is a second leading case in the development of the fundamental fairness test. In *Twining*, the U.S. Supreme Court rejected Albert Twining's claim that his due process rights had been violated by the trial judge's instruction that the jury could consider the defendant's failure to testify at his trial in determining his guilt or innocence. There was little question that this instruction in a federal trial would be considered to be in violation of the Fifth Amendment right against self-incrimination. The Supreme Court, however, held that the right against self-incrimination at trial was not "an immutable principle of justice which is the inalienable possession of every citizen of a free government." The people of New Jersey were free to change the law in the event that they found the judge's instruction to be fundamentally unfair.

The Supreme Court in *Twining* encouraged lawyers to continue to bring cases claiming that various protections contained within the Bill of Rights were included in the Due Process Clause of the Fourteenth Amendment when it observed that it is "possible that some of the personal rights safeguarded by the first eight amendments against national action may also be safeguarded against state action, because a denial of them would be a denial of due process of law." The Court stressed that these rights are protected "not because those rights are enumerated in the first eight amendments, but because they are of such a nature that they are included in the conception of due process" (*Twining v. New Jersey*, 211 U.S. 78, 99, 113 [1908]).

The world was beginning to change. President Woodrow Wilson had led America into a European conflict in World War I and had proclaimed in his famous "Fourteen Points" that he aspired to bring liberty, freedom, and the rule of law to all the peoples of the world. In Wilson's speech, he called for the formation of a League of Nations to settle international disputes through negotiation and understanding rather than through war. This American commitment to liberty and justice was in stark contrast to the newly developing European fascist movements in Italy, Germany, and Spain, which illustrated the dangers posed to democracy by mob rule, racism, and intolerance.

The Supreme Court took a small step toward recognizing that the Fourteenth Amendment protected individuals against abuse by state authorities in *Moore v. Dempsey*. In *Moore*, a meeting of African American farmers to discuss discriminatory practices in Phillips County, Arkansas, was attacked by white residents. One of the attackers was killed during the exchange of gunfire. Seventy-nine African Americans were prosecuted and convicted, and twelve received a death sentence. In the prosecutions, African Americans were excluded from the juries, the judges rushed through the trials, and threatening mobs surrounded the courthouse. The Supreme Court, based on the totality of the circumstances, held that the murder convictions of five of the defendants violated due process. The Court stressed that it was compelled to intervene to correct the trial court's verdict given that the "whole proceeding" had been a "mask" in which lawyers, judge, and jury had been "swept to the fatal end by an irresistible wave of public opinion" and the Arkansas appellate courts had failed to correct the "wrongful sentence of death" (*Moore v. Dempsey*, 261 U.S. 86, 91 [1923]).

Moore was followed in 1932 by the famous case of *Powell v. Alabama*. The Supreme Court held in *Powell* that the failure of the trial court to ensure that indigent, illiterate, and youthful African American defendants confronting the death penalty in a hostile community were represented by an "effective" lawyer constituted a violation of due process of law under the Fourteenth Amendment. The judgment stressed that "this is so . . . not because [this right is] enumerated in the first eight Amendments, but because [it is of] such a nature that [it is] included in the 'conception of due process of law'" (*Powell v. Alabama*, 287 U.S. 45, 67–68 [1932]).

In *Powell*, five Caucasian homeless men reported that they had been attacked and thrown off a freight train by a group of African Americans. The sheriff deputized every man who owned a firearm, and as the train pulled into Paint Rock, Alabama, the forty-two cars were searched, and the sheriff seized nine African Americans between 13 and 20 years of age as well as two Caucasian females. The two women were dressed in men's caps and overalls. One of the women, Ruby Bates, informed a member of the posse that the African American suspects had raped her along with her companion, Victoria Price.

The nine "Scottsboro Boys" were brought to trial on April 6, 1932, twelve days following their arrest. The courthouse was ringed by armed national guardsmen to protect the defendants from the angry crowd, which at times numbered several thousand. Judge Alfred E. Hawkins initially appointed the entire local bar to represent the defendants at their arraignment. On the morning of the trial, Judge Hawkins named Stephen R. Roddy to represent the defendants. Roddy was a semi-alcoholic Tennessee lawyer who had been sent to observe the trial by the defendants' families. He protested that he was unfamiliar with Alabama law, and Judge Hawkins responded by appointing a local 70-year-old senile lawyer, Milo Moody, to assist him. Roddy was given roughly thirty minutes to meet with his clients before the opening of the trial. He immediately filed an unsuccessful motion to change the location of the proceedings to ensure his clients received a fair trial, which he argued was impossible given the inflammatory newspaper coverage and threatened lynching of his clients. The trial opened on a Monday, and by Thursday, eight of the defendants had been convicted and sentenced to death. The jury divided over whether

13-year-old Roy Wright should receive a death sentence or life imprisonment, and Judge Hawkins declared a mistrial in his case. The Alabama Supreme Court affirmed the verdicts.

By the time that the case came before the U.S. Supreme Court, the Scottsboro Boys had become the central cause for political progressives and civil rights activists in the United States and in Europe. The Supreme Court focused on the single issue of denial of counsel. Justice Arthur Sutherland, citing *Twining,* held that the defendants had been deprived of legal representation in violation of the Due Process Clause of the Fourteenth Amendment. Sutherland based his judgment on the lack of time provided to the defendants "to retain a lawyer" as well as the trial judge's appointment of a "less than competent attorney."

The Supreme Court avoided criticism that they were assuming the role of a "super legislator" by narrowly limiting the judgment to the specific facts that confronted the Scottsboro Boys. Justice Sutherland stressed that the trial court's failure to provide the defendants with "reasonable time and opportunity to secure counsel was a clear denial of due process" in light of the "ignorance and illiteracy of the defendants, their youth, the circumstances of public hostility, the imprisonment and . . . the fact that their friends and families were . . . in other states . . . and above all that they stood in deadly peril of their lives." The trial court's obligation to provide a lawyer to defendants confronting capital punishment was not satisfied by an "assignment at such time or under such circumstances as to preclude the giving of effective aid in the preparation and trial." This ruling, according to Justice Sutherland, was based on "certain immutable principles of justice which inhere in the very idea of free government which no member of the Union may disregard" (*Powell,* 287 U.S. at 70).

Powell was followed by several cases in which the Supreme Court overturned the convictions of young African American defendants whose confessions had been obtained through abusive and coercive interrogations by Southern police officers. The Court condemned these practices as reminiscent of the totalitarian policies of Nazi Germany and as having no place in a democratic society. In *Brown v. Mississippi,* which is discussed in Chapter Sixteen, confessions were extracted from three African American defendants through "physical torture." The Supreme Court held that it "would be difficult to conceive of methods more revolting to the sense of justice than those taken to procure the confessions . . . and the use of confessions thus obtained as the basis for conviction and sentence was a clear denial of due process" (*Brown v. Mississippi,* 297 U.S. 278, 285 [1936]).

In summary, although *Hurtado* and *Twining* affirmed the respective defendants' convictions, these cases established that the Due Process Clause of the Fourteenth Amendment protected individuals against practices that are contrary to the "immutable principles of liberty and justice." The Supreme Court held that due process had been violated and overturned convictions when confronted with poor, rural, African American defendants who had been subjected to "sham judicial hearings," who had been denied access to effective counsel in a capital punishment case, or whose confessions had been extracted through physical coercion. Keep the following four points in mind in regard to the fundamental rights approach to the Fourteenth Amendment Due Process Clause.

- *Fundamental rights.* The Due Process Clause prohibits state criminal procedures and police practices that violate fundamental rights. Justice Felix Frankfurter observed that the Fourteenth Amendment "neither comprehends the specific provisions by which the founders deemed it appropriate to restrict the federal government nor is it confined to them. The Due Process Clause . . . has an independent potency" (*Adamson v. California,* 332 U.S. 46, 66 [1947]).

- *Bill of Rights.* The Due Process Clause protects rights because they are fundamental, not because they are in the Bill of Rights.

- *Legal test.* The Supreme Court has employed various tests to determine whether a right is fundamental. In 1937, in *Palko v. Connecticut,* the Supreme Court held that the right against double jeopardy was not violated by a Connecticut law that authorized the state to retry a defendant in the event of a successful appeal of a criminal conviction. The Court held that rights are fundamental only if they are of the "very essence of the scheme of ordered liberty," if "a fair and enlightened system of justice would be impossible without them," or if they are based on "principle[s] of justice so rooted in the traditions and conscience of our people as to be ranked as fundamental" (*Palko v. Connecticut,* 302 U.S. 319, 325 [1937]).

- *Procedures.* States are free to establish criminal procedures that do not violate fundamental rights protected under the Due Process Clause of the Fourteenth Amendment. The Supreme Court noted that in those instances in which it holds that a state law does not violate due process, the law may be changed through the democratic process.

■ TOTAL INCORPORATION

The fundamental fairness doctrine continued to hold sway in the Supreme Court until the 1960s. Justice Hugo Black was one of the most prominent critics of fundamental fairness. In 1947, Justice Black, in his dissenting opinion in *Adamson v. California*, explained that he had studied the history of the Fourteenth Amendment and that the intent of the drafters of the amendment was to totally incorporate and to protect the principles contained within the Bill of Rights (*Adamson v. California*, 332 U.S. 46 [1947]). Justice Black made the following points in his criticism of the fundamental fairness approach.

- *Decision making.* Fundamental fairness does not provide definite standards to determine the rights that are protected by the Fourteenth Amendment Due Process Clause.
- *Bill of Rights.* The Bill of Rights includes the rights that the founders struggled to achieve and believed were essential to liberty and freedom. The Fourteenth Amendment is intended to make these rights available to individuals in their relations with state governments.
- *Textual language.* The drafters of the Fourteenth Amendment would have used the phrase "rights essential to liberty and justice" if this were their intent.

Justice Black concluded by expressing doubts whether his fellow judges were "wise enough to improve on the Bill of Rights. . . . To hold that this Court can determine what, if any, provisions of the Bill of Rights will be enforced, and if so to what degree, is to frustrate the great design of the written Constitution" (89–90). Justice Black's "total incorporation" approach never succeeded in attracting a majority of the Supreme Court. Justices Frank Murphy, Wiley Rutledge, and William O. Douglas at various times went so far as to endorse a **total incorporation plus** approach, which extended the Bill of Rights to the states along with additional rights, such as the right to a clean environment and health care. As observed by Justice Murphy in his dissent in *Adamson,* "the specific guarantees of the Bill of Rights should be carried over intact into the . . . Fourteenth Amendment. But I am not prepared to say that the latter is entirely and necessarily limited by the Bill of Rights. Occasions may arise where a proceeding falls so far short of . . . fundamental standards of procedure as to warrant constitutional condemnation in terms of a lack of due process despite the absence of a specific provision in the Bill of Rights" (124). The total incorporation approach is straightforward and involves three simple steps.

- *Due process.* Due process is shorthand for the Bill of Rights.
- *Bill of Rights.* Identify the rights protected by the Bill of Rights.
- *Incorporation.* These rights are incorporated into the Fourteenth Amendment and must be followed by the states to the same extent that the rights are followed by the federal government.

Critics of total incorporation asked Justice Black to explain why the drafters of the Fourteenth Amendment did not explicitly state that their intent was to extend the protections of the Bill of Rights to the states. The total incorporation approach, although never endorsed by a majority of the U.S. Supreme Court, nevertheless is important for making a strong case for extending most of the rights available to defendants in the federal system to defendants in the fifty state criminal procedure systems.

■ SELECTIVE INCORPORATION

By 1962, the U.S. Supreme Court included five judges who favored incorporation and who provided the votes that resulted in the Supreme Court's adopting the incorporation doctrine. The majority of judges, rather than embracing total incorporation, endorsed a *selective incorporation* approach, first articulated by Justice William Brennan. Justice Brennan wrote the majority opinion in *Malloy v. Hogan* incorporating the Fifth Amendment right against self-incrimination into the Fourteenth Amendment. Justice Brennan "rejected the notion that the Fourteenth Amendment applies to the States only a watered-down . . . version of the individual guarantees of the Bill of Rights. . . . It would be incongruous to have different standards determine the validity of a claim of privilege . . . depending on whether the claim was asserted in a state or federal court. Therefore, the same standards must determine whether an accused's silence in either a federal or state proceeding is justified" (*Malloy v. Hogan*, 378 U.S. 1, 10 [1964]).

An example of selective incorporation, *Duncan v. Louisiana* (391 U.S. 145, 148–158 [1968]) incorporated the Sixth Amendment right to a jury trial into the Fourteenth Amendment. Justice Byron "Whizzer" White wrote the majority opinion and relied on the selective incorporation doctrine to hold that trial by jury in criminal cases is "fundamental to the American scheme of justice" and that the Fourteenth Amendment "guarantees a right of jury trial in all criminal cases which . . . would come within the Sixth Amendment guarantee." Justice White noted that by the time the U.S. Constitution had been drafted, the jury trial had been in existence in England for several centuries. The jury was part of the legal system of the American colonies and then was incorporated into the constitutions of the new states and included in the Sixth Amendment. Justice White concluded by noting that the jury continued to be an important feature of federal and state criminal justice systems and provided a check on the abuse of power. He stressed that while a criminal justice process that is "fair and equitable but used no juries is easy to imagine," the jury is "fundamental" to the organization and philosophy of the American criminal justice system. Justice Black, in his concurring opinion, remained steadfast in his advocacy of total incorporation, while Justice John M. Harlan provided a passionate defense of fundamental fairness (*Duncan v. Louisiana*, 391 U.S. 145 [1968]). *Duncan* provides the opportunity to review your understanding of the relationship between the Fourteenth Amendment Due Process Clause and the Bill of Rights as we turn our attention to the important topic of equal protection under the law.

The elements of the selective incorporation approach may be easily summarized.

- *Fundamental rights.* The Fourteenth Amendment incorporates those provisions of the Bill of Rights that are "fundamental principles of liberty and justice which lie at the base of all our [American] civil and political institutions." The entire amendment rather than a single portion of the amendment is incorporated into the Fourteenth Amendment ("jot-for-jot and case-for-case").
- *Application.* The amendment that is incorporated is applicable to the same extent to both state and federal governments. Justice Douglas characterized this as "coextensive coverage."
- *Federalism.* States are free to design their own systems of criminal procedures in those areas that are not incorporated into the Fourteenth Amendment.

The U.S. Supreme Court has incorporated a number of the fundamental rights included in the Bill of Rights into the Fourteenth Amendment Due Process Clause. The rights that are incorporated are listed in Table 1.2. The Court has not incorporated the following five provisions of the Bill of Rights into the Fourteenth Amendment, and therefore, a state is free to adopt a law or include a provision in its constitution that extends these five protections to its citizens.

- *Third Amendment.* Prohibition against quartering soldiers without consent of the owner.
- *Fifth Amendment.* Right to indictment by a grand jury for capital or infamous crimes.
- *Seventh Amendment.* Right to trial in civil law cases.
- *Eighth Amendment.* Prohibition against excessive bail and fines.

■ RULES OF EVIDENCE

The United States initially relied on the rules of evidence transported from England. American courts and legislatures, however, quickly developed new rules and procedures. Any description of the law of evidence is complicated by the fact that the systems of evidence differ in the federal and state legal systems and the states differ from one another. Some of the states that have adopted the federal rules often have slightly modified the federal rules.

Table 1.2 ■	Bill of Rights Provisions Related to Criminal Procedure Incorporated Into the Fourteenth Amendment

First Amendment

Fiske v. Kansas, 274 U.S. 380 (1927)
[freedom of speech]

Second Amendment

McDonald v. Chicago, 561 U.S. 3025 (2010)
[right to bear arms]

Fourth Amendment

Wolf v. Colorado, 338 U.S. 25 (1949)
[unreasonable searches and seizures]

Mapp v. Ohio, 367 U.S. 643 (1961)
[exclusionary rule]

Fifth Amendment

Malloy v. Hogan, 378 U.S. 1 (1964)
[compelled self-incrimination]

Benton v. Maryland, 395 U.S. 784 (1969)
[double jeopardy]

Sixth Amendment

Gideon v. Wainwright, 372 U.S. 335 (1963)
[right to counsel]

Klopfer v. North Carolina, 386 U.S. 213 (1967)
[speedy trial]

In re Oliver, 333 U.S. 257 (1948)
[public trial]

Pointer v. Texas, 380 U.S. 400 (1965)
[right to confront witnesses]

Duncan v. Louisiana, 391 U.S. 145 (1968)
[impartial jury]

Washington v. Texas, 388 U.S. 14 (1967)
[right to compulsory process for obtaining favorable witnesses at trial]

Eighth Amendment

Robinson v. California, 370 U.S. 660 (1962)
[cruel and unusual punishment]

Federal Rules of Evidence

The variation in the approach to the law of evidence in various states and between states and federal courts prompted various efforts to create a uniform system of evidence. For example, states differed in whether a wife could be compelled to testify against her husband. An early effort to develop uniform rules of evidence was undertaken in 1942 by the American Law Institute (ALI), a prestigious private group of lawyers, judges, and professors.

In the 1960s, the Supreme Court created an advisory committee to draft a code of evidence for federal courts. The committee spent eight years developing a draft set of regulations on evidence.

In 1972, the United States Supreme Court adopted the Rules of Evidence for United States Courts and Magistrates and transmitted them to Congress for approval. The Congressional Judicial Committee of the House of Representatives debated these rules for almost a year before transmitting slightly amended rules to the floor of the House of Representatives, which approved the new rules of evidence in early 1975.

In 1994, the Supreme Court appointed an Advisory Committee on Evidence Rules to review the **Federal Rules of Evidence** and to propose amendments to Congress. The rules have continued to undergo slight modification, and the current version became effective in December 2011. The purpose of the Federal Rules of Evidence (FRE) and approach to their interpretation are set forth in Federal Rule 102.

> These rules shall be construed to secure fairness in administration, elimination of unjustifiable expense and delay, and promotion of growth and development of the law of evidence to the end that truth may be ascertained and proceedings justly determined.

The federal rules apply to trial and appellate proceedings in federal courts including district and appellate courts. They apply to all types of criminal, civil, bankruptcy, and maritime cases.

The Federal Rules of Evidence are a comprehensive set of rules on evidence that attempted to combine the common law with more recent developments in the law of evidence. In discussing the Federal Rules of Evidence, the text at times refers to the observations of the Advisory Committee and the legislative history from Congress, which are helpful in understanding the meaning of the rules. Thirty years has passed since the drafting of the rules, and the most authoritative source for interpreting the rules is federal court decisions, particularly the decisions of the U.S. Supreme Court.

Uniform Rules of Evidence

The National Conference of Commissioners on Uniform State Laws in an effort to standardize state laws of evidence drafted new **Uniform Rules of Evidence** (URE). State legislatures were encouraged to adopt the uniform rules.

The Uniform State Laws follow the same text and numbering system as the Federal Rules and in virtually all instances have adopted the text.

State Rules of Evidence

States have the sovereign power to adopt their own rules of evidence. The majority of states have adopted the Federal Rules of Evidence, and forty-two states have adopted the Federal Rules in whole or in part. These states are not bound by the interpretation of the federal rules by U.S. district or appellate courts or the Supreme Court, although in most instances they follow the precedent established by these federal courts. Several states, including California, have adopted their evidentiary rules that follow most of the basic principles of the Federal Rules of Evidence. Even those states that have not accepted the federal rules look to federal court decisions in interpreting the meaning of their own evidentiary codes.

■ DO WE NEED RULES OF EVIDENCE?

It is important that trials are viewed as fair. We all want to believe that if we find ourselves prosecuted for a criminal offense we will be dealt with in a respectful and equitable fashion. This sense of fairness ensures that individuals accept and respect the outcome of trials and avoid resorting to self-help to resolve disputes.

The rules of evidence are important for ensuring the fairness of trials.

Equality. The rules of evidence ensure that both the prosecution and defense follow the same rules and that neither the defense nor the prosecution has an advantage over the other by, for example, introducing hearsay evidence.

Values. The rules of evidence promote important societal values. The rules, for example, establish testimonial privileges that safeguard the relationship between spouses, clergy and penitent, and doctor and patient.

Fairness. The rules of evidence ensure that one side does not have an unfair advantage over the other side at trial. One side of a case generally can present evidence so long as the other side has the opportunity to cross-examine the witness and to test the witness's truthfulness.

Efficiency. The rules of evidence exclude evidence that is cumulative (repeats) and that does not add additional information to the case and therefore constitutes an unnecessary expenditure of time and resources.

Quality. The rules of evidence help ensure that the "best evidence" is presented at trial by, for example, encouraging the use of original documents rather than copies of documents or testimony about the content of documents.

Emotion. The rules of evidence limit the evidence presented to jurors to ensure that evidence is not introduced that will result in decisions being made on the basis of emotion rather than based an analysis of the facts.

Improper conduct. The rules of evidence limit the ability of lawyers to influence the outcome of trials through the verbal abuse of witnesses, or misrepresentation of the facts presented at trial in opening and closing arguments.

There is criticism that the adversarial legal system in which two lawyers argue for their point of view does not always result in the emergence of the truth. Lawyers are more concerned with winning than with finding the truth.

In the inquisitorial system used in Europe, Latin America, the Middle East, and Asia, the judge controls the trial and questions witnesses. Because the judge is a sophisticated legal practitioner, there is little restriction on the type of evidence that may be introduced in England.

CHAPTER SUMMARY

Section 140 of the California Evidence Code defines "evidence" as "testimony, writings, material objects, or other things presented to the senses that are offered to prove the existence or nonexistence of a fact." This definition makes clear that along with the testimony of witnesses a number of items, objects, and documents may constitute evidence. The definition also suggests that what is considered evidence in a specific case depends on the facts involved.

Evidence introduced at trial may include testimony, firearms and other instrumentalities, documents, and forensics. Items seized in violation of the Fourth Amendment to the U.S. Constitution may be excluded from evidence based on the exclusionary rule.

The prosecution has the burden of proof in a criminal case. This means that each and every element of a crime must be established beyond a reasonable doubt. The defendant is presumed not guilty. The prosecution in most cases has the burden of production, the burden of presenting evidence ("moving forward"), and the burden of persuasion or the obligation to persuade the jury of the defendant's guilt beyond a reasonable doubt. The defendant has no obligation to present a defense, and unless the prosecution presents evidence that establishes the defendant's guilt beyond a reasonable doubt, the defendant should be found not guilty.

An important role for the judge is to rule on what evidence will be introduced at trial. Some of these decisions involve a fairly straightforward application of the law of evidence. Other situations, such as whether a prosecutor's closing argument to the jury was inflammatory and potentially prejudiced the jury against the defendant, call for an exercise of judicial discretion and are less clear cut. The judge also is the "traffic cop" in the courtroom. He or she is responsible for ensuring that the lawyer's questions are asked in the appropriate form and that the witness's answers are responsive to the question.

The origins of the law in the United States can be traced to England. The decisions of local courts gradually were compiled into a system of law common to the English people and formed the basis of the common law that was shared by the English people. The judges' decisions formed the precedent (*stare decisis*) that was to be followed by other judges. A system of trial by jury also gradually developed. The common law had a strong emphasis on individual rights and liberties. The Magna Carta of 1215, known as the "Great Charter," was a significant step in the development of the common law. A second important event in the development of civil rights and liberties was the Glorious Revolution of 1689, which resulted in the installation of King William II and Mary II and led to the adoption of the Bill of Rights.

In 1787, representatives from twelve of the original thirteen states met in Philadelphia and drafted a Constitution, which contains various provisions that address individual rights in the criminal justice system. The Supreme Court in 1803 in *Marbury v. Madison* claimed the authority of judicial review, the right to define the meaning of the Constitution and to throw out federal, state, and local laws as unconstitutional that do not conform to the Constitution. The federal judicial system is based on a pyramid. At the lowest level are ninety-four district courts. These are federal trial courts of general jurisdiction that hear every type of case. District courts are the workhorses of the federal system and are the venue for prosecutions of federal crimes. A single judge presides over the trial. The ninety-four district courts, in turn, are organized into eleven regional circuits and the District of Columbia. Appeals may be taken from district courts to the court of appeals in each circuit.

Each of the fifty states has a constitution, and virtually all of these constitutions contain a "declaration of rights." In most cases, the provisions are the same as the criminal procedure provisions in the Bill of Rights to the U.S. Constitution. In some instances, state constitutions have provided for additional rights or have clarified the meaning of particular rights.

There is significant variation among the states in the structure of their state court systems. Most state court systems include courts of original jurisdiction, which include courts of limited jurisdiction and courts of general jurisdiction. Appeals as a matter of right are taken from courts of general jurisdiction to intermediate appellate courts.

Discretionary appeals may be taken to the state supreme court.

Federal and state courts follow *stare decisis*, which means that once a court has established a legal principle, this rule constitutes a precedent that will be followed by courts in future cases that involve the same legal issue. The advantage of precedent is that courts do not have to reinvent the wheel each time that they confront an issue and, instead, are able to rely on the opinion of other judges.

The last half of the twentieth century witnessed the *nationalization* or what law professors refer to as the constitutionalization of criminal procedure. This involved interpreting the Fourteenth Amendment Due Process Clause to extend most of the protections of the Bill of Rights to the states. There now is a single standard of criminal procedure that all levels of government must satisfy. You may be prosecuted in Indiana, in Iowa, or in the federal system, and your rights are fundamentally the same. This *constitutionalization* or development of a single standard that applies to the federal government as well as to the states marked a true revolution in the law.

There are strong arguments that the individuals who drafted the Bill of Rights intended that the Due Process Clause incorporate the Bill of Rights and extend these protections to state governments. Judges favoring the total incorporation approach argue that these rights were viewed as fundamental by the drafters of the U.S. Constitution and clearly were intended to be guaranteed to African American citizens by the congressional sponsors of the Fourteenth Amendment.

A second approach contends that the Due Process Clause left states free to conduct criminal trials so long as the procedures are consistent with fundamental fairness.

Other judges favored selective incorporation. A small number of judges advocated selective incorporation plus and contended that there are rights that are not part of the Bill of Rights that also applied to the states. The challenge confronting the selective incorporation approach is to identify what parts of the Bill of Rights are essential.

In 1972, the United States Supreme Court adopted the Rules of Evidence for United States Courts and Magistrates and transmitted them to Congress for approval. The Congressional Judicial Committee of the House of Representatives debated these rules for almost a year before transmitting the slightly amended rules to the floor of the House of Representatives, which approved the new rules of evidence in early 1975. States have the sovereign power to adopt their own rules of evidence.

The majority of states have adopted the Federal Rules of Evidence in entirety, and forty-two states have adopted the Federal Rules in whole or in part. These states are not bound by the interpretation of the federal rules by U.S. district or appellate courts or the Supreme Court, although in most instances they follow the precedent established by these courts. Several states, including California, have adopted their evidentiary rules, which follow most of the basic principles of the Federal Rules of Evidence.

CHAPTER REVIEW QUESTIONS

1. Discuss the relationship between the burden of proof and guilt beyond a reasonable doubt and differing roles of the judge and the jury at trial.

2. Outline the development of trial by jury in England.

3. Discuss the significance of the U.S. Constitution and role of the Supreme Court in maintaining constitutional standards through the exercise of judicial review.

4. What is the role of state courts in interpreting state constitutions?

5. Explain the significance of precedent.

6. Discuss the Fourteenth Amendment, the Due Process Clause, and the various approaches to incorporation.

7. What is the relationship between the federal rules of evidence and state rules of evidence?

8. Do we need rules of evidence?

LEGAL TERMINOLOGY

appellant

appellee

bench trial

beyond a reasonable doubt

binding authority

brief

burden of persuasion

burden of production

burden of proof

certiorari

collateral attack

concurring opinion

constitutionalization of the Bill of Rights
courts of general jurisdiction
courts of limited jurisdiction
courts of original jurisdiction
dissenting opinion
Due Process Clause
en banc
Federal Rules of Evidence
Fourteenth Amendment
fundamental fairness
guilt beyond a reasonable doubt

information
intermediate appellate courts
judicial review
majority opinion
ordeals
original jurisdiction
per curiam
persuasive authority
petitioner
plurality opinion
respondent

rule of four
selective incorporation
selective incorporation plus
stare decisis
supervisory authority
Supremacy Clause
total incorporation
total incorporation plus
trial *de novo*
Uniform Rules of Evidence

REFERENCES

Abramson, Jeffrey. 2000. *We the Jury*. Cambridge, MA: Harvard University Press.

Blackstone, William. 1979. *Commentaries on the Laws of England: A Facsimile of the First Edition of 1765–1769*. Chicago: University of Chicago.

Chemerinsky, Erwin. 2002. *Principle and Policies*, 2nd ed. New York: Aspen.

Friedman, Lawrence. 1993. *Crime and Punishment in American History*. New York: Basic Books.

Green, Thomas Andre. 1985. *Verdict According to Conscience*. Chicago: University of Chicago Press.

Visit the Student Study Site at **http://study.sagepub.com/lippmance** to access additional study tools, including mobile-friendly eFlashcards and Web quizzes as well as links to SAGE journal articles and hyperlinks for *Criminal Evidence* on the Web.

CHAPTER 2

THE CRIMINAL JUSTICE PROCESS

CHAPTER OUTLINE

Introduction
The Criminal Complaint
First Appearance
Preliminary Hearing
Grand Jury
Arraignment
Suppression Hearings and Pretrial Motions
Discovery
Plea Bargaining

Jury Selection
The Trial
The Judicial Sentencing Process
Sentencing Guidelines and the Role of the Jury in Sentencing
Criminal Appeals
Habeas Corpus
Chapter Summary
Chapter Review Questions
Legal Terminology

TEST YOUR KNOWLEDGE

1. Are you able to describe the functions of the first appearance, the preliminary hearing, and the arraignment?

2. Can you describe the role of the grand jury and why it is called the prosecutor's "little darling"?

3. What is the role of a motion to suppress?

4. Can you define *voir dire* and distinguish between peremptory challenges and challenges for cause?

5. Are you able to identify the purpose of the lawyers' opening and closing statements at trial?

6. Can you list the policy arguments for and against plea bargaining? What constitutional issues are presented by the plea-bargaining process? Describe the conditions that must be satisfied before a trial court judge may accept a defendant's guilty plea.

7. Can you describe the role of the judge and jury in fixing criminal sentencing?

8. Do you know the importance of the plain error exception, the harmless error exception, and the automatic reversal rule?

9. Are you able to describe the importance writ of *habeas corpus* for protecting rights and liberties?

■ INTRODUCTION

In this chapter, we examine the pretrial, trial, and appeal phases of the criminal justice process. During this portion of the criminal justice process, there is an effort to strike a balance between the interest in convicting the guilty and the fact that defendants are presumed innocent until proven guilty. The procedures during this phase of the criminal justice process also reflect the interest in public participation in the criminal justice system.

The government is required to establish that there is probable cause to bring the case to trial. There are two procedures that are relied on to determine whether the government may proceed to trial.

1. *Preliminary hearing.* The prosecutor files an information or written formal charge that is reviewed by a judge at the preliminary hearing.

[handwritten margin note: really just to check the govt]

2. *Grand jury.* The prosecutor files a criminal complaint, and a grand jury composed of ordinary citizens decides whether to issue an indictment.

This is followed by the formal charging of a criminal offense at the arraignment and the defendant's entry of a formal plea.

Prior to trial, the defendant may file **pretrial motions** challenging violations of his or her constitutional rights. These motions include speedy trial; improper venue; double jeopardy; the discovery of potentially exonerating evidence in the possession of the prosecution; and the filing of motions to suppress unlawfully obtained evidence. The next step is the selection of the jury. Due process procedures are designed to ensure that the jury-selection process is free from discrimination and that the jury reflects a cross section of the community. Keep in mind the important role played by the jury in protecting defendants against unfair prosecution and prosecutorial abuse.

The next phase of the process is the trial itself. As you read about opening statements, presenting evidence, closing arguments, and jury decision-making, pay attention to how trial procedures are organized to strike a balance between the efficient criminal prosecution of offenders and the interest in ensuring that defendants are treated in accordance with due process of law and that their guilt or innocence is determined by the evidence rather than on the basis of unfounded accusations. The chapter also discusses plea bargaining and determining guilt without a formal trial. The vast majority of criminal cases are decided by a defendant's plea of guilty, and the question arises whether this is desirable.

Following a criminal conviction, the attention of the defendant, the lawyers, and the judge shifts to the sentencing phase of the trial. The sentencing decision will determine the nature and length of the defendant's punishment.

Despite the fact that every effort is made to ensure that a defendant is fairly treated throughout the pretrial and trial phases of the criminal justice system, there always is the possibility that a defendant's conviction has been significantly influenced by an error. This might involve a judge's mistake in admitting unlawfully obtained evidence or a judge's failure to tell the jury to disregard a prosecutor's improper and inflammatory remarks during the closing argument. As a result, the federal government and the states provide individuals with an appeal to review the lawfulness of their convictions. Defendants who have exhausted their appeals are provided with yet another safeguard in the writ of *habeas corpus*. This civil action permits a defendant to petition federal courts to examine whether the trial court and appellate courts have reasonably interpreted the law in upholding his or her conviction. (See Figure 2.1.)

■ THE CRIMINAL COMPLAINT

[handwritten margin note: - might be complaining about cop - ? cop doesn't do anything when they complain]

A criminal case is initiated by the filing of a **complaint** by a police officer, prosecutor, or private citizen. If an individual is arrested prior to the filing of a complaint, the complaint is sworn by the officer following the arrest.

The complaint is a legal document that lists the charges, the legal elements of the crime, and the supporting facts against the individual and possible penalties.

The police may decide to obtain an arrest warrant based on probable cause that an individual has committed a crime. The officer must swear an affidavit under oath. In the event a judge is satisfied there is probable cause for an arrest, the warrant will be issued for the arrest of the individual. Several states provide that an arrest warrant can take the place of the complaint following the arrest. The police also may obtain a search warrant to search a designated location for items connected to the criminal case against the individual.

Figure 2.1 ■ Criminal Justice Process Chart

What is the sequence of events in the criminal justice system?

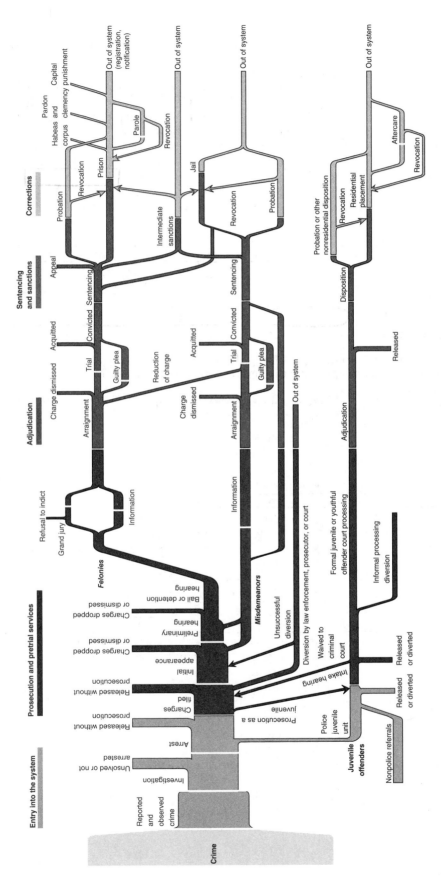

Source: Department of Justice.

Note: This chart gives a simplified view of caseflow through the criminal justice systems. Procedures vary among jurisdictions. The weights of the lines are not intended to show actual size of caseloads.

The **booking** follows the individual's arrest. This is an administrative procedure in which the suspect's name, arrest time, offense charged, fingerprinting, and photographs are recorded.

[handwritten annotation: might take 48 hrs: • over the weekend • natural disaster (hurricane) • need to sober up | if over 48 hrs... court sees the reason for the delay and excuses it]

■ FIRST APPEARANCE

The next step following an arrest is the **first appearance** or the *initial appearance*. The first appearance is triggered by the filing of a complaint. The Federal Rules of Criminal Procedure and most states specify that a defendant is to be brought before a magistrate or judge "without unnecessary delay." States differ on the permissible time between the arrest and the first appearance. The Supreme Court has set the outside limit at forty-eight hours (*County of Riverside v. McLaughlin*, 500 U.S. 44 [1991]). The Court has held that a confession obtained after failing to promptly present a defendant to a magistrate is inadmissible in evidence (*McNabb v. United States*, 318 U.S. 332 [1943]; *Mallory v. United States*, 354 U.S. 449 [1957]).

The initial appearance is an important part of the process because the judge informs the defendant of the charges and of his or her rights. These rights include the right to remain silent, the right to an attorney and the availability of a public defender if the accused is indigent, the right to a jury, the right to bail if the defendant is charged with a bailable offense, and the right to a preliminary hearing. Bail is set in some jurisdictions at a bail hearing and will be denied if the defendant is determined to be a flight risk or presents a risk of harm to other individuals.

Most defendants charged with a misdemeanor offense plead guilty to the charges against them and pay a fine. Felony defendants may not enter a plea of guilty because the initial appearance customarily occurs in a court of limited jurisdiction without authority to accept a plea.

[handwritten annotation: govt isn't having people arrested for no reason → not all evidence is presented, and don't need to present evidence that person didn't do it]

■ PRELIMINARY HEARING

[handwritten annotation: evidence viewed in light most favorable to the govt — based on probable cause]

The next step is the **preliminary hearing**. This is a mini-trial in which the defendant has the right to counsel. The purpose is for a judge to determine if there is probable cause that an offense was committed and that the defendant committed the crime. Some states combine the initial appearance with the preliminary hearing in those instances in which an arrest warrant was not issued by a judicial official. The defendant may waive the preliminary hearing although the preliminary hearing gives the defendant an idea of the prosecution's case because the prosecution presents witnesses whose testimony establishes probable cause.

As observed by the Wisconsin Supreme Court, the purpose of the preliminary hearing is to prevent "hasty, malicious, improvident, and oppressive prosecutions" that subject individuals to the "humiliation and anxiety involved in public prosecution" and to "avoid the [unnecessary] expense of a public trial" (*Thies v. State*, 189 N.W. 539, 541 [Wis. 1922]).

The preliminary hearing is a "critical stage" of the criminal justice system in which a defendant possesses the right to counsel. The defendant in most instances will not put on witnesses because the best strategy is to discover the prosecution's case while revealing as little as possible about the defense. The defense attorney has the opportunity to cross-examine witnesses who take an oath to testify truthfully and to determine the strength of the prosecution's case. A defendant confronting a strong case may conclude that a plea bargain is in his or her best interest. Defendants avoid taking the stand because testimony at the preliminary hearing may be used at trial. *[handwritten annotation: first time they hear evidence against them]*

The judge at the conclusion of the preliminary hearing determines if there is sufficient evidence to proceed to trial on the charges. The prosecution must establish that it is more likely than not that the defendant committed the crime or crimes with which he or she is charged. The judge must evaluate the testimony and credibility of each witness.

Courts follow one of two standards in determining whether to bind over a defendant for trial. The basic question is whether a crime was committed and whether the defendant committed the crime. Most states adhere to the probable cause standard, while a minority of states adhere to the *prima facie* approach.

Probable cause. The judge determines whether there is a "fair probability" based on the evidence presented during the preliminary hearing that the government will succeed in convicting the defendant at trial. The issue is whether there is probable cause to believe that a defendant may be convicted.

Prima facie. The judge determines whether the prosecution's evidence, if believed by the jury, is sufficient to convict the defendant at trial.

police tells the jury what happened and charges against → then defendant is indicted.

■ GRAND JURY

★Also screening for prosecution →

★not recorded★

The Fifth Amendment provides that "no person shall be held to answer for a capital, or otherwise infamous crime, unless on presentment or indictment of a grand jury." The *Grand Jury Clause* does not apply to states, and state law determines whether a **grand jury** is required to be conducted. The Supreme Court has held that states have the option of relying either on a preliminary hearing or on a grand jury.

States are categorized as either **indictment states**, **information states**, or **modified indictment states** based on the role of the preliminary hearing.

The federal grand jury is composed of twenty-three people, and the proceedings are not open to the public. The only individuals present are the prosecutors, witnesses, and grand jurors. State grand juries may range from six to twenty-three members.

The rules of evidence are inapplicable to grand jury proceedings, although a suspect's testimony is admissible at trial. As a result, defendants customarily invoke the privilege against self-incrimination if subpoenaed to testify. The testimony of other witnesses also may be used for various purposes at trial.

There are two functions of the grand jury. The first is the charging function. The prosecutor is the only party presenting evidence before the grand jury, which in contrast to the preliminary hearing is a non-adversarial proceeding. The suspect has no right to attend the proceedings, testify, or present evidence. In theory, the grand jury may ask questions of the witnesses and request the prosecutor to call particular witnesses. Although the purpose of the grand jury is to check overzealous prosecutions, defense attorneys remark that because of the prosecutor's dominance of the proceedings, the grand jury is the prosecutor's "little darling" and a prosecutor could get a grand jury to indict a ham sandwich.

The grand jury functions in secrecy to avoid drawing attention to an individual where there are found to be no grounds to indict. Individuals in most cases are not informed that they are the target of a grand jury. Indictments require a two-thirds rather than unanimous vote although some states provide for a majority vote. Another unique aspect of the grand jury is that witnesses have no right to legal representation by a lawyer during their testimony.

A grand jury returns an **indictment** also known as a **true bill** if they conclude that there are grounds for bringing the suspect to trial. Charges that are found sufficient result in a **no bill**. → *not indicted*

The second function of a grand jury is to carry out investigations. Grand juries have the power to compel the attendance of witnesses through the issuances of *subpoenas ad testificandum,* and to compel the production of evidence through *subpoenas duces tecum.* The grand jury can persuade individuals to testify by granting immunity from prosecution. In *transactional immunity,* the prosecutor agrees not to prosecute the witness for any crimes the individual admits. The government under *use immunity* agrees not to use a witness's grand jury testimony to prosecute him or her. A witness who refuses to testify may be held in contempt of court and jailed. Following the completion of a grand jury investigation, the grand jury may provide a **presentment**, or report on criminal activity, to a court.

★govt doesn't need to present all the evidence they have★

↳ investigate monsters, 911 people...

■ ARRAIGNMENT

Once the decision is made to indict an individual or to bind him or her over for trial, the next step is an **arraignment**. At the arraignment, a defendant is brought before a judge, is informed of the charges filed against him or her, and is required to enter one of four possible pleas.

- *Not guilty.* "I did not commit the crime."
- *Not guilty by reason of insanity.* "I did not know the nature and quality of my act." → *defendant must prove insane, might need to go to mental hospital*
- *Nolo contendere.* "I do not want to contest the criminal charge."
- *Guilty.* "I committed the crime."

A plea of **nolo contendere**, or "no contest," requires the permission of the court. This plea is used when a defendant while not admitting guilt does not dispute the charge. The plea carries all the consequences of a guilty plea with one exception. The exception is that unlike a guilty plea or criminal conviction, a plea of nolo contendere may not be admitted into evidence in a civil trial to establish that the defendant committed an act that injured the victim and therefore is civilly liable to pay damages to the victim. Ordinarily, a criminal conviction for a crime like aggravated assault can be introduced in a civil trial to prove that the defendant injured the plaintiff and now should be held liable for medical expenses and monetary damages. A plea of nolo contendere prevents the plaintiff at a civil trial from pointing to the criminal conviction as evidence that he or she was assaulted by the defendant. *Standing mute* or refusing to plead results in a court entering a "not guilty" plea for the defendant preserving the defendant's right to trial.

The judge at the arraignment is responsible for ensuring that a plea of nolo contendere or guilty is voluntary. In the event that the defendant pleads not guilty at the arraignment and indicates that he or she plans to proceed to trial, the defense lawyers may file various pretrial motions that are discussed in the next section of the chapter.

■ SUPPRESSION HEARINGS AND PRETRIAL MOTIONS

The exclusionary rule prohibits the introduction at trial of unlawfully obtained evidence. A **motion to suppress** generally is required prior to trial when the defense is aware of possible legal grounds to object to evidence seized as a result of an unlawful search and seizure, an unlawful confession, or an illegally conducted lineup. Motions to suppress are conducted following the preliminary hearing because a suppression hearing will not be required if the case is dismissed at the preliminary hearing. The preliminary hearing also may reveal grounds to pursue motions to suppress evidence.

The rules of evidence apply to a suppression hearing, and both sides have the right to call and to cross-examine witnesses. The defendant's testimony at a suppression hearing cannot be used as evidence at trial because a defendant cannot testify about unconstitutional seizure of narcotics or about an unlawful confession without admitting guilt and incriminating him- or herself. In some jurisdictions, the defense may support the motion to suppress by submitting the transcript of the preliminary hearing if the defense believes that the testimony supports the claim that the evidence was unlawfully seized. The prosecution may respond to call witnesses to rebut the defense attorney's motion.

The judge will issue his or her ruling immediately following the hearing or take the matter "under advisement" and issue a ruling at a later date. A successful motion to suppress will result in the exclusion of the material from evidence. *→exclude or admit evidence into the case*

There are other matters that may be filed in a pretrial motion. One of the most significant is called a **motion in limine**. In limine ("at the threshold") means that the motion is filed in the pretrial stage. A prosecutor or defense attorney files such a motion to exclude evidence from trial or to obtain permission to introduce an item of evidence into trial. For example, the defense attorney may want to exclude a defendant's earlier convictions from evidence or obtain permission to introduce the victim's prior sexual history at trial.

Motions in limine are based on the rules of evidence unlike motions to suppress, which are based on conduct in violation of the U.S. Constitution. Filing an evidentiary motion before trial gives the attorney the time to make an in-depth argument that may be difficult to make during the trial. An early decision on the evidence may assist the defense attorney to plan his or her trial strategy.

There are various other motions that may be filed prior to trial.

Motion for a dismissal of charges. The defense may file a motion to dismiss the charges on the grounds that there is insufficient evidence as a matter of law to support the charges. This is unlikely to be successful because probable cause already has been found to exist to proceed to trial.

Double jeopardy. The defendant claims that he or she is being subjected to a second prosecution for the crime with which he or she is charged. **Double jeopardy** is not violated by prosecuting an individual for separate crimes committed during a single transaction. An individual who commits a criminal act that violates two criminal statutes may be charged with a violation of each law.

Change of venue. A defense attorney may file a motion for a change of venue if the defense attorney believes that there is a "reasonable likelihood" that the defendant cannot receive a fair trial.

Motion for severance. Co-defendants typically are tried together. A defendant may make a motion for a separate trial on the grounds that severance is "necessary to achieve" a fair determination of the defendant's guilt or innocence. The court considers whether the jury in its deliberations will be able to separately consider the guilt of each of the defendants or whether each defendant will be prejudiced by standing trial with his or her co-defendant(s).

Speedy trial. The Sixth Amendment to the U.S. Constitution provides that "[i]n all criminal prosecutions, the accused shall enjoy the right to a speedy . . . trial." The Fourteenth Amendment Due Process Clause incorporates the right to **speedy trial**, which also is guaranteed by law in each of the fifty states. Scholars point to the English Magna Carta of 1215, one of the most famous human rights documents in history, as the first clear statement of the right to a speedy trial. The U.S. Supreme Court has recognized that the "history of the right to a speedy trial and its reception in this country clearly establish that it is one of the basic rights preserved by our Constitution" (*Klopfer v. North Carolina*, 386 U.S. 213, 223, 226 [1967]). Courts in making this determination consider the length and reason for the delay and whether the defendant has been prejudiced by the delay in the prosecution of the defendant (*Barker v. Wingo*, 407 U.S. 514 [1972]). → If it takes too long you can ask for case to be thrown out

■ DISCOVERY

Discovery is the right for each side to have warning of the evidence that the other side will present at trial. Discovery is based on the notion that each side in a case should be informed of what the other side will present at trial. The idea is to allow the defense and prosecution to fully prepare for trial and to avoid being surprised by evidence that they did not know would be introduced at trial. This promotes a fair, efficient, and truthful trial and prevents the prosecution from withholding evidence that could result in the conviction of an innocent individual.

The underlying philosophy is that a trial is a search for truth rather than a competitive sporting contest.

In *Brady v. Maryland*, the Supreme Court held that the Due Process Clause requires prosecutors, when requested by the defense, to disclose exculpatory (exonerating) evidence (*Brady v. Maryland*, 373 U.S. 83 [1963]). The Supreme Court has held that evidence is "material" and must be handed over when "there is a reasonable probability" that it "undermines confidence in the outcome of the trial" (*Smith v. Cain*, 565 U.S. __ [2012]).

The **Brady rule**, the constitutional requirement to hand over exculpatory information, is binding on both state and federal prosecutors.

State statutes and state rules of procedure adopt varying positions on disclosure of other evidence ranging from virtually no disclosure to complete disclosure. Rule 16 of the Federal Rules of Criminal Procedure addresses disclosure in federal courts. Discoverable evidence is limited to (1) the defendant's statements, (2) the defendant's criminal record, (3) documents and tangible evidence, and (4) reports of medical examinations and tests. A discovery request by the defense under the federal rules results in the prosecution's right to make a reciprocal discovery request.

Several examples of state and federal approaches to discovery are outlined below.

Names and addresses of witnesses. One-half of the states provide for discovery of the names and addresses of all persons known to have relevant information. A number of other jurisdictions and the federal government do not make this information available because of a fear of intimidation of witnesses. A third group requires disclosure only of individuals "intended" to be called at trial.

Witness statements. A majority of states either do not permit discovery of the statements of interviewed witnesses or leave this to the discretion of the judge. Roughly fourteen states and the federal government do not require pretrial disclosures of the statements of witnesses. The federal policy is based on the interest in protecting witnesses from harassment.

Police officers. Police personnel records generally are not discoverable. Some states require disclosure in the event that the records are likely to contain information relevant to the officer's credibility.

Most jurisdictions provide for the disclosure by both sides of medical and physical examinations and scientific tests, documents and tangible objects, and statements made by the accused to the government. A co-defendant's statements that are to be introduced into evidence generally are not discoverable, because this might lead to the intimidation of witnesses.

A number of jurisdictions require a defendant to provide notice that he or she plans to offer an alibi defense and to provide the name of the alibi witnesses. This requirement allows the prosecution to investigate the background of alibi witnesses. Various statutes also require the state to disclose that an insanity plea will be entered or that expert witnesses will be called.

Neither the prosecution nor the defense is required to disclose internal research on the law or trial strategy or other privileged information. Statements made by a defendant to a lawyer are exempt from discovery.

Discovery may be formal or informal. Lawyers customarily turn over required material to the other side because they know the court will order the material to be turned over in any event. Formal discovery motions are filed when lawyers on one side resist turning over material because they question whether they are obligated to provide the material, or the lawyers have developed a difficult relationship with one another.

A prosecutor's failure to comply with a judge's discovery order to turn information over to the defense may result in the material being declared inadmissible at trial or may result in the dismissal of the case. A prosecutor is responsible for knowing what is in his or her files and police files. A statement by a prosecutor that information in the files does not exist also may result in the dismissal of a case.

■ PLEA BARGAINING →keeps the system moving

Plea bargaining involves an agreement between the prosecution and defense in which the defendant agrees to enter a guilty plea (or, in some cases, nolo contendere) and waives his or her right to a trial in return for a "benefit" from the prosecution. The Federal Rules of Criminal Procedure identify the types of plea bargains.

Charges. The prosecutor dismisses some of the charges against the defendant or charges the defendant with a less serious offense or offenses. This results in a less severe prison sentence, and the defendant avoids a conviction for a more serious offense.

Sentence recommendation. The prosecutor agrees not to oppose the defendant's request for a specific sentence with the understanding that the judge is free to impose whatever sentence he or she views as appropriate.

The American Bar Association Standards for Criminal Justice, Section 14-1.8 (3rd ed., 1997), lists four considerations that explain why it is good social policy for prosecutors to offer a benefit to defendants who plead guilty.

1. *Responsibility.* The guilty plea indicates that a defendant is taking responsibility for his or her actions and is expressing regret for the crime.

2. *Flexibility.* The guilty plea creates the opportunity for the judge to engage in creative sentencing alternatives such as drug treatment or probation.

3. *Victims.* The defendant's guilty plea avoids subjecting victims to the painful experience of a trial.

4. *Cooperation.* The defendant may agree to cooperate with the police or prosecutor in other investigations and prosecutions.

Plea bargaining also permits the prosecution to focus resources on those cases in which there is a strong public interest in bringing a defendant to trial or in which a defendant refuses to enter into a plea bargain. Critics, however, point to several troubling aspects of plea bargaining.

Disparity. Defendants who plead guilty typically receive less severe sentences than defendants who are convicted at trial. The result is that individuals are perceived to be punished for exercising the constitutional right to a public trial. There also may be a disparity between the sentences handed out to individuals who enter into plea bargains. This means that the penalty that is imposed on individuals as a result of the plea-bargaining process may not fit the crime.

Innocent defendants. There is a risk that innocent individuals will plead guilty to avoid the uncertainty of trial.

Administrative convenience. A defense lawyer may persuade a defendant to bargain because the lawyer wants to avoid taking the time to prepare the case for a criminal trial. There also is the temptation for defense lawyers to persuade clients to plead guilty in an effort to maintain a good working relationship with the prosecutor's office in hopes of being offered attractive bargains in future cases.

Plea bargaining has been successfully eliminated in Alaska and in some counties in Arizona, Iowa, Louisiana, Michigan, Oregon, and Texas.

The U.S. Supreme Court has upheld the constitutionality of plea bargains entered into by defendants and by prosecutors who are seeking the "mutuality of advantage" of avoiding trial. The Court noted that the Constitution does not prohibit a defendant from waiving his or her rights when motivated by a "desire to accept the certainty or probability of a lesser penalty rather than face a wider range of possibilities extending from acquittal to conviction and a higher penalty authorized by law for the crime charged" (*Brady v. United States*, 397 U.S. 742, 751–752 [1970]). In *Santobello v. New York*, the U.S. Supreme Court observed that plea bargaining is "essential to the administration of justice," and "[p]roperly administered, it is to be encouraged" (*Santobello v. New York*, 404 U.S. 257, 260 [1971]).

There are a number of steps that must be satisfied as a condition for a court's accepting a guilty plea. In *Brady v. United States*, the U.S. Supreme Court held that "[w]aivers of constitutional rights not only must be voluntary but must be knowing, intelligent acts done with sufficient awareness of the relevant circumstances and likely consequences" (*Brady v. United States*, 397 U.S. 742, 748 [1970]). The Court ruled that it is unconstitutional for a judge to accept a guilty plea without an affirmative statement by a defendant indicating that he or she has met the constitutional standard for waiver (*Boykin v. United States*, 395 U.S. 238, 242 [1969]).

The constitutional standard is fully articulated in Rule 11 of the Federal Rules of Criminal Procedure. Rule 11 requires that before accepting a plea of guilty or a plea of nolo contendere, the judge must address the defendant personally in open court and ensure that the defendant understands the consequences of a guilty plea. The judge is required to cover the following points.

Nature of the criminal charges. The judge is required to explain the charges to which the defendant is pleading guilty and the possible criminal sentence (*McCarthy v. United States*, 394 U.S. 454, 467 [1969]). In *Henderson v. Morgan*, the Supreme Court held that Morgan's guilty plea to second-degree murder was not an intelligent and voluntary admission of guilt because the court never explained to Morgan that second-degree murder required a specific intent to kill and Morgan's guilty plea to second-degree murder was inconsistent with his statement that he had not intended to kill the victim (*Henderson v. Morgan*, 426 U.S. 637 [1976]).

Factual basis of the plea. The judge should explain how the specific facts of the defendant's case fit the requirements of the criminal charge to which the defendant is pleading guilty. This is intended to ensure that the defendant does not plead guilty to a criminal charge that does not fit the facts of the case. In *North Carolina v. Alford*, Henry Alford was indicted for first-degree murder and pled guilty to second-degree murder in order to avoid the possibility of receiving the death penalty. Alford insisted that he was innocent but was sentenced to thirty years in prison. The U.S. Supreme Court held that the trial court judge had properly accepted Alford's guilty plea in light of the "strong factual" support from witnesses that Alford had killed the victim (*North Carolina v. Alford*, 400 U.S. 25 [1970]).

Voluntary. Courts may not accept a plea of guilty without first determining that the plea is voluntary and is not the result of force or threats or of promises that are not explicitly set forth in the plea bargain. A prosecutor who offers a defendant a choice between alternatives that the defendant is free to accept or to reject is not considered to have coerced a guilty plea. In *Bordenkircher v. Hayes,* Paul Lewis Hayes was indicted for attempting to cash a forged check in the amount of $88.30, an offense punishable by a term of two to ten years in prison. The prosecutor offered to recommend a sentence of five years in prison in exchange for Hayes pleading guilty. He warned that in the event that Hayes refused to plead guilty and save the court the inconvenience and necessity of a trial, he would return to the grand jury and seek an indictment under the Kentucky Habitual Criminal Act based on Hayes's two prior felony convictions. Hayes chose to stand trial and was sentenced under the habitual offender law to life in prison. Hayes contended that the prosecutor had acted vindictively in an effort to force him to plead guilty. The U.S. Supreme Court held that the "course of conduct engaged in by the prosecutor . . . which no more than openly presented the defendant with the unpleasant alternatives of forgoing trial or facing charges on which he was plainly subject to prosecution, did not violate the Due Process Clause of the Fourteenth Amendment" (*Bordenkircher v. Hayes,* 434 U.S. 357, 365 [1978]).

The trial court judge also is required to inform the defendant that a guilty plea will result in the waiver of a defendant's right to raise constitutional violations committed prior to the entry of the plea. This includes challenges based on the lawfulness of arrest, unlawful searches and seizures, coerced confessions, denial of a speedy trial, and entrapment.

In recent decisions, the U.S. Supreme Court has taken the first steps toward setting constitutionally required standards to be followed by defense attorneys in the plea-negotiating process (*Missouri v. Frye,* 566 U.S. __ [2012]; *Lafler v. Cooper,* 566 U.S. __ [2012]).

■ JURY SELECTION

Following the pretrial motions, the case proceeds to trial. A criminal defendant confronting a charge that may result in incarceration has a constitutional right to have his or her guilt or innocence decided by a jury of his or her peers. A defendant my waive this right and have the case heard by a judge. In those instances in which the criminal charge does not carry a penalty of incarceration, the defendant is not entitled to a jury trial (*Duncan v. Louisiana,* 391 U.S. 145 [1968]). Assuming the defendant wants a jury trial, the next step is the selection of the jury.

The jury pool, or **venire** (i.e., master list or jury list), from which a petit panel is selected typically is based on names drawn from voter registration lists, lists of taxpayers, or lists of licensed drivers over 18 years of age. Several states continue to rely on the key-man system. Under the key-man system, the individuals who serve on juries are drawn from a master list compiled by community notables. Individuals who are to serve on juries typically receive a summons directing them to appear at a designated time and place for jury service. In most jurisdictions, individuals will be asked to complete an information form that will help to determine their eligibility for jury service.

The federal Jury Selection and Service Act of 1968, 28 U.S.C. §§ 1861–1862, 1865–1867, regulates the selection of grand juries and petit juries in the federal courts. Most state statutes follow this federal statute in proclaiming that all eligible individuals are to have the opportunity to be considered for jury service and have the obligation to serve when summoned for service. Several principles guide selection of the jury pool. The jury pool in the federal courts is drawn from the district in which the crime is committed, and within states, the jury pool is drawn from the geographic area in which the crime is committed. The following are some other basic guidelines for the selection of the jury venire.

- *Random selection.* Individuals are to be selected in a random fashion.
- *Discrimination.* Individuals shall not be excluded from service based on race, color, religion, sex, national origin, or economic status.
- *Fair cross section.* The individuals who are called to serve on the jury should reflect a fair cross section of the community.
- *Exemption.* Various individuals are ineligible to serve on a petit jury. This includes noncitizens; individuals less than 18 years of age; individuals who are unable to read, write, and understand or speak English; individuals whose mental or physical condition prevents their service; and convicted felons. Various states exempt law enforcement officers, firefighters, and other individuals who serve a vital public function. Individuals may be temporarily excused as a result of illness or personal obligations.

Individuals who are called for jury service appear at the courthouse and are randomly assigned to courtrooms. The questioning of individuals to determine who is to serve on the jury is called *voir dire,* or "to speak the truth." The prosecutor and defense attorney may remove individuals from the jury pool based on a **peremptory challenge** (without offering a reason) or based on a **challenge for cause** (based on bias or prejudice). A lawyer is not required to offer a reason for exercising a peremptory challenge. A challenge for cause requires a reason. The grounds for a challenge for cause typically are stated in a statute. This ordinarily includes a prohibition against individuals serving on the jury who sat on the grand jury, who are acquainted with an individual involved in the case, or who are related to an individual in the case. A defense attorney or prosecutor also may strike an individual for cause when the lawyer satisfies the judge that the individual cannot be fair (actual bias) or when an individual's background or experience indicates that he or she likely will not be impartial (implied bias). An example of actual bias is an individual who states on *voir dire* that he or she cannot be fair to a defendant. Implied bias may arise in a criminal case when a potential juror recently has been the victim of the same crime with which the defendant is charged.

The Equal Protection Clause of the Fourteenth Amendment provides that "[n]o State shall . . . deny to any person within its jurisdiction the equal protection of the law." The U.S. Supreme Court has interpreted the Equal Protection Clause as prohibiting the intentional exclusion of individuals from jury service because of their race, ethnicity, gender, or religion. In *Strauder v. West Virginia,* the Supreme Court held a statute unconstitutional that limited jury service to "white male persons." The Court, however, also held that the diversity of the American population made it unrealistic to obligate the state to take affirmative steps to ensure that each jury is composed of members of various racial, religious, ethnic, and gender groups (*Strauder v. West Virginia,* 100 U.S. 303 [1879]). In 1881, the Supreme Court held that the Equal Protection Clause was violated by a Delaware County jury-selection system that, although not listing race as a criterion for jury service, was administered in a discriminatory fashion and resulted in only Caucasian citizens being called to serve on local juries (*Neal v. Delaware,* 143 U.S. 370 [1881]).

The Court, in *Glasser v. United States,* held that the Sixth Amendment requires that a federal jury be drawn from a fair cross section of the community in which a crime has been committed (*Glasser v. United States,* 315 U.S. 60 [1942]). The federal Jury Selection and Service Act of 1968, 28 U.S.C. §§ 1861–1869, repeats the requirement that a jury is to be drawn from a "fair cross-section of the community."

The fact that a jury pool is created in a nondiscriminatory fashion and reflects a cross section of the community does not guarantee that every member of the venire is willing and able to fairly and objectively weigh and balance the evidence at trial. The Supreme Court has recognized that voir dire is of the utmost importance in ensuring the protection of a criminal defendant's Sixth Amendment right to an impartial jury. The voir dire involves questioning the potential jurors to determine whether they should be excluded for cause or whether the lawyer should exercise a peremptory challenge and exclude the juror "without cause." Keep in mind that lawyers also use voir dire to establish a personal connection with potential jurors who will be asked to weigh and to evaluate the evidence presented by the lawyer during the trial.

Rule 24 of the Federal Rules of Criminal Procedure provides that a judge may examine prospective jurors or may permit the lawyers to conduct the voir dire. In the event that the judge conducts the voir dire, he or she may permit the lawyers to ask additional questions or to submit questions. States adopt various approaches to the role of judges and lawyers during voir dire. It is argued that lawyers are so concerned about the impartiality of jurors that they ask more questions than is necessary and consume valuable time selecting the jury. Lawyers, on the other hand, typically argue that judges do not take the time required to fully explore a potential juror's background and attitudes.

The courts, other than in cases in which race or ethnicity is a prominent part of a trial, have established very few legal rules regarding the questions that may be asked on voir dire. This is based on the belief that the trial court judge is in the best position to evaluate the questions that are required to reveal whether a juror is fair and impartial and that the lawyers or judge should be free to ask whatever questions the judge believes will be helpful in revealing the jurors' attitudes and beliefs.

The selection of jurors in death penalty cases has been of particular concern to the U.S. Supreme Court. The jury first determines whether an individual is guilty or not guilty of the criminal charge. The next step is the sentencing phase at which the jury determines whether to impose a sentence of death or to impose a sentence of life imprisonment. The Court has held that potential jurors may be excluded *for cause* who during voir dire state that they are unwilling to vote for the death penalty. These jurors, according to the Supreme Court, have indicated that they are unwilling to follow the judge's instructions to impose capital punishment in those cases in which the statutory standard is satisfied (*Witherspoon v. Illinois,* 391 U.S. 510 [1968]). The Supreme Court later broadened the grounds for excluding jurors for cause and authorized the exclusion of individuals whose views would "prevent or substantially impair" their willingness to impose capital punishment (*Wainwright v. Witt,* 469 U.S. 412 [1985]).

The exclusion of individuals who state that they are unwilling to impose the death penalty is only one example of the exclusion of individuals for cause. The thinking is that a juror who has his or her "mind made up" cannot fairly and impartially weigh the evidence, should not serve on the jury, and should be struck for cause. In other cases, an once jury has sworn, double jeopardy attaches

individual's background and personal relationships may lead a judge to agree with a lawyer that a potential juror cannot be fair. This may arise when an individual is married to a police officer, has a child who is a police officer, or has been the victim of the same crime with which the defendant is charged. Once individuals have been removed for cause, the lawyers may exercise their peremptory challenges. A peremptory challenge is a challenge that is "exercised without a reason stated, without inquiry, and without being subject to the court's control." Peremptory challenges, although not required by the U.S. Constitution, historically have been considered fundamental to a fair trial and "one of the most important of the rights secured to the accused" (*Swain v. Alabama,* 380 U.S. 202, 219, 220 [1965]).

Rule 24(b) of the Federal Rules of Criminal Procedure provides both the prosecution and the defense with twenty peremptory challenges in a death-penalty case. In a trial for an offense punishable by imprisonment for more than one year, the government may exercise six peremptory challenges, and the defendant or defendants may exercise ten peremptory challenges. The defense and prosecution each are provided with three peremptory challenges in the case of an offense punishable by no more than one year in jail, by a fine, or both. State statutes and state rules of procedure generally provide both the defense and the prosecution with an equal number of peremptory challenges. Why are peremptory challenges viewed as essential to a fair trial?

Impartial trial. Both the defense and prosecution should be permitted to exclude people who they believe will be unfair despite the fact that they cannot point to specific facts and circumstances to support this conclusion. Peremptory challenges also promote the perception that the jury is fair.

Voir dire. A lawyer or judge may closely question a juror who, in the end, is not excluded for cause. This may lead the juror to become irritated or frustrated, and the lawyer may conclude that the best course is to remove the individual from the jury panel.

Judges historically placed very few limitations on peremptory challenges by lawyers. In 1965, in *Swain v. Alabama,* Robert Swain challenged the selection of the jury in Talladega County, Alabama, that sentenced him to death. He alleged that peremptory challenges had been used in the county to exclude every African American called for jury service since 1950. The Supreme Court held that lawyers were free to exclude jurors based on race, religion, gender, ethnicity, or hair or eye color. The belief was that a lawyer had the right to act in the "best interest" of his or her client and that the lawyer properly may conclude that minorities would be unsympathetic to his or her client and exclude them from the jury. The only limitation was that the Equal Protection Clause prohibited excluding jurors based on an intent to discriminate on account of race, gender, or ethnicity. In the case of Talladega County, there simply was not enough information to determine the reason for excluding African Americans from jury service. Do you agree with the decision in *Swain* that the Equal Protection Clause does not prohibit a prosecutor from relying on peremptory challenges to strike African Americans or Hispanics from a jury? (*Swain v. Alabama,* 380 U.S. 202 [1965]).

In 1986, in *Batson v. Kentucky,* the Supreme Court reconsidered its decision in *Swain* and changed course. In *Batson,* the prosecutor used his peremptory challenges to remove all four African Americans from the jury venire, and Batson was convicted by an "all-white jury" of second-degree burglary and of receipt of stolen goods. The Supreme Court held that the Equal Protection Clause prohibits a prosecutor from challenging potential jurors "solely on account of their race . . . on the assumption that black jurors as a group will be unable to impartially consider the State's case against a black defendant." In other words, a peremptory challenge must be based on a factor other than race, and a lawyer may not exclude potential jurors on account of their race (*Batson v. Kentucky,* 476 U.S. 79 [1986]).

In 1994, in *J.E.B. v. Alabama ex rel.,* the Supreme Court held that lawyers are prohibited from using peremptory challenges to exclude jurors based on gender. The Court reasoned that the Equal Protection Clause "prohibits discrimination in jury selection on the basis of gender . . . on the assumption that an individual will be biased in a particular case for no reason other than the fact that the person happens to be a woman or happens to be a man." As with race, the "core guarantee of equal protection ensuring citizens that their State will not discriminate . . . would be meaningless were we to approve the exclusion of jurors on the basis of such assumptions, which arise solely from the jurors' gender" (*J.E.B. v. Alabama ex rel.,* 511 U.S. 127, 146 [1994]).

In 2005, in *Miller-El v. Dretke,* the Supreme Court majority concluded that African American jurors in Dallas, Texas, had been improperly challenged by prosecutors and removed from juries based on their race. On two occasions, the prosecution rearranged the order of voire dire to avoid questioning African Americans. A majority of African Americans and only 3 percent of "nonblack" jurors were read a graphic account of the death penalty meant to "induce qualms" about it before being questioned on their opinion of capital punishment. One hundred percent of African Americans and 27 percent of "nonblacks" were asked what the Court majority termed a "trick question" intended to "induce" them to make a "disqualifying response." The Court majority concluded that "the prosecutors took their cues from a 20-year old [Dallas, Texas] manual of tips on jury selection," which provided suggestions on how to limit the participation of African Americans on juries. By the time the jury was selected in *Miller-El,* the prosecutors had "peremptorily challenged 12% of qualified nonblack panel members, but eliminated 91% of the black ones" (*Miller-El v. Dretke*, 543 U.S. 231 [2005]).

Once the jury is selected, the jurors take an oath to decide the case fairly in accordance with the evidence presented in court. The jurors are reminded not to speak to any other individual about the case and that they are prohibited from engaging in independent investigation of the case. The judge reminds the jury that they are the finders of fact and that the case is to be decided in accordance with the law as given to them by the judge.

■ THE TRIAL

The criminal trial, although only involving roughly 10 percent of cases, affirms that we live in a society that functions in accordance with the rule of law. Individuals accused of crimes will be prosecuted in open court in a fair fashion and will not be arbitrarily and unfairly incarcerated. The trial typically involves the following steps.

Opening statements →defense can waive opening statement

Prosecution's case-in-chief

Defense's case-in-chief

Prosecution's rebuttal

Defendant's surrebuttal

*only evidence comes from witness stand

Closing arguments

Jury instruction

Jury deliberations

Jury unanimity

Verdict

Opening Statements

>not evidence, just what the jury will expect to hear.

Following the judge's preliminary instructions to the jurors, the defense attorney and the prosecutor can address the jury in their *opening statements*. An **opening statement** provides a road map of a lawyer's case. Each attorney will tell the jury about the witnesses he or she plans to present and about the evidence that the witnesses will present. The lawyer will explain how this evidence supports the defendant's guilt or the defendant's innocence. The opening statement is particularly important in complicated cases in which the jury needs to connect complicated evidence.

The judge will inform the jury that the lawyers' opening statements are not to be considered as evidence in the case. Evidence is presented by witnesses testifying under oath at trial. These statements only introduce the type of evidence that the lawyers plan to introduce in the case. There are strict limitations on the opening statements. Judges will interrupt an opening statement to remind a lawyer that an opening statement is intended to be a description of the evidence to be introduced and is not meant to be used to argue or to persuade the jurors. A lawyer could not attack an adverse witness and denounce him or her as a liar. On the other hand, a skilled lawyer may note that he or she plans to present a witness who will testify that the defendant was playing poker at the time of the murder and could not possibly have shot the victim.

The prosecutor customarily gives the first opening statement followed by the defense attorney. The defense has the option of giving an opening statement, delaying its statement until after the prosecution has concluded the presentation of its case, or waiving an opening statement. Lawyers generally believe an opening statement is important in shaping the jurors' initial perception of the case. There is an argument for delaying the opening statement until the prosecution has presented its case. This allows the defense attorney to tailor its opening statement to the prosecution's case and to wait to reveal his or her defenses. On the other hand, the lawyer runs the risk that the jurors already have accepted the prosecution's version of the facts.

Lawyers are allowed to use charts, diagrams, and other visual aids during the opening statement to help in conveying their story of the case.

Prosecution's Case-in-Chief →convict beyond reasonable doubt →show they committed crime

The prosecution presents its case followed by the defense rebuttal. Each prosecution witness will be given an oath and testify on the witness stand in response to the questions asked by the prosecutor. In other words, testimony proceeds through questions and answers. The prosecutor's questions during the prosecution's case-in-chief are termed **direct examination**.

Questions are required to be relevant or directly related to the case. The prosecutor may not ask a **leading question** or questions that suggest an answer to the witness. The prosecutor may ask a witness, "Who was with you at the time of the robbery?" but may not ask, "Now you were with your friends Bill and Bob at the time of the robbery, were you not?"

Federal and state rules of evidence recognize that there are situations in which a leading question is permitted on direct examination. Examples are when the lawyer is examining children, experts, or mentally challenged individuals or when examining a hostile witness. A *hostile witness* "in fact" is a witness who is resistant or uncooperative. A hostile witness "in law" is a witness who identifies with the adverse party such as the widow of an individual allegedly to have been killed by the defendant.

The examination of a witness typically entails a series of questions that ask for a short and precise answer. A **narrative question** that asks a witness to "tell me what happened on the day of the robbery" is not permitted because it leads to incoherent answers that are difficult to follow and to understand. A lawyer as a practical matter should avoid asking narrative questions because of the risk that the witness will offer a disjointed response, not provide the desired information, or contradict him- or herself. Lawyers also may not ask an **argumentative question** that intimidates or harasses a witness. An example of an argumentative question would be to ask, "Isn't it true you, Bill, and Bob stood on the corner with the specific intent to commit a robbery, and isn't it true that you were prepared to kill if necessary?" The thinking is that a witness who testifies should not be treated in a rude or hostile manner and that questions can be asked in a polite though assertive manner.

The defense attorney may object to the questions being asked by the prosecutor. Objections pursuant to the contemporaneous objection rule are to be made to the judge immediately after the question is asked and before the witness has the opportunity to answer.

The Contemporaneous Objection Rule

The **contemporaneous objection rule** allows the judge to decide whether a question is permissible before the jury hears the witness's answer. The lawyer who makes the objection is required to state the precise legal rule that makes the question improper (e.g., as leading). The lawyer who asked the question may be given the opportunity to explain why the question is permissible before the judge makes his or her ruling. The judge may find the question proper and state that the "objection is overruled" and instruct the witness to answer the question. In the alternative, the judge may find the question improper and hold that the "objection is sustained." The witness will be instructed not to answer the question. A creative lawyer after an objection is sustained will modify the question so as to comply with the rules of evidence.

Evidence is introduced by calling witnesses to testify on the stand. Physical evidence is introduced by a witness who testifies where the object was found and that the "chain of evidence" was followed. This ensures that the object to be introduced is the same object found at the crime scene and was not altered or modified. For example, the witness will testify about the steps followed to protect the integrity of a knife found next to the victim's body. This is referred to as *laying the foundation,* which will be discussed later in the text. Once it is established that the object is relevant to the case and authenticated (it has not been modified), it is given an identification number or letter. Items introduced by one side typically are given numbers, and objects introduced by the other side are given letters. The knife in our example may be marked "People's Exhibit 1" and subsequent objects introduced into evidence will receive the next applicable numbers. The defense later may introduce blood type evidence indicating that the defendant was not at the crime scene. The blood evidence will be marked "Defense Exhibit A," and subsequent items will be designated by other letters.

Cross-Examination

The Sixth Amendment right to confront witnesses is interpreted to mean that a defendant has the right to be present and to confront the witnesses who testify against him or her. Following the prosecution's questioning of a witness, the Sixth Amendment Confrontation Clause gives the defendant the constitutional right to cross-examine the witness. Cross-examination is limited to topics covered on direct examination.

Cross-examination may involve questions about the witness's statements on direct examination. This may involve asking a witness who stated he or she was drinking about how much alcohol he or she consumed (follow-up questions). In a situation in which the defendant is relying on self-defense, the witness may be asked on cross-examination about questions not asked on direct examination. A defendant who is relying on self-defense may be asked on cross-examination whether he or she initiated the physical confrontation with the victim.

Another purpose of cross-examination may be to demonstrate that the witness should not be believed by the jury. This is called *impeachment*, which is discussed later in the text.

Impeachment may involve:

- *Inconsistent statements.* Demonstrating that the witness has made statements in the past that contradict his or her testimony.
- *Dishonesty.* Calling other witnesses who testify about the witness's reputation for a lack of honesty or conviction of a crime of dishonesty.

The attorney who called the witness originally now has the opportunity to ask the witness more questions. This is known as **redirect examination**. The attorney may attempt to demonstrate that the witness should be believed. This is termed **rehabilitation** of the witness. Redirect examination also is used to clarify the witness's testimony on cross-examination. The attorney, however, is not permitted to explore areas that were not covered on direct examination. At this point, the opposing counsel has the opportunity for *re-cross examination*. Re-cross examination is limited to questions intended to clarify the witness's testimony during redirect examination. Neither redirect nor re-cross examination is required and may be waived by the lawyers.

The prosecutor now continues with his or her case. The prosecutor will call witnesses who are examined on direct examination and cross-examined by the defense attorney. The prosecutor will continue to call witnesses until he or she is satisfied that each element of the crime is established beyond a reasonable doubt. At the completion of direct examination, the prosecutor will "rest its case."

The defense attorney may file a motion for a **directed verdict** after the prosecution "rests its case." In a motion for a directed verdict, the defense attorney argues that the prosecution failed to prove an element of the offense and that the case should be dismissed without the defense counsel needing to present evidence of the defendant's innocence. Keep in mind that the prosecution has the burden of establishing the defendant's guilt beyond a reasonable doubt. These motions are rarely successful because to be successful the prosecution generally must have failed to put on any evidence to prove a criminal intent or a criminal act.

Defense's Case-in-Chief

The defense attorney and his or her client may decide not to call any witnesses and to rely on cross-examination of the prosecution to poke holes in the witness's testimony. The defense attorney may believe that the prosecution's case is weak and that it is unnecessary to rebut the prosecution's case. The defense attorney also may doubt the persuasiveness of the defense witnesses, including the defendant if he or she testifies, or may believe that their testimony will be weakened on impeachment.

Once the defense attorney calls witnesses, the defense attorney will examine them, and they will be subject to cross-examination by the prosecution. The defense may introduce character witnesses demonstrating that the defendant has a reputation for honesty or another relevant trait such as nonviolence. The hope is that the jury will believe that the defendant could not have committed the crime. Character witnesses may be cross-examined on the defendant's character and on their own credibility. The prosecution on *rebuttal* will have the opportunity to call witnesses attacking the defendant's character.

After the defense has called all its witnesses and they have been cross-examined, the defense rests.

Prosecution's Rebuttal and Defendant's Surrebuttal

The prosecution following the presentation of the defendant's **case-in-chief** is provided the opportunity to rebut any evidence that was presented in the defendant's case. The prosecution's **rebuttal** may not be used to strengthen the prosecution's case-in-chief; the purpose is to challenge the defendant's case. The defense, for example, may have raised a self-defense claim in its case-in-chief, and the prosecution's rebuttal is limited to challenging the evidence of self-defense. Rebuttal witnesses are subject to cross-examination by the defense. The defendant now may present evidence on **surrebuttal** (called *rejoinder* in some jurisdictions) refuting new evidence on the issue of self-defense introduced by the prosecution. These witnesses, in turn, are subject to cross-examination. The judge has the discretion to provide for additional rounds of rebuttal and surrebuttal.

Closing Arguments → not evidence, what they think the jury should have gotten at

Following the presentation of evidence by the prosecutor and the defense, the lawyers make their **closing arguments** (also referred to as summations). The prosecutor goes first, and the defense then replies. The prosecutor is permitted to respond to the defense. The thinking behind this arrangement is that the prosecutor bears the burden of proving guilt beyond a reasonable doubt and should be provided with the opportunity to rebut the defendant's closing arguments.

In *Herring v. New York,* U.S. Supreme Court Justice Potter Stewart noted that the closing argument is a vital part of the adversarial process because it permits both sides to submit their complete case to the jury (*Herring v. New York,* 422 U.S. 853 [1975]).

The prosecutor and defense attorney are expected to adhere to the same standard of conduct in their closing statements. Trial courts tend to be more concerned about the conduct of prosecutors, who possess a special responsibility as representatives of the government to ensure that their authority is exercised in a fair and just fashion and is not employed to abuse and to convict the innocent (*Berger v. United States,* 295 U.S. 78 [1935]). The U.S. Supreme Court has stressed that while the lawyers should be given significant freedom in making their closing arguments, these arguments may be limited to ensure that a trial is orderly and fair. Section 3.5 of the American Bar Association Standards for Criminal Justice (1980) sets forth several types of prohibited arguments:

can't ask jury to sit in the shoes → "imagine if it was you...."

- Intentional misstatement of evidence or misleading of the jury
- Arguments that are not supported by the evidence that was introduced at trial
- Expressions of personal beliefs or opinions in regard to the truth or falsity of the evidence or in regard to the defendant's guilt
- Reference to issues beyond the trial itself or speculation on the social consequences of a conviction or of an acquittal
- Appeals that are calculated to inflame emotions and prejudices
- Comments that draw negative inferences from the defendant's assertion of his or her constitutional rights including a failure to testify or to consent to a search

The U.S. Supreme Court has recognized that in the heat of a trial, lawyers occasionally may breach these standards (*Dunlop v. United States,* 165 U.S. 486 [1897]). The Court has held that a prosecutor's argument violates due process in those instances that the argument "so infected the trial with unfairness as to make the resulting conviction a denial of due process" (*Donnelly v. DeChristoforo,* 416 U.S. 637 [1974]). In other words, courts require that the defense demonstrate that the remark likely prejudiced or had an impact on the verdict. Professors LaFave, Israel, and King (2004) list various factors that are considered by courts in evaluating the impact of a closing argument. This analysis is based on the totality of the circumstances and considers the following:

- Whether the remarks are particularly inflammatory or likely to incite the jury
- Whether the remarks are isolated or extensive
- Whether the remarks were provoked by the closing argument of the other side
- Whether the defense lawyer made an objection to the remarks thereby indicating a fear of prejudice
- Whether the trial court judge issued instructions to the jury in an effort to limit the prejudice
- Whether the remarks are combined with other errors at trial
- Whether there is overwhelming evidence of guilt

I don't need to know...

The **invited response** doctrine is used by courts to evaluate the impact of a prosecutor's remarks. In those cases in which the prosecutor's closing argument is a response to the arguments made by the defense attorney, courts are inclined to rule that the prosecutor's remarks were balanced by the defense lawyer's closing argument and were an effort to "right the scale" and thereby were not prejudicial to the defendant (*United States v. Young*, 470 U.S. 1 [1985]). Appellate courts increasingly have expressed frustration over the trend toward the abuse of the closing argument and have hinted that lawyers who persist in such conduct risk a suspension of their licenses to practice law (*United States v. Modica*, 663 F.2d 1173 [2d Cir. 1981]).

Courts rarely reverse a conviction based on a prosecutor's closing argument. In *Darden v. Wainwright*, the prosecutor in seeking the death penalty blamed the Department of Corrections in Florida for granting the defendant a weekend furlough and referred to him as an "animal" who should not have been permitted to leave his cell without a "leash." The prosecutor, in his closing argument, expressed regret that the victim had not been armed so that she could have "blown" the defendant's "face off." The prosecutor also stated he wished that when the defendant changed his appearance following the killing he had "cut his throat." The Supreme Court held that the prosecutor's argument did not "manipulate" or "misstate" the evidence, and the trial court judge had instructed the jurors that their decision should be made on the basis of the evidence. The weight of the evidence against the defendant was "heavy" and "overwhelming," and much of the "objectionable content" was "invited by or was responsive" to the defense attorney's summation (*Darden v. Wainwright*, 477 U.S. 168 [1986]).

Jury Instructions

The judge issues **jury instructions** before they begin to discuss the defendant's guilt or innocence. These instructions typically are given following the closing arguments, but the judge usually gives a copy of the instructions to the lawyers beforehand to enable them to refer to the instructions during their closing arguments. A judge's instructions usually include the following:

- The judge decides the law, and the jury is the finder of fact.
- The defendant is presumed innocent until proven guilty beyond a reasonable doubt.
- The burden is on the prosecution to establish guilt beyond a reasonable doubt.
- The jury is required to find each of the elements of the crime with which the defendant is charged beyond a reasonable doubt.
- The jury is told the procedures that are to be followed in deliberating the defendant's guilt or innocence.

In most jurisdictions, there are standard **pattern jury instructions** that a judge follows. The lawyers are permitted to ask the judge to submit particular instructions and may object to a judge's instructions and appeal the verdict in those instances in which the judge's instructions are alleged to be in error. Jury instructions are a controversial area. The instructions often are given in technical legal language. Studies indicate that jurors understandably have a difficult time fully understanding instructions in complex areas of criminal law such as insanity defense or white-collar crime.

Jury Deliberations →based on what they want to do

During the jury deliberations, jurors ordinarily are provided with copies of the charges and of the judge's jury instructions. The judge also may allow the jurors to view the exhibits that were introduced into evidence. Judges have the discretion to permit jurors to take notes during the trial and to bring the notes into the jury room during their deliberations. In most jurisdictions, the jury may ask to examine specific portions of the trial testimony. The jury, at the end of their deliberations, may return a verdict of guilty or not guilty and, where relevant, not guilty by reason of insanity.

I can't make a decision

In those instances in which a jury is unable to reach a verdict and is "deadlocked," the judge may order the jurors to deliberate for a reasonable period of time before dismissing the **hung jury.** The U.S. Supreme Court has approved of a trial court judge issuing a so-called *Allen* or **dynamite charge** when a jury is deadlocked. This charge is named after the judge's instruction in *Allen v. United States* in which the judge instructed the jury that if a significant number of jurors favor a conviction, the dissenting juror or jurors "ought to reconsider whether your doubt is a reasonable one." On the other hand, "if a majority or even a lesser number . . . favor . . . an acquittal, the rest of you should ask . . . whether you should accept the weight and sufficiency of evidence which fails to convince your fellow jurors beyond a reasonable doubt" (*Allen v. United States*, 164 U.S. 492 [1896]).

The next issue to be examined is jury decision-making on the verdict.

Jury Unanimity

The requirement that juries consist of twelve individuals became accepted practice in England in the fourteenth century. The origins of this rule are unclear, but it appears to be based on the notion that an individual should not be held criminally liable unless twelve of his or her neighbors are all persuaded of his or her guilt. The unanimity requirement, by the eighteenth century, had been firmly established as the practice in the American colonies and was subsequently enshrined in the Sixth Amendment to the U.S. Constitution.

In 1970, in *Williams v. Florida*, the Supreme Court held that the twelve-person requirement cannot be regarded as an indispensable component of the Sixth Amendment that is incorporated into the Due Process Clause of the Fourteenth Amendment. The Court held that Florida's six-person jury is able to perform the same functions as the common law twelve-person jury (*Williams v. Florida*, 399 U.S. 78 [1970]). Eight years later in *Ballew v. Georgia*, the Supreme Court concluded that a jury of fewer than six is less likely to represent the diversity of the community and is less likely to engage in vigorous debate and discussion than a six-person jury (Ballew v. Georgia, 435 U.S. 223 [1978]).

Today, forty-eight states follow the requirement in Rule 31 of the Federal Rules of Criminal Procedure and require that a "verdict shall be unanimous." In *Apodaca v. Oregon*, the U.S. Supreme Court held that the Sixth Amendment requirement of unanimity is not incorporated into the Fourteenth Amendment and upheld the constitutionality of an Oregon statute that provided that a verdict of guilty may be based on the vote of ten out of twelve jurors. Justice Byron White explained that permitting a conviction to be based on ten or eleven votes rather than on unanimity does not interfere with the jury's ability to reflect the "commonsense judgment of the community" and to safeguard the defendant against prosecutorial abuse. The Supreme Court also dismissed the notion that a conviction based on less than a unanimous verdict will allow the majority of jurors to disregard the views of "minority elements" and thereby undermine the requirement that the jury verdict reflect a cross section of the community. The Court noted that the Constitution requires that diverse groups be provided with the opportunity to be represented on juries and that there is no evidence that nonunanimous verdicts result in the views of "minority jurors" being ignored or overlooked (*Apodaca v. Oregon*, 406 U.S. 404 [1972]).

In *Johnson v. Louisiana*, decided the same day as *Apodaca*, the Supreme Court upheld a 9-to-3 guilty verdict in a robbery case. The Court rejected the contention that the fact that Johnson was convicted on a less-than-unanimous vote indicated that the jury had failed to find the defendant guilty beyond a reasonable doubt. The fact that three jurors did not agree with the majority did not establish the existence of reasonable doubt regarding the defendant's guilt, "particularly when such a heavy majority of the jury . . . remains convinced of guilt. That rational men disagree . . . is not . . . equivalent to a failure of proof . . . nor does it indicate infidelity to the reasonable doubt standard." Justice William O. Douglas, in his dissenting opinion, questioned whether due process permits states to apply a "watered-down" version of the Sixth Amendment and pointed out that research indicates that in roughly 10 percent of cases requiring a unanimous verdict, the minority of jurors succeed in changing the minds of the majority. Justice Douglas concluded that the decision in *Johnson* undermines an essential safeguard of individual freedom and liberty. Do you agree? (*Johnson v. Louisiana*, 406 U.S. 456, 361–362, 383, 387 [1972]).

The question remained at what point a majority vote is not sufficiently strong to meet the requirements of due process. Justice Harry Blackmun, for example, noted that a "system employing a 7–5 standard, rather than a 9–3 or a 75% minimum, would afford me the greatest difficulty" (366). In *Burch v. Louisiana*, the U.S. Supreme Court was confronted with a Louisiana statute that provided that misdemeanors punishable by imprisonment of more than six months are to be tried by a jury of six persons, five of whom "must concur to enter a verdict." The Court announced without a lengthy explanation that "lines must be drawn somewhere if the substance of the jury trial right is to be preserved" and that permitting six-person juries to reach nonunanimous verdicts threatens the ability of the jury to represent the community and to safeguard defendants. The Court noted that Louisiana was one of two states that permitted six-person juries to decide cases based on nonunanimous verdicts and that Louisiana's interest in saving time and money by providing for nonunanimous verdicts is outbalanced by the need to protect the constitutional role of the jury and due process of law (*Burch v. Louisiana*, 441 U.S. 130, 138–139 [1979]).

In some isolated instances, a jury may find that the prosecutor proved a defendant guilty beyond a reasonable doubt but nonetheless may refuse to return a guilty verdict. This situation may arise where the jury believes that a law is unfair or that it is unfair under the circumstances to convict a defendant. A jury's disregard of the law and decision to acquit a defendant is termed **jury nullification**.

Verdict

The jury notifies the judge when they have reached a verdict. The judge, lawyers, and defendant are all present in the courtroom and listen to the verdict. Each charge is read aloud, and the verdict on each charge is announced by the foreperson.

Following the verdict, the defense and prosecution may request that the judge poll the jury. This **jury poll** involves asking each juror whether he or she agrees with the verdict. In the event that the poll reveals that the jury in fact has failed to reach a verdict, the judge may order the jurors to continue their deliberations or may dismiss the jury. A defendant's ability to attack a jury verdict on the grounds of juror misconduct is limited by the fact that jurors are prohibited by law in most jurisdictions from testifying regarding jury deliberations. For example, the U.S. Supreme Court prohibited a defense attorney from interrogating jurors regarding the consumption of alcohol and unlawful narcotics during a trial (*Tanner v. United States*, 484 U.S. 107, 121 [1987]). There are two situations in which a juror may testify as to what occurred during jury deliberations:

1. *Prejudicial information.* Prejudicial information was improperly brought to the attention of a juror or jurors.

2. *Outside influences.* Outside influences and pressures were brought to bear on a juror.

The information must be demonstrated to have had an impact on the jury verdict.

■ THE JUDICIAL SENTENCING PROCESS

The judge in most jurisdictions is required to order a probation officer to conduct a presentence investigation and to compile a report. The **presentence report** contains information regarding the defendant, including his or her criminal record and financial condition and other circumstances that may influence the defendant's future behavior. The report addresses aggravating and mitigating circumstances, including the impact of the crime on the victim. The document concludes by providing the judge with the types of sentences that are available. A report typically is required in most jurisdictions in the cases of first offenders, for offenders under 21 years old, and for felonies. The judge in various jurisdictions may waive the report in the event that the trial record contains enough information on which to base the sentence. In the federal system and in most states, the defendant has a right to inspect the sentencing report to ensure accuracy. A defendant in a capital case has a constitutional right to inspect the presentence report (*Gardner v. Florida*, 430 U.S. 349 [1977]). Portions of the report that are considered sensitive may be withheld from the defendant. This includes information that might disrupt the defendant's rehabilitation program or lead to the physical harm of defendants or other persons as well as the name of and impact of the crime on a juvenile victim and information provided upon a promise of confidentiality (*Williams v. New York,* 337 U.S. 241 [1949]).

Following the preparation of the presentence report, the judge conducts a **sentencing hearing**. In 1967, in *Mempa v. Rhay* (389 U.S. 128 [1967]), the U.S. Supreme Court held that a sentencing hearing is a "critical stage" of the criminal justice process and that a defendant at this point in the process has a Sixth Amendment right to a lawyer. The lawyers are given the opportunity to describe aggravating or mitigating circumstances and to make arguments in support of one of the various sentencing alternatives that are available (e.g., probation as opposed to incarceration). The defendant also is provided the opportunity to make a statement. This is called the **right of allocution**. The U.S. Supreme Court has recognized that a defendant at sentencing may assert the right to remain silent and that no negative inference may be drawn from his or her silence (*Mitchell v. United States*, 526 U.S. 314 [1999]). The federal courts and most state courts also allow victim impact statements. The purpose is to provide the judge with information on the impact of the crime on the victim and the victim's family (*Payne v. Tennessee*, 501 U.S. 808 [1991]). The judge considers the presentence report and other relevant information and pronounces the sentence in open court. In the case of misdemeanors, sentences typically are announced immediately following the sentencing hearing. Felony sentencing typically is delayed until the judge has had the opportunity to consider all relevant information.

The judge in most jurisdictions is entitled to consider a broad range of information in setting the sentence (*Williams v. New York*, 337 U.S. 241 [1949]). For example, the Constitution protects the right of a defendant to testify truthfully (*United States v. Grayson*, 438 U.S. 41 [1978]), and a judge may consider the fact that a defendant testified falsely during the trial as indicating that the defendant possesses an antisocial attitude that will interfere with his or her rehabilitation. In some states, the judge is obligated to provide a written statement of the reasons for the sentence. Federal court judges are required to advise the defendant of his or her right to an appeal.

An individual convicted of multiple crimes may be given *consecutive sentences*, meaning that the sentences for each criminal act are served one after another. In the alternative, an individual may be subjected to *concurrent sentences*, meaning that the sentences for all criminal acts are served at the same time.

Governors and the president of the United States, in the case of federal offenses, may grant an offender **clemency**, resulting in a reduction of the individual's sentence or in the *commutation* of a death sentence to life in prison. A **pardon** exempts an individual from additional punishment. The U.S. Constitution, in Article II, Section 2, authorizes the president to pardon "offenses against the United States." Former Illinois governor George Ryan, in 2004, concluded that the problems in the administration of the death penalty risked the execution of an innocent, and he responded by pardoning four individuals on death row and commuting the sentences of over one hundred individuals on death row to life in prison.

In the next sections, we will examine two of the more important and controversial types of sentencing schemes: sentencing guidelines and determinate sentencing.

mandatory sentencing for certain charges

■ SENTENCING GUIDELINES AND THE ROLE OF THE JURY IN SENTENCING

At the turn of the twentieth century, most states and the federal government employed indeterminate sentencing. The legislature established the outer limits of sentences, and parole boards were provided with the authority to release individuals prior to the completion of their sentences in the event that they demonstrated that they had been rehabilitated. This approach is based on the belief that an individual who is incarcerated will be inspired to demonstrate that he or she no longer poses a threat to society and deserves an early release. Disillusionment with the notion of rehabilitation and the uncertain length and extreme variation in the time served by different offenders for similar crimes led to the introduction of determinate sentencing.

In 1980, Minnesota adopted **sentencing guidelines** in an effort to provide for uniform proportionate and predictable sentences. Currently over a dozen states employ guidelines. In 1984, the U.S. Congress responded to this movement by passing the Sentencing Reform Act. The law went into effect in 1987 and established the U.S. Sentencing Commission, which drafted binding guidelines to be followed by federal judges in sentencing offenders. The Sentencing Commission is composed of seven members appointed by the president with the approval of the U.S. Senate. At least three of the members must be federal judges. The Sentencing Commission monitors the impact of the guidelines on sentencing and proposes needed modifications (18 U.S.C. §§ 3531–3626, 28 U.S.C. §§ 991–998).

The Sentencing Reform Act abandoned rehabilitation as a primary purpose of imprisonment. The goals are retribution, deterrence, incapacitation, and the education and treatment of offenders. All sentences are determinate, and an offender's term of imprisonment may be reduced only by credit for good behavior earned while in custody.

Sentences under the federal guidelines are based on a complicated formula that reflects the seriousness and characteristics of the offense and the criminal history of the offender. The judge employs a sentencing grid and must sentence an offender within the narrow range where the offender's criminal offense and criminal history intersect. In formulating the appropriate sentence within the range authorized under the guidelines, a judge is to consider a number of factors, including the basic aims of sentencing and the need to avoid unwarranted disparities. The commission, in developing the guidelines, examined tens of thousands of sentencing decisions and enlisted the assistance of law enforcement.

Judges are required to document the reasons for criminal sentences and are obligated to provide a specific reason for an upward or downward departure from the sentence authorized by the guidelines. The prosecution may appeal a sentence below the presumed range, and the defense may appeal any sentence above the presumed range. The process of applying the guidelines can be incredibly complicated and may require a judge to undertake as many as seven separate steps. The federal guidelines also specify that a judge must approve plea bargains or negotiated agreements between defense and prosecuting attorneys to ensure that any sentence agreed upon is within the range established by the guidelines. The impact of the guidelines is difficult to measure, but studies suggest that the guidelines have increased the percentage of defendants who receive prison terms.

Several Supreme Court decisions have held that it is unconstitutional to enhance a sentence based on facts found to exist by the judge by a preponderance of the evidence (a probability) rather than by a jury beyond a reasonable doubt. According to the Supreme Court, excluding the jury from the fact-finding process constitutes a violation of a defendant's Sixth Amendment right to trial by a jury of his or her peers. The result is that any enhancement of a sentence is to be determined by the jury rather than by a judge. In *Apprendi v. New Jersey*, the U.S. Supreme Court explained that to

> guard against . . . oppression and tyranny on the part of rulers, and as the great bulwark of [our] . . . liberties, trial by jury has been understood to require that "the truth of every accusation . . . should . . . be confirmed by the unanimous suffrage of twelve of [the defendant's] equals and neighbors." (*Apprendi v. New Jersey*, 530 U.S. 466, 477 [2000])

In *Blakely v. Washington*, decided in 2004, Ralph Howard Blakely pled guilty to kidnapping his wife. The judge followed Washington's sentencing guidelines and determined that Blakely had acted with "deliberate cruelty" and imposed an "exceptional" sentence of ninety months rather than the standard sentence of fifty-three months. The U.S. Supreme Court ruled that a judge's sentence is required to be based on "the facts reflected in the jury verdict or admitted by the defendant" and that a judge may not enhance a sentence based on facts that a jury did not find beyond a reasonable doubt to exist (*Blakely v. Washington*, 542 U.S. 296 [2004]).

In *United States v. Booker*, the U.S. Supreme Court held that the enhancement of sentences by a judge under the Federal Sentencing Guidelines unconstitutionally deprives defendants of their right to have facts determined by a jury of their peers. Freddie Booker was convicted of possession with intent to distribute at least fifty grams of crack cocaine. His criminal history and the quantity of drugs in his possession required a sentence of between 210 and 262 months in prison. The judge, however, concluded that a preponderance of the evidence showed that

Booker had possessed an additional 556 grams of cocaine and that he also was guilty of obstructing justice. These findings required the judge to select a sentence of between 360 months and life, and the judge sentenced Booker to thirty years in prison. The Supreme Court ruled that the trial judge had acted unconstitutionally and explained that Booker, in effect, had been convicted of possessing a greater quantity of drugs than was charged in the indictment and that the determination of facts was a matter for the jury rather than for the judge.

Justice Stephen Breyer concluded that the best course under the circumstances was for judges to view the guidelines as advisory and to use their own judgment in sentencing a defendant. Why? An advisory system enables judges to formulate a sentence without consulting the jury. On the other hand, mandatory guidelines under the Supreme Court decisions require the jury to find each fact on which a sentence enhancement is based beyond a reasonable doubt. A judge under advisory guidelines is unrestricted by the guidelines, which merely constitute one factor among many to be considered by the judge (*United States v. Booker*, 543 U.S. 220 [2005]).

In summary, in the past several years, the U.S. Supreme Court has firmly established that federal and state sentencing guidelines are advisory rather than mandatory. An appellate court, in reviewing the sentence, is to ask whether the sentence is reasonable under the circumstances. In 2007, Justice Ruth Bader Ginsburg, in her majority opinion in *Kimbrough v. United States*, wrote that the guidelines, "formerly mandatory," now are "one of many factors" that a court may consider in establishing an appropriate sentence. The judge may determine in a particular case that a within-guidelines sentence is "greater than necessary" to serve the objectives of sentencing or, alternatively, that it is "less than is required." In other words, a judge should start by calculating the sentence under the guidelines and then may consider other factors that may justify departing from the sentence under the guidelines. Justice Ginsburg affirmed that reasonableness is the standard to be applied on appellate review (*Kimbrough v. United States*, 552 U.S. ___ [2007]). In 2009, in *Nelson v. United States*, the Supreme Court once again stressed that a sentencing court is not required to follow the guidelines. The Court stressed that the trial court should not presume that the guidelines provide the sentence that the defendant "reasonably" should receive. An appellate court in reviewing the sentence is to ask whether the sentence handed out by the trial court judge is "reasonable" (*Nelson v. United States*, 555 U.S. ___ [2009]).

The significance of recent developments is that the U.S. Supreme Court has resisted imposing a straightjacket on sentencing decisions and has returned sentencing decisions to the authority of judges. All sentences, whether inside or outside the guidelines, are to be reviewed by appellate courts based on whether they are "reasonable."

■ CRIMINAL APPEALS

The U.S. Supreme Court has followed the common law rule and has held that there is no due process right to a criminal appeal, and the decision as to whether to provide defendants a right to an appeal is a question to be decided by the legislative branch. Despite the fact that there is no requirement that an individual be provided any appeal whatsoever, various justices have expressed the belief that a defendant who is convicted of a crime should have the opportunity to have the judgment reviewed by an appellate court (*Ross v. Moffitt*, 417 U.S. 600, 609 [1974]). The consequences of a criminal conviction are too serious to have an individual's fate decided by a single judge and jury (*Jones v. Barnes*, 463 U.S. 745 [1983]). The federal government and all fifty states accordingly provide an appeal as a matter of right for a felony conviction. This appeal in most cases is to an intermediate appellate court. A discretionary appeal (optional) to a state supreme court also is available. An appeal of a conviction for a misdemeanor usually involves a new trial (trial *de novo*) before an intermediate court. A number of claims may be raised on the appeal of a felony conviction. These issues typically include one or more of the following:

- *Motion to suppress.* The trial court improperly permitted the prosecution at trial to introduce a coerced or involuntary confession or evidence seized as a result of an unlawful search.
- *Self-incrimination.* There was a violation of the defendant's right against self-incrimination.
- *Exonerating evidence.* The prosecutor failed to disclose exculpatory evidence to the defense.
- *Double jeopardy.* The defendant was previously tried for the same crime.
- *Speedy trial.* The defendant was not provided with a speedy trial.
- *Jury.* The petit jury selection process was discriminatory.
- *Judge.* The judge's instructions to the jury were wrong.

- *Defense attorney.* The defendant was represented by an ineffective counsel.
- *Prosecutor.* The judge improperly permitted the prosecutor to introduce prejudicial evidence at trial or to engage in an inflammatory closing argument to the jury.
- *Verdict.* The facts at trial were insufficient to establish the defendant's criminal conviction.

The U.S. Supreme Court has held that a defendant who files an appeal as a matter of right possesses various constitutional rights. In 1956, in *Griffin v. Illinois*, the Supreme Court held that although Illinois is not required to provide an appeal as a matter of right, once it has provided the opportunity for an appeal, it is required to provide a free transcript of the criminal trial to indigents to avoid discriminating against individuals based on their economic status (*Griffin v. Illinois*, 351 U.S. 12 [1956]). Seven years later, the Supreme Court condemned the denial of legal representation to an indigent defendant who had filed an appeal as a matter of right. The Court held that the equality of treatment required by the Fourteenth Amendment is lacking where the "rich man" enjoys the benefit of a lawyer and a "meaningful appeal" while the "indigent" is forced to "shift for himself" and has an appeal that is little more than a "meaningless ritual." The right to "effective legal representation" does not extend to the discretionary appeal (*Wainwright v. Torna*, 455 U.S. 585 [1982]). An individual who files a successful appeal also may not be subjected to a vindictive prosecution (more serious charges) on retrial or vindictive sentencing (a longer sentence) following a reconviction (*North Carolina v. Pearce*, 395 U.S. 711 [1969]). One limitation on an appeal is that courts will not review a case that is *moot*. An example is the death of a defendant that makes it unnecessary for an appellate court to decide an appeal.

May a defendant file an appeal at any point during the trial when he or she believes that the judge has committed an error? The **final judgment rule** provides that a defendant ordinarily may appeal only following a guilty verdict and sentencing. There are several reasons for the final judgment rule:

- *Respect.* An appeals court should not interfere with the trial process by deciding questions in the middle of the trial.
- *Delay.* An appeal during the trial will delay the proceedings.
- *Efficiency.* Delaying an appeal until the end of the trial allows the appeals court to issue a single judgment that addresses all of the errors alleged to have been committed at trial.

[handwritten: taken while the case is proceeding—before case goes to trial]

The federal and state courts recognize an **interlocutory appeal** exception. This is limited to issues that cannot be effectively corrected by waiting until the final judgment and do not affect the determination of a defendant's guilt or innocence at trial (*Cohen v. Beneficial Industrial Loan Corporation*, 337 U.S. 541 [1949]). The U.S. Supreme Court has recognized four situations in which a defendant may file an interlocutory appeal.

Bail. In *Stack v. Boyle*, the Court recognized that a defendant may appeal excessive bail. A judgment following trial that an individual has been subjected to excessive bail would not provide remedy for a defendant who has not met bail and who has been incarcerated for many months (*Stack v. Boyle*, 342 U.S. 1 [1951]).

Double jeopardy. The proscription against double jeopardy protects individuals against being convicted more than once for the same crime as well as being subjected to a second trial for the same crime. The defendant who is required to wait for a final judgment to appeal already would have been subjected to a second trial in violation of the right not to be subjected to double jeopardy (*Abney v. United States*, 431 U.S. 651 [1977]).

Competency. An individual who is to be forcibly medicated in order to be competent to stand trial may file an interlocutory appeal (*Sell v. United States*, 539 U.S. 166 [2003]).

Speech or Debate Clause. The Speech or Debate Clause of the U.S. Constitution protects a member of Congress from standing trial and being held legally responsible for statements made in Congress (*Helstoski v. Meanor*, 442 U.S. 500 [1979]).

The general rule is that in order to appeal, an individual must first raise an objection at trial. The reason for the "raise or waive" rule is that this provides the trial court judge with the opportunity to correct an error and to avoid a reversal of a trial verdict on appeal. A reversal may lead to a second trial and result in considerable time and expense. The federal courts and most state courts provide for a **plain error exception**. Federal Rule of Criminal Procedure 52(b) states that there are plain errors "affecting substantial rights" that may be reviewed by an appellate court though not raised in the trial court. The purpose of the plain error exception is to prevent a miscarriage of justice. The U.S. Supreme Court defined a plain error as a clear error under existing law that "affects substantial rights" and that "seriously affects the fairness, integrity, or public reputation of judicial proceedings" (*United States v. Olano*, 507 U.S. 725 [1993]; *Johnson v. United States*, 520 U.S. 461 [1997]). An example of plain error may be a prosecutor's inflammatory and potentially prejudicial closing argument to the jury (*United States v. Young*, 470 U.S. 1 [1985]).

What is the standard of review on appeal? The fact that the trial court committed an error does not necessarily mean that the verdict will be reversed. Trial errors are reviewed under a **harmless error** standard. The appellate court must be convinced "beyond a reasonable doubt that the error complained of did not contribute to the conviction obtained." In other words, is the court convinced that the error did not influence the jury's guilty verdict? In *Chapman v. California*, the U.S. Supreme Court concluded that it was "impossible" to conclude beyond a reasonable doubt that the prosecutor's and trial judge's comments to the jury that they could infer that the defendant was guilty from the fact the defendant did not take the stand in his or her own defense "did not contribute to petitioner's convictions." In other words, this was "a case in which, absent the constitutionally forbidden comments, honest, fair-minded jurors might very well have brought in not-guilty verdicts" (*Chapman v. California*, 386 U.S. 18 [1967]).

The Supreme Court decision in *Chapman* recognized that there are some constitutional errors that are so serious that they cannot be considered harmless under any circumstances. The **automatic reversal rule** is limited to what the Supreme Court has described as "structural defects" that are fundamental to a fair trial. These constitutional errors are restricted to a "very limited class of cases" and include the denial of a lawyer at trial, a biased judge, racial discrimination in the selection of a jury, a rejection of the right to self-representation, denial of a public trial, inaccurate reasonable-doubt instruction to a jury, denial of a speedy trial, and a violation of double jeopardy (*Neder v. United States*, 527 U.S. 1 [1999]).

The Supreme Court has been concerned that permitting prosecutors to appeal will subject defendants to costly and lengthy appeals and may violate the defendants' rights against double jeopardy. The Double Jeopardy Clause was thought to prohibit appeals by the prosecution until the Supreme Court held in 1892 that the Congress and state legislatures might provide for limited categories of government appeals (*United States v. Sanges*, 354 U.S. 394 [1892]). Federal and state statutes accordingly recognize a narrow set of instances in which the prosecutor may file an appeal. The U.S. Supreme Court has characterized these situations as "something unusual, exceptional," and "not favored" (*Carroll v. United States*, 354 U.S. 394, 400 [1957]). For example, a prosecutor may file an interlocutory appeal contesting a pretrial order to suppress evidence and to exclude the evidence from trial. The reason is that at this point, the defendant's double jeopardy rights have not yet "attached," and the Double Jeopardy Clause would prohibit a second trial if the appeal were taken after the case proceeded to trial and the defendant was acquitted. The prohibition on a second trial would be particularly harmful in those instances in which the trial judge's exclusion of the evidence has resulted in the acquittal of a defendant who should have been convicted (18 U.S.C. § 3731).

The last issue in regard to criminal appeals is the **retroactivity of judicial decisions**. A U.S. Supreme Court ruling that breaks new constitutional ground, such as the right of a defendant to be represented at trial by a lawyer, applies to all other defendants with cases on appeal as well as to defendants whose cases are in "midstream," and to all cases that are brought to trial following the judgment. The reason for "retroactivity" is that the fact that a defendant's case was selected for review and that the appeal proved successful should not mean that this particular defendant should benefit while other defendants should not benefit from the decision (*Griffith v. Kentucky*, 479 U.S. 314 [1987]).

In the next section, we discuss *habeas corpus*. *Habeas* is a collateral remedy or an appeal that is available after a defendant has exhausted his or her direct state and federal appeals.

■ HABEAS CORPUS

State and federal judicial systems all provide for so-called **collateral remedies** or appeals that are available following the exhaustion of *direct appeals* or in some instances are available following a failure to take advantage of direct appeals. Federal ***habeas corpus*** review is the most important collateral remedy for both federal and state inmates.

An application for *habeas corpus* is a noncriminal (civil) lawsuit in which the defendant (now called the petitioner or plaintiff) asks the court for a writ on the grounds that he or she is being unlawfully detained. The writ of habeas corpus (literally "you have the body") is an order issued by a judge to a government official (usually the warden of a correctional institution) who has a person in custody to bring the person to court and to explain why the individual is in detention. In the event that the court finds that the plaintiff was unlawfully convicted or is being held without justification, the judge will order the individual released from custody.

The famous English jurist William Blackstone termed the writ of *habeas corpus* "the most celebrated writ in the English law." The "Great Writ of Liberty" has an important place in English and American history as a mechanism to protect individual rights. In 1677, in *Bushel's Case*, the writ was used to release Edward Bushel, a juror who was imprisoned for refusing to convict Quakers William Penn and William Mead for practicing their religion. In 1867, the U.S. Supreme Court held that President Abraham Lincoln improperly suspended *habeas corpus* without the approval of Congress and had unlawfully established military courts with jurisdiction over civilians (*Ex parte Milligan*, 71 U.S. 2 [1866]). In recent years, *habeas corpus* has been relied on by individuals who claim that they have been improperly detained as part of the "war on terror" (*Hamdi v. Rumsfeld*, 542 U.S. 507 [2004]).

The importance of the writ of *habeas corpus* is apparent from the fact that Article I, Section 9, Paragraph 2 of the U.S. Constitution provides that "[t]he Privilege of the Writ of Habeas Corpus shall not be suspended, unless when in Cases of Rebellion or Invasion the Public Safety may require it." In 1789, the First Judiciary Act authorized federal courts to grant writs of *habeas corpus* to federal prisoners. The Habeas Corpus Act of 1867 extended federal *habeas* review to state inmates. This law was intended to protect former African American slaves and northern activists who found themselves harassed by local law enforcement officials in the post–Civil War American South. In 1996, the U.S. Congress significantly limited the availability of *habeas corpus* in the Antiterrorism and Effective Death Penalty Act (AEDPA). This legislation was a response to the Oklahoma City terrorist bombing and was an effort to combat domestic terrorism by limiting the ability of individuals to challenge their death sentences. The basic language of the 1867 act was incorporated into the AEDPA, which authorizes federal courts to issue a writ of *habeas corpus* when a prisoner is in custody pursuant to the judgment of a state or federal court "in violation of the Constitution or laws or treaties of the United States" (28 U.S.C. §§ 2241–2266). An application for a writ of *habeas corpus* customarily is filed with the federal district court in which an individual is incarcerated or convicted. There is provision for an additional appeal to a court of appeals and a discretionary appeal to the U.S. Supreme Court. Keep in mind that in a *habeas* petition filed by a state prisoner, a federal court reviews the judgment of a state trial court and of state courts of appeals, including the state supreme court.

The writ of *habeas corpus* is a topic of intense debate among judges and legal commentators and is a complicated and technical area of the law that even most lawyers do not fully understand. The Warren Court (1953–1969) in the 1960s viewed the writ as a mechanism for federal courts to ensure that state courts protected the criminal procedural rights that the Court led by Earl Warren had incorporated into the Fourteenth Amendment. The next two chief justices, Warren Burger (1969–1986) and his successor, William Rehnquist (1986–2005), headed courts that adopted a more limited view of federal *habeas* review of state court judgments.

Fay v. Noia is the most frequently cited example of the Warren Court's view that *habeas* review is required to ensure that the constitutional rights of defendants are being protected by state courts. The U.S. Supreme Court ruled that Noia's failure to exhaust his appellate remedies in New York did not prevent federal courts from examining the voluntariness of his confession. Justice William Brennan wrote that the history of the writ of *habeas corpus* is

> inextricably intertwined with the growth of fundamental rights of personal liberty. . . . Its root principle is that, in a civilized society, government must always be accountable to the judiciary for a man's imprisonment: if the imprisonment cannot be shown to conform with the fundamental requirements of law, the individual is entitled to his immediate release. (*Fay v. Noia*, 372 U.S. 391, 401–402 [1963])

Brennan later stressed that "conventional notions of finality of litigation have no place where life or liberty is at stake and infringement of constitutional rights is alleged" (*Sanders v. United States*, 373 U.S. 1, 7 [1963]).

The majority of judges on the Burger and Rehnquist Courts questioned whether federal courts should actively intervene in state court decision-making. A particular concern was whether the federal courts should review a case like *Noia,* in which the defendant had not exhausted his state remedies.

The Supreme Court's desire to limit the growth of *habeas* is illustrated by the Court's judgment in 1976 in *Stone v. Powell*. The Court majority held that where a state has provided an opportunity for "full and fair litigation of a Fourth Amendment claim," the Constitution does not require federal *habeas corpus* relief on the grounds that evidence obtained from an unconstitutional search and seizure was introduced at the individual's trial. Justice Powell explained that the deterrent effect of the exclusionary rule is achieved by the threat that evidence will be excluded from trial and that little additional deterrent effect is provided by the possibility that the evidence will be excluded on *habeas* review. He argued that

> the view that the deterrence of Fourth Amendment violations would be furthered rests on the dubious assumption that law enforcement authorities would fear that federal *habeas* review might reveal flaws in a search or seizure that went undetected at trial and on appeal. Even if one rationally could assume that some additional incremental deterrent effect would be present in isolated cases, the resulting advance of the legitimate goal of furthering Fourth Amendment rights would be outweighed by the acknowledged costs to other values vital to a rational system of criminal justice. (*Stone v. Powell*, 428 U.S. 465, 493, 494 [1976])

The AEDPA and the U.S. Supreme Court in recent years have combined to restrict the access of state prisoners to federal *habeas corpus* review. In developing the law of *habeas corpus*, the Supreme Court has employed the familiar balancing approach, in which the Court has attempted to strike a balance between the interest in finality of judgments and respect for state judges ("comity") on the one hand and the protection of the rights of the accused on the other hand. The federal courts now play the role of "quality control" and review *habeas* petitions to ensure that the state trial and appeal courts provide defendants with a fair and reasonable consideration of their claims. Federal courts will intervene where there is clear evidence that the defendant's rights have been disregarded or where there is new evidence that the defendant is innocent.

The U.S. Supreme Court has recognized that *habeas corpus* may be relied on to remedy a number of constitutional violations. Various examples are listed below.

- *Evidence at trial.* A defendant was denied due process of law by being convicted based on insufficient evidence (*Jackson v. Virginia*, 443 U.S. 307 [1979]).
- *Confessions.* A defendant's conviction was based on statements obtained in violation of *Miranda v. Arizona* (*Withrow v. Williams*, 507 U.S. 680 [1993]).
- *Ineffective assistance of counsel.* Claims were made of racial discrimination in the selection of a grand jury (*Rose v. Mitchell*, 443 U.S. 545 [1979]).
- *Jury instructions.* Faulty jury instructions relieved the prosecution of proving elements of a crime or improperly placed the burden of proof on the defendant (*Engle v. Isaac*, 456 U.S. 152 [1982]; *United States v. Frady*, 456 U.S. 132 [1982]).
- *Prosecutorial misconduct.* It was alleged that prosecutors withheld exculpatory evidence or made prejudicial comments during the trial (*Kyles v. Whitley*, 514 U.S. 419 [1995]).
- *Actual innocence.* A defendant claims that newly discovered evidence supports his or her claim of "actual innocence" (*Schlup v. Delo*, 513 U.S. 298 [1995]).

In the U.S. Supreme Court's *habeas* rulings, the Court has attempted to balance the interests in finality of state court judgments and comity (respect) toward state court judges against the interest in ensuring that criminal convictions have not resulted from a disregard for constitutional rights. It certainly is the case that courts are overwhelmed with *habeas* petitions from imprisoned individuals, only a very small percentage of which result in an individual's release from prison. The Congressional Research Service, in 2006, reported that since 1997 an average of roughly 18,600 noncapital petitions were filed with federal courts, each of which required an average of five to seven months to consider. An average of 198 *habeas* petitions regarding capital punishment cases were filed each year. On the other hand, every judge would agree that there is an interest in reviewing claims of actual innocence based on new evidence.

In summary, *habeas corpus* historically has protected individuals against unfair and arbitrary criminal convictions. Federal courts employ *habeas* today to ensure that criminal convictions have not resulted from constitutional errors. *Habeas* also is available to review newly discovered or newly available evidence to guard against miscarriages of justice that result in the criminal conviction of the innocent. The question remains whether the benefits of *habeas* review are outweighed by the resources required to protect the rights of individuals.

CHAPTER SUMMARY

Following the first appearance, the next step typically is the preliminary hearing. The purpose of the preliminary hearing is to determine whether there is sufficient evidence to bind the defendant over for trial or, in the alternative, whether there is sufficient evidence to send the case to a grand jury. The preliminary hearing is conducted as a "mini-trial" in which the defendant has a right to be represented by a lawyer. The basic question is whether a crime was committed and whether the defendant committed the crime. Most states adhere to the probable cause standard, while a minority of jurisdictions adhere to the *prima facie* approach. A preliminary hearing is not constitutionally required.

The grand jury constitutes between sixteen and twenty-three persons who provide a check on the prosecutor and determine whether there is sufficient evidence to proceed to trial. At the conclusion of the grand jury's investigation, the grand jury may return a true bill and issue an indictment or refuse to indict and return a no bill, or the grand jury may decide to undertake an independent investigation of criminal activity and file a presentment, a report on criminal activity, with the court. The grand jury is, in theory, independent of prosecutors and judges but, in practice, possesses several powers that make it a particularly powerful arm of the prosecutor in investigating criminal activity.

Once the decision is made by the grand jury to indict an individual or by a preliminary hearing to bind a defendant over for trial, the next step is an arraignment. At the arraignment, a defendant is brought before a trial court judge and is informed of the charges filed against him or her and is asked to enter one of four possible pleas: guilty, not guilty, nolo contendere, or not guilty by reason of insanity.

Prior to trial, the defense attorney may file a number of pretrial motions including double jeopardy, speedy trial, venue, discovery, and motion to suppress.

Evidence seized in violation of the Fourth Amendment as well as unconstitutionally obtained confessions and identifications may be excluded from evidence.

The Sixth Amendment provides that "in all criminal prosecutions, the accused shall enjoy the right to a . . . public trial by an impartial jury." In 1968, in *Duncan v. Louisiana*, the U.S. Supreme Court held that the right of a jury trial in "serious criminal cases" is "fundamental to the American scheme of justice" and is protected under the Due Process Clause of the Fourteenth Amendment and "must therefore be respected by the States." The Court held that a jury trial is required for "serious crimes" that carry a sentence of more than six months. The federal government and a majority of states require twelve-person juries. In 1970, in *Williams v. Florida*, the U.S. Supreme Court reversed course and held that the twelve-person requirement is not an indispensable component of the Sixth Amendment as incorporated into the Due Process Clause of the Fourteenth Amendment. Eight years later, in *Ballew v. Georgia*, the Supreme Court held that Georgia could not constitutionally conduct criminal trials with juries of fewer than six persons.

The jury pool, or venire from which a petit panel is drawn, typically is based on names drawn from voter registration lists or lists of licensed drivers, and several states rely on the key-man system. Individuals in the jury venire are subject to *voir dire* and may be struck from the jury based on a challenge for cause or based on a peremptory challenge. The Fifth Amendment Equal Protection Clause prohibits intentional discrimination based on race, ethnicity, gender, or religion in the jury-selection process. The Sixth Amendment requires that a jury be drawn from a fair cross section of the community. Individuals may be excluded during *voir dire* for cause based on an inability to fairly and impartially weigh the evidence. A peremptory challenge is a challenge that is exercised "without a reason." In 1986, in *Batson v. Kentucky*, the U.S. Supreme Court held that the Equal Protection Clause prohibits a prosecutor from challenging potential jurors "solely on account of their race . . . on the assumption that black jurors as a group will be unable to impartially consider the State's case against a black defendant." In 1994, the U.S. Supreme Court held in *J.E.B. v. Alabama ex rel.* that lawyers also are prohibited from using peremptory challenges to exclude jurors based on gender. Judges with a conflict of interest should remove themselves from a case (or recuse themselves), and a defendant may file a motion requesting that a judge remove himself or herself from the case on the grounds that the judge is unable to be fair and impartial.

The criminal trial has a number of stages.

Opening statements. The lawyers may make brief opening statements.

Presentation of evidence. The prosecution presents the case-in-chief, and the defense responds with its case-in-chief. Witnesses may be cross-examined. The defendant has a Sixth Amendment right to confront the witnesses against him or her and to cross-examine these individuals.

Reasonable doubt. Each element of the offense must be established beyond a reasonable doubt, or by a "near certitude" of guilt.

Closing argument. The prosecution and the defense have the opportunity to summarize their cases.

Jury instructions. The judge instructs the jury on the law, and the jury must apply the law to the facts in deciding whether the defendant is guilty beyond a reasonable doubt.

Jury deliberations. The jury generally is permitted to examine a copy of the charges and the judge's instructions, and in most cases, the jurors may view items introduced into evidence. The U.S. Supreme Court has approved nonunanimous verdicts based on a 9-to-3 vote on the grounds that a "heavy majority" of the jury remains "convinced of guilt." The jury possesses the power of nullification: the ability to disregard the law and to acquit a defendant despite overwhelming evidence of guilt.

The vast majority of criminal cases do not reach trial and are disposed of by guilty pleas. These cases typically are plea-bargained. The U.S. Supreme Court has upheld this practice, although it has required that a guilty plea be knowing, intelligent, and voluntary.

The federal government and the states have initiated a major shift in their approach to sentencing. The historical commitment to indeterminate sentencing and to the rehabilitation of offenders has been replaced by an emphasis on deterrence, retribution, and incapacitation. This primarily involves presumptive sentencing guidelines and mandatory minimum sentences. Several recent U.S. Supreme Court cases have resulted in sentencing guidelines that are advisory rather than binding on judges. An appellate court is required to find only that a sentence, whether inside or outside the guidelines, is "reasonable."

The U.S. Supreme Court has followed the common law rule and has held that there is no due process right to a criminal appeal, and the decision whether to provide defendants a right to an appeal is to be decided by the legislative branch. The federal government and all fifty states provide an appeal as a matter of right for a felony conviction. This appeal in most cases is to an intermediate appellate court. A discretionary appeal (optional) to the U.S. Supreme Court and to state supreme courts also is available. An appeal of a conviction for a misdemeanor usually involves a new trial (trial *de novo*) before an intermediate court. A number of claims may be raised on the appeal of a felony conviction. These typically include issues such as the denial of a motion to suppress, a prejudicial process of jury selection, double jeopardy, ineffectiveness of counsel, and a judicial error in the instructions to the jury.

There are several points to keep in mind in regard to criminal appeals.

Interlocutory appeal. The federal and state courts recognize an interlocutory appeal exception in the case of issues that cannot be effectively corrected by waiting until the final judgment and that do not affect the determination of a defendant's guilt or innocence at trial.

Plain error rule. The general rule is that in order to file an appeal, an individual must first raise an objection at trial. The federal courts and most state courts recognize a plain error exception that allows appellate courts to review an error that was not raised in the trial court. The purpose of the plain error exception is to prevent a miscarriage of justice. The U.S. Supreme Court defined a plain error as a clear error under existing law that "affects substantial rights" and that "seriously affects the fairness, integrity, or public reputation of judicial proceedings."

Harmless error standard. Trial errors are reviewed under a harmless error standard. The appellate court asks whether the court is convinced "beyond a reasonable doubt that the error complained of did not contribute to the conviction obtained." The question is whether the court is convinced that the error did not influence the jury's guilty verdict.

Automatic reversal rule. The Supreme Court has recognized that there are some constitutional errors that are so serious that they cannot be considered harmless under any circumstances. The automatic reversal rule is limited to what the Supreme Court has described as "structural defects" that are fundamental to a fair trial. These constitutional errors are restricted to a "very limited class of cases" and include the denial of a lawyer at trial, a biased judge, racial discrimination in the selection of a jury, a rejection of the right to self-representation, denial of a public trial, inaccurate reasonable-doubt instruction to a jury, denial of a speedy trial, and violation of double jeopardy.

Retroactivity of judicial decisions. The last issue in regard to criminal appeals is the retroactivity of judicial decisions. A U.S. Supreme Court ruling that breaks new constitutional ground, such as the right of a defendant to be represented at trial by a lawyer, applies to all other defendants with cases on appeal as well as to defendants whose cases are in "midstream" and to all cases that are brought to trial following the judgment.

A writ of habeas corpus is a noncriminal (civil) lawsuit in which the plaintiff asks the court for a writ on the grounds that he or she is being unlawfully detained. The importance of the writ of *habeas corpus* is apparent from the fact that Article I, Section 9, Paragraph 2 of the U.S. Constitution provides that "the Privilege of the Writ of Habeas Corpus shall not be suspended, unless when in Cases of Rebellion or Invasion the Public Safety may require." In 1996, the U.S. Congress significantly limited the availability of *habeas corpus* in the Antiterrorism and Effective Death Penalty Act. This legislation was a response to the Oklahoma City terrorist bombing and was an effort to combat domestic terrorism by limiting the ability of individuals to challenge their death sentences.

CHAPTER REVIEW QUESTIONS

1. What is the purpose of a preliminary hearing?

2. Discuss the role of the grand jury. Why is the grand jury such a powerful institution?

3. Describe the function of an arraignment.

4. Outline the purpose of the pretrial motions raising issues of double jeopardy, speedy trial, change of venue, discovery, and the suppression of evidence.

5. When is a defendant entitled to a jury trial?

6. Discuss the constitutional requirements regarding the size of the jury.

7. What are the limitations on the selection of jurors imposed by the Equal Protection Clause and the Sixth Amendment cross-section-of-the-community requirement?

8. What is *voir dire*? Discuss challenges for cause and death-qualified juries. Describe the *Batson* requirement and peremptory challenges.

9. What is the purpose of the opening statement?

10. What is the significance of the burden of proof? Why is the prosecution required to prove guilt beyond a reasonable doubt? In your own words, describe the beyond-a-reasonable-doubt standard.

11. What information is included in a judge's instructions to the jury? What are the limitations on the closing arguments at trial?

12. Discuss whether jury unanimity is required. When may a jury engage in jury nullification?

13. What are the policy arguments for and against plea bargaining and the disposing of a defendant's criminal charges through a guilty plea? What constitutional issues are presented by the plea-bargaining process? Describe the conditions that must be satisfied before a trial court judge may accept a defendant's guilty plea.

14. Describe sentencing guidelines. How do recent U.S. Supreme Court decisions modify the role of state and federal sentencing guidelines in judicial sentencing practices?

15. Why are defendants provided with criminal appeals? Define and discuss the final judgment rule and interlocutory appeals. What is the importance of the plain error exception, the harmless error exception, and the automatic reversal rule?

16. Describe the importance of the writ of *habeas corpus* for the protection of rights and liberties. What are the requirements for filing a petition for a writ of *habeas corpus*?

LEGAL TERMINOLOGY

argumentative question

arraignment

automatic reversal rule

booking

Brady rule

case-in-chief

challenge for cause

clemency

closing argument

collateral remedies

complaint

contemporaneous objection rule

cross-examination

direct examination

directed verdict

discovery

double jeopardy

dynamite charge

final judgment rule

first appearance

grand jury

habeas corpus

harmless error

hung jury

indictment

indictment states

information states

interlocutory appeal

invited response

jury instructions

jury nullification

jury poll

leading question

modified indictment states

motion in limine

motion to suppress

narrative question

no bill

nolo contendere

opening statement

pardon

pattern jury instructions

peremptory challenge

plain error exception

plea bargain

preliminary hearing

presentence report

presentment

pretrial motions

rebuttal

redirect examination

rehabilitation

retroactivity of judicial decisions

right of allocution

sentencing guidelines

sentencing hearing

speedy trial

subpoena ad testificandum

subpoena duces tecum

surrebuttal

true bill

venire

voir dire

REFERENCE

LaFave, Wayne, Jerald H. Israel, and Henry J. King. 2004. *Criminal Procedure*, 4th ed. St. Paul, MN: Thomson/West.

Visit the Student Study Site at **http://study.sagepub.com/lippmance** to access additional study tools, including mobile-friendly eFlashcards and Web quizzes as well as links to SAGE journal articles and hyperlinks for *Criminal Evidence* on the Web.

CHAPTER 3

TYPES OF EVIDENCE

Did the prosecutor's questioning of defense witnesses about their gang membership create undue prejudice against the defendant?

Leo Morgan, Larry Blacksmith, and Steve Van Mierlo (Steve) were working in a 7-Eleven store at 6 p.m. one evening when a man with a gun entered and ordered all three men to lie face-down on the floor. Morgan (the store manager) and Blacksmith saw the man for five to ten seconds before complying with his order. . . . The man commanded Steve to open the store safe, and Steve complied. However, Morgan was shot in the back, and a struggle ensued between Blacksmith and the intruder, who eventually dropped his gun and fled. . . .

Appellant was arrested for the robbery attempt five days after its commission. . . .

The prosecutor was permitted to attack the credibility of the defense witnesses by eliciting testimony from them that they and appellant were members of a youth gang or "group" known as El Monte Flores. Two of the male witnesses were asked to exhibit to the jury their gang tattoos on their forearms and hands. . . .

The evidence was offered to establish possible bias of the defense witnesses in favor of appellant. The prosecution sought to prove that the witnesses and appellant "live[d] in the same neighborhood" and "had the same circle of friends." . . . [T]hese facts had already been amply established by other testimony before the prosecutor began his inquiries into the witnesses' gang affiliations. . . .

In Southern California, Chicano youth gangs have received widespread media publicity for their purported criminal activities. In this case, the prosecutor did not specifically refer to the El Monte Flores as a youth gang. However, the jury undoubtedly identified the group as such, either from their personal knowledge or from their in-court observations of the witnesses' age, ethnicity, and tattoos. (*People v. Cardenas*, 647 P.2d 569 [Cal. 1982])

CHAPTER OUTLINE

Introduction
Relevance
Competence
Exclusion of Relevant Evidence Based on
    Prejudice and Other Concerns
Direct and Circumstantial Evidence
Testimonial and Real Evidence
Substitutes for Evidence

Stipulations
Judicial Notice
Presumptions
Presumptions and Criminal Law
Case Analysis
Chapter Summary
Chapter Review Questions
Legal Terminology

TEST YOUR KNOWLEDGE

1. Do you understand the relationship among relevant evidence, material evidence, probative value of evidence, and competent evidence?

2. Can you explain when relevant evidence may be excluded because of the risk of unfair prejudice?

3. Are you aware of the difference between direct and circumstantial evidence and between testimonial and real evidence?

4. Can you define and explain the legal tests for stipulations, judicial notice, and presumptions?

■ INTRODUCTION

We all collect evidence or facts and opinions to help us make decisions. Consider what you want to know before buying a car, purchasing a computer, deciding what movie to see, or whether to eat at a new restaurant. The law of evidence determines what type of facts and opinions a judge or jury may consider in making a decision on a defendant's guilt or innocence. As noted in Chapter One, the California Evidence Code, Section 140, defines evidence as follows:

> [E]vidence means testimony, writings, material objects, or other things presented to the senses that are offered to prove the existence or nonexistence of a fact.

A lawyer under this definition can rely on oral testimony, written documents, and physical objects to prove a fact in a legal proceeding. There are several reasons why only **relevant evidence**, or evidence directly connected to the issues in a criminal case, is admitted at trial.

Preparation. The prosecution and defense only is required to prepare for the issues involved in the case. A defense attorney only need prepare to rebut the criminal charges against the defendant. In a robbery prosecution, the defense lawyer does not have to worry about an allegation that the property was obtained through fraud.

Decision-making. The judge and jury only are asked to focus on a limited number of issues.

Bias. Limiting the evidence helps to guard against decisions based on bias or personal prejudice. A jury if informed of a defendant's entire criminal arrest record may be reluctant to acquit the defendant.

Legitimacy. The public has confidence that the outcome of cases is decided on evidence relating to the crime with which the defendant is charged rather than on factors that are not strictly relevant to the charge such as the celebrity status or wealth of the defendant.

Efficiency. Limiting the trial to relevant evidence conserves judicial time and resources and allows for the processing of a large number of cases. Consider the negative reaction to the outcome of a trial when we believe that the outcome was not based on the evidence presented to the jury. On the other hand, limiting the trial to relevant evidence requires a relatively complicated set of procedures and is subject to criticism. These criticisms include the following:

Lack of logic. Rules may appear to be unfair or make little sense to the public. You may think a jury should be informed about the entire background of a defendant at trial rather than waiting for a defendant's criminal record to be considered at sentencing.

Legal representation. The party with access to money and resources has an advantage in complicated trials requiring expert representation, experts, and scientific investigation.

Guilty pleas. A number of commentators note that trials are so complicated, expensive, and unpredictable that the average defendant is encouraged to plead guilty.

There are several key Federal Rules of Evidence addressing relevance that will form the basis for our discussion in this chapter.

■ RELEVANCE *does the evidence add to proving someone guilty*

Relevance is the key to the courtroom door. A central principle of the law of evidence is that only relevant evidence is admissible in a trial. Federal Rule of Evidence 402 provides that "relevant evidence is admissible . . . [i]rrelevant evidence is inadmissible."

What is relevant evidence? Federal Rule of Evidence 401 defines relevance as evidence that has any tendency to make a fact more or less probable than it would be without the evidence; and the fact is of consequence in determining the action."

Rule 401. Test for Relevant Evidence

Evidence is relevant if

(a) it has any tendency to make a fact more or less probable than it would be without the evidence, and

(b) the fact is of consequence in determining the action.

↳ *evidence adds to what you are proving*

Commentators note that Rule 401 includes two different tests for relevance:

1. *Materiality.* The evidence must relate to a "fact of consequence to the determination of the action."

2. *Probative value.* Evidence must make a "fact of consequence more probable or less probable than it would be without the evidence." The evidence must be logically related to establishing a fact of consequence.

The trend today as indicated by Rule 401 is to talk in terms of relevant evidence rather than to treat materiality and probative value as separate categories of analysis. We take a closer look at Rule 401 below.

Fact "of consequence." What is a fact of consequence? The facts of consequence are the elements required to prove the criminal charge and the elements of any affirmative defenses relied on by the defendant. In other words, the facts of consequence are determined by the criminal charges and affirmative defenses available to a defendant in each case.

First-degree murder requires the intentional, premeditated (planning), and deliberate (calm and cool state of mind) killing of another (criminal act). An item of evidence is termed **material fact** if it assists in proving or disproving a fact of consequence.

Evidence that is *material* to establishing the facts of consequence of the intentional, premeditated, and deliberate killing of another might include the defendant's purchase of a firearm shortly before the killing, the defendant's motive to kill the victim, whether the killing was carried out in a methodical and organized fashion (e.g., lying in wait), the defendant's familiarity with the type of weapon used in the killing, the entry point of the bullet, and statements made by the defendant before or following the killing. Can you explain based on the definition of relevant evidence why the evidence listed above is relevant to a first-degree murder charge?

These items of evidence also would be of consequence or relevant to the prosecution overcoming the defendant's claim of self-defense. A claim of the use of deadly force in self-defense requires that the defendant reasonably believed he or she confronted an imminent and immediate threat of death or serious bodily harm and responded in a proportionate fashion and, in some jurisdictions, retreated or attempted to retreat before resorting to deadly force. An item of evidence would be material if it assisted in proving or disproving self-defense. Evidence that is material in evaluating the reasonableness of a defendant's belief that he or she confronted an imminent threat of harm might include the number of assailants, the comparative physical size and strength of the assailant and victim, the victim's knowledge of the assailant's past violent behavior, and the threatening words uttered by the assailant.

The fact the defendant had tickets to a rock concert on the night of the attack would not be relevant to a claim of self-defense although it would be relevant if the defendant offered an alibi defense and claimed he or she was not at the bar at the time the shooting took place. That the deceased left behind a heartbroken spouse and child might be relevant in a civil suit for wrongful death although it would not be relevant in determining whether the defendant was guilty of first-degree murder.

In a rape prosecution, a lack of consent is a fact of consequence of the crime of rape, and evidence of the victim's consent is an affirmative defense. What facts might be material in establishing consent or a lack of consent?

A demonstration of a lack of consent is not of consequence to a charge of sexual relations with a minor child, and evidence of consent would be irrelevant to a charge of statutory rape, which generally is defined as a sexual relationship between an individual under 14 years of age and an individual four or more years older than the victim.

Any tendency to make a fact "more probable or less probable." Evidence is relevant if it helps establish a fact at issue in the case. *The test is whether the material fact is more probable with the evidence than without the evidence.* Returning to our homicide example, evidence the alleged killer was angry over the victim's affair with the defendant's spouse makes it more probable the defendant possessed the motive and the intent to kill the victim than would be the case absent evidence of the alleged killer's motive. On the other hand, if the defendant did not know about the victim's affair with his or her spouse, evidence of the affair would not make it more probable the defendant possessed the motive and intent to kill the victim than would be the case without the evidence.

Professor Gianelli (2006) observes that a single piece of evidence only need "get on base" and need not "hit a homerun." In other words, the defendant's knowledge of the affair in the example above helps to establish that the defendant had the motive and thus the intent to kill although it does not definitively establish that the defendant was the killer. Keep in mind the determination of the relevancy of a piece of evidence is not a scientific process. A judge in determining the relevancy relies on his or her experience and logic. It is the challenge of determining whether evidence is relevant that makes the law of evidence such an interesting topic to study.

Once again, a single piece of evidence is not required to establish a material fact on its own. As various commentators observe, a fact of consequence may be proven one brick at a time and need not constitute a "wall." The question is whether a piece of evidence makes a fact of consequence "more or less probable." Scholars of evidence advise that relevance (a brick) is different from sufficiency (a wall). At the end of the prosecution's case, the issue is whether all of these pieces of evidence combine to establish the defendant's guilt beyond a reasonable doubt.

The logical connection between an item of evidence and the fact of consequence to be proved is the **probative value** of the evidence. Think of the probative value of an item of evidence as the explanatory power of an item of evidence or the weight to be placed on an item of evidence. Probative value is a matter of logic. A jury may logically place more weight on the fact that the defendant threatened the victim the day before the killing than on the fact that the defendant threatened the victim a year before the killing.

3.1 YOU DECIDE

David Ogden is described as "nice sober, nasty drunk." He boasted to his girlfriend Audry James that he killed a man and had stabbed another man to death who complained about Ogden having sold him a "fake watch." He also stated he once ripped a side-view mirror off a car and beat a man unconscious with it and on another occasion he had held a man down at knifepoint and threatened to tear out his eyes. James was aware that Ogden carried a knife in his sock. Ogden on one occasion verbally attacked James when she refused to have sexual relations with him.

Jaylene, James's daughter, had beaten Ogden on three occasions, and Ogden would never fight back and allegedly was scared of her although she only was 14. Ogden following a party hit Jaylene's boyfriend in the face. Jaylene chased Ogden and

returned to the car and asked James for a gun. James reached into her purse and handed Jaylene a firearm, which she used to shoot and kill Ogden. James was charged and convicted of aiding and abetting Jaylene's manslaughter of Ogden based on her handing Jaylene the firearm.

James pled that she gave Jaylene the gun because she believed that she and her daughter were in danger of serious bodily harm from Ogden based on her knowledge of Ogden's stories of previous acts of violence. James unsuccessfully sought to introduce court documents corroborating Ogden's previous acts of violence. The trial judge allowed James and her daughter to testify about their knowledge of Ogden's previous acts of violence. The judge refused to allow the trial records to be introduced into evidence because James and Jaylene had not seen these documents at the time of the killing. Why did James want to introduce the court documents? How would you rule? See *United States v. James* (169 F.3d 1210 [9th Cir. 1999]). Would you allow the prosecution to introduce court documents indicating that the stories Ogden told James were untrue and that he never physically attacked another person? See *Knapp v. State* (168 Ind. 153 [Ind. 1907]).

You can learn what the court decided by referring to the study site, **http://study.sagepub.com/lippmance.**

3.2 YOU DECIDE

Charles Holden was charged and convicted of the murder of Cora Smith in a Pennsylvania court. The police took Holden to the home of Ralph Jones, who had been with Holden for several hours prior to the time the police concluded Smith had been killed. Jones testified at Holden's trial that during his questioning by the police Holden winked at him although he did not know what Holden "meant" and he might merely have had something in his eye. Jones also testified that when interrogated by the police a second time he stated that "I think he was trying to get me to make an alibi for him to cover up some of his actions and I don't know nothing about any of his actions." The defense attorney objected to Jones's testimony and argued that Jones's interpretation of Holden's "wink" did not constitute evidence relevant to the prosecution's rebuttal of Jones's alibi defense. See *Commonwealth v. Holden* (134 A.2d 868 [1957]).

You can learn what the court decided by referring to the study site, **http://study.sagepub.com/lippmance.**

Legal Equation

Relevance = The evidence makes a fact of consequence more or less probable.
Relevance = Materiality + probative value.

See Table 3.1 for examples of relevant evidence.
We next look at the requirement that evidence must be competent.

■ COMPETENCE

As stated above, Federal Rule 402 provides that "relevant evidence is admissible . . . [i]rrelevant evidence is inadmissible." Rule 402 also recognizes that relevant evidence is excluded from trial if obtained in violation of a defendant's constitutional rights or if in violation of the rules of evidence such as hearsay or a privileged communication. **Competent evidence** is defined as evidence that is relevant and material and admissible in court.

Rule 402. General Admissibility of Relevant Evidence

Relevant evidence is admissible unless any of the following provides otherwise:

- the United States Constitution,
- a federal statute,
- these rules, or
- other rules prescribed by the Supreme Court.

Irrelevant evidence is not admissible.

Table 3.1 ■ Examples of Relevant Evidence

Relevant Evidence in a Murder Prosecution

Blood type and/or DNA at murder scene matches suspect.

Suspect owns type of firearm used in killing.

Defendant has motive to kill victim.

Defendant threatened victim in the past.

Defendant was with victim on night of the murder.

Relevant Evidence in a Burglary Prosecution

Defendant was in possession of burglar tools.

Defendant was in possession of items stolen from the home.

Witness observed defendant surveying the home.

Defendant was in possession of diagram of home.

Defendant has committed other burglaries employing techniques used to burglarize the home.

Constitutional rights. A firearm used in a killing may be seized by the police during an unlawful search and seizure. The gun although relevant to establishing the defendant's identity as the killer is excluded from evidence at trial because it was seized in violation of the Fourth Amendment to the U.S. Constitution prohibiting unlawful searches and seizures.

Rules of evidence. Various provisions of the Federal Rules of Evidence specifically exclude evidence from trial. Lawyer-client communications, for example, are privileged, and a defendant and lawyer may not be required to disclose the content of their discussions. Another example is statements made in the course of negotiations over guilty pleas or withdrawn guilty pleas. The relevance of this evidence is substantially outweighed by the risk the jury will interpret the evidence as an admission of the defendant's guilt, and it will discourage defendants from entering into discussions with the prosecution over whether to plead guilty.

Other grounds for exclusion. Various congressional statutes exclude evidence from trial. An example of a statute that excludes evidence is federal law excluding evidence obtained through an unlawful wiretap or eavesdropping (18 U.S.C. § 215). The Federal Rules of Criminal Procedure and various Supreme Court decisions also provide for the exclusion of this type of evidence under certain conditions (*Taylor v. Illinois*, 484 U.S. 400 [1988]).

The judge has the discretion to exclude another category of relevant evidence under Federal Rule of Evidence 403. Rule 403 provides that relevant evidence may be excluded "if its probative value is substantially outweighed by the danger of unfair prejudice, confusion of the issues, or misleading the jury, or by considerations of undue delay, waste of time or needless presentation of cumulative evidence."

prejudice, waste of time, misleading the jury

Legal Equation

Competent evidence **=** Relevant evidence is admissible, except as otherwise provided by the Constitution of the United States, by acts of Congress, by the Federal Rules of Evidence, or by rule prescribed by the Supreme Court.

■ EXCLUSION OF RELEVANT EVIDENCE BASED ON PREJUDICE AND OTHER CONCERNS

A judge has the discretion to exclude certain categories of relevant evidence from trial whose probative value is substantially outweighed by the dangers of unfair prejudice. This discretionary authority of the judge provides a safeguard against the possible negative impact of relevant evidence on the fairness of a trial. Relevant evidence also may be excluded based on confusion of the issues, if there is risk of confusing the jury, or by considerations of undue delay, waste of time, or unnecessary presentation of cumulative evidence.

Rule 403. Excluding Relevant Evidence for Prejudice, Confusion, Waste of Time, or Other Reasons

The court may exclude relevant evidence if its probative value is substantially outweighed by a danger of one or more of the following: unfair prejudice, confusing the issues, misleading the jury, undue delay, wasting time, or needlessly presenting cumulative evidence.

nickname is "killer" cannot call him killer in trial

The prosecution and defense will present arguments to the judge as to whether evidence is prejudicial or falls within another ground for exclusion under Rule 403. The question of the admissibility of relevant evidence posing a "danger" or involving "considerations" involves three steps:

1. *Probative value.* The judge determines the probative value of the evidence.

2. *Dangers.* The judge must find one of the specified dangers (unfair prejudice, confusion, misleading the jury) or considerations (undue delay, wasting time, or needlessly presenting cumulative evidence).

3. *Balance.* The court balances the probative value of the relevant evidence against the risk of prejudice to the defendant, confusion, or misleading the jury or considerations of delay, waste of time, or needlessly cumulative evidence and "may" (has the discretion to) exclude the evidence if the dangers or considerations listed in Rule 403 substantially outweigh the probative value of the evidence.

The judge has broad discretion to admit or to exclude evidence under Rule 403. His or her decisions only may be overturned based on an "abuse of judicial discretion." This standard is so high that judicial rulings under Rule 403 rarely are appealed.

Virtually every item of evidence introduced by the prosecution damages the opponent's case. Rule 403 is directed at safeguarding the judicial process against unfair prejudice and other specific types of *dangers* and considerations that *substantially interfere* with the ability of jurors to make a reasoned decision and that as a result undermine respect for the justice system.

Commentators note the requirement that a ground for exclusion under Rule 403 substantially outweighs the probative value of the evidence is a high standard and means that Rule 403 in most instances will result in the admission of evidence. The judge, for example, may not exclude evidence if the prejudicial character of the evidence is precisely offset by the probative value of the evidence or if the danger of prejudice from the evidence slightly outweighs the probative value of the evidence. Keep in mind that items of evidence have differing probative values. DNA evidence and fingerprints have greater probative value than evidence of a defendant's flight. This may prove important in balancing probative value against the danger of prejudice, confusion, or misleading the jury.

Prejudicial, Misleading, and Confusing Evidence

nickname killer
swastica tattoos on defendant } *can't show this*

Prejudicial evidence is singled out because the evidence runs the risk that the jury will unfairly decide a case based on emotion or prejudice rather than based on an objective analysis of the evidence. An example of evidence considered prejudicial is photographs of the body of a murder victim. Such photos corroborate the death of the victim and may be helpful in illustrating the entry point of bullets or the aggravated nature of the crime. On the other hand, photos may inflame the passion of jurors and cause them to disregard or selectively analyze the evidence and convict the defendant. Judges in a number of cases involving what is termed *punishing/rewarding prejudice* have tried to strike a balance between the value of photographic evidence and possible prejudice to the defendant by limiting the number of photographs, requiring black-and-white photos, or restricting the size of photos. A family photograph of a crime victim surrounded by his or her children and spouse would be both irrelevant and prejudicial to the defendant.

There also is the danger of what is termed *bad logic prejudice.* This happens when a jury disregards the evidence and convicts the defendant based on a factor that is only marginally relevant or irrelevant to the case, such as dislike of a defendant because of his or her gang affiliation or membership in a racist organization. There is a risk the jury will find the defendant guilty of a murder because of the belief that individuals who are members of these types of organizations engage in violent crime.

In 2004, the Supreme Judicial Court of Maine overturned the murder conviction of Brandon Thongsavanh. The prosecution had been allowed by the judge in its opening statement and in witness testimony to refer to the T-shirt Thongsavanh wore on the night of the murder, which read, "Jesus is a cunt." The Maine appellate court held that the phrase on Thongsavanh's T-shirt presented an "extremely high danger of prejudice" and it is "difficult to conceive of a more inflammatory and prejudicial expression" that possessed an "undue tendency to move the tribunal to decide on an improper basis." The phrase on the T-shirt worn by Thongsavanh possessed "slight" probative value and did not advance the prosecution's case beyond what was introduced by witness testimony (*State of Maine v. Brandon Thongsavanh*, 861 A.2d 29 [Me. 2004]).

In *United States v. Felton*, the defendants denied charges they planned to construct an explosive device. The government argued the defendants were motivated by a desire to advance their racist ideology and introduced photographs of one of the defendants giving a Nazi salute standing next to a well-known racist leader previously convicted of criminal activity and articles written by the other defendants expressing racist views. The government claimed the evidence was required to establish the defendants' motives. How would you rule? See *United States v. Felton* (417 F.3d 97 [1st Cir. 2005]).

There also is a risk the jury is unable to limit evidence to the proper purpose. Keep in mind evidence may be relevant for one issue in a case but prejudicial and excluded from evidence for other purposes. A judge confronting this situation should either exclude the evidence from trial or issue a **limiting instruction** advising the jury to limit their consideration of the evidence to a single purpose. An example is a situation in which a robber tells the victim to "hand over your money or I will kill you! I am a convicted felon and have nothing to lose." The statement is relevant for the requirement that to convict a defendant of robbery the prosecution is required to establish the money was taken by force or threat of force. On the other hand, the defendant's reference to his or her prior felony conviction may prove prejudicial to the defendant. The judge may either exclude the defendant's statement from evidence or instruct the jury to limit their consideration of the defendant's statement to whether the money was taken by force or threat of force and not to consider the defendant's status as an ex-felon in determining the defendant's guilt or innocence.

Another example is the ability of the prosecution to rely on an unlawfully obtained confession to cross-examine a defendant who takes the stand at trial and asserts his or her innocence. The jury is instructed by the judge that the unlawfully obtained confession may be considered in evaluating the defendant's credibility (believability), but it may not be considered in terms of the defendant's guilt or innocence. Is it realistic to believe jurors are able to limit their consideration of the confession to the defendant's credibility and to avoid viewing the confession as an admission of guilt? See *Harris v. New York* (401 U.S. 222 [1971]).

3.3 YOU DECIDE

Stephen McRae was charged with the murder of his wife Nancy. He claimed that the shooting was an accident. His attorney objected to the introduction of two photographs that the judge noted "were not pretty." The first showed Nancy in her bloody clothes with an exit wound in her skull. Another photo showed the entry point of the bullet in the front of Nancy's "broken head" with a disfigured left eye. The government argued the photos were relevant to rebut Stephen's claim the shooting was an accident. Would you admit the photos at trial? See *United States v. McRae* (593 F.2d 700 [5th Cir. 1979]).

You can learn what the court decided by referring to the study site, **http://study.sagepub.com/lippmance.**

3.4 YOU DECIDE

Rex Dewayne Cutchall was charged with the 1989 murder of Cathern Young, age 80. The trial court judge permitted the prosecutor to present evidence that following Cutchall's discovery of Cathern's body Cutchall immediately fled the crime scene, leaving his apartment in disarray. Cutchall's attorney objected to the evidence. Cutchall took the stand at trial and testified he fled because he feared he would be arrested for the murder based on his 1977 criminal conviction for unarmed robbery and service of six years in prison. Cutchall subsequently was convicted of murder. Cutchall's attorney contended the probative value of the flight evidence was outweighed by the unfair prejudice of the evidence. How would you rule? See *People v. Cutchall* (299 Mich. App. 396 [1993]).

You can learn what the court decided by referring to the study site, **http://study.sagepub.com/lippmance.**

Confusing and misleading evidence also may be excluded under Rule 403.

Confusing evidence. Evidence may *confuse* the jury. Showing a videotaped reenactment runs the risk that jurors will view the reenactment as a recorded version of the crime itself.

Misleading evidence. *Misleading* evidence is evidence that the jury may give undue importance. An example is lie detector or polygraph evidence, which has been held by courts to lack scientific accuracy. The Tenth Circuit Court of Appeals noted in *United States v. Call*, "there is the danger . . . the jury may overvalue polygraph results as an indicator of truthfulness because of the polygraph's scientific nature . . . the evidence was more prejudicial than probative" (*United States v. Call*, 129 F.3d 1402 [10th Cir. 1997]).

Courts rather than excluding evidence may require the prosecution or defense to rely on a less prejudicial *evidentiary alternative* such as a chart or diagram to illustrate the nature of the victim's injuries rather than a potentially inflammatory photo.

Consider the court's limiting of evidence at the trial of Dennis Kozlowski, the former head of Tyco International convicted of misuse of $81 million of the firm's funds along with the expenditure of $14.7 million for an art collection. The government wanted to introduce a video of a $2 million birthday party Kozlowski gave for his wife on the island of Sardinia, $1 million of which was paid for by Tyco. Judge Michael J. Obus required the government to omit various scenes from the video including an ice sculpture of Michelangelo's David urinating vodka, and a birthday cake in the shape of a woman's body with sparklers on her breasts, a guest mooning the camera, a waitress feeding grapes to a male guest, an exotic dancer, and a video clip of Mrs. Kozlowski carried around by models dressed as gladiators. Judge Obus explained the scenes he ordered to be omitted contributed very little to the government's case and risked prejudicing the jury against Kozlowski. Do you agree with the judge's ruling?

Old Chief v. United States is a well-known case applying Rule 403. Johnny Lynn Old Chief was charged with various offenses including the felony of being a convicted felon in possession of a firearm. This charge was based on Old Chief's prior conviction for a criminal assault causing serious bodily injury. The trial court judge rejected the defense attorney's request to instruct the jury that Old Chief had a prior felony conviction, leaving the only issue whether he had possessed a firearm. The United States Supreme Court held the judge should have instructed the jury Old Chief had a prior felony conviction that fell within the category of felons prohibited from possessing a firearm. Allowing the jury to hear the details of Old Chief's prior conviction created the risk that the jury, once having heard the details of his prior conviction, would conclude he possessed a "violent disposition" and was guilty of the other crimes with which he was charged (*Old Chief v. United States*, 519 U.S. 1972 [1997]).

How would you rule in a case in which a defendant during the course of an aggravated battery and robbery shouted anti-gay epithets at the victim? In balancing the probative value of the evidence against the prejudicial impact of the statement, would you admit these statements into evidence to demonstrate a specific intent to injure the victim? What if the defendant was charged with a hate crime?

Other Grounds for Excluding Evidence Under Rule 403

Rule 403 also allows the exclusion of evidence to encourage the efficient presentation of evidence.

Concerns. The exclusion of relevant evidence causing undue delay or a waste of time is based on the need to conserve the time and resources of the judge and jurors and to avoid the risk that cases will be decided in a hurried fashion by jurors frustrated by the length of the trial. Judges in most instances rule against taking jurors to visit a crime scene on grounds that the visit will likely have limited probative value because there is nothing about viewing the site of a crime that will assist jurors in their deliberations. The probative value of the visit is substantially outweighed by the resulting undue delay and waste of resources.

Rule 403 also allows a court to exclude "needless" evidence. This is aimed at **cumulative evidence** or evidence which repeats evidence already admitted at trial. The evidence adds nothing that has not already been heard by the jury and for that reason does not improve the jurors' understanding. A judge likely would hold that three or four eyewitnesses to a crime is sufficient and would not allow the prosecution to present eight or nine eyewitnesses to a crime.

Cumulative evidence restates evidence already introduced into evidence. **Corroborative evidence** adds new information that confirms prior testimony. An eyewitness may testify that he or she saw the defendant discard a firearm at the crime scene. A forensic expert may testify that the defendant's fingerprints were found on the weapon.

As we end our discussion of relevancy, consider the problem posed by Professor Gianelli (2006), who asks whether the following items of evidence are relevant: Type AB blood is found at the murder scene. The victim is type O. The defendant is type AB. In a local population of several million people, roughly sixty thousand people are likely to have type AB blood. As a judge, would you allow the prosecution to introduce the AB blood type into evidence? What about evidence that a witness saw a "white man" fleeing the scene of the crime and the defendant is a Caucasian?

Legal Equation

Admissibility	=	Relevant evidence.
Inadmissibility of relevant evidence within discretion of the judge	=	Probative value substantially outweighed by the danger of unfair prejudice, confusion of the issues, or misleading the jury, or by considerations of undue delay, waste of time, or needless presentation of cumulative evidence.

CRIMINAL EVIDENCE IN THE NEWS

A little noticed aspect of the murder trial of neighborhood watch volunteer George Zimmerman for the February 2012 murder of 17-year-old Trayvon Martin in Florida was Judge Debra Steinberg Nelson's pretrial denial of defense motions asking the judge to admit fifteen tweets and photographs from Martin's cell phone. These included tweets in the months preceding of a photograph of a handgun expressing his intent to get a gun, a photograph that appeared to be him smoking marijuana, a tweet mentioning the purchase and use of marijuana, and text messages discussing him getting in fights, his mother "kicking him out of the house," and his expulsion from school for marijuana. Other photographs pictured Martin smiling into the camera with a gold tooth and "flipping the bird." The defense also unsuccessfully filed a motion to admit a toxicology report that Martin had traces of marijuana in his blood at the time of his death. Judge Steinberg Nelson also rejected as a "logistical nightmare" a site visit by the jury to the townhouse complex where Martin had been shot.

One exchange read:

"So you just turning into a lil hoodlum."

Martin: "Naw, I'm a gangsta," the text message read.

Mark O'Mara, Zimmerman's lead defense counsel, argued the evidence was central to the defense theory that Martin was a troubled and aggressive young man who had attacked Zimmerman, who responded by killing Martin in self-defense.

The defense attorneys had leaked this information to the press prior to trial. Benjamin Crump, the lawyer who represented the Martin family, accused the defense of attempting to influence potential jurors prior to trial. He pronounced that none of the photographs and tweets provided insight into the events on the night Zimmerman was shot.

The social media evidence presumably was not admitted because it did not establish a fact "at issue" in the charge of murder against Zimmerman and his claim of self-defense. Would you have admitted this evidence at trial?

■ DIRECT AND CIRCUMSTANTIAL EVIDENCE

One approach to classifying types of evidence divides evidence into **direct evidence** and **circumstantial evidence** (see Chapter Four for a detailed discussion). A prosecutor at trial in a murder case is required to establish beyond a reasonable doubt that the defendant killed the victim. The identity of the killer may be established either by direct evidence or by circumstantial evidence or by a combination of direct and circumstantial evidence.

Direct evidence. Direct evidence is evidence that if believed by the jury establishes a fact at issue (the identity of the killer). A witness, for example, may testify he or she saw the defendant stab the victim. The eyewitness's testimony if accepted by the jury conclusively proves the defendant killed the victim. Commentators have described direct evidence as evidence that "speaks for itself." Direct evidence typically is based on a witness's observations (eyewitness) or knowledge (e.g., knowledge of a defendant's admission or a confession of guilt) and always is relevant.

Circumstantial evidence. Circumstantial evidence is the evidence from which a fact at issue may be inferred. The evidence *indirectly establishes a fact*, or in other words establishes a fact in a *roundabout fashion*. Commentators note that the jurors must decide for themselves whether the circumstantial evidence if believed is evidence of the defendant's guilt or innocence.

The important evidence book *McCormick on Evidence* (Broun 2008) notes testimony that the defendant fled the scene of a stabbing would be circumstantial evidence of the defendant's guilt. Testimony that the witness saw the defendant stab the victim with a knife would be direct evidence.

In the previous example, the jury must determine whether to infer a defendant's guilt from his or her flight from the crime scene. It is reasonable to infer a defendant fled because he or she wanted to escape apprehension. On the other hand, the defendant may have fled because he or she was fearful for his or her life or was innocent and feared being accused of stabbing the victim.

The circumstantial evidence would be even stronger if there also was testimony that the suspect was apprehended with blood on his or her clothes and was in possession of a bloody knife that appeared to be the type of weapon used in the killing.

Circumstantial evidence may have differing weight or significance (e.g., differing probative value). A judge exercises his or her discretion whether to admit circumstantial evidence at trial and may find a threat to kill a victim made two years before the killing, although relevant, is too remote to be considered relevant.

In general, the law of evidence gives equal weight to direct and circumstantial evidence. A criminal conviction may be based on direct or circumstantial evidence or a combination of direct and circumstantial evidence.

Keep in mind that these categories are not always entirely distinct. How would you categorize a witness's testimony that the masked assailant was the same height and weight as the defendant and walked with a limp like the defendant?

In thinking about direct and circumstantial evidence, consider *State v. Forrest*. The defendant John Forrest was convicted of the premeditated and intentional killing of his father and was sentenced to life imprisonment despite the fact that there was no eyewitness to the killing.

Forrest's father was hospitalized and near death. Two days later, on Christmas Eve, Forrest visited his father in the hospital, and a nurse testified that Forrest was crying and visibly upset. He told the nurse his father was dying. The nurse left the room, and Forrest pulled a small pistol from his pants pocket, placed it against his father's temple, fired four times, and walked out of the hospital room and threw the gun on the ground. Forrest stated, "I killed my daddy. . . . I promised my dad I wouldn't let him suffer." The gun was a single action, .22-caliber revolver that had to be cocked each time it was fired and contained four empty shells and one live round (*State v. Forrest*, 362 S.E.2d 252 [N.C. 1987]).

The North Carolina Supreme Court affirmed Forrest's conviction for premeditated murder based on bringing the pistol to the hospital, his statements to the nurse, and firing four times at point-blank range. As a truck driver, Forrest carried the pistol when on the job and might have killed his father as an impulsive, emotional response to his father's condition. The North Carolina Supreme Court, however, found the circumstantial evidence was determinative of Forrest's premeditated plan to kill his father (direct evidence).

See Table 3.2 for a comparison of direct and circumstantial evidence.

Table 3.2 ■ Direct and Circumstantial Evidence	
Direct evidence	**Circumstantial evidence**
Eyewitness viewed killing	Eyewitness saw defendant running from scene of crime
Surveillance camera recorded defendant killing victim	Defendant's blood, DNA, fingerprints found at crime scene
Defendant confessed murder to police	Defendant threatened to kill victim

Justin Sullivan / Stringer / Getty Images

spoken or written evidence

■ TESTIMONIAL AND REAL EVIDENCE

A second approach to classifying evidence is based on presentation of the evidence at trial. Evidence is divided between testimonial evidence and real evidence. These two types of evidence overlap with direct and circumstantial evidence; evidence, for example, may be testimonial and direct or testimonial and circumstantial.

When thinking about a trial, we immediately think about oral or **testimonial evidence**. Testimonial evidence is oral communication by a competent witness given under oath or affirmation in a judicial proceeding. An affirmation is a formal declaration by individuals whose religious obligations prohibit oath-taking.

Testimonial evidence also encompasses written statements made out of court under an oath to testify truthfully or affirmation as well as oral statements made in pretrial depositions. A deposition is the pretrial statement primarily used in civil cases. The witness is placed under oath and is questioned by the lawyers. The proceedings are recorded by a court stenographer. Lawyers during the deposition may confer with their client, object to questions, and present their own witnesses. The transcript of the examination may be introduced into evidence if the witness is unavailable to testify in person.

Deborah Jones Merritt and Ric Simmons (2012) note that there are various categories of witnesses, which are listed below.

Fact witnesses. Individuals who testify about facts related to the crime are called fact witnesses. These witnesses may be eyewitnesses to the crime, individuals who overheard the defendant make an incriminating statement, or individuals who testify about circumstantial evidence such as a mechanic who repaired the damaged automobile of an individual charged with a "hit-and-run accident."

Expert witnesses. Expert witnesses are used to help the jury understand the significance of facts presented at trial. Experts possess specialized knowledge and expertise that is not commonly possessed by the average person. For example, a defendant relying on the insanity defense will retain an expert psychiatrist to support his or her claim that he or she did not know the difference between right and wrong. The prosecution will counter with experts challenging the testimony of the defense expert.

talk about someone else

Character witnesses. Character witnesses testify about the character of a party or witness and do not testify about the facts of the case. They are required to have knowledge about the background of the defendant and are not required to have knowledge about the facts of the case.

usually not about defendant → just an opinion and not really relavant if you think he is a good guy

Real evidence is a second way of presenting evidence. Real evidence is physical evidence that is directly related to the case, such as a firearm, a bloody shirt, fingerprints, or narcotics.

Real evidence typically is defined as evidence you can see, feel, or smell.

Real evidence must be **authenticated** by a witness who testifies to the genuineness of the evidence (e.g., the same gun seized at the crime scene). A witness who testifies about a shooting is providing testimonial evidence, and the gun if introduced in evidence at trial is real evidence. The object introduced into evidence must be in "substantially the same condition" at the time of the crime.

See Table 3.3 for examples of real evidence.

The next two approaches to categorizing evidence are **documentary evidence** and **demonstrative evidence**, both of which are considered by some commentators as forms of real evidence.

Table 3.3 ■ Real Evidence
Physical evidence: clothing, firearms, guns, bullets, maps
Documents: letters, diaries, maps, drug prescriptions, medical records
Visual images: photographs, videos, medical imaging

Documentary evidence. Documentary evidence includes written information as well as video and audio recordings. This may take the form of written confessions, fingerprint cards, notes, reports prepared by experts, X-rays, e-mails, photographs, and recordings from surveillance cameras.

Demonstrative evidence. Demonstrative evidence includes visual aids intended to assist the fact finder to understand the facts involved in the case. Lawyers may present charts, tables, graphs, anatomical models, computer simulations, and PowerPoint slides. Demonstrative evidence also may include objects similar to those used in a crime, such as displaying a gun of the same type used in a robbery. Lawyers at times use literal "demonstrations," such as reenacting the circumstances surrounding a killing. Trial judges need to ensure that the demonstrative evidence accurately re-creates or imitates the crime.

Real evidence involves objects connected to a case, and demonstrative evidence illustrates facts involved in the crime.

Some commentators include a fourth type of evidence, real-testimonial evidence.

Real-testimonial evidence. This category includes testimonial evidence presented in a tangible form, such as copies of affidavits, depositions, and transcripts of a witness's prior testimony that is introduced at trial.

CRIMINAL EVIDENCE AND PUBLIC POLICY

Jurors in high-profile cases may have been bombarded before the trial by an avalanche of print and electronic accounts and comments on a crime and on the defendant's guilt or innocence. Judges, although able to exclude prejudicial evidence from trial, confront the challenge of ensuring that jurors put aside their preconceived notions and fairly and impartially determine a defendant's guilt or innocence. This becomes a particular challenge in an age of social media and multiple media platforms.

The question is how to balance the defendant's right to a fair and impartial trial against the First Amendment freedom of the press and the right of the public to be informed.

In the 2011 trial of Casey Anthony for the killing of her 2-year-old daughter, Judge Belvin Perry Jr. determined that an impartial jury could not be obtained in Orlando. The judge responded by importing a jury from Clearwater, Florida, a hundred miles away. The jurors were sequestered in a hotel for over forty days and were prohibited from using the Internet and social media or watching the news on television, and their newspapers were closely edited. They were allowed closely monitored visits by relatives on weekends.

What if a defendant believes he or she cannot obtain a fair trial in the physical location or venue of the judicial district in which the prosecution is to occur? Rule 21(a) of the Federal Rules of Criminal Procedure requires that the court, on the motion of the defendant, shall transfer the trial to another district in the event that the court is "satisfied" that there exists "so great a prejudice" against the defendant that "the defendant cannot obtain a fair trial." Similar provisions exist at the state level. This may require witnesses and lawyers to travel to distant locations and is contrary to the interest in selecting a jury from the area in which the crime has been committed.

The most famous case of pretrial publicity prejudicing a case is the prosecution in Cleveland, Ohio, in 1954 of Dr. Sam Sheppard for bludgeoning to death his pregnant wife. The pretrial coverage of the trial was "massive and pervasive. . . . For months the virulent case publicity about Sheppard and the murder made the case notorious" and "bedlam reigned at the courthouse at the time of the trial." The

(Continued)

(Continued)

news media were described by the Supreme Court as having created a "carnival atmosphere" that "influenced and prejudiced" the public, witnesses, and jurors.

The U.S. Supreme Court held that due process "requires that the accused receive a trial before an impartial jury free from outside influences." The Court recognized the difficulty of eliminating the impact of prejudicial publicity from the minds of jurors given the "pervasiveness of modern communication" and held that in those instances in which there is a "reasonable likelihood" that prejudicial news coverage will prevent a fair trial, courts should grant a continuance (suspension) of the trial until the "threat abates" or should transfer the trial to another county "not so permeated with publicity." In the event the trial is not transferred, courts also can limit the impact of publicity by placing "gag orders" on statements by lawyers to the media, sequestering the jury to prevent jurors from being exposed to the media, advising the jury to remain impartial, and prohibiting the media from interviewing witnesses. A more drastic approach is the Court's solution in the Casey Anthony case, keeping the trial in the judicial district and selecting a jury from another location.

The Sheppard "presumption of prejudice" approach to pretrial publicity was adopted by the Supreme Court in *Rideau v. Louisiana*. In *Rideau*, two months prior to trial, a local television station broadcast Wilbert Rideau's twenty-minute confession to the police on three occasions over a three-day period. It is estimated that roughly two-thirds of the 150,000 people in the Louisiana parish had viewed the confession. The Supreme Court held that despite the fact that the three jurors who had watched the confession testified they were capable of objectively weighing the broadcast of the confession, the Court held the broadcast had reduced the trial to a "hollow formality." The Court held that the judge's failure to grant Rideau's motion for a change of venue denied him due process of law (*Rideau v. Louisiana*, 373 U.S. 723 [1963]).

The recent trend is toward an *actual-prejudice standard* in deciding whether a change of venue is required. The trial court judge, before granting a change of venue under this standard, is to determine whether the jurors are able to act in an objective and fair fashion. The fact that a juror is exposed to prejudicial publicity is not the test. In fact, it is desirable that jurors should be interested in the news and well informed. The question is whether a juror is able to make a decision based solely on the evidence presented in court and "can lay aside his impression or opinion." The burden is on the defendant to demonstrate "the actual existence of such an opinion in the mind of the juror[s] as will raise the presumption of partiality." In other words, the defendant must demonstrate that based on the totality of circumstances, the jurors are predisposed to find the defendant guilty (*Irvin v. Dowd*, 366 U.S. 717 [1961]).

In a world saturated by information from the Internet, social media, cable and satellite television, professional trial consultants and media-savvy lawyers, and leaks to the press, it increasingly is the case that members of the jury pool likely will have been exposed to pretrial coverage of a case. Jurors are in the unenviable position once a trial has ended of returning to a community that may have strong views on a defendant's guilt or innocence.

The research on the impact of pretrial publicity is divided on whether media coverage has an impact on jury decision-making although it seems to result in harsher sentences for defendants. The research does seem to indicate that the impact of pretrial coverage on juror attitudes lessens with the passage of time.

A related problem is publicity during the trial, which judges can address through "gag orders" on lawyers or holding lawyers in contempt of court who make provocative comments. The Supreme Court has held that lawyers have a responsibility to ensure a fair and impartial trial and may not engage in speech or conduct that has a "substantial likelihood" of threatening to influence the outcome of the trial (*Gentile v. State Bar of Nevada*, 501 U.S. 1030 [1991]).

A recent development is laws such as those in California that instruct judges to direct jurors they are not to use social media during the trial. A juror who disregards this instruction may be held in contempt of court. In *Dimas-Martinez v. State*, the Arkansas Supreme Court threw out a murder conviction because a juror despite warnings from the judge continued to post messages on his Twitter account. The court explained that the possibility of "prejudice" from individuals outside the courtroom is simply too high. In other cases, jurors during trials have conducted research about the law, "friended" defendants, or communicated with lawyers during the trial. In *Dimas-Martinez*, the court explained that the slightest hint that jurors are being influenced by external factors undermines faith in the legal system (*Dimas-Martinez v. State*, 385 S.W.3d 249 [Ark. 2011]).

Would you favor restrictions on pretrial coverage and coverage of trials? What about restrictions on the use of social media by jurors, lawyers, witnesses, and defendants? In 2013, Jodi Arias was convicted of the first-degree murder of her boyfriend. An Arizona jury was unable to decide whether she should receive the death penalty. The judge prohibited cameras in the courtroom for her resentencing hearing. A jury consultant in arguing that a jury could not be found in Phoenix able to fairly adjudicate whether Arias should receive the death penalty found in addition to national news coverage of the trial there were

- 2,450 TV news reports on the trial in the Phoenix area;
- 205 print stories in Maricopa County, Arizona;
- 503 Internet photos that generated 9,600 links;
- 233,000 links to videos;
- 524,000 tweets about Arias; and
- a made-for-TV movie that attracted 3.1 million viewers.

■ SUBSTITUTES FOR EVIDENCE

The jury ordinarily is responsible for deciding the facts of a case. There are three situations in which the jury is instructed by the judge to accept certain facts as true. The next sections of the chapter discuss stipulations, judicial notice, and presumptions.

■ STIPULATIONS →prior to trial admit they weren't supposed to have a gun.

A **stipulation** is a voluntary agreement between opposing parties in a trial to accept a fact as true for purposes of the trial. Stipulations agreed upon before trial typically are in writing. Stipulations reached during trial usually involve an oral agreement. The judge based on the stipulation between the parties will instruct the jury that they are to accept the stipulated facts as true, and the stipulated facts are to be given the same weight as facts established during the trial.

There is no requirement that a party enter into a stipulation although judges encourage the parties to enter into stipulations where possible. There are several interests advanced by stipulations:

- *Efficiency*. Stipulations save judges time and resources.
- *Focus*. Stipulations allow the parties to focus on the main issues presented by the criminal charges.
- *Credibility*. A lawyer may believe that it is in his or her client's interest to enter into a stipulation. Jurors may grow frustrated by a lawyer who extends the length of the trial by challenging every fact at trial.

Stipulations, though most often used for factual matters, also may be used to agree on the content of the testimony of an absent witness and to accept the admissibility of otherwise inadmissible evidence. The parties, for example, may stipulate that a lie detector test to be taken by the defendant is admissible into evidence.

There are several reasons why parties enter into factual stipulations.

Minor factual points. Minor details such as whether it was dark outside or the defendant's weight or height can be agreed upon by the parties and avoid wasting time.

Facts easily established. One side knows the other attorney easily can establish a fact. A prior conviction, for example, can be established by entering a certified copy of the conviction into evidence.

Prejudice. A defense attorney may want to avoid facts that may prejudice the jury against the defendant. The defendant may have committed a prior violent and bloody felony. A stipulation allows the jury to be informed of the prior felony without providing the details of the offense. An example is the *Old Chief* case previously discussed in this chapter in which the defense attorney unsuccessfully attempted to avoid the jury hearing the details of the defendant's felony conviction. There also may be a stipulation that the defendant possessed narcotics without identifying the narcotic as heroin.

The judge enforces stipulations although a judge may allow a party to be released from a stipulation under certain compelling circumstances. A defense attorney, of course, will not stipulate to all of the prosecution's factual allegations because this would result in the defendant's conviction and would constitute ineffective assistance of counsel.

In *United States v. Grassi*, Dante Angelo Grassi was prosecuted for the distribution of five obscene films. The government asked the court for permission to show the films to the jury. The defense unsuccessfully asked the prosecutor to agree to stipulate the films were obscene. The government refused the stipulation on the grounds the films were necessary to establish that Grassi knew of the obscene content of the films he was distributing. Grassi next unsuccessfully argued the judge should not allow the jury to view the films because their probative value was substantially outweighed by the prejudice arising from showing the films. The judge recognized the films were "bizarre and repulsive" and allowed three of the films to be viewed by the jury in entirety. Can you understand why the prosecutor would not stipulate the films were obscene? Do you agree with the judge's ruling? See *United States v. Grassi* (602 F.2d 1192 [5th Cir. 1979]).

■ JUDICIAL NOTICE

Judicial notice allows a judge to recognize a fact as true without the need to hear from a witness or to view an exhibit. In other words, this "legal shortcut" permits a judge on his or her own initiative to notice a fact as true that has not been established through ordinary evidentiary procedures.

Judicial notice is a mechanism for achieving efficiency. Absent judicial notice, trials would drag on interminably because every minor fact in the case would have to be established through the evidentiary process. Consider a case in which the defendant is charged with shooting and killing the victim with a revolver. The prosecutor would have to establish the characteristics and functioning of the "gun," the types of injuries that may result from the gun, and the precise process by which a bullet causes death. Judicial notice allows a court to merely recognize guns are dangerous weapons that can cause death.

State statutes and rules of evidence all recognize judicial notice, and most adopt the text in Federal Rule 201. Federal Rule 201 provides that a court may take judicial notice of an adjudicative fact that is not subject to reasonable dispute because it is generally known within the territorial jurisdiction of the trial court or is capable of accurate and ready determination by resort to sources whose accuracy cannot reasonably be questioned.

Rule 201. Judicial Notice of Adjudicative Facts

(a) **Scope.** This rule governs judicial notice of an adjudicative fact only, not a legislative fact.

(b) **Kinds of Facts That May Be Judicially Noticed.** The court may judicially notice a fact that is not subject to reasonable dispute because it
   (1) is generally known within the trial court's territorial jurisdiction or
   (2) can be accurately and readily determined from sources whose accuracy cannot reasonably be questioned.

(c) **Taking Notice.** The court
   (1) may take judicial notice on its own or
   (2) must take judicial notice if a party requests it and the court is supplied with the necessary information.

(d) **Timing.** The court may take judicial notice at any stage of the proceeding.

(e) **Opportunity to Be Heard.** On timely request, a party is entitled to be heard on the propriety of taking judicial notice and the nature of the fact to be noticed. If the court takes judicial notice before notifying a party, the party, on request, is still entitled to be heard.

(f) **Instructing the Jury.** In a civil case, the court must instruct the jury to accept the noticed fact as conclusive. In a criminal case, the court must instruct the jury that it may or may not accept the noticed fact as conclusive.

Adjudicative Facts

An adjudicative fact is a fact that is part of the trial.

Indisputable Facts

Judicial notice is limited to "self-evident truths that no reasonable person could question" (*United States v. Bourque*, 541 F.2d 290 [1st Cir. 1976]). A judge presiding over a terrorism trial could recognize that al Qaeda is a terrorist organization with a history of attacks on civilians or that the World Trade Center and Pentagon were attacked on September 11, 2001.

Common Knowledge

The indisputable fact must generally be known to the general public. Knowledge by members of a particular religion, race, or group is not sufficient. Courts also may take judicial notice of facts widely known within the court's local jurisdiction though not known to the larger public. This includes the residential character of neighborhoods, the location of local landmarks, and major roadways and mass transit systems. Residents of South Florida may have a fairly detailed knowledge of hurricanes, and the residents of rural areas in the western United States reasonably may be expected to know about farming or ranching or hunting and fishing.

Facts within common knowledge include virtually all significant historical figures and events; state boundaries; the political institutions and structure of federal, state, and local governments; the fact that smoking contributes to cancer; the dangerous nature of guns; abbreviations (e.g., Dr. for *doctor*); the meaning of slang expressions (e.g., a "john" or "turning a trick" in prostitution); the fact that beer is an intoxicant; the explosive capacity of various chemicals; and the laws of physics and other scientific principles. Judges typically take judicial notice of the fact that fingerprints and DNA have been established as scientifically valid and reliable.

Matters Capable of Accurate Determination

A court may take judicial notice of a fact that can be established by consulting an unquestioned source. This includes the days of the week, the dates of World War I and World War II, the meaning of foreign language words, and the state capital of Missouri and other states. These facts all are easily found and verified in a source whose accuracy cannot reasonably be questioned, such as a dictionary, an encyclopedia, or a map. A police officer who seized an individual for investigation and seized narcotics might testify that his or her suspicions were aroused because the defendant was a known gang member and was in an area known for drug trafficking and was wearing a heavy coat. The judge could take judicial notice of the warm temperatures on the day in question.

Personal Knowledge of the Judge

A judge only may take judicial notice of facts generally known or subject to determination through an accurate and reliable source. A judge may not take judicial notice based solely on his or her personal experience or expertise.

Procedure

A judge may take judicial notice on his or her own without consulting the lawyers and is required to take judicial notice on the request of a party so long as the request meets the requirements of Rule 201. The judge may refuse to take judicial notice of a fact that does not meet the standard of Rule 201. See Table 3.4 for examples of judicial notice.

The court on the request of the prosecution or the defense must allow a party to address the court requesting the court to take judicial notice. The opposing party is entitled to argue that a fact is not "generally known" and should not be judicially noticed. A court may take judicial notice of a fact anytime during the trial or on appeal. In a criminal case, the jury is the fact finder and must find that the prosecution established each element of a crime beyond a reasonable doubt. The judge as a result instructs the jurors that they are not required to accept facts judicially noticed as conclusive.

Courts observe that judicial notice is to be used with caution because of the risk that a court by recognizing a fact will relieve the prosecution of the burden to present evidence of the defendant's guilt beyond a reasonable doubt. On the other hand, a jury is not required to accept a judicially noted fact as true.

In *United States v. Dior*, the defendant was charged with transportation of stolen merchandise worth $5,000 or more across the Canadian border into the United States. A federal appellate court found that the district court had properly declined to find that based on the exchange rate the furs were worth at least $5,000 in American dollars. Judicial notice improperly would have violated the defendant's right to have each and every element of the criminal charge established beyond a reasonable doubt (*United States v. Dior*, 671 F.2d 351 [9th 1982]).

Rule 201 only addresses adjudicative facts. Keep in mind that judges also may take judicial notice of **legislative facts** which are facts relating to the larger

Table 3.4 ■ Judicial Notice
Stolen airline tickets are redeemable for their face value. Theft of tickets valued at more than $200 constitutes first-degree theft (*State v. Mayo*, 623 P.2d 898 [Hawaii App. 1981]).
Court takes judicial notice that a .22-caliber gun under state law is a pistol that may not be in the possession of a convicted felon (*State v. McGuire*, 124 Ariz. 64 [1978]).
Court takes judicial notice that a military academy is a school for purposes of a law prohibiting sale of narcotics within a thousand feet of a school (*Haley v. State*, 736 N.E.2d 1250 [Ind. App. 2000]).
Court takes judicial notice of National Highway Traffic Safety Administration standards governing administration of a field sobriety test (*State v. Stritch*, 205 WL 678938 [Ohio 2005]).

context of the case. Legislative facts might include the fact that drugs are a serious social problem or that a city is marked by gang violence or that women earn less money than men and have been subject to discrimination.

→If A is true, B is true

■ PRESUMPTIONS   *→If A is true, B doesn't need to be true.*

Conclusive and Rebuttable Presumptions

You see an individual late at night kicking and breaking a large backdoor window of a nearby home and alert the police to a burglary. An officer arrives and arrests the individual for burglary, the breaking and entering of a dwelling house at night with the intent to commit a felony. You have relied on a legal **inference**, logical reasoning through which you rely on one fact or facts (a break-in at night) to establish the existence of another fact (the individual possesses the intent to commit a felony within the home). Inferential reasoning regularly is used by jurors to evaluate a defendant's guilt or innocence.

A presumption is different. The judge instructs the jurors that, as a matter of law, if they believe an eyewitness account, they are required to reach a specific conclusion. In our burglary hypothetical, the jury would be told if they believe the eyewitness's account that he or she saw the defendant breaking down the back door at night ("basic facts"), they are required to conclude the defendant possessed the required intent to commit a burglary ("presumed fact"). In other words, if the jury believes the "basic fact," they are required to reach the "presumed fact" (*State v. Jackson*, 774 P.2d 1211 [1989]).

Note that in contrast to judicial notice and stipulations a presumption depends on the establishment of the "basic fact."

There are a number of presumptions recognized in civil and criminal law. Several states list presumptions in their legal codes although other states rely on the common law or on state court decisions to define presumptions. There are two broad categories of presumptions, **conclusive presumptions** and **rebuttable presumptions**.

Conclusive presumptions. The judge instructs the jurors that, if they believe the "basic fact," they are required to accept the "presumed fact." This also is referred to as an irrebuttable presumption. A failure by the defense to challenge the "basic fact" by attacking the credibility of the witness or to counter evidence of the "basic fact" results in the jury being required to find proof of the "presumed fact."

Rebuttable presumptions. The jurors are instructed that, even if they believe the "basic fact" has been established, they are not required to accept that proof of the "basic fact" establishes the presumed fact. The jurors instead will weigh and balance all of the evidence at trial before deciding whether to apply the presumption. This also is referred to as a **permissive presumption.** *ex: child in the house, man of the house doesn't mean its his father*

In other words, the primary difference between conclusive and rebuttable presumptions is that a conclusive presumption requires that the jury conclude that proof of the basic fact establishes the presumed fact. A rebuttable presumption permits although does not require the jury to infer the presumed fact from the basic fact.

A defendant in a criminal prosecution may follow various strategies in challenging a presumption.

Basic fact. The opposing party can attempt to persuade the jury that the "basic fact" did not occur by attacking the credibility of the witness who testified about the basic fact or by presenting witnesses who question whether the basic fact occurred. Returning to our burglary hypothetical, the defense attorney may attack the credibility of the eyewitness testimony by challenging the accuracy of the eyewitness account ("basic fact").

Presumed fact. In the case of a rebuttable presumption, the opposing party may also attack whether the presumed fact follows from the basic fact. Although the defendant was kicking and breaking the back door, the defense attorney may present evidence indicating the defendant's intent was to vandalize rather than burglarize the home ("presumed fact"). In contrast, in the case of a conclusive presumption, once the jury accepts the basic fact, the opposing party cannot challenge the presumed fact.

Absence of rebuttal. Jurors may find against a rebuttable presumption although the defendant offers no evidence challenging either the basic fact or the presumed fact. In the case of a conclusive presumption, the jury would be required to find the presumed fact if the defendant fails to challenge the basic fact.

Presumptions and Social Policy

Presumptions are based on a number of considerations, only some of which apply to each and every presumption.

Efficiency. The use of presumptions expedites trials by making it easier to establish a fact or element of a crime. This relieves judges of the need to untangle complicated factual situations.

Probability. Presumptions are based on a close and demonstrated connection between the basic fact and the presumed fact.

Social policy. Various presumptions are based on the promotion of a desirable social policy.

Fairness. One of the parties has greater access to evidence, and the presumption assists the party who lacks access to information by placing the burden of producing evidence on the more informed party.

Jury decision-making. Presumptions help guide jury decision-making.

Consider the so-called mailbox rule and the presumption that a properly addressed and stamped letter has been delivered. The judge instructs the jury that, if the recipient does not claim the letter failed to arrive, the jury is to conclude the letter reached the recipient. This rebuttable presumption is based on the experience that letters generally reach the recipient (probability). The individual mailing the letter also would experience difficulty establishing the delivery of a letter (fairness).

Another example is the conclusive presumption that a child born to a married couple who live together was fathered by the husband, assuming the husband is neither impotent nor sterile. The presumption reflects a strong social policy in protecting a child from being considered "illegitimate" (social policy).

The law also presumes undue influence when a lawyer who drafts a will is listed as a beneficiary. Lawyers have a duty of loyalty to their clients and should not take advantage of a professional relationship by making themselves a beneficiary (social policy).

Another presumption is that a person missing for a period of five to seven years depending on state law is presumed dead unless there is evidence he or she is alive. The purpose is to allow the distribution of the "missing person's" property and proceeds from life insurance and to allow the individual's spouse and family to move on with their lives (social policy). The judge or jury must presume the individual is dead unless there is evidence the individual was seen or heard from or he or she possessed motive to "disappear," such as fleeing criminal prosecution. Another presumption provides an individual who suffered a violent death died as a result of an accident.

■ PRESUMPTIONS AND CRIMINAL LAW

Mandatory Presumptions and Criminal Law

Presumptions are treated differently in civil and criminal law, and we will limit our discussion for the sake of clarity to criminal presumptions. In reading about presumptions in criminal law, keep three concerns in mind.

Prosecutor. The prosecution must prove each and every element of a crime (the intent and the act) beyond a reasonable doubt.

Jury. The jury is the ultimate fact finder (unless there is a bench trial before a judge) and must be free to make a judgment on guilt or innocence. A rebuttable presumption does not prevent the jury from evaluating for itself whether the prosecution established every element of the crime beyond a reasonable doubt.

Fundamental fairness. There must be a logical connection between the basic fact and the presumed fact.

The Supreme Court has reasoned that a conclusive presumption conflicts with the requirement that the prosecution to convict a defendant prove each element of a crime beyond a reasonable doubt. The jury, if they find the prosecutor has established the basic fact in a conclusive presumption, is required to find the prosecutor established the presumed fact. This presumption prevents the jury from fulfilling their obligation to evaluate the evidence to determine whether the prosecution has established every element of a criminal charge beyond a reasonable doubt (*County Court of Ulster County v. Allen*, 442 U.S. 140 [1979]).

In *Sandstrom v. Montana*, David Sandstrom confessed to a killing and was convicted. Sandstrom contended that he suffered from a mental illness that, when he was inebriated, prevented him from distinguishing "right from wrong" and as a result he did not "purposely and knowingly" kill Annie Jensen. The United States Supreme Court held as unconstitutional the jury instruction at Sandstrom's trial providing the "law presumes that a person intends the ordinary consequences of his voluntary acts."

The Court explained that the jury could have interpreted the instruction as requiring the jury once finding Sandstrom killed Annie ("basic fact") to conclude he possessed the required criminal intent (presumed fact). An irrebuttable presumption of criminal intent based on the defendant's act of killing Annie relieved the prosecution of the burden of establishing the defendant's criminal intent beyond a reasonable doubt. In the alternative, the Supreme Court explained the jury could have interpreted the instruction as directing the jury to find a criminal intent unless Sandstrom produced evidence beyond a reasonable doubt negating intent. This would impermissibly shift the burden of persuasion from the prosecutor to the defense. The Court stated that the judge should have told the jurors they were not required to find that Sandstrom possessed the required criminal intent based on his confession to killing the victim and that the prosecution possessed the burden of proving criminal intent beyond a reasonable doubt. Consider that the jury, even if they did not accept Sandstrom's version of the facts based on their own evaluation of the evidence, may have concluded that Sandstrom killed negligently or recklessly or in the heat of passion rather than intentionally or knowingly (*Sandstrom v. Montana*, 442 U.S. 510 [1979]).

In *Carella v. California*, Eugene John Carella was convicted of grand theft for failing to return a rental car. The jury instructions provided for two statutory presumptions. The first required the jury to find a fraudulent theft if the rental car was not returned within twenty days following a demand to return the auto. The jury instruction also required the jury to find embezzlement if the rental car was not returned within five days of the expiration of a lease. The Supreme Court held that these instructions "relieved the State of its burden . . . [of] proving by evidence every essential element of Carella's crime beyond a reasonable doubt" and "directly foreclosed" independent jury consideration of the evidence (*Carella v. California*, 491 U.S. 263 [1989]).

In *Leary v. United States*, Harvard psychology professor Timothy Leary was convicted of marijuana possession "knowing it was imported into the United States." The federal statute under which Leary was convicted contained the conclusive presumption that individuals in possession of marijuana know the marijuana was unlawfully imported into the United States. The Supreme Court in *Leary v. United States* held that a significant proportion of marijuana is grown within the United States, and there was little indication that most users of marijuana were aware of the origins of the marijuana they consumed (*Leary v. United States*, 395 U.S. 1 [1969]).

Contrast the conclusive presumptions in *Sandstrom*, *Carella*, and *Leary* with the Supreme Court decision in *County Court of Ulster County v. Allen*. Three adult males and a 16-year-old, Jane Doe, were jointly prosecuted and convicted of the possession of two large-caliber handguns, which together with their ammunition weighed approximately six pounds. The firearms were in Jane Doe's handbag in the front seat or front floor on the passenger side where Jane Doe was sitting. The jury was instructed they were "entitled to infer possession from the defendants' presence in the car." The trial court judge, however, stressed this permissive inference "could be ignored by the jury even if there was no affirmative proof offered by the defendants in rebuttal."

The United States Supreme Court examined the specific facts and found the presumption that the three adults possessed the firearm was rational despite the fact the firearm was in Jane Doe's purse. The gun was too large to fit easily in the handbag, the bag was in easy reach of the adult occupants of the auto, and it therefore was reasonable to presume that the adults in the auto "were fully aware of the presence of the guns and had both the ability and intent to exercise dominion and control over the weapons" (*County Court of Ulster County v. Allen*, 442 U.S. 140 [1979]).

We next look at examples of rebuttable presumptions in the criminal law.

Rebuttable Presumptions and Criminal Law

The law establishes a number of rebuttable presumptions in criminal cases.

The presumption of innocence. The rebuttable presumption of innocence requires the prosecution prove the defendant's guilt beyond a reasonable doubt. The judge instructs that the defendant is not required to prove his or her innocence or even produce any evidence, and a negative inference may not be drawn from the defendant's failure to testify.

The presumption of sanity. Individuals who are prosecuted are presumed to be mentally sound and sane. Once the defendant produces some credible evidence proving his or her insanity at the time of the offense, the prosecution has the burden of proving the defendant's insanity beyond a reasonable doubt. In the federal system, the defendant possesses the burden of demonstrating insanity by clear and convincing evidence.

The presumption of knowledge of the law. Individuals are presumed to know the law. This presumption is based on the fact that absent this presumption individuals would plead a lack of awareness of the law. There are isolated cases in which individuals relied on an inaccurate statement of the law by government officials and were acquitted based on a lack of criminal intent.

The presumption against suicide. There is a presumption that "an unexplained death by violence" is the result of an accident rather than a "self-imposed" death by suicide. The presumption is based on the belief that most individuals embrace life and would not intentionally take their own life.

The presumption of the regularity of official acts. The presumption is that government officials acted in a lawful fashion in good faith. Absent evidence to the contrary presented at trial, it is presumed that prosecutors did not discriminate in bringing charges against a defendant, the police seized evidence in a lawful fashion, and the analysis of fingerprints and DNA was carried out in a procedurally correct fashion.

The resumption of criminal intent of juveniles. Most states follow the common law approach to whether juveniles are capable of forming the requisite criminal intent to be held liable for criminal acts. Children under 7 years old are conclusively presumed to be incapable of criminal intent although there is a rebuttable presumption that juveniles between 7 and 14 are capable of criminal intent. Juveniles 14 and older are presumed to be capable of forming criminal intent.

Legal Equation

Stipulations	=	Voluntary agreement between opposing parties to accept that a fact is true for purposes of the trial.
Judicial notice	=	An adjudicative fact **+** not subject to reasonable dispute **+** that is generally known within the territorial jurisdiction of the trial court or is capable of accurate and ready determination by resort to sources whose accuracy cannot reasonably be questioned.
Presumptions		
Conclusive presumptions	=	Jurors believe the "basic fact" **+** required to accept the "presumed fact."
Rebuttable presumptions	=	Jurors are instructed that even if they believe the "basic fact" has been established **+** they are not required to accept proof that the "basic fact" establishes the presumed fact.

 ## 3.5 YOU DECIDE

Luis Parrilla, together with Wendell Semeina, Pierre Larichere, and five other men, went on a robbery spree. Joseph Duggan was driving his motor scooter and was forced off the road by a car driven by Larichere containing a group of masked men. Semeina testified that the group had decided to rob Duggan, and Parrilla was seated in the back seat of the car, behind the passenger

(Continued)

seat. Duggan attempted to escape, but in the process, he fell off the bike into the bushes next to the side of the road. Parrilla and one of his companions, Papito, fired shots at Duggan. One bullet hit Duggan in the foot. The assailants fled but were subsequently chased by the police and arrested. As a consequence of the shooting, Duggan now walks with a limp.

Parrilla was charged with assault with intent to commit mayhem as a result of the attack on Duggan and the injury to his foot. An individual commits mayhem when he or she willfully and with intent to commit a felony or to injure,

disfigure, or disable inflicts upon another person any injury that destroys or disables any member or organ of his body. The infliction of injury is presumptive evidence of the intent required to commit mayhem. The federal Third Circuit Court of Appeals held that this was a mandatory presumption. Was the presumed fact that Parrilla intended to commit mayhem upon Duggan more likely than not to flow from the basic fact that Duggan's foot was injured and consistent with due process of law? See *Virgin Islands v. Parrilla* (7 F.3d 1097 [3rd Cir. 1993]).

You can learn what the court decided by referring to the study site, **http://study.sagepub.com/lippmance.**

■ CASE ANALYSIS

In *United States v. Yahweh*, federal district court Judge Norman Roettger decided whether the probative value of enlarged autopsy photographs of homicide victims was substantially outweighed by the danger of unfair prejudice.

Were the enlarged autopsy photos admissible at trial?

United States v. Yahweh Ben Yahweh,
792 F.Supp. 104 (S.D. Fla. 1992), Roettger, C.J.

Defendants objected to introduction of enlarged autopsy photographs of homicide victims.

Violent crime cases are the exception in federal courts. The instant case is arguably the most violent case ever tried in a federal court: the indictment charges the sixteen defendants on trial with fourteen murders by means such as beheading, stabbing, and occasional pistol shots, plus severing of body parts such as ears, to prove the worthiness of the killer. Plus, they are charged with arson of a slumbering neighborhood by Molotov cocktails with the perpetrators under orders to wait outside the innocent victims' homes wearing ski masks and brandishing machetes to deter the victims from fleeing the flames. In the course of the trial, the government sought to introduce into evidence medical examiners' photographs of the victims. Defendants objected to the admission of these photographs into evidence on the grounds that the photographs were not relevant pursuant to Federal Rule of Evidence 401 and prejudicial in effect pursuant to Federal Rule of Evidence 403. Specifically, the defendants contended that the size of the photographs, which were roughly 30 × 40 inches, was designed to inflame the passions of the jury.

The relevance of these photographs is without question. Photographs of homicide victims are relevant in showing the identity of the victim, the manner of death, the murder weapon,

or any other element of the crime. In addition to identifying the victims and the means of death, the photographs in this case corroborated the testimony of witnesses, Lloyd Clark, Ricardo Woodside, and Robert Rozier, whose credibility was central to the government's case.

With reference to the beating of Aston Green, Clark testified that he "saw somebody jump on his [Green's] chest." [Further, Woodside testified that there were "people jumping up and down on his chest. . . .]" Government Exhibit 7 showed the outline of a footprint on the chest of Green. Dr. Charles Wetli, the medical examiner who performed the autopsy on Green, stated that this injury was consistent with someone jumping on the deceased's chest.

Woodside testified concerning the decapitation of Green. He estimated that he heard approximately fifteen to thirty "chops" as if a knife was coming down on flesh. He also heard the attention-riveting statement: "Damn. This blade is dull." This testimony at first seemed incredible. However, it was corroborated by Government Exhibit 9, which clearly showed that a number of "chops" were necessary for the decapitation.

Prior to the admission of Exhibits 7 and 9 in the enlarged size, this court reviewed the same photographs in the 8 × 10–inch size. The latter did not show the detail necessary to corroborate the witnesses' testimony. The footprint could not be seen clearly on the 8 × 10 of Exhibit 7, and the number of lacerations on the top of Green's torso were not clearly visible on the 8 × 10 of Exhibit 9. Discussing the enlarged photographs of Green, Dr. Wetli testified, and the court concurred, that 8 × 10 photographs did not reveal the contusions on the deceased's face, the machete marks on his neck, or the footprint on his chest.

Relevant evidence can be excluded pursuant to Federal Rule of Evidence 403 if "its probative value is substantially outweighed by the danger of unfair prejudice." The subject matter of the photographs in question—decapitation, slit throat, removed ears, repeated stabbing, and gunshot wounds—is both difficult to view as well as disturbing and distasteful. However, so were the crimes alleged. Murder, particularly "murder most foul" by methods such as decapitation or stabbing and the removal of body parts, is inherently offensive. However, these exhibits are not flagrantly or deliberately gruesome depictions of the crimes.

Displaying an enlarged photograph while the medical examiner testified to facts illustrated in the photograph enabled all members of the jury simultaneously to follow the witness's testimony. The probative value of the enlarged autopsy photographs substantially outweighed the danger of unfair prejudice, and therefore the objections to the photographs were overruled. Although enlargements may have magnified certain wounds, they by no means distorted the nature of the wounds in this case. The court attempted to keep the photographs to about life size. However, in certain instances, larger blow-ups were permitted as necessary to illustrate the medical examiner's testimony, such as with reference to severed ears and a severed trachea and carotid artery. Even with an enlargement larger than life size, the court found the enlargement did not distort the subject. Additionally, arguments as to size cut both ways. Photographs many times smaller than life size do minimize the wounds inflicted but, as was the case with the footprint in Exhibit 7, may not accurately reflect injuries that were present.

CHAPTER SUMMARY

Evidence is comprised of "testimony, writings, material objects, or other things presented to the senses that are offered to prove the existence or nonexistence of a fact."

Evidence to be admissible must be relevant. "Relevant evidence" means evidence having any tendency to make the existence of any fact that is of consequence to the determination of the action as more probable or less probable than it would be without the evidence. Material evidence is evidence that is directed at establishing a "fact of consequence."

Relevant evidence is inadmissible at trial if obtained in violation of a defendant's constitutional rights or if in violation of a statute or the rules of evidence such as hearsay or a privileged communication.

Relevant evidence also may be excluded if its probative value is substantially outweighed by the danger of unfair prejudice, confusion of the issues, or misleading the jury, or by considerations of undue delay, waste of time, or needless presentation of cumulative evidence.

Evidence may be divided into direct and circumstantial evidence. Direct evidence is evidence that if believed by the jury establishes a fact at issue (the identity of the killer). The evidence "speaks for itself." Direct evidence typically is based on a witness's observations (eyewitness) or knowledge (e.g., an admission or a confession) and always is relevant. Circumstantial evidence is evidence from which a fact at issue may be inferred. This includes evidence that the defendant had the ability, opportunity, motive, and means to commit the crime.

Evidence also may be categorized as either real or testimonial. Real evidence is physical evidence that is directly involved in the case, such as a firearm, a bloody shirt, fingerprints, or narcotics. Testimonial evidence is oral communication by a competent witness given under oath or affirmation in a judicial proceeding.

The chapter concluded with a discussion of three "substitutes for evidence." A stipulation is a voluntary agreement between opposing parties to accept that a fact is true for purposes of the trial. Judicial notice allows a judge to recognize a fact as true without the need to hear from a witness or to view an exhibit.

There are two types of presumptions. In a conclusive presumption, the judge instructs the jurors that, if they believe the "basic fact," they are required to accept the "presumed fact." The jurors are instructed in the case of rebuttable presumption that, even if they believe the "basic fact" has been established, they are not required to accept proof that the "basic fact" establishes the "presumed fact". Conclusive presumptions in criminal cases are considered to intrude unconstitutionally on the role of the jury as the fact finder in a case.

In Chapter Four, we examine circumstantial evidence.

CHAPTER REVIEW QUESTIONS

1. What is the test for relevant evidence?

2. Explain the requirement that evidence must be material.

3. Why do different items of evidence differ in terms of their probative value?

4. Define the requirement that evidence must be competent.

5. Discuss the legal standard for the exclusion of relevant evidence based on prejudice.

6. Give an example of evidence excluded because of the risk of confusion.

7. Distinguish between direct and circumstantial evidence.

8. Give examples of testimonial and real evidence.

9. Define stipulations.

10. What are the procedural steps for judicial notice? When may a judge exercise judicial notice?

11. Explain the difference between an inference and a presumption.

12. Distinguish between conclusive and irrebuttable presumptions. What are the concerns that arise in the use of presumptions in criminal cases?

13. Give three examples of rebuttable presumptions in criminal law.

14. Why do courts rely on various "substitutions for evidence"?

LEGAL TERMINOLOGY

circumstantial evidence
competent evidence
conclusive presumption
corroborative evidence
cumulative evidence
demonstrative evidence
direct evidence
documentary evidence

inference
irrebuttable presumption
judicial notice
legislative facts
limiting instruction
material fact
permissive presumption
prejudicial evidence

probative value
real evidence
rebuttable presumption
relevant evidence
stipulations
testimonial evidence

REFERENCES

Broun, Kenneth S., ed. 2008. *McCormick on Evidence,* 6th ed. St Paul, MN: West.

Gianelli, Paul C. 2006. *Understanding Evidence,* 2nd ed. Newark, NJ: Matthew Bender.

Merritt, Deborah Jones, and Ric Simmons. 2012. *Learning Evidence From the Federal Rules to the Courtroom,* 2nd ed. St. Paul, MN: West.

Visit the Student Study Site at **http://study.sagepub.com/lippmance** to access additional study tools, including mobile-friendly eFlashcards and Web quizzes as well as links to SAGE journal articles and hyperlinks for *Criminal Evidence* on the Web.

CHAPTER 4

find lots of evidence of selling drugs ⟹ believe they are selling drugs/not using.

DIRECT AND CIRCUMSTANTIAL EVIDENCE

Direct = see it first hand
circumstantial = down the street, hear gun, then see → criminal intent and criminal act

Would it violate the rape shield statute for the defendant to cross-examine the victim on her acts of prostitution and for the defendant to testify he knew the rape "victim" was a prostitute and reasonably believed she consented to sexual relations?

Tina C. went to the defendant's residence . . . seeking employment as a day laborer. The defendant operated a roofing business and, approximately one and one-half to two years earlier, he had employed the victim as a day laborer for a period of one day when he first met her. Since that time, the victim had interacted socially with the defendant several times, including visiting his home. On at least one occasion, the victim had engaged in consensual sexual activity with the defendant. . . .

When the defendant expressed an interest in engaging in sexual activity with the victim, she indicated that she wanted to go home. . . . The defendant then [according to the victim] forced the victim to submit. . . . When the victim returned from the bathroom, the defendant gave her $30, and she left the apartment. . . .

The victim then counted the money and suggested that she would return for the balance of the $50 that she had requested. The defendant told the victim not to do so because his wife would be home. The victim stated, "I warned you". . . . [T]he primary issue was whether the sexual intercourse was consensual. (*State v. De Jesus*, 856 A.2d 345 [Conn. 2004])

CHAPTER OUTLINE

Introduction
Jury Decision-Making
Circumstantial Evidence of Ability to Commit the Crime
Circumstantial Evidence of an Inference of
    Consciousness of Guilt and of Guilt
Circumstantial Evidence That an Individual Is the Victim of Rape
Character Evidence
Other Acts Evidence

Other Acts Evidence and Circumstantial Evidence of
    Identity
Other Acts Evidence and Circumstantial
    Evidence of Intent
Case Analysis
Chapter Summary
Chapter Review Questions
Legal Terminology

 TEST YOUR KNOWLEDGE

1. Can you give examples of how circumstantial evidence may create an inference that a suspect possesses the capacity to commit the crime with which he or she is charged? In your answer, think about specialized skill, possession of the means to commit the crime, and physical and mental capacity.

(Continued)

2. Do you know how circumstantial evidence may be used to demonstrate consciousness of guilt? Consider evidence of flight, concealing evidence, and offers to plead guilty. Explain how possession of stolen property and sudden wealth are circumstantial evidence of guilt.

3. Do you understand what types of character evidence about a defendant are admissible at trial and what types of character evidence are admissible by the prosecutor in rebuttal?

4. Can you explain what types of character evidence about victims may be offered by the defense and by the prosecution?

5. Do you know when "other acts" evidence is admissible?

6. Are you able to distinguish character evidence from evidence of habit?

7. Can you explain rape shield laws?

■ INTRODUCTION

In a criminal case, the prosecutor is required to prove the defendant's guilt beyond a reasonable doubt. The defense attorney typically responds by attempting to create a reasonable doubt in the mind of the finder of fact, either the judge or the jury. This may be accomplished by presenting an alternative version of the facts presented by the prosecutor, calling the credibility of the prosecution witnesses into question, or offering affirmative defenses such as self-defense.

The prosecution and defense may rely on direct and circumstantial evidence or a combination of both types of evidence.

In Chapter Three, we distinguished between direct and circumstantial evidence. As you recall, *direct evidence* is based on personal knowledge or observation. The evidence if believed by the jury directly and conclusively establishes the fact or facts, and no inference is required. In contrast, *circumstantial evidence* indirectly establishes a fact. The trier of fact must use an inference or presumption to establish the fact "at issue." A witness may directly view a killing (direct evidence) or testify that he or she viewed the defendant flee from the crime scene (circumstantial evidence).

Direct evidence always is relevant and admissible so long as it is material and competent and not privileged (e.g., a doctor-patient relationship). The judge exercises discretion in the admission of circumstantial evidence and determines whether the evidence is relevant and whether despite the relevance of the evidence the admission of the evidence will waste time, will create confusion, or is unduly prejudicial.

In the classic story used to distinguish direct evidence from circumstantial evidence, an eyewitness watches the defendant bite off the ear of the victim in a fight. This direct evidence contrasts with the testimony of a second witness who did not see the assailant bite off the victim's ear but recounts watching the assailant spit out the victim's bloody ear.

Keep in mind that circumstantial evidence may be used to establish criminal intent as well as a criminal act. In *People v. Conley*, a high school student at a party hit another student with a wine bottle, breaking the victim's upper and lower jaws, nose, and cheek and permanently numbing his mouth. The attacker was convicted of committing an aggravated battery that "intentionally" or "knowingly" caused "great bodily harm or permanent disability or disfigurement." An Illinois appellate court held that the "words, the weapon used, and the force of the blow . . . the use of the bottle, the absence of warning and the force of the blow are facts from which the jury could reasonably infer the intent to cause permanent disability." In other words, the defendant's actions revealed his intent (*People v. Conley*, 543 N.E.2d 138 [Ill. App. Ct. 1989]).

As noted, the general view is that direct and circumstantial evidence are of equal significance and that guilt or innocence may be determined based on either direct or circumstantial evidence or by a combination of both types of evidence. However, a number of states require judges in prosecutions based wholly on circumstantial evidence to provide the so-called Webster-type charge "that where the Government's evidence is circumstantial it must be such as to exclude every reasonable hypothesis other than that of guilt." The Webster charge was first given by Justice Lemuel Shaw in the famous 1850 Webster-Parkman murder case in Massachusetts.

■ JURY DECISION-MAKING

The judge has sole responsibility for matters of law, and the jury is the finder of fact; in a bench trial without a jury, however, the judge determines the law and the facts. The judge issues instructions to the jury stating the law to be applied in evaluating the facts.

The jury must sort through the evidence presented at trial and, where there is a conflict, decide which version to believe. This may involve an evaluation of the credibility (or believability) of witnesses offering different versions of events. Jurors are able to observe the demeanor of a witness. Demeanor includes body language and whether the witness acted in a cooperative or evasive fashion. Lawyers on cross-examination attempt to attack the credibility or believability of witnesses. Impeachment may involve cross-examination of a witness's inconsistent statements, motive to fabricate evidence, specific acts or reputation for untruthfulness, felony convictions, and criminal convictions for crimes of dishonesty or false statement.

job of attorney→ to show they aren't credible

Each juror in his or her own mind assigns weight or importance to various items of evidence. In a trial for financial fraud, the jurors may give little significance to the defendant's comment to a friend denying responsibility and give more weight to the defendant's unexplained destruction of documents. The jurors must decide what inference to draw from evidence. For example, they must determine whether the defendant's flight is an admission of guilt or a justifiable reaction based on the fear he or she would be unfairly implicated in the crime.

Juror deliberations may involve multiple ballots and intense disagreements. The judge may intervene to encourage the jurors to reach a verdict.

In the next sections of the chapter, we review several categories of circumstantial evidence.

■ CIRCUMSTANTIAL EVIDENCE OF ABILITY TO COMMIT THE CRIME

Specialized Skill

→auto mechanic can hot wire a car.
worked for locksmith - can pick lock

Some crimes require skills and abilities that are not possessed by the average individual. The prosecutor may demonstrate the defendant has the type of aptitudes required to commit the crime. The defense may take the opposite approach and attempt to establish that the defendant lacks the skills required to commit the crime.

Examples of crimes requiring special knowledge include art forgery, cybercrime, accounting fraud, and terrorist offenses involving the construction of sophisticated explosives.

In *United States v. Barrett*, Arthur Barrett was convicted of the theft and sale of valuable postage stamps stolen from a museum. The court admitted evidence of Barrett's sophisticated knowledge of burglar alarms and ability to "bypass" the alarm system.

In affirming the district court's admission of this evidence, the First Circuit Court of Appeals stressed:

> Barrett's expertise with alarms indicated that he had the skill to wire off the alarm system prior to the break-in and accordingly helped identify him as one of the guilty parties. . . . One of the stamp burglars had to have sufficient knowledge of the intricacies of burglar alarm systems to locate the alarm wires, which were mingled with other wires inside a telephone cable, and to loop them off. The ordinary person or even burglar would be unlikely to possess the skill to do this. Where the bypassing of the alarm was so distinctive a feature of the stamp burglary, evidence that Barrett had expertise with alarms, while not by itself conclusive of guilt, reinforced the evidence that linked him to the burglary, and thereby to the crimes charged. (*United States v. Barrett*, 539 F.2d 244 [1st Cir. 1976])

Means to Commit the Crime

- possess stolen card
- tools in trunk

The defendant's possession of the equipment to commit a crime, which is not possessed by a large cross-section of the public, may be used as circumstantial evidence that the defendant committed a crime. Possession of scales, plastic Baggies, cell phones, beepers, a firearm, and a large amount of cash may be circumstantial evidence of involvement in narcotics trafficking. A stolen credit card may provide circumstantial evidence to prove the individual was responsible for the unauthorized charges on the card. Possession of a firearm found by ballistics evidence to have been involved in a crime also would constitute circumstantial evidence of the means to accomplish a crime. Burglar tools may constitute circumstantial evidence of involvement in a burglary.

In *People v. Hall*, the defendant, an escaped inmate, was identified by the victim of an armed robbery. Two days after the crime, the defendant was arrested in possession of a loaded handgun. The victim testified that during the robbery a pistol had been fired into the ground as a warning. The victim was not certain of the color or caliber of the gun; "[a]ll I knew was that it was a gun." A Michigan Court of Appeals nonetheless held the firearm was circumstantial evidence of the defendant's ability to carry out the crime.

> [W]here weapons or tools were used to commit a crime, weapons or tools that might have been used to commit the crime found in the accused's possession at the time of the arrest may be introduced without proof that they were the very weapons or tools in fact so used. (*People v. Hall*, 172 N.W.2d 473 [Mich. App. 1969])

On the other hand, the Oregon Supreme Court held the probative value of a 22-caliber revolver seized from a defendant's home seventy-five miles from the crime scene, two months after the crime, was outweighed by the risk of prejudice to the defendant. There was no testimony that the gun was "similar to the gun that had been seen by the robbery victim. . . . There was nothing to tie this revolver to the crime alleged other than it was found in the home of the man charged with committing the crime" (*State v. Thompson*, 364 P.2d 783 [Ore. 1961]).

→someone bigger than someone else —bigger person with little old lady

Physical Capacity

A defendant's physical capacity to commit a crime also may be relied on by the prosecution as circumstantial evidence of guilt. The defense may present evidence that a defendant lacked the strength to commit the crime with which he or she is charged, arguing, for example, that the defendant was impotent and could not have raped the victim.

An assailant's physical strength has been relied on by the prosecution to demonstrate that the victim in a rape case reasonably feared a physical assault if she did not consent or that the victim's will was overborne by the defendant. A New York Family Court decision noted a number of criminal decisions relying on the relative difference in strength between a male defendant and a female victim to demonstrate an absence of consent.

> Forcible compulsion by physical force has also been found where the defendant, taking advantage of his superior physical size and strength, engages in a physical act directed against the victim . . . forcible compulsion was established by evidence that defendant, who was 35 years old and 6 feet, 2 inches tall, entered the victim's bedroom while she was sleeping and tried to put his penis into her vagina, that she told him to stop and tried to move, but he covered her mouth and held her down; . . . forcible compulsion was established by evidence that defendant was approximately seven inches taller and 70 pounds heavier than the victim, and he stopped an elevator between floors, thereby trapping her inside the elevator. . . . forcible compulsion established where the medical evidence showed bruising of the victim's genitalia and there was large disparity in size and age between the victim and defendant . . . evidence was sufficient to establish forcible compulsion where defendant overcame the victim's physical resistance with his superior size and strength, by pinning her down and the medical examination showed deep vaginal abrasions; . . . evidence was sufficient to establish forcible compulsion where the victim was pulled into a bedroom by her brother-in-law who was older, bigger and stronger, and the victim's injuries were severe and painful. (*Matter of Rosaly S. v. Ivelisse T.*, 910 N.Y.S.3d 408 [Fam. Ct., Kings County, 2010])

people who can't understand nature of crime

Mental Capacity

A defendant may claim that he or she lacked the mental capacity to commit the crime because of legal insanity typically defined as a lack of capacity to appreciate the nature and quality of his or her act or a lack of appreciation of right and wrong as a result of mental disease or defect. Several states recognize the "diminished responsibility" defense in which a defendant establishes an incapacity to form the requisite guilt or innocence.

A jury cannot look into an individual's brain to determine mental capacity. Mental incapacity is established by expert psychiatric testimony along with circumstantial evidence including a lack of remorse and a bizarre explanation for the criminal act such as the fact the victim was a witch or space alien (*Moler v. State*, 782 N.E.2d 454 [Ind. App. 2003]).

Involuntary intoxication as a result of drugs or alcohol is a complete defense where the defendant meets the state's legal test for insanity. Voluntary intoxication in most states is a defense that negates a finding of a specific intent to commit a crime.

In 2003, in *State v. Kruger*, Daniel Kruger attempted to strike an officer with a beer bottle and, during a struggle, "head butted" the officer. He was arrested and charged with third-degree assault and convicted of intentionally touching or striking an officer in a harmful or offensive manner with intent to inflict bodily harm. A Washington appellate court overturned Kruger's conviction on the grounds that the jury should have received an instruction that it may consider whether the defendant's intoxication prevented the defendant from forming the required intent. The court concluded that the record contains substantial circumstantial evidence of "Mr. Kruger's drinking and level of intoxication. And there is ample evidence of his level of intoxication on both his mind and body, e.g., his 'blackout,' vomiting at the station, slurred speech, and imperviousness to pepper spray. He was entitled to the instruction" (*State v. Kruger*, 57 P.3d 147 [Wash.App. 2003]).

■ CIRCUMSTANTIAL EVIDENCE OF AN INFERENCE OF CONSCIOUSNESS OF GUILT AND OF GUILT

behavior that someone did something criminal

An individual's behavior following a crime may constitute circumstantial evidence of a consciousness of his or her guilt of a crime. This post-arrest behavior may include escape, flight to avoid trial, the concealment or destruction of evidence, and intimidation of witnesses.

An inference of guilt may not be drawn against individuals invoking their constitutional rights. *Miranda v. Arizona* established that under the Fifth Amendment right against self-incrimination individuals under arrest or whose freedom of movement is restricted in a significant fashion by the police have the right to silence and the right to an attorney and are to be informed that anything they say may be used against them (*Miranda v. Arizona*, 384 U.S. 436 [1966]). In *Doyle v. Ohio*, the U.S. Supreme Court held that a prosecutor may not cross-examine a defendant on the invocation of his or her involved Fifth Amendment right to silence during police interrogation (*Doyle v. Ohio*, 426 U.S. 610 [1976]).

why are they running?—they did something | reasons against... | ·scared

Flight *can be before or after arrest → skip bail*

Flight to avoid arrest or prosecution, "jumping bail," and flight following a conviction to avoid a prison sentence all raise the inference the defendant is guilty and wants to avoid a criminal trial, appeal, or incarceration. An individual who is innocent presumably would want to be exonerated and to clear his or her name. A Kentucky court noted the "rule is based on the inference that the guilty run away but the innocent remain" (*Rodriguez v. Commonwealth*, 107 S.W.3d 215 [Ky. 2003]).

The jury is to decide in light of the other evidence the weight to be accorded to flight. The length of time between the crime and the flight and the circumstances of the flight clearly are important in evaluating the probative value of flight.

Judges on occasion have questioned the probative value of flight and whether the evidence is unduly prejudicial. Flight may be motivated by fear or panic, a belief the defendant will not obtain a fair trial, or an existing plan to move to another state.

In *Commonwealth v. Johnson*, Jamar Johnson was wanted for attempted murder. As he was approached by two officers, he fled and before stopping discarded a jar of marijuana. Johnson unsuccessfully claimed the evidence of flight should have been excluded because he was forced to incriminate himself by taking the stand to explain that he fled to avoid arrest for marijuana rather than because of a fear of apprehension for homicide (*Commonwealth v. Johnson*, 910 A.2d 60 [Pa. Super. 2006]).

Armed resistance to arrest and attempt to commit suicide are other acts admissible as evidence of consciousness of guilt.

Concealing Evidence

The concealment or destruction of evidence is admissible to prove an individual's consciousness of guilt. This category includes a range of acts, including shredding of documents, disposing of evidence in the trash, erasing files, modifying photographs, and falsifying documents. In *United States v. Hanson*, the Sixth Circuit Court of Appeals approved of the instructions issued by a trial court in Hanson's trial for conspiracy to distribute methamphetamines.

[Y]ou find that the defendant attempted to conceal evidence in connection with the crime charged in this case, you may consider such evidence in light of all the other evidence. You may consider whether this evidence shows a consciousness of guilt and determine the significance, if any, to be attached to such conduct. (*United States v. Hanson*, 2000 U.S.App.LEXIS 1351)

In *People v. Yeoman*, the California Supreme Court affirmed the trial court instructions that the defendant's wiping his fingerprints off the automobile that he allegedly used to commit a robbery-murder was admissible to establish consciousness of guilt (*People v. Yeoman*, 31 Cal. 4th 93 [Cal. 2003]).

statements made during plea bargain → not admissible

Offers to Plead Guilty

★ If you make a deal ex. we let you out if you do this after getting out — never hear from them after letting them out.

Offers to plead guilty or to plead nolo contendere and statements made during negotiations over a guilty plea or plea of nolo contendere are inadmissible. Admission of this evidence at trial would be highly prejudicial to a defendant and would discourage individuals from plea bargaining. Defendants who ultimately decided to go to trial would be reluctant to testify in their own defense if this evidence could be used to impeach their credibility if they testified in their own defense at trial. The prohibition on the introduction of offers to plead guilty includes situations in which a defendant pled guilty and later withdrew and proceeded to trial. Keep in mind that statements made during plea negotiations are admissible in situations in which the plea agreement between the defendant and the prosecutor stipulates that plea agreements and statements made during plea agreements are admissible if the defendant fails to meet agreed-upon conditions and the prosecutor proceeds to trial. This situation arises in cases in which the defendant pledged to provide information or to testify against other individuals or to work as an undercover informant (*United States v. Verrusio*, 803 F.2d 885 [7th Cir. 1985]).

Possession of Stolen Property

The possession of stolen property in a prosecution for theft is circumstantial evidence that the defendant was responsible for the theft. An individual may be charged with receiving stolen property without being charged with theft where there is a relatively lengthy period of time between the theft and the possession of stolen goods.

The Indiana Supreme Court observed:

[P]ossession of recently stolen property may provide "an inference the possessor either was the thief or knew the property was stolen." . . . Indeed in *Barnes v. United States,* 412 U.S. 837 (1973) the United States Supreme Court noted that "[f]or centuries courts have instructed juries that an inference of guilty knowledge may be drawn from the fact of unexplained possession of stolen goods." (*Fortson v. State*, 919 N.E.2d 1136 [Ind. 2010])

Sudden Wealth

Evidence of sudden unexplained wealth may be considered to be probative of criminal activity. The defendant may respond to this evidence by documenting the legitimate source of these funds.

Leandro Salas-Galaviz and two co-defendants were convicted in federal court of drug trafficking and money laundering and of conspiracy to carry out these crimes. The federal district court noted the defendants' sudden increase in wealth. Salas-Galaviz, for example, between 2005 and 2009 had a reported total income of $30,000 and yet accumulated a bank account of over $750,000. His wife, Mayra Lopez, reported an income of $12,000 during this period and was inexplicably able to accumulate a bank account of over $350,000. The defendant's import-export business in 2008 reported a loss of roughly $48,000 and yet received wire transfers of over $61,000. The couple between 2002 and 2008 went from a small rental apartment to a $500,000 home, and their combined income during this period was $50,000 (*United States v. Alaniz*, 2013 WL 389878 [5th Cir. 2013]).

■ CIRCUMSTANTIAL EVIDENCE THAT AN INDIVIDUAL IS THE VICTIM OF RAPE

[handwritten: sexual activities/needs]

[handwritten: can test against injuries]

The common law definition of rape requires proof of the carnal knowledge of a female without her consent. Injury and bruising of a victim provides circumstantial evidence of the use of physical force and the lack of consent. This definition continues to be followed by a number of states. In a Massachusetts case, the defendant's claim that his sexual interaction with the victim was consensual was challenged by the prosecutor who noted

> [t]he treating physician described the bruising to the victim's knees as significant. The physician testified that there had been excessive force and trauma to the [vaginal] area based on his observation that there was a lot of swelling in her external vaginal area and her hymen had been torn and was still oozing. The doctor noted that in his experience it was fairly rare to see that much swelling and trauma. (*Commonwealth v. Lopez*, 745 N.E.2d 961 [Mass. Sup.Jud.Ct. 2001])

A prosecutor may rely on an expert witness to establish that the multiple injuries to a child resulted from physical assaults and are not the result of an accident (*Estelle v. McGuire*, 502 U.S. 62 [1991]).

Most courts accept that rape victims may introduce expert testimony on "**rape trauma syndrome**" to educate the jury of the post-traumatic behavior of the victims of sexual assault, some of which may appear inconsistent with victimization. A number of courts provide that the jury, based on this testimony and other evidence, can draw an inference that the defendant raped the victim.

The Indiana Supreme Court in *Simmons v. State* held "that the trial court's finding that the testimony of the experts was admissible [and] was not an abuse of discretion because they . . . merely [were] showing that her inability to recall certain events was consistent with the 'clinically observed behavior pattern.' Thus, it tended to show that the victim had suffered a rape and was not a direct opinion of an expert that the victim was telling the truth" (*Simmons v. State*, 504 N.E.2d 575 [Ind. 1987]). The defense attorney may call his or her own expert to counter expert evidence on rape trauma syndrome (*Henson v. State*, 546 N.E.3d 189 [Ind. 1989]). Other courts limit expert evidence on rape trauma syndrome to explaining to the jury why the calm demeanor following the crime or failure to immediately report the attack is characteristic of sexual victimization (*People v. Bledsoe*, 681 P.2d 291 [Cal. 1984]).

The so-called battered spouse and battered child syndromes are two additional psychological profiles that are admissible at trial to explain the behavior of the victims of alleged abuse. The "battered spouse syndrome" typically is relied on by women accused of killing their husbands. In some instances, the woman is considered the aggressor because her husband was sleeping and did not pose an imminent threat of death or of great bodily harm. The question arises why the female remained in the home throughout the abuse rather than retreating to safety. Expert testimony on the battered spouse syndrome educates the jury on the fear, helplessness, and lack of confidence suffered by a battered spouse and on her psychological inability to flee the home. The "battered child syndrome" applies the framework of the battered spouse syndrome to abused children to explain their assault or murder of their alleged abusers (*State v. Edwards*, 60 S.W.3d 602 [Mo.App. 2001]).

A last important syndrome is child sexual abuse accommodation syndrome (CSAAS), which is relied on in prosecutions for the sexual abuse of children. Experts may offer evidence on this syndrome to explain the conduct of the child that may appear to the jury as inconsistent with abuse and to bolster the child's credibility.

[handwritten: identifies a trait that someone has. → court doesn't like this → highly prejudice]

■ CHARACTER EVIDENCE

[handwritten: ★stop talking about the facts and talk about what type of person defendant is ★]

Character and Public Policy

Character evidence is considered highly prejudicial, and as a result, the Federal Rules of Evidence limit the circumstances in which character evidence may be introduced at trial. The thinking is that character evidence diverts attention from the criminal charge, wastes time, and creates a risk of prejudice. The fear is the defendant or victim's "bad character" may lead the jury to return a verdict based on the accused's negative character trait rather than based on the evidence presented at trial (*Whitty v. State*, 159 N.W.3d 557 [Wis. 1967]). A jury in a criminal assault case, for example, may be influenced to convict a defendant who the prosecution demonstrates is a "bad person" who has failed to pay child support to his or her economically dependent former spouse.

The rules of evidence strike a compromise by permitting character evidence on a limited basis. This so-called *mercy rule* is based on recognition that the defendant is entitled to defend him- or herself at trial and in some instances may want to introduce character evidence. Character evidence is regulated by a series of complicated rules that the Supreme Court has called illogical and confusing (*Michelson v. United States*, 335 U.S. 469 [1948]).

Federal Rule 404(a)(2)(A) permits a defendant to introduce evidence of a "pertinent" character trait as evidence he or she acted consistent with the "pertinent trait" on a particular occasion. Character evidence includes evidence of a wide variety of human traits including trustworthiness, honesty, law-abidingness, nonviolence, and attention to detail. This often is referred to as *propensity evidence*. A *pertinent trait* is a trait relevant to the charge against the defendant. Honesty and trustworthiness, for example, are pertinent to a charge of fraud or embezzlement. On the other hand, character evidence that the defendant is a devoted and responsible parent is not pertinent to fraud or embezzlement. Character evidence is circumstantial evidence because it does not directly prove the defendant acted in accordance with his or her character. The jury instead must infer that the defendant did not commit the criminal offense with which he or she is charged because he or she acted in a fashion consistent with his or her character and as a result is not guilty of the criminal offense with which he or she is charged.

Federal Rule 405(a) and most states provide proof of character "may be made by testimony" as to *reputation in the community* at the time charges are filed against the defendant or by the witness's *personal opinion*. Reputation is what other people believe about an individual's character. Character typically is established through the testimony of character witnesses. A witness testifying as to a defendant's reputation is reporting what he or she has heard from other people about the defendant's reputation for a specific trait. The jury may infer that the actions of a defendant with a reputation for nonviolence were consistent with this trait and that he or she did not initiate a fight.

Federal Rule 405(a) also provides proof of character "may be made by testimony" by the personal opinion of a witness. A witness may not testify about specific acts of a defendant's conduct. The thinking is that this evidence is time-consuming and may divert the jury's attention from the facts of the case. The jury also may place too much weight on the defendant's past conduct.

In *United States v. Staggs*, an FBI agent who arrested Lonnie Paul Staggs for desertion from the Marine Corps contended Staggs pointed a firearm at the agent. Staggs denied threatening the officer. The Seventh Circuit Court of Appeals held the trial court improperly had excluded the expert testimony of a therapist who would have testified Staggs was nonviolent and would rather "hurt himself than to think about directing his aggressions towards others." The Seventh Circuit Court of Appeals held the therapist's opinion testimony made it more likely than not the defendant was telling the truth when he denied pointing a firearm at the FBI agent (*United States v. Staggs*, 553 F.2d 1073 [7th Cir. 1977]).

The prosecution is barred from attacking the character of the accused unless the defendant "opens the door" by offering evidence of a "pertinent" character trait. Once the defendant introduces evidence of his or her character, the door is opened for the prosecutor to rebut this evidence with evidence of the same trait. The defendant's presentation of honesty in a theft case may be rebutted by prosecution character witnesses offering reputation or opinion evidence of dishonesty or by opinion evidence the defendant lacks the character trait of honesty.

The prosecutor also may impeach a defendant's character witness on cross-examination and inquire into the witness's knowledge of specific, relevant instances of a defendant's conduct. The cross-examination may focus on arrest, criminal acts, and other bad acts, including the act with which the defendant is charged. The thinking is a witness who does not know about a specific act either has exercised poor judgment in assessing the defendant's character or has been poorly informed about the defendant's reputation.

In *Michelson v. United States*, the defendant was charged with bribery of an Internal Revenue Service agent. The Supreme Court held the prosecution on cross-examination properly asked the defendant's character witnesses about the defendant's arrest for a property crime that occurred over twenty-seven years earlier. The Court reasoned that the prosecutor had a right to test the witnesses' knowledge of the defendant on a crime related to a character for honesty and truthfulness and law-abidingness (*Michelson v. United States*, 335 U.S. 469 [1948]).

Legal Equation

Defense	=	Evidence of good character on pertinent trait at issue + reputation and opinion.
Prosecution	=	Evidence of negative character on pertinent character trait + reputation and opinion.

4.1 YOU DECIDE

Randall Dahlin was charged with bank robbery. He testified he was babysitting his infant niece at the time of the robbery and was "deeply devoted to his niece and his family" and never would have left her alone. The prosecutor responded by asking the district court judge to admit two types of evidence: (1) Dahlin did not get along with his family; (2) Dahlin took things that did not belong to him. Would you admit this evidence? See *United States v. Dahlin* (734 F.2d 393 [8th Cir. 1984]). *yes. it is pertinent evidence*

You can learn what the court decided by referring to the study site, **http://study.sagepub.com/lippmance.**

4.2 YOU DECIDE

Boston police officer Richard Nazzaro was convicted of purchasing questions and answers to a civil service exam administered to officers applying for promotion. The trial court judge ruled that Nazzaro could not introduce evidence of the military and police commendations he had received, including a medal for "special valor." How would you rule? See *United States v. Nazzaro* (889 F.2d 1158 [1st Cir. 1989]).

You can learn what the court decided by referring to the study site, **http://study.sagepub.com/lippmance.**

Character as an Essential Element of a Crime

Federal Rule 405(b) provides that in cases in which the character or character trait of a person is an essential element of a charge or defense, "proof may be made of specific instances of that person's conduct" in addition to reputation and opinion evidence. This situation is presented infrequently. One instance is in entrapment cases in which a defendant may rely on specific instances of conduct to demonstrate he or she was not "predisposed" to commit a crime and the defendant's criminal activity was a product of the creative activity of the government.

Victim's Character in a Criminal Case

The defense attorney under Federal Rule 404(a)(2)(B) may introduce character evidence about the alleged victim. The character of the victim of an assault may be at issue in a case in which the accused claims to have acted in self-defense. The victim's violent character trait may support the reasonableness of the defendant's belief that he or she confronted a threat of imminent and immediate harm and was justified in acting in self-defense. This evidence also is intended for the jury to draw the inference that the victim was the aggressor. The prosecution may rebut the defendant's evidentiary claim that he or she acted in self-defense by offering evidence of the victim's character for peacefulness. The prosecutor also may introduce evidence of the defendant's violent character trait. Evidence of the victim's character is limited to reputation or opinion evidence.

In *State v. Everett*, a North Carolina appellate court held the trial court was in error in preventing a wife who claimed she killed her husband in self-defense from introducing evidence of his violent character. On one occasion, he had been angry at a car dealer and broke windows of autos on the lot. The appellate court reasoned that the husband's violent character was relevant to the reasonableness of the wife's claim she was in reasonable fear of imminent harm and "it tends to shed some light upon who was the aggressor since a violent man is more likely to be the aggressor than a peaceable man" (*State v. Everett*, 630 S.E.2d 703 [2006]).

Victim's Character in a Homicide Case

There is a special rule of evidence in homicide cases that expands the ability of the prosecution to offer evidence of the victim's character. Federal Rule 404(a)(2)(C) provides that "in a homicide case, the prosecutor may offer evidence of the alleged victim's trait of peacefulness to rebut any evidence that the alleged victim was the first aggressor." The prosecutor does not have to wait for the defendant to place the character of the victim at issue. Returning to our bar brawl scenario, an eyewitness may testify the victim assaulted the defendant without provocation. The testimony *suggesting* that the alleged victim was the aggressor entitles the prosecutor to respond by introducing character evidence of the victim's peacefulness. Once again, the prosecutor does not have to wait for the defendant to introduce character evidence regarding the alleged victim.

Legal Equation

Defense	=	Evidence of victim's bad character **+** evidence of reputation and/or opinion.
Prosecution	=	Evidence of victim's good character for same trait and/or defendant's bad character for same trait + evidence of reputation and/or opinion.
Defense	=	Evidence in homicide case victim was aggressor **+** evidence of reputation and/or opinion.
Prosecution	=	Evidence of victim's peaceful character **+** evidence of reputation and/or opinion.

4.3 YOU DECIDE

Ronald Keiser alleged he shot and paralyzed Victor Romero in self-defense. During a recess, Romero encountered Keiser's brother in the hallway outside the courtroom. Romero, in the presence of his family and court security, angrily shouted, "There he is, that's the f___'s brother. And I want you to remember his face, remember his face." The trial court refused to permit the defendant's lawyer to offer evidence of this confrontation to demonstrate Romero's violent nature and circumstantial evidence that Romero was the aggressor. As a judge, how would you rule? See *United States v. Keiser* (57 F.3d 847 [9th Cir. 1995]).

You can learn what the court decided by referring to the study site, **http://study.sagepub.com/lippmance.**

CRIMINAL EVIDENCE IN THE NEWS

On November 23, 2012, Michael Dunn and his girlfriend Rhonda Rouer pulled into a service station. Rouer exited the car to buy chips and wine while Dunn waited in the automobile. Rouer later would testify Dunn, a 47-year-old computer programmer, remarked he "hated" the "thug music" loudly playing in an adjacent SUV. Dunn claimed he "calmly and politely" requested the teens to lower the volume of the music. He reportedly quickly became embroiled in a "war of words" with the four teens in the SUV after they turned down and then resumed the volume of what he testified was their "rap-crap" music. He testified that he feared for his life when he saw through the rearview mirror Jordan Davis display what he believed was the barrel of a 12-gauge or 20-gauge shotgun or a pipe, believed the teens were staring at him with "menacing expressions," heard one of the teens utter a profanity-laced threat to kill him, and saw Davis begin to exit the SUV. Dunn, who possessed a concealed carry weapons permit, removed his semiautomatic pistol from the glove compartment, inserted a clip, and fired three shots, which penetrated the SUV and killed 17-year-old Davis. He fired another seven shots as the car sped from the parking lot. Dunn testified he believed this was "life or death," my "death was imminent," and I was "fighting for [my] life. . . . He's showing me a gun and he's threatening me."

Dunn quickly drove off as Rouer entered the car and Dunn explained to Rouer that he acted in self-defense because the teens were "advancing" and he feared for his life. She would testify at trial that he only referred to having seen a firearm on one occasion during the remainder of the evening. They hurried back to their bed-and-breakfast, walked their dog Charlie, drank rum and coke, and ordered a pizza. Both Dunn and Rouer testified they did not know anyone in the car was hurt until they turned on the television news and learned 17-year-old Davis was dead. The next day, they drove two and a half hours back home without calling the police. An eyewitness recorded Dunn's license number, and Dunn was contacted by the police.

Rouer testified that Dunn was an "easygoing guy" and she had never "seen him lose his cool" although he was passionate in conversations about politics and gun control.

The police failed to uncover a weapon in the SUV although Dunn's attorney later pointed out Dunn had the right to exercise self-defense even if the teens did not possess a weapon if he reasonably believed he was confronted with an imminent and immediate threat of physical bodily harm. Dunn had no duty to retreat under Florida's so-called stand-your-ground law.

The forensic evidence indicated Davis had been shot while lying in the backseat of the SUV, and there was no evidence at any point that he had exited the car. Witnesses testified Dunn had shouted at Davis, "You can't talk to me that way!" and that he had opened his door to get a better shooting angle.

Dunn was convicted of attempted second-degree murder, which requires a substantial step toward the taking of the life of another person. The jury included four white women, two African American women, one Asian woman, a Hispanic man, and four white men. Ten of the twelve jurors found sufficient evidence to convict on a first-degree murder charge although two jurors argued Dunn acted in self-defense in killing Davis. The jurors after thirty minutes told the judge they were unable to return a verdict on the charge that Dunn deliberately and intentionally and with premeditation killed Davis, and a mistrial was declared on the first count in the indictment. Dunn was sentenced to sixty years and likely will spend the rest of his natural life in prison. Prosecutor Angela Corey, who had handled the Trayvon Martin case, pledged to prosecute Dunn a second time for first-degree murder.

Corey was criticized for bringing a first-degree rather than second-degree charge for the killing of Jordan Davis although certainly there was enough evidence to support a finding that Dunn reflected and planned to kill Davis.

The prosecution also was criticized for failing to educate the jury about the character of Davis who, in the words of his father, "was a good kid" who along with the other good kids "should have a voice" in the courtroom.

The prosecution avoided interjecting race into the trial and did not ask Dunn about the letters he had written from prison blaming the teenagers for having brought this onto themselves by "embracing the gang culture." He wrote his experience in prison had made him "more prejudiced" and if more people "would arm themselves and kill those . . . idiots when they're threatening you, eventually they may take the hint and change their behavior." In October 2014, Dunn was convicted of first-degree murder by a Florida jury and sentenced to life in prison without parole, and his sentence for attempted murder was increased.

Character and Habit

Habit evidence is admissible to demonstrate that the defendant acted in accordance with his or her habit on a particular occasion. Federal Rule 406 provides that "[e]vidence of a person's habit or an organizational routine practice" may be admitted to establish that on a "particular occasion the person or organization acted in accordance with the habit or routine practice." In other words, a habit is a specific behavior that is repeated over and over again when confronted with a specific situation. The Federal Rules of Evidence give the example of an auto mechanic who follows the same steps in changing the oil in an automobile.

What is the difference between character evidence, which is subject to restrictions on admissibility, and habit evidence, which always is admissible? Character is general, and habit is specific. You may have the reputation of being a safe and careful driver and possess the habit of fastening your seat belt.

Character evidence refers to an individual's general tendencies such as honesty, violence, trustworthiness, and peacefulness. Habit evidence refers to a regular response to a repeated specific situation, such as eating the same food for lunch at the same time each and every day, or parking in the same parking space. Habit is required to be specific, routine, and continuous. Most commentators refer to habit as an act that is virtually automatic. Habit is admissible because it is limited to specific behavior and is considered to possess greater probative value than character and has less capacity to create prejudice against a defendant.

Rule 406 does not define habit. In *United States v. Angwin*, the Ninth Circuit Court of Appeals identified the central characteristics of habit as a specific behavior repeated for a lengthy period of time and carried out in a "semi-automatic" fashion (*United States v. Angwin*, 271 F.3d 786 [9th Cir. 2001]).

Courts have adopted a broad notion of what constitutes habit. In *State v. Allen*, the defendant in a murder prosecution claimed the victim was alive when he left her house. His fingerprints were found on a drinking glass. The court admitted evidence that the victim was an obsessive housekeeper as circumstantial evidence that she likely would have wiped the defendant's fingerprints off the glass had she been alive (*State v. Allen*, 653 N.E.2d 674 [Ohio, 1995]).

The federal rules leave it to the trial court judge to determine the type of evidence that is admissible to prove habit. Most courts hold that habit may be established through opinion testimony and through specific instances of conduct and may be established through the defendant or through witnesses familiar with the defendant's habit. A defendant or the individuals who eat lunch with the defendant each and every day may testify that the defendant had the habit of drinking two beers.

Legal Equation

Habit = Admissible to prove individual acted on a particular occasion in accordance with specific behavior.

4.4 YOU DECIDE

The defendant was convicted in 1977 of various offenses including contributing to the delinquency of a minor. The minor female testified the defendant regularly would beat her and that she wrote worthless checks because she was afraid of additional beatings. The defendant denied beating her. The prosecution responded by calling his former wife who claimed he had beaten her three or four times during the one month they lived together in 1975. His former girlfriend testified he had beaten her on a "number of times" between 1974 and 1976. The trial court admitted this testimony as "evidence of the habit of a person . . . relevant to prove that the conduct of the person . . . on a particular occasion was in conformity with the habit." The defendant claimed the beating of the minor occurred under different circumstances from the beatings alleged by the prosecution "habit-witnesses." What is your view? See *State v. Gardner* (573 P.2d 236 [N.M. Ct. App. 1977]).

You can learn what the court decided by referring to the study site, **http://study.sagepub.com/lippmance.**

Rule 404(a). Character Evidence; Crimes or Other Acts

(a) Character Evidence.

   (1) *Prohibited Uses.* Evidence of a person's character or character trait is not admissible to prove that on a particular occasion the person acted in accordance with the character or trait.

   (2) *Exceptions for a Defendant or Victim in a Criminal Case.* The following exceptions apply in a criminal case:

   (A) a defendant may offer evidence of the defendant's pertinent trait, and if the evidence is admitted, the prosecutor may offer evidence to rebut it;

   (B) subject to the limitations in Rule 412, a defendant may offer evidence of an alleged victim's pertinent trait, and if the evidence is admitted, the prosecutor may

   (i) offer evidence to rebut it; and

   (ii) offer evidence of the defendant's same trait; and

   (C) in a homicide case, the prosecutor may offer evidence of the alleged victim's trait of peacefulness to rebut evidence that the victim was the first aggressor.

Rule 405. Methods of Proving Character

(a) By Reputation or Opinion. When evidence of a person's character or character trait is admissible, it may be proved by testimony about the person's reputation or by testimony in the form of an opinion. On cross-examination of the character witness, the court may allow an inquiry into relevant specific instances of the person's conduct.

(b) By Specific Instances of Conduct. When a person's character or character trait is an essential element of a charge, claim, or defense, the character or trait may also be proved by relevant specific instances of the person's conduct.

■ OTHER ACTS EVIDENCE

Admission of evidence of prior criminal acts generally is not admissible because it is prejudicial. There is a risk the defendant will be convicted because of his or her past acts rather than based on the crime with which he or she is charged, which violates the defendant's right to be tried solely for the offense for which he or she is standing trial. **Other acts evidence** because of its prejudicial character is not admissible to prove the defendant is the type of person with a bad character or criminal predisposition who more than likely committed the crime with which he or she is charged.

There is an exception to the prohibition on other acts evidence. Federal Rule 404(b) provides that the "other crimes, wrongs, or acts" of a defendant are admissible by the prosecution to establish "motive, opportunity, intent, preparation, plan, knowledge, identity, absence of mistake, or lack of accident." Other acts evidence, however, "is not admissible to prove the character of a person in order to show action in conformity therewith." An act under the "other acts" exception may occur prior to or following the commission of the crime with which the defendant is charged.

Rule 404(b) allows admission of evidence of "a crime, wrong, or other act." In other words, the prosecutor may introduce evidence of a crime for which the defendant was not arrested or convicted. The standard for admissibility is flexible, it is sufficient the act is relevant to an "issue in dispute," and the prosecutor submits enough evidence in the view of the judge for a reasonable juror to conclude it occurred (*Huddleston v. United States*, 485 U.S 681 [1988]).

Keep in mind other acts evidence always may be excluded under Rule 403 because the probative value of the evidence is outweighed by the risk of prejudice. Another important point is that "motive, opportunity, intent, preparation, plan, knowledge, identity, absence of mistake, or lack of accident" may be established by all types of circumstantial evidence and proof is not limited to other acts evidence. For example, the inference that an individual was responsible for a murder may be established by the defendant's conviction of similar crimes as well as by items belonging to the defendant left at the crime scene.

Some of these exceptions are discussed in the next section of the text. Keep in mind that the judge in admitting other acts evidence will weigh the probative value of this type of evidence against its prejudicial effect on the jury.

Legal Equation

Crimes, wrongs, or other acts	=	(may be used for) Motive, opportunity, intent, preparation, plan, knowledge, identity, absence of mistake, or lack of accident.
Crimes, wrongs, or other acts	≠	(may not be used for) Action in conformity with prior act.

■ OTHER ACTS EVIDENCE AND CIRCUMSTANTIAL EVIDENCE OF IDENTITY

Modus Operandi *crime is committed the same each time*

The so-called *signature modus operandi* rule is an exception to the rule that prior crimes generally are excluded from evidence. *Modus operandi* evidence is admissible to prove the defendant's identity as the perpetrator of a crime or may be used to rebut a defendant's denial that he or she committed the crime with which he or she is charged. The crimes must be "so nearly identical" to "earmark them as the handiwork of the accused. . . . [M]uch more is demanded than the mere repeated commission of crimes of the same class, such as repeated burglaries or thefts. The device used must be so unusual and distinctive as to be like a signature" (*State v. Sladek*, 835 S.W.2d 308 [Mo. Ct. App. 1999]).

In *Jones v. State*, the defendant was charged with leading his victim into an empty barn where the victim was robbed by a confederate who used a "long-barreled pistol" and wore a Halloween mask and a black wig. The court heard testimony from a criminal investigator who recounted that two weeks following the robbery he went with another investigator to the farm and posed as a cattle buyer. The defendant took him to a barn where the investigator was robbed at gunpoint by a man holding a long-barreled pistol and wearing a Halloween mask and a black wig. The second offense was admitted to identify the defendant as the perpetrator of the robbery with which he was charged (*Jones v. State*, 460 So.2d 1384 [Ala. Cr. App. 1984]).

In *State v. Vorhees*, Shane A. Vorhees was charged and convicted of the sodomy of his 13-year-old stepdaughter. S. W. testified that beginning when she was 13 years of age Vorhees, her stepfather, repeatedly assaulted her sexually during a two-year period. S. W. testified that during the assaults Vorhees would use his saliva as a lubricant by spitting on his hand, rubbing his penis, and then placing his penis in S. W.'s anus or vagina. On one occasion, Vorhees placed his penis in S. W.'s mouth and urinated, and on other occasions, he ejaculated in her mouth. Vorhees appealed the trial court judge's admission of evidence from another young woman who testified a number of years ago when she was 6 years old that Vorhees had engaged in precisely the same behavior in molesting her. The Missouri Supreme Court held the testimony was admissible to identify Vorhees as the perpetrator of the molestation of his stepdaughter (*State v. Vorhees*, 248 S.W.3d 585 [Mo. 2008]).

■ OTHER ACTS EVIDENCE AND CIRCIRCUMSTANTIAL EVIDENCE OF INTENT

Intent

Other acts evidence is relevant to prove intent and also is relevant in those instances in which the defendant denies his or her criminal intent. In *State v. Brewster*, the defendant was convicted of harassment based on his threatening to kill a child support enforcement officer of the New Hampshire Division of Child Support Services. Brewster claimed the trial court improperly admitted evidence of an incident following a child support hearing two years prior to the threatening statement in which Brewster angrily pointed his finger at the officer and proclaimed "this is why people like you get shot."

The New Hampshire Supreme Court held that Brewster's statement was relevant to establish the defendant's intent to "intimidate" and "annoy or alarm" the officer. Although the incidents were two years apart, both events were logically connected because they were provoked by Brewster's resentment over being required to pay child support (*State v. Brewster*, 147 A.2d 158 [N.H. 2002]).

> We will find sufficient support for a reliable inference of intent only if the defendant's intent in committing other bad acts and the defendant's intent in the charged offenses is closely connected by logically significant factors. . . . In both instances, the defendant's threatening behavior was directed toward the same person. Both of the defendant's statements were similar, involving [the officer] being shot. Also, the defendant made the statements in circumstances where he was having problems with his child support payments. Therefore, although the prior act occurred two years earlier, these factors provide a sufficient logical connection to the charged act.

Knowledge

Prior criminal convictions are admissible to establish the intent of knowledge. Donovan New drove at a speed of eighty-five miles per hour, lost control of the car, and crashed, killing his father and cousin. A blood alcohol test indicated New's alcohol content was measured at .320. He was charged with involuntary manslaughter, which requires that New was aware or reasonably should have been aware that his conduct posed a threat to others. His two prior convictions for drunk driving were admitted to establish New's knowledge that driving under the influence of alcohol both was illegal and posed a substantial risk of harm to him and to other individuals (*United States v. New*, 491 F.3d 375 [8th Cir. 2007]).

a house was foreclosed— rob a bank

Motive *hatred of people*

Conviction of a crime requires the prosecution to establish the required criminal intent beyond a reasonable doubt.

Motive, although not an element of a crime, may be important in proving the intent of an individual to batter or to kill and may be used to rebut the defendant's claim that an injury or death resulted from an accident. Motive also may constitute circumstantial evidence of the defendant's identity as the perpetrator of a crime.

The defendant's hatred of another individual may constitute circumstantial evidence of an intent to kill. Individuals motivated to kill by financial considerations include the beneficiary of a life insurance policy, an individual who stands to inherit a large sum of money, and an individual who owes a large gambling debt. The owner of a failing restaurant may be viewed as having a motive to hire an arsonist to burn down the restaurant or the restaurant of a competitor.

Jealousy of another individual also may provide a motivation to kill. A disappointed lover, a former spouse, or an individual who wants to eliminate a romantic rival all may be viewed as possessing a motive to kill or to injure or maim.

An individual's expression of racial or religious hatred or anger toward women or same-sex couples may provide circumstantial evidence that an individual criminal attack constituted a hate crime.

One individual's motive to kill another may be used to counter a defendant's claim of self-defense or murder in the heat of passion. This would demonstrate an individual intended to kill rather than responded to provocation from the deceased.

In *State v. Kim*, the defendant's significant gambling debt and financial distress were evidence of his motive to rob and to kill the two victims from whom he had unsuccessfully sought a loan.

> There is a sufficient logical connection between [the defendant's] declining financial situation and his motive to rob and kill the victims. Evidence of the defendant's debt and financial difficulties establish a motive for [the defendant] to not only rob the Joseph brothers but also to kill them in order to eliminate any potential witnesses. The defendant's dire financial position has further relevance in assessing the motive to kill witnesses to the robbery when viewed in light of his failed attempt to obtain a [twenty thousand dollar] loan from Theodore Joseph immediately prior to the homicides. (*State v. Kim*, 847 A.2d 968 [N.H. 2006])

admissible ✔

Threats

The threat to commit a crime is admissible as circumstantial evidence the defendant committed the crime. The weight to be accorded to the threat depends on the nature and context of the threat, the length of time between the threat and the criminal act, and whether witnesses can testify to the threat (*State v. Dukette*, 761 A.2d 442 [N.H. 2000]).

In *State v. Sawtell*, the defendant shot and killed his girlfriend because of his unhappiness over her having given birth to a child two months earlier. The defendant's threats with a firearm directed against the victim five and ten months prior to the murder were held to be admissible to establish intent to kill (*State v. Sawtell*, 872 A.2d 1013 [2005]).

A defendant's threats against prosecutors, co-defendants, and witnesses generally are considered probative of consciousness of guilt. The reasoning is that these threats are an effort to affect the outcome of the case and are probative of the defendant's awareness that the government likely will obtain a conviction. The jury determined the weight to be accorded to this evidence because threats against prosecutors and other criminal justice personnel may reflect frustration or anger at the government. In *United States v. Copeland*, the Sixth Circuit Court of Appeals determined that the probative value of evidence of threats against the prosecutor was outweighed by the risk that the jury would make the impermissible inference that the defendant possessed a violent nature. The trial court reasoned that the fact the defendant made threats against the prosecutor had little relevance to the charge of conspiracy to distribute a controlled substance. Do you agree with the trial court judge's holding? (*United States v. Copeland,* 321 F.3d 582 [6th Cir. 2003]).

suspect had access to the crime scene before crime happened

Opportunity

In *Huang v. McEwen*, the defendant discovered two men entering his house, accused them of attempting to steal his marijuana, and was charged and convicted of holding them captive overnight and killing them and disposing of their bodies in the desert. A number of individuals testified to witnessing the defendant's confinement of the individuals. The federal district court stressed there was circumstantial evidence that the defendant murdered the two hostages and took them captive at knifepoint, killed them, and disposed of their bodies in the desert. The circumstantial evidence supporting the defendant's guilt included the opportunity presented by the defendant's detention of the individuals at his house following their apprehension (*Huang v. McEwen*, 2012 U.S. Dist. LEXIS 86965).

Act Not Performed Inadvertently, Accidentally, Involuntarily, or Without Guilty Knowledge

It has been noted that the death of one spouse in the bath might be accidental; three drownings, however, are not so easily explained (Broun 2000).

The classic example is the Australian case *Makin v. Attorney General of New South Wales*. The bodies of thirteen infants were discovered in the home and former home of John and Sarah Makin. They were charged and convicted of the murder of two of the children and claimed the court had improperly permitted the introduction of the evidence of the eleven other infants. The English Privy Council, with jurisdiction over appeals from British possessions, held that the "recurrence of the unusual phenomenon of bodies of babies having been buried in an unexplained manner in a similar part of the premises, previously occupied" implied that the deaths were "willful and not accidental" (*Makin v. Attorney General of New South Wales*, [1894] App. C. 57 [P.C. 1893]).

Prior False Claims

The filing of a false complaint raises the inference that a present complaint also is false. This type of circumstantial evidence is particularly persuasive in those instances in which an individual is being prosecuted for filing a fraudulent insurance claim.

In *United States v. Jackson*, the defendant received nine checks for educational benefits from the Veterans Administration (VA). The VA later found the defendant had dropped out of college during the 1979–1980 academic year and never should have received the checks. In 1982, Jackson claimed he had never received the checks and filed a claim for the checks. The VA produced evidence that the checks had been cashed. The defendant responded the next year by filing another claim for the checks (*United States v. Jackson*, 845 F.2d 880 [9th Cir. 1988]).

Jackson was convicted of making false claims against the United States for the proceeds of government checks and claimed the court improperly admitted evidence of his first, false claim for the checks. The trial court, however, held that "the fact that Jackson submitted prior false claims involving the same nine VA checks is probative on issues of intent, knowledge, good faith and absence of mistake in his later dealings with the Treasury Department."

A complaining witness may be discredited by evidence he or she has made a false complaint for the same crime in the past. The inference is that the present complaint also is false. This "false complaint" evidence typically is brought out on cross-examination of the complainant by the defense attorney. In *State v. Stevenson*, the defendant appealed his rape convictions based on the court's refusal to allow him to cross-examine the victim on her prior claims against him for sexual assault. A Connecticut appeals court held

> Courts have recognized that prior false claims of sexual assault may be relevant to a complainant's credibility. These claims must, however, be proven false. "Without evidence of the falsity of the prior accusation . . . the defendant cannot show the relevance of the proposed cross-examination." In this case, the defense attorney had no information that J's [the victim's] prior sexual assault claims were false. . . . The questioning proposed by the defendant is improper in the absence of proof of any false accusations made by the victim. (*State v. Stevenson*, 686 A.2d 500 [Conn. App. 1996])

Evidence of false claims of victims may have the greatest probative value when involving the same type of offense for which the defendant is being prosecuted and when the same victim is involved and these false complaints have been filed on a number of occasions.

Plan

Gary DeCicco was charged with setting his commercial warehouse on fire in July 1995 and fraudulently collecting insurance proceeds on the building. The prosecutor alleged DeCicco planned to use the money to pay off more than $1 million in back taxes. The trial court judge excluded government evidence that a 1992 warehouse fire was set in the same manner as one of the 1995 fires. The fire department was able to extinguish the fire. The government argued the 1992 fire demonstrated an ongoing plan to burn the warehouse and to collect insurance proceeds.

The First Circuit Court of Appeals held the trial court was in error in excluding the evidence of the fire set in 1992, reasoning that the jury could infer a plan from three suspicious fires in the same building. DeCicco's insurance had been canceled, and the 1995 fires occurred two months after his insurance resumed (*United States v. DeCicco*, 370 F.3d 206 [1st Cir. 2004]). The First Circuit Court of Appeals reasoned that

> [t]he degree of resemblance of the crimes . . . favors inclusion of the evidence. Both the 1992 fire and the final fire were set in the same manner: an accelerant was poured on the base of the support pillars on the first floor of the Heard Street warehouse. They are the same type of crime, and, more importantly, the object of all fires was the same property. These factors tend to show that the previous offense leads in progression to the two charged fires, or, put more simply, that DeCicco had one common scheme to burn the Heard Street warehouse, which had previously proven financially unsuccessful. . . . Therefore, the district court erred in not considering whether the 1992 fire was relevant to a common scheme or plan to burn the Heard Street warehouse for the insurance proceeds. The evidence is probative of a common scheme or plan and should be introduced to that effect.

 blue prints

Preparation

In *State v. Ayer*, the New Hampshire Supreme Court held a number of firearms seized from the defendant's automobile immediately following the killing were admissible at trial. The weapons, though not used in the killing, were admissible as the defendant's truck was "probative of his intent, plan or preparation to commit a violent act." In other words, the weapons provided circumstantial evidence of the defendant's preparation and planning and an intent to murder the victim (*State v. Ayer*, 917 A.2d 219 [N.H. 2006]).

⚖ 4.5 YOU DECIDE

Two Caucasian Air Force police officers were robbed walking back to Fort Dix, New Jersey. They were robbed, and one was sexually assaulted by an African American male wearing a wool cap and a tan nylon jogging suit and brandishing a small, silver handgun. Both men identified Richard Stevens in a lineup as the assailant. Stevens, in his defense, unsuccessfully attempted to introduce "reverse" Rule 404(b) evidence. An African American member of the Air Force, three days after the two Air Force officers were attacked, suffered a similar assault. Tyrone Mitchell, however, stated that Stevens was not his assailant.

A court of appeals noted that similarities between them are significant. Both crimes: (1) took place within a few hundred yards of one another; (2) were armed robberies; (3) involved a handgun; (4) occurred between 9:30 p.m. and 10:30 p.m.; (5) were perpetrated on military personnel; and (6) involved a black assailant who was described similarly by his victims. Indeed, based on these similarities, the United States Army Criminal Investigation Division came to believe, initially, that the same person had committed both crimes. As a judge, would you admit the "reverse" Rule 404(b) evidence? See *United States v. Stevens* (935 F.2d 1380 [3rd Cir. 1991]).

You can learn what the court decided by referring to the study site, **http://study.sagepub.com/lippmance.**

CRIMINAL EVIDENCE AND PUBLIC POLICY

The common law defined rape as the forcible carnal knowledge of a woman against her will. Carnal knowledge for purposes of rape is defined as vaginal intercourse by a man with a woman who is not his wife. The vaginal intercourse is required to be carried out by force or threat of severe bodily harm without the victim's consent.

(Continued)

sexual behavior of victim is admissible ⌐] does make rape harder
ex: had prior consentual relations with defendant in the past] to prove
→ other behavior is not
ex: tinder relationships not admissible

(Continued)

The common law of rape reflects a distrust of women, and various requirements were imposed to ensure that the prosecutrix (victim) was not engaged in blackmail or in an attempt to conceal a consensual affair or was not suffering from a psychological illness. There was a fear that a judge and jury would be emotionally carried away by the seriousness of the charge and convict a defendant based on false testimony. The prosecution was required to overcome a number of hurdles under the common law in order to convict the defendant:

Immediate Complaint. The absence of a prompt complaint by the victim to authorities was evidence that the complaint was not genuine.

Corroboration Rule. The victim's allegation of rape required corroboration, evidence such as physical injury or witnesses.

Sexual Activity. The victim's past sexual conduct or reputation for chastity was admissible as evidence of consent or on cross-examination to attack her credibility.

Judicial Instruction. The judge was required to issue a cautionary instruction to the jury that the victim's testimony should be subject to strict scrutiny because rape is a crime easily charged and difficult to prove.

Consent. The victim's lack of consent was demonstrated through outward resistance. The victim was required to "resist to the utmost."

During the 1970s and 1980s, a number of states abolished the special procedures surrounding the common law of rape. A number of states adopted new sexual assault statutes that fundamentally changed the law of rape. These statutes treated rape as an assault against the person rather than as an offense against sexual morality. These statutes refer to "criminal sexual conduct" or "sexual assault" rather than rape. The modified statutes widely differ from one another although they typically incorporate one or more of the following provisions:

Gender Neutral. A male or female may be the perpetrator or victim of rape.

Degree of Rape. Several degrees of rape are defined that are distinguished from one another based on factors such as the degree of force and use of a weapon.

Sexual Intercourse. Sexual intercourse is expanded to include forced sexual activity or forced intrusion into a person's body, including oral and anal intercourse, and the insertion of an object into the genital or anal opening of another.

Consent. State statutes provide that consent requires free, affirmative, and voluntary cooperation or that resistance may be established by either words or actions.

Coercion. There is recognition that coercion may be achieved through fraud or psychological pressure as well as through physical force.

As part of rape reform in the 1970s, the states and federal government adopted so-called **rape shield laws**, which restricted the cross-examination of alleged victims and the admissibility of their reputation for sexual "virtuosity." The thinking was that this evidence was irrelevant to the adjudication of the alleged rape at issue in the trial, diverted the attention of jurors and the court to irrelevant events, and discouraged women from coming forward with complaints of rape. The basic framework of rape shield statutes is set forth in Federal Rule of Evidence 412.

The rape shield protections at times may conflict with the defendant's constitutional right to confront his or her accusers. Federal Rule 412 accordingly recognizes certain limited exceptions to the rape shield law. Evidence of past sexual activity with the defendant is admissible as evidence of consent. Courts interpret sexual behavior to include all varieties of intimate contact between the complainant and the accused.

Sexual activity with individuals other than the defendant is admissible to prove that "a person other than the accused was the source of semen, injury or other physical evidence." A final provision provides the judge discretion to admit evidence to protect the right of a defendant to confront his or her accusers. This so-called catchall provision was unsuccessfully relied on in arguing that the defendant reasonably, though mistakenly, believed the victim consented because she was a prostitute (*United States v. Saunders*, 943 F.2d 388 [4th Cir. 1991]).

Prior to the admission of evidence under Rule 412, the judge is required to hold an in-camera (closed to the public) hearing to afford all the parties to the case the opportunity to be heard.

Greg Matoesian (2001) finds that the rape shield statute has provided limited protection to women because of the skill of talented lawyers in getting around the limitations of rape shield laws. Matoesian demonstrates how a talented defense lawyer like Roy Black is able to indirectly infer the female victim consented to the alleged rape. Black represented William Kennedy Smith, a doctor and member of the highly respected and revered Kennedy family, who was charged with the 1991 rape of a young woman in Florida. Black persuaded the judge to exclude the testimony of three rape employs because the allegations were too dissimilar to constitute *modus operandi*.

Matoesian documents how Black's questioning suggests the victim's inability to recall when she removed her pantyhose after leaving the bar with William Kennedy Smith calls her character into question. The victim alleged she drove Smith home, took a tour of the historic Kennedy compound, and took a walk on the beach with Smith, and that he later raped her on the front lawn. Black asked whether the victim was wearing her pantyhose in the car when she drove Smith home. He then asked whether she had them on when she went into the house, walked through the kitchen, walked through the house, walked across the lawn, and walked on the beach. The victim in each instance responded that "I'm not sure." Matoesian notes that the victim's removal of her pantyhose is a normal act before walking on the beach and irrelevant to whether she consented to the sexual interaction with the defendant. Black, however, based his cross-examination on the premise that jurors believed that decent women do not lose track of their underwear when they are with a man. Smith was acquitted by a jury within five minutes of their consideration of the case.

There are two other federal rules addressing sexual offenses. Federal Rule 413 provides that in a criminal case in which a defendant is accused of sexual assault, the court may admit evidence "that the defendant committed any other sexual assault." This evidence may be introduced to support an inference that the defendant's commission of a sexual assault in the past increases the probability he or she committed the offense with which he or she is charged. The prosecutor must disclose to the defendant beforehand his or her intent to introduce this evidence at trial along with the testimony in support of the prior sexual assault. Federal Rule 414 provides in a prosecution of an individual for molestation of a child under 14 that the court may admit evidence the defendant "committed any other child molestation."

Rule 412. Sex Offense Cases: The Victim's Sexual Behavior or Predisposition

(a) **Prohibited Uses.** The following evidence is not admissible in a civil or criminal proceeding involving alleged sexual misconduct:

(1) evidence offered to prove that a victim engaged in other sexual behavior, or

(2) evidence offered to prove a victim's sexual predisposition.

(b) **Exceptions.**

(1) *Criminal Cases.* The court may admit the following evidence in a criminal case:

(A) evidence of specific instances of a victim's sexual behavior, if offered to prove that someone other than the defendant was the source of semen, injury, or other physical evidence;

(B) evidence of specific instances of a victim's sexual behavior with respect to the person accused of the sexual misconduct, if offered by the defendant to prove consent or if offered by the prosecutor; and

(C) evidence whose exclusion would violate the defendant's constitutional rights.

4.6 YOU DECIDE

The defendant Korey Fells contended that the trial court erred in refusing to allow him to present evidence that the rape victim, S. H., was HIV-positive. Fells argued that this evidence demonstrated that S. H. had a motive to lie about being raped because it is a crime for a person to knowingly expose another to HIV, and S. H. "knew that if she did not say she was raped, it would be consensual sex and she'd be charged with a crime." Fells argued that the evidence of the victim's HIV status was not subject to the rape shield law because it did not address any prior sexual activity, merely that S. H. was HIV-positive. How would you rule? See *Fells v. State* (207 S.W.2d 498 [Ark. 2005]).

You can learn what the court decided by referring to the study site, **http://study.sagepub.com/lippmance.**

CASE ANALYSIS

In *State v. Kirsch*, the New Hampshire Supreme Court addressed whether in a prosecution for sexual assault the testimony of three other young women who testified to similar activity was properly admitted under Rule 404(b).

Was the prosecution's other acts evidence of molestation admissible under Rule 404(b)?

State v. Kirsch, 662 A.2d 937 (N.H. 1995)

The defendant was tried on thirteen indictments charging sexual assaults . . . between 1984 and 1987. In addition to the three victims named in the indictments, three other young women testified, pursuant to Rule 404(b), about sexual abuse committed against them by the defendant from the late 1970s to the mid-1980s. With minor variations, each young woman testified to similar activity and association with the defendant. During that time period, the defendant led pre-teen church groups at the Granite State Baptist Church in Salem, occasionally driving the church bus that transported the children from their homes to the church. In addition to leading a group called Alpha-Teens that provided recreational activities, the defendant was one of several church staff members who monitored sleep-overs at the church. He also hosted church sleep-overs at his home in Salem and, later, at his home in Plaistow. Each of the victim/witnesses testified to having been approximately seven to ten years old when she met the defendant through her association with the church and to having become close to him through the church groups she attended. Each rode on the bus or in his van with the defendant and spent the night at the church or at his home. Some remembered sitting in the defendant's lap, and all remembered the defendant's inappropriate touching, from fondling of the breasts and vaginal area to digital penetration, fellatio, cunnilingus, and sexual intercourse. . . .

Prior to trial the State moved to introduce evidence of other uncharged sexual assaults as evidence of the defendant's motive, intent, and common plan or scheme. According to the State's proffer to the trial court, the evidence would show that the defendant "selected and seduced each victim by always choosing as his victims young girls, who lived well below the poverty line, in dysfunctional households, without any real father figure." It would further show, according to the State, that the defendant "positioned himself," through his role in the church, as a trusted father figure who occasionally fed and clothed them and "then seduced each of the little girls in the same manner." After a hearing, the trial court ruled that the evidence was relevant to prove motive, intent, and common plan or scheme, that there was clear proof the defendant committed the acts, and that the probative value of the evidence was not substantially outweighed by prejudice to the defendant.

In ruling that the probative value of the evidence was not substantially outweighed by the prejudice, the court found that the victims all met the defendant through the church, that most of them had no father, came from broken homes, were poor, and that the defendant "offered emotional support to the victims and became a father figure to them," taking them out to eat and to amusement parks. "In this manner," the court explained in its order, "the State seeks to prove that the defendant gained the trust and confidence of the victims to lure them into his home and into his life."

Motive is generally understood to refer to the "reason that nudges the will and prods the mind to indulge the criminal intent". . . . The crux of the State's argument appears to be that the other incidents show the defendant's desire for sexual activity with a certain type of victim. This, however, "is proof of propensity, not motive."

The second reason advanced by the State for admitting the other acts was that they were probative of the defendant's intent. To argue that evidence of the defendant's other similar assaults tends to prove his guilt of the charged offenses is to seek to show "propensity, pure and simple; calling it relevant to prove 'state of mind' does not make it so."

With respect to the State's common plan or scheme rationale for relevance, the State argued to the trial court that the defendant's "routine used in assaulting any one of the victims is similar, if not identical, to the manner in which he assaulted other victims." The common plan exception to the Rule 404(b) prohibition requires more. . . . Showing that the defendant had a pre-existing "plan" to gain the trust of young girls from deprived homes in order to seduce and sexually assault them does not demonstrate a common plan or scheme. . . .

Whether . . . labeled motive, intent or common plan, the ostensible purpose for which the prosecution sought to admit evidence of a multitude of other uncharged sexual assaults was to show the defendant's predilection for molesting young females over whom he was able to gain control through engendering trust. At most, this is evidence of the defendant's disposition to commit the offenses with which he was charged, impermissible under Rule 404(b). Because it was not relevant for a permissible purpose, the evidence should have been excluded, and its introduction was an abuse of discretion.

CHAPTER SUMMARY

Direct and circumstantial evidence are of equal significance, and guilt or innocence may be determined based on either direct or circumstantial evidence or by a combination of both types of evidence. However, a number of states require judges in prosecutions based wholly on circumstantial evidence to provide the so-called Webster-type charge.

Circumstantial evidence commonly is used to establish a defendant's consciousness of guilt and to establish that an individual is the victim of the crime with which the defendant is charged.

Character evidence is considered prejudicial and prohibited from being introduced at trial. Federal Rule 404(b) creates an exception and permits a defendant to introduce evidence of a "pertinent" character trait as evidence he or she acted consistent with the "pertinent trait" on a particular occasion. Character evidence includes evidence of a wide variety of human traits including trustworthiness, honesty, law-abidingness, violence, and attention to detail. A pertinent trait is a trait relevant to the charge against the defendant. Honesty and trustworthiness, for example, are pertinent to a charge of fraud or embezzlement. A pertinent character trait may be established by either reputation or opinion evidence.

The prosecution is barred from attacking the character of the accused unless the defendant "opens the door" by offering evidence of a "pertinent" character trait. Once the defendant introduces evidence of his or her character, the door is opened for the prosecutor to rebut this evidence with evidence of the same trait. The prosecutor also may impeach a defendant's character witness on cross-examination and inquire into the witness's knowledge of specific, relevant instances of a defendant's conduct. The cross-examination may focus on arrest, criminal acts, and other bad acts, including the act with which the defendant is charged.

Federal Rules of Evidence 405(b) provides that in cases in which the character or trait of character of a person is an essential element of a charge or defense, "proof may be made of specific instances of that person's conduct" in addition to reputation and opinion evidence. This evidence must be based on reputation or on opinion.

There is a special rule of evidence in homicide cases that expands the ability of the prosecution to offer evidence of the victim's character. Federal Rule 404(a)(2) provides that in a homicide case the prosecutor may offer evidence of the alleged victim's trait of peacefulness to rebut "evidence" that the alleged victim was the first aggressor. The prosecutor does not have to wait for the defendant to place the character of the victim at issue.

Habit evidence is admissible to demonstrate that the defendant acted in accordance with his or her habit on a particular occasion. Federal Rule 406 provides that "[e]vidence of a person's habit or an organizational routine practice" may be admitted to establish that on a "particular occasion the person or organization acted in accordance with the habit or routine practice." Admission of evidence of prior criminal acts generally is not admissible because it violates the defendant's right to be tried for the offense for which he or she is standing trial. This evidence may not be admitted to prove a defendant's character or predisposition. In other words, it may not be admitted to prove the defendant is the type of person who commits criminal acts.

Federal Rule of Evidence 404(b) provides that the prior acts of a defendant may be admissible by the prosecution to establish "motive, opportunity, intent, preparation, plan, knowledge, identity, absence of mistake, or lack of accident." Other acts evidence, however, "is not admissible to prove the character of a person in order to show action in conformity therewith." An act under the "other acts" exception may occur prior to or following the commission of the crime with which the defendant is charged.

As part of rape reform in the 1970s, the states and federal government adopted so-called rape shield laws, which restricted the cross-examination of alleged victims and the admissibility of their reputation for sexual "virtuosity." The thinking was that this evidence was irrelevant to the adjudication of the alleged rape at issue in the trial, diverted the attention of jurors and the court to irrelevant events, and discouraged women from coming forward with complaints of rape.

CHAPTER REVIEW QUESTIONS

1. Are circumstantial and direct evidence of equal value? Can an individual be convicted solely on the basis of circumstantial evidence?

2. What are some examples of how circumstantial evidence may create an inference of a defendant's ability to commit a crime?

3. Give examples of how circumstantial evidence may be offered to create an inference of a defendant's consciousness of guilt or an inference of a suspect's guilt.

4. How is circumstantial evidence used to create an inference that an individual was the victim of a crime?

5. Why is character evidence prohibited from being introduced at a criminal trial? Discuss the exception for a defendant's character evidence and the prosecution's rebuttal under Federal Rule 404(b) and Federal Rule 405.

6. May a defendant introduce character evidence regarding a victim?

7. What is the rule regarding the ability of the prosecutor to introduce character evidence about the defendant in a homicide case?

8. Distinguish between character and habit evidence. When is habit evidence admissible?

9. Outline the requirements of rape shield statutes.

LEGAL TERMINOLOGY

character	habit	rape trauma syndrome
credibility	impeachment	weight
demeanor	other acts evidence	
flight	rape shield laws	

REFERENCES

Broun, Kenneth, ed. 2000. *McCormick on Evidence*, 6th ed. St. Paul, MN: Thomson/West.

Matoesian, Greg. 2001. *Law and the Language of Identity Discourse in the William Kennedy Smith Trial*. New York: Oxford University Press.

Visit the Student Study Site at **http://study.sagepub.com/lippmance** to access additional study tools, including mobile-friendly eFlashcards and Web quizzes as well as links to SAGE journal articles and hyperlinks for *Criminal Evidence* on the Web.

WITNESSES

witness = how you prove your case.

used to be → only white men who owned land can testify
    ↳now everyone can unless they can't

Should the judge have allowed the witness to testify about posthypnotic recollections?

Defendant Wesley Allen Tuttle appeals from his jury conviction of first-degree murder, for which he received a life sentence. He contends that the trial court erred in admitting hypnotically enhanced testimony and in excluding expert testimony that hypnotically enhanced testimony is unreliable.

On the afternoon of September 26, 1983, Sydney Ann Merrick traveled up Parley's Canyon in her white Datsun on an errand for her employer. Her body was discovered later that day in her car on the off-ramp of the Summit Park exit. She had been stabbed several times. . . .

Records of telephone calls that Tuttle, a truck driver, made to his employer placed him in the area of the murder at about 2:30 p.m. on the date in question. He was driving a black Chevrolet one-ton truck without a bed that was pulling a thirty-foot flatbed trailer. The truck was equipped with a bug screen bearing the word "Apache," the name of Tuttle's employer. This was the only such truck owned by Apache. The truck carried a chain with hooks that could be used for towing. . . .

Before he was hypnotized, the witness in question gave a statement indicating that he had seen a glossy black flatbed truck with something written on its doors towing a small car with an uncomfortable-looking girl in it. He also said that he saw the truck pulled off at the Summit Park exit and that the truck driver was a "scroungy" man wearing a dark baseball cap and a light blue shirt, clothing similar to what Tuttle was wearing when he arrived in Evanston. Under hypnosis, the witness stated that the truck's bug screen had the word "Apache" on it, gave a more complete description of the car and Tuttle, and "recalled" many additional details that were conflicting and internally inconsistent. . . .

At trial, Tuttle's counsel objected to the witness's testifying to any information "recalled" for the first time after being hypnotized; he sought to limit the witness's testimony to his prehypnotic statements. The trial judge overruled this objection and admitted the testimony. The witness testified to details from both his pre- and post-hypnotic recollections. The witness also identified Tuttle as the driver of the truck, even though he had never done so before the trial.

Would you have allowed the witness to testify about facts that he only recalled following being hypnotized? See *State v. Tuttle* (780 P.2d 1203 [Utah 1989]).

CHAPTER OUTLINE

Introduction
Competency Hearings
Hypnosis
Child Testimony
Judges as Witnesses
Jurors as Witnesses
Spousal Competence
Religion
Mental Incapacity
Impeachment
Bias
Prior Felony Convictions
Crimes Involving a Dishonest Act or False Statements

Character for Truthfulness
Uncharged Crimes and Immoral Acts
Prior Inconsistent Statements
Specific Contradiction
Physical and Psychological Incapacity
Rehabilitation
Corroboration
Recorded Recollection
Case Analysis
Chapter Summary
Chapter Review Questions
Legal Terminology

1. Do you know what is meant by competence to testify? List and explain the requirements that must be met for a witness to be competent to testify.

2. Can a witness testify who has been hypnotized?

3. Can you discuss the special procedures courts use in determining whether children are competent to testify?

4. Do you know whether judges and jurors may be called as witnesses at a trial?

5. Does the law of evidence allow a spouse to prevent his or her partner from testifying against him or her at a criminal trial?

6. May an individual be disqualified to testify at a trial because of his or her religious beliefs?

7. Do judges allow individuals with felony convictions to testify? What of individuals with severe mental challenges?

8. Explain the purpose of impeachment. When may a witness be impeached by the opposing attorney?

9. Can you explain what is involved in impeaching a witness based on bias? A prior inconsistent statement? Do you know some other grounds on which to impeach a witness?

10. Are you able to explain the difference between present recollection refreshed and past recollection recalled?

■ INTRODUCTION

Evidence at a criminal trial in most instances is introduced through the testimony of witnesses. The prosecution relies on the testimony of witnesses to establish the elements of the criminal charge beyond a reasonable doubt. This testimony helps develop a story that tells the jury who, what, where, and why a crime was committed. The defense responds with the testimony of witnesses to raise a reasonable doubt in the minds of jurors.

In 1967, the Supreme Court noted that both the defendant and the prosecution have the right under the Sixth Amendment to the United States Constitution to present the testimony of witnesses.

The right to offer the testimony of witnesses and to compel their attendance, if necessary, is in plain terms the right to present a defense and the right to present the defendant's version of the facts, as well as the prosecution's, to the jury so it may decide where the truth lies (*Washington v. Texas*, 388 U.S. 14 [1967]).

Under the common law, there were strict qualifications on who was entitled to be a witness based on age, race, religion, conviction of a crime, mental capacity, marriage, and whether an individual was a party to the case. The thinking was that certain categories of individuals either were unable or could not be trusted to be truthful. Permitting these individuals to testify was thought to risk rampant falsehoods and threatened the trustworthiness of the legal system. Perjury was both a crime and a mortal sin, and the best policy was to prevent these individuals from testifying at trial. As early as 1918, the United States Supreme Court abandoned the restrictive qualifications on witness testimony established by the "dead hand of the criminal law."

> [T]he conviction of our time [is] that the truth is most likely to be arrived at by hearing the testimony of all persons of competent understanding who may seem to have knowledge of the facts involved in a case, leaving the credit and weight of such testimony to be determined by the jury or the court. (*Rosen v. United States*, 245 U.S. 467 [1918])

The Federal Rules of Evidence and state rules of evidence take the approach that virtually any witness whose testimony is relevant to the case should be allowed to testify unless the testimony is prohibited by another federal rule. Federal Rule 601 states that "[e]very person is competent to be a witness unless these rules provide otherwise." The Advisory Committee involved in drafting the federal rules notes that "[n]o mental or moral qualifications for testifying as a witness are specified." The witness's accuracy, believability, and motive to fabricate can be brought out on cross-examination, and the jury is to evaluate the "weight and credibility" to be accorded to a witness's testimony.

There are a limited number of restrictions on what the Federal Rules of Evidence refer to as **competency to testify**. These restrictions are listed below.

[handwritten: oath = hand on bible]
[handwritten: affirmation = same but no bible]

- Oath or affirmation
- Personal knowledge
- Mental capacity
- Narration

Rule 601. Competency to Testify in General

Every person is competent to be a witness unless these rules provide otherwise. But in a civil case, state law governs the witness's competency regarding a claim or defense for which state law supplies the rule of decision.

[handwritten: swearing to God] *[handwritten: understanding to tell the truth → just a statement, no specific language]*

Oath or Affirmation

Every witness is required to take an **oath or affirmation that he or she will "testify truthfully."** The purpose is to reinforce the duty and obligation to tell the truth. In theory, there is **no difference between an oath and an affirmation although a jury may discount the testimony of a witness who offers an affirmation.**

Federal Rule of Evidence 603 stipulates that a "witness must give an oath or affirmation to testify truthfully. It must be in a **form designed to impress that duty on the witness's conscience.**" An oath or affirmation also **reminds the witness that he or she is subject to prosecution for perjury for intentional false statements.** All states have adopted similar rules. **An oath involves swearing to God to tell the truth. An affirmation is "a solemn undertaking to tell the truth"** and uses the term *affirm* rather than *swear to God.*

The common form of an **oath is to swear to "tell the truth, the whole truth, so help me God."** The affirmation only is required to **include a statement that the individual will tell the truth and is not required to include any specific language.** The Advisory Committee note to Rule 603 explains that the rule is intended to afford "the flexibility required in dealing with religious adults, atheists, conscientious objectors, mental defectives and children." The affirmation is based on the First Amendment right to freedom of religion and a recognition that individuals may not believe in God or may adhere to a religion that prohibits an oath.

In general, as stated in the California Evidence Code, "[a] person is disqualified to be a witness if he or she is . . . [i]ncapable of understanding the duty of a witness to tell the truth." **A court may waive an oath or affirmation in the case of a child-witness.** The California Evidence Code, in Section 710, provides that a child under the age of 10 or a person with a "substantial cognitive impairment" may be "required only to promise to tell the truth." **In practice, the lawyer must satisfy the judge that the child demonstrates an awareness of the importance to tell the truth.**

An individual who refuses to swear an oath or make an affirmation **may be prevented from testifying.** Defendant E. L. Fowler as part of his antigovernmental views rejected the language of the oaths presented to him by the judge, including the statement "I state that I will tell the truth in my testimony." Fowler only was willing to state that "I am a truthful man" and "I would not tell a lie to stay out of jail." The Fifth Circuit Court of Appeals upheld the decision of the district court judge to refuse him permission to testify (*United States v. Fowler*, 605 F.2d 181 [5th Cir. 1979]).

On the other hand, the Fifth Circuit Court of Appeals overturned a district court judge's refusal to accept an oath by a religious objector that read, "I, [Betty Ann Ferguson], do hereby declare that the facts I am about to give are, to the best of my knowledge and belief, accurate, correct, and complete." The plaintiff was open to incorporating a statement that she recognized that she was subject to prosecution for perjury in the event she testified falsely (*Ferguson v. Commissioner*, 921 F.2d 688 [5th Cir. 1991]).

The Fourth Circuit Court of Appeals in *United States v. Looper* stressed that "any form of statement that impressed on the mind and conscious of the witness the necessity for telling the truth would suffice as an oath" (*United States v. Looper*, 419 F.2d 1405 [4th Cir. 1969]).

In *United States v. Ward*, Wallace Ward insisted on substituting the phrase "fully integrated honesty" for the word *truth*. The District Court rejected Ward's version of the oath and held that the oath or affirmation, which had been administered throughout the United States to "millions of witnesses for hundreds of years," should not be "required to give way to the defendant's idiosyncratic distinctions between truth and honesty." The Court of Appeals reversed the decision of the district court and held the form of the oath is less important than the fact the witness swears to tell the truth (*United States v. Ward*, 989 F.2d 1015 [9th Cir. 1993]).

In an unusual California case, a prosecution witness refused to take an oath or to swear to tell the truth. The prosecution proceeded to question the witness who answered the questions despite failing to swear to tell the truth. A California appellate court held the defendant by failing to object had waived his or her grounds to complain (*People v. Prentiss*, 2008 Cal. App. Unpub. Lexis 8119 [Cal. 2008]).

Rule 603. Oath or Affirmation to Testify Truthfully

Before testifying, a witness must give an oath or affirmation to testify truthfully. It must be in a form designed to impress that duty on the witness's conscience.

can't be what someone told you

Personal Knowledge

A witness is required to have personal knowledge about the subject of his or her testimony. This is best understood to be knowledge based on one of an individual's five senses. You may witness a murder, hear a gun being fired, smell marijuana, or feel a firearm on your back during a robbery.

The personal knowledge requirement ensures that testimony is not based on conjecture, speculation, or secondhand information (this is the problem of hearsay discussed in Chapter Nine). A judge, if a motion is filed to exclude a witness's testimony on the grounds of Rule 602, only is required to confirm the testimony is based on "personal knowledge."

The weight to be accorded the evidence is a matter for the jury. A witness is not required to be absolutely certain about the accuracy of his or her statement.

A witness who observes a portion of a transaction may draw the inference or opinion that a "normal person would form on the basis of the facts he observed and heard." In *Marks v. State*, the witness saw two assailants beat the victim. One of the assailants announced he was going to run the victim over and got into his car and began driving. As the assailant got into his car, the witness turned and ran and heard a loud crash. His testimony that the assailant ran over the victim with his car was challenged on appeal on the grounds he had not witnessed the vehicle run over the body. The Arkansas Supreme Court held the "common experience of most persons when coupled with the facts [the witness] observed . . . reasonably leads to the inference [the witness] made in regard to the source of the sound" (*Marks v. State*, 289 S.W.3d 923 [Ark. 2008]).

An emergency room doctor, in a Texas case, was permitted to testify that he concluded the victim's wounds were consistent with an individual fleeing a fight although he had not actually witnessed the fight (*Vasquez v. State*, 2006 Tex. App. Lexis 500 [2006]). A witness also may testify about circumstantial evidence and need not witness the crime itself.

In *McCrary-El v. Shaw*, Jerry McCrary-El claimed three prison guards beat him. The trial court held that Antonio Jones, who was housed in a neighboring cell, could not have been able to watch the beating through an inch-and-a-half crack at the corner of his cell door and therefore lacked personal knowledge of the beating and barred his testimony. The Eighth Circuit Court of Appeals affirmed the trial court's ruling noting that "no reasonable person could conclude that Jones was able to see anything of relevance" (*McCray-El v. Shaw*, 992 F.2d 809 [8th Cir. 1993]).

In *State v. Ranieri*, Eric Ranieri was arrested for burglary and for an assault with a dangerous weapon based on his alleged entry into the apartment of Elsie M. and beating of Elsie, aged 73 years. Elsie maintained for the eighteen months prior to trial that she was unable to identify her assailant although on the evening before the trial she informed the prosecutor she was able to identify her assailant. Elsie explained that she previously was afraid to testify because she feared the defendant despite the fact he had been incarcerated for the past eighteen months. The Rhode Island Supreme Court found that "without any basis, Elsie . . . maintains that 'she knew' it was Ranieri who was spying on her" through the shades of a neighboring apartment. She "readily admits she never saw Ranieri or anyone else actually enter her home." The Rhode Island Supreme Court concluded that "it was clearly erroneous for the trial justice to find that sufficient evidence was introduced that Elsie had personal knowledge of her assailant's identity. Accordingly Elsie was not competent under Rule 602 of the Rhode Island Rules of Evidence to testify as to her assailant's identity, and her out-of-court and in-court identifications should have been suppressed."

A neighbor, William Picard, intervened during the assault on Elsie and identified the defendant as the perpetrator based on his viewing the assailant's "upper lip." The court questioned whether the neighbor could identify Ranieri's face based on a brief view of a defendant's upper lip, and the neighbor "admittedly had no personal knowledge of the overall facial characteristics of the assailant." The Rhode Island Supreme Court held that Picard's testimony should have been barred by the trial court judge based on Rule 602 of the Rhode Island rules of evidence (*State v. Ranieri*, 586 A.2d 1094 [R.I. 1991]).

Keep in mind that even if a witness is allowed to testify, his or her ability to observe events may be attacked on cross-examination. This questioning may focus on factors such as an individual's physical disability that prevented a clear view of events, the configuration of the crime scene, the absence of sufficient light, distractions, or the witness's physical distance from events that impeded his or her ability to accurately view events.

Rule 602. Need for Personal Knowledge

A witness may testify to a matter only if evidence is introduced sufficient to support a finding that the witness has personal knowledge of the matter. Evidence to prove personal knowledge may consist of the witness's own testimony. This rule does not apply to a witness's expert testimony under Rule 703.

very low standard — just need some recall of what happened and some how communicate it

Mental Capacity

Courts recognize an implicit requirement that an individual who observes events is capable of recalling what occurred (*United States v. Lightly*, 677 F.2d 1027 [4th Cir. 1982]).

The rule, as you recall, is that "every person is competent to be a witness" unless specifically barred by an evidentiary rule. As a result, a mental disability does not automatically prevent an individual from testifying at trial. The burden will be on the party challenging the witness to demonstrate the witness's capacity to remember events. The jury evaluates the weight to be accorded to the testimony.

In *United States v. Peyro*, a government witness in a prosecution for conspiracy to distribute cocaine testified on the stand that she had "some very substantial memory problems" and was "emotionally unbalanced," and that "I don't remember anything very well." The Eighth Circuit Court of Appeals upheld the district court judge's decision to allow her to testify holding that the trial court judge had not abused his discretion in refusing to strike her testimony. The jury had the opportunity to evaluate the witness's psychological problems in evaluating her testimony (*United States v. Peyro*, 786 F.2d 826 [8th Cir. 1986]).

In *United States v. Phibbs*, the defense challenged the competence of two prosecution witnesses, one of whom previously had been found to lack the mental capacity to stand trial, had a history of auditory delusions, and had spent time in a mental health facility. The treating psychiatrist of the other witness testified that the witness suffered from "confusion, agitation, paranoia and hallucinations." The Sixth Circuit Court of Appeals held that Rule 601 disfavors barring witnesses due to mental incapacity and that the trial court judge had found no indication the witnesses were incapable of understanding the oath or obligation to testify truthfully or to remember events (*United States v. Phibbs*, 999 F.2d 1053 [6th Cir. 1993]). The court wrote:

As long as a witness appreciates his or her duty to tell the truth, and is minimally capable of observing, recalling, and communicating events, his or her testimony should come in for whatever it is worth. It is then up to the opposing party to dispute the witness's powers of apprehension, which well may be impaired by mental illness or other factors. As we are persuaded that [the witnesses] were at least minimally capable of offering reliable evidence, the possible weaknesses in their testimony went to its credibility, and so were to be assessed by the jury.

Narration → communicate somehow (self or translator)

A witness must be able to narrate or to communicate to the judge and to the jury what happened. Challenges may arise with children or with individuals with severe mental challenges. Individuals who do not speak English are able to communicate through qualified translators who themselves are under oath, and individuals who suffer from speech challenges may communicate through sign language or the written word.

The central consideration is whether the defendant has the capacity to communicate in some fashion. In *Byndom v. State*, the Arkansas Supreme Court affirmed the competency to testify of a rape victim who suffered from cerebral palsy and a mental challenge. The court noted the victim was able to testify through "gestures, facial expressions, [and] the ability to use sign language and to articulate 'yes' and 'no,' and [that she] possessed the limited use of the yes/no function on her computer." The court recognized that ruling the victim incompetent would eliminate the ability to testify of individuals who rely on alternative modes of communication because they cannot communicate in the same manner as the average person (*Byndom v. State*, 39 S.W.3d 781 [Ark. 2001]). A speech-impaired rape victim was recognized as competent who communicated through pointing to an anatomically correct doll, gestures, and pointing to the alphabet (*People v. Vandiver*, 468 N.E.2d 454 [Ill. App. 1984]).

The witness must be able to respond to cross-examination; otherwise, the defendant is being deprived of the right to confront his or her accusers. In *Illinois v. White*, Mrs. Idelle Broday and Mrs. Mickey Kallick were roommates in a nursing home. Kallick allegedly observed a nurse steal a ring from Broday's finger. Broday was incompetent to testify. Kallick was too ill to be moved, and her testimony was taken in the nursing home. She could not speak although her hearing was normal. Mrs. Kallick was found by the judge to be competent and communicated during her testimony by raising her right knee for "yes" and remained still if her answer was "no." The head nurse testified that when she asked Kallick whether the defendant, Anita White, had stolen the ring, Kallick answered "yes" by moving her right knee. Kallick raised her right knee when White was brought into the room. The Illinois Supreme Court reversed White's conviction, reasoning the witness was unable to "state what she saw nor could she describe the ring or the person who took it. Cross-examination was necessarily limited. . . . It is practically impossible to gauge the influence which [the head nurse] may have exerted upon the witness" (*Illinois v. White*, 238 N.E.2d 389 [Ill. 1968]).

need all

Legal Equation

Competency to testify = Oath or affirmation + Personal knowledge + Mental capacity + Narration.

(person who says they aren't) they must prove witness isn't competent

■ COMPETENCY HEARINGS

A judge in those instances in which there is an issue whether a witness is competent will conduct a hearing outside the presence of the jury. The questioning of the individual to establish competency to testify before he or she is sworn as a witness is termed *voir dire*. This term also is used to examine potential jurors. In most instances, the party challenging the competency of a witness to testify must do so before he or she is sworn in as a witness. The party calling the witness has the burden of persuading the judge that the witness is competent to testify. The opposing lawyer may cross-examine the witness. The judge may conduct a hearing after an individual has taken the stand. ★a person doesn't need to remember everything★ ↳ can say "I don't remember" and its fine

5.1 YOU DECIDE

Esker Dodson was a government witness in a drug conspiracy trial. Dodson engaged in substantial use of heroin over a number of years and injected heroin within two days of his testimony. Following his first day of testimony, Dodson was taken to the hospital to receive medication and received 75 mg of Demerol and 50 mg of Phenergan. In several instances during Dodson's testimony, he was asked to "speak up and on several occasions during the testimony, Dodson was observed to be bouncing or nodding." An expert witness for the defense testified Demerol was for pain relief and the normal dosage is 50 mg, which may be raised to 75 mg or, in an extreme case, to 100 mg. A person who receives the dosages administered to Dodson would experience some clouding of consciousness and difficulty in pinpointing accurate thoughts and would experience difficulty thinking for roughly eighteen hours after receiving the medication. The defense attorney following the first day of Dodson's testimony claimed, "This guy is flying now." The trial court judge replied that this "is not my opinion" and allowed Dodson to testify. Was the judge's ruling correct? See *United States v. Harris* (542 F.2d 1283 [7th Cir. 1976]).

You can learn what the court decided by referring to the study site, **http://study.sagepub.com/lippmance.**

depends on what state you're in and what state of hypnosis you're in
→ some allow to come in while hypnotised
or attest to things said before you were hypnotised.

■ HYPNOSIS

On occasion, hypnosis is used to refresh the memory of witnesses. Courts are divided on whether to admit this type of testimony. States permitting hypnotically refreshed evidence generally require videotaping of the hypnosis, detailed records, and the examination by a qualified hypnotist.

The theory behind hypnosis is that this places an individual in an altered and relaxed state in which the psychological barriers to release of painful, repressed memories are removed.

In *Rock v. Arkansas*, Vickie Rock shot her husband after he attacked her. She did not remember the details of the shooting and submitted to hypnosis with a neuropsychologist. Vickie recalled under hypnosis that she did not have her hand on the trigger and the gun fired when her husband grabbed her. A test confirmed the gun was at risk of accidentally firing when hit or dropped (*Rock v. Arkansas*, 479 U.S. 1079 [1987]).

The United States Supreme Court held that Arkansas' absolute prohibition on the use of hypnotically refreshed evidence because the evidence "always is . . . untrustworthy" unconstitutionally interferes with a defendant's right to testify in his or her defense. A defendant's testimony can be tested on cross-examination, and the jury can be equipped to evaluate hypnotically induced testimony through expert testimony or the judge's instructions to the jury. The Court held that Arkansas was free to prohibit nondefendant witnesses from offering hypnotically refreshed testimony (*Rock v. Arkansas*, 479 U.S. 1079 [1987]).

The Supreme Court recognized the problems with hypnotically refreshed testimony. An individual may try to please the hypnotist by telling the hypnotist the information he or she believes the hypnotist wants to hear, the hypnotist(s) may manipulate the responses of the suspect, and hypnotism may give the witness a false sense of confidence in his or her memory. The subject also may fill in the details he or she cannot remember to make his or her testimony appear detailed and coherent. Despite these risks, the opposing side is free to raise questions about the reliability of hypnotically induced testimony. *problems*

State courts rejecting hypnotically refreshed testimony have found this testimony to be unreliable and to have the potential to powerfully influence juries. A compromise approach permits the police to hypnotize witnesses to assist their investigation, but it limits witnesses' testimony to prehypnosis recollections. States admitting testimony obtained under hypnosis typically require that a number of safeguards are followed by the therapist (*People v. Schreiner*, 573 N.E.2d 1077 [1991]).

■ CHILD TESTIMONY

not explain full case to help this

The competency of child-witnesses has posed a continuing challenge for courts, particularly in childhood abuse cases in which the credibility of the child-victim is central to the case. The fear is that children will be coached into

PHOTO 5.1

Police testimony is crucial for documenting how the criminal investigation led to the defendant's arrest.

[handwritten: demonstrate they know the diff from right/ wrong]

offering false testimony or that they may not understand the obligation to tell the truth or may lack the ability to recall what they witnessed.

There are several approaches to child-witnesses. The traditional approach declared children 10 years of age or older presumptively competent. Children under 10 were required to be found competent following *voir dire* by the judge.

Federal law (18 U.S.C. § 3508) follows Rule 601, which states that "[e]very person is competent to be a witness except as otherwise provided in these rules." Section 3508 provides that a child is presumed to be competent and that a competency examination regarding a child may be conducted only if the court determines that compelling reasons *[handwritten: now]* exist. A child's age alone is not a compelling reason to conduct a competency examination (*voir dire*).

Alabama, Connecticut, and Utah, along with most other states, follow the federal rule and also presume that children under 10 are competent to testify, and it is left to the jury to evaluate the weight and credibility of the child's testimony. A Utah statute provides that a child-victim of sexual abuse under the age of 10 is "a competent witness and shall be allowed to testify without prior qualification in any judicial proceeding. The trier of fact shall determine the weight and credibility of the testimony."

Another group of states allows children under 10 to testify even when the child does not understand the significance of an oath. Delaware provides that "[n]o child under the age of 10 years may be excluded from giving testimony for the sole reason that such child does not understand the obligation of the oath. Such child's age and degree of understanding of the . . . oath may be considered by the trier of fact in judging the child's credibility."

New York State, on the other hand, provides that a witness under 9 years of age may not testify unless the court is satisfied he or she understands the oath. Individuals who do not understand the oath may give an unsworn statement if the court is satisfied they possess sufficient intelligence and understanding.

Ohio allows a child under 10 to testify in those instances in which the judge is satisfied the child is competent to testify. In *State v. Armstrong*, the defendant argued the trial court improperly allowed the 7-year-old female victim to testify against him in a sexual abuse case in which he was charged with sexually abusing the witness and taking photos of her on his cell phone. An Ohio appellate court stated that a judge is to consider various factors in determining whether a child is competent to testify:

> (1) the child's ability to receive accurate impressions of fact or to observe acts about which he or she will testify, (2) the child's ability to recollect those impressions or observations, (3) the child's ability to communicate what was observed, (4) the child's understanding of truth and falsity and (5) the child's appreciation of his or her responsibility to be truthful. (*State v. Armstrong*, 2011 Ohio 6265 [2011])

The appellate court upheld the ruling of the trial court judge to allow the victim to testify based on the child-victim's ability to testify accurately about her age, school, identification of her favorite teacher, favorite book, and ability to explain the difference between being truthful and untruthful.

In Washington State, children are to be considered incompetent if they "appear incapable of receiving just impressions of the facts, respecting which they are examined, or of relating them truly." The party challenging the child's competency has the burden of establishing that the child-witness is incompetent. In *State v. Swan* (114 Wash. 2d 613 [1990]), the Washington Supreme Court held the trial court properly found R. T. incompetent to testify in a child abuse case.

> R.T. said that her birthday was in "higher June." She also said she had been in the courtroom 40 times (although she had never been there before) and that it was Saturday, although it was not. When asked if she recognized anyone, she pointed to defense counsel and said she had seen him 4 days ago, which she had not. She did not say that she recognized her father or the defendants. . . . When the court asked R.T. if she knew the difference between the truth and a lie, R.T. said "not telling the truth" is telling a lie. The court then asked R.T. if it would be the truth or a lie if she said she was wearing a pink dress. Though her dress was pink, R.T. said it would be a lie because her dress was long. R.T. then said her dress was "blue, sort of, but it's pink." The court excused R.T. and found her incompetent to testify on the basis she did not understand the obligation to tell the truth on the witness stand and because she did not have a sufficient memory to speak truly about past events.

A child's testimony also may be challenged on the grounds that the child's testimony is tainted. A party alleging the testimony of the child is "tainted" has the burden of establishing by clear and convincing evidence that the child has been subject to outside influence that has shaped his or her testimony. These examinations typically take place in the privacy of the judge's chambers (in camera), and the prosecutor and defense counsel may be provided with the opportunity to ask questions. In taint hearings, the court considers the age of the child, hostility by the child's guardian against the defendant, whether the child was subjected to numerous interviews by adults, and the interview techniques and methods employed.

Courts have adopted special procedures for child testimony in recognition of the emotional difficulties experienced by children confronting an abuser. Courts attempt to balance the need to protect the child against the defendant's right to confront his or her accuser.

One court authorized a child to sit on a relative's lap while testifying (*State v. Johnson*, 528 N.E.2d 567 [Ohio App. 1986]). A federal statute on child-witnesses allows child testimony by two-way closed-circuit television. The Supreme Court, in *Maryland v. Craig*, upheld a Maryland procedure for one-way closed-circuit television in a sexual abuse case based on the court's finding that requiring the child to confront the accused would cause severe emotional distress (*Maryland v. Craig*, 497 U.S. 836 [1990]).

Federal law also allows a court to permit a child to give a videotape testimony (e.g., recorded testimony). Another provision permits the judge to order the exclusion from the courtroom of all individuals who do not have a direct interest in the case. Federal courts also may appoint a guardian to accompany the child throughout the justice process to protect the child and to serve as an advocate for the child throughout the process. A number of state statutes provide for the use of anatomically correct dolls in child abuse cases to ease the trauma associated with recounting abuse.

The important point to remember is that the general policy under Rule 601 is to allow individuals to testify and to rely on cross-examination to test the credibility and weight of the testimony. The jury is instructed to evaluate the testimony of a child who is found to be competent like any other witness. In *United States v. Snyder* (189 F.3d 640 [7th Cir. 1999), the Seventh Circuit Court of Appeals upheld the trial court judge's refusal to examine the competency of the 11-year-old victim of horrible child abuse. The court reasoned:

> First, the fact that some of Doe's [the victim] statements were unfounded [e.g., that one of the perpetrators showed him guns and had taken him to a museum and gotten into a fight with a biker] does not show that he was unable to differentiate between reality and fantasy. Second, . . . Doe was taking medication that could render him incompetent to testify; [there was no evidence that] the medication had in fact made Doe incompetent. Finally, the reliability of Doe's testimony was predictably (and effectively) called into question on cross examination, when [the defense] attorney elicited detailed descriptions of imaginary events from Doe. Indeed, we have found no abuse of discretion in situations where the competency of a witness was much more questionable.

5.2 YOU DECIDE

The defendant was charged with the abuse of two 5-year-old children in day care. The appellate court was asked to decide whether the trial court judge was in error for not conducting a competency hearing and whether the testimony of the children was improperly introduced at trial.

Turning to T. W.'s testimony, the beginning colloquy is as follows:

Q: Can you tell me your name?
A: [T.]
Q: Wow. What's your last name?
A: [W.]
Q: How do you spell your first name?
A: I don't know.
Q: You don't know. Okay. How old are you?
A: Five.
Q: When is your birthday?
A: June 18th.
Q: What year were you born in?
A: I don't know.
Q: You don't know. 2001 maybe? But you're five now, right?
A: Yes.
Q: When will you be six?
A: I don't know.
Q: How about on your birthday? Do you think you'll turn six on June 18th?
A: Yes.
Q: All right. What grade are you in?
A: Kindergarten.
Q: What's the name of your school?
A: I don't know.
Q: You don't know. What's [your] teacher's name?

A: Mrs. Sowa.
Q: Do you know the difference between telling the truth and a story or a lie?
A: I don't know.
Q: Do you know what it means to tell the truth?
A: No.
Q: No? Is it a good thing to tell the truth?
A: Yes.
Q: All right. Is it a bad thing to tell a lie?
A: No.
Q: No? Do you think people should tell lies?
A: No.
Q: All right. You wouldn't lie to your mommy or anyone if they asked you something, would you?
A: No.
Q: Why not?
A: I don't know.

During the course of her testimony, T.W. did not know where she lived or the name of her street, she did not remember talking to the social worker about this case, she was inconsistent in identifying her body parts, and she did not recall anyone talking about her private parts. She testified that C.R. touched her private parts with her hand, and not the back scratcher; appellant never touched her; she did not see appellant touch C.R.; and she did not tell anyone that someone touched her private parts. She also did not recall having a conversation with her grandmother about touching C.R.'s private parts.

Was T.W. competent to testify? See *State v. Holland* (2008-Ohio-3450 [Cuyahoga Co. Ohio]).

You can learn what the court decided by referring to the study site, **http://study.sagepub.com/lippmance.**

CRIMINAL EVIDENCE IN THE NEWS

In 2013, Elizabeth Ramirez, Cassandra Rivera, Kristie Mayhugh, and Anna Vasquez, the so-called San Antonio Four, were released from prison on bail for the crime of child abuse, when a Houston judge agreed with the state of Texas that the case was seriously flawed. The judge recommended that the Texas Court of Criminal Appeals vacate the women's sentence.

In 1998, the women, all self-identified lesbians, were convicted of child abuse. Rivera, Mayhugh, and Vasquez were sentenced to fifteen years in prison. Ramirez was described as the moving force behind the ritual abuse and was sentenced to thirty-seven and a half years in prison.

In the summer of 1994, Ramirez's nieces, 7 and 9, lived with her and with her roommate Mayhugh. At the time, Ramirez was 20 and pregnant, and Mayhugh was 21. Ramirez's 9-year-old niece accused Ramirez and Mayhugh and two of their friends, Rivera, a 19-year-old mother of two children, and Vasquez, 19, of abusing her and her sister. The four women were accused of forcing the children to participate in an orgy, holding them down by the wrists and ankles, and raping them with various objects.

Texas prosecutors overlooked the young girls' inconsistent and incoherent testimony. The girls changed their stories on the number of days they were abused, whether they were held at gunpoint, whether they were separate or together when molested, whether they were threatened with a gun or knife, and whether all four women participated in the molestation at the same time. The girls told the police they screamed although there is no report that the neighbors heard their cries for help.

The primary evidence supporting abuse was a small white scar on the hymen of the older sister, a mark that a medical expert inaccurately testified was consistent with sexual abuse. The girls allegedly were encouraged to make the allegations by their father Javier Limon, who vowed to hurt Ramirez because she had rejected Limon's desire to marry her. Limon had been married to Ramirez's sister and had a history of using his daughters to make false accusations of sexual abuse against individuals.

The four women continued to insist on their innocence, and three of them passed two polygraph tests. They were so confident in their innocence that they refused to plead guilty in exchange for a sentence of ten years' probation.

Individuals involved in the case claim that the women were suspected of abuse because of antigay hysteria in San Antonio and the prevailing mythology that lesbians were involved in child abuse. The foreperson of the jury in Ramirez's trial was a local minister who viewed homosexuality as a sin, and the prosecutor was allowed to question Ramirez about whether she had a relationship with each of the other women.

The prosecution expert, a board-certified pediatrician, examined the girls in 1994 after they reported to their grandmother they had been abused. She testified the white scar on the hymen of the older girl was evidence of "satanic ritual abuse." The *San Antonio Express-News* in 2010 reported that medical reports available to the doctor at the time of the trial indicated that the older child's vagina was normal in appearance. In 2013, the doctor filed an affidavit admitting her testimony was wrong. In 2012, the younger of the two girls recanted her testimony and also reported the older sister was not telling the truth. A key development relied on by the lawyers for the San Antonio Four was a new Texas law allowing defendants to file appeals based on the use of "junk science" to convict them.

The women have yet to be declared innocent, which would result in the payment of compensation by the state of Texas. Clearly, in the vast majority of cases, child testimony is accurate. The moral of the story of the San Antonio Four is that a number of extralegal factors can combine to result in the conviction of innocent individuals. Child-witnesses are susceptible to pressure from adults and may want to please adults by alleging abuse. There often is little physical evidence of abuse, and cases often are filed many months after the incident. On the other hand, a significant number of children are embarrassed or scared and retract accusations.

The University of Michigan Law School and the Center on Wrongful Convictions at Northwestern University School of Law created the National Registry of Exonerations. A report recording exonerations between 1989 and 2012 found 102 exonerations for child abuse cases. Close to 75 percent involved perjury or a false accusation. Other factors contributing to false accusations were mistaken witness identification, false or misleading forensic evidence, and official misconduct, and a small number involved a false confession.

■ JUDGES AS WITNESSES

The Federal Rules of Evidence disqualify two categories of individuals from testifying as a witness, judges and jurors. Rule 605 prohibits a judge from testifying as a witness in a trial in which he or she is presiding. There are numerous reasons for prohibiting a judge from testifying. A judge who testifies for the prosecution or defense likely will not be viewed as impartial in the outcome of the case, which undermines respect for verdict. There also is the problem of who will rule on objections to the lawyer's questions or to the judge's responses. Lawyers likely will be reluctant to aggressively question and risk alienating the judge. Most important, a judge's testimony will carry significant weight with the jury and prejudice the position of the other party to the case.

The bar on testifying has been extended to other court personnel involved in a case, such as the judge's law clerk. The Code of Conduct for United States Judges states that a judge who knows ahead of time he or she may be a witness should recuse (step down) him- or herself before the trial. A lawyer who fails to object to a judge's testimony is not prohibited from raising the issue on appeal. This is because the lawyer confronts the dilemma that an objection risks alienating the judge. States like Nebraska have adopted statutes prohibiting judges from testifying in a trial in which the judge is presiding.

In *United States v. Nickl*, Marc Nickl was charged with aiding and abetting Paula Steward, the head bookkeeper at the National Bank of Andover, in the misapplication of close to $1 million in bank funds. Steward pled guilty although Nickl proceeded to trial. The government had the burden of establishing at Nickl's trial that Steward specifically intended to injure or to defraud the bank. At trial, Steward gave "conflicting testimony as to her intent to injure the bank." Nickl's attorney in cross-examining Steward suggested that Steward lacked the required intent and posed the question whether she had pled guilty "just to 'get it over with.'" The trial judge interrupted the defense attorney and proclaimed: "Well, I'll answer that question because I took her plea. . . . I would never have accepted her guilty plea unless she would have convinced me that . . . she intended [to injure the bank] . . . [a]nd that's why I accepted her plea. And that's why she's in prison."

The Tenth Circuit Court of Appeals held the judge's comment constituted "impermissible testimony in violation of Rule 605." The prosecution experienced difficulty establishing Steward's intent at Nickl's trial, and the judge "introduced evidence the government was not able to otherwise establish . . . and . . . almost certainly affected the jury's conclusions." The judge interrupted Steward and did not allow her to answer the question posed to her. The judge's comment "did not summarize Steward's testimony, it reshaped it. It converted Steward's equivocations into a definitive answer on the question of intent and improperly addressed an ultimate factual issue to be decided by the jury" (*United States v. Nickl*, 426 F.3d 1286 [10th Cir. 2005]).

Rule 605. Judge's Competency as a Witness

The presiding judge may not testify as a witness at the trial. A party need not object to preserve the issue.

- outside influence

■ JURORS AS WITNESSES

Federal Rule 606 disqualifies a juror from being a witness in the case in which he or she is impaneled. The thinking is that a juror may have an overly strong influence on the other jurors and may be in a position to share information that the trial court judge excluded from evidence. A judge when impaneling a jury asks individuals about possible connections to the case to avoid the possibility that an individual chosen for the jury will be asked to testify.

A far more frequent issue arises when a defendant convicted at trial wants to question jurors about what occurred during the jury deliberations. Rule 606 covers the jury room with a veil of secrecy. The rule is that jurors may not testify about votes, statements, or events during jury deliberations or the impact of arguments or evidence on their own thinking or on the thinking of other jurors. The reason for this rule is to ensure that jurors feel free to express their viewpoint during deliberations without fear that they later will be required to testify about the deliberations. There are three situations in which jurors are allowed to testify about events inside the jury room:

1. Outside prejudicial information was improperly brought to the jurors' attention.

2. Outside influences were brought to bear on a juror or jurors.

3. A mistake was made in entering the verdict on the verdict form.

As you can see, Rule 606 limits the testimony of jurors to outside influences such as bribes, threats, evidence excluded from trial, outside research conducted by jurors, and media coverage. In other words, jurors can testify about influences that enter the jury room that are not part of trial or jury deliberations.

Jurors following the trial also are free to make extrajudicial statements to the press, friends, acquaintances, or anyone about the jury deliberations or jury verdict.

A number of cases discuss whether a juror's testimony relates to internal matters inside the jury room, which may not be the subject of testimony, or relates to external influences outside the jury room, which may be the subject of a juror's testimony.

In *Tanner v. United States*, the defense attorney filed a motion for a new trial. The attorney alleged that several jurors reportedly drank two or three pitchers of beer during lunch breaks, had mixed drinks, and slept through afternoon portions of the trial. A juror described himself as "flying" during the trial. Two jurors stated they ingested cocaine, and three other jurors "regularly" smoked marijuana during the trial. The Supreme Court noted the use of alcohol and drugs "seems no more an 'outside influence' than a virus, poorly prepared food, or a lack of sleep." A juror only may testify about influences outside the jury room; intoxication arises from the jurors themselves. The Court noted that although examination of what transpired in the jury room may uncover "reprehensible conduct," the jury system could not survive a "barrage" of judicial investigations of jury decision-making (*Tanner v. United States*, 483 U.S. 107 [1987]).

What about expressions of racial prejudice in the jury room based on past experience with members of a group? In *United States v. Benally*, Kerry Dean Benally was convicted of forcibly assaulting a Bureau of Indian Affairs officer with a dangerous weapon. The next day, a juror came forward and alleged that the jury deliberations had been tainted by two discussions in which racist remarks were made about Native Americans. During the judge's *voir dire* of potential jurors, all of the individuals impaneled on the jury stated that their consideration of the case would be uninfluenced by the fact the defendant was of Native American descent (*United States v. Benally*, 546 F.3d 1230, 1233 [10th Cir. 2008]).

The trial court judge found that two jurors had lied on *voir dire* when they failed to reveal past experiences and biases against Native Americans, and a third juror had introduced outside evidence when the juror remarked that members of his family in law enforcement believed it was important to "send a message" to the "reservation" that there were consequences for assaulting government officials.

The Tenth Circuit Court of Appeals reversed the trial court judge's overturning of the jury verdict and order of a new trial.

> We do not deny that the jurors' alleged statements were entirely improper and inappropriate. The statements about Native Americans in particular were gross generalizations built upon prejudice. . . . Impropriety alone, however, does not make a statement extraneous. That would unravel the internal/external distinction and make anything said in jury deliberations "extraneous information". . . . [J]uror testimony regarding the possible subjective prejudices or improper motives of individual jurors has been held to be within the rule [rather than outside the rule].

The Tenth Circuit Court of Appeals while condemning the juror misconduct stressed that postverdict investigations into jury decision-making should be limited to a narrow set of allegations. Postverdict investigations disrupted the finality of jury verdicts, made jurors reluctant to speak openly and honestly during jury deliberations, may lead to the harassment of jurors by the lawyers seeking to overturn the verdict, result in endless appeals, and cause individuals to question the objectivity of jurors and the criminal justice system. Allowing courts to explore the basis for the jury's decision would shift power away from the ordinary citizens sitting on a jury to appellate court judges. The appellate court recognized jurors may at times engage in misconduct although in the overwhelming number of cases they are more objective and fair than professional jurists.

What about jurors who disregard the law in reaching a verdict? In *Fulghum v. Ford*, two jurors contacted Thomas A. Fulghum's lawyer and stated that they had believed Fulghum was legally insane at the time of the murder for which he was convicted although they had reached the guilty verdict because they feared a verdict of not guilty by reason of insanity "would have been less effective in assuring Fulghum's removal from society." The Eleventh Circuit Court of Appeals invoked Federal Rule of Evidence 606(b) and held jurors were disqualified from testifying about the mental process and considerations that led them to "assent or dissent" from the verdict. Rule 606(b) also prohibits a juror from testifying about coercion or pressure placed on a juror by other jurors or testifying about misunderstanding the law (*Fulghum v. Ford*, 850 F.2d 850 F.2d 759 [11th Cir. 1988]).

Should the jury room be insulated from judicial examination in instances when the decision-making process is tainted by coercion or a lack of understanding?

Rule 606. Juror

(a) **At the Trial.** A juror may not testify as a witness before the other jurors at the trial. If a juror is called to testify, the court must give a party an opportunity to object outside the jury's presence.

(b) **During an Inquiry into the Validity of a Verdict or Indictment.**

(1) *Prohibited Testimony or Other Evidence.* During an inquiry into the validity of a verdict or indictment, a juror may not testify about any statement made or incident that occurred during the jury's deliberations; the effect of anything on that juror's or another juror's

(Continued)

(Continued)

vote; or any juror's mental processes concerning the verdict or indictment. The court may not receive a juror's affidavit or evidence of a juror's statement on these matters.

(2) *Exceptions.* A juror may testify about whether:

(A) extraneous prejudicial information was improperly brought to the jury's attention;

(B) an outside influence was improperly brought to bear on any juror; or

(C) a mistake was made in entering the verdict on the verdict form.

5.3 YOU DECIDE

John Dioguardi was convicted of stock manipulation, and ten days after the trial, he received a letter from one of the jurors, Genena Rush. The letter was written on stationery with the zodiac sign of Libra along with the legend, "the heavenly house under which I was born." She urged Dioguardi to repent. She stated "she has 'eyes and ears that . . . see things before [they] happen.' But that her eyes 'are only partly open' because 'a curse was put upon them some years ago.'" Dioguardi's lawyers sent copies of the letter to seven psychiatrists, all of whom concluded Miss Rush's letter indicated hallucinatory tendencies; symptoms of possible psychosis, paranoia, and grandiosity; and an inability to appreciate reality without fantasizing. The judge refused to inquire into Rush's competence to have served as a juror and denied the motion for a new trial. At the time of *voir dire*, Rush had worked for the past four years as a medical attendant at a local hospital, and there was no indication that her reasoning or mental abilities were deficient. May the judge conduct an inquiry into Rush's mental competence? See *United States v. Dioguardi* (492 F.2d 70 [2d Cir. 1974]).

You can learn what the court decided by referring to the study site, **http://study.sagepub.com/lippmance.**

today: spouse can refuse to testify unless its about spouse leaving family or not paying... faithful in marriage

■ SPOUSAL COMPETENCE

At common law, husbands and wives were incompetent to testify against one another because it was thought that an individual had an interest in supporting and protecting his or her spouse and could not provide unbiased and truthful testimony. The United States Supreme Court also noted the prohibition on spousal testimony protects against conflict within a family and promotes family harmony and stability (*Hawkins v. United States*, 358 U.S. 73 [1958]).

An early exception to the prohibition on spousal testimony was made in those instances in which one spouse committed a crime against the person or property of the other spouse or against the person or property of the couple's child (*Stein v. Bowman*, 38 U.S. 209 [1839]).

In 1933, the United States Supreme Court rejected the rule prohibiting one spouse from testifying against the other in federal courts, explaining that the policy of disqualifying various categories of individuals from testifying had given way to a policy of allowing individuals to testify and leaving it to juries to evaluate the credibility and weight to be accorded the testimony. The Court explained that the disqualification of spousal testimony interfered with the pursuit of "truth" at trial (*Funk v. United States*, 390 U.S. 371 [1933]).

The contemporary federal law of spousal privilege was established in 1980, in *Trammel v. United States*. The defendant and his wife had been arrested for dealing in narcotics. She entered a plea agreement to testify against her husband in exchange for having the charges dropped against her. The Supreme Court held that under federal law the witness-spouse was the holder of the privilege and possessed the privilege of refusing to testify although if the witness desired to testify the defendant could not prevent his or her spouse from testifying (*Trammel v. United States*, 445 U.S. 40 [1980]).

States and the federal government all recognize **spousal competence** to testify against one's spouse although, as we shall see in Chapter Ten, a spouse may refuse to testify based on the spousal testimony privilege and the marital communications privilege. These privileges against testifying are subject to exceptions involving crimes against the person or property of the spouse or children. Recognition of the spousal privilege in domestic abuse cases would be contrary to public policy and would allow a spouse to pressure the other spouse into refusing to testify. In a number of states, a spouse may be compelled to testify in criminal prosecutions for bigamy and child abandonment or murder or rape outside of the marriage.

The Pennsylvania statute on spousal competence reads as follows (42 § 5913):

Spouses as witnesses against each other.

Except as otherwise provided in this subchapter, in a criminal proceeding a person shall have the privilege, which he or she may waive, not to testify against his or her then lawful spouse except that there shall be no such privilege:

(1) in proceedings for desertion and maintenance;] not paying bills/child support

(2) in any criminal proceeding against either for bodily injury or violence attempted, done or threatened upon the other, or upon the minor children of said husband and wife, or the minor children of either of them, or any minor child in their care or custody, or in the care or custody of either of them;

(3) applicable to proof of the fact of marriage, in support of a criminal charge of bigamy alleged to have been committed by or with the other; or

(4) in any criminal proceeding in which one of the charges pending against the defendant includes murder, involuntary deviate sexual intercourse or rape.

doesn't have to if...

The question is whether the interest in spousal harmony should outweigh the social interest in the presentation of material and relevant evidence at trial.

■ RELIGION

Early common law proclaimed that belief in a divine being who punished false swearing was a prerequisite to taking an oath. Followers of disfavored religions, atheists, and agnostics were disqualified from testifying.

This restriction was abandoned in the United States because it is inconsistent with American democracy and with the First Amendment prohibition on the establishment of a religion. As noted above, an individual who possesses a religious objection to swearing an oath may affirm under penalty of perjury. The only requirement for swearing an oath is whether the witness understands the obligation of the oath and consequences of failing to truthfully testify. ⭐

The Advisory Committee on Rules of Evidence notes that among the grounds abolished for competence is "religious belief." Federal Rule 610 also prohibits the use of religious beliefs or opinions to impeach a witness's credibility. This rule, although not directly related to competency, reflects a strong policy against using religion to evaluate an individual's truthfulness.

Michigan explicitly provides:

No person may be deemed incompetent as a witness, in any court, matter or proceeding, on account of his opinions on the subject of religion. No witness may be questioned in relation to his opinions on religion, either before or after he is sworn. (Mich. Comp. Laws § 600.1436 [2011])

5.4 YOU DECIDE

Federal Rule 610 states that "[e]vidence of a witness's religious beliefs or opinions is not admissible to attack or support the witness's credibility." Bedros Kalaydjian and Akram Hayat were brought to trial for distributing heroin. They both testified against their co-conspirators at trial. Kalaydjian and Hayat, both of whom were practicing Muslims, withdrew their initial request to be sworn on the Koran rather than the Bible and made affirmations of truthfulness. The defense counsel for their co-conspirators argued he was entitled to cross-examine Kalaydjian and Hayat about their decision to rely on an affirmation. He asserted as practicing Muslims the witnesses should swear on the Koran and their decision to rely on an affirmation demonstrated a lack of credibility. What is your view? See *United States v. Kalaydjian* (784 F.2d 53 [2nd Cir. 1986]).

You can learn what the court decided by referring to the study site, **http://study.sagepub.com/lippmance.**

Criminal Convictions

English common law provided that an individual convicted of a felony was incompetent to testify as a witness. The large number of crimes considered felonies meant that virtually every individual convicted of a crime was disqualified from testifying. This rule was part of American law until the late nineteenth century. The states and federal courts and legislatures eventually eliminated the disability on testimony because of conviction of a felony based on the realization that a criminal conviction did not mean an individual would be untruthful at trial. The Advisory Committee on Rules of Evidence in the notes to Rule 601 observes that conviction of a crime has been abolished as a disqualification to testify.

Rosen v. United States in 1918 was the most important decision rejecting the disqualification of felons (*Rosen v. United States*, 245 U.S. 467 [1918]). The United States Supreme Court held it was time to remove the "dead hand" of the common law rule prohibiting felons from testifying as witnesses in trials.

State statutes today specify that an individual may not be prevented from testifying because he or she has been accused, indicted, or convicted of a crime. There are any number of situations in which a prosecutor is forced to depend on convicted criminals to provide the evidence required to obtain a conviction. In discussing the use of a paid informant to arrest individuals involved in narcotics trafficking, the Eleventh Circuit Court of Appeals noted that "the government cannot be expected to depend exclusively upon the virtuous in enforcing the law." A witness's felony conviction, however, may be used to impeach his or her credibility (*United States v. Richardson*, 764 F.3d 1514 [11th Cir. 1985]).

■ MENTAL INCAPACITY *understand oath.*
mental disability can be questioned in cross-examination

In 1882, the United States Supreme Court in *District of Columbia v. Armes* held that an individual's mental incapacity did not automatically disqualify him or her from testifying as a witness at trial. Instead, a judge was to evaluate individuals' capacity to understand the obligation of an oath and the consequences of violating the oath, to observe and remember, and to narrate events.

> [A] lunatic or a person affected with insanity is admissible as a witness if he has sufficient understanding to apprehend the obligation of an oath, and to be capable of giving a correct account of the matters which he has seen or heard in reference to the questions at issue and whether he has that understanding is a question to be determined by the court, upon examination of the party himself, and any competent witnesses who can speak to the nature and extent of his insanity. (*District of Columbia v. Armes*, 107 U.S. 519 [1882])

The defendant in *Armes* held a severely depressed individual who was confined to a mental asylum and who attempted suicide several times by sticking a fork in his neck was competent to testify. The Court explained that "the existence of partial insanity" does not prevent individuals from giving an "accurate" and clear statement of "what they have seen or heard."

The burden of establishing incompetence is on the party challenging the witness's competence. The Advisory Committee on Rules of Evidence notes that a "witness wholly without [mental] capacity is difficult to imagine and the issue of mental capacity is best left to the jury in determining the credibility and weight to be accorded to testimony."

In *United States v. Bloome*, a witness had a documented history of "psychological disturbance" and suffered from the traumatic effect of bullet wounds to his head and the remaining bullet fragments in his head. A federal district court found the witness competent to testify and held that "the competence of a witness depends upon a capacity to observe, to remember, to communicate and to understand the nature of an oath and the duty it imposes to tell the truth" (*United States v. Bloome*, 773 F. Supp. 545 [E.D.N.Y. 1991]). Applying this standard, the Fourth Circuit Court of Appeals found a prosecution witness competent to testify who was a drug addict, smoked crack cocaine on the day she witnessed the crimes involved at the trial, and suffered from a gunshot wound to her head and auditory and visual hallucinations. The witness also was under a doctor's care and was being treated with various psychiatric medications (*United States v. Williams*, 445 F.3d 724 [4th Cir. 2006]).

Incompetent to testify as witnesses	=	Judges **+** jurors.
Competent to testify	=	May not be prohibited to testify based on marital status
	+	religious belief, felony arrest, prosecution, conviction, or mental disability.

■ IMPEACHMENT

The evidentiary rules of impeachment address the methods by which a party may discredit the testimony of a witness. Impeachment refers to evidence intended to create doubts about the credibility of a witness. This may entail calling into question the accuracy of the witness's description or memory of events or pointing out the witness's bias or intoxication or lack of objectivity or his or her character trait for dishonesty. The goal of impeachment is to create doubts about the believability or accuracy of the witness's testimony, whether he or she is lying or merely mistaken.

An individual who promises under oath to testify truthfully subjects his or her credibility to cross-examination. As we have seen, there are very few limitations on the competency of individuals to testify. The ability of the jury to intelligently evaluate the credibility and weight of a witness's testimony requires that the rules of evidence allow lawyers to subject witnesses to flexible rules of impeachment. A judge possesses the discretion to exclude impeachment that is prejudicial or that would waste time to present at trial or is collateral (nonessential) to the charge.

Federal Rule 607 permits a party to impeach adverse witnesses or their own witnesses. Most commentators list five principal forms of impeachment, only some of which are covered in the Federal Rules of Evidence.

Bias or interest. "Is it true you were offered a reduced sentence if you testified for the government against the defendant?"

Sensory or mental defects. "You identified the defendant as the perpetrator of the crime although you were not wearing your glasses?"

Character for untruthfulness. "Were you previously convicted of perjury?"

Specific contradiction. "You told the police you killed the victim, and now you deny killing the victim?"

Prior inconsistent statement. "You are testifying you were playing cards at the time of the crime although you previously told the police you went by yourself to the movies." *in → part of prior statement*

Impeachment proceeds in two phases. A witness in most instances is impeached by the opposing lawyer on cross-examination. The witness is asked about the discrediting facts on cross-examination. In certain types of impeachment, the attack on the witness is limited to this *intrinsic evidence*, and as the expression goes, "You must take his answer." Certain categories of impeachment evidence may be undertaken in a second stage through *extrinsic evidence*. This is evidence presented in a second step through documents or through an additional witness rather than through questioning the witness on cross-examination. Extrinsic evidence typically is used when the principal witness resists responding to a question, which may impeach his or her credibility. A witness claiming self-defense may not be able to "recall" on cross-examination being tossed out of a bar as a result of a fight several years ago. The lawyer may call the owner of the bar to testify about the fight or show a video that recorded the incident. Extrinsic evidence typically is permitted for those categories of impeachment that have strong probative value and when the extrinsic evidence can be efficiently presented.

The common law prohibited a party from impeaching his or her own witness. The theory was that a party who called a witness to testify was "vouching for" the witness's credibility and character. There also was the notion that it was "foul play" to call a witness and then attack his or her truthfulness or accuracy. This rule gradually was abandoned because a party at times may call a witness with whom he or she is not well acquainted because he or she is believed to be knowledgeable about the facts. The Advisory Committee on Rules of Evidence notes that a party

ex → use from other evidence show they are lying

"rarely has a free choice" in selecting witnesses, and denial of the right to cross-examination leaves the party at the "mercy of the witnesses."

In *United States v. Carter*, the prosecutor called Cedric Scott, a conspiracy member who had pled guilty in exchange for a promise to testify against Mark Carter. At trial, Scott denied Carter was a member of a gang and denied ever giving him cocaine to sell. The judge allowed the prosecutor to impeach his own witness by introducing statements Scott had made to the police implicating Carter in a drug conspiracy (*United States v. Carter*, 973 F.3d 1509 [11th Cir. 1992]).

Rule 607. Who May Impeach a Witness

Any party, including the party that called the witness, may attack the witness's credibility.

■ **BIAS** *relationship between ~~victim/defendant~~ witness and what they are talking about → relationships (sexual/friend/family)*

A witness may be impeached on bias, interest, partiality, or corruption (e.g., bribery). In *United States v. Booty*, the Eleventh Circuit Court of Appeals defined bias as a "relationship between a party and a witness which might lead the witness to slant, unconsciously or otherwise, his testimony in favor of or against a party." The Federal Rules of Evidence do not explicitly address bias although a number of state jurisdictions have rules on bias. The United States Supreme Court held that it is "permissible to impeach a witness by showing bias under the Federal Rules of Evidence. . . ." (*United States v. Booty*, 621 F.2d 1291 [5th Cir. 1980]). The Court explained that "proof of bias is almost always relevant because the jury, as finder of fact and weigher of credibility, has historically been entitled to assess all evidence which might bear on the accuracy and truth of a witness' testimony" (*United States v. Abel*, 469 U.S. 45 [1984]).

There are two types of bias. The first is a relationship between the witness and the prosecution or the defense. The relationship may be a bias in favor of a party based on family, friendship, business, or romance, or a bias against a party based on anger, disagreement, or jealousy. The second type of bias is based on a connection between the witness and the litigation. Examples are a witness who is offered a reduced charge in his or her criminal case in exchange for his or her testimony against the defendant and an expert witness who is paid to testify at trial. The cross-examiner is not obliged to take the witness's response to a question on bias and if dissatisfied may prove bias through the extrinsic evidence of other witnesses or documents.

In *United States v. Abel*, John Abel was charged with robbery. His two accomplices had pled guilty, and one of them, Kurt Ehle, agreed to testify against Abel and implicated him in the robbery. Abel called Robert Mills who had spent time in prison with Ehle to testify. Mills claimed that Ehle had told him he planned to falsely implicate Abel in the bank robbery. On cross-examination, Mills denied he was a member of the Aryan Brotherhood prison gang. The prosecution called Ehle back to the stand who testified that all three of them were members of a secret prison gang whose members were required to "lie, cheat [and] steal" to protect one another. It would have been a death sentence for Ehle to confide in Mills that he planned to falsely testify against Abel. Abel's conviction before a jury was upheld by the United States Supreme Court, which explained that the "evidence showing Mills' and respondent's membership in the prison gang was sufficiently probative of Mills' possible bias towards respondent [Abel] to warrant its admission into evidence" (*United States v. Abel*, 469 U.S. 45 [1984]).

→ for impeaching someone

■ **PRIOR FELONY CONVICTIONS** *→ for felony → must be within 10 years of release of prison* / *→ crimes of dishonesty → can show lying + have value*

At early common law, an individual convicted of a felony or any misdemeanor involving dishonesty was disqualified from testifying. A criminal conviction no longer bars an individual from testifying although conviction of various crimes may be used to impeach a witness. States differ on what offense may be used for impeachment. The majority view is that any felony may be used for impeachment.

The thinking behind impeachment by prior convictions is that a person convicted of a crime involving untruthfulness may act in conformity with this character trait in testifying in court. An individual's conviction of a crime may indicate a lack of respect for legal rules. There clearly are limits to the category of criminal offenses that reasonably may be viewed as indicating a propensity to distort or shade the truth. What of a five-year-old drunk driving conviction? Some offenses may be so prejudicial they should not be admissible on impeachment. Should the same standard be used for defendants as is used for other witnesses?

Federal Rule 609 strikes a balance between the interest in using prior criminal convictions to challenge a witness's truthfulness and the risk that a prior conviction will portray a witness as a "bad person" and prejudice the jury against the witness, particularly in the case of a defendant-witness. There is the risk that the jury's negative view of a witness will taint their view of the witness as well as prejudice their view of the defendant for whom the witness is testifying. A defendant's anticipation he or she or witnesses will be impeached on a prior criminal conviction may convince him or her not to testify in a case, impeding his or her ability to present a defense.

Keep in mind that prior convictions under Rule 609 serve a different purpose than "other acts" admissible under Rule 404(b) as proof of motive, opportunity, intent, preparation, plan, knowledge, identity, absence of mistake, or lack of accident. Remember Rule 609 allows lawyers to introduce evidence of a prior conviction to evaluate the witness's character for truthfulness. This evidence may not be used as evidence of a defendant's guilt. The thinking is that a witness or defendant-witness taking the stand to testify opens him or her to impeachment. This assists the jury in evaluating the credibility and weight to be accorded to the testimony.

We can best understand Rule 609 by going through the rule's provisions in a step-by-step fashion.

Felony Convictions to Impeach Nonparty Witnesses

A witness other than the accused may be impeached by criminal convictions if two conditions are satisfied. First, the crime was punishable by death or imprisonment in excess of one year. The drafters of Rule 609 believed that the commission of any felony was sufficiently serious to impeach a nonparty witness's truthfulness. Second, the judge may exercise discretion under Rule 403 to prevent the crime being used to impeach the witness if the probative value is "substantially outweighed" by the danger of unfair prejudice.

Felony Convictions to Impeach Defendant-Witnesses

Federal Rule 609(1)(B) anticipates the risk that evidence of a criminal defendant's prior criminal convictions will lead the jury to conclude the defendant is guilty of the crime with which he or she is charged at trial. As a result, it is somewhat more difficult to introduce crimes punishable by death or imprisonment in excess of one year to impeach a defendant-witness than other witnesses. This higher bar for impeaching defendants is based on the risk the crime will prejudice the jury against the defendant and lead jurors to convict the defendant because of his or her past behavior rather than based on the evidence at trial. Rule 609(a)(1)(B) prohibits the use of evidence of a prior conviction to impeach the accused whenever the prejudicial impact *equals or is greater than the probative value*. Note Rule 403 excludes this evidence if the probative value is *substantially outweighed* by the danger of unfair prejudice (see Table 5.2).

A persistent issue is whether an offense that is similar to the crime charged against the defendant is prejudicial and should be employed for impeachment. In *United States v. Sanders*, the defendant was convicted of assault with a dangerous weapon with the intent to commit bodily harm and for possession of contraband (a shank used in the assault). The trial court admitted impeachment evidence of Carlos Sanders's prior convictions for assault and possession of contraband (a shank), and Sanders was convicted. The Fourth Circuit Court of Appeals held that Sanders's prior convictions were not admissible under Rule 609(a).

> Admission of evidence of a similar offense often does little to impeach the credibility of a testifying defendant while undoubtedly prejudicing him. The jury . . . can hardly avoid drawing the inference that the past conviction suggests some probability that defendant committed the similar offense for which he is currently charged. The generally accepted view, therefore, is that evidence of similar offenses for impeachment purposes under Rule 609 should be admitted sparingly if at all. (*United States v. Sanders*, 964 F.2d 295 [4th Cir. 1992])

Federal courts look at five factors to guide judicial decision-making in regard to the relevant prior criminal convictions under Federal Rule 609(a)(1)(B) (*United States v. Hall*, 486 F.2d 613 [9th Cir. 1978]; see also Table 5.1).

Table 5.1 ■ Impeachment of a Defendant by Evidence of a Criminal Conviction

Impeachment value of the former crime. Crimes of violence such as robbery, arson, and murder possess low probative value for demonstrating dishonesty. Convictions for crimes such as perjury, false pretenses, and embezzlement have a high probative value for demonstrating dishonesty and are admitted under Rule 609(a)(2).

Timing of the prior conviction and subsequent criminality. The more remote the crime, the less the probative value in demonstrating a lack of truthfulness.

Similarity between the prior crime and the charged crime. The offense used for impeachment should be sufficiently different from the offense with which the defendant is charged so as not to risk prejudicing the jury's consideration of the charges against the defendant.

Importance of the defendant's testimony. The more important the defendant's testimony, the greater the interest in allowing the defendant to testify without the risk of impeachment of the defendant's testimony.

Centrality of credibility. The more central the defendant's credibility is to a case, the greater the interest in admitting evidence to impeach his or her testimony.

The government, when using a criminal conviction to impeach a defendant's testimony, bears the burden of demonstrating that the probative value of the felony conviction outweighs its prejudicial effect.

Table 5.2 ■ Prejudice and Evidence of Prior Crimes to Impeach a Witness		
Prejudicial Effect	**Rule 403**	**Rule 609(a)(1)(B)**
Less than probative value	Admit evidence	Admit evidence
Equals probative value	Admit	Exclude
Slightly outweighs probative value	Admit	Exclude
Substantially outweighs probative value	Exclude	Exclude

■ CRIMES INVOLVING A DISHONEST ACT OR FALSE STATEMENT

Federal Rule 609 allows the use of any conviction of *any crime* of dishonesty or a crime involving a false statement to impeach the character of *any witness* regardless of the criminal sentence. The thinking is these offenses are considered probative of a witness's character for truthfulness. This category refers to crimes involving deception, falsehood, and untruthfulness and includes embezzlement, forgery and uttering, counterfeiting, false pretenses, larceny by trick, and tax evasion. Most judges will examine whether a crime was committed using deception rather than make a judgment based on the name of the crime. A conviction for larceny, for example, may involve the physical taking of property and fall within Rule 609(a)(1), or it may fall within the terms of Rule 609(a)(2) when committed through verbal deceit.

It is important to keep in mind that prior convictions involving dishonesty and false statements are admissible for impeachment and may not be excluded by the judge on the grounds of prejudice.

Time Limits

Rule 609(b) requires that a conviction used for impeachment ordinarily may not be more than ten years old, measured by the later of the witness's criminal conviction or release from confinement. A conviction more than ten years old is admissible only if "its probative value . . . substantially outweighs its prejudicial effect."

Pardons, Annulments, and Certificates of Rehabilitation

Criminal convictions may not be used for impeachment when the individual has been pardoned by the chief executive, when the conviction has been annulled (e.g., removed from the individual's record), or when a certificate of rehabilitation has been issued (e.g., attests to the good character of an individual with a criminal record). These convictions may be used on impeachment in those instances in which an individual has been convicted of a later crime punishable by death or by imprisonment for more than a year.

Juvenile Adjudications

Juvenile adjudications are not available to impeach the defendant. They only may be used in other circumstances when the offense would be admissible against an adult and the evidence is necessary to impeach a witness in those circumstances in which the conviction is necessary to fairly determine guilt or innocence.

Appeals

A pending appeal does not bar use of a conviction to impeach a witness. The witness also may introduce a pending appeal when impeached on a criminal conviction.

Rule 609. Impeachment by Evidence of a Criminal Conviction

(a) In General. The following rules apply to attacking a witness's character for truthfulness by evidence of a criminal conviction:

  (1) for a crime that, in the convicting jurisdiction, was punishable by death or by imprisonment for more than one year, the evidence:

    (A) must be admitted, subject to Rule 403, in a civil case or in a criminal case in which the witness is not a defendant; and

    (B) must be admitted in a criminal case in which the witness is a defendant, if the probative value of the evidence outweighs its prejudicial effect to that defendant; and

  (2) for any crime regardless of the punishment, the evidence must be admitted if the court can readily determine that establishing the elements of the crime required proving—or the witness's admitting—a dishonest act or false statement.

(b) Limit on Using the Evidence after 10 Years. This subdivision (b) applies if more than 10 years have passed since the witness's conviction or release from confinement for it, whichever is later. Evidence of the conviction is admissible only if:

  (1) its probative value, supported by specific facts and circumstances, substantially outweighs its prejudicial effect; and

  (2) the proponent gives an adverse party reasonable written notice of the intent to use it so that the party has a fair opportunity to contest its use.

(c) Effect of a Pardon, Annulment, or Certificate of Rehabilitation. Evidence of a conviction is not admissible if:

  (1) the conviction has been the subject of a pardon, annulment, certificate of rehabilitation, or other equivalent procedure based on a finding that the person has been rehabilitated, and the person has not been convicted of a later crime punishable by death or by imprisonment for more than one year; or

  (2) the conviction has been the subject of a pardon, annulment, or other equivalent procedure based on a finding of innocence.

(d) Juvenile Adjudications. Evidence of a juvenile adjudication is admissible under this rule only if:

  (1) it is offered in a criminal case;

  (2) the adjudication was of a witness other than the defendant;

  (3) an adult's conviction for that offense would be admissible to attack the adult's credibility; and

  (4) admitting the evidence is necessary to fairly determine guilt or innocence.

(e) Pendency of an Appeal. A conviction that satisfies this rule is admissible even if an appeal is pending. Evidence of the pendency is also admissible.

5.5 YOU DECIDE

On January 24, 1992, four armed men robbed a bank in Victorville, California. The employees and customers were ordered to lie facedown on the floor, and they ordered the employees to empty the cash from the vault into a duffle bag. They fled with over $300,000 in cash. The police responded to the robbery and pursued the two cars containing the robbers. One of the cars stalled, and the two men inside fled. The police arrested Anthony Hicks nearby to the vehicle. At trial, Hicks chose to take the stand and present an alibi defense. He testified that he was in the area of the arrests on the day of the robbery because he was meeting a friend there. He claimed to have fled when he heard sirens and saw police cars because he was fearful of being arrested on two outstanding warrants for traffic violations. This is the reason he gave the arresting officer a false name. On cross-examination, the prosecution impeached Hicks by questioning him on his prior convictions for residential robbery and possession of rock cocaine for sale. As a judge, would you have permitted Hicks to be impeached by these felony convictions? See *United States v. Alexander* (48 F.3d 1477 [9th Cir. 1955]).

You can learn what the court decided by referring to the study site, **http://study.sagepub.com/lippmance.**

if someone raises character trait about dishonesty→ can use this

■ CHARACTER FOR TRUTHFULNESS

The Federal Rules of Evidence permit a lawyer to impeach an opposing witness's character for truthfulness in three different ways. We already have discussed Rule 609(a)(b). In this section, we discuss Rules 608(a) and 608(b).

Rule 608(a) provides that a witness's credibility may be attacked or supported by testimony about the witness's reputation for "truthfulness or untruthfulness."

Rule 608(b) allows a judge to permit questions on cross-examination about specific instances of conduct that are probative of the character for truthfulness or untruthfulness of the witness or of "another witness whose character the witness being cross-examined is being questioned about."

Rule 609(a)(b) allows evidence on cross-examination of a witness's prior criminal convictions.

You may recall that Rule 404(a)(1) provides that character evidence generally is inadmissible as evidence that an individual committed a crime. Rule 404(a)(3), however, provides an exception for character evidence used for impeachment purposes under Rules 607, 608, and 609.

Rule 608(a) provides that a witness's credibility may be attacked or supported by testimony about the witness's reputation for "truthfulness or untruthfulness." As we shall soon see, this testimony must be in the form of reputation or opinion. In other words, Rule 608(a) restricts the purpose for which character evidence may be used (impeachment), the type of character evidence (truthfulness), and the method of presenting character evidence (opinion or reputation). The reasoning behind Rule 608(a) is that an individual who takes the stand and swears an oath to tell the truth "opens the door" for his or her credibility to be impeached. The question is whether the witness is the type of person who tells the truth.

Commentators distinguish between *fact witnesses* or *content witnesses* who testify about the facts of the crime and *impeaching witnesses* who testify about the character for truthfulness of fact witnesses. Once a fact witness testifies, the adverse party may introduce character witnesses to impeach the character of the fact witness. A character witness may testify as to the character of the fact witness by opinion or reputation and may not testify regarding specific acts of the testifying witness.

A foundation must be established before admitting reputation or opinion evidence. The witness testifying about reputation must demonstrate a knowledge of the witness's reputation in the community. The concept of community is flexibly interpreted in recognition of the mobility of modern society to mean the witness's neighborhood, place of employment, or school.

The witness offering reputation evidence will be asked how he or she knows the testifying witness, whether he or she participated in discussions about the testifying witness's character for truthfulness for untruthfulness, and about the testifying witness's reputation among other people for truthfulness and untruthfulness. A witness who offers opinion evidence on a witness's character for truthfulness is required to demonstrate a personal relationship with the witness being impeached. A character witness will be asked how he or she knows the testifying witness, how long he or she has known the testifying witness, and whether he or she has "formed an opinion" of the testifying witness (*Wilson v. City of Chicago*, 6 F.2d 1233 [7th Cir. 1993]).

Keep in mind that Rule 608(a) limits impeachment to a witness who has testified at trial. In *United States v. McGauley*, the defendant claimed the police lacked grounds to stop him and search his luggage for narcotics. The Eighth Circuit Court of Appeals held the trial court had acted properly in excluding evidence about the lack of truthfulness of the detective who directed a drug bust who did not testify at the trial. The prosecutor had put other officers on the stand to avoid the risk that the detective would be impeached.

As a trial court judge, would you allow a defense lawyer to testify that a police officer had a reputation for a lack of truthfulness among the lawyer's clients whom the officer had testified against at trial and among other defense attorneys who had interacted with the police officer in criminal cases? What about the testimony of a reporter who had written an article documenting multiple complaints from citizens about several officers in their police district whom they viewed as "liars"? Should the credibility and weight of this testimony be left to the jury? (*United States v. McGauley*, 786 F.2d 888 [8th Cir. 1986]).

> **Rule 608. A Witness's Character for Truthfulness or Untruthfulness**
>
> **(a) Reputation or Opinion Evidence.** A witness's credibility may be attacked or supported by testimony about the witness's reputation for having a character for truthfulness or untruthfulness, or by testimony in the form of an opinion about that character. But evidence of truthful character is admissible only after the witness's character for truthfulness has been attacked.

* you can use uncharged crimes to impeach but usually doesn't happen.

■ UNCHARGED CRIMES AND IMMORAL ACTS

The common law allowed impeachment for misconduct that did not result in a criminal conviction on the theory that the details of an individual's personal background are "open season" for cross-examination. Several states limit impeachment to criminal convictions based on the belief cross-examination on misconduct that did not result in criminal convictions raises too many collateral matters that distract the jury.

A number of state courts accept that judges may exercise their discretion to allow impeachment by criminal acts with which an individual was charged that did not result in either an acquittal or a conviction. This includes cases that were dropped by the prosecutor due to procedural errors such as an unlawful search and seizure. Immoral acts that are not contrary to criminal law also may be used in some states for impeachment.

The same types of considerations involved in evaluating the probative value of criminal convictions are used by judges in evaluating whether to allow impeachment by uncharged crimes and immoral acts. The acts should be relevant to truthfulness, misdemeanors generally are inadmissible, and a crime that occurred some years ago has less probative value than a more recent criminal act. Uncharged crimes and immoral acts should be prohibited from being used for impeachment if they involve an unreasonable risk of prejudice and confusion. The judge also must consider the importance of the credibility of the witness to the case. In those instances in which a witness's credibility is a central aspect of the case (e.g., an alibi witness), cross-examination on uncharged crimes and immoral acts likely should be permitted.

Federal Rule 608(b) allows the introduction of "specific instances of misconduct" by a witness to attack or to support a witness's "character for truthfulness" or "character for truthfulness" of another witness about whose character the witness has testified. The cross-examiner must ask the question in a "good faith factual belief" the incident occurred and must accept the answer provided by the witness. A good faith belief is a belief that is supported by some evidence and a basis in fact, and the cross-examination may not be based on wild speculation.

The cross-examiner may not rely on extrinsic evidence to establish "specific instances of conduct." The thinking is that relying on extrinsic evidence would consume valuable time and divert the attention of the jury.

An example of a court limiting cross-examination to truthfulness or untruthfulness is the impeachment in *United States v. Nosov*. Alexander Spitchenko was the central witness in the prosecution of the defendants for kidnapping and murder. The judge prohibited the defendants to cross-examine Spitchenko on the content of his scheme to produce pornographic films. They were allowed to cross-examine Spitchenko on parts of the scheme involving dishonesty, the bribing of officials in Estonia to allow the women to emigrate to the United States, and seizing the women's passports to ensure they fulfilled their contracts (*United States v. Nosov*, 221 F.Supp.2d 445 [S.D.N.Y. 2002]).

An exception arises when the defendant-witness "opens the door" by volunteering information on his or her direct testimony. In *United States v. Benedetto*, Carl Benedetto, a federal agricultural inspector, was charged with taking bribes from the operators of meat plants. On direct testimony, he denied ever receiving a bribe, and the Second Circuit Court of Appeals held his testimony was properly impeached by two witnesses who testified he had accepted two uncharged criminal bribes (*United States v. Benedetto*, 571 F.2d 1246 [2d. Cir. 1978]).

A persistent question is whether a "specific instance of misconduct" raises a question about a witness's truthfulness. One court held that a police officer could not be impeached with evidence he had employed false statements to elicit a confession based on the fact this was a routine practice and did not undermine an officer's credibility under oath. Do you agree with the notion that because this is standard procedure among the police it should not be used for impeachment? (*Minnesota v. Martinez*, 657 N.W.2d 600 [Minn. App. 2008]). Certain uncharged crimes clearly fall within Federal Rule 608(b), including forgery, perjury, bribery, and false income tax returns.

In *United States v. Whitmore*, the defendant was convicted of possession of a firearm and claimed the arresting officer planted the gun on him at the time of the arrest. The District of Columbia Court of Appeals held the trial court improperly had prohibited cross-examination of the officer based on a judge's statement from the bench in another case that the officer had "lied" and also had improperly prohibited cross-examination on the officer's failure to pay child support and on his failure to inform his superiors of his suspended driver's license (*United States v. Whitmore*, 359 F.3d 609 [D.C. Cir. 2004]).

Rule 608. Specific Instances of Conduct

(b) **Specific Instances of Conduct.** Except for a criminal conviction under Rule 609, extrinsic evidence is not admissible to prove specific instances of a witness's conduct in order to attack or support the witness's character for truthfulness. But the court may, on cross-examination, allow them to be inquired into if they are probative of the character for truthfulness or untruthfulness of:

(1) the witness; or

(2) another witness whose character the witness being cross-examined has testified about.

By testifying on another matter, a witness does not waive any privilege against self-incrimination for testimony that relates only to the witness's character for truthfulness.

5.6 YOU DECIDE

Stephanie, a midshipman at the Merchant Marine Academy, accused a fellow midshipman, Francis, of sexual assault. At trial, the judge prohibited the cross-examination of Stephanie on complaints she filed against other students for cheating on exams at the Merchant Marine Academy. The judge first heard the cross-examination of Stephanie outside the presence of the jury. Francis's lawyer asked Stephanie a number of times whether she had "lied" about these complaints and "falsely accused" the other midshipmen. On each occasion, she responded, "No." The judge examined the files from the academy, and although student officials did not find that Stephanie had been untruthful, they also found insufficient evidence to support Stephanie's claims. Stephanie's truthfulness was a crucial aspect of the case. The trial court judge, however, exercised his discretion and ruled that because Stephanie would have denied her allegations of cheating against other students were false and because Francis was prohibited from relying on extrinsic evidence to refute Stephanie's denial, the cross-examination would have created a "confusing" and "distracting" "sideshow." "The prejudicial impact of engendering speculation about the subject outweighed the minimal probative value of permitting the jury to evaluate [Stephanie's] demeanor during the question and answer." Do you agree? See *United States v. Crowley* (318 F.3d 401 [2d Cir. 2003]).

You can learn what the court decided by referring to the study site, **http://study.sagepub.com/lippmance.**

■ PRIOR INCONSISTENT STATEMENTS

A witness may be impeached by a prior verbal or written statement inconsistent with his or her testimony at trial. The **prior inconsistent statement** may be a verbal statement or signed, written document such as a confession to the police. The purpose of demonstrating the two statements are at odds with one another is to call attention to the inconsistency of the two statements rather than to prove one of the statements is true and the other statement is false. The goal is for the jury to consider whether the witness is credible and whether his or her testimony is to be believed.

Prior inconsistent statements are not required to be directly contradictory. It is sufficient if the facts in the defendant's testimony under oath at trial are slightly different from the facts asserted in the prior statement. "To be received as a prior inconsistent statement, the contradiction need not be in plain terms. It is enough if the 'proffered testimony, taken as a whole, either by what it says or by what it omits to say' affords some indication that the fact was different from the testimony of the witness whom it sought to contradict" (*United States v. Gravely*, 840 F.2d 1156 [4th Cir. 1988]). For example, the defendant may have made an earlier statement he or she killed the victim and at trial may deny he or she killed the victim or assert that he or she killed in self-defense or as a result of an accident. A judge has the ability to exercise a degree of discretion in determining whether a statement is inconsistent. Consider whether an immediate inability to recall what occurred is inconsistent with a detailed statement offered at trial. What about the opposite situation?

The cross-examiner is required to have a reasonable basis for believing the earlier statement was made by the witness. The statement under the federal rules must be disclosed to the adverse party's lawyer on request before asking about the inconsistent statement on cross-examination. The purpose is to allow the opposing lawyer to anticipate what is about to transpire at the trial so as to allow the lawyer to prepare to counter the impeachment of the witness.

The traditional approach is that in the event the witness denies or is unable to recall the statement or tries to explain why the statement is not inconsistent with the witness's testimony or offers an explanation why he or she made the inconsistent statement, the cross-examiner may offer extrinsic evidence (a witness or document) to support the statement was made. Rule 613(b) provides that the witness must be given the opportunity to "explain or deny" the inconsistent statement before or after the extrinsic evidence is introduced. Extrinsic evidence typically may not be introduced when the inconsistent statement is about a minor (collateral) matter, such as the color of a bank robber's shirt or shoes, which is not a central issue in the case.

The United States Supreme Court has addressed prior inconsistent statements in several Fifth Amendment interrogation cases. In *New York v. Harris*, the Court held confessions made in violation of a suspect's *Miranda* rights may be used to impeach a defendant who takes the stand and contradicts the confession by denying having committed the crime (*New York v. Harris*, 495 U.S. 14 [1990]).

What of a suspect's failure to speak? Can silence be considered to be inconsistent with a claim of innocence at trial? In *Doyle v. Ohio*, the Supreme Court held that an individual's invocation of silence following the reading of the *Miranda* rights may not be used against him or her because this would burden the defendant's assertion of his or her constitutional right against self-incrimination (*Doyle v. Ohio*, 426 U.S. 610 [1976]).

The Supreme Court also has held a suspect charged with a fatal stabbing could be impeached by the fact he waited two weeks to turn himself into the police and to assert he killed in self-defense. The Court stressed that "no governmental action induced petition to remain silent before arrest. . . . Consequently, the fundamental unfairness present in *Doyle* is not present in this case" (*Jenkins v. Anderson*, 447 U.S. 231 [1980]).

In *Fletcher v. Weir*, the Supreme Court allowed a defendant who testified he killed in self-defense at trial to be impeached by his silence in failing to offer this explanation before the police read him his *Miranda* rights (*Fletcher v. Weir*, 455 F.2d 603 [1982]). This is consistent with the general rule that pre-*Miranda* silence may be used to impeach the individual if he or she takes the stand and offers an alibi or denies his or her guilt (*Jenkins v. Anderson*, 447 U.S. 231 [1980]).

Joe came to the victim's home while intoxicated looking for the victim's mother, whom he was dating. The victim (who was then 17 years old) and her sister answered the door and told Joe to leave. The sister pushed Joe out of the house and locked the door.

Shortly thereafter, the victim left her home, and Joe approached, hit her in the face, fractured her nose, and pulled her into alley. He threatened to kill her and sexually assaulted her. During the assault he choked her and bit her chin and arm. The victim's injuries were consistent with nonconsensual vaginal and anal intercourse. The night of the assault she provided a detailed statement to the police during a two-hour interview. Joe was charged with kidnapping, aggravated assault, and sexual assault. The trial because of procedural delays did not take place until nearly three years following the assault.

At trial, when asked during direct examination by the prosecutor about the assault, the victim responded on several occasions: "I don't remember." In response, the state asked: "You don't remember, or you would rather not say?" Each time, the victim answered: "I would rather not say." The victim added that it was difficult to testify, stating she "tried forgetting" the assault but it was "hard to get over it."

The victim admitted giving a detailed statement to the police following the attack. The prosecutor argued these statements were admissible as prior inconsistent statements. The prosecutor identified the inconsistency as "she's told us that she doesn't want to talk about it, and I'm saying she knows about it but she's not willing to say. So I'm impeaching her with the statements made to the police." The judge over the defendant's objection allowed the prosecutor to ask the victim whether she had made specific statements to Detective Sutton on the night of the incident, and the victim consistently testified that she had made those statements. "After the court allowed such questioning, the victim answered a number of similar questions without reference to her prior statements to Detective Sutton."

Joe argues the victim "never gave testimony that was inconsistent with her prior statements. It cannot be claimed that the [victim] could not recall the events because when questioned by the state she did not claim she could not remember only that she did not want to talk about it." See *State v. Joe* (316 P.3d 615 [Ariz. App. 2014]).

You can learn what the court decided by referring to the study site, **http://study.sagepub.com/lippmance.**

Rule 613. Witness's Prior Statement

(a) **Showing or Disclosing the Statement during Examination.** When examining a witness about the witness's prior statement, a party need not show it or disclose its contents to the witness. But the party must, on request, show it or disclose its contents to an adverse party's attorney.

(b) **Extrinsic Evidence of a Prior Inconsistent Statement.** Extrinsic evidence of a witness's prior inconsistent statement is admissible only if the witness is given an opportunity to explain or deny the statement and an adverse party is given an opportunity to examine the witness about it, or if justice so requires. This subdivision (b) does not apply to an opposing party's statement under Rule 801(d)(2).

■ SPECIFIC CONTRADICTION

A witness may be impeached by a specific contradiction although there is no provision of the Federal Rules addressing this method of impeaching a witness's testimony. Specific contradiction involves directly contradicting a witness's testimony by evidence at trial. A prior inconstant statement, in contrast, typically involves an inconsistent statement made outside of court.

First, a witness may be impeached by his or her own statements at trial. The prosecutor may point out that the witness's admission that he or she was high on marijuana at the time he or she witnessed the crime is in contradiction to earlier testimony that he or she was not a "drug user." Second, the prosecutor may directly challenge the witness's testimony that he or she never used narcotics by presenting a witness who directly challenges the defendant's account. Third, the prosecution may challenge the witness's statement he or she never used unlawful narcotics by introducing narcotics into evidence seized lawfully or unlawfully from the suspect's home or office. Evidence introduced based on specific contradiction is intended to challenge a witness's credibility and is not considered substantive evidence of guilt.

CRIMINAL EVIDENCE AND PUBLIC POLICY

Jailhouse informant Timothy Villalba testified in 2000 that Roy Garcia had confessed to a murder while both were incarcerated in California. Six years before, in an earlier trial, Villalba, a convicted murderer, had implicated another inmate in a killing. A federal judge on appeal held that Villalba "entirely" lacked credibility and overturned the conviction of Glen "Buddy" Nickerson in a 1984 double homicide. Nickerson was released after DNA evidence and a co-defendant implicated another individual in the killings.

Garcia after eight years in prison was exonerated after a second judge held that Villalba was unreliable and had fabricated Garcia's confession in an effort to gain release from prison.

Villalba, a heroin user, had pled guilty after beating a robbery victim to death with a baseball bat and was serving twenty-five years to life in prison. In prison, he joined the Nuestra Familia gang and was known to have ordered prison stabbings and had been disciplined for drugs on several occasions.

Villalba's testimony was crucial in Garcia's conviction because although Garcia had feuded with the victim, Deborah Gregg, the firearms in his home did not match the murder weapon, and there were no eyewitnesses and no fingerprint or DNA evidence. In 1999, Villalba had approached authorities and claimed Garcia had confessed during a chance encounter.

In 2011, California Governor Jerry Brown signed legislation that along with Texas, Illinois, and Massachusetts prohibited reliance on the uncorroborated testimony of jailhouse informants. This legislation was based on evidence that prosecutors rely on jailhouse informants even when there is a basis to doubt the reliability of their story. There also was a pattern of informants who testified receiving favorable treatment beyond the promises revealed to jurors at trial. In many instances, promises are not made to informants, and only later are charges dropped or recommendations made to state parole boards.

In one instance, former inmate Leslie White had obtained his release from jail after providing authorities with information in as many as forty prosecutions over the course of a decade. White subsequently revealed how he had sent his girlfriend to preliminary hearings to learn details of a fellow inmate's crime and background and fabricated confessions. In reaction to the scandal, Los Angeles had virtually stopped relying on jailhouse informants.

The difficulty is that some informants undoubtedly are telling the truth, and jurors are trusted to evaluate the credibility of jailhouse informants. There are instances in which disregarded informants have come forward to report that an innocent person has been convicted. Should prosecutors rely on jailhouse informants?

■ PHYSICAL AND PSYCHOLOGICAL INCAPACITY

An individual may be impeached by his or her physical or psychological incapacity to accurately observe, recall, or narrate events. These challenges may involve a temporary disability such as a failure to wear glasses or a hearing aid or may involve a total incapacity such as color blindness, blindness, or deafness. Other disabling conditions may include intoxication, drug use, psychological delusions, amnesia, a debilitating disease, lack of sleep, or a blackout. The conditions may have interfered with an individual's observation at the time of the event or may have arisen before trial.

Courts are reluctant to allow a witness to be impeached through the use of an expert witness who is able to testify on the impact of a physical or psychological limitation. This type of testimony is thought to be collateral to the primary issues at trial and to unnecessarily lengthen the trial.

Legal Equation

Impeachment   =   Bias + prior felony conviction + crime involving dishonest act or false statement + character for truthfulness + uncharged crimes and immoral acts + prior inconsistent statements + specific contradiction + physical and psychological incapacity.

■ REHABILITATION

A witness who is impeached may be rehabilitated by the party who called the witness. Rehabilitation involves repairing the witness's credibility in the eyes of the jury. This typically is accomplished on redirect examination although in certain circumstances a judge will permit a *rehabilitation witness* to testify. The rehabilitation testimony is required to directly respond to the attack directed against the witness. A witness simply may deny that a disability impedes his or her ability to see or hear or to fully function, or may point to the fact his or her vision is perfect with glasses. If possible, an expert witness may be used to support the accuracy of the witness's vision with glasses.

Rehabilitation in the law of evidence usually is used to describe (1) restoring a witness's character for truthfulness through character evidence and (2) restoring a witness's credibility through a prior consistent statement.

Rule 608(a) provides that once an individual's character for truthfulness is attacked, the individual may introduce evidence of good character for truthfulness. Evidence for truthfulness is limited to reputation and opinion evidence. Specific acts may not be introduced to establish a character for truthfulness.

The credibility or believability of a witness may be rehabilitated by a statement that is consistent with his or her trial testimony. In *Tome v. United States*, the Supreme Court held that the consistent statement must have been made before the witness's motive to fabricate developed. The logic of this requirement is that a consistent statement made before the motive to fabricate arose "is a square rebuttal of the charge that the testimony was contrived as a consequence of that motive" (*Tome v. United States*, 513 U.S. 150 [1995]).

Consider the following hypothetical example. An individual's trial testimony against a drug kingpin may be impeached by the defense attorney's allegation that the testimony was fabricated in return for the prosecutor's promise to drop the criminal charges against the witness in another case. The co-conspirator may be rehabilitated by the witness's denial that he or she has been offered a plea bargain as well as by character or opinion evidence supporting the witness's truthfulness.

Another approach would be to present a witness who testifies the co-conspirator told him or her several months ago that he or she was upset over the impact of drugs on the community and that he or she was eager to testify against the defendant. As a result, the witness's testimony was not based on a motive to fabricate the evidence against the drug dealer. The same statement made after the witness entered into a plea agreement would not be admissible to rehabilitate the witness's credibility because it would have been made after rather than before the witness had a motive to fabricate the evidence.

Table 5.3 compares and contrasts the impeachment and rehabilitation of witnesses.

Table 5.3 ■ Impeachment and Rehabilitation of Witnesses		
	Impeachment	**Rehabilitation**
Reputation	Character witness on reputation/opinion evidence of dishonesty	Character witness on reputation/opinion evidence of truthfulness
Felony Conviction	Felony conviction for fraud	Law-abiding behavior over a period of years
Bias	Reason to distort truth	Deny bias motive to distort the truth and express commitment to objectivity
Prior Inconsistent Statement	Statement inconsistent with testimony	Introduce statements that are consistent with trial testimony
Incapacity	Physical/mental disability	Demonstrate fully functions with hearing aid, glasses, and prescription drugs

■ CORROBORATION

Corroborative evidence is evidence that supports without repeating the testimony of a witness. A witness's testimony that he or she observed the defendant shoot the victim in the course of an armed robbery may be corroborated by a witness who saw the defendant flee from the site of the attack or discard a wallet in the trash. Another method of corroborating evidence may be real evidence such as a video of the armed robbery that shows the defendant robbing the store or evidence that the defendant's fingerprints were on a firearm discarded at the crime scene or a letter in which the defendant admits committing the crime.

Corroboration, though typically not required, strengthens a case because multiple witnesses may support an individual's testimony. There are certain crimes that require corroboration. Article III, Section 3 of the United States Constitution provides that "[n]o Person shall be convicted of treason unless on the testimony of two Witnesses to the same overt Act or on Confession in open Court."

Treason is defined as levying war against the United States or providing aid and comfort to the enemy. Both witnesses must testify to the identical act of treason. In most cases, corroboration only requires "some evidence" in support of the defendant having committed a criminal act with the requisite criminal intent, and there is no requirement that every element of the crime is corroborated.

The Model Penal Code provision on perjury, which is followed by federal statutes and by most state statutes, follows the "two witness rule." The rule provides that a conviction for perjury is required to be based on the testimony of two witnesses or must be based on the testimony of one witness and supporting evidence such as a confession or a document. The reason for this rule is that courts want to avoid a "swearing contest" between a defendant who asserts he or she was truthful and a witness who alleges the defendant's statement was false.

False pretenses, or the fraudulent misrepresentation of a material fact that causes another to transfer ownership, also requires corroboration in a few jurisdictions. The reason is that, as with perjury, courts want to avoid a "swearing contest" between two individuals.

Most jurisdictions also require corroboration of the testimony of an accomplice to a crime. The reason is that an accomplice may have a motive to testify falsely against the other party or parties to a crime. For example, an accomplice may portray the defendant as playing a dominant role in the crime in order to reduce his or her own criminal responsibility.

The risk of false confessions or coerced confessions has led to the requirement that a confession must be supported by corroborating evidence. The corroborating evidence is not required to be sufficient standing alone to convict the defendant and may be an extrajudicial admission of guilt to another individual, an eyewitness who observed the crime, or physical evidence gathered at the crime scene.

Corroboration often is a matter of good trial strategy. It makes sense for a prosecutor to corroborate that the defendant's act resulted in property damage or physical injury to a victim rather than relying on the testimony of a single witness.

Model Penal Code, Section 213 provides that rape, statutory rape, sexual assault, and sexual imposition on an underage person all require corroboration. The Model Penal Code justifies this requirement as a safeguard against false accusations, the risk that a jury will be tempted to convict based on the emotional nature of the crime, and the difficulty of defending against a false accusation of rape. The Model Penal Code explains that the corroboration requirement is not intended to discount the testimony of the victim or to be insensitive to the harm to the victim. Instead, the corroboration requirement is part of the "general policy that uncertainty should be resolved in favor of the accused." Corroborating evidence of rape under the laws of various states only need constitute a "basis for believing" that the testimony of the complaining witness is "worthy of credit and belief." This may include physical injury, medical testimony, eyewitness testimony, or a victim's display of the rape trauma syndrome.

As you recall, corroboration is distinct from cumulative evidence, which repeats the evidence already introduced at trial and which may be excluded from trial. Cumulative evidence would involve testimony by another witness who testifies to having observed an armed robbery.

can use almost anything — photographs, videos, documents

■ **RECORDED RECOLLECTION**

Present Recollection Refreshed

Individuals may only dimly recall the events they are called on to testify about at trial. The witness may be nervous and unable to think clearly, the incident may have occurred some months ago, or the individual may find the events too painful to recall. A police officer may be involved in any number of criminal investigations and may have a difficult time recalling the details of the crime. He or she may remember some details and may have only an incomplete recollection of other details. The law of evidence provides two procedures to revive a witness's memory although a total lapse of memory is not required. A witness who experiences a complete failure of memory clearly is not competent to testify.

The two methods of assisting a witness to jog his or her memory are **present recollection refreshed** and **past recollection recorded**. We will return to this topic when we discuss hearsay.

A witness may find him- or herself unable to answer a question because of a failure of memory. The lawyer will try to *refresh* the witness's *recollection* either before trial or on the stand.

The rule is that anything may be used to refresh the witness's memory. A lawyer may use a document prepared by the witness, a photo, a video, or the individual's notes to refresh his or her memory. A police officer, for example, may have his or her memory refreshed by his or her field notes. One federal judge remarked that "a song, a face, or a newspaper item" may be used to refresh memory. Note that the item used to refresh the witness's memory is not itself introduced into evidence (*Jewett v. United States*, 15 F.2d 955 [9th Cir. 1926]).

There are several requirements for refreshing a witness's memory:

- The witness has incomplete or no memory of events.
- The document is presented to the court and to the opposing lawyer.
- The document is shown to the witness.
- After examining the document and the witness's memory is refreshed, the witness puts the document aside and testifies without reading from the document.

As noted, the adverse party has the right to inspect the document and has the discretion to introduce all or part of the document into evidence and to cross-examine the witness on the document. The thinking is the adverse lawyer may want to attack the credibility of the witness by pointing out that the witness's testimony was based on the document rather than on independent memory. Consider a witness who recalls the license plate number of the bank robbers' car after examining the piece of paper on which he or she wrote down the number and a description of the automobile and of the bank robbers. An adverse party may want to cross-examine the witness to point out that the witness's testimony was limited to precisely what was written and that the witness lacked an independent memory of the events. Another approach to discrediting the reliability of the witness's testimony is to point out that the witness repeated facts in the document used to refresh his or her memory that are inaccurate.

A lawyer may prefer to refresh a witness's memory before the witness takes the stand. The adverse party has a right under the Federal Rules to ask and to receive a copy of the document to cross-examine the witness. Most state courts do not recognize the right of an adverse party to inspect documents used to refresh a witness's memory before trial on the grounds that this may be used as a "fishing expedition" to inspect everything a witness looked at prior to trial to prepare his or her testimony.

Rule 612. Writing Used to Refresh a Witness

(a) Scope. This rule gives an adverse party certain options when a witness uses a writing to refresh memory:

  (1) while testifying; or

  (2) before testifying, if the court decides that justice requires the party to have those options.

(b) Adverse Party's Options; Deleting Unrelated Matter. Unless 18 U.S.C. § 3500 provides otherwise in a criminal case, an adverse party is entitled to have the writing produced at the hearing, to inspect it, to cross-examine the witness about it, and to introduce in evidence any portion that relates to the witness's testimony. If the producing party claims that the writing includes unrelated matter, the court must examine the writing in camera, delete any unrelated portion, and order that the rest be delivered to the adverse party. Any portion deleted over objection must be preserved for the record.

(c) Failure to Produce or Deliver the Writing. If a writing is not produced or is not delivered as ordered, the court may issue any appropriate order. But if the prosecution does not comply in a criminal case, the court must strike the witness's testimony or—if justice so requires—declare a mistrial.

Past Recollection Recorded

In some instances, a witness has a limited memory of events, and his or her memory cannot be refreshed. Rule 803(5) allows a lawyer to rely on *past recollection recorded* in those instances in which the witness testifies he or she no longer is able to remember the information recorded in a document "well enough to testify fully and accurately."

The requirements for admissibility under past recollection recorded are as follows:

- The statement is embodied in a memorandum, report, or compilation of data.
- The document was prepared or adopted by the witness at a time when the matter was fresh in the witness's memory.

The document in some jurisdictions must have been drafted by the witness. The modern trend is to consider the document admissible when drafted by another individual so long as the witness read the document when fresh in his or her memory, found the text correct, and adopted the document as an accurate record. Some jurisdictions require that the witness directed preparation of the document.

- The document was prepared or adopted when fresh in the witness's memory and the witness had first-hand knowledge of the facts. →*can't just write down the correct answer.*

The witness must testify that he or she once knew about the information in the document and adopted the document at the time he or she possessed this knowledge. The key is that the accurate account of events was prepared while the events were fresh in the victim's mind.

- The document when prepared accurately reflected the witness's knowledge.
- The document is authentic and has <u>not been modified</u>.

Rule 803(5) requires that the document is read into the record by the witness and only may be introduced as an exhibit by the adverse party. The thinking is that the jury may give a written document a great deal of importance and lawyers may be tempted to encourage witnesses to testify that they are unable to recall events. An adverse party may want a document that is revealed to be inaccurate or appears to have been hurriedly and sloppily prepared brought to the attention of the jury. The jury may consider the document as evidence going to guilt or to innocence.

In *Commonwealth v. Galvin*, the defendant appealed his conviction of operating a motor vehicle so as to endanger, leaving the scene of an accident after causing personal injury, and speeding. Robert Lee observed the accident in the rearview mirror of his car. He pursued the Camaro to within about twenty feet and observed its registration plate number. He repeated the number in his mind until his wife located a pen. Lee then wrote the number on his hand. Lee returned to the scene of the accident and repeated the number to a police officer who Lee testified correctly recorded the number in his notebook. The next day, the officer testified he correctly copied the number in his police report and discarded his notes. Officer Walter Bevis was allowed over the defendant's objection to rely on the police report as past recollection recorded. A Massachusetts appellate court held that the court had properly allowed the officer to rely on the police report as "double application of the principle of past recollection recorded." Can you explain the reasoning of the Massachusetts court? (*Commonwealth v. Galvin*, 27 Mass. App. Ct [1989]).

Why should the law of evidence distinguish between present recollection refreshed and past recollection recorded? Consider *United States v. Riccardi*. In *Riccardi*, the defendants, rather than moving the victim's valuable linens, silverware, and household items to the victim's new home, unlawfully moved the victim's belongings to Arizona. The victim testified she made notes that she later typed. Only one of the original notes was produced at trial along with items listed in the criminal indictment, which the government used to refresh the victim's memory. The victim-witness testified that her "recollection was refreshed and that she presently recognized and could identify each item. She was then permitted to read the lists aloud, and testified that she knew that the items were loaded on the truck or station wagon." An antique dealer who had examined the items on numerous occasions in preparation for an auction also testified after his memory was refreshed. The defendant argued the lists had not been made at the time of the transaction and the victim had read the list out loud in court, calling into question whether her memory in fact was refreshed or recollected. A federal court of appeals upheld the trial judge's decision to allow the lists to revive the witness's memory. Was this more appropriately viewed as a past recollection recorded? Why did the court not analyze the notes and indictment as a past recollection recorded? See *United States v. Riccardi* (174 F.2d 883 [3rd Cir. 1949]).

Rule 803. Exceptions to the Rule Against Hearsay

The following are not excluded by the rule against hearsay, regardless of whether the declarant is available as a witness:

(5) Recorded Recollection. A record that:

(A) is on a matter the witness once knew about but now cannot recall well enough to testify fully and accurately;

(B) was made or adopted by the witness when the matter was fresh in the witness's memory; and

(C) accurately reflects the witness's knowledge.

If admitted, the record may be read into evidence but may be received as an exhibit only if offered by an adverse party.

Table 5.4 compares and contrasts refreshed and recorded memory.

Table 5.4 ■ Refreshing Memory and Recorded Recollection		
	Refreshing Memory	**Recorded Recollection**
When:	Witness cannot recall details	Witness cannot recall details
What:	Looks at document to refresh memory	Reads document out loud
Form:	Any items that will refresh memory	Any item "made or adopted' by witness that reflects personal knowledge at time drafted
Introduce into evidence:	Adverse party	Adverse party

■ CASE ANALYSIS

In *People v. Thomas*, an Illinois appellate court considers whether the trial court was correct in allowing the witness to be impeached by his membership in a gang.

Should the court have allowed the witness to be impeached by his membership in a gang?

People v. Thomas, 821 N.E.2d 628 (Ill. App. 2004), Cahill, J.

Defendant Duel Thomas was convicted of first degree murder and aggravated kidnapping after a jury trial. He was sentenced to 60 years' imprisonment for murder and 30 years for aggravated kidnapping, to be served concurrently. Defendant appeals, claiming . . . the trial court erred in admitting the statement of a witness as a prior inconsistent statement; the trial court erred in admitting evidence linking defendant to a gang. . . .

Quinton Kirkwood's body was found on March 27, 1999, in a rear basement stairwell. . . . He had been shot to death. Jeff

Henderson was arrested on March 28, 1999, in connection with the murder. The next day, he gave Assistant State's Attorney Luke Sheridan a statement, implicating defendant in the shooting. Henderson said he and several other people, including defendant, defendant's brother Antonio Thomas (Antonio) and Linord Thames were in the apartment of Frederick Laws at 8 p.m. on March 26, 1999. Thames told defendant and Antonio that Kirkwood was playing dice in another apartment, had won about $9,000 and was a good target for a robbery. Antonio gave Henderson a set of keys and told him to go get a car that was parked nearby. Henderson got the car and parked it in front of the building where the dice game was taking place. About 10 minutes later, Henderson saw Antonio walking Kirkwood at gunpoint from the building. Antonio pushed Kirkwood into the trunk of the car and closed the lid. Antonio ordered defendant and Henderson to get inside the car. Henderson said Antonio drove to an alley where he stopped and opened the trunk. Defendant and Antonio grabbed the victim and walked him to a cemented area under a porch behind a building. When defendant and Antonio demanded money, Kirkwood used a cellular phone to call relatives and ask for money. Henderson then went to Kirkwood's relatives' house but they refused to give him money. . . . When Henderson told defendant and Antonio that no money was given to him, Kirkwood asked to call his relatives again. Antonio dialed the number and handed the phone to Kirkwood as defendant shot Kirkwood multiple times with an automatic weapon. . . . Henderson was acquitted [in a previous trial and repeated his statement to the police]. Defendant, Antonio and Williams then were tried concurrently before separate juries.

The State called Henderson to testify. Henderson testified that he could not recall seeing defendant on the night of the murder, contrary to his testimony at his own trial, and stated that his entire testimony at his own trial was untrue. The State then examined Henderson on the basis of the transcript of his trial, impeaching his statements that his trial testimony was untrue. Defendant did not object. Henderson said he was not with defendant on the night of the murder and he knew defendant "just from around the neighborhood, that's all." Henderson admitted to testifying at his own trial that he was with defendant that night, but claimed "the whole transcript you're reading is a lie." . . . Henderson testified that, contrary to his earlier accounts of the murder, he alone forced Kirkwood at gunpoint into the trunk of a car and tried to rob him. He said that when he failed to get money from Kirkwood's relatives, he drove to the scene of the murder and shot Kirkwood, firing a .38-caliber weapon with one hand and a .45-caliber weapon with the other hand.

After a discussion with the parties outside the presence of the jury, the trial court decided to allow the introduction of gang evidence despite its earlier refusal to do so. Over defendant's objection, the trial judge instructed the jury as to gang-related evidence:

"You are going to be hearing evidence and testimony that is being admitted for a limited purpose, and the testimony involves the mention of gang membership. There is no evidence or inference or argument that this homicide in any way was gang related. So it is being offered for the limited purpose only of evaluation of the credibility of this witness as well as the consideration of any arguments concerning his motivation."

When questioning resumed, Henderson denied ever being a member of the Black Souls street gang, of which defendant was the chief, but Henderson admitted that he so testified at his own trial. Henderson admitted that he testified that the number one law

of the Black Souls was "to never disown one of your brothers" and "to always look up to your older brothers and never disobey the mob, never go against the grain."

The State claimed Henderson falsified his testimony to exonerate defendant because Henderson feared defendant, his gang's chief:

"This man [defendant] and his brother [Antonio Thomas] were the muscle men behind [Kirkwood's] murder. And still their muscle power can be felt, his muscle power, not just in how he . . . used these powerful guns to plug bullet after bullet after bullet into [Kirkwood's] body; no, the way in which his power is still being felt can be seen by the way you saw 19-year-old Jeff Henderson, substantially younger than him . . . come in here and lie on his behalf.

After defendant was convicted and sentenced, he filed motions for a new trial and to reconsider sentencing, which were denied. Defendant appeals. . . .

Defendant first argues that the State failed to establish proof of his guilt beyond a reasonable doubt because its case depended entirely on the "incredible" testimony of Henderson. Defendant claims Henderson's testimony was fatally discredited because he was an accomplice, he had been immunized from prosecution, he had recanted his earlier statement and he appeared to be a habitual perjurer.

Defendant . . . argues the trial court erred in allowing the State to impeach Henderson with gang evidence. Defendant argues that the evidence should have been barred because gang testimony is unduly prejudicial due to society's disapproval of gangs. . . . In his petition for rehearing, defendant asserts that the State "failed to connect the dots" to show that the gang affiliation common to Henderson and defendant caused Henderson to recant his earlier accounts that implicated defendant. Defendant argues that no evidence showed that gang threats were communicated to Henderson or "animated" Henderson to recant.

The State contends that evidence of the men's common gang membership was relevant to Henderson's bias and motivation to recant because there was a potential threat of physical reprisal against Henderson for implicating his gang's chief, defendant.

The trial court's function is to weigh the probative value and prejudicial effect of evidence in determining its admissibility. Our review of a decision to admit gang evidence is deferential, that is, reversal requires a showing that the trial court clearly abused its discretion, resulting in manifest prejudice to the defendant.

Gang evidence is relevant "if it tends to make the existence of any fact that is of consequence to the determination of the action more probable or less probable than it would be without the evidence." Bias describes the "relationship between a party and a witness which might lead the witness to slant, unconsciously or otherwise, his testimony in favor of or against a party. . . . Proof of bias is almost always relevant because the jury . . . has historically been entitled to assess all evidence which might bear on the accuracy and truth of a witness' testimony." . . . The common

(Continued)

membership of a witness and a party in an organization is probative of bias.

Here, the evidence of Henderson's and defendant's common gang affiliation was not admitted to show defendant's motive for killing the victim, but to show Henderson's bias and motive to lie at the trial of his gang's leader, defendant. The evidence was relevant because it made the question of whether Henderson was lying more probable than it would have been without the evidence. It would be reasonable to conclude that the relationship between Henderson and defendant, his superior in the gang, could have led Henderson on the stand at defendant's trial to recant his earlier statements that implicated defendant and to implicate himself instead. Impeaching Henderson with gang-related evidence revealing his possible bias was relevant to the jury as it assessed all the evidence bearing on the truth of Henderson's recantation. Here, the common gang membership and respective gang ranks of Henderson and defendant were probative of bias. The record, including the trial court's initial refusal to admit gang-related evidence, supports the conclusion that the trial court properly weighed the probative value of the evidence against its prejudicial effect. We cannot say that the trial court abused its discretion in admitting the evidence, particularly in light of the fact that a limiting instruction was given. The

gang evidence—Henderson's admission that he was a Black Souls member and defendant was the Black Souls' chief—was admissible to support the State's theory that Henderson told the truth in his earlier statements and lied to exculpate his gang chief when the chief was on trial. The prosecutor's comments represented a fair and reasonable inference from the fact that defendant had "seniority over" Henderson in the street gang whose mottos were "never disown one of your brothers" and "always look up to your older brothers."

Defendant argues that even if the gang evidence were admissible, it was "so highly prejudicial, and so weakly warranted, that the error in its admission is palpable, and its use in summations overwhelmingly improper." The State responds that defendant was not prejudiced by Henderson's testimony because the court provided a limiting instruction to the jury before the introduction of gang testimony. A trial court does not abuse its discretion where it offers a limiting instruction to the jury and takes other precautions to ensure that highly probative evidence does not unduly prejudice the respondent. Here, the fact that the trial judge gave a limiting instruction to the jury, along with the probative value of gang testimony to show Henderson's bias and motivation to change his testimony in favor of defendant, prevented undue prejudice to defendant.

CHAPTER SUMMARY

Under the common law, there were strict qualifications on who was entitled to be a witness based on age, race, religion, conviction of a crime, mental capacity, marriage, and whether an individual was a party to the case. The federal rule is that virtually any witness whose testimony is relevant to the case should be allowed to testify unless the testimony is prohibited by another federal rule. Federal Rule 601 states that "[e]very person is competent to be a witness unless these rules provide otherwise."

A witness is considered competent to testify who is able to understand the meaning and consequences of an oath or affirmation, possesses personal knowledge, and has the capacity for memory and narration. States are divided over the competence of a witness whose testimony is based on hypnosis. The competency of child-witnesses has posed a continuing challenge for courts, particularly in childhood abuse cases in which the credibility of the child-victim is central to the case. Most states stipulate that children over 10 are competent to testify. Children under 10 may testify who are found by the judge after examination to be able to accurately and truthfully testify. The Federal Rules of Evidence disqualify two categories of individuals from testifying as a witness, judges and jurors.

Most states and the federal government recognize spousal competence although a spouse may refuse to consent to testify based on the spousal testimony privilege and the marital communications privilege. These privileges against testifying are subject to exceptions involving crimes against the person or property of the spouse or children. Recognition of the spousal privilege in domestic abuse cases would be contrary to public policy and would allow a spouse to pressure the other spouse into refusing to testify. In some states, a spouse may be compelled to testify in criminal prosecutions for bigamy and child abandonment or murder or rape outside of the marriage. A witness is not incompetent to testify based on religion, criminal conviction, or mental incapacity.

The credibility of a witness may be impeached based on various grounds including bias, prior felony conviction, crimes involving a dishonest act or false statement, character for truthfulness, uncharged crimes and immoral acts, prior inconsistent statements, and physical and psychological incapacity. A witness who is impeached may be rehabilitated by the party who called the witness.

Rehabilitation testimony is required to directly respond to the attack directed against the witness. The two methods of assisting a witness's memory on direct examination are present recollection refreshed and past recollection recorded.

CHAPTER REVIEW QUESTIONS

1. How does the traditional approach to witness competency differ from the approach in the Federal Rules of Evidence? Discuss the requirements of an oath or affirmation, personal knowledge, mental capacity, and narration.

2. What are the concerns about the competency to testify of child-witnesses? Discuss some of the different judicial approaches to the competency of young children to testify.

3. Why are judges and jurors in most cases prohibited from testifying as witnesses at trials? What about spouses?

4. May an individual be found incompetent to testify based on religion? What about based on a mental challenge?

5. What is the purpose of the impeachment of witnesses?

6. Discuss the specific purpose and process of impeaching a witness based on bias; on a prior felony conviction of a nonparty witness and of a defendant-witness; and on crimes involving a dishonest act or false statement.

7. Give some examples of impeachment based on a character for truthfulness, uncharged crimes and immoral acts, prior inconsistent statements, and physical and psychological incapacity.

8. Compare and contrast present recollection refreshed and past recollection recorded.

LEGAL TERMINOLOGY

competency to testify

corroboration

oath or affirmation

past recollection recorded

present recollection refreshed

prior inconsistent statement

spousal competence

Visit the Student Study Site at **http://study.sagepub.com/lippmance** to access additional study tools, including mobile-friendly eFlashcards and Web quizzes as well as links to SAGE journal articles and hyperlinks for *Criminal Evidence* on the Web.

THE OPINION RULE AND EXPERT TESTIMONY

May the witnesses give their opinion about the defendant's reaction to the fire engulfing his home containing his wife and children?

Appellant's neighbor, David Burton, received a phone call from another neighbor that Appellant's house was on fire. Burton immediately went to Appellant's house, which was engulfed in flames. Approximately thirty minutes after the fire department arrived at the scene, Appellant drove up, watched the fire for a few minutes, spoke with the firemen, and thereafter drove away. During the course of extinguishing the fire, firemen discovered three bodies, an adult and two children. The victims were later identified as Appellant's wife, Shirley Bowles McKinney, and her two children, 11-year-old Brian and 3-year-old Amy.

An autopsy of the three victims subsequently revealed that they had died as a result of gun shot wounds prior to the fire being set in the house. Kentucky State Police inspected the remains of the house and found not only numerous .22 caliber shell casings which were consistent with having been fired from Appellant's gun, but also discovered trace amounts of an accelerant used to start the fire. Following a trial, a jury found Appellant guilty on all charges and recommended three death sentences. . . .

[T]he Commonwealth offered the testimony of ten witnesses who described how Appellant acted on the day of the fire. A neighbor testified that Appellant seemed "calm" and that he "acted normal" at the fire scene. Martha Owens, Shirley McKinney's sister, testified that when she broke the news to Appellant about the fire, he "just had his head down and his hands in his pockets," which she said was normal for him. Charles Bowles, Shirley's brother, stated that Appellant had "no reaction," did not "act any different that day than he had any other day," and did not "seem concerned." Several firemen who did not know Appellant testified that his demeanor was "nothing out of the ordinary," "non-emotional," and "like a normal person." Finally, Pulaski County Sheriff Sam Catron . . . stated that Appellant was "calm, [and] didn't show any emotion" at the fire scene.

Appellant argues that the lay witness testimony was irrelevant and prejudicial. He contends that the only purpose of the testimony was to create an implication that he did not show any emotion because he was not saddened by the death of his family and that he was not surprised because he already knew they were dead, presumably because he had killed them prior to setting the fire. (*McKinney v. Commonwealth*, 60 S.W.3d 499 [Ky. 2001])

CHAPTER OUTLINE

Introduction
Unavailable Witnesses
Opinion Rule
Lay Witnesses
Expert Testimony
Qualifying an Expert Witness
Testimony on Ultimate Issues

Scope of Expert Testimony
Court-Appointed Experts
Case Analysis
Chapter Summary
Chapter Review Questions
Legal Terminology

■ INTRODUCTION

The common meaning of *witness* is an individual who observes an event. A witness at trial is an individual who has been sworn and takes the stand. There generally are thought to be two types of witnesses, **lay witnesses** and **expert witnesses**.

Most of the witnesses at trial are lay witnesses. Lay witnesses testify about any event relevant to the criminal case they observed with one of their five senses. They may have viewed the killing, talked to the killer, or observed the events leading up to the killing or following the killing. A lay witness obviously can have a variety of professional backgrounds ranging from construction worker to real estate agent to teacher, businessperson, and scientist.

An expert witness performs a different role at trial. This witness's professional expertise will help explain things to the jury they otherwise could not understand. Federal Rule 702 establishes two foundation requirements for an expert. First, the expert is "qualified as an expert by knowledge, skill, experience, training, or education." Second, "the expert's scientific, technical, or other specialized knowledge will help the trier of fact to understand the evidence or to determine a fact in issue." The party calling an expert is required to lay the foundation for the witness to testify. A hearing will be held before the judge if the adverse party challenges qualifications or need for an expert or contends the expert's proposed testimony is not based on principles and methods recognized as scientifically valid. An expert who is permitted to testify may be challenged on cross-examination based on a lack of scientific competence, errors in testing procedures, or reliability of equipment or errors in carrying out the tests.

A lay witness is limited to a factual report on what he or she perceived, heard, or smelled with one of the five senses, and his or her testimony is not based on scientific, technical, or other specialized knowledge.

Federal Rule 702 recognizes that it is possible for the same person to testify both as a lay witness and as an expert witness and, for this reason, distinguishes between expert testimony and lay testimony.

■ UNAVAILABLE WITNESSES

A witness may not be available to testify for various reasons, such as illness, death, flight, or a desire to avoid the trial. The hearsay rule provides that statements under oath at a prior court hearing on the same matter may be introduced at trial if the witness is unavailable. The party against whom the evidence is introduced must have had the opportunity to cross-examine the witness. The Sixth Amendment to the U.S. Constitution protects the right of an individual to confront his or her accusers in a criminal case. We will return to this topic when we discuss hearsay in Chapter Nine.

There are various mechanisms to preserve the testimony of a material witness who it is believed may be unavailable at trial. This includes videotaping sworn testimony and sworn testimony on the record subject to cross-examination by the opposing party.

A radical approach to ensure the availability of a witness is the use of a material witness warrant to arrest and detain a material witness until trial. A judge typically is authorized to require the material witness to post an appearance bond that will be forfeited in the event the witness fails to appear to testify.

■ OPINION RULE

An opinion is an inference from the perceived facts such as a conclusion based on facts that a defendant killed in a reckless fashion. The jury, or judge if the jury is waived, is the trier of fact at trial. Witnesses testify as to facts at trial, and the fact finder—the jury or judge—analyzes facts and draws conclusions such as whether the defendant killed in a premeditated fashion.

The common law **opinion rule** limited the testimony of witnesses to facts, perceived through the five senses. Witnesses were prohibited from offering opinions because this was the province of the jury. The prohibition on witnesses offering opinions, in part, reflected a concern that jurors would give too much credit to the opinions of witnesses and complicate their reaching an independent conclusion.

This description is somewhat misleading because the line between fact and opinion is not always clear, and expert witnesses are permitted to offer professional opinions.

■ LAY WITNESSES

The Federal Rules of Evidence modified the common law prohibition on witnesses offering opinions. The Advisory Committee on the Advisory Rules of Evidence noted that people typically express themselves by offering a combination of facts and opinions. A witness may testify that a defendant acted aggressively, seemed angry, slurred his or her speech, was driving unsafely, or seemed unsteady on his or her feet.

Federal Rule 701 lists three requirements that a lay witness must satisfy before offering an opinion. First, the opinion must be logically based on the witness's perception, meaning that there must be a relationship between the facts and the inference drawn from the facts. It may be logical to draw the inference that an individual who is shouting at a police officer who has issued him or her a ticket is "angry" or "aggressive."

Second, lay opinion must help the fact finder to understand the witness's testimony. The jury may find it helpful for the witness to inform them that the assailant was "big and powerful, and spoke with a nasty tone of voice" rather than merely describing the assailant's height, estimated weight, and words used. A witness may find it difficult to be more precise than to offer the testimony that the defendant seemed "threatening." On the other hand, a description of an individual as looking like a "gang banger" or "homeless person" or "prostitute" should be excluded from evidence as unhelpful and as needlessly prejudicial.

Last, lay opinion should be straightforward and nontechnical and may not rely on "scientific, technical, or other specialized knowledge." The idea behind this requirement is to prohibit lawyers from using lay witnesses to sneak in expert testimony such as testimony that the defendant appeared to be a "borderline personality."

Johnny Yazzie Jr., age 20, was convicted of the statutory rape of a 15-year-old neighbor. He presented the defense that he reasonably believed that the female was at least 16. Yazzie explained that be believed this because the victim smoked cigarettes, drove a car, used makeup, and looked "mature" enough to be at least 16. He knew the victim because he had previously dated her older sister but claimed that the minor never told him her age. Yazzie called a number of witnesses who were permitted to testify as to their perceptions of the minor's physical appearance and behavior although they were prohibited from stating in their opinion that the minor was at least 16 years of age. The Court of Appeals held the district court judge was in error in refusing to allow these non-expert witnesses to voice their opinions.

The excluded testimony of Yazzie's witnesses may have assisted the jury in assessing the reasonableness of Yazzie's belief that the victim was at least 16 years old on the night of the incident. By the time the case came to trial, the victim was well past 16 years of age. An impression of an individual's age is dependent on a range of subtle considerations and does not merely depend on objective considerations like height, weight, or clarity of expression. "Because of the trial court's restrictions the witnesses testified in large part only to facts that the prosecution did not deny: that the minor smoked, drank, and drove a car" (*United States v. Yazzie*, 976 F.2d 1253 [9th Cir. 1992]).

There are a number of areas on which judges customarily admit lay opinion.

Smell

Identity (e.g., recognition of voice, handwriting)

Age

- Conduct (e.g., trying to get away)
- Dimension (e.g., length, size)
- Physical condition
- Emotional condition (e.g., insane, happy, sad)
- Owner's estimation of value of land or other objects
- Suspicious conduct (e.g., witnessing drug transaction)
- Weight, distance, color
- Time and duration
- Speed

The issue that is most challenging for courts is to determine the dividing line between lay and expert opinion. A lay witness, unlike experts, may not offer opinions based on "scientific, technical, or other specialist knowledge." Some issues are easy to resolve; a snowy and slippery sidewalk, a dangerously driven automobile, a substance that appears to be blood, and the fact an individual is drunk are the type of opinions that reflect everyday experience. These opinions are very different from the scientific background required to conduct a ballistics analysis of a bullet or laboratory analysis of DNA, or to know that bruising around the eyes is suggestive of skull trauma.

Despite the prohibition in Rule 701 against lay witnesses relying on "specialized knowledge," "judges allow lay witnesses to provide opinions based on their background and experience so long as the opinions do not require specialized education and training" and a "process of reasoning which can be mastered only by specialists."

Courts flexibly apply the rule on opinion evidence by lay witnesses because witnesses possess a broad range of experiences and backgrounds that qualify them to offer an opinion. A lawyer offering lay opinion is required to first establish the foundation that the witness had personal knowledge of the facts and the knowledge to offer an opinion. In *United States v. Huddleston*, Isaac S. Huddleston was convicted of distributing cocaine. The court allowed an experienced drug trafficker, over the objection of Huddleston, to testify about the quality of cocaine he sold. The court explained that an experienced narcotics trafficker is able to assess the quality of cocaine without applying scientific expertise or specialized expertise (*United States v. Huddleston*, 810 F.2d 751 [8th Cir. 1987]).

In another case, a co-conspirator charged with selling cocaine was allowed to testify on the meaning of various expressions used by a co-conspirator that were common to the drug trade and helpful to the jury. The First Circuit Court of Appeals stressed the witness had firsthand experience and background in the drug trade and was a participant in many of the conversations he analyzed (*United States v. Lizardo*, 445 F.3d 73 [1st Cir. 2006]). Courts also have permitted law enforcement officers who briefly observed a defendant to testify that they believed the defendant was legally sane (*United States v. Lawson*, 653 F.2d 299 [7th Cir. 1981]).

6.1 YOU DECIDE

Christina Christo, the 21-year-old daughter of James Earl Paiva's former wife, testified that in 1983 she discovered a plastic bag containing white powder in one of Paiva's shoes. Christina testified that she had regularly used cocaine in the past and at age 14 developed an addiction to the drug.

Christina testified that based on the appearance and taste of the substance it was cocaine. The defense appealed the trial court's admission of Christina's testimony. Do you agree? See *United States v. Paiva* (892 F.2d 148 [1st Cir. 1989]).

You can learn what the court decided by referring to the study site, **http://study.sagepub.com/lippmance** .

Rule 701. Opinion Testimony by Lay Witnesses

If a witness is not testifying as an expert, testimony in the form of an opinion is limited to one that is:

(a) rationally based on the witness's perception;

(b) helpful to clearly understanding the witness's testimony or to determining a fact in issue; and

(c) not based on scientific, technical, or other specialized knowledge within the scope of Rule 702.

■ EXPERT TESTIMONY

We have seen that opinion by lay witnesses must be rationally based on the witness's perception, must be helpful to the understanding of the jury, and may not be based on scientific, technical, or other specialized knowledge.

 Expert testimony can be of central importance in criminal prosecutions. Expert witnesses are witnesses who are qualified by "knowledge, skill, experience, training, or education" and may testify in the form of an opinion in their area of expertise. Expert witnesses include a ballistic expert qualified to report on ballistic testimony linking a bullet taken from the victim to a firearm owned by the defendant, a forensic scientist whose testimony links DNA at the crime scene to the defendant, and a doctor whose medical testimony explains how the blow to the victim's head caused his or her death. Expert testimony may be based on experience or training as well as on education. An individual trained in the military in munitions may testify on the structure of a bomb and how the structure links the bomb to a terrorist group. A police gang crimes investigator may testify on how the defendant's killing furthered the goals of the gang and merits an enhanced penalty. In *United States v. Webb*, the defendant claimed that he was unaware that there was a gun concealed in the engine compartment of his automobile. The Ninth Circuit Court of Appeals affirmed the trial court's qualification of a police officer as an expert who had worked in the county jail and had talked to fifty or sixty inmates a day about "where, how, and why criminals conceal their weapons." What is your view? (*United States v. Webb*, 115, F.3d 711 [9th Cir. 1997]).

On the one hand, courts want to rely on experts to help jurors learn as much as possible about the case. On the other hand, expert testimony may confuse jurors and consume considerable time at trial. Jurors may be ill equipped to understand expert testimony and may be overly influenced by it. There also may be an unequal situation in which one side has the money to hire impressive experts while the other side only has the resources to mount a bare-bones case. There is the additional possibility that each side will hire multiple experts who will cancel one another out without clarifying matters for the jury.

A central issue with experts in American courts has been how to determine the reliability of an expert's "scientific" expertise. The so-called *Frye* test developed by federal courts was the predominant approach for roughly seventy years. In *Frye*, the defendant James Alphonzo Frye wanted to introduce the results of an early form of lie detector test. The court in *Frye* rejected introduction of the systolic blood pressure test on the grounds that a scientific principle will not be recognized in federal courts unless it has "gained general acceptance in the particular field in which it belongs." In other words, courts asked whether the scientific community "generally accepted" a methodology such as DNA as reliable before accepting that individuals with competence in this area could testify as experts (*Frye v. United States*, 293 F. 1013 [D.C. Cir. 1923]).

Frye meant that newly developed techniques had to be fully embraced by the scientific community before they were recognized as "science" for purposes of expert testimony. On the other hand, abandoning *Frye* and loosening standards of evaluating expert testimony risked the recognition of "junk science."

In 1993, in *Daubert v. Merrell Dow Pharmaceuticals Inc.*, the United States Supreme Court adopted a middle ground for recognizing "scientific expertise." The Court explained that the *Frye* test was incompatible with the newly drafted Federal Rules of Evidence. The trial judge under *Daubert* rather than the scientific community was the main gatekeeper for expert testimony. The judge is charged with ensuring that the evidence is "reliable" (valid) and "relevant" (addresses an issue at trial). The judge is to look with a flexible mind-set at a number of factors, none of which should be determinative. These factors include whether the theory or technique has been tested; whether the technique has been peer reviewed and published; the technique's error rate; and whether the technique has been generally accepted in the relevant scientific community (*Daubert v. Merrell Dow Pharmaceuticals*, 509 U.S. 579 [1993]). The *Daubert* approach and the judge's gatekeeper role later were extended to "technical or other specialized knowledge" (*Kumho Tire Co., Ltd. v. Carmichael*, 526 U.S. 137 [1999]).

Frye continues to be followed in roughly twelve states and for this reason remains an important test.

Federal Rule 702 lists four factors in addition to the witness's qualifications as an expert that are required to be satisfied before an individual my qualify as an expert.

First, the expert's testimony based on his or her "knowledge, skill, experience, training, or education" must be helpful to the jury. In other words, the expert must help the jury understand an area they otherwise would have difficulty understanding. An expert, for example, may testify on the potential health hazards created by the defendant's dumping toxic chemicals in a landfill.

Second, the expert's opinion must be based on "sufficient facts or data" to undertake a meaningful analysis.

Third, the expert must employ reliable principles and methods in his or her analysis.

The last requirement is that the analysis must follow the accepted way of carrying out the analysis or test.

Rule 702. Testimony by Expert Witnesses

A witness who is qualified as an expert by knowledge, skill, experience, training, or education may testify in the form of an opinion or otherwise if:

(a) the expert's scientific, technical, or other specialized knowledge will help the trier of fact to understand the evidence or to determine a fact in issue;

(b) the testimony is based on sufficient facts or data;

(c) the testimony is the product of reliable principles and methods; and

(d) the expert has reliably applied the principles and methods to the facts of the case.

Expert witnesses prior to the drafting of the Federal Rules of Evidence were required to describe the data on which they based their opinion or to respond to a hypothetical question setting forth facts. Experts still may be asked hypothetical questions although the Federal Rules have eased the burden on experts by allowing them to base their testimony on one of four sources. Experts according to Federal Rule 703 may base their opinions on facts or data from the following sources.

Perception. The expert's analysis is based on his or her actual perceptions. An example is a psychiatrist who analyzes a defendant's mental sanity.

Information. An expert may base his or her analysis on information provided by another individual. A doctor may rely on X-rays and medical scans to analyze the cause of death, and a laboratory technician may rely on DNA collected at the crime scene.

Trial. An expert may base his or her opinion on testimony of other witnesses at trial.

Experts in the field. An expert may rely on facts or data that are not admissible in evidence if they are the "type reasonably relied upon by experts in the particular field." For example, an expert may base his or her opinion on consultation with other experts or on scientific articles and books.

The admission of expert testimony is conditioned on Federal Rule of Evidence 403. Highly prejudicial evidence will not be admitted into evidence. An example is polygraphs (lie detector tests) that are likely to be overvalued by jurors or bloody photos of the victim relied on by an expert to report on the cause of death (*United States v. Scheffer*, 523 U.S. 303 [1998]).

Rule 703. Bases of Opinion Testimony of Experts

An expert may base an opinion on facts or data in the case that the expert has been made aware of or personally observed. If experts in the particular field would reasonably rely on those kinds of facts or data in forming an opinion on the subject, they need not be admissible for the opinion to be admitted. But if the facts or data would otherwise be inadmissible, the proponent of the opinion may disclose them to the jury only if their probative value in helping the jury evaluate the opinion substantially outweighs their prejudicial effect.

PHOTO 6.1

Each individual has a distinctive set of teeth in form, arrangement, and dental work. Perpetrators of crimes may leave bite marks on the victim and an expert witness may connect a defendant to the wound.

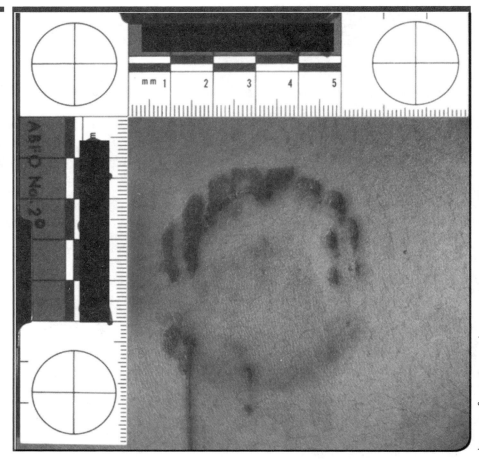

University of Texas Health Science Center at San Antonio—Center for Education and Research in Forensics, www.utforensic.org/bitemark.asp

■ QUALIFYING AN EXPERT WITNESS

A judge must be satisfied that Rules 703 and 403 are satisfied before admitting an expert witness at trial. The burden of proof is on the party requesting the appointment of an expert. The opposing party may challenge the expert's qualifications, the helpfulness of the testimony, the reliability of the data, and the expert's analysis, as well as the prejudicial impact of the expert's testimony.

In *United States v. Powers*, Grady William Powers was convicted of the repeated aggravated sexual assault of his daughter when she was 9 and 10 years old. The Fourth Circuit Court of Appeals held the trial court had properly excluded the testimony of a clinical psychologist who would have testified about the results of a penile plethysmograph test that measured Powers's sexual response to pictures of nude females in various age groups. The Court of Appeals noted that the scientific literature does not regard the test as a valid diagnostic tool. The majority of incest offenders who do not admit their guilt, such as Powers, demonstrate a normal response to the test. These false negatives render the test unreliable (*United States v. Powers*, 59 F.4d 1460 [4th Cir. 1995]).

The appellate court also affirmed the decision of the trial court judge to exclude the testimony of an expert who would have testified that Powers did not demonstrate the psychological profile of a fixated pedophile. The court noted that the testimony only would have demonstrated that Powers did not belong to a group that comprised 40 percent of incest abusers. Powers was charged with statutory rape of his daughter rather than with being a fixated pedophile. The testimony did not demonstrate that those who are not pedophiles are less likely to commit incest abuse.

■ TESTIMONY ON ULTIMATE ISSUES

The common law prohibited an expert from offering an opinion on the ultimate issue in a case. This was considered to interfere with the prerogative of the jury or judge sitting without a jury. Federal Rule 704 states that an opinion is not automatically excluded because it "embraces an ultimate issue." Nonetheless, testimony that the defendant had the intent to kill or was reckless or negligent likely would be excluded from evidence on the grounds that it involved an ultimate issue to be litigated at trial.

In *Hygh v. Jacobs*, William C. Hygh sued William Jacobs, a police officer, for the use of excessive force in arresting him. Terry C. Cox, a professor and expert on police use of force, testified that Jacobs's hitting Hygh in the face with a flashlight was not "warranted under the circumstances" and that Jacobs's conduct was "totally improper." The Second Circuit Court of Appeals concluded that Cox's testimony "regarding the ultimate legal conclusion entrusted to the jury crossed the line and should have been excluded" (*Hygh v. Jacobs*, 961 F.2d 359 [2d Cir. 1992]).

Congress in reaction to the use of experts in cases of legal insanity prohibited experts from testifying on whether a defendant possessed the mental state or condition constituting an element of the crime. This is a matter for the jury alone. Experts despite this provision continue to testify on issues of criminal intent by avoiding giving an opinion on an "ultimate issue" such as whether a defendant pleading legal insanity is able to distinguish between right and wrong. The expert instead testifies the defendant suffered from a mental disease or defect that would affect the defendant's ability to evaluate whether his or her actions are acceptable.

Rule 704. Opinion on an Ultimate Issue

(a) **In General—Not Automatically Objectionable.** An opinion is not objectionable just because it embraces an ultimate issue.

(b) **Exception.** In a criminal case, an expert witness must not state an opinion about whether the defendant did or did not have a mental state or condition that constitutes an element of the crime charged or of a defense. Those matters are for the trier of fact alone.

At common law an expert had to disclose prior to testifying the facts or data he or she relied on reaching his or her conclusion. Rule 705 eliminates this requirement. An expert is required to testify about the underlying facts if asked by the court or asked on cross-examination. The idea is to save time. In those instances in which the opposing attorney believes the expert's testimony lacked a solid foundation, he or she may explore this on cross-examination.

Rule 705. Disclosing the Facts or Data Underlying an Expert's Opinion

Unless the court orders otherwise, an expert may state an opinion—and give the reasons for it—without first testifying to the underlying facts or data. But the expert may be required to disclose those facts or data on cross-examination.

An expert witness may base his or her opinion on facts or data "made known to the expert" at trial. This is accomplished through the use of a hypothetical question in which the lawyer asks the expert to assume certain facts and asks the expert whether he or she has formed an opinion based on the assumed facts.

6.2 YOU DECIDE

Lewis "Scooter" Libby, chief of staff to Vice President Richard "Dick" Cheney, was charged with perjury and other crimes based on his lying to FBI investigators and a grand jury about conversations in 2003 with various journalists. Libby contended that he lacked a criminal intent and that his false statements to the FBI were based on a faulty memory. Libby attempted to offer the expert testimony of Dr. Robert A. Bjork, a memory science expert. He would testify that it is entirely reasonable given memory scientific research that Libby "innocently confused or misremembered the conversation on which this case turns."

Dr. Bjork was prepared to testify about various causes of memory error. Should the court allow Dr. Bjork to testify? See *United States v. Libby* (461 F.Supp.2d 3 [D.D.C. 2006]).

You can learn what the court decided by referring to the study site, **http://study.sagepub.com/lippmance.**

6.3 YOU DECIDE

Jeanne Dunne, a bank teller, provided a description of a bank robber "moments" following the robbery. The robber was identified as an African American with dark skin, a wide nose, and medium build. Dunne was unable to select defendant Johannes Hines from a book of photographs. Working with a police artist, she constructed a sketch of the robbery and selected Hines from eight photographs of men who "resembled the robber." She stated that Hines "looked like him" but remained unsure. Hines offered the expert testimony of Dr. Saul Kassin, a psychologist studying human perception at Williams College. Kassin's testimony was offered to document the "decreased accuracy of cross-racial identification, the effect of time on memory . . . the absence of any correlation between the amount of confidence expressed by an eyewitness in his or her memory, and the accuracy of that witness identification, the suggestiveness of subtle aspects of the identification process, such as the darkness of a particular photo as compared to others in the array [and] the fact that the eyewitness knows there is a suspect in the mix, the transference phenomenon by which a witness may believe that a face looks familiar but is unable to say whether her familiarity comes from seeing a previous mug shot, or from the robbery" and other elated issues. The government expert questioned whether Kassin's studies of college students could be applied to "a real life setting." Should Kassin be qualified as an expert and be permitted to testify? See *United States v. Hines* (55 F.Supp.2d 2 [D. Mass 1999]).

You can learn what the court decided by referring to the study site, **http://study.sagepub.com/lippmance.**

■ SCOPE OF EXPERT TESTIMONY

Experts commonly are used in several areas in criminal trials:

Fingerprint identification

DNA evidence

Handwriting analysis

Ballistics evidence

Footprint analysis

Neutron activation analysis (gunpowder residue testing)

Testimony relating to common practices of drug trafficking

Gang organization and functioning

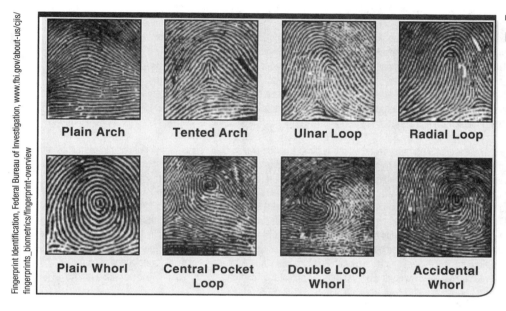

Fingerprint Identification, Federal Bureau of Investigation, www.fbi.gov/about-us/cjis/fingerprints_biometrics/fingerprint-overview

Plain Arch　　Tented Arch　　Ulnar Loop　　Radial Loop

Plain Whorl　　Central Pocket Loop　　Double Loop Whorl　　Accidental Whorl

PHOTO 6.2

Fingerprints can be classified on the basis of the pattern of ridges that constitute the print. Patterns are classified as loops, whorls or arches. Sixty-six percent of the population has loop prints, thirty-three percent whorls, and only one percent arches.

Courts also have recognized expert testimony on syndromes, which explains behavior and symptoms characteristic of "typical" victims of abuse and rape. This evidence is intended to help the jury understand why an alleged victim's behavior may be contrary to what a jury may anticipate. This assists the jury in evaluating the evidence, which the defense may claim is inconsistent with the behavior expected of a victim of abuse or rape. For example, studies indicate victims of rape by an acquaintance because of their sense of guilt, shame, and trauma tend to delay reporting the rape and may be more likely to report the attack first to a friend rather than to an intimate partner. Another important insight is that the victims of spousal abuse lose confidence and a sense of self-efficacy and are likely to remain in the home rather than to flee.

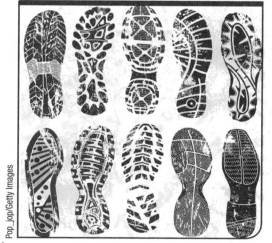

Pop_jop/Getty Images

PHOTO 6.3

Analysts overlay a suspect's shoe prints with impressions left at the crime scene to determine whether the suspect was at the crime scene.

Rape trauma syndrome, battered spouse syndrome, battered child syndrome, and child sexual abuse accommodation syndrome all are variants of post-traumatic stress disorders and are well documented in the social science literature. The basic insight is that severe traumatic experiences affect the human psyche and result in certain identifiable symptoms and patterns of behavior. There is the risk that the jury will use this evidence to conclude a rape occurred rather than to understand that the reaction of the alleged victim is consistent with the behavior of a victim of abuse.

CRIMINAL EVIDENCE IN THE NEWS

In a controversial Texas case, Cameron Todd Willingham, age 23, was convicted of the arson murder of his three young daughters in Corsicana, Texas, on December 2, 1991. Arson investigators testified that Willingham spread accelerant on the floor of the house and ignited a fire with the intent of killing his young daughters. The assistant prosecutor who was assigned to prosecute the case told the newspapers that Willingham's motive was to rid himself of his young children because they interfered with his "beer drinking and dart throwing." In the past, Willingham had experienced minor scrapes with the law and had been known to drink and to abuse his wife, Stacie. It later was alleged that Willingham had killed the children to conceal Stacie's abuse of the children.

The prosecutor wanted to avoid a trial and offered Willingham's two assigned attorneys life imprisonment in return for a guilty plea to murder. One of the attorneys was a former state trooper and the other a local general practitioner. Willingham refused to listen to his lawyers' advice and insisted on his innocence and turned down the plea bargain. Murder charges were filed in January 1992, and the case proceeded to trial.

At trial in August 1992, the prosecutor primarily relied on the testimony of the two arson investigators. A jailhouse informant awaiting trial for robbery testified Willingham had confessed to him in prison. The informant who later was diagnosed as a bipolar personality subsequently recanted his testimony and then turned around and affirmed his original testimony. The informant subsequently was sentenced to fifteen years in prison and five years later was released based on the recommendation of the prosecutor in the Willingham case. Other witnesses modified their earlier statements to the police. One witness initially told the police Willingham was devastated and had to be restrained from risking his life by reentering the burning house to save his daughters. The same witness later testified Willingham's emotional reaction appeared inauthentic and that he had a gut feeling Willingham "had something to do with the setting of the fire." Willingham's lawyers presented a single defense witness, a babysitter who could not believe Willingham would kill his children.

The prosecutor, in his argument to the jury, read from a bible that had been in Willingham's home. He concluded his closing argument by reciting a passage spoken by Jesus that whoever harmed one of his children is to be cast in the seas with a millstone around his neck.

Following Willingham's conviction, the prosecutor in the sentencing phase of the trial highlighted Willingham's tattoo of a skull encircled by a serpent, which together with other evidence allegedly fit the profile of a sociopath. The prosecutor presented two psychological expert witnesses. Tim Gregory, a family counselor, analyzed the posters of rock groups like Iron Maiden and Led Zeppelin that had hung on Willingham's wall and suggested they were indicative of an interest in violence and Satanism and cult activities. The primary psychological expert, Dr. James Grigson, a forensic psychiatrist, had testified so frequently for the prosecution in Texas capital punishment cases that he commonly was referred to as "Dr. Death." Grigson concluded Willingham was an "extremely severe sociopath" who was beyond treatment. Dr. Grigson previously had been expelled from the American Psychiatric Association for unethical conduct in testifying regarding the psychological state of defendants who he had not personally examined and for having claimed he could predict dangerousness with 100 percent accuracy.

Willingham was sentenced to death. An independent examination of the forensic evidence by Dr. Gerald Hurst, a leading world expert on explosives and fires, concluded the forensic report was flawed on all of the twenty indicators that allegedly supported the conclusion that Willingham was guilty of arson. The Texas Board of Pardons and Paroles four days before Willingham's execution rejected a plea for clemency based on Hurst's report, and Texas Governor Rick Perry refused to stay the execution. On February 17, 2004, Willingham was executed by lethal injection. He insisted that "I am an innocent man convicted of a crime I did not commit. I have been persecuted for twelve years for something I did not do."

In 2005, a report by outside experts submitted to a Texas commission established to investigate allegations of error and misconduct by forensic scientists concluded the arson investigation in the case of Willingham was flawed. Governor Perry continued to insist that Willingham was a "monster," and Perry allegedly pressured the head of the commission to decide against pursuing the investigation of the Willingham case. Governor Perry subsequently removed the head of the commission and two other members of the commission in a step critics alleged was intended to prevent the continuing investigation of Willingham's conviction. The *Chicago Tribune* reported in August 2009 that nine of the country's top fire analysts concluded the investigation of the Willingham fire had been based on outmoded theories and folklore. Consider how some of the points discussed in this chapter contributed to what may have been the wrongful conviction of Willingham.

Source: Grann, David. "Trial by Fire." *The New Yorker* (September 7, 2009), pp. 42–51.

■ COURT-APPOINTED EXPERTS

The Advisory Committee on Rules of Evidence expressed dissatisfaction over the practice of parties to a case "shopping" for favorable experts, the dishonesty of some experts, and the reluctance of many skilled experts to involve themselves in litigation. A jury also may be overly influenced by experts and, at the same time, may be easily confused by the contest between competing prosecution and defense experts.

A trial court as recognized in Federal Rule 706 has the inherent right to call expert witnesses. An expert appointed by the court may take on the aura of infallibility, and the judge may choose not to disclose the appointment of the expert to the jury.

Judges under Federal Rule 706 may on their own motion or on the motion of any party enter an order appointing any expert witnesses agreed upon by the parties or selected by the court. Judges are reluctant to take this step because it undercuts the ability of the adversarial nature of the trial. This does not affect the rights of the opposing parties to call their own experts. The expert is subject to cross-examination by each party to the case.

6.4 YOU DECIDE

Roy Dale Ryan was charged with the murder of his spouse, Keri Ryan. They had a tumultuous marriage characterized by physical abuse. Ryan attempted to control Keri and demanded to know where she was and who she was with at all times. He called her as often as ten times a day at work. He constantly accused her of extramarital affairs. Keri left Ryan in November 1996 and obtained a family violence protection order against him. During the separation, Keri began seeing another man and intended to return to school. Ryan became depressed. The prosecutor called Rosemary Bratton as an expert on the subject of battered woman syndrome (BWS). Bratton described a phenomenon she described as "separation violence." She stated the time a victim is planning to leave or has left a relationship is "the time more homicides are committed . . . and it happens because perpetrators . . . who need to maintain power and control over their partner become extremely upset." Batterers typically attempt to isolate their spouses, make constant calls to their places of employment, limit their access to other individuals, threaten suicide, engage in constant criticism, and often accuse their spouses of having adulterous affairs with strangers. Bratton states that a majority of women involved were killed with guns. Should the judge have permitted Bratton to testify as an expert at Ryan's trial? See *Ryan v. State* (988 P.2d 46 [Wyo. 1999]).

You can learn what the court decided by referring to the study site, **http://study.sagepub.com/lippmance.**

Legal Equation

Opinion evidence = Lay witness + inferences drawn from facts + help fact finder + nontechnical.

Expert witness = Qualified as an expert by knowledge, skill, experience, training, or education + may testify in the form of an opinion or otherwise if + the expert's scientific, technical, or other specialized knowledge will help the trier of fact + to understand the evidence or to determine a fact in issue + the testimony is based on sufficient facts or data + the testimony is the product of reliable principles and methods and + the expert has reliably applied the principles and methods to the facts of the case.

CRIMINAL EVIDENCE AND PUBLIC POLICY

In February 2008, Barbara Sheehan, a Queens, New York, school secretary, shot her husband of twenty-four years eleven times while he was shaving. At Sheehan's trial, a number of witnesses testified on how her husband, a former sergeant in the New York Police

(Continued)

(Continued)

Department, would make regular death threats against his wife by showing her crime scene photos of dead bodies and taking his loaded semiautomatic handgun with him into the bedroom and threatening and forcing her to engage in bizarre sexual rituals such as compelling her to watch him masturbate while wearing a diaper or talking to him about a sexual encounter with another couple. There was evidence her husband had doused her with scalding pasta sauce and hit her in the head with a telephone when she tried to call 9-1-1. He grew increasingly angry at her when she refused to go with him on vacation in Florida. Even his own children despised him. His 25-year-old daughter recalled "millions" of violent outbursts from her father as she was growing up. "It happened every day."

Sheehan pled self-defense, claiming she reasonably feared an imminent threat to her life. The defense explained her passivity and failure to flee when confronted with abuse as battered woman syndrome (BWS). This psychological variant of post-traumatic stress disorder is based on psychological studies and explains that a woman subjected to constant violence and threats of violence feels helpless, captive, and confined, and has a lack of confidence to combat her husband's abuse. Jacquelyn C. Campbell of Johns Hopkins University testified as an expert witness that an abused woman is like an animal that receives a shock every time she tries to leave the cage and in the end remains paralyzed in place even when the cage door is left open.

BWS became a widely accepted legal defense in the 1990s, and several state governors granted clemency to women imprisoned for killing their spouse. BWS modifies the law of self-defense by recognizing that deadly force in self-defense is a justified response to an ongoing pattern of violent abuse rather than being limited to an imminent and immediate threat. The victim finds him- or herself in the home with his or her assailant and is not required to retreat before resorting to deadly force. Sheehan's trial was popularly seen as a referendum on the legitimacy of the defense.

The prosecutor, Debra Pomodore, called BWS a "pseudoscience" relied on by Sheehan to avoid imprisonment. There was no good explanation for why she remained in the home, and at the time she killed her husband, he did not pose a threat. Pomodore noted that as many as four million women are subject to abuse in the United States although only five hundred to six hundred women kill their husbands. Sheehan was characterized as a vindictive, manipulative, and money-hungry woman who was relying on BWS to justify the killing of her husband.

The prosecution asked why Sheehan after so many years of marriage killed her husband at this point in their relationship. Did she genuinely feel unable to leave the relationship? The prosecution pointed out that Sheehan had told her daughter a week before the shooting that she wanted a divorce. The prosecution suggested her true motivation was not physical fear, but her belief her husband was cheating on her. The prosecution also pointed out Sheehan profited from her husband's death—her kids sent her over $220,000 they had received in insurance payments following the death of their father.

Sheehan was acquitted, but she was sentenced to five years in prison on a weapons charge, the jury finding that she continued to fire her husband's firearm at him after he no longer posed a threat.

BWS was first recognized in 1981 by the Ohio Supreme Court in *State v. Thomas* (423 N.W.2d 137). The thinking is that "only by understanding these unique pressures that forced battered women to remain with their mates, despite their long-standing and reasonable fear of severe bodily harm and the isolation that being a battered woman creates, can a battered woman's state of mind be accurately and fairly understood" (*State v. Kelly*, 478 A.2d 364 [N.J. 1984]). The syndrome today is recognized by most state courts.

What is your view of reliance on "syndrome evidence" to explain a victim's pattern of behavior? Should the law of self-defense be relaxed in recognition of BWS?

■ CASE ANALYSIS

In *Winfrey v. State*, a Texas appeals court ruled on the scientific reliability of dog-scent evidence to identify the identity of a murderer.

Winfrey v. State, 323 S.W.3d 875 (Crim. App. Tex. 2010), Hervey, J.

On August 7, 2004, Murray Wayne Burr was found murdered in his home. Evidence at trial indicated that the victim had been stabbed twenty-eight times and had received multiple blunt-force injuries, including a broken right-eye orbit and a broken jaw. There was no evidence of forced entry into the victim's home. The

evidence indicated that the victim was dragged from his living room to his bedroom where his body was found. Family members reported that the only item missing from the victim's home was a Bible. . . . Investigators collected a variety of forensic evidence from the crime scene including a partial bloody fingerprint, a bloody shoe print, and several hair samples. Neither the prints nor the hair samples matched appellant. Investigators were able to obtain a DNA profile from evidence at the crime scene, however, the profile excluded appellant and his family members. . . . During the interview, appellant stated that he had known the victim, that he had never been in the victim's house, that he had not seen the victim in four to five years, and that he assumed he was the number one suspect.

Appellant was convicted and complained on direct appeal that the evidence is legally and factually insufficient to support a conviction of murder. . . . The court appeals found that the evidence was legally and factually sufficient. . . .

At the request of the Texas Rangers, Deputy Keith Pikett performed the dog-scent lineup. Deputy Pikett, a certified peace officer who specializes in canine handling, testified that he had been training bloodhounds since 1989. At trial, Deputy Pikett explained the scent lineup procedure:

"We use 6-quart paint cans that have numbers on them. They're just clean paint cans, and I put a piece of wood on the bottom of them so they are more stable and they're numbered. I set the paint cans out. I typically go like ten walking steps, put a can down; ten walking steps, put a can down. The cans are placed so there—with a crosswind—so if the can is here and the next can is here, the wind is going either this way or this way. We don't want the scent from can 2 blowing toward 3 or toward can 1. We want the wind to be blowing away, so it's not going to cross-contaminate that way. So we check that. Then I set the cans out."

On August 22, 2007, a scent lineup was conducted, and appellant's scent was placed in paint can number four. Deputy Pikett had no knowledge where appellant's scent was placed. He used three bloodhounds during this scent lineup: James Bond, Quincy, and Clue. All three alerted to appellant's scent in paint can number four.

This however, is not proof positive that appellant came in contact with the victim. Even when viewed in the light most favorable to the verdict, the dog-scent lineup proves only that appellant's scent was on the victim's clothes, not that appellant had been in direct contact with the victim, as the court of appeals decided.

During his testimony, Deputy Pikett acknowledged, "It's possible to transfer scent. . . . If I shake hands with you, I can give you the scent on my hand." The ease of transferring scents is well documented and is also accepted by law enforcement agencies such as the FBI. ("Because human scent is easily transferred from one person or object to another, it should not be used as primary evidence. However, when used in corroboration with other evidence, it has become a proven tool that can establish a connection to the crime.")

At oral argument, the State conceded that "dog scent alone is not enough [to convict the defendant]." Deputy Pikett also recognized the limitations of the scent lineup in his testimony when he stated that: "We never convict anybody solely on the dog. It is illegal in the State of Texas. . . . You cannot convict solely on

the dog's testimony." However, the record indicates, and the State acknowledged, that the jury gave significant weight to the canine-scent evidence. The jury submitted a note asking, "Is it illegal to convict solely on the scent pad evidence?" No eye witnesses put the appellant at the crime scene. The State was unable to match the appellant to the fingerprint or to any of the footprints found at the crime scene. The appellant did not match the DNA profile obtained from the crime scene. Criminologists microscopically compared seventy-three hairs recovered from the crime scene, yet none of the hairs were consistent with appellant's. None of the victim's belongings were found in appellant's possession. Not a Bible, a gun, or a knife collection.

Based on our review of this record, we find that the evidence, even when viewed in the light most favorable to the verdict, merely raises a suspicion of guilt and is legally insufficient to support a conviction of murder beyond a reasonable doubt. Because we find the evidence legally insufficient, we need not address appellant's factual-sufficiency claim.

We note, however, that the science underlying canine-scent lineups has been questioned; thus, we think it proper to briefly address the issue. Law-enforcement personnel have long utilized canines in crime management. For example, dogs have been employed for detecting narcotics and explosives, for tracking trails, in search-and-rescue operations, for locating cadavers, and for discriminating between scents for identification purposes. In thousands of cases, canines and their handlers have performed with distinction. Despite this success, we acknowledge the invariable truth espoused by Justice Souter that "[t]he infallible dog, however, is a creature of legal fiction" (Illinois v. Caballes, 545 U.S. 405 [2005].

This case pertains to canines used to discriminate among human scents in order to identify a specific person in a lineup. This process is often referred to as human-scent discrimination. Some courts, including the Fourteenth Court of Appeals, have determined that for purposes of admissibility, "there is little distinction between a scent lineup and a situation where a dog is required to track an individual's scent over an area traversed by multiple persons."

Like our sister courts across the country, we now hold that scent-discrimination lineups, whether conducted with individuals or inanimate objects, to be separate and distinct from dog-scent tracking evidence. . . . Accordingly, we conclude that scent-discrimination lineups, when used alone or as primary evidence, are legally insufficient to support a conviction. Like the Supreme Court of Washington, we believe that "[t]he dangers inherent in the use of dog tracking evidence can only be alleviated by the presence of corroborating evidence."

In 2007, three different dogs alerted only to appellant's scent. But, the question essentially presented in this case is whether dog-scent lineup evidence alone can support a conviction beyond a reasonable doubt. And, while this evidence may raise a strong suspicion of appellant's guilt, we nevertheless decide that, standing alone, it is insufficient to establish a person's guilt beyond a reasonable doubt.

CHAPTER SUMMARY

The Federal Rules of Evidence modified the common law prohibition on witnesses offering opinions. Opinion evidence by a lay witness must be based on the witness's perception, must assist the jury, and must be nontechnical and straightforward.

Expert testimony can be of central importance in criminal prosecutions. Expert witnesses are witnesses who are qualified by "knowledge, skill, experience, training, or education" and may testify in the form of an opinion in their area of expertise. A trial court has the inherent right as recognized in Federal Rule 706 to call expert witnesses.

CHAPTER REVIEW QUESTIONS

1. Are lay witnesses limited to testifying on the facts of a case?

2. Compare and contrast the *Frye* and *Daubert* approaches to scientific evidence.

3. What requirements must be met by an expert witness?

4. List some areas in which an expert witness typically is relied on during a criminal trial.

LEGAL TERMINOLOGY

expert testimony

expert witness

lay witness

opinion rule

Visit the Student Study Site at **http://study.sagepub.com/lippmance** to access additional study tools, including mobile-friendly eFlashcards and Web quizzes as well as links to SAGE journal articles and hyperlinks for *Criminal Evidence* on the Web.

7

CRIME SCENE EVIDENCE AND EXPERIMENTS

May the footprint evidence be introduced against the defendant at trial?

Defendant was arrested and as he was getting ready to go with the police, his mother handed him a pair of wet, blue tennis shoes saying, "Put on your shoes." Defendant's jeans were wet from the knees down. [Henry] Niedbala was brought over to defendant's house in a police car and identified defendant as the person who had assaulted him earlier that evening. The police made a further investigation of the footprints outside defendant's house. One of the officers had been trained in footprint comparison methods . . . He stated that his opinion was based on a visual comparison of the footprints in which he noted the particular pattern of the shoe sole and the individual markings left by the bottom of the shoe. . . .

The officer testified that his sole basis of comparison was his visual comparison made at night with the aid of a flashlight and that further measurements were impossible due to the snow that was falling. . . .

Defendant further argues that there was no proof that he actually owned the blue tennis shoes he put on when he was arrested which were used as the basis of comparison with the footprints in the snow. The police officer testified that defendant was not wearing shoes when he was apprehended and that the officer did not know who owned the blue tennis shoes. . . .

In this case, the police officer stated that he based his comparison of the footprints on the particular diamond pattern of the shoe sole and the individual markings on the sole showing where it was worn. He testified that he observed these specific markings in the footprints he saw in the snow near defendant's residence and that the same diamond pattern and wear markings were present on the sole of the blue tennis shoes and in the footprints which defendant made after he was arrested. (*McNary v. State*, 460 N.E.2d 145 [Ind. 1984])

CHAPTER OUTLINE

Introduction	Other Judicially Recognized Tests
Crime Scene Evidence	Tests Not Accepted by the Courts
Chain of Custody	Experiments
Scientific Evidence	Case Analysis
Laying the Foundation for Scientific Evidence	Chapter Summary
Right to Defense Experts	Chapter Review Questions
Judicially Accepted Scientific Tests	Legal Terminology

1. Do you know the steps in marking evidence?

2. Can you discuss how to authenticate crime scene evidence?

3. What is the importance of the chain of custody of evidence? How is the chain of custody established?

4. Do you know the steps in establishing the foundation for scientific evidence?

5. Are defendants provided access to expert witnesses?

6. Can you describe the process of gathering fingerprint evidence?

7. How does blood alcohol testing work?

8. What is the significance of a ballistics test?

9. Why are the results of polygraph examinations generally not admissible at trial?

■ INTRODUCTION

Real evidence, as you may remember, includes any tangible item that may be perceived with the five senses. This category of evidence includes documents, exhibits, photos, videos, clothing, and firearms. This chapter covers evidence seized from the crime scene such as fingerprints along with experiments, models, and diagrams.

There are two preliminary steps involved in real evidence. First, the evidence must be marked. Second, the lawyer introducing real evidence must lay a foundation for the admissibility of the evidence.

There are four steps involved in marking evidence. First, the material must be shown to the opposing lawyer before the witness takes the stand to testify. The purpose is to inform the opposing counsel and provide him or her the opportunity to examine the material and to formulate questions for cross-examination. Second, the lawyer intending to introduce the evidence asks the clerk of the court to number the item for purposes of identification. The third step is to establish a foundation for the admissibility of evidence.

Laying the foundation of real evidence as discussed in Chapter Three requires authentication of the evidence. **Authentication** involves demonstrating that the evidence is "what it claims to be." In other words, the party seeking to introduce the item must demonstrate that the item before the court is the same item removed from the crime scene or seized from the defendant's home or automobile or is an accurate representation of the crime scene. Federal Rule 901 provides that "[t]o satisfy the requirement of authenticating or identifying an item of evidence, the proponent must produce evidence sufficient to support a finding that the item is what the proponent claims it is." In the fourth step, the lawyer makes a formal request to admit the material into evidence.

Evidence that is not authentic is inadmissible at trial. Keep in mind that authenticated real evidence before being introduced at trial also must be found to be relevant and nonprejudicial and may not be hearsay or privileged, and its seizure must have been obtained in compliance with the law (e.g., the Fourth Amendment prohibition on unreasonable searches and seizures). Evidence that surmounts all these hurdles may be challenged by the adverse party at trial who is free to question the accuracy of a scientific test or whether the evidence has been modified or altered.

In the event the judge finds the material admissible, it is assigned an exhibit number and admitted as evidence in the case. The purpose of numbering for identification and as exhibits is to keep the trial record organized and to allow items to be quickly identified by referring to the item's number (e.g., "People's exhibit number one"). Typically, one side's exhibits are assigned numerical identification and the other side is assigned alphabetical identification, or each side is assigned a block of numbers (e.g., 1–100).

Once admitted into evidence, exhibits may be examined by the jury and taken by them into the jury room during their deliberations over the defendant's guilt or innocence. Keep in mind that evidence that surmounts all the hurdles described above may be challenged by the adverse party on various grounds. An example is arguing that a firearm seized at the crime scene does not belong to the defendant or that there is an innocent explanation for the defendant's fingerprints on the firearm.

■ CRIME SCENE EVIDENCE

Items seized from a crime scene must be *authenticated* or shown to be genuine. Authentication in addition to demonstrating that an object "is what the proponent claims it is" also assists the jury by linking the item to the case. A bag of narcotics is relevant because it is seized from the defendant's home, an area under his or her constructive control. The burden for establishing authenticity is low. The lawyer only is required to introduce evidence "sufficient to support a finding" of authenticity. The question in authentication is whether a reasonable jury could find the object authentic.

PHOTO 7.1

Police investigators secure a crime scene and collect physical evidence and document the crime scene through photographs and sketches.

The party seeking to authenticate real evidence from a crime scene is required to demonstrate the item is substantially in the same condition it was in when seized by police.

There is no required method for authenticating crime scene evidence, but there are two common methods of authentication. First, a witness may identify the object. Second, a chain of custody may be established.

Real evidence with distinctive characteristics may be authenticated by a witness's testimony without establishing a chain of custody. A police officer in a murder prosecution may testify that the knife shown to him or her by a lawyer is the knife seized from the defendant following the killing based on the unusual shape of the blade and carving on

PHOTO 7.2

O. J. Simpson was acquitted in 1995 of the murder of Nicole Brown Simpson and Ron Goldman. Forensic experts reconstructed the crime by analyzing footprints, blood splatter, the position of bodies, and the location of wounds on the bodies.

the handle of the knife. Police officers often will take steps to ensure that an ordinary item has unique and distinctive visual properties by scratching or writing their initials on an object or securely attaching a label. The officer then is able to testify that the knife is the same knife he or she seized from the defendant.

In *United States v. Mahecha-Onofree*, the defendant was arrested for possession of cocaine bonded chemically within two suitcases with intent to distribute. The arresting officer authenticated the luggage based on its unusual shape, color, distinctive rivets, and scratches made on the suitcases by the officer (*United States v. Mahecha-Onofree*, 936 F.2d 623 [1st Cir. 1991]).

Federal Rule 901(b)(1) also recognizes authentication based on "Testimony of a Witness with Knowledge." A crime victim may identify a stolen watch because it is engraved with his or her father's initials and date of birth. An eyewitness may identify the gun used in the robbery because of its distinctive, shiny, metallic appearance (*United States v. Stewart*, 98-CF-904, 02-CO-1177 [D.C. Ct. App. 2005]).

Rule 901. Authenticating or Identifying Evidence

(a) In General. To satisfy the requirement of authenticating or identifying an item of evidence, the proponent must produce evidence sufficient to support a finding that the item is what the proponent claims it is.

■ CHAIN OF CUSTODY

A **chain of custody** must be established by the party seeking to authenticate real evidence in those instances in which the evidence cannot be readily identified by a witness or may be easily modified, tampered with, or misplaced. Examples of items requiring a demonstration of a chain of custody include blood samples, narcotics, and items of clothing. The proponent of the evidence must demonstrate there is a strong probability that the evidence presented at trial has been protected and preserved and is the same item that was seized by the police and has not been interfered with or tainted.

The two goals of chain of custody are to demonstrate the item (1) is the same item seized by the police and (2) is in substantially the same condition as when it was seized by the police.

Consider the chain of custody of a firearm. A prosecutor can demonstrate that the serial number on a firearm introduced as evidence in court is the same as the serial number on the firearm seized from the defendant by the police and the serial number, in turn, matches the serial number on the gun analyzed by the ballistics expert. Establishing a chain of custody as is apparent requires the maintenance of reliable records by the police and prosecutor.

Chain of custody is particularly important when items are subject to undetectable alteration or replacement. In the case of narcotics, it is crucial that each individual with custody accounts for the security of the item to ensure that the substance has not been tampered with or altered. The police officer who seized the package of powder from the defendant must immediately place the cocaine in a sealed envelope, which he or she signs and places in a safe and secure location with limited access by other individuals. The envelope should clearly indicate the contents, and there should be room for each individual with custody over the narcotics to indicate the time, date, and reason for possessing the drugs. The prosecutor next must establish that the same envelope was delivered to the forensic laboratory and an analyst opened the envelope, examined the powder, and determined it was cocaine. The laboratory chemist who examined the item must testify in court about the safeguards and procedures that were employed to analyze the powder and to store the powder in a safe and secure location. Different types of material require different types of packaging for storage. Bloodstained clothing needs to be air-dried because otherwise mold and mildew can interfere with various chemical tests.

Once the chain of custody is established, the burden shifts to the opposing party to demonstrate an irregularity or that the evidence was tampered with and tainted. The chain of custody is not required to be "perfect." Rule 901(a) provides that it is sufficient if the chain of custody supports "a finding that the matter in question is what its proponent claims." The common refrain is that so long as the chain of custody satisfies Rule 901(a), any problem goes to weight rather than to admissibility.

In *United States v. Ladd*, the First Circuit Court of Appeals held there was an unexplained break in custody that resulted in the exclusion of a blood sample from evidence. The state lab assigned the number T87-1938-BBO to a blood sample. The private laboratory received and analyzed a blood sample labeled T87-1936-BBO (note the numerical-digit discrepancy). The 6 later was modified to look like an 8. There was no explanation offered at trial for the difference in the numbers assigned to the two samples. Absent an explanation, there was the possibility, however remote, that the wrong blood sample was introduced as evidence at trial. The First Circuit Court of Appeals concluded that "[d]ue to the missing link, the . . . test results should not have been admitted into evidence" (*United States v. Ladd*, 885 F.2d 854 [1st Cir. 1989]). In an Indiana case, the deposit of narcotics in the police evidence room and the failure of lab technicians to testify about the location and safeguarding of the sample over a six-day period resulted in the exclusion of the narcotics from evidence (*Graham v. State*, 255 N.E.2d 652 [Ind. 1970]). In *Wilson v. State*, a Georgia appellate court found a break in the chain of custody where the envelope containing the narcotics was unsealed, it did not carry an identification number, and the lab technicians failed to track their receipt and custody over the narcotics (*Wilson v. State*, 609 S.E.2d 704 [Ga. App. 2005]). Are courts overly concerned about tampering or the replacement of evidence by the police and prosecutors?

7.1 YOU DECIDE

Danny Zink took his car to a business for installation of a car stereo. Mark Lawless, a company employee, removed a brown paper bag from the glove compartment during installation of the radio and tossed the paper onto the floor. His assistant, Ronald Barajas, picked up the sack and threw the bag into a trash can. When Zink returned for his car, he found the sack was missing. Visibly upset, he told employee Larry Vasquez that $400 was in the sack and he needed to recover it immediately. Zink approached Lawless, who retrieved the bag from the trash can

and gave it to his supervisor, Gerald Robinson. Robinson "began counting the money and noticed that the serial numbers were identical, that several bills were double printed and that the color was abnormal." Store manager Lester Dale Howell called the police, who marked the bag and bills with identifying numbers in order to track the chain of custody of the bag and bills. Zink challenges the admissibility of the counterfeit money based on a break in the chain of custody See *United States v. Zink* (612 F.2d 511 [10th Cir. 1980]).

You can learn what the court decided by referring to the study site, **http://study.sagepub.com/lippmance.**

The next section explores the next step after an exhibit of forensic evidence has been admitted into evidence.

■ SCIENTIFIC EVIDENCE

Forensic laboratory analysis of **scientific evidence** is a crucial component of modern criminal investigation. Evidence found at the crime scene may be sent to a crime lab for evaluation. This may involve DNA and blood testing; hair, fiber, and footprint and ballistics analysis; fingerprints; and speed detection radar. Individual suspects also may be subjected to testing to determine whether there is a match with material seized at the crime scene. Forensic evidence, though only a small percentage of the evidence introduced at trial, may prove vital in the determination of guilt or innocence in prosecutions for crimes such as murder, drug possession, driving under the influence, and sexual molestation. A number of these forensic tests are well established, and judges take judicial notice of their scientific reliability. Other tests such as handwriting and footprint analysis and analysis of various syndromes are less well established, and judges may require that a foundation is laid for the admissibility of this type of evidence. Keep in mind that the authentication of the results of a scientific test does not prevent the adverse party from attacking the reliability of the test on cross-examination.

■ LAYING THE FOUNDATION FOR SCIENTIFIC EVIDENCE

The foundation for the introduction of scientific evidence involves three questions: first, whether the test was scientifically valid; second, whether the equipment was accurate; and third, whether the test was performed in the required fashion by a qualified analyst.

Judges, as noted, will accept the scientific validity of established scientific tests like fingerprinting by judicial notice. A radar gun typically is accepted by judicial notice although when challenged by the defense attorney the prosecution must demonstrate the radar was accurately calibrated and working properly and that the gun was operated by a qualified officer.

The validity of less well-established tests in most instances is established through expert testimony on *voir dire*. First, the expert witness must possess the required training, knowledge, and skill to qualify as an expert. Second, the expert must establish that the test will be helpful to the jury and satisfies either the *Frye* or *Daubert* test, whichever is applicable in the jurisdiction. As you recall, under the *Frye* "general acceptance" test, the question is whether the test is "sufficiently established to have gained general acceptance in the particular field in which it belongs." *Daubert* allows the judge to decide the scientific validity of the test and examines whether the theory or technique has been tested, whether it has been examined by peer review and published in professional journals, the error rate of the methodology, and whether standard operating procedures have been established. The third step for the expert witness is to establish that required methods of analysis were followed in conducting the test using appropriate equipment.

The United States Supreme Court has held that the party introducing a DNA test and presumably other scientific laboratory tests is required to call the analyst who conducted the test to testify. The analyst will be asked to testify about his training experience and adherence to established procedures and the working order of the equipment (*Melendez-Diaz v. Massachusetts*, 557 U.S. 305 [2009]; *Bullcoming v. New Mexico*, 54 U.S. __ [2011]).

The opposing lawyer on cross-examination will attempt to demonstrate that the analyst lacked training or experience, highlight the error rate of the laboratory, and point to the failure of the analyst to follow required procedures and question the accuracy of the equipment. An expert also may be called to impeach the scientific acceptance and credibility of the scientific test (*Melendez-Diaz v. Massachusetts*, 558 U.S. 305 [2009]; *Bullcoming v. New Mexico*, 54 U.S. __ [2011]).

■ RIGHT TO DEFENSE EXPERTS

In *Ake v. Oklahoma*, the accused was charged with first-degree murder, carrying the death penalty. His behavior was so "bizarre" at the arraignment that the trial court judge ordered a mental examination. Glen Burton Ake was determined to be incompetent to stand trial although he later recovered as a result of psychotropic drugs. Ake's attorney at trial decided to rely on the insanity defense. The trial court judge refused Ake's attorney's request that his client be provided a psychiatric examination at state expense, and he was convicted. At the sentencing stage, the prosecution presented psychiatric testimony that Ake posed a danger to society (*Ake v. Oklahoma*, 470 U.S. 68 [1985]).

The United States Supreme Court reversed Ake's conviction and noted that "when a State brings its judicial power to bear on an indigent in a criminal proceeding, it must take steps to ensure that the defendant has a fair opportunity to present his defense." This "fair opportunity" to present a defense requires the "basic tools" to present an adequate defense. The Court held that when a defendant makes a preliminary showing that "his sanity at the time of the offense is likely to be a significant factor at trial, the Constitution requires that a State provide access to a psychiatrist's assistance on this basis, if the defendant cannot otherwise afford one."

The scope of this holding is uncertain. Some courts have limited a defendant's access to experts to cases in which a defendant relies on the insanity defense although other courts have limited access to experts to death penalty cases. Another unresolved issue is whether the expert is to be appointed by the defense or is to be court-appointed as a neutral expert. The federal Criminal Justice Act establishes a $1 million cap on expenditures for experts although the judge may certify that additional expenditures are required. State laws also provide for compensation for experts although the funding is significantly more limited.

CRIMINAL EVIDENCE IN THE NEWS

On July 5, 2011, 25-year-old Casey Lee Anthony was acquitted of first-degree murder, aggravated manslaughter, and aggravated child abuse stemming from the death of her 2-year-old daughter, Caylee Anthony. The jury convicted Casey of four misdemeanor charges of "lying" to the police, and she was released from custody on July 17, 2011.

Prosecutors alleged that Casey drugged Caylee with chloroform and then suffocated her by placing duct tape over her mouth and nose. The prosecutor alleged that Anthony hid Caylee's body in the trunk of her car before disposing of the body in the woods.

Statements by the jurors following the trial indicated that they concluded that the prosecution failed to establish Casey's guilt beyond a reasonable doubt on the felony counts. Caylee's two years' decomposed body was discovered in a park. There was no DNA or blood or fingerprint evidence linking the body to the killer. As a result, the government relied on circumstantial evidence along with controversial scientific evidence, which some observers dismissed as "junk science."

The government introduced controversial expert evidence that linked the smell in the trunk of Casey's car to the smell of a decomposed body. A "sniffer dog" linked the smell in the trunk to Caylee. Experts also testified that bugs in the trunk were the type of bugs associated with the decomposition of a body. There was additional DNA evidence connecting hair fibers found in the trunk of Casey's car to Caylee. Critics asserted that the mitochondrial DNA pattern could have been from Casey or from her mother or her grandmother or any other relative from the maternal side of her family. An analysis of the computer in the Anthony home indicated that there were eighty-four computer searches for chloroform, a chemical used to render an individual unconscious. The defense dismissed most of this evidence as "fantasy forensics" and as "junk science," and it was called into question following the trial.

There was duct tape over Caylee's skull. The prosecution's theory was that Casey had placed the duct type over Caylee's mouth and nose and suffocated Caylee to death and then disposed of the body. Prosecutors used a video demonstration of an image of Caylee's decomposing duct-taped skull superimposed over a photo of Caylee cheek-to-cheek with her smiling mother. Defense lawyers contended that the demonstration evidence was prejudicial. The judge ruled that the video was necessary to demonstrate that the tape was large enough to cover Caylee's nose and mouth. The jury also heard evidence about a "phantom sticker" that allegedly left residue in the shape of a heart on the duct tape. There was no sticker on the duct tape although prosecutors introduced a sheet of heart stickers found in the Anthony home in an attempt to link Casey to the death.

The testing of the air in the trunk of Casey's automobile was particularly controversial. This was the first time the technique had been used in a criminal trial and involved extracting an air sample with a syringe and comparing it with four hundred chemical compounds identified with decomposing bodies. The prosecution put Arpad Vass, who pioneered the air-sample method, on the stand. The defense presented experts who testified it was impossible to know the vapor that existed in the trunk at the time of the experiment. One expert testified the chemicals found in human remains also are found in the spoiled cheese and salami found in Casey's trunk. Studies of juries in death penalty cases indicate they find scientific evidence presented by the prosecution to be persuasive. As a juror, would you have been persuaded by the scientific tests performed on the air in the trunk of Casey's car or by the other scientific evidence introduced by the prosecution?

■ JUDICIALLY ACCEPTED SCIENTIFIC TESTS

The validity of various well-established scientific tests, as noted above, are accepted without challenge. Courts may take judicial notice of the validity of the tests. The opposing party nonetheless may challenge the accuracy of the equipment or the procedures used by the analyst. The next several sections discuss several of the tests.

Fingerprints

Fingerprint evidence has a long history, although the reliability of this technique of identification was not always fully accepted. Fingerprinting was first accepted in 1901 when the New York City Civil Service Commission employed fingerprints to keep track of applicants for city employment. The FBI established a centralized fingerprint file, which, in 1924, was formally named the National Crime Information Center.

Fingerprints are employed in the criminal justice system for two primary purposes: first, to identify the name and pertinent details of a detainee, and second, to link an individual to a criminal offense by matching his or her fingerprints with the fingerprints found at the crime scene or found on evidentiary items in the case, such as a firearm or bag used to carry one.

Fingerprints ordinarily are taken as a regular part of the booking procedure. An individual has no constitutional right to avoid the taking of a properly administered fingerprint, and a court may order an individual to submit to fingerprinting. Fingerprints are not considered to be in violation of the Fifth Amendment right against self-incrimination. They are not verbal expressions and do not violate the right to privacy because of their brief and nonintrusive character and the limited information that is revealed. The fingerprints of an individual arrested by the police may be taken without reasonable suspicion or probable cause.

In a criminal case, the foundation for fingerprints found at the crime scene or on a firearm is laid by the testimony of the police officer who obtained the fingerprints. A qualified expert would compare the fingerprints to the fingerprints of the defendant. There is no legal requirement that the police dust for fingerprint evidence or retain the fingerprint evidence.

Fingerprint evidence is useful because fingerprints are unique to each individual, remain constant throughout a lifetime, and possess physical characteristics that make them easy to analyze and distinguish from one another. It is noted that there is no recorded case in which different individuals have been shown to have identical fingerprints. The work of fingerprint comparison in most instances may be completed through computers although an analyst is required to interpret the results.

A fingerprint is an impression left by the "friction ridges" of the human finger. A fingerprint typically is based on the last joint of fingers and thumbs. Fingerprint impressions may be left on a surface by secretions of sweat from the eccrine glands or may be obtained by ink transferred on the skin to a fingerprint card.

A typical fingerprint may have as many as 150 ridge characteristics. A match in most instances is based on between 8 and 16 ridge patterns although there is no set number of patterns that must be compared for a match to be declared.

There are four basic types of fingerprints:

Exemplar prints. Prints intentionally collected following an arrest for a suspected criminal offense.

Latent prints. Chance or accidental impressions not visible to the naked eye left on a surface.

Patent prints. Impressions visible to the human eye left as a result of the transfer of material such as flour, wet clay, or blood from a finger onto a surface.

Plastic. An impression left in a material such as wet clay that reflects the shape of the friction ridge.

The process of recovering prints is exacting and precise, and the print may be "lifted" onto another surface or recorded in a photograph, or if possible the object with the print may be seized. Investigators typically are cross-examined in an effort to determine whether the prints may have been contaminated or tainted by human error. Courts also have recognized palm prints and footprint identification.

Blood Alcohol

Blood alcohol testing is used when an individual is arrested and charged with driving with an unlawful blood alcohol level (DUBAL). DUBAL laws hold individuals liable for driving while their blood alcohol level was too high, despite the fact that their driving may be unaffected. Every state gradually lowered the required blood alcohol level from 0.10 in the bloodstream in the 1960s to 0.08 in the 1990s. States typically impose harsher punishment on individuals with higher blood alcohol levels, typically between 0.15 and 0.20 percent.

Individuals also may be charged with driving while intoxicated (DWI), which prohibits an individual from driving an automobile while affected by alcohol. In the 1970s, DWI was expanded to punish driving under the influence (DUI), which punishes driving under the influence of liquor or narcotics. Individuals may be convicted of these offenses based on testimony that their driving was impacted by alcohol or narcotics. Individuals also may be charged with drunk and disorderly conduct in public. Alcohol testing also may be undertaken in circumstances in which an individual's intoxication has a bearing on criminal intent.

The United States Supreme Court has upheld the constitutionality of implied consent laws that provide that individuals who obtain a driver's license impliedly have consented to the administration of a urine or blood test or breathalyzer to determine their blood alcohol content. The Court further held that it does not violate the Fifth

Amendment right against self-incrimination for a state to provide that a refusal to submit to a blood test under the implied consent law will result in suspension of an individual's driver's license and that a refusal to submit to a blood test may be introduced as evidence of the individual's guilt of DUBAL or other criminal offenses. In some states, refusal to take a test to determine your blood alcohol content also may result in a fine and a brief jail term (*South Dakota v. Neville*, 459 U.S. 58 [1983]). In 2013, in *Missouri v. McNeely*, the Supreme Court held that a nonconsensual drawing of blood ordinarily requires a warrant (*Missouri v. McNeely*, 569 U.S. ___ [2013]).

Alcohol is absorbed into the body's blood and circulation system and distributed throughout the body, and it is possible to estimate the total alcohol content of the body based on a small sample of blood. The testing for alcohol must follow strict requirements to guard against contamination of the needle by the alcohol swab, guard against deterioration of the sample, and prevent the intermingling of drug samples. Testing for alcohol also may be undertaken by a breathalyzer.

Blood Typing

Forensic serology is relied on to answer various questions in a criminal investigation. The initial question at a crime scene is whether the substance is blood and whether the blood is from a human being or from an animal. The next issue is the blood type of the blood to determine if this matches the blood type of the suspect. DNA analysis (see below) can be used to determine conclusively whether the DNA drawn from the blood matches a suspect although this analysis can be time-consuming and expensive.

Blood typing is performed to categorize human blood. The ABO system is relied on by most analysts and categorizes blood as either A (roughly 41 percent of the U.S. population), B (10 percent of the U.S. population), AB (4 percent of the U.S. population), or O (45 percent of the U.S. population). Two other categorization systems are used by analysts, the Rh and MN systems.

All of these systems are limited to excluding individuals who do not possess the blood type. They cannot, as DNA analysis can, definitively determine that an individual committed a crime even if he or she possesses the blood type found at the crime scene. Blood evidence nonetheless can be of value. In a prosecution for kidnapping and child abuse, blood evidence on the victim's clothing matched the defendant's blood type, and an expert witness concluded there was a high probability it came from the defendant. DNA analysis of semen on the victim's shirt matched the defendant's DNA (*California v. Funston*, 2002 Cal. App. Unpub. Lexis 3513 [2002]).

DNA

DNA or deoxyribonucleic acid is a molecule that stores an individual's genetic code. An individual exhibits the same unique genetic code in each cell whether the cell is extracted from bones, teeth, saliva, semen, hair, or blood. Every individual has a distinct genetic code (other than genetic twins).

DNA analysis can be compared to looking at the pages in a book. You can examine the first word in the first sentence on four pages of a book (a suspect's DNA) and compare this to the first word in the first sentence on four pages of another book (DNA at the crime scene). In the event both patterns are the same, there is a genetic "match." At trial, the expert in DNA expresses this match in statistical terms and, for example, will testify that only 0.0015 percent of the population, or one in one hundred thousand people, will exhibit such a match. On the other hand, the DNA may exclude a match in those instances in which the patterns are not the same. DNA may be obtained from the saliva on a stamp, cigarette, or bite mark; fluids excreted in a rape; hair on a pillow; sweat from a glove; or blood at a crime scene.

DNA has a number of applications in the criminal process:

Detection. DNA may be used to connect an individual to a criminal act.

Investigation. DNA includes or excludes an individual as a suspect.

Guilt or innocence. DNA may establish guilt or innocence at trial. Individuals who have been convicted may discover DNA evidence that establishes their innocence. DNA is not always a "magic bullet" that will reliably indicate whether an individual is guilty or innocent.

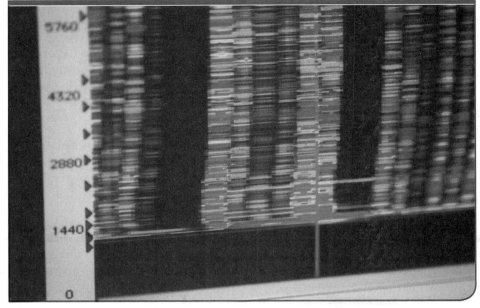

PHOTO 7.3

DNA is an important advance in criminal investigation. Each individual other than identical twins has a unique DNA which makes DNA analysis a powerful tool for identifying the perpetrators of crimes.

Contamination. A defendant's DNA sample may be mixed up with another individual's DNA. DNA also may deteriorate as a result of a failure to safeguard the sample.

Laboratory procedures. The laboratory may make a mistake in analysis or in calculating statistical probabilities.

Significance. There may be numerous explanations for the presence of a suspect's DNA at the crime scene, and this may lead to the prosecution and possible conviction of an innocent individual. In other instances, a jury may become so confused about DNA evidence that they either fail to take into account or exaggerate its significance.

Relevancy. DNA is not always relevant to the issue in a case. For instance, in a rape prosecution, the issue may be whether there was consent rather than whether the defendant was the perpetrator.

The West Virginia Supreme Court was the first court to accept DNA analysis. The court in affirming a rape conviction noted that the reliability of DNA tests is generally accepted. DNA could be challenged by calling into question the procedures used to collect, preserve, and analyze the DNA (*State v. Woodall*, 385 S.E.235 [W.V.A. 1989]). Three years later, the Second Circuit Court of Appeals in *United States v. Jakobetz* took the first step toward admissibility of DNA evidence in federal courts by holding that the "general theories of genetics which support DNA profiling are unanimously accepted within the scientific community" (*United States v. Jakobetz*, 95 F.2d 784 [2nd Cir. 1992]).

DNA now is considered admissible by virtually every state and federal court. This evidence has been excluded only when the DNA sample has been contaminated or when there has been a failure to follow accepted procedures. In 2006, the U.S. Supreme Court fully embraced DNA evidence in *House v. Bell* when it ruled that Paul Gregory House was entitled to a new trial in federal court based in large part on DNA evidence that was not available at the time of his 1985 trial, which, together with other evidence, supported his "actual innocence." The Supreme Court majority found that the "central forensic proof connecting House to the crime—the blood and the semen—has been called into question [by the DNA], and House has put forward substantial evidence pointing to a different suspect. Accordingly, and although the issue is close, we conclude that this is the rare case where—had the jury heard all the conflicting testimony—it is more likely than not that no reasonable juror viewing the record as a whole would lack reasonable doubt" (*House v. Bell*, 547 U.S. 518 [2006]).

In 2009, in *District Attorney's Office v. Osborne*, the United States Supreme Court held that William G. Osborne, who had been convicted in 1994 of kidnapping and sexual assault, did not have a right under the Due Process

Clause of the U.S. Constitution to be given access to evidence for the purpose of DNA testing. Justice John G. Roberts recognized that DNA possessed an "unparalleled ability" to exonerate the innocent and to convict the guilty but stressed that the policy of permitting inmates following their conviction to gain access to DNA testing was a matter for the state legislatures. Alaska law did not leave Osborne without a remedy. Alaska permits inmates to obtain access to, or to test, any type of newly discovered or newly available evidence that the petitioner is able to demonstrate by "clear and convincing evidence" will establish his or her innocence (*District Attorney's Office v. Osborne*, 557 U.S. 52 [2009]). Other state statutes specifically provide convicted felons with access to DNA while prohibiting access to DNA by certain categories of felons, such as offenders who have confessed to a crime. Massachusetts and Oklahoma along with Alaska do not have laws that specifically address postconviction DNA testing although Alabama provides access to DNA evidence to individuals on death row.

All states and the federal government collect DNA from felons. Judgments upholding this practice have relied on offenders' diminished expectations of privacy. In the leading case of *United States v. Kincade*, six judges of the Ninth Circuit Court of Appeals sitting *en banc* affirmed the constitutionality of the mandatory extraction of blood for DNA analysis from a recently released armed robber who was under supervised release and receiving treatment in a residential drug program. Five judges reasoned that the limited expectation of privacy of individuals who have committed a "qualifying offense" under the DNA Analysis Backlog Elimination Act is clearly outweighed by the "overwhelming interest" in ensuring that individuals on conditional release comply with the conditions of their supervision and do not engage in further criminal activity (*United States v. Kincade*, 379 F.3d 813 [9th Cir. 2004]).

In 2013, in *Maryland v. King*, the U.S. Supreme Court held that the police may take DNA samples from people arrested and not yet prosecuted for serious crimes. The federal government and twenty-eight states authorize the collection of DNA from arrestees for felonies. Justice Anthony Kennedy reasoned that "[w]hen officers make an arrest supported by probable cause to hold for a serious offense and they bring the suspect to the station to be detained in custody . . . taking and analyzing a cheek swab of the arrestee's DNA is, like fingerprinting and photographing, a legitimate police booking procedure that is reasonable under the Fourth Amendment. . . . [T]here can be little reason to question 'the . . . interest of the government in knowing for an absolute certainty the identity of the person arrested, in knowing whether he is wanted elsewhere, and in ensuring his identification in the event he flees prosecution'" (*Maryland v. King*, 569 U.S. ___ [2014]).

There are various methods of DNA testing that commonly are used. Two of the most widely used are Restriction Fragment Length Polymorphism (RFLP) and Polymerase Chain Reaction (PCR). The primary threats to DNA analysis are contamination of a sample by bacteria or by laboratory equipment. The most controversial aspect of DNA analysis is the estimation of the probability that the DNA belongs to the defendant. In those instances in which the database is limited to a small insular group such as a Native American tribe, the probability that the DNA is from the defendant appears much greater than when a database of a larger population is employed. Jurors also are felt to be overly influenced by the mathematical probabilities.

Analysis of Controlled Substances

The increasing number of arrests for narcotics possession and trafficking has led forensics laboratories to devote significant resources to the chemical analysis of drugs seized by federal and state law enforcement.

Laboratories frequently test a sample or a percentage of the narcotics when confronted with a large quantity of drugs. The three primary tests are listed below.

Ultraviolet spectrophotometry. This test analyzes the reaction of a substance to ultraviolet (UV) and infrared (IR) light. A spectrophotometry machine measures how the sample reflects or absorbs these rays, which provides a sense of the composition of the material.

Microcrystalline test. A drop of the material is added to a chemical on a slide. A crystal begins to form. Each drug has a specific crystal pattern when viewed under a polarized light microscope.

Gas chromatography/mass spectrometry. A small amount of the substance is injected into the gas chromatograph. The sample is funneled into a mass spectrometer and is hit with an electron beam and breaks apart. The breaking apart of the substance helps to identify the type of substance.

Ballistics

Ballistics analysis is used for firearms analysis. The question is whether a specific bullet was fired from a specific firearm. Pistols, rifles, automatic assault rifles, machine guns, and submachine gun weapons all are termed rifled firearms. The barrels of these weapons leave scratches or striations on the bullets fired from the firearm. There are certain striations found in all guns of a particular type, which are termed "class characteristics." Other "individual characteristics" are specific to an individual firearm.

The primary purpose of the analysis is to identify the type of firearm that fired a bullet. A 9-mm bullet cannot be fired from a 10-mm firearm. The testing of several bullets may reveal whether more than a single firearm was involved.

Forensic experts also may be asked to determine the firing distance. Distances between the muzzle and the target may be measured through an examination of gunpowder residue. This analysis can be important in situations in which an individual is claimed to have committed suicide or when a defendant claims to have acted in self-defense. An individual's hands also may be examined for gunpowder residue to determine whether he or she recently fired a weapon.

The more sophisticated aspect of ballistics analysis involves matching a test bullet fired from a rifled firearm seized from a suspect with a bullet found at the crime scene to determine whether the bullet was fired from the weapon. The manufacturing process along with wear and tear from the use of a firearm can cause grooves specific to a particular firearm. Sophisticated criminals may attempt to modify a firearm's striations by modifying or changing a rifle or scrubbing the barrel. A gun recovered some time after the crime for which it was used poses a challenge because the striations may have changed as a result of the gun having been fired a number of times.

A third aspect of ballistics analysis involves matching the marks on the cartridge case of a bullet to marks in the chamber and breech of a firearm. This is a somewhat easier analysis because cartridge case marks are less likely to deteriorate although bullets may be mangled on impact, making marks difficult to analyze. The examiner will test fire a bullet into a "bullet trap" and match the characteristics of the test-fired bullet with the bullet recovered at the crime scene.

A weapon that is uncovered will be tested for fingerprints, fibers, blood, samples of skin, and other evidence that may link the firearm to the shooter. An analysis of gunpowder burns found on clothing or on skin may allow a determination of the distance from which a gun was fired. Powder burns also may allow a determination whether an individual recently fired a weapon.

A number of reputable scientific studies and federal court opinions have called the reliability of ballistics testing into doubt. After discussing this evidence, a federal district court in New Mexico placed strict limits on an expert's testimony on the match between a bullet and a firearm.

> Accordingly, Mr. [Ron G.] Nichols will be permitted to give to the jury his expert opinion that there is a match between the .30-.30 caliber rifle recovered from the abandoned house and the bullet believed to have killed Mr. [Jimmy S. "Bo"] Chunn. However, because of the limitations on the reliability of firearms identification evidence discussed above, Mr. Nichols will not be permitted to testify that his methodology allows him to reach this conclusion as a matter of scientific certainty. Mr. Nichols also will not be allowed to testify that he can conclude that there is a match to the exclusion, either practical or absolute, of all other guns. He may only testify that, in his opinion, the bullet came from the suspect rifle to within a reasonable degree of certainty in the firearms examination field. (*United States v. Taylor*, 663 F.Supp.2d 1179 [D.N.M. 2009])

■ OTHER JUDICIALLY RECOGNIZED TESTS

There are a number of other scientific tests.

Toxicology. Toxicology tests are used for the identification of poisonous substances.

Breathalyzer. A machine analyzes the breath to determine the alcohol content of the blood. The foundation for admission of the test result requires that the equipment has been properly determined to be in working order and the test must be properly administered.

Urine tests. Courts admit the results of urine tests to measure blood alcohol content or drug metabolites.

Hair analysis. Radioimmunoassay hair analysis is admissible to determine drug use so long as proper procedures are followed.

Horizontal gaze nystagmus. Police employ this test in the field to determine whether there is probable cause to arrest an individual driving under the influence of alcohol. The test is based on the inability of the eye to maintain "visual fixation."

Vehicle speed detection. The speed of an automobile may be measured by radar.

Spectrographic voice identification. Spectrographic voice identification or voice prints may be introduced to link an individual to a voice recording although a significant number of courts view this technique as unreliable.

■ TESTS NOT ACCEPTED BY THE COURTS

Polygraph

Polygraphs or lie detector tests are premised on the understanding that an individual who "lies" will exhibit physiological responses in blood pressure, heart rate, and respiration. The **polygraph** is based on the assumption that lying leads to internal conflict that causes fear and anxiety that, in turn, cause a measurable physical reaction.

There are two primary approaches to polygraph tests. The "relevant-irrelevant" test compares an individual's truthful responses to simple and straightforward (irrelevant) questions with his or her response to questions relevant to the investigation (relevant). If the physiological response is the same, then the subject is determined to be telling the truth. If the responses differ, then the individual is considered to be untruthful. In the control question method, a general question about illegal activity ("Have you ever committed a robbery?") is paired with questions on the criminal event in question. Innocent individuals are thought to be more aroused by the control questions than by the relevant questions. The opposite is true of the guilty.

In *Frye v. United States* in 1923, the District of Columbia Court of Appeals held that the results of polygraph testing lacked a sound scientific basis and were inadmissible in evidence. The Court held that that polygraph testing had "not yet gained such standing and scientific recognition among physiological and psychological authorities." There also can be no reference to whether an individual agreed to take or refused to take a polygraph test (*Frye v. United States*, 293 F. 1013 [D.C. Cir. 1923]). Twenty-seven states adhere to the precedent in *Frye* and exclude polygraph results, offers to take a polygraph, and refusal to take a polygraph from evidence on the grounds that the test is unreliable and has not been accepted in the scientific community. Another group of states authorize the parties to stipulate or agree that the results of polygraph tests are admissible in evidence in criminal trials. A handful of states, along with an increasing number of federal courts, leave to the trial court judge the decision whether to admit polygraph evidence. The primary objection to the use of polygraph evidence at trial is that potential for prejudice to the trial outweighs its evidentiary value (*Lee v. Martinez*, 96 P.3d 291 [N.M. 2004]).

In *United States v. Scheffer*, the United States Supreme Court held Military Rule of Evidence 707's exclusion of polygraph evidence did not violate individuals' constitutional right to offer a criminal defense. Military Rule of Evidence 707 guaranteed that only reliable evidence would be introduced at trial and protected the right of the jurors to determine the credibility of a witness for themselves without being influenced by the alleged "scientific results" of a polygraph exam. *Scheffer* in upholding the military court's exclusion of the results of polygraph exams held that individuals do not possess a constitutional right to have the results of polygraph evidence introduced at trial. The case did not prohibit a federal judge from allowing the introduction of this type of evidence (*United States v. Scheffer*, 523 U.S. 303 [1998]).

In 2002, the National Research Council of the National Academy of Sciences issued a report concluding there was weak scientific support for the accuracy of polygraphs.

CRIMINAL EVIDENCE AND PUBLIC POLICY

In 2013, a chemist for a Boston state drug laboratory was indicted on twenty-seven counts for obstructing justice, tampering with evidence, perjury, and other related charges based on her mishandling of tens of thousands of cases and defendants over a nine-year period. "Little Annie" Dookhan was accused of faking test results, contaminating drug samples, and forging signatures of co-workers on lab reports. This led to the closing of the lab, the release of hundreds of drug offenders, and the resignation of various criminal justice officials. The laboratory was run by a police sergeant who lacked a scientific background, lacked written procedures, did not clean instruments, allowed unrestricted access to the drug vault, and did not monitor the work of technicians.

A 2013 review of New York City's handling of rape cases found that in more than eight hundred rape cases over a ten-year period, analysts failed to detect the DNA evidence in twenty-six cases, and DNA evidence was commingled with DNA evidence from other cases.

The Saint Paul, Minnesota, police department crime laboratory suspended its drug and fingerprint analysis after an investigation disclosed significant problems, including dirty equipment, a lack of written procedures, inaccurate testing, and a lack of scientific expertise. Problems earlier were found with drug testing at Texas laboratories.

The Nassau County crime lab was closed in February 2011 after serious problems emerged with drug analysis. Even the famed FBI crime laboratory has experienced problems in explosives, DNA, comparative bullet-lead analysis, and hair microscopy.

The problems with these crime laboratories pale in comparison to the issues with the North Carolina crime laboratory. An independent examination found 230 cases over a sixteen-year period in which analysts withheld or misrepresented evidence, including three cases resulting in an execution. An individual was exonerated after serving sixteen years for murder. The Raleigh *News & Observer* found training materials advising analysts how to tailor their testimony to improve conviction rates and found evidence that analysts were distorting the results of their analysis.

These types of scandals first emerged in 1993 when a West Virginia forensic scientist was found to have falsified results in 134 cases over a ten-year period. This level of corruption was matched by an Oklahoma City police department analyst who was referred to as "Black Magic" because of her ability to help convict defendants through her laboratory results. She testified as an expert in twenty-three death penalty cases, including twelve inmates who later were executed.

There is no way to know how many fraudulent laboratory results or failures to test DNA or other evidence have resulted in false convictions. The integrity of laboratories is vital because in most cases defendants cannot afford to hire experts and crime laboratories become crucial in the criminal process.

In 2009, the National Academy of Sciences found serious problems with crime laboratories. Control and supervision over the laboratories is complicated by the fact that there are hundreds of crime laboratories located in cities, counties, and states with varying standards and procedures. Analysts often are overworked and lack academic training, and labs are underfunded and lack modern equipment. There is too much confidence placed by criminal justice officials in certain areas of analysis that have yet to be proven reliable.

One reform proposal is that laboratories should be independent and should not be administered by police departments or by prosecutor's offices. Only accredited laboratories that are subject to periodic inspection by outside examiners should be qualified to submit results in criminal cases, and only laboratories meeting professional standards should receive federal funding.

■ EXPERIMENTS

The results of experiments are admissible to assist the trier of fact to resolve an issue in the trial. The threshold issue is whether the conditions of the experiment are "substantially similar" to the circumstances surrounding the original event. The experiment also must be conducted by qualified experts employing procedures and methods determined to be reliable by the judge. An experiment because of the power of visual representations also may be considered overly prejudicial or involve undue delay and confusion and excluded from evidence. An **experiment** may be undertaken during trial inside the courtroom or outside the courtroom. Experiments conducted outside of the courtroom often are videotaped and shown to the jury in court.

A well-known example of an experiment outside the courtroom involves efforts to establish whether President John F. Kennedy could have been assassinated by a single sniper.

Another example involved Dr. Henry Lee, a well-known forensic scientist known for his experiments. He testified on behalf of William Kennedy Smith who was charged with the rape of a woman on the Kennedy family estate. Dr. Lee, to establish the alleged victim consented to sex on the lawn, testified there were none of the expected grass stains on the woman's pantyhose. He illustrated his point by rubbing a grass-stained handkerchief in the grass of his own yard. Critics pointed out the handkerchief was composed of different fabric than the victim's dress and that the conditions were dissimilar.

Murray Wayne Burr was found murdered in his home in August 2004. In 2007, Deputy Keith Pikett, a police officer involved with training bloodhounds since 1989, conducted a "dog-scent" lineup using three bloodhounds: Quincy, James Bond, and Clue. Pikett prescented the dogs with scent samples obtained from the clothing the victim was wearing at the time of his death. Each dog then walked by a line of six paint cans spaced ten paces apart, one of which contained a scent sample from the defendant, Richard Lynn Winfrey.

All three dogs responded to can number four containing Winfrey's scent sample. Pikett concluded the defendant's scent was on the victim's clothing. He testified on cross-examination that "an alert only established some relationship between the scent and objects and that scent detection does not necessarily indicate the defendant was at the murder scene when the scent was transferred and the transfer of a scent may occur with casual contact." Pikett for these reasons conceded that an individual could not be convicted based on dog scent alone. Concluding that the evidence was legally and factually sufficient, the court of appeals specifically found (1) Deputy Pikett's canine-scent testimony provided direct evidence placing the appellant in direct contact with Burr's clothing;

and (2) the jury could have reasonably concluded that the appellant was in Burr's house at the time of the murder and that he had significant physical contact with Burr. There was no eyewitness who saw the defendant at the crime scene, and his fingerprints, footprints, hair, and DNA did not match those found at the crime scene. The Texas appellate court noted:

Cases involving the use of dogs, usually bloodhounds, to track humans are abundant and the law is well settled in regards to admissibility of such evidence with only a minority of courts outright rejecting bloodhound evidence. . . . Law-enforcement personnel have long utilized canines in crime management. For example, dogs have been employed for detecting narcotics and explosives, for tracking trails, in search-and-rescue operations, for locating cadavers, and for discriminating between scents for identification purposes. In thousands of cases, canines and their handlers have performed with distinction. Despite this success, we acknowledge the invariable truth . . . that "[t]he infallible dog, however, is a creature of legal fiction."

As a judge, would you allow the jury to hear Pikett's expert testimony? See *Winfrey v. State* (323 S.W.3d 875 [Tex. App. 2010]).

You can learn what the court decided by referring to the study site, **http://study.sagepub.com/lippmance.**

■ CASE ANALYSIS

In *State v. Guilbert*, the Connecticut Supreme Court held that an expert witness was admissible on the reliability of eyewitness identification.

May an expert witness testify on the reliability of eyewitness testimony?

State v. Guilbert, 206 Conn. 218 (Conn. 2012)

The jury found the defendant, Brady Guilbert, guilty of capital felony, two counts of murder and assault in the first degree. The trial court rendered judgments in accordance with the jury verdicts and sentenced the defendant to a term of life imprisonment without the possibility of release, plus twenty years. On appeal, the defendant . . . contends that the trial court improperly precluded him from presenting expert testimony on the fallibility of eyewitness identification testimony.

At approximately 11:30 p.m. on October 8, 2004, Cedric Williams and Terry Ross arrived at a bar in New London known as Ernie's Café (bar). Before arriving at the bar, Ross had parked his Volvo station wagon in a nearby municipal parking lot. At approximately 11:45 p.m., William Robinson arrived at the bar. About one hour later, as Robinson walked to the restroom, he was shot in the face and suffered a life-threatening wound. . . .

(Continued)

(Continued)

At approximately 12:51 a.m., the New London police department received a 911 call about a shooting at the intersection of Hope and Hempstead Streets in New London. Police officers responding to the call found Ross' Volvo station wagon crashed into a tree. Ross and Williams were inside the vehicle, and both had been shot in the head. Williams was pronounced dead at the scene and Ross was taken to Lawrence Memorial Hospital in New London, where he was pronounced dead. An examiner with the state forensic science laboratory ultimately determined that Ross and Williams had been shot with the gun that had been used to shoot Robinson.

Detective Keith Crandall and Officer George Potts of the New London police department visited Robinson at Rhode Island Hospital. When Potts asked Robinson who had shot him, Robinson responded . . . "Fats did it." Potts and Crandall then showed Robinson several photographic arrays, and Robinson identified the defendant as the person who had shot him. Robinson gave a statement to Crandall indicating that he had known the defendant "for a while" and had "had words" with him "a couple of months" earlier. . . . Crandall prepared a written statement, and Robinson signed it. At trial, Robinson denied knowing who had shot him, denied having signed the statement, and denied that the reason why he had picked the defendant's photograph from the array was that the defendant had shot him.

Nine days after the shooting, Lashon Baldwin saw the defendant's photograph in a newspaper and gave a statement to the New London police about the incident at the intersection of Hope and Hempstead Streets. . . . Baldwin recognized the defendant and knew him as "Fats" because she had seen him as a "regular customer" in a donut shop where she had worked for more than one and one-half years. . . . [Jackie] Gomez gave a statement to the police nine days after the shooting. . . . Gomez knew the defendant because they previously had lived together for "quite some time. . . ." Ten days after the shootings, Scott Lang, who had been at the bar when Robinson was shot, saw the defendant's photograph in a newspaper and recognized him as the person who had shot Robinson.

On October 14, 2004, police apprehended the defendant in New York. Thereafter, the defendant was tried before a jury and convicted of two counts of murder in connection with the shooting deaths of Williams and Ross, capital felony arising out of that double killing, and assault in the first degree for the shooting of Robinson.

We agree that expert testimony on eyewitness identification is admissible upon a determination by the trial court that the expert is qualified and the proffered testimony is relevant and will aid the jury. . . . Before trial, defense counsel indicated that he intended to call Charles A. Morgan III as an expert on eyewitness identifications. The state filed a motion to preclude Morgan's testimony on the ground that the reliability of eyewitness identifications is within the knowledge of the average juror. The trial court then conducted an evidentiary hearing on the state's motion at which Morgan proffered testimony that he is a medical

doctor with "specialty training" in psychiatry and that, for the last seventeen years, he has spent 50 percent of his time researching how stress affects thought processes and memory.

Although Morgan observed that, if an eyewitness is familiar with a person, the eyewitness' identification of that person is likely to be more accurate, he explained that an identification's accuracy may be adversely affected by such factors as the length of time during which the eyewitness was able to observe the person, lighting, distance, and whether the eyewitness was paying attention.

Morgan testified that the effect of stress on memory is not a matter of common knowledge. . . . Morgan also testified that studies have shown that most jurors mistakenly believe that the more confident someone is of an identification, the more likely the identification is to be accurate.

At the conclusion of the hearing, the trial court granted the state's motion to preclude Morgan's testimony. . . . Morgan's study involving the deleterious effects of stress on the memories of military personnel in an interrogation setting did not meet the standard for the admission of scientific evidence. . . . The court seemed to find that Morgan's theory had not been sufficiently tested, had no known or potential rate of error, lacked consistent standards, and was not generally accepted in the scientific community. The court also appeared to conclude that Morgan's general opinions about the effects of stress on memory, the lack of a correlation between confidence and accuracy of identifications, and the risk of retrofitting were all inadmissible because these matters generally were within the common knowledge of jurors. . . . Ultimately, the trial court instructed the jury that stress and the receipt of postevent information can reduce the accuracy of an eyewitness identification and that confidence often is not a reliable indicator of accuracy.

"This court recently articulated the test for the admission of expert testimony, which is deeply rooted in common law. Expert testimony should be admitted when: (1) the witness has a special skill or knowledge directly applicable to a matter in issue, (2) that skill or knowledge is not common to the average person, and (3) the testimony would be helpful to the court or jury in considering the issues. . . . In other words, [i]n order to render an expert opinion the witness must be qualified to do so and there must be a factual basis for the opinion. . . .

"Beyond these general requirements regarding the admissibility of expert testimony, [t]here is a further hurdle to the admissibility of expert testimony when that testimony is based on . . . scientific [evidence]. In those situations, the scientific evidence that forms the basis for the expert's opinion must undergo a validity assessment to ensure reliability. . . .

"[W]e set forth . . . a number of different factors, nonexclusive and whose application to a particular set of circumstances could vary, as relevant in the determination of the threshold admissibility of scientific evidence. . . . In particular, we recognized the following considerations: general acceptance in the relevant scientific community; whether the methodology underlying the scientific evidence has been tested and subjected to peer review; the known or potential rate of error; the prestige and background of the expert witness supporting the evidence; the extent to which the technique at issue relies [on] subjective judgments made by the expert rather than on objectively verifiable criteria; whether the expert can present and explain the data and methodology underlying the testimony in a manner that assists the jury in drawing conclusions therefrom; and whether the technique or methodology was developed solely for purposes of litigation. . . .

"We stated that the proposed scientific testimony must be demonstrably relevant to the facts of the particular case in which it is offered, and not simply be valid in the abstract. . . ."

We now conclude that . . . [there is] widespread judicial recognition that eyewitness [I]dentifications are potentially unreliable in a variety of ways unknown to the average juror. This broad based judicial recognition [I]acks a near perfect scientific consensus. The extensive and comprehensive scientific research, as reflected in hundreds of peer reviewed studies and meta-analyses, convincingly demonstrates the fallibility of eyewitness identification testimony and pinpoints an array of variables that are most likely to lead to a mistaken identification. "[T]he scientific evidence . . . is both reliable and useful." . . . "Experimental methods and findings have been tested and retested, subjected to scientific scrutiny through peer-reviewed journals, evaluated through the lens of meta-analyses, and replicated at times in real-world settings. . . . [C]onsensus exists among the experts . . . within the . . . research community." . . . "[T]he science abundantly demonstrates the many vagaries of memory encoding, storage and retrieval; the malleability of memory; the contaminating effects of extrinsic information; the influence of police interview techniques and identification procedures; and the many other factors that bear on the reliability of eyewitness identifications." Courts across the country now accept that (1) there is at best a weak correlation between a witness' confidence in his or her identification and its accuracy, (2) the reliability of an identification can be diminished by a witness' focus on a weapon, (3) high stress at the time of observation may render a witness less able to retain an accurate perception and memory of the observed events, (4) cross-racial identifications are considerably less accurate than same race identifications, (5) a person's memory diminishes rapidly over a period of hours rather than days or weeks, (6) identifications are likely to be less reliable in the absence of a double-blind, sequential identification procedure, (7) witnesses are prone to develop unwarranted confidence in their identifications if they are privy to postevent or postidentification information about the event or the identification, and (8) the accuracy of an eyewitness identification may be undermined by unconscious transference, which occurs when a person seen in one context is confused with a person seen in another. This list is not exhaustive; courts have permitted expert testimony on other factors deemed to affect the accuracy of eyewitness identification testimony.

Although these findings are widely accepted by scientists, they are largely unfamiliar to the average person, and, in fact, many of the findings are counterintuitive. For example, people often believe that the more confident an eyewitness is in an identification, the more likely the identification is to be accurate. Similarly, the average person is likely to believe that eyewitnesses held at gunpoint or otherwise placed in fear are likely to have been acutely observant and therefore more accurate in their identifications. Most people also tend to think that cross-racial identifications are no less likely to be accurate than same race identifications. Yet none of these beliefs is true. Indeed, laypersons commonly are unaware of the effect of the other aforementioned factors, including the rate at which memory fades, the influence of postevent or postidentification information, the phenomenon of unconscious transference, and the risks inherent in the use by police of identification procedures that are not double-blind and sequential. Moreover, although there is little if any correlation between confidence and accuracy, an eyewitness' confidence "is the most powerful single determinant of whether . . . observers . . . will believe that the eyewitness made an accurate identification." . . .

As a result of this strong scientific consensus, federal and state courts around the country have recognized that the methods traditionally employed for alerting juries to the fallibility of eyewitness identifications—cross-examination, closing argument and generalized jury instructions on the subject—frequently are not adequate to inform them of the factors affecting the reliability of such identifications.

Cross-examination, the most common method, often is not as effective as expert testimony at identifying the weaknesses of eyewitness identification testimony because cross-examination is far better at exposing lies than at countering sincere but mistaken beliefs. An eyewitness who expresses confidence in the accuracy of his or her identification may of course believe sincerely that the identification is accurate. Furthermore, although cross-examination may expose the *existence* of factors that undermine the accuracy of eyewitness identifications, it cannot effectively educate the jury about the *import* of these factors. "Thus, while skillful cross-examination may succeed in exposing obvious inconsistencies in an [eyewitness'] account, because nothing is obvious about the psychology of eyewitness identification and most people's intuitions on the subject of identification are wrong . . . some circumstances undoubtedly call for more than mere cross-examination of the eyewitness."

Defense counsel's closing argument to the jury that an eyewitness identification is unreliable also is an inadequate substitute for expert testimony. In the absence of evidentiary support, such an argument is likely to be viewed as little more than partisan rhetoric. This is especially true if the argument relates to a factor that is counterintuitive.

Finally, research has revealed that jury instructions that direct jurors in broad terms to exercise caution in evaluating eyewitness

(Continued)

(Continued)

identifications are less effective than expert testimony in apprising the jury of the potential unreliability of eyewitness identification testimony. "[Generalized] instructions given at the end of what might be a long and fatiguing trial, and buried in an overall charge by the court, are unlikely to have much effect on the minds of [the jurors]. . . . [Moreover], instructions may come too late to alter [a juror's] opinion of a witness whose testimony might have been heard days before. [Perhaps most important], even the best cautionary instructions tend to touch only generally on the empirical evidence. The judge may explain that certain factors are known to influence perception and memory . . . but will not explain how this occurs or to what extent."

We now recognize that . . . expert testimony on the reliability of eyewitness identifications does not [invade] the province of the jury to determine what weight or effect it wishes to give to eyewitness testimony." An expert should not be permitted to give an opinion about the credibility or accuracy of the eyewitness testimony itself; that determination is solely within the province of the jury. Rather, the expert should be permitted to testify only about factors that generally have an adverse effect on the reliability of eyewitness identifications and are relevant to the specific eyewitness identification at issue.

[M]istaken eyewitness identification testimony is by far the leading cause of wrongful convictions. A highly effective safeguard against this serious and well documented risk is the admission of expert testimony on the reliability of eyewitness identification.

In light of the numerous scientifically valid studies cited previously in this opinion, we also conclude that, as a general matter, competent expert testimony predicated on those studies' findings satisfies the threshold admissibility requirement . . . at least with respect to the following propositions: (1) there is at best a weak correlation between a witness' confidence in his or her identification and the identification's accuracy; (2) the reliability of an identification can be diminished by a witness' focus on a weapon; (3) high stress at the time of observation may render a witness less able to retain an accurate perception and memory of the observed events; (4) cross-racial identifications are considerably less accurate than identifications involving the same race; (5) memory diminishes most rapidly in the hours immediately following an event and less dramatically in the days and weeks thereafter; (6) an identification may be less reliable in the absence of a double-blind, sequential identification procedure; (7) witnesses may develop unwarranted confidence in their identifications if they are privy to postevent or postidentification information about the event or the identification; and (8) the accuracy of an eyewitness identification may be undermined by unconscious transference, which occurs when a person seen in one context is confused with a person seen in another.

CHAPTER SUMMARY

Forensic laboratory analysis is a crucial component of modern criminal investigation. These tests include DNA, blood analysis, fingerprints, and ballistics. Evidence found at the crime scene typically is sent to a crime lab for evaluation. Individual suspects also may be subjected to testing to determine whether there is a match with material seized at the crime scene.

Forensic evidence, though only a small percentage of the evidence introduced at trial, may be vital in the determination of guilt or innocence in cases ranging from drug possession to driving under the influence and sexual molestation. A number of these forensic tests are well established, and judges typically take judicial notice of their scientific reliability. In other instances, a foundation must be laid for admission of the results of the forensic evidence. A key aspect is establishing a chain of custody.

The foundation for the introduction of scientific evidence involves three questions: first, whether the test was scientifically valid; second, whether the equipment was accurate; and third, whether the test was performed in the required fashion by a qualified analyst.

Judges will accept the scientific validity of established scientific tests like fingerprinting by judicial notice. The validity of less well-established tests in most instances is established through expert testimony on *voir dire*.

A fingerprint is an impression left by the "friction ridges" of the human finger. A fingerprint typically is based on the last joint of fingers and thumbs. Fingerprint impressions may be left on a surface by secretions of sweat from the eccrine glands or may be by ink transferred on the skin to a fingerprint card. Fingerprints left at the crime scene are compared to fingerprints on a database to identify the perpetrator of a crime or to identify the name of a suspect in detention.

Blood tests may be used to measure the alcohol concentration in the blood to determine whether an individual is intoxicated. Blood type evidence also is used to determine whether there is a match between blood evidence at the crime scene and the blood type of the alleged perpetrator. DNA analysis provides definitive analysis of the perpetrator's identity.

Various tests are used to identify whether a substance is an unlawful narcotic. Ballistics analysis may be employed for various purposes including whether a bullet was fired from a particular firearm.

Most courts hold that the results of polygraph examinations are inadmissible because they are considered unreliable and are thought to confuse jurors.

Experiments are used to replicate conditions to test the credibility of testimony.

CHAPTER REVIEW QUESTIONS

1. Describe the four steps in marking evidence. What are the two methods of authenticating real evidence?

2. How is the foundation laid at the crime scene for the admission of evidence?

3. Why is the chain of custody of evidence important? How is the chain of evidence established?

4. Are expert witnesses on scientific tests only available to the prosecution?

5. How is evidence relating to fingerprints, the content of blood alcohol, and blood types and ballistics used in criminal trials?

6. What is the role of DNA in criminal trials?

7. Why is polygraph evidence inadmissible in criminal trials?

8. What is the purpose of using experiments at trial? What foundation must be established for the introduction of experiments?

LEGAL TERMINOLOGY

authentication	chain of custody	laying the foundation
ballistics	DNA	polygraph
blood alcohol testing	experiment	scientific evidence
blood typing	fingerprint evidence	

Visit the Student Study Site at **http://study.sagepub.com/lippmance** to access additional study tools, including mobile-friendly eFlashcards and Web quizzes as well as links to SAGE journal articles and hyperlinks for *Criminal Evidence* on the Web.

DOCUMENTARY EVIDENCE, MODELS, MAPS, AND DIAGRAMS

Was the computer printout from the social media site properly authenticated?

We . . . hold that the pages allegedly printed from Griffin's girlfriend's MySpace profile were not properly authenticated . . . and shall, therefore, reverse the judgment of the Court of Special Appeals and remand the case for a new trial.

Griffin was charged in numerous counts with the shooting death, on April 24, 2005, of Darvell Guest at Ferrari's Bar in Perryville, in Cecil County. During his trial, the State sought to introduce Griffin's girlfriend's, Jessica Barber's, MySpace profile to demonstrate that, prior to trial, Ms. Barber had allegedly threatened another witness called by the State. The printed pages contained a MySpace profile in the name of "Sistasouljah," describing a 23-year-old female from Port Deposit, listing her birthday as "10/02/1983" and containing a photograph of an embracing couple. The printed pages also contained the following blurb:

FREE BOOZY!!!! JUST REMEMBER SNITCHES GET STITCHES!! U KNOW WHO YOU ARE!! . . .

The identity of who generated the profile may be confounding, because "a person observing the online profile of a user with whom the observer is unacquainted has no idea whether the profile is legitimate." . . . The concern arises because anyone can create a fictitious account and masquerade under another person's name or can gain access to another's account by obtaining the user's username and password. (*Griffin v. State*, 19 A.3d 415 [Md. App. 2010])

CHAPTER OUTLINE

Introduction	Application of the Best Evidence Rule
Authentication of Documents	Models, Maps, Diagrams, and Charts
Methods of Authenticating Documents	In-Court Exhibitions
Self-Authenticating Documents	Case Analysis
Visual Images	Chapter Summary
Authentication of Objects	Chapter Review Questions
Authentication of Voice Communication	Legal Terminology
The Best Evidence Rule	

■ INTRODUCTION

We have referenced several types of evidence in a trial: *testimonial evidence*, *real evidence* (tangible items, e.g., a knife or a gun), and *scientific evidence* (e.g., DNA). Scientific evidence typically is considered a form of real evidence. In this chapter, we turn our attention to other categories of real evidence. Documentary evidence includes photographic evidence, medical images, and voice identification. The last section of the chapter covers several forms of demonstrative evidence, which includes graphs, maps, charts, and models designed to assist the jury to visualize the facts of the case, such as a crime scene.

TEST YOUR KNOWLEDGE

1. Do you know what is meant by authentication? Why are documents authenticated?

2. Are you aware of the various methods for authenticating documents?

3. Can you explain why some documents are considered self-authenticating?

4. Do you know the requirements for authenticating photographs, and videos from surveillance cameras? What about medical images?

5. Are you aware of the purpose of using models, maps, diagrams, and charts and how to authenticate these items?

6. Can you explain how to authenticate that a defendant made a phone call to the victim?

7. Do you know requirements of the best evidence rule and why it is difficult to determine when the rule applies?

8. Are you aware of the primary requirement that must be met for in-court exhibitions?

party that introduces something must authenticate it
↳ doesn't mean its true

Keep in mind that documentary evidence includes paper documents as well as various electronic and visual depositories of information. Federal Rule 1001(1) provides that "[w]ritings" and "recordings" consist of "letters, words, or numbers, or their equivalent, set down by handwriting, typewriting, printing, photostating, photographing, magnetic impulse, mechanical or electronic recording, or other form of data compilation."

Photographs also are broadly defined. Federal Rule 1001(2) defines photographs as "photographs, X-ray films, video tapes, and motion pictures." Documents may be private documents such as letters, home videos, contracts, wills and diaries, or public documents such as birth, marriage, death, police, or court records.

The chapter is centered on two central concepts of particular relevance to documentary evidence: authentication and the best evidence rule.

→ show that what you're showing in court is what it is → burden is very low – judge has lots of discretion.

■ AUTHENTICATION OF DOCUMENTS

Documents like other types of evidence must be relevant, and a document's probative value must outweigh any resulting prejudice. The party introducing the documentary evidence must authenticate the document. As we have seen in Chapter Six, this simply means that the party that wants to admit the document at trial has the burden of establishing the document is genuine. This does not mean that the document is accurate or truthful. A police arrest report may be inaccurate or falsified although it is an official account of the arrest that appears to have been written by a police officer. A jury also may decide after listening to the adverse party's impeachment of the document that it is a forgery and therefore lacks probative value.

A party introducing the document only is required to meet the low legal standard of introducing sufficient evidence for a judge to conclude that a jury reasonably could conclude that the document is genuine (what the proponent claims it to be). In a bench trial, the standard is whether the judge believes the evidence is genuine.

Why must documents be authenticated? The purpose is to ensure that documents introduced at trial meet a minimum standard of reliability and trustworthiness and are not forgeries. Authentication also guards against a claim based on a document that, in fact, does not exist. A defendant might be falsely accused of threatening the victim in a letter. Authentication establishes that there is a letter to the victim that appears to be signed by the defendant. Once again, authentication establishes that a letter exists; authentication does not establish that the letter contains an unlawful threat or even was written by the defendant.

Keep in mind that under the common law authentication was limited to documents. Federal Rule 901(a) expands authentication and requires that an "item of evidence" as well as a document must be authenticated or shown "the item is what the proponent claims it is." Rule 901 provides a list of possible methods for authenticating documents

PHOTO 8.1 A, B, & C

Three letters containing deadly anthrax were sent in September and October 2001. Experts examined the writing and language in an effort to identify the perpetrator.

FBI/DOJ

and other items of evidence. The rule explicitly states that the methods of authentication included in the rule are "by way of illustration only" and are "not by way of limitation." In other words, a lawyer can propose ways to authenticate a document to the judge at trial that are not listed in Rule 901.

Rule 901. Authenticating or Identifying Evidence

(a) **In General.** To satisfy the requirement of authenticating or identifying an item of evidence, the proponent must produce evidence sufficient to support a finding that the item is what the proponent claims it is.

(b) **Examples.** The following are examples only—not a complete list—of evidence that satisfies the requirement:

(1) **Testimony of a Witness With Knowledge.** Testimony that an item is what it is claimed to be.

(2) **Nonexpert Opinion About Handwriting.** A nonexpert's opinion that handwriting is genuine, based on a familiarity with it that was not acquired for the current litigation.

(3) **Comparison by an Expert Witness or the Trier of Fact.** A comparison with an authenticated specimen by an expert witness or the trier of fact.

(4) **Distinctive Characteristics and the Like.** The appearance, contents, substance, internal patterns, or other distinctive characteristics of the item, taken together with all the circumstances.

(5) **Opinion About a Voice.** An opinion identifying a person's voice—whether heard firsthand or through mechanical or electronic transmission or recording—based on hearing the voice at any time under circumstances that connect it with the alleged speaker.

(6) **Evidence About a Telephone Conversation.** For a telephone conversation, evidence that a call was made to the number assigned at the time to:

(A) a particular person, if circumstances, including self-identification, show that the person answering was the one called; or

(B) a particular business, if the call was made to a business and the call related to business reasonably transacted over the telephone.

(7) **Evidence About Public Records.** Evidence that:

(A) a document was recorded or filed in a public office as authorized by law; or

(B) a purported public record or statement is from the office where items of this kind are kept.

(8) **Evidence About Ancient Documents or Data Compilations.** For a document or data compilation, evidence that it:

(A) is in a condition that creates no suspicion about its authenticity;

(B) was in a place where, if authentic, it would likely be; and

(C) is at least 20 years old when offered.

(9) **Evidence About a Process or System.** Evidence describing a process or system and showing that it produces an accurate result.

(10) **Methods Provided by a Statute or Rule.** Any method of authentication or identification allowed by a federal statute or a rule prescribed by the Supreme Court.

■ METHODS OF AUTHENTICATING DOCUMENTS

The authentication of documents may be accomplished through various ways.

Witness testimony. A witness can testify about the making of the document. A co-conspirator may testify for the prosecution and testify he or she saw the defendant write the ransom note or forge a tax form. → *witness show that its true/theirs*

Lay opinion on handwriting. An individual's handwriting may be authenticated by anyone familiar with the individual's handwriting or by anyone who observed the document being written or signed. A close friend who regularly corresponded with the author of the letter or a family member may authenticate the signature on a letter. Other examples are a coauthor who collaborated on a manuscript. → *someone can say thats my/their handwriting*

Handwriting expert. A handwriting expert or what is termed a forensics document examiner may authenticate handwriting on a document. The expert compares the handwriting on a document with a handwriting exemplar (e.g., sample) of the individual's handwriting. The expert compares the handwriting on a letter written by the defendant with the handwriting on a ransom note, forged check, or forged document. Keep in mind that compelling an accused to produce a handwriting exemplar does not violate the right against self-incrimination, which is limited to testimonial evidence.

A forensic documents examiner may be used to analyze impressions to determine whether they were produced by a particular typewriter, computer printer, or Xerox machine. In older documents, forensic examiners may be asked to analyze the type and age of ink on a document and the composition of the paper, and to detect erasures and modifications of documents.

Unique characteristics. A document may be authenticated by distinctive characteristics such as words, phrases, punctuation, or physical appearance. A letter, for example, may contain information only known to the maker or to a very small group of persons. → *special stamp/symbol*

PHOTO 8.2

The ransom note left in 1996 by the murderer of 6-year-old Jon Benet Ramsey in Boulder, Colorado. Analysts studied the note in an effort to identify the type of individual who may have been responsible for the killing.

[handwritten note in margin:] other party can always question the contents of the document

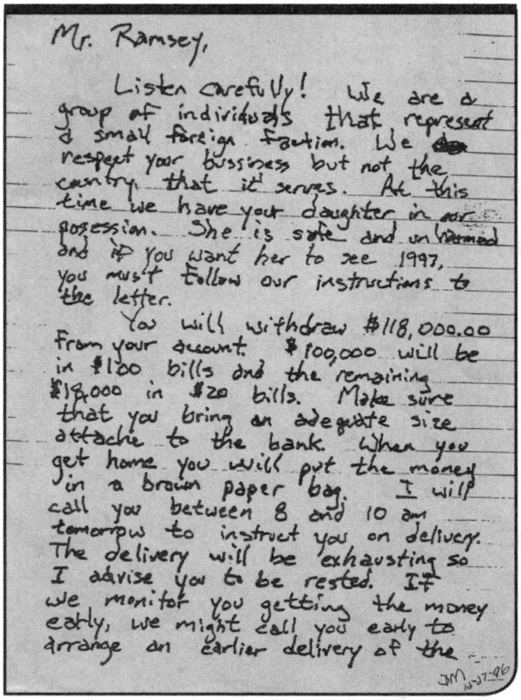

[handwritten ransom note reproduced in image:]

Mr. Ramsey,

Listen carefully! We are a group of individuals that represent a small foreign faction. We respect your bussiness but not the country that it serves. At this time we have your daughter in our posession. She is safe and unharmed and if you want her to see 1997, you must follow our instructions to the letter.

You will withdraw $118,000.00 from your account. $100,000 will be in $100 bills and the remaining $18,000 in $20 bills. Make sure that you bring an adequate size attache to the bank. When you get home you will put the money in a brown paper bag. I will call you between 8 and 10 am tomorrow to instruct you on delivery. The delivery will be exhausting so I advise you to be rested. If we monitor you getting the money early, we might call you early to arrange an earlier delivery of the

JM²⁷⁷⁹⁶

Reply letter doctrine. A writing may be authenticated by evidence that it was received in response to a letter sent to the author. This might entail reference to the contents of the original letter in the letter written by the author. A letter also may be authenticated by evidence that it is one in a series of letters between individuals.

Admissions. The party against whom the writing is offered has admitted its authenticity in the past.

Process or system used. Various documents are authenticated by the fact a reliable process or system was used to produce them. Courts have authenticated information obtained by surveillance cameras, global satellites, X-ray machines, and scans to authenticate the image that is produced. In most instances, these images are recognized by judicial notice.

Public records. Documents legally required to be filed may be authenticated by evidence they were retrieved from the required custodian. An example may be a police report of a crime or a doctor's filing of a report of the abuse of a child. A customs document submitted by an individual may provide evidence the defendant failed to declare items he or she unlawfully brought into the United States. As noted, in some instances, these documents may be self-authenticating. Keep in mind that certified copies rather than original documents typically are introduced at trial.

[handwritten note:] (Federal: govt documents over 20 yrs old.

Ancient documents. Ancient documents are admitted without authentication if they appear to be genuine and there is no indication of modification or forgery. The document also must have been handled as an original document and kept in a safe and secure location such as a museum or safe deposit box. At common law, a document was required to be at least thirty years old to be considered an ancient document. Some states adopted a shorter period.

The Federal Rules of Evidence require a document to be twenty years old. Federal Rule 901(b)(8) provides that any document at least twenty years old and "fair on its face" is presumed to be authentic. "Fair on its face" means that the condition of the document creates no suspicion about the document's authenticity and the document was found in a place where an authentic document is likely to be found. Most states have more limited rules. An interesting application of the **ancient documents rule** involves documents and identification cards linking individuals who emigrated to the United States following World War II to involvement in Nazi war crimes. These documents provide grounds to deprive these individuals of their American citizenship and to deport them or to extradite them to stand trial abroad. Courts require the prosecution to provide testimony that the documents are reliable, have not been modified, and were found in files where such documents may be expected to be located (*United States v. Stelmokas*, 100 F.3d 302 [3d Cir. 1996]).

Keep in mind that after a letter has been admitted, the defense attorney may argue the defendant did not write the letter, the letter has been altered, or the letter contains various falsehoods. The jury in adjudicating the defendant's guilt or innocence will be asked to weigh and evaluate the probative value of the letter.

■ SELF-AUTHENTICATING DOCUMENTS

Self-authenticating documents are documents that require no independent proof of their authenticity. Rule 902 lists twelve types of self-authenticating documents. Producing the document establishes its authentication. These documents typically display a seal or other visual display of authenticity that appears on the document. The justification is that the authenticity of the document is clear from the face of the document. Self-authentication is an important time-saving device at trial. Keep in mind the other party may demonstrate the document is inauthentic.

1. Domestic public documents under seal
2. Domestic public documents not under seal → copied and certified (copy of a birth certificate)
3. Foreign public documents
4. Certified copies of public records
5. Official publications
6. Newspapers and periodicals

   these documents can be forged but other party can question it

7. Trade inscriptions and the like
8. Acknowledged documents
9. Commercial paper and related documents
10. Presumptions under Acts of Congress
11. Certified domestic records of a regularly conducted activity
12. Certified foreign records of a regularly conducted activity

The most important of these categories are discussed below.

Government Documents

Government documents and records typically are self-authenticating.

Domestic public documents under seal. Public documents include documents made by federal, state, and local governments and are self-authenticating so long as they contain an official seal of the relevant government agency and are signed by an authorized government official indicating that the document is a true copy of the original. Birth and death certificates and a judge's order convicting an individual of a crime are documents under seal.

Domestic public documents not under seal. In most instances, a copy of a government document rather than the original is introduced into evidence. A government document without a seal is self-authenticating if accompanied by a certificate that the attached document is a correct copy of the original. The certificate typically states that the original is recorded or filed with the government and is signed by the custodian of the public record, and the government seal appears on the certificate. A death certificate typically is signed by the attending physician or by a coroner and is filed with the relevant government agency. A clerk when asked to provide the death certificate attaches a certification to a photocopy indicating the document is a true copy of the original.

Foreign government records. Government documents from foreign countries are self-authenticating if they have a seal or include a certificate of genuineness that is signed by a responsible official.

Notarized documents. A notary public is an individual appointed by a government official to serve various functions, the most important of which is attesting to the authenticity of a document or of a signature. You may sign a document stating that you have received money from a friend and promise to pay back the money. The notary may ask to see your identification, witness the signature on the promissory note, and on the same document or on a certificate indicate that he or she witnessed the signature and include the notary's official seal and signature.

Acknowledged documents. An acknowledged document is a document in which an individual's signature is witnessed by another person who also signs the document.

The signatory before signing the document tells the witness the nature of the document the signatory is signing. An example may be a will or an agreement to accept a financial settlement and to drop a legal action for damages. The purpose of the witness is to corroborate that the signatory knew the nature of the document he or she was signing and to ensure that undue influence was not used to obtain the signatory's signature on the document.

Official publications. Official government publications also are self-authenticating. This category includes officially issued civil and criminal codes and case reports. The volume can be brought to court and given to a judge. Because a judge can take judicial notice of state and local statutory provisions, it typically only is necessary to present a judge with copies of the law of other states.

Other self-authenticating documents. Various other documents are viewed as having a limited likelihood of forgery and are self-authenticating. This includes newspapers, brand-name labels affixed to merchandise in the course of doing business to identify the manufacturer of an item, and various commercial documents such as an invoice that records work performed or merchandise sold or received. Keep in mind that authentication does not mean the newspaper story is accurate or that the merchandise is genuine.

Legal Equation

Authentication	=	Produce evidence sufficient to support a finding that the item is what the proponent claims it is.
Self-authenticating document	=	Document that requires no independent proof of its authenticity.

8.1 YOU DECIDE

In *United States v. Samet*, the Second Circuit Court of Appeals was asked to decide whether U.S. Postal Inspector Patricia Thornton possessed sufficient familiarity with Mordechai Samet's handwriting to authenticate his signature and handwriting on twenty-five fraudulent documents. Inspector Thornton had spent 80 percent of her time over three years on the case and had viewed Samet's signature and handwriting on his passport, driver's license, check register, and other documents. As a judge, how would you rule? See *United States v. Samet* (466 F.3d 251 [2d Cir. 2006])

You can learn what the court decided by referring to the study site, **http://study.sagepub.com/lippmance.**

■ VISUAL IMAGES →must accurately show what happened

Photographs, X-rays, and video and tape recordings must be authenticated and demonstrated to be accurate reproductions of the individuals or objects portrayed.

Authentication of Photographs and Videos

Testimony by a witness may not always effectively communicate the facts of a case to a jury, and a photograph may assist the jury to understand the facts of the case. The threshold question is the relevance of the photo to an issue in the case. The admission of a photograph or video is within the discretion of the court.

[handwritten at top: 1. is it accurate and does it accurately show what it is supposed to show?]
[handwritten: 2. is it prejudice — will it cause prejudice/distract the jury?]

Federal Rule 901 requires that the photograph should be authenticated as an accurate portrayal of what it purports to show. This might be accomplished by the testimony of the photographer or by the testimony of a witness who viewed the area or events portrayed in the photo and who testifies that the picture is an accurate image. The photo must capture the view at the time of the crime or shortly thereafter and may not have been taken following a change in circumstances.

A photograph may constitute direct proof of a crime and show the defendant engaged in a crime, such as photos of child pornography. Other photographs may help the jury understand the nature of the crime by portraying the victim's wounds. An example is the physical injuries to a rape victim, which corroborate the rape victim's resistance to a sexual assault.

An additional step prior to the authentication of the photograph is for the judge to determine whether the prejudicial impact of the photo substantially outweighs the photo's probative value. A judge might rule that a particularly gruesome photograph is inadmissible or limit the size or number of photographs. In other words, the key is whether the photograph is accurate and does not create undue prejudice.

The opposing party may challenge a photograph on various grounds, including a claim the photo was taken at an angle that distorts the view or is overly prejudicial. A gruesome photograph of a crime scene, though relevant to demonstrating that a crime was committed, may interfere with the capacity of jurors to objectively evaluate the evidence.

The mounting of video cameras on squad cars has led to the availability of videos to establish a driver's inebriated condition and inability to successfully complete a field sobriety test or to coherently express him- or herself. The so-called silent witness theory allows the authentication of a video from a surveillance camera in those instances in which there is no individual able to testify that based upon his or her personal knowledge the tape fairly and accurately portrays events. In these circumstances, a tape may be authenticated where there is an indication of the time and date of the tape, a clear chain of evidence, an absence of evidence of editing or tampering, testimony supporting the accuracy and reliability of the video system, and testimony identifying the individuals depicted in the photo. In *Wagner v. State*, the court relied on the "silent witness" theory to admit a video captured by a camera mounted in the car of an informant who purchased narcotics as she drove down the street (*Wagner v. State*, 707 So.2d 827 [Fla. Ct. App. 1998]).

Authentication of Medical Images *[handwritten: → show process is accurate + chain of custody]*

A medical image, unlike a photograph, is not authenticated by testimony that it is an accurate representation of a patient's condition. Authentication of X-rays, scans, and electrocardiograms requires a demonstration that the process is accurate, that the machine was in functioning order and was operated by a qualified technician, and finally that there was a clear custodial chain of evidence. These images may be relevant to the nature of the victim's injuries.

[handwritten: ↳ that is the persons x ray]

■ AUTHENTICATION OF OBJECTS

Objects can be authenticated through many of the same methods as documents. The owner of a stolen bike could identify the bike based on an identification number on the frame of the bike, and a firearm seized by the police could be authenticated based on a serial number or prominent feature.

[handwritten: - use friends/family of the voice]
[handwritten: - detective who interviewed him]
[handwritten: speaker discloses facts that only the speaker would know]

■ AUTHENTICATION OF VOICE COMMUNICATION

Authentication of voice communication is required when a legal team wants to establish that a statement was made by a particular person. This requires the presentation of sufficient evidence that the person claimed to have made the statement was responsible for making the statement. This may entail authentication that the defendant left a message on voice mail or recorded a confession to the police on audiotape or authentication that it was the defendant's voice that was recorded by electronic surveillance. Federal Rule 901(5) provides that an individual's voice may be authenticated by any individual familiar with the individual's voice. Rule 901(4) allows authentication based on the fact that the speaker disclosed knowledge of specific facts within the particular knowledge of an individual. An expert witness was allowed to testify in the Trayvon Martin murder case that the recorded voice calling for assistance belonged to the defendant George Zimmerman.

8.2 YOU DECIDE

Dean D. Small was charged with the aggravated murder of Robel Medhin. Small's wife testified at trial he was angry with Medhin because Medhin owed Small money. Tesfalem Ellos, a friend of Medhin, testified Medhin believed his life was in danger because he owed an unnamed person $900 and Medhin had asked Ellos for a gun. Medhin made a phone call on Ellos's phone on the evening of his murder and told the person who answered the phone he did not have the money. Following Medhin's death, Ellos called the phone number from which the call had been made to Medhin. The person who answered the phone had a Jamaican accent and said his name was Dominique. Ellos and Dominique discussed Ellos paying Medhin's debt. There was testimony that Small was known as Dominque. Small was convicted and claimed that the evidence did not authenticate that the defendant Small was the individual to whom Ellos had talked. See *State v. Small* (2007 Ohio 6771).

You can learn what the court decided by referring to the study site, **http://study.sagepub.com/lippmance.**

CRIMINAL EVIDENCE IN THE NEWS

In 2007, police and prosecutors had little to rely on in solving the murders of Christopher Horton, 16, and Brian Dean, 20. In 2011, a detective newly assigned to the case stumbled upon the YouTube video of local rapper Twain Gotti. Local authorities concluded that Gotti's song "Ride Out" contained incriminating lyrics. The lyrics printed below along with other language were interpreted as Gotti boasting of the killings.

"But nobody saw when I [expletive] smoked him," Gotti sang on the video. "Roped him, sharpened up the shank, then I poked him, 357 Smith & Wesson beam scoped him."

Although the prosecutors relied on the video to indict Gotti, they failed to introduce the lyrics at Gotti's trial and relied on witnesses who viewed Gotti at the crime scene. In May 2014, Gotti was acquitted on second-degree murder charges but convicted on weapons charges.

Gotti's case is an example of the roughly three dozen prosecutions in the past several years in which prosecutors have relied on rap lyrics to support their prosecution or to establish a defendant's guilt. Defense attorneys express concern that the lyrics prejudice judges and jurors against defendants. Critics assert that judges and jurors often do not appreciate that gangsta rappers assume exaggerated, personal, and violent identities that have very little relationship to their daily lives. There is little difference between gangsta rappers and authors who write violent stories.

Gotti allegedly had been fighting with one of the victims, and two eyewitnesses identified Gotti with a gun near the crime scene around the time of the shootings. Gotti pointed out there were no eyewitnesses to the actual shootings, that the knife mentioned in the lyrics was not involved in the crime, that the rap lyrics mention only a single murder, and that the shell casings found at the crime scene were of a different caliber than the gun mentioned in the song.

Lyrics as in Gotti's case at times are relied on as confessions and more often are relied on to establish the defendant's motive and intent. More recently, two Pittsburgh rappers were indicated based on lyrics that were interpreted as a criminal threat against the two police officers who arrested them for gun possession. The New Jersey Supreme Court has heard a challenge to a trial court's admission in a murder trial of thirteen pages of lyrics including lines like "four slugs drillin' your cheek to blow your face off and leave your brain caved in the street."

In Kansas, a rapper is being prosecuted for a double murder based on lyrics from his song "Prove Me Guilty" in which he mentions that "a couple bitches got killed."

Critics of the use of lyrics against defendants contend that the lyrics are a form of artistic expression and that courts should require prosecutors to meet a high standard of proof before using lyrics against defendants at trial. What is your view?

■ **THE BEST EVIDENCE RULE** — *using original is prefered ⟹ doesn't really matter in trial today*

The **best evidence rule** in Federal Rule 1002, or what often is referred to as the "original writing rule," requires that an "original writing, recording, or photograph is required in order to prove its content unless these rules or a federal statute provides otherwise." The term *writing* in Rule 1002 includes artwork, architectural designs and GP displays, and inscribed objects such as tombstones.

Commentators observe that the best evidence rule has lost much of its significance today because of the broad notion of what constitutes an "original" document.

Certified copies are substituted for original

Rule 1001(d) provides that an original of a writing or recording is the writing or recording "itself or any counterpart intended to have the same effect by a person who executed or issued it." "Counterpart" is defined to include the negative of a photograph "or any print from it" as well as a computer printout or carbon copy. In a prosecution for credit card fraud, the copy of the bill retained by the restaurant and the copy given to the customer both would qualify as the original writing.

Because of the impracticality of removing originals of public documents from agency files and taking them to court, certified copies of public records may be admitted into evidence as originals. This includes police records, birth certificates, and applications for professional licenses and passports.

Duplicates today can be accurately and reliably produced. Rule 1003 accordingly stipulates in most instances a "duplicate" may be admitted to the same extent as the original. What is a duplicate? Rule 1001(e) defines a duplicate as a "counterpart produced by the same impression as the original, or from the same matrix, or by means of photography, including enlargements and miniatures, or by mechanical or electronic re-recording, or by chemical reproduction, or by other equivalent technique which accurately reproduces the original." A duplicate under Rule 1001(e) includes a matrix (printing plate or stencil), a photographic enlargement or reduction (photocopy, microfilm, microfiches), and computer printouts. In other words, any reproduction that does not risk mistakes from human reproduction is considered a duplicate.

There are at least two instances in which the original is required under the Federal Rules of Evidence. Rule 1003 provides that a "duplicate is admissible to the same extent as an original unless a genuine question is raised as to the original's authenticity or the circumstances make it unfair to admit the duplicate." The original may be required, for example, where the duplicate only reproduces a part of the original.

Keep in mind the core principle behind the best evidence rule is that a party who intends to prove the content of a document is required to introduce the original rather than rely on human recollection. Rule 1002 states that the original or duplicate is required to prove the *content of these items*. The question is whether the witness is attempting to prove the content of a writing, in which case an original is required, or whether the writing merely happens to record the subject of the witness's testimony, in which case an original is not required.

Courts struggle with whether the best evidence rule is required to be followed. The question is whether the document is being introduced to prove a fact. Take the example of a videotape that captures an armed robbery. A witness who identifies the defendant in court as the individual he or she saw rob a bank is testifying based on his or her personal observation of the robbery. The best evidence rule is not involved, and there is no requirement that the prosecution introduce the videotape into evidence. In the alternative, the best evidence rule is involved if the witness testifies that the robber is the same person who appears on the videotape or the only witness has died and the videotape is introduced to prove the identity of the robber. In these cases, the prosecution is required to introduce the original or a duplicate.

A police officer may testify about the details of the defendant's confession to a crime, and the original copy is not required to be introduced into evidence. The written document, of course, would strengthen the police officer's testimony although the original copy need not be introduced. An original copy of the written confession would be required to be introduced into evidence if the police officer testified that he or she was testifying about the details of the defendant's confession as recorded in a written document signed by the defendant.

In an Arkansas case, a store clerk detected a theft by watching a surveillance tape in the store. The appellate court held that the store was required to introduce the original tape (*Bradley v. State*, 2003 Ark. App. LEXIS 756 [2003]).

What if the tape in the Arkansas case was lost or misplaced? Federal Rule 1004 provides that the original is not required and other evidence of the contents of a writing, recording, or photograph is admissible under four circumstances.

Lost or destroyed. The best evidence rule does not apply and secondary evidence is admissible if the original writing has been lost or destroyed unless the party required to produce the document intentionally destroyed the documents "in bad faith." A business may have a policy of destroying documents to avoid being swamped by paper and would not be considered to have acted in bad faith if in the process a document was destroyed. → house fire (birth certificate in their)

Original not obtainable by judicial process. The original is not required where the party in possession of the document is outside the jurisdiction of the court and the document cannot be obtained by any available judicial process (e.g., subpoena *duces tecum*). This is unlikely to arise in a criminal case because courts can subpoena documents anywhere within the United States.

Possession of opponent. The party against whom the document is to be admitted has the document in his or her possession and fails to produce the original. In this instance, the proponent may rely on secondary evidence. The logic of this requirement is that the opponent always can attack the secondary evidence by relying on the original.

Collateral matters. The document is not important to the case. A witness may testify that the defendant was drinking and driving and texting before his or her car went out of control and killed a pedestrian. The content of the text is not central to establishing the defendant's reckless driving.

Evidence other than the original that may be relied on to prove the content of an original document is termed **secondary evidence**. This may entail the rough draft of a document, notes on the content of a document, or oral testimony.

Courts pursuant to Rule 1006 have waived the best evidence rule and allowed for the introduction of a summary of the document when the writings are so lengthy that it would be impractical to produce the document in court. The original or duplicates must be made available to be inspected or copied by the opposing party. The "admissions doctrine" in Rule 1007 establishes that the original also is not required to be produced when the party against whom the writing is being offered waives the requirement that the original be introduced.

Rule 1005 notes that, because original public records cannot be removed from the government files, the content of an official record or of a recorded document (e.g., a marriage certificate) may be proven by certified copy.

The trial court judge decides whether the document is an original or a duplicate and whether the best evidence rule and various exceptions to the best evidence rule apply. The party offering the document has the burden of establishing a document's admissibility. Keep in mind that the opposing party may challenge the accuracy of a duplicate or summary, whether the document or another document is the original or whether an original ever existed.

Rule 1002. Requirement of the Original

An original writing, recording, or photograph is required in order to prove its content unless these rules or a federal statute provides otherwise.

■ APPLICATION OF THE BEST EVIDENCE RULE

The question is whether the best evidence rule is required to be followed in a particular situation. Federal Rule 1002 provides that an original writing, recording, or photograph is required in order to "prove its content."

Commentators note the best evidence rule only applies to the content of "writings." The rules of evidence do not require the introduction of the "best" physical evidence. In a murder prosecution, the government is not required to introduce the murder weapon. A photograph of the weapon may be introduced into evidence, or the arresting officer may testify about the weapon that was seized when the defendant was arrested. The homicide may be proved through wounds, DNA, hair samples, and other evidence.

Legal Equation

Best evidence rule	=	"To prove the content of writing, recording, or photograph, the original writing, recording, or photograph is required" unless an exception applies.
Original required	=	Witness testifies as to content of document.
Duplicate admissible	=	Unless question raised about authenticity of original or unfair to admit duplicate.

8.3 YOU DECIDE

The complainant was working as the manager of a Laundromat. The defendant and the manager became involved in a fight in which

the complainant suffered a severe injury. The prosecution offered the testimony of the owner of the Laundromat who had watched a videotape of the fight on the store's surveillance camera. The videotape had been lost, and the owner's testimony was offered to establish what the videotape showed about the fight. May the owner testify? See *People v. Jimenez* (796 N.Y.S.2d 232 [2005]).

You can learn what the court decided by referring to the study site, **http://study.sagepub.com/lippmance.**

8.4 YOU DECIDE

Vincent Bennett was charged with importing marijuana into the United States. Government agents boarded his boat traveling north of the Mexican border along the California coastline. An X-ray examination revealed more than 1,500 pounds of marijuana in the hull of the ship. The federal prosecution was based on Bennett's transport of marijuana into the United States from Mexico. A customs offer testified at Bennett's trial that he activated the "back track feature" of a global positioning system on board the boat, which showed that Bennett had traveled from Mexico into American waters. Bennett appealed his conviction based on the fact that the GPS display was a writing or recording and that the best evidence rule required the introduction of the original into evidence. It was not sufficient to rely on the testimony of the customs agent who had activated the GPS. Is Bennett correct? See *United States v. Bennett* (363 F.3d 947 [9th 2004]).

You can learn what the court decided by referring to the study site, **http://study.sagepub.com/lippmance.**

> *[handwritten: as long as material put on here is accurate and accurately shows the evidence]*

■ MODELS, MAPS, DIAGRAMS, AND CHARTS

> *[handwritten: made up of admissible evidence]*

Courts typically allow lawyers and witnesses to use replica models, maps, diagrams, and charts to visually illustrate testimony. A drawing or map may help the jurors visualize the crime scene. The lawyer will ask the witness questions to explain the drawing. Anatomical models frequently are used to explain impact of a bullet or physical attack.

The trend today is for lawyers to use sophisticated computer-generated three-dimensional images and re-creations. The requirement for the introduction of these materials is that they are reasonable replicas of the object to be portrayed and are created to scale, meaning that although the drawing or object is of a smaller size, the height and distance and dimensions must be the same as the actual object.

A replica of a gun used in robbery or the use of a ski mask has been held to be properly permitted to be used in a criminal prosecution (*United States v. Towns*, 913 F.2d 434 [7th Cir. 1990]). The Maryland Supreme Court held a trial court had improperly permitted a demonstration of the circumstances causing "shaken baby syndrome": where the dimensions of the doll including the strength of the neck muscles were not substantially similar to the dimensions of the child (*Andrews v. State*, 811 A.2d 282 [Md. 2002]).

8.5 YOU DECIDE

Rogelio Trevino Reyna was convicted of aggravated sexual assault and indecency with a child. Reyna objected on appeal to the prosecution's use of an "anatomically correct" doll to enable the 8- and 4-year-old victims to illustrate the molestation they experienced.

"B.J.F. testified that [Reyna] had put her hands on his penis, and when asked what that was, she pointed to the genital area of the male doll. C.F. testified that he put his 'thing' 'behind her,' when asked what she meant when she said his 'thing' she pointed to the male sex organ of the male doll, and when asked what she meant by her 'thing' and 'behind her' she pointed to the genitalia and anus of the female doll."

As a judge, would you have allowed the use of the doll? *See Reyna v. State* (797 S.W.2d 189 [Tex. Crim. App. 1990]).

You can learn what the court decided by referring to the study site, **http://study.sagepub.com/lippmance.**

CRIMINAL EVIDENCE AND PUBLIC POLICY

In 2010, neo-Nazi John Ditullio, then 24, was convicted of first-degree murder and attempted second-degree murder by a Florida court. His court-appointed lawyer successfully petitioned the trial court judge to pay a cosmetologist $125 per day to cover the indigent Ditullio's tattoos, the most prominent of which were the large swastika and the words "f--- you" on his neck along with the barbed wire running down the side of his face. Ditullio had attempted to kill a next-door neighbor whom the prosecution alleged Ditullio disliked because she had an African American friend and gay son. Her son's friend was killed during the knife attack.

Ditullio's lawyer contended that the tattoos might prejudice the jury against his client. On the other hand, the prosecutor contended that tattoos are a statement of an individual's opinions and views. In any event, the prosecutor pointed out that a judge who concludes the tattoos are prejudicial could instruct the jury to disregard the tattoos.

Courts are divided on whether defendants are entitled to coverage of their tattoos. Lawyers asserting the right of their clients to cover their tattoos rely on *Estelle v. Williams* (425 U.S. 501 [1976]), in which the United States Supreme Court held that forcing defendants to wear a prison uniform when appearing in court before a jury is contrary to the presumption of innocence. The Ninth Circuit Court of Appeals held that *Estelle* does not require a trial court judge to order a defendant's tattoos to be covered although the appellate court recognized that "a particular tattoo" could cause prejudice against a defendant (*United States v. Quinteros,* 933 F.2d 1017 [9th Cir. 1991]).

Prosecutors may petition the court to order a defendant to reveal his or her tattoo when a witness testifies that the perpetrator of the crime had a specific visible tattoo. The Fifth Amendment right against self-incrimination only extends to testimony and does not protect individuals against display of physical evidence (*Schmerber v. California*, 383 U.S. 757 [1966]). Defendants also may display their tattoo or lack of a tattoo to establish that they were not the perpetrator of the crime without waiving their Fifth Amendment right against self-incrimination (*United States v. Bay*, 762 F.2d 1314 [9th Cir. 1984]).

A defendant also does not have a Fifth Amendment right to refuse to display a tattoo that communicates information. This is because the defendant was not compelled by the government to have a tattoo. In *United States v. Greer* (631 F.3d 608 [2d Cir. 2011]), a rental car was used in the commission of a robbery. Prosecutors tied the defendant to the crime, in part, by showing that the name of the woman who had rented the auto was on the defendant's arm.

A defendant always can argue that the prosecution is misinterpreting the meaning of a tattoo. Teardrop tattoos may have various meanings including the number of victims the individual has murdered or the honoring of fellow gang members who have been killed.

The defendant may challenge the introduction of a tattoo into evidence on the grounds that it is irrelevant. In *Dawson v. Delaware* (503 U.S. 159 [1992]), the United States Supreme Court held that the "Aryan Brotherhood" tattoo of a white defendant was irrelevant to the charge that the defendant had killed a white victim. A gun tattoo was held irrelevant to establish unlawful gun possession (*United States v. Thomas,* 321 F.3d 627, 633 [7th Cir. 2003]). Courts in other instances have found that the "probative value" of a tattoo is "substantially outweighed by danger of unfair prejudice" (*United States v. Irvin,* 87 F.3d 860 [7th Cir. 1996]).

A proper foundation for the introduction of a tattoo into evidence must be established. The prosecutor typically calls a witness to establish the design of the defendant's tattoo to establish that the defendant possessed the incriminating tattoo on the date of the crime. A defendant seeking to display his or her tattoo in order to retain his or her right against self-incrimination would want to establish the tattoo existed at the time of the crime and may call a close acquaintance or the tattoo artist who inscribed the tattoo.

The defense can request jury instructions instructing the jury against drawing a prejudicial inference based on the tattoo. The prosecutor also may allow the defendant to stipulate to the existence of the tattoo in exchange for an agreement not to present the tattoo to the jury.

What is your view about whether defendants should be required to display their tattoos?

■ IN-COURT EXHIBITIONS *detective or someone takes person into other room and checks.*

A judge may exercise his or her discretion to require the defendant to reveal identifying physical characteristics. The right against self-incrimination protects individuals against "testimonial" evidence and does not extend to the display of physical characteristics during **in-court exhibitions**. In those instances in which this may prove embarrassing, a court may direct that an impartial individual observe an individual's physical features outside of court and testify about what he or she observed. An Ohio appellate court used this approach to determine whether the defendant accused of rape possessed a scar on his sexual organ (*State v. Minkner*, 627 N.E.2d 973 [Ohio App. 1994]).

■ CASE ANALYSIS

In *United States v. McGlory*, the Third Circuit Court of Appeals addressed the authentication of notes seized by the police from the trash.

Was there a foundation for the admission of the notes found in the trash?

United States v. McGlory, 968 F.2d 309 (3rd Cir. 1992), Hutchinson, J.

After two years of investigation by agents of the DEA [Drug Enforcement Administration] and the Pittsburgh Police, including personal observation in Pittsburgh, Los Angeles and Thailand, as well as electronic surveillance and searches of [Reginald D.] McGlory's garbage in Pittsburgh, the government concluded it had pieced together a major heroin conspiracy involving defendants McGlory, [Vira] Kulkovit, [Charles] Cotton, [Melvin] Hauser, Norman Gomez (Gomez) and others. . . .

From the evidence admitted at trial, the jury found that McGlory operated a large heroin distribution business in the Pittsburgh area from about July 1986 to September 1989. The heroin was imported from Thailand to Los Angeles and then brought to Pittsburgh for distribution. Kulkovit was McGlory's supplier. Defendants Cotton, Hauser and others helped McGlory distribute it. Whether the jury was justified in these findings is the issue before us.

Notes and scraps of paper seized during searches of McGlory's known residences and from the trash outside in 1988 and 1989 indicate that McGlory was keeping track of transactions involving large sums of money with an individual named "BroMel" on a regular basis. Agent Rotter testified that in his opinion these notes were records of drug transactions. Government informants [Roland] Slade and [Vernon] Williams testified that they would use the nicknames "Brother Melvin" "Brother Mel" or "Abdul" in speaking with Hauser. McGlory's personal phone book contained an entry for "BroMelvin" and a number listed to Hauser.

It is undisputed that there was overwhelming evidence linking McGlory to heroin trafficking, and he does not contest the sufficiency of the evidence against him. The evidence showed that Kulkovit met with McGlory on numerous occasions, exchanged large sums of money with him, and that the two were clearly involved in some illegal conspiracy, the object of which Kulkovit knew. That McGlory was so heavily engaged in heroin trafficking and so deeply involved in trafficking something with Kulkovit, coupled with the fact that when Kulkovit came to Pittsburgh he called Hauser, a known drug dealer, is sufficient to establish that Kulkovit participated in the heroin conspiracy.

McGlory objected at trial to the introduction of handwritten notes seized from his garbage and residences for lack of authentication because the handwriting expert had insufficient handwriting exemplars to determine the author of some of the writings. The district court, nevertheless, found the notes were properly authenticated. We review the district court's ruling as to proper authentication for abuse of discretion. "The admission or exclusion of evidence is a matter particularly suited to the broad discretion of the trial judge."

Under Federal Rule of Evidence 901 "the requirement of authentication or identification as a condition precedent to admissibility is satisfied by evidence sufficient to support a finding that the matter in question is what its proponent claims." For authentication or identification of the notes the government could rely on "comparison by the trier of fact or by expert witnesses with specimens which have been authenticated," Fed. R. Evid. 901(b)(3), or on "appearance, contents, substance, internal patterns, or other distinctive characteristics, taken in conjunction with circumstances." Fed. R. Evid. 901(b)(4).

The showing of authenticity is not on a par with more technical evidentiary rules, such as hearsay exceptions, governing admissibility. Rather, there need be only a prima facie showing, to the court, of authenticity, not a full argument on admissibility. Once a prima facie case is made, the evidence goes to the jury and it is the jury who will ultimately determine the authenticity of the evidence, not the court. The only requirement is that there has been substantial evidence from which they could infer that the document was authentic.

Viewing the record in its entirety, there was sufficient evidence from which the jury could find that McGlory authored the notes in question despite the government's inability to establish fully McGlory's authorship by expert opinion. The evidence showed that the notes were seized from the trash outside of McGlory's known residences during the course of the charged conspiracy or during the September 9, 1989 search of his residences. Some of the notes from the trash were torn from a notebook found in one of his residences. Some of the notes were contained in the same garbage bag as other identifying information. Some of the notes were written on note paper from hotels at which McGlory stayed during the course of the conspiracy. Although he could not be conclusive, the government's handwriting expert did testify to numerous similarities between the writing on several of the notes and a handwriting exemplar McGlory had provided. Finally, the notes were similar in form and contained similar amounts as well as initials of persons listed in McGlory's private phone books known to associate with him.

The evidence demonstrated that Exhibits 100 and 110, which were seized from the trash at 236 South Negley Avenue on May 1, 1989, were torn from government Exhibit 113, a notebook seized from the same property on September 8, 1989. Exhibit 101 is written on a bank deposit slip which corresponds to an account utilized by McGlory. A wire transfer receipt dated April 12, 1989 showing the transfer of money from McGlory to Kulkovit was found in the same garbage bag as Exhibits 100 and 101. Exhibit 102 is a piece of notepaper with the message "tell We I never called because the newspaper never came in." The evidence shows "We" is the appellant Kulkovit. Although the handwriting expert

(Continued)

(Continued)

testified that McGlory did not write Exhibit 102, McGlory had his mother take and relay messages between himself and Kulkovit.

Exhibits 103, 103A and 103B, recovered from the trash at 4267 Bryn Mawr Road, were written on notepaper from a Stouffer's tablet. McGlory stayed at a Stouffer's hotel on several occasions when he travelled to Los Angeles during the course of the conspiracy. Exhibits 136 and 138 were also written on Stouffer's note paper. Exhibits 104, 104A and 104B, obtained from the trash at 4267 Bryn Mawr Road, were written on notepaper obtained from the Westin Hotel in Detroit. McGlory stayed at this hotel in July 1988. The handwriting on Exhibits 104 and 104A was identified by the government's handwriting expert as being similar to McGlory's.

Exhibits 105, 105A and 105B were taken from the trash at 4267 Bryn Mawr Road. The names and initials contained on these three exhibits are similar to those that appear on the exhibits discussed above. The handwriting on Exhibit 105 was identified as being similar to that of McGlory. Exhibit 106 was seized from the trash at 4267 Bryn Mawr Road. The initials on this exhibit are similar to the ones on the exhibits discussed above. Exhibit 107, recovered from the trash at 4267 Bryn Mawr Road, consists of notes written on notepaper taken from Bally's Hotel in Las Vegas. Other evidence indicates that McGlory made trips to Las Vegas during the relevant time period. The initials in columns on the back of Exhibit 107 are similar to the initials on the other exhibits. A notation on the front of Exhibit 107 refers to "Cellular One." A bill from Cellular One was found in McGlory's trash in April 1989.

Exhibit 108 is a note recovered from the trash at 4267 Bryn Mawr Road. The initials and notations written on it are similar to the ones that appear on the exhibits discussed previously. Exhibit 109 is a note seized from the trash at 236 South Negley Avenue. The initials written on it are similar to the initials that appear on the other exhibits. The handwriting expert testified that the handwriting on Exhibit 109 is similar to the handwriting exemplar provided by McGlory.

Exhibit 111 was also obtained from the trash at 236 South Negley Avenue and contains numbers, initials and notes in the same format as the other notes. Exhibit 112 is a spiral notebook found during the search of 4267 Bryn Mawr Road. Several of the pages in Exhibit 112 contain lists of initials and numbers similar to that found in the other notes. The handwriting expert testified that there were similarities between the handwriting in Exhibit 112 and that of McGlory.

Exhibit 113 is a spiral notebook found during the search at 236 South Negley Avenue. Several pages contain columns of names and numbers similar to those found on the other notes. Other pages in the notebook contain handwritten references to Precision Doors, KYE and "Peice [sic] on car Ted McWm." Other evidence showed McGlory's association with Precision Doors and KYE and that he had his Porsche repaired at Ted McWilliams' garage. Government Exhibit 114 is a business card for a furrier, which was found during the search at 236 South Negley Avenue. The list of initials on the back is similar to those found on the other exhibits. Exhibit 115 was found during the search at 236 South Negley Avenue and contains lists of initials and figures similar to the other exhibits.

In addition, Special Agent Rotter testified that the numbers in the various documents, when considered each along with the others, show that McGlory was paying approximately $6,000.00 an ounce for heroin and selling it for $10,000.00. He also testified that the notes referred to ounce quantities purchased by various individuals and the amount of profit McGlory realized from the sale. The initials and names contained in the documents also link them to McGlory. "[A] document . . . may be shown to have emanated from a particular person by virtue of its disclosing knowledge of facts known particularly to him." Fed. R. Evid. 901 advisory committee's note. . . . As discussed above, Exhibits 101, 104, 104B, 106, 107, 108, 109, 112, 113, 114, and 115 contain similar lists of from five to ten names with corresponding notations. For example, Exhibit 100 referred to seven salesman in a column of initials: K, CC, BM, D, MC, MK and Go. Exhibit 103A contains the initials Kil, BM, M, Go, S (illegible) and CC in column form. Exhibit 103 contains the names Cerly, BroMel, Charley C, GooGoo, Killer, G(illegible) and Norma in column form. The jury could infer from the other evidence set out in our analysis of Hauser and Cotton's sufficiency arguments that some of these names and initials referred to Cotton and Hauser. Other evidence showed McGlory's association with "Killer," "Go-Go" and Norma Pruitt and their names were listed in his personal phone book.

Exhibit 136, a sheet of Stouffer's notepaper, was seized from the trash at 4267 Bryn Mawr Road residence. It contained the name "We" and a Bangkok telephone number. Exhibit 137 is a piece of notepaper seized on January 31, 1989 from McGlory's trash containing the name We and a Bangkok telephone number. Evidence introduced at trial indicated that We (Kulkovit) was in Thailand just prior to the time this note was seized and that McGlory called this number during that time. Exhibit 138 is another piece of Stouffer's notepaper with the name Yongyos Thauthong written on it. The evidence showed that McGlory met with Thaut[h]ong in Pittsburgh, wired money to him, and that Thauthong was associated with Kulkovit in Los Angeles.

Considering all the surrounding circumstances, the documents in this case (Exhibits 100-15, 136-138) could be authenticated by their contents, and thus precise handwriting [331] identification is not required. In *United States v. Reyes*, 798 F.2d 380 (10th Cir. 1986), the defendant objected to the admission of handwritten notes on authenticity grounds. The notes were seized from the defendant's residence and their contents included the name of the defendant, initials of his coconspirators, notations of numbers and ounces and phone numbers. The court found no abuse of discretion in the admission of the notes. It stated: "The source of the notes and the correspondence of information contained in the notes to members of the conspiracy provided ample foundation for their admissibility." As in this case, "the contents of the notes indicated that they were written by someone involved in the conspiracy."

Similarly, in *United States v. Wilson*, 532 F.2d 641 (8th Cir. 1976), the court admitted the contents of two notebooks found in a house that an informer said was being used in a narcotics operation. Although the author was unknown, the court found that the contents of the books, nicknames of the defendants and code terms referring to heroin, were sufficient for authentication purposes. And in *United States v. Luschen*, 614 F.2d 1164 (8th Cir. 1980), a prosecution for conspiracy to distribute cocaine, the trial court allowed expert testimony as to the meaning of notations in a notebook found in the defendant's bedroom. The court allowed the contents of the writing to be used in determining the identity of the declarant for purposes of Rule 901 since dates and prices listed in the notebook corresponded to the dates of drug transactions in the case. Handwriting analysis was not required.

More directly on point, in *United States v. Baker*, 855 F.2d 1353 (8th Cir. 1988), the defendant objected, on the grounds of authenticity, to the admission of items collected from a coconspirator's garbage. The court held that a proper foundation had been laid for their admission. All of the contested items came from large trash bags. Some of the items "such as bills, notes and receipts contained distinctive characteristics linking the items to the" coconspirators. Further, some of the documents in the garbage contained one of the coconspirator's address. The court also found persuasive the testimony of a police officer that the garbage came from the coconspirator's house.

Here, there was testimony concerning the procedures used to pick up and search the trash. Although the handwriting on the notes was not definitively identified as that of McGlory, all of the notes contained distinctive characteristics linking them to him. Other items found in the trash such as letters, plane tickets and bills linked the trash to McGlory. Additional handwritten notes from the trash besides the owe sheets referred to Armand's Art Gallery, McGlory's Porsche, C&E Fashions, Timothy Reed and Linda Jewelry. The evidence linked McGlory to all of these references. Since the notes were likely to be what the government said they were, we cannot say that the district court abused its discretion in deciding that Exhibits 100-15 and 136-38 were authenticated.

CHAPTER SUMMARY

This chapter addressed the admission into evidence of documentary evidence. Documentary evidence is broadly defined to include written documents, photographs, videos, medical images, and voice identification. The last section of the chapter covered the admission of demonstrative evidence including graphs, maps, charts, and models designed to assist the jury to visualize the facts of the case.

Documents like other types of evidence must be relevant, and their probative value must not be substantially outweighed by the danger of unfair prejudice. The party introducing the documentary evidence must authenticate the document. This simply means that the party that wants to admit the document at trial has the burden of establishing the document is genuine, meaning the document is what the moving party claims it to be. This does not mean that the document is accurate or truthful.

Self-authenticating documents are documents that require no independent proof of their authenticity. These documents typically display a seal or other visual display of authenticity that appears on the document. The justification is that the authenticity of the document is clear from the face of the document. Self-authentication is an important time-saving device at trial. Keep in mind the other party during the trial may demonstrate the document is inauthentic.

Other documents require authentication. There are various ways to authenticate a document including lay testimony, expert testimony, jury comparison, distinctive characteristics of a document, and ancient documents.

Photographs, X-rays, and video and tape recordings must be authenticated and demonstrated to be accurate reproductions of the individuals or objects portrayed. Objects can be authenticated through many of the same methods as documents.

A medical image, unlike a photograph, is not authenticated by testimony that it is an accurate representation of a patient's condition. Authentication of X-rays, scans, and electrocardiograms requires a demonstration that the process is accurate, that the machine was in functioning order and operated by a qualified technician, and finally that there was a clear custodial chain of evidence.

Authentication of oral statements is required when the statement was made by a particular person. This requires the presentation of sufficient evidence that the person claimed to have made the statement was responsible for making the statement. An individual's voice may be authenticated by any individual familiar with the individual's voice. Rule 901(b)(4) allows authentication based on the fact that the speaker disclosed knowledge of specific facts within the particular knowledge of an individual.

The best evidence rule, or what often is referred to as the "original writing rule," requires that "to prove the content of writing, recording, or photograph, the original writing, recording, or photograph is required" unless an exception applies. The term *writing* also includes artwork, architectural designs and GP displays, and inscribed objects such as tombstones. In most instances, a "duplicate" may be admitted to the same extent as the original. A duplicate is a "counterpart produced by the same impression as the original, or from the same matrix, or by means of photography, including enlargements and miniatures, or by mechanical or electronic re-recording, or by chemical reproduction, or by other equivalent technique which accurately reproduces the original." Any reproduction that does not risk human reproduction mistakes is a duplicate. The "best evidence" rule applies when a witness is testifying about the content of a document.

Courts typically allow lawyers and witnesses to use replica models, maps, diagrams, and charts to visually illustrate testimony. The requirement for the use of these materials is that they are reasonable replica of the object to be portrayed and are created to scale, meaning that, although the drawing or object is of a smaller size, the height and distance and the dimensions must be the same as the actual object.

A judge may exercise his or her discretion to require the defendant to reveal identifying physical characteristics. The right against self-incrimination protects individuals against "testimonial" evidence and does not extend to the exhibit of physical characteristics during in-court exhibitions.

CHAPTER REVIEW QUESTIONS

1. Explain the purpose of the authentication of evidence.

2. Why are some documents self-authenticating? Give examples of documents that are self-authenticating.

3. Discuss some methods of authenticating documents that are not self-authenticating.

4. What is the rule for authenticating ancient documents?

5. How are photographs, videos, and medical images authenticated?

6. What is the purpose of the "best evidence" rule? Distinguish an original document from a duplicate document. When is an original not required?

7. What is the requirement for the use of maps, charts, and diagrams at trial?

LEGAL TERMINOLOGY

ancient documents rule

best evidence rule

in-court exhibitions

secondary evidence

self-authenticating documents

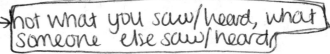

not what you saw/heard, what someone else saw/heard

HEARSAY

statement not made at trial – witness says "my friend told me..."

most of the time not admissible except for the exceptions

Was the victim's statement admissible as an excited utterance?

Caruso was hospitalized for seven weeks following the assault, during which time she underwent two brain operations. There was testimony that she suffered brain damage which rendered her unable to comprehend the significance of an oath and therefore incapable of testifying at trial. It was also testified, although her memory was intact, that her communication with others was restricted to isolated words and simple phrases, often precipitated by situations of stress and strain. Approximately one week after Caruso returned home from the hospital, her sister, Eileen Moore, showed her a newspaper article containing a photograph of the defendant. Moore testified that Caruso looked at the photograph (but did not read the accompanying article), and her "immediate reaction was one of great distress and horror and upset," and that Caruso "pointed to it and she said very clearly, 'He killed me, he killed me.'" Moore also testified that no member of the family had attempted to discuss the incident with Caruso prior to the display of the photograph. The court admitted the statement, over defendant's objection that it was inadmissible hearsay, as a "spontaneous exclamation" (*United States v. Napier*, 518 F.2d 316 [9th Cir. 1975]).

CHAPTER OUTLINE

Introduction
The Development of the Rule Against Hearsay
The Definition of Hearsay
The Reasons for the Hearsay Rule
Hearsay Objections
The Sixth Amendment and Hearsay
Exceptions to the Hearsay Rule
Admission and Confessions
Prior Statements
Hearsay Exceptions When Declarant Is
    Not Required to Be Available
Present Sense Impression
Excited Utterance
Then-Existing Mental, Emotional, or Physical Condition
Medical Treatment-Diagnosis
Business Records

Absence of Business Records
Public Records
Vital Statistics
Unavailability of Declarant
Former Testimony
Statement Under Belief of Impending Death
Declaration Against Interest
Statement of Personal or Family History
Statement Offered Against a Party That Wrongfully
    Caused the Declarant's Unavailability
Residual Exception
Hearsay Within Hearsay
Case Analysis
Chapter Summary
Chapter Review Questions
Legal Terminology

1. Do you know the definition of hearsay and the reason for excluding hearsay evidence from trial?

2. Can you summarize the U.S. Supreme Court cases that analyze the relationship between the Sixth Amendment Confrontation Clause and the hearsay rule?

3. Are you able to explain the relationship between admissions, adoptive admissions, admission by an agent, and admission by a co-conspirator?

4. Do you know the difference between admissions and statements against interest?

5. Are you able to describe the distinction between a present sense impression and an excited utterance?

6. Can you explain the difference between then-existing mental, emotional, or physical conditions and a statement made for medical treatment?

7. Do you know the requirements that must be met for the business records exception? When is the absence of a business record admissible in evidence?

8. Can you explain why there is a hearsay exception for public records?

9. Are you able to discuss why there is a hearsay exception when a party wrongfully causes the absence of a witness?

10. Do you know the reason for a residual exception?

■ INTRODUCTION

The presentation of facts at trial is communicated through witnesses. Witnesses typically testify to what they observed through their own observations.

Cross-examination traditionally relies on four types of examination:

1. *Memory.* The attorney explores the witness's ability to recall what transpired.

2. *Perception.* The lawyer tests the accuracy of the witness's observations.

3. *Narration.* The attorney examines whether the witness is able to clearly and coherently relate what he or she observed.

4. *Sincerity.* The lawyer explores whether the witness has a motive to fabricate or to misrepresent the facts.

An eyewitness may testify that he or she saw the defendant approach the victim and pull out a dark object that he pointed at the victim's head and that the witness heard a loud noise and then saw the victim collapse on the street. The opposing lawyer on cross-examination can ask how far the eyewitness was from the events described above, ask whether there were streetlights illuminating the crime scene, explore the condition of the witness's eyesight, and ask about whether the eyewitness knows the defendant and possessed a motive to misrepresent the facts.

This scenario is dramatically changed if the witness admits that he or she was not present at the crime scene and that his or her testimony is based on what his or her friend Cynthia said took place. This is a problem for the lawyer cross-examining the witness because Cynthia is not on the stand and the lawyer cannot test Cynthia's memory, perception, narration, or sincerity through cross-examination. As a result, the general rule is that hearsay, which occurs when one person testifies in court about what another person stated outside of court, is inadmissible in court. Federal Rule 802 provides that "[h]earsay is not admissible except as provided by these [federal] rules or by other rules prescribed by the Supreme Court . . . or by act of Congress."

■ THE DEVELOPMENT OF THE RULE AGAINST HEARSAY

John Henry Wigmore (1863–1943), an important scholar of the law of evidence, proclaimed that the **hearsay** rule was one of the greatest contributions of the common law to the advancement of trial procedure.

Before the development of the hearsay rule in the late seventeenth century, defendants found themselves convicted based on oral hearsay and later on the basis of written depositions. The declarant whose oral or written statement was relied on by the prosecution did not swear to an oath before making the statement and was not subject to cross-examination.

In extreme cases, jurors relied on information they obtained on their own before or during trial by individuals who did not appear as witnesses at trial. Defendants found themselves convicted on the basis of rumor, gossip, and popular opinion.

In the famous English trial of Sir Walter Raleigh in 1603, Raleigh was convicted of entering a conspiracy to overthrow King James I. He was convicted based on the testimony and written statement of Lord Cobham, an alleged co-conspirator who did not appear in court. The judge refused to allow Raleigh to confront his accuser, and he was sentenced to death.

As jurors began to be chosen who had no familiarity with the case or with the defendant, hearsay evidence started to be excluded from English trials. By the late seventeenth century, English courts began to limit the admission of hearsay in criminal cases.

Hearsay initially was accepted by courts in the United States. This trend was reversed in 1813 when Supreme Court Chief Justice John Marshall declared that hearsay was inconsistent with the adversary system of justice and created the risk of false and fabricated evidence. "Its intrinsic weakness, its incompetency to satisfy the mind of the existence of the fact, and the frauds which might be practiced under its cover, combine to support the rule that hearsay evidence is totally inadmissible" (*Mima Queen and Child v. Hepburn* 7 U.S [3 Cranch] 290 [1813]).

■ THE DEFINITION OF HEARSAY

There is a commonly accepted definition of hearsay. Federal Rule 801 provides that

"'Hearsay' means a statement that:

(1) the declarant does not make while testifying at the current trial or hearing; and

(2) a party offers in evidence to prove the truth of the matter asserted in the statement."

There are three components to the legal definition of hearsay.

1. A statement → *includes things people said, nonverbal or action intended for communication* [*shrugging*]

2. A declarant

3. Offered in evidence to prove the truth of the <u>matter asserted</u>

Federal Rule 801 provides definitions of these three components of the hearsay rule, which are discussed below.

A *statement* is an oral, written, or recorded assertive statement and also includes nonverbal movements undertaken with an intent to communicate, such as a shrug of the shoulders, pointing of a finger, gesture indicating disrespect, or nod of the head in agreement. Think about written statements in broad terms—they may include a letter, diary, will, or contract.

What do we mean by an *assertive statement*? This is a statement that is intended to communicate an individual's thoughts, beliefs, or observations.

A *declarant* is a person who makes the out-of-court statement (e.g., a statement not made under oath). The statement of a testimonial witness as to what another individual (declarant) said is hearsay. One technical wrinkle on this rule to keep in mind is that a witness who testifies about what he or she previously said is considered to be offering hearsay evidence. In other words, the testimonial witness also is the declarant. Why? Because the testimonial witness is repeating an out-of-court statement in court. Keep in mind that machines, such as computers and clocks and surveillance cameras, and the physical and verbal responses of animals, such as tracking dogs, are not hearsay. This evidence may be excluded from evidence by a judge because it is unreliable but not because it is hearsay.

The third prong of the hearsay rule is summed up in the phrase that the statement is "*offered in evidence to prove the truth of the matter asserted*." What does this mean? The statement is being used to establish that an event occurred. Jose tells Samantha at the crime scene that he saw Moses reach into his bulging pocket to get what Jose thought was a gun and that Jose responded by shooting and killing Moses. The defense attorney places Samantha on the stand and asks Samantha to repeat Jose's statement in order to establish that Jose shot and killed Moses because Jose thought Moses was in possession of a gun. Why is this hearsay? It is hearsay because Samantha is repeating Jose's out-of-court assertion that the victim was in possession of a gun to "*prove the truth of the matter asserted*."

Keep in mind that the same statement may not be hearsay if the defense attorney introduces Jose's statement to establish the reasonableness of Jose's belief that Moses possessed a gun and that, as a result, Jose acted in self-defense. In this instance, the statement is not being introduced to establish the truth of the matter asserted (e.g., that Moses in fact possessed a gun). Jose is entitled to self-defense based on a reasonable belief that the assailant was armed and posed an imminent threat of serious bodily harm. The judge will offer a *limiting instruction* and instruct the jury to consider the statement on the reasonableness of Jose's belief that he was in imminent threat of bodily harm.

Consider the following example. Jose, as a practical joke in a crowded theater, shouts, "There is a terrorist with a gun!" People panic, and several individuals are trampled to death as the crowd runs from the theater. Jose is charged with malicious mischief. Witnesses at trial testify that Jose shouted, "There is a terrorist with a gun!" This is not hearsay because the prosecutor is not attempting to establish that there was a terrorist with a gun in the theater. The purpose was to demonstrate that the statement was made by Jose and that in response to the statement there was panic in the theater that resulted in several people being trampled to death.

Legal Equation

Hearsay = A statement
+ A declarant
+ Offered in evidence to prove the truth of the matter asserted.

■ THE REASONS FOR THE HEARSAY RULE

The United States Supreme Court in *Williamson v. United States* noted that the hearsay rule is based on the assumption that out-of-court statements are subject to various "hazards" because of the inability to cross-examine the individual who made the statement (*Williamson v. United States*, 512 U.S. 594 [1994]).

Cross-examination. The inability to cross-examine the declarant prevents an examination of whether the declarant might be lying, have misperceived the event, or have a faulty memory or whether the listener misunderstood the declarant's words or took the declarant's words out of context. →won't be there

Safeguards. The safeguards available at trial to minimize the "hazards" associated with in-court statements are not available for out-of-court statements. This includes the oath that highlights the solemnity of the proceedings and carries the threat of a prosecution for perjury, the awareness of a witness who testifies at a trial of the seriousness of the proceedings, cross-examination, and the jury's ability to observe the witness on the stand.

Constitutional protections. Hearsay evidence violates the Confrontation Clause of the Sixth Amendment to the U.S. Constitution, which gives a defendant in a criminal trial the right to confront and cross-examine his or her accusers.

There are a number of exceptions to the hearsay rule that we will cover in the chapter.

■ HEARSAY OBJECTIONS *must be right away*

An attorney must lodge an immediate objection to hearsay and specify the specific grounds on which the objection is based. A failure to object in a timely and specific fashion may result in the admission of the hearsay. The best approach is to object to a question by the adverse attorney that calls for a hearsay response before the witness answers the question. Otherwise, although the jury may be instructed to disregard the witness's response, the jury may have a difficult time disregarding the answer (e.g., what did Jim tell you about whether or not he fired the pistol?).

→ before the jury hears the answer

■ THE SIXTH AMENDMENT AND HEARSAY *→ defendant has the right to confront the accuser*

The introduction of hearsay statements is subject to the requirements of the U.S. Constitution. The most important limitation is the **Confrontation Clause** of the Sixth Amendment. The Confrontation Clause provides that "in all criminal prosecutions, the accused shall enjoy the right . . . to be confronted with the witnesses against him." This clause extends to both federal and state prosecutions (*Pointer v. Texas*, 389 U.S. 805 [1965]). The Court continues to struggle to define the relationship between the Confrontation Clause and hearsay and in recent years avoided interpreting the Confrontation Clause so as to prevent the introduction into evidence of the traditional exceptions to the hearsay rule. At this point, we only have a limited number of decisions that address the relationship between the Confrontation Clause and hearsay.

The Court's decisions on the Confrontation Clause for many years were based on *Ohio v. Roberts*. In *Roberts*, the Supreme Court held that hearsay evidence may be used in those instances in which the declarant, whose statements are to be used against the defendant, is unavailable. In other words, a judge may admit into evidence testimony regarding the content of another person's statement because the declarant is unavailable. The hearsay statement must have been made under circumstances providing sufficient "indicia of reliability" that the statement actually was made.

The Supreme Court in *Roberts* held that the trial court had properly permitted the prosecution to introduce the statement of an unavailable witness at trial. The witness had testified at the preliminary hearing and had been cross-examined at the hearing by the defense counsel, and the statement was found to carry the indicia of reliability. The Court also affirmed that hearsay meets the indicia of reliability in those instances in which a statement is within one of twenty "firmly rooted" categories of hearsay testimony that historically have been recognized as reliable by the common law (*Ohio v. Roberts*, 448 U.S. 56 [1980]).

The U.S. Supreme Court in *Crawford v. Washington* held that the essence of the Confrontation Clause is the prohibition on the use of testimony by an unavailable declarant who is not subject to cross-examination. *Roberts* was rejected because it allowed a jury to hear evidence "untested by the adversary process based on a mere judicial determination of reliability." The Supreme Court accordingly held that out-of-court statements that are "*testimonial*" are inadmissible unless the declarant has been cross-examined earlier by a lawyer representing the defendant. The court did not define *testimonial* and merely noted that examples of testimonial statements are statements made at a

→ prohibits hearsay unless one of the exceptions

preliminary hearing or before a grand jury or statements made during a previous trial or during police interrogation (*Crawford v. Washington*, 41 U.S. 36 [2004]).

In 2006, in *Davis v. Washington*, the U.S. Supreme Court held that statements made that are intended to respond to an ongoing emergency are "nontestimonial" and are admissible in a prosecution against the accused. The declarant in this situation is not a "witness" and is not "testifying" against the accused. The Supreme Court in *Davis* accordingly held that an audiotape of the statements made by an unavailable victim of domestic violence to an operator during a 911 emergency call were nontestimonial and admissible in evidence. "Statements are nontestimonial when made in the course of police interrogation under circumstances objectively indicating that the primary purpose of the interrogation is to enable police assistance to meet an ongoing emergency" (*Davis v. Washington*, 547 U.S. 813 [2006]).

In *Michigan v. Bryant*, in 2011, the police responded to a radio dispatch and found Anthony Covington severely wounded in a parking lot. In response to police questioning, Covington stated that he had been shot by Richard Bryant. The conversation ended after five to ten minutes when Covington was taken to the hospital where he died within several hours.

At Bryant's trial, the police officers took the stand and repeated what Covington had told them. The jury convicted Bryant of second-degree murder, being a felon in possession of a firearm, and possession of a firearm during the commission of a felony.

Justice Sonia Sotomayor noted that *Bryant* differed from earlier Confrontation Clause cases because it involved a "nondomestic dispute," a "victim found in a public location suffering from a fatal gunshot wound," and a potentially dangerous perpetrator "whose location was unknown." This situation presented an "ongoing emergency" that extended "beyond an initial victim to a potential threat to the responding police and the public at large."

The Court concluded that the circumstances of the encounter, as well as the statements and actions of Covington and the police, objectively indicated that the "primary purpose of the interrogation" was "to enable police assistance to meet an ongoing emergency." As a result, Covington's identification and description of the shooter and the location of the shooting were nontestimonial, and the Confrontation Clause did not bar the admission of Covington's statements at Bryant's trial (*Michigan v. Bryant* 562 U.S. __ [2011]).

In 2009, the U.S. Supreme Court held that analysts who create crime laboratory reports that are used at trial are required to testify and to subject themselves to cross-examination. This rule provides the defense with the opportunity to probe whether the test was conducted in accordance with established procedures and whether the test results support the analyst's conclusion. In the past, a sworn affidavit recording the results of the test was considered sufficient in most state and federal courts. Defendants could challenge the test results through their own experts or by conducting their own test (*Melendez-Diaz v. Massachusetts*, 557 U.S. 305 [2009]).

In *Bullcoming v. New Mexico*, the U.S. Supreme Court affirmed the holding in *Melendez-Diaz* and stated that the "Confrontation Clause prohibits the prosecution from introducing a forensic laboratory report through the in-court testimony of an analyst who did not personally perform or observe the performance of the test" (*Bullcoming v. New Mexico*, 54 U.S. __ [2011]).

In summary, the Confrontation Clause permits the introduction of testimonial statements where the declarant is unavailable and when, at an earlier time, he or she was subject to cross-examination by the accused. Commentators have speculated how the Court since deciding *Crawford* would address various exceptions to the prohibition on hearsay evidence.

The Supreme Court also has recognized that nontestimonial statements made by unavailable declarants may be introduced at trial when the statements are made in response to an ongoing emergency and were not obtained for the purposes of gathering evidence for trial.

Legal Equation

Confrontation Clause

Testimonial statements (admissible)	=	Declarant unavailable + subject to earlier cross-examination by accused.
Nontestimonial statements (admissible)	=	Response to an ongoing emergency + not obtained to gather evidence.

■ EXCEPTIONS TO THE HEARSAY RULE

The Federal Rules of Evidence list the hearsay exceptions in three separate rules. Rule 803 lists twenty-three exceptions that may be used whether or not the declarant is available to testify. Rule 804 lists five exceptions that may not be used unless the lawyer demonstrates to the judge that the declarant is unavailable as a witness. Rule 807 is a so-called residual or catch-all exception that provides for the recognition of other exceptions that are not specifically listed in those instances in which there are "equivalent circumstantial guarantees of trustworthiness" to the exceptions recognized in the Federal Rules.

Two other exceptions to hearsay, prior inconsistent and prior consistent statements (801[d][1][A]) and admissions (801[d][1][B]), are recognized by as many as ten states as exceptions to the hearsay rule but are not included as an exception to hearsay under the Federal Rules of Evidence and by the rules of evidence in other states. Commentators often refer to these statements as *exemptions* from the hearsay rule because under the federal rule they are exempt from the rule on hearsay evidence.

Most of the hearsay exceptions were first recognized in the common law and refined throughout the years. How do we square the introduction of exceptions to the hearsay rule with the threats of insincerity, faulty perception, deficiencies in memory, and errors in narration?

One answer is that most of these exceptions possess some degree of reliability or trustworthiness. For example, Rule 803(2) permits the introduction into evidence of statements provoked by an exciting event so long as the declarant speaks while under the influence of the event. The time between the event and the statement typically is short, reducing the threat of a faulty memory. The fact the declarant spoke excitedly and with little or no time for thought reduces concern that the statement was an intentional falsehood. Rule 804(4) is another example; according to Lilly (2006), most people likely will be truthful in statements about their medical condition made for diagnosis or treatment.

A second explanation for hearsay exceptions is necessity. A victim's "dying declaration" (Rule 804[b][2]) about the cause of his or her imminent death may be necessary in a murder prosecution. This statement also is thought to be reliable because the law assumes an individual confronting imminent death will be truthful. Necessity also arises when a witness is absent, either physically absent or absent because of a testimonial privilege, a loss of memory, or a refusal to testify.

In the last analysis, the exceptions to hearsay are the product of the evolution of the common law, and there likely is no single unifying explanation for each and every exception.

An attorney desiring to introduce hearsay evidence has the challenge of finding the exception that applies to the testimony he or she wants to get admitted into evidence. In some instances, more than one exception may apply. The lawyer then must persuade the judge that the statement falls within one of the exceptions. The jury determines how much weight or importance to give the evidence.

At times, lawyers may encounter double hearsay (discussed below). Jessica tells you what Natasha said to her. In this example, Jessica's statement to you is hearsay. We have double hearsay if Natasha told Jessica what Maeve said to Natasha. Each statement in a double hearsay statement must be admissible under an exception to the hearsay rule. In other words, there must be an exception that covers both Natasha's statement to Jessica and Jessica's statement to you.

Roughly half of the states follow the hearsay rules listed in the Federal Rules of Evidence. The others follow their own rules, which at times may be similar to the Federal Rules.

The remainder of the chapter discusses some of the most frequently relied upon exceptions to the hearsay rule. We first need to look at admissions and confessions.

[handwritten: admit that they were in the area → should be truthful → doesn't have to be]

■ ADMISSIONS AND CONFESSIONS *[handwritten: → usually reliable and they can contest]*

An admission of a party-opponent is a statement or conduct outside of the courtroom (e.g., extrajudicial) by a party to the litigation that is inconsistent with the party's claim at trial. Audiotapes of a defendant's narcotics sales to a confidential informant were admitted as admissions of a party-opponent (*United States v. Tolliver*, 454 F.3d 660 [7th Cir. 2006]).

The traditional approach is that admissions are an exception to the hearsay rule. The thinking is that an admission typically is reliable and an individual who made the admission has the option of taking the stand and explaining the

[handwritten: confession = admission by party opponent ↳ defendant in criminal case]

statement. A second reason for admitting admissions is that people should be held responsible for their statements. The Federal Rules (801[d][2]) categorize admissions as nonhearsay, and they are freely admissible as an "exemption" from the hearsay rule.

California and other states follow the traditional approach and treat admissions as an "exception" to the hearsay rule rather than as an "exemption." There are various explanations for the Federal Rules exemption of admissions by a party-opponent. The Advisory Committee on Rules of Evidence appeared to reason that the use of admission against a party-opponent is a traditional part of the adversary process.

As you read this chapter, pay attention to the difference between an admission and a declaration against interest. See also Table 9.1.

Admissions by a Party

A defendant's confession and other admissions may be admitted into evidence as an **admission by party-opponent**. An admission is not required to be a statement of guilt. A damaging statement that undercuts the defendant's case also qualifies as an admission.

An admission may be a verbal expression or conduct. Consider an individual who immediately after a hit-and-run accident tells a bystander that he or she "did not see the red light." Removing his or her fingerprints from the crime scene and painting the car hours after the hit-and-run accident are acts that may qualify as an admission.

There may be an admission through silence. An example is a failure to respond to a bystander's remark that "you ran a red light and caused the accident." The question is whether a reasonable person would have denied the statement under the circumstances. The defendant at trial may explain his or her failure to reply.

Keep in mind that the defendant may take the stand and deny or clarify the statement. An admission, like other evidence, also may be excluded from evidence because it is prejudicial. Consider a statement by the driver that this is the "third time I ran a red light this month." A judge may consider the reference to the other incidents prejudicial.

A confession is admissible as an admission. A confession is a direct statement of guilt by an accused. The confession only is admissible if the police follow the steps set forth in the *Miranda* decision and in Supreme Court cases elaborating on the requirements of *Miranda*. Statements made to the police before an individual is read the *Miranda* rights may be admissible as an admission. The fact an individual relied on his or her right against self-incrimination and invoked his or her right to an attorney and/or right to silence may not be used against him or her at trial. The reason is that this type of evidence would penalize an individual for relying on his or her constitutional rights and that invoking the *Miranda* rights does not necessarily mean that an individual had something to hide. He or she may merely have thought it best to avoid speaking to the police without the presence of a lawyer (*Doyle v. Ohio*, 426.U.S. 610 [1976]).

[handwritten annotations: ρ defendant / Someone makes a statement and you agree/affirm it → that is admissible]

Adoptive Admissions *[handwritten: "you killed him" → *you hang your head down* ↳ communicative behavior]*

An **adoptive admission** occurs when a person reacts to a statement made by another person that may reasonably be interpreted as an affirmation that the statement is true. In other words, the individual through words or actions accepts the statement of another person. The theory is that individuals will not agree with a statement that is false, particularly when the statement suggests that they are guilty of a crime.

The typical situation involving an adoptive admission is when an individual alleges that another person committed a crime and the alleged offender admits his or her guilt, nods his or her head in agreement, remains silent, or gives an ambiguous response ("I may have committed the crime"). What if the alleged offender says "I am not talking" or walks away? Think about how you react when you agree with a statement by another person.

Let us return to our hit-and-run example. If the bystander says to the driver that "you clearly went through a red light" and the defendant replies, "I am sorry; you are right," the defendant has adopted the initial statement. The defendant's silence in response to the bystander's question also would be an admission.

A judge must determine if a statement was heard and understood and whether a reasonable person would have objected to the statement. The purpose of the judge making a preliminary determination whether the statement was adopted is to prevent the jury from considering a statement that was not adopted by the defendant. The jury then may be asked to determine the probative value of the adopted statement. *The test for the jury is whether a reasonable person in the individual's position would have denied or protested the statement if he or she believed the statement was untrue.*

A number of courts only apply the adoptive admission exception when the individuals are physically face-to-face and do not apply the exception if an individual does not respond to an accusation or question in a phone call, e-mail, text, or written note.

Another adoptive admission exception arises when an individual is confronted by the police or another authority figure. The law assumes most people will remain silent in this situation. Why? As noted, a refusal to talk to the police following the reading of the *Miranda* rights does not constitute an admission because an individual is entitled to exercise his or her right against self-incrimination. How far should we extend the adoptive admission exception? What about an employer, coach, or parent?

Authorized Admissions *you give someone authority to speak on your behalf.*

An authorized admission is a statement by an individual authorized to speak on behalf of a party to a legal case. This may arise when the head of a corporation accused of selling a defective product that results in serious injury or death admits or denies that the defect was covered up by corporate officials. The question is whether the individual is authorized to speak on behalf of the organization or is only authorized to speak for him- or herself. In other instances, statements by a lawyer or by an accountant handling financial matters may be introduced as adoptive admissions.

Admissions by an Agent → *employee who works for you in a big company* *has liability* *↳ will talk*

An admission by a "party's agent or servant" is a statement concerning a "matter within the scope of the agency or employment made during the existence of the relationship." An example is a truck driver who makes a statement to the police that he or she drove in an irresponsible and reckless fashion. This statement is admissible against the employer because it concerns a matter within the driver's responsibilities.

Admissions by a Co-Conspirator → *"we" did this together*

Most states and the federal government recognize a hearsay exception for statements made by co-conspirators. Statements by a co-conspirator may be used against other conspirators. The statement must be made during the course of the conspiracy and in furtherance of the purpose of the conspiracy.

Table 9.1 ■ Admissions
A statement may be admissible under the Federal Rules of Evidence, under various state rules, or as an admissions exception to the hearsay rule if used against a party and the statement falls within one of the following situations.

Admissions of a Party

Statement by a party to a legal action

Adoptive Admission

Party to the legal action adopts the statement as true

Authorized Admission

Statement made by person authorized to make a statement regarding the subject matter of a legal action

Admission by Agent

Statement made by agent of a party to the lawsuit within the scope of agency or employment during the existence of the relationship

Admission by Co-conspirator

Statement made by co-conspirator of a party during the conspiracy and in furtherance of the conspiracy

9.2 YOU DECIDE

Harry Guzman was charged with acting along with Juan Cruz to burn a building that killed two people. Guzman sought to introduce two statements by Cruz to establish that Cruz acted alone in burning the building. In the first statement, Cruz and an informant drove past the site of the fire. The informant asked Cruz whether he committed the arson. Cruz responded that "I didn't have anything to do with that." Shortly thereafter in response to another question from the informant, Cruz stated that "[t]hey wanted me to do it but I didn't do it because you know two people died there." Cruz also told the informant that "[the guy] that did it, he didn't even get paid for it." Cruz was unavailable at trial. Was this statement to the informant against Cruz's penal interest?

A state trooper walked into the park to offer a reward for information about the fire. Five minutes after the trooper left the park, Javier Rodriguez heard Cruz comment in Spanish to a friend that "I just told you that I started the fire, how do I know that you . . . won't rat me out." The prosecution wanted to introduce the testimony of the "third" person to whom Cruz was speaking who would testify that Cruz was "joking." Should the judge allow the jury to hear the statement of Cruz's friend in considering whether Cruz's statement is an admission? See *United States v. Guzman* (603 F.3d 99 [1st Cir. 2010]).

You can learn what the court decided by referring to the study site, **http://study.sagepub.com/lippmance.**

CRIMINAL EVIDENCE IN THE NEWS

In 2006, U.S. Supreme Court Justice Antonin Scalia pronounced that opponents of the death penalty could not point to a single instance in which a guilty individual had been executed. In August 2014, evidence emerged that Texas may have put an innocent man to death in executing Cameron Todd Willingham in February 2004.

Cameron was executed after being convicted of the arson death of his three children, 2-year-old Amber and 1-year-old twins Karmon and Kameron. His conviction rested on two pillars, forensic analysis of the fire and the testimony of jailhouse informant Johnny E. Webb. The forensic evidence relied on at trial was discredited by leading forensic experts whose analysis was endorsed by the Texas Forensic Science Commission. Governor Rick Perry declared Willingham a "monster" and refused to stay his execution. The Texas Board of Pardons and Paroles appointed by Governor Perry as recently as March 2014 refused to grant Willingham a posthumous pardon.

The discrediting of the forensic report did not deter John H. Jackson, the prosecutor in the Willingham case and now a judge, from declaring that Willingham was a "psychopathic killer" and there was "overwhelming" evidence of guilt independent of the "undeniably flawed forensic report." Based on Willingham's lengthy criminal history, there was a natural predisposition to view him as guilty. But, in August 2014, Webb in two lengthy interviews described that he had only talked to Willingham on one occasion in the county jail. He then had been encouraged by prosecutor Jackson to testify that Willingham had confided in him that he was responsible for the fire that killed his children. Jackson had shown Webb photos of the dead children and told him that his testimony would help keep a dangerous man off the street. Jackson promised Webb that he would help to make his first-degree robbery charge "disappear" and that even if Webb was convicted he would "help him later." Webb subsequently pled guilty to robbery.

The highly respected Innocence Project conducted two lengthy interviews with Webb a decade after Willingham's death and in July 2014 based on their findings filed a grievance with the Texas Bar Association against Jackson alleging that Jackson "fabricated and concealed evidence" and that Webb had received special favors in exchange for his testimony, which both Jackson and Webb were aware was false.

The Marshall Project, a media site dedicated to criminal justice reform, uncovered documents that record that Jackson made efforts to reduce the severity of the robbery charge for which Webb was convicted, to have him transferred to a less dangerous and disciplined correctional institution, to obtain his early release, and to provide him with financial support from a wealthy, local businessman while in prison as well as following his release from prison.

In a 1996 letter, Jackson urged a criminal justice official to afford Webb an "out of sequence" parole hearing because of Webb's cooperation in Willingham's prosecution and because of the threats against him. Webb was granted parole in 1998 but almost immediately returned to prison on drug charges.

A number of state rules of evidence require judges to give jurors special instructions when a jailhouse informant testifies. The jury in weighing the credibility of the informant is instructed to consider

- the extent to which the informant's testimony is confirmed by other evidence;
- the specificity of the testimony;
- the extent to which the testimony contains details known only by the perpetrator;
- the extent to which the details of the testimony could be obtained from a source other than the defendant;
- the informant's criminal record;
- any benefits received in exchange for the testimony;
- whether the informant previously has provided reliable or unreliable information; and
- the circumstances under which the informant initially provided the information to the police or the prosecutor, including whether the informant was responding to leading questions.

previously made @ oath

■ PRIOR STATEMENTS

There are three types of prior statements by a witness that are not considered hearsay and are admissible for the truth of the matter asserted (substantive proof). The first is prior inconsistent statements, the second is prior consistent statements, and the third is prior identifications.

"it was night when crime occured" — "it was day time when crime occured"

Prior Inconsistent Statements *↳used to impeach credibility*

Federal Rule 801(d)(1)(A) categorizes prior inconsistent statements as exempt nonhearsay although as noted above a number of states categorize prior inconstant statements as an exception to hearsay. Inconsistent statements are statements made outside of court before the witness testifies at trial that are inconsistent with the witness's direct testimony. A specific provision addressing these statements was necessary because under the common law a witness's own out-of-court statements are hearsay if introduced for the truth of the matter asserted. The thinking is that these statements should not be considered hearsay because the declarant is available to testify at trial and the jury is able to observe the declarant and his or her response.

Inconsistent statements are admissible under the federal rules:

Trial. The declarant testifies at the trial or hearing and is subject to cross-examination about the statement.

Inconsistent. The statement is inconsistent with the witness's current testimony.

Oath. The inconsistent statement was given under oath subject to the penalty of perjury at a trial, hearing, other proceeding or deposition. Various states do not require that the inconsistent statement was made under oath.

Testimony. The witness is given opportunity to admit, explain the inconsistency, or deny making the statement.

Under the Federal Rules of Evidence, an inconsistent statement that is not made under oath is admissible to impeach a witness's lack of credibility. The statement is not offered for truth of the matter asserted and is not hearsay.

Consider the following example. A testifying witness testifies at trial that he or she has no idea which gang member shot the victim. The prosecutor may introduce the witness's prior statement made under oath at an earlier trial that the defendant committed the crime. Once again, under the Federal Rules to be exempt from hearsay, the witness's prior statement is required to have been made under oath and subject to the penalty of perjury. The requirement that the prior testimony was given under oath provides proof that the statement was made, and the witness may be cross-examined on the prior statement.

In *United States v. Scruggs*, Travis Friend implicated James Wilbur Scruggs in a murder in several sworn statements. At trial, he denied any knowledge of the murder. The prosecutor introduced Friend's prior statements at trial as proof of Scruggs's involvement in the killing (*United States v. Scruggs*, 356 F.3d 539 F.3d 539 [5th Cir. 2004]).

Some states allow an unsworn prior inconsistent statement to be offered into evidence as substantive evidence. There are several reasons. First, the prior statement is closer in time to the events and may be more accurate and reliable than the testimony offered at trial. Second, jurors have difficulty with the notion that testimony should be considered for impeachment purposes only and likely will consider the testimony as substantive evidence in any event.

Prior Consistent Statements

Prior consistent statements are admissible to *rehabilitate* a witness. Prior consistent statements are introduced on redirect examination after the witness has been impeached by a prior inconsistent statement or by allegations that his or her testimony recently was fabricated or is based on a motive such as friendship or a bribe.

Federal Rule 801(d)(1)(B) and various states consider prior consistent statements to be exempt from the hearsay rule although other states consider these statements to be exceptions to the hearsay rule.

A prior consistent statement is not required to be given under oath and subject to the penalty of perjury.

There also is a *premotive rule* requirement for prior consistent statements intended to ensure the trustworthiness of these statements. The United States Supreme Court has ruled that a prior consistent statement may be admitted to "rebut a charge of recent fabrication or improper influence or motive" if the statement was made before an individual developed a motive to lie about making the statement. A prior consistent statement made after the allegation of the declarant's motive to lie arose is inadmissible in evidence (*Tome v. United States* 64 U.S. 150 [1995]).

In *Tome*, Matthew Wayne Tome was charged with the sexual abuse of his 4-year-old daughter. Tome was divorced and shared joint custody with the child's mother. The prosecution's evidence indicated that the young girl disclosed the abuse to her mother when on vacation. The defense contended the child's statements about her abuse were influenced by the mother and fabricated by the mother in an effort to achieve sole custody. The U.S. Supreme Court held that the judge improperly permitted into evidence the statement made by the child to her mother and to other individuals after a motive to fabricate arose.

Consider the following illustrations of prior consistent statements. Juan testifies at trial that Pierre killed the victim. The defense attorney may impeach Juan by suggesting that he testified in return for the plea bargain he entered into with the government in another case. A statement by Juan to Joanne before he entered into the plea bargain that Pierre was the killer may be used to rebut the charge that Juan's testimony that Pierre was the killer was influenced by the plea agreement. On the other hand, if Juan's statement to Paula took place after Juan entered into the plea bargain, his statement to Paula may be excluded from evidence by the judge because Juan had a motive to pin the killing on Pierre.

Identifications—that the person who robbed the bank ⇒ NOT hearsay

Rule 801(d)(1)(C) provides that a witness's identification of a "person made after perceiving the person" is admissible as an exemption to the hearsay rule. Witnesses typically are asked to make an in-court identification of the offender. This understandably may be dismissed by the jury as a formality because the defendant is sitting at the defense table. A prior identification made closer to the time of the crime during a lineup, confrontation, photographic display, police report, or related hearing may be more reliable, particularly since the defendant's personal appearance may have changed.

Under the Federal Rules, prior **identifications** are admissible as substantive evidence. Prior identifications are admissible regardless of whether the witness makes an in-court identification so long as the witness is "subject to cross-examination concerning the statement [earlier identification]" at trial (*United States v. Anglin*, 169 F.3d 154 [2d Cir. 1999]).

In *United States v. Lewis*, an eyewitness identified the perpetrator in a photo array following a robbery. She was unable to identify the offender in court and instead picked out a deputy U.S. marshal. She then was shown the photographic display and picked out the photograph of the offender that she had selected earlier. The Second Circuit Court of Appeals affirmed the trial court judge's ruling that the FBI agent should be permitted to testify that Norma Sharpe had selected the same photo following the bank robbery (*United States v. Lewis*, 565 F.2d 1248 [2nd Cir. 1977]). A similar situation arose in *United States v. Salameh*. The appellate court in this terrorism trial affirmed that a "prior identification is admissible . . . regardless of whether the witness confirms the identification in court" (*United States v. Salameh*, 152 F.3d 88 [2d Cir. 1988]).

In criminal cases, identifications must satisfy the Sixth Amendment to the Constitution and the requirements of the Due Process Clause, topics discussed in Chapter Seventeen on lineups.

9.3 YOU DECIDE

John Foster, a correctional counselor at a federal prison, was brutally attacked with a metal pipe and suffered a skull fracture. The victim was hospitalized, and initially his memory was impaired and he was unable to remember his attacker's name. Roughly five weeks later, the victim identified the defendant James Owens as the assailant and selected the defendant's photo from a photo array. On direct examination at Owens's trial for attempted murder, Foster stated "he clearly remembered identifying" the defendant as the offender. On cross-examination, Foster testified that he had no memory of "seeing his assailant" or even if he "had the opportunity to see" his assailant he "could not remember" any visitors other than the FBI agent and could not recall whether any of his visitors suggested that Owens was the assailant. The defendant was convicted and sentenced to twenty years' imprisonment. Was Foster's identification to the FBI of Owens admissible? Was Foster "subject to cross-examination" about his identification of Foster? See *United States v. Owen* (484 U.S. 553 [1988]).

You can learn what the court decided by referring to the study site, **http://study.sagepub.com/lippmance.**

Legal Equation

Prior inconsistent statement	=	The declarant testifies at the trial or hearing
	+	Is subject to cross-examination concerning a statement that is inconsistent with the witness's testimony
	+	The inconsistent statement was given under oath subject to the penalty of perjury at a trial, hearing, other proceeding, or deposition
	+	The witness is given opportunity to admit, explain the inconsistency, or deny making the statement.
Prior consistent statement	=	Offered to rebut express or implied charge of recent fabrication or improper influence or motive
	+	Statement made before the motive to fabricate or improper influence or motive.
Identifications	=	Prior identification of a person
	+	Subject to cross-examination at trial.

■ HEARSAY EXCEPTIONS REGARDLESS OF WHETHER THE DECLARANT IS AVAILABLE

The Federal Rules of Evidence under Rule 803 provide that twenty-three of the twenty-eight hearsay exceptions are not excluded by the hearsay rule, even though the declarant is unavailable to testify. The thinking is that these statements are so reliable that they may be introduced into evidence even when a live witness is available to take the stand.

■ PRESENT SENSE IMPRESSION

when you describe as you see it happening "did you just see that guy punch her?"

Federal Rule 803(1) defines a **present sense impression** as a "statement describing or explaining an event or condition made while or immediately after the declarant perceived it." The statement must describe or explain rather than analyze the event and must be made immediately or within a brief period following the event. The exception is based on the notion that an individual's narration of an event that he or she is observing will be both accurate and reliable because there is no threat that the declarant's memory will fail in recounting the events and the declarant's account is given at the same time he or she is observing the event.

Keep the following in mind in considering present sense impressions.

Participant. The declarant may be an observer and is not required to be involved in the event. The declarant is required to speak from his or her own sensory perceptions.

Subject matter. The declarant must describe or explain an event or condition. The thinking is that a statement that involves analysis indicates that the declarant had a sufficient opportunity to reflect on the event.

Contemporaneous. The statement is required to be made at the precise moment the declarant is observing the event. The Advisory Committee on Rules of Evidence notes that in most instances "precise contemporaneity is not possible" and a "slight lapse is allowable." Courts have held that there is a requirement of "substantial contemporaneity" although the determination of how much time may pass is within the discretion of the judge. The longer the period between the observation and the statement, the less reliable the statement.

In *United States v. Hawkins*, the police received a 911 call complaining about a disturbance in a nearby apartment. Seven minutes later, Louise Hawkins called 911 from a convenience store stating that her husband pointed a gun at her and describing the gun. The court found that despite the lapse in time between Hawkins's call and the altercation with her husband, her ability to describe the gun provided confidence in the reliability of her account (*United States v. Hawkin*s, 58 F.2d 723 [8th Cir. 1995]).

Declarant. The present sense exception applies to both identified and unidentified declarants. The declarant is not required to be available.

Knowledge. The declarant must directly experience the events and may not rely on the account of another individual.

Corroboration. There is no requirement that the declarant's description is corroborated by another individual.

Legal Equation

Present sense expression	=	Declarant must describe or explain an event or condition based on own sensory perception
	+	Made at precise moment of observed event.

 ## 9.4 YOU DECIDE

State Trooper Jeffrey Jones of the Maryland State Police stopped an automobile because Jones wanted to determine whether the vehicle was displaying a rear license plate. The Ford Pinto was operated by a female who was accompanied by Willie Hooks, the owner of the vehicle. Jones directed the female to enter his squad car to discuss the fact she was in violation of the conditions of her New Jersey learner's permit. Jones allegedly handcuffed and sexually molested the female driver. She returned to her vehicle and instructed Hooks to get the officer's license plate number. Jones, however, allegedly sped off at a rapid speed without lights. Hooks tried to give chase, but his car was no match for Jones's squad car. Hooks stopped at the first roadside emergency phone, and the female victim reported the incident to the police. Jones denied physical contact with the female and denied operating his vehicle without headlights.

State Trooper William Byrd stated he was monitoring the radio in his squad car when he heard two CB radio transmissions.

1st Speaker: Look at Smokey Bear southbound with no lights on at a high rate of speed.

2nd Speaker: Look at that little car trying to catch up with him.

The trial court judge held the CB accounts were admissible as present sense impressions, and Jones was convicted of sexual offense battery and misconduct in office. Was the trial court correct in admitting the CB transmissions? See *State v. Jones* (532 A.2d 169 [Md. Ct. App. 1987]).

You can learn what the court decided by referring to the study site, **http://study.sagepub.com/lippmance.**

Rule 803. Exceptions to the Rule Against Hearsay—Regardless of Whether the Declarant Is Available as a Witness

The following are not excluded by the rule against hearsay, regardless of whether the declarant is available as a witness:

(1) Present Sense Impression. A statement describing or explaining an event or condition, made while or immediately after the declarant perceived it.

[handwritten: "Holy Shit" reacting immediatly—what ever comes out of your mouth]

■ EXCITED UTTERANCE

An **excited utterance** is a "statement relating to a startling event or condition made while the declarant was under the stress of excitement caused by the event or condition." There are three primary requirements for an excited utterance:

Startling event. There was a startling event that resulted in the observer's shock and excitement.

Time. The statement was made while the observer was under the stress of the event either contemporaneously or immediately following the event.

Scope. The statement was related to the event.

There must be an event that is sufficiently startling to elicit a sense of excitement in the declarant. The statement must be made while the individual is overwhelmed and excited. It is this state of excitement that helps to ensure the truthfulness of the spontaneous statement because there is little possibility that the statement is fabricated. The risk of memory loss is reduced by the fact that the declarant's statement is proximate to the event. Of course, an argument may be made that an individual's perception may be distorted by the thrill and excitement of witnessing the event. On balance, the policy is that the search for truth is advanced by the admission of this evidence.

The statement must "relate" to the exciting event that the individual has observed although unlike present sense impression it need not explain or describe the event. Courts are divided on whether an opinion is admissible (e.g., "that guy was crazy"). The declarant is not required to be identified or present at trial although he or she must have personal knowledge of (witnessed) the events. A declarant may contact the police after seeing an assailant rob and shoot a victim. The police officer would then testify about the declarant's statement (*United States v. Luciano*, 414 F.3d 174 [1st Cir. 2005]).

There is no specific time within which the statement is required to be made although the statement must be made while the individual remains excited as a result of the event. A Wisconsin court admitted a statement made by a victim ten minutes after being hit in the head by a tire iron during a robbery. The fact that the victim knew the assailant undoubtedly increased the trial court judge's confidence in the accuracy of the identification.

Judges exercise their discretion in determining whether a statement made after an event is a spontaneous utterance. In a Florida case, the defendant tried to grab the victim and push her into his van and threatened her with a firearm. The victim managed to reach her house and call 911. It took fifteen or twenty minutes before the distraught and terrified victim was able to speak to the police. The victim's statements to the police were admitted as spontaneous utterances because there was a startling event that resulted in statements made under stress with little possibility of fabrication (*Bell v. State*, 847 So.2d 558 [Fla. App. 2003]). The statement to a police officer by an eyewitness to a shooting who fled the scene, was shot, and subsequently collapsed was admitted by a trial court judge although the statement was made forty minutes after the shooting (*United States v. Delvi*, 275 F.Supp.2d 412 [S.D.N.Y. 2003]). At some point, the time between the crime and the individual's account is too lengthy for the court to conclude that the statement is spontaneous with little threat that the statement was fabricated (*North Carolina v. Riley*, 472 S.E.2d 857 [N.C. App. 2002]).

Legal Equation

Excited utterance **=** Startling event
          + Statement under stress of event
          + Statement related to event.

9.5 YOU DECIDE

Jacqueline LaMothe saw Bonnie Eaton leave the bar with three men. She testified that she heard a shot and then a scream, and that then someone ran into the bar and told her to telephone for an ambulance because Sharon Ann Snow had been mistakenly shot. LaMothe testified that after making the telephone call she went outside and "asked who had shot the gun once, and nobody answered me.". . . LaMothe testified that Eaton then "yelled out" in response to her inquiry. . . . The judge allowed the prosecutor to ask LaMothe, "What did Bonnie Eaton say?" LaMothe responded, "Joe Puleio." Was Eaton's statement admissible in evidence? Should the judge consider that Puleio apparently considered Eaton his girlfriend and after arriving at the bar Puleio had gotten into two arguments with the men and at one point threatened to shoot one of them? See *Commonwealth v. Puleio* (394 Mass. 101 [1985]).

You can learn what the court decided by referring to the study site, **http://study.sagepub.com/lippmance.**

Rule 803. Hearsay Exceptions: Availability of Declarant Immaterial

The following are not excluded by the hearsay rule, even though the declarant is available as a witness:

(2) **Excited utterance.** A statement relating to a startling event or condition made while the declarant was under the stress of excitement caused by the event or condition.

■ THEN-EXISTING MENTAL, EMOTIONAL, OR PHYSICAL CONDITION

The last two sections discussed a declarant's perceptions of an external event. The exception for **then-existing mental, emotional, or physical condition** is concerned with a declarant's internal (personal) view of his or her own state of mind and emotional, sensory, or physical condition. The statement is admissible to establish what the declarant truthfully believed about his or her condition.

The Advisory Committee on Rules of Evidence notes that the extemporaneous and immediate expression of an individual's personal condition, like present sense impressions and excited utterances, is reliable because these statements do not allow for an opportunity to fabricate or craft a response. A current statement of a declarant's state of mind or emotional or physical condition does not risk a faulty memory or inaccuracy and as noted is likely to be reliable. The risk, of course, is self-characterization, which in many instances is subjective. One person's intense pain may be another individual's discomfort. Jurors, however, can assess the statement based on their own experience.

The drafting committee of the Federal Rules concluded that the immediate expression of an internal state is similar to an immediate statement about an external event that the declarant observed. A statement that "I am afraid" or "I am nervous" or "I am in pain" or "I am starving" or "I plan to marry my girlfriend tomorrow" is a report of an individual's emotional or physical condition that reflects the declarant's mental or physical condition at the time of the statement.

Rule 803(3) articulates the requirements for statements of mental, emotional, or physical condition. Note that the rule is limited to a "then-existing state of mind." This is because statements of past condition risk a faulty memory or a fabricated response. Consider the statement that "I acted in self-defense yesterday when I shot the intruder because I was frightened to death." Rule 803(3) also excludes statement of belief. The statement that "I believe I felt an overwhelming sense of fear" is not admissible because the word *believe* introduces a measure of uncertainty and is not a clear statement of state of mind. One more confusing observation is that the United States Supreme Court held that statements of a present state of mind are admissible to prove the declarant's future conduct.

Keep in mind that a witness may testify on behalf of a defendant's claim of self-defense that she stated that "she was afraid of her husband." This statement is a statement about the defendant's state of mind. On the other hand, the witness likely could not testify that the victim stated that her husband was "out of control and violent." This is a statement about her husband's behavior rather than her state of mind. Nonetheless, this might be admissible as circumstantial evidence that the defendant acted in self-defense.

Legal Equation

Then-existing mental, emotional, or physical condition   **=**   Statement
  +   Existing mental, emotional, or mental condition.

9.6 YOU DECIDE

James Boyden Jr. was at his sister's apartment. He left the apartment about 8 p.m. informing his sister Marie Boyden Connors that he was going out "to meet Billy Herd." Boyden's dead body was found on a nearby street several hours later.

William "Billy" Herd was charged with the murder. May Connors testify about Boyden's statement to prove that Herd killed Boyden? See *United States v. Houlihan* (871 F.Supp. 1495 [D. Mass. 1994]).

You can learn what the court decided by referring to the study site, http://study.sagepub.com/lippmance.

Rule 803. Exceptions to the Rule Against Hearsay—Regardless of Whether the Declarant Is Available as a Witness

The following are not excluded by the rule against hearsay, regardless of whether the declarant is available as a witness: . . .

(3) **Then-Existing Mental, Emotional, or Physical Condition.** A statement of the declarant's then-existing state of mind (such as motive, intent, or plan) or emotional, sensory, or physical condition (such as mental feeling, pain, or bodily health), but not including a statement of memory or belief to prove the fact remembered or believed unless it relates to the validity or terms of the declarant's will.

■ MEDICAL TREATMENT-DIAGNOSIS

Federal Rule 803(4) recognizes a broad hearsay exception for **medical treatment-diagnosis**. The hearsay exception allows for "[s]tatements made for . . . medical diagnosis or treatment and describing medical history, or past or present symptoms, pain, or sensations." The rule also states that the cause or source of the declarant's medical condition is admissible "insofar as reasonably pertinent to diagnosis or treatment."

Statements made for medical treatment or diagnosis are considered reliable because individuals have an interest in ensuring effective diagnosis or treatment. Statements made for diagnosis may involve a crime victim's statements to a doctor describing the physical or psychological impact of the crime. Some commentators are skeptical about the reliability of statements made for diagnosis because an individual may exaggerate his or her symptoms or injuries in order to appear more sympathetic at trial. A second reason for the medical treatment-diagnosis exception is efficiency. The medical treatment-diagnosis exception avoids the need to require doctors, nurses, and other medical professionals to testify about the patient's condition.

The medical treatment exception does not allow for the admission of fault or blame or the identity of the individual responsible for the injury. However, a statement about the cause of the injury, such as that the declarant was hit over the head, is important for medical treatment and considered reliable. Attributing the act to a specific individual is not considered reliable.

An exception recognized by various courts involves child abuse cases in which statements identifying the perpetrator are admissible in court because this information is considered to be a necessary part of the physician's treatment. This is due to the fact that if a perpetrator is a member of the family the treatment may include removal of the victim from the home. The identity of a perpetrator may be important information for a therapist treating a victim of abuse although this is of little significance to a medical doctor.

There are several conditions for the admission of statements made for medical diagnosis or treatment:

Purpose. The statement is made for medical diagnosis or treatment. This is a subjective test. The patient must be seeking medical diagnosis or treatment.

Scope. The statement must fit into one of three categories: (1) accounts of medical history, (2) descriptions of past or present symptoms or sensations, or (3) the inception of the condition or its general cause. Statements about the cause of an injury (e.g., "I was hit over the head") are admissible although statements attributing the condition to the act of another do not fit within the exception. "John hit me over the head" is not admissible to establish that John was the perpetrator although the statement is admissible to establish the cause of injury.

9.7 YOU DECIDE

Hazel Chatfield and Judith Moen were found dead as a result of gunshot wounds to the head. The defendant, Moen, was charged and convicted of aggravated murder and sentenced to death. Dr. Daniel Davis Mulkey was permitted to testify about statements of Chatfield describing the behavior of her son-in-law, Ronald Howard Moen.

"Dr. Daniel Mulkey testified that he treated Hazel Chatfield from August 1985 up to and including visits on February 11 and March 11, 1986. During the latter two visits, Mrs. Chatfield complained of depression and despondency since her daughter and son-in-law (defendant) had moved into her home. Mrs. Chatfield appeared agitated, anxious, nervous, very tearful, and crying. Dr. Mulkey attempted to treat her for a potentially fatal lesion but, because

of her situation at home, was unable to convince her that she needed treatment. Dr. Mulkey further testified that Mrs. Chatfield told him that she was upset about her daughter and son-in-law, that her son-in-law had been physically abusive to her daughter, and that 'she felt he might kill them both.' Dr. Mulkey diagnosed her condition as situational depression and recommended that defendant be removed from the home. A former husband of Judith Moen testified that defendant was pursuing a dissolution of his marriage with Judith and quoted the defendant as saying, "I'm finally going to get rid of the b–ch one way or the other."

Should the trial court judge have allowed the jury to hear Dr. Mulkey's account of his treatment of Mrs. Chatfield? See *State v. Moen* (786 P.2d 111 [Ore. 1990]).

You can learn what the court decided by referring to the study site, **http://study.sagepub.com/lippmance.**

Rule 803. Hearsay Exceptions; Availability of Declarant Immaterial

The following are not excluded by the hearsay rule, even though the declarant is available as a witness.

    (4) Statements for purposes of medical diagnosis or treatment. Statements made for purposes of medical diagnosis or treatment and describing medical history, or past or present symptoms, pain, or sensations, or the inception or general character of the cause or external source thereof insofar as reasonably pertinent to diagnosis or treatment.

■ BUSINESS RECORDS

The Federal Rules of Evidence and state rules recognize a **business records** exception to hearsay. There are a mass of documents potentially relevant to a criminal case including police reports and medical and hospital records, bank documents, and computer printouts. These records are hearsay when introduced for the truth of the matter asserted because they reflect the recorded statements of the individual who created the document. Business records nonetheless are an exception to hearsay because they are considered reliable. Organizations follow a standardized approach in creating accurate records on which they can rely in making decisions. Doctors depend on accurate records in making medical decisions.

Business records may be introduced by the organization's "custodian of the records" who testifies about the methods used to collect, draft, record, and safeguard the reports. The testimony should include the steps taken to ensure the accuracy of the records.

There are several elements to the business records exception. The cross-examination will attempt to undermine the accuracy of the business records in order to challenge their admissibility.

Scope. The business records exception is broadly drafted to admit almost any type of information. This includes an "act, event, condition, opinion, or diagnosis."

Personal knowledge. The record must be recorded by an individual with personal knowledge of the data or by a person who received information from an individual or individuals with personal knowledge. Police crime reports are compiled by analysts who receive reports from police officers who record their activities on the beat.

Time. The information needs to be recorded within a reasonable period of time. This is designed to ensure that the information is trustworthy.

Regular course of business. The record must be made in the customary course of business. This is intended to ensure that the record is recorded in regular and standardized procedure and accurate. Confidence in the accuracy of the information is enhanced when the document is relied on by the organization. A related requirement is that making the record was a "regular practice of the organization." Documents prepared on a regular basis likely are based on standardized practice, which also increases the likelihood of the document's accuracy.

Witness. These conditions must be demonstrated by the testimony of the person in charge of maintaining the records ("custodian") or by a certification by the custodian that the records meet the requirements of Rule 803(6).

The custodian is not required to have knowledge of who collected or compiled the records. The issue is whether the custodian is able to testify about the organization's record-keeping practices.

Trustworthiness. A business record is not admissible if the "source of information [or] the method or circumstances of preparation indicate a lack of trustworthiness." This is intended to exclude from evidence an internal investigation of misconduct drafted to insulate criminal justice professionals in an agency from civil and criminal liability rather than to objectively identify misconduct.

Business. The term *business* is broadly defined to include a broad range of organizations, including "business, organization, occupation or calling of every kind, whether or not for profit." Courts have interpreted this to include self-employed individuals. The records of a blackjack dealer in Las Vegas were held to be admissible to establish that an individual underreported his tips on his tax return (*Keogh v. Commissioner*, 713 F.2d 496 [9th Cir. 1983]).

9.8 YOU DECIDE

Christopher Pless was convicted of violating an animal control ordinance based on his failure to control his five pit bulls. He appealed the trial court's ruling that he could not introduce various prior police reports in which he reported that unidentified persons had "trespassed on his property . . . during which trespasses they took pictures, opened doors, killed animals and let animals loose." Does the police report containing his statement qualify under the business record exception? See *Pless v. State* (633 S.E.2d 340 [Ga. App. Ct. 2006]).

You can learn what the court decided by referring to the study site, **http://study.sagepub.com/lippmance.**

Rule 803. Exceptions to the Rule Against Hearsay—Regardless of Whether the Declarant Is Available as a Witness

The following are not excluded by the rule against hearsay, regardless of whether the declarant is available as a witness: . . .

(6) Records of a Regularly Conducted Activity. A record of an act, event, condition, opinion, or diagnosis if:

(A) the record was made at or near the time by—or from information by—someone with knowledge;

(B) the record was kept in the course of a regularly conducted activity of a business, organization, occupation, or calling whether or not for profit;

(C) making the record was a regular practice of that activity;

(D) all these conditions are shown by the testimony of the custodian or another qualified witness, or by a certification that complies with Rule 902(11) or (12) or with a statute permitting certification; and

(E) neither the source of information nor the method of circumstances of preparation indicate a lack of trustworthiness.

if it existed they would have a copy

■ ABSENCE OF BUSINESS RECORDS

Rule 803(7) recognizes a hearsay exception for the absence of a business record. It must be established that it is the regular practice of the business to maintain records of all transactions. The Advisory Committee on Rules of Evidence notes that the "[f]ailure of a record to mention a matter which would ordinarily be mentioned is satisfactory evidence of its nonexistence." In *United Sates v. De Georgia*, the court admitted the computer record of a rental car company that indicated there was no record of the vehicle being rented during the time in which it was stolen. The court concluded that "if a business record designed to note every transaction of a particular kind contains no notation of such a transaction between specified dates, no such transaction occurred between those dates." The reliance on the absence of a record as evidence is termed **negative hearsay** (*United States v. De Georgia*, 420 F.2d 889 [9th Cir. 1969]). There are three foundation requirements for the admissibility of the absence of a record as an exception to hearsay:

1. *Regular course of business.* The proponent is required to show that records are kept in the course of regular activity and that the business regularly kept the records.

2. *Scope of records.* The absence of the records concerns matters that regularly were recorded by the business.

3. *Reliability.* The judge must be confident that the absence of a record is a reliable indicator that an event did not occur.

Rule 803. Exceptions to the Rule Against Hearsay—Regardless of Whether the Declarant Is Available as a Witness

The following are not excluded by the rule against hearsay, regardless of whether the declarant is available as a witness.

(7) Absence of a Record of a Regularly Conducted Activity. Evidence that a matter is not included in a record described in paragraph (6) if:

(A) the evidence is admitted to prove that the matter did not occur or exist;

(B) a record was regularly kept for a matter of that kind; and

(C) neither the possible source of the information nor other circumstances indicate a lack of trustworthiness.

Legal Equation

Business record	=	Record must be recorded by a person with personal knowledge of the data or by an individual who received information from an individual or individuals with personal knowledge
	+	The information needs to be recorded within a reasonable period of time
	+	The record must be made in the regular course of business
	+	These conditions must be demonstrated by the testimony of the person in charge of maintaining the records ("custodian") or by a certification by the custodian
	+	A business record is not admissible if the "source of information [or] the method or circumstances of preparation indicate a lack of trustworthiness"
	+	The term *business* is broadly defined to include virtually any organization, including "business, organization, occupation or calling of every kind, whether or not for profit."

■ PUBLIC RECORDS

The **public records** of agencies include the courts, police, correctional institutions, and every other part of the government. Public records under the Federal Rules of Evidence 803(8)(A) are divided into three categories: acts of the agency, an agency's required observations and reports, and results of investigations. The hearsay exception for public records is based on the interest in the efficient presentation of information without interfering with the work of all the government officials involved in compiling the information. The public records exception is based on the assumption that public officials will accurately and responsibly carry out their responsibilities.

Subsection (A)(i) admits the activities of an office or agency. This includes records of all of an organization's activities including budgetary expenditures, the hiring of employees, and the organization of the agency. This exception is limited to matters reported by agency personnel, which the agency has a duty to report. Individuals outside the agency who submit information to the agency or who issue reports on the activities of an agency do not possess the same legal duty to accurately report information.

Subsection (A)(ii) covers matters "observed" by a public agency "while under a legal duty to report." This might include data on the number of inches of rain, cars traveling on a state highway, or students expelled from school; agricultural records; or the incidence of domestic violence. Once again, information obtained from individuals outside the agency is not included in the hearsay exception.

Observations of law enforcement personnel are excluded from this exception to the hearsay rule because law enforcement personnel may not be neutral because of their interest in obtaining a conviction. Another explanation is that police reports typically rely on victims and eyewitnesses, individuals who are not under the same legal duty as the police to be accurate and ethical. These reports also are inadmissible because of the difficulties of cross-examination of individuals responsible for making the statements in the document. Courts frequently limit this provision to the prosecution in a criminal case and allow the admission of these reports by the defense attorney.

Subsection (A)(iii) allows the admission of "factual findings from a legally authorized investigation." This may involve a government report on the causes of an accident, an agency report on whether an individual was the victim of discrimination, or an autopsy report on the causes of death. A criminal report may discuss the causes and extent of gang violence or police abuse of citizens or the results of an investigation of a police shooting or police corruption. The results of a government investigation are not admissible in a criminal case against a defendant for the reasons discussed above in regard to Subsection (A)(ii).

Subsection (B) provides that a public record is inadmissible if a trial judge determines there is a "lack of trustworthiness." A report prepared in investigating a police shooting may not be admissible in a civil case if prepared in anticipation of litigation.

Federal Rule 803(10) provides that the absence of a record also may be introduced to prove a matter. The lack of a record in the files of the Department of Motor Vehicles of an individual's driver's license may be introduced to demonstrate that an individual does not possess a driver's license.

Rule 803. Exceptions to the Rule Against Hearsay—Regardless of Whether the Declarant Is Available as a Witness

The following are not excluded by the rule against hearsay regardless of whether the declarant is available as a witness:

(8) **Public Records.** A record or statement of a public office if:

  (A) it sets out:

    (i) the office's activities:

    (ii) a matter observed while under a legal duty to report, but not including, in a criminal case, a matter observed by law-enforcement personnel; or

    (iii) in a civil case or against the government in a criminal case, factual findings from a legally authorized investigation; and

  (B) neither the source of information nor other circumstances indicate a lack of trustworthiness. . . .

(10) **Absence of a Public Record**. Testimony—or a certification under Rule 902—that a diligent search failed to disclose a public record or statement if the testimony or certification is admitted to prove that:

  (A) the record or statement does not exist; or

  (B) a matter did not occur or exist, if a public office regularly kept a record or statement for a matter of that kind.

■ VITAL STATISTICS

Birth, death, and marriage records are admissible. These government records are based on the reports of various individuals (e.g., doctors, clergy) and are considered reliable because individuals are under a duty to report these events and they are required to be reported immediately following the occurrence of the event. These individuals are not viewed as possessing a motive to misrepresent the facts. There also is the practical consideration that this information may not be easily available absent these records. Even when the custodian of the records is available to testify as to the authenticity of the records, a certified copy typically is required.

Each state legislature has adopted statutes that establish the forms that are to be completed and the procedures for recording births, deaths, and marriages. Birth certificates typically are filled out by the doctor and sent from the hospital to the county department and then to the state department concerned with compiling **vital statistics**.

Rule 803. Hearsay Exceptions; Availability of Declarant Immaterial

The following are not excluded by the hearsay rule, even though the declarant is available as a witness.

(9) Records of Vital Statistics. Records of data compilations, in any form, of births, fetal deaths, deaths, or marriages, if the report thereof was made to a public office pursuant to requirements of law. . . .

(12) Marriage, Baptismal, and Similar Certificates. Statements of fact contained in a certificate that the maker performed a marriage or other ceremony or administered a sacrament, made by a clergyman, public official, or other person authorized by the rules or practices of a religious organization or by law to perform the act certified, and purporting to have been issued at the time of the act or within a reasonable time thereafter.

---

assert a privilage – don't want to test (husband wife, church w/ sins)

■ UNAVAILABILITY OF DECLARANT

The five hearsay exceptions listed in Federal Rule 804 only are available when the declarant is unavailable. The fact that this evidence is admissible when the declarant is unavailable reflects the judgment that it is better that the evidence be admitted at trial than that the evidence be unavailable at trial.

Rule 804(a) provides a list of circumstances in which a witness is considered to be "unavailable." These circumstances do not exhaust the situations in which a declarant is considered unavailable, and a judge may determine that a witness is unavailable based on reasons not listed in Rule 804(a).

Privilege. The declarant is exempted from testifying based on a privilege. The assertion of a privilege like the attorney-client privilege furthers the social interest in effective legal representation for the defendant.

Refusal. The declarant disregards a court order and refuses to testify. The witness may want to protect the defendant or may fear retaliation if he or she testifies. The judge may hold the witness in contempt and impose a fine or even jail term on an individual who refuses to testify.

Memory. The declarant testifies to a lack of memory of the subject matter. Note that the witness may have a clear memory of matters other than the specific issue on which he or she is being interrogated.

Death. The declarant is unable to testify because of death or because of an existing physical or mental illness or infirmity. The infirmity must result in the witness being incompetent to testify.

Absence. The declarant is absent from the hearing, and the proponent has been unable to procure the declarant's attendance by process or other reasonable means. This typically arises when a party cannot locate the declarant after a good faith search or the declarant refuses to appear and is outside the court's jurisdiction. In the latter situation, the party must attempt to serve a subpoena on the witness and make efforts to persuade the declarant to testify. In the case of statements under the belief of impending death, statements against interest, and statements of personal and family history, an effort must be made to take the individual's deposition if he or she refuses to attend the trial.

Wrongdoing. A party cannot cause a witness to be unavailable in order to prevent the witness from testifying and then rely on the hearsay exceptions in Federal Rule 804 to admit the witness's prior statement.

→ find out witness forced person not to show up @ trial ⇒ hearsay is automatically admissible

■ FORMER TESTIMONY

The **former testimony** exception to the hearsay rule in Federal Rule 804 (b)(1) refers to transcripts of a witness's testimony at an earlier deposition or proceeding in the same case or in another case. Why is this considered hearsay by commentators? Former testimony is hearsay because it is a statement made in an earlier proceeding offered for the truth of the witness's testimony. The jury was not at the earlier hearing and therefore is not able to evaluate the witness's demeanor when testifying at the earlier proceeding.

Former testimony hearsay evidence presents few of the risks presented by other types of testimony. The testimony is recorded under oath in a formal proceeding, and there is no concern about a secondhand version of the statement. Most importantly, the adverse party had an opportunity for cross-examination or examination of the declarant. This type of hearsay evidence may be particularly important because the witness may be crucial to the prosecution or to the defense.

The majority view is that this former testimony is an exception to the hearsay rule under certain circumstances:

Unavailability. The declarant is unavailable.

Identity of motive and of issues. There is sufficient identity of the issues to have provided a motive at the earlier hearing to examine or to cross-examine the individual on issues substantially the same as the issues presented at the trial. In *United States v. Koon*, the appellants had a full opportunity to examine the witness at an earlier state trial, and because the issues were the same at the later federal trial, the defense had a "similar motive they would have had in the later proceeding. . . . The operative facts and legal issues in the state and federal trials were substantially similar" (*United States v. Koon*, 34 F.3d 1416 [9th Cir. 1994]).

Type of proceeding. The proceeding may be in a court of law, legislative committee hearing, or administrative hearing in which testimony was given under oath and was subject to cross-examination.

Examination. It is sufficient that the adverse party had the opportunity or motive to "develop" the declarant's testimony either by cross-examination, by examination, or by redirect examination. The earlier opportunity to "develop" the declarant's testimony satisfies the federal rule regardless of whether the adverse party actually took advantage of the opportunity to examine the declarant.

Establishing prior testimony. The prior testimony is established by offering a certified transcript of the testimony in the previous trial. Absent a transcript, the proponent typically establishes the prior testimony though the testimony of the presiding judge or by another reliable person who attended the prior proceeding. This testimony may be based on notes or on recollection.

The Federal Rules adopt a narrow set of circumstances in which former testimony is admissible as an exception to hearsay. The Federal Rules require the witness's testimony from an earlier trial, deposition, or proceeding is admissible only if the party against whom it is now is being offered was a party to an earlier trial or proceeding, had an opportunity to examine the witness at that time, and had a similar motive to develop the witness's testimony either by direct or by cross-examination. The reasoning is that it may be unfair to impose upon the current party testimony developed by another party in an earlier proceeding.

The trend in state courts in criminal and in civil trials is to reject the "identity of the parties" requirement so long as there is an identity of interest and motive between the parties at the two proceedings. In theory, a declarant may have been cross-examined by a lawyer at a civil trial for damages attempting to establish the individual's fault for an accident. This same testimony under a state evidentiary rule may be introduced by the prosecution at criminal trial because the prosecutor shared the motive of the private attorney to establish the defendant's criminal intent.

Note that the involvement of the same parties in a prior and in the present proceedings does not mean that there was a similar motive. A clear example of a similar motive is when there is a hung jury in the first prosecution and the prosecution decides to prosecute the defendant a second time for the same crime. In a case in which the defense focused on the pretrial identification of the defendant by an eyewitness, the defense was allowed to introduce the transcript of a hearing to suppress the identification. The appellate court reasoned that the defendant had a motive to challenge the accuracy of the identification at the motion-to-suppress hearing and that the defendant was motivated by the same goal at trial (*United States v. Poland*, 659 F.2d 584 [4th Cir. 1981]).

Legal Equation

Former testimony	=	The declarant is unavailable.
	+	There is sufficient identity of the issues to have provided a motive to examine or to cross-examine the individual on issues substantially the same as the issues at trial.
	+	Adverse party had the opportunity or motive to "develop" the declarant's testimony either by cross-examination, by examination, or by redirect examination.
	+	Prior testimony is established by offering a certified transcript of the testimony in the previous trial. Absent a transcript, the proponent typically establishes the prior testimony through the testimony of the presiding judge or by another reliable person who attended the prior proceeding.

9.9 YOU DECIDE

Defendant Dwayne Reed was charged with bank robbery along with his co-defendant Frank Simmons, who cooperated with the government. The trial ended with a hung jury and a mistrial. At the second trial, Simmons, who already had been sentenced under his plea agreement, refused to testify a second time. The court admitted Simmons's testimony from the first trial, and Reed was convicted. During the first trial, Simmons testified and was cross-examined by Reed's lawyer who impeached Simmons's credibility by pointing out that he was being tried for bank robbery and was subject to imprisonment and tried to establish Reed's alibi. Is Simmons's prior testimony admissible? If Reed contended that the government persuaded Simmons to refuse to testify at Reed's second trial, would this make a difference in your answer? What of the fact that Reed could not point out that Simmons bargained with the government? See *United States v. Reed* (227 F.3d 763 [7th Cir. 2000]).

You can learn what the court decided by referring to the study site, **http://study.sagepub.com/lippmance.**

Rule 804. Exceptions to the Rule Against Hearsay—When the Declarant Is Unavailable as a Witness

(b) The Exceptions. The following are not excluded by the rule against hearsay if the declarant is unavailable as a witness.

(1) *Former Testimony.* Testimony that:

(A) was given as a witness at a trial hearing, or lawful deposition, whether given during the current proceeding or a different one;

(B) is now offered against a party who had—or, in a civil case, whose predecessor in interest had—an opportunity and similar motive to develop it by direct, cross- or redirect examination.

usually true

■ STATEMENT UNDER BELIEF OF IMPENDING DEATH

A **statement under belief of impending death**, or what is commonly referred to as a dying declaration, is one of the oldest hearsay exceptions. The assumption is that a person who is on the verge of dying will speak truthfully and has little reason to lie, and for that reason, these statements are more reliable than other out-of-court hearsay statements. The dying declaration also is based on the practical consideration that the deceased is unavailable to testify.

Commentators in addition trace the dying declaration to the religious belief that individuals will not want to "meet their maker" with a "lie upon their lips." There also is the emotional appeal to the notion that a dying individual identifies a killer with the last words that he or she utters.

On the other hand, there is a persuasive argument that a dying declaration may not be entirely accurate if the victim has suffered a traumatic injury and/or may not have accurately witnessed or recalled or clearly narrated the event. These points, however, may be used to impeach the reliability of the declarant's statement.

A statement under the belief of impending death under Federal Rule 804(b)(2) must meet the following requirements:

Unavailable. The declarant must not actually die but must be unavailable. This is intended to ensure that the declaration is reliable.

Type of cases. The dying declaration exception is limited to civil cases and homicide prosecutions. As a result, a dying declaration is inadmissible in most criminal cases. This helps to preserve the defendant's right to confront his or her accusers.

Facts. Dying declarations are limited to the cause or circumstances of the declarant's death, statements that are likely to be accurate. Other factual statements are inadmissible.

Declarant's belief. The declarant must personally and actually believe that death is imminent and certain (at most several hours away) and that death is inevitable.

Personal knowledge. The Advisory Committee notes that the declarant must possess firsthand knowledge of the facts. The declarant is subject to impeachment by pointing out that he or she was in a delirious condition or made a prior inconsistent statement.

At what point is death considered "imminent" for purposes of a dying declaration? In *Shepard v. United States*, the Supreme Court stated that the declarant must possess "a settled hopeless expectation that death is near at hand" and the declarant "must have spoken with the consciousness of a swift and certain doom." The focus is on how long the declarant believed he or she would live rather than on how long the declarant actually lived. Note that the dying declaration hearsay exception would not apply to a situation in which an individual believed he or she *likely* or *probably* would die (*Shepard v. United States*, 290 U.S. 96 [1933]).

The proponent of a dying declaration must establish that the declarant possessed a sincere and settled belief in his or her imminent death by a preponderance of the evidence. The declarant's sincere belief may be established by the totality of the circumstances. This might be accomplished by the victim's statements, statements made to the victim by medical professionals, the extent of the declarant's wounds, and the length of time between the statement and the victim's death. Several state evidence codes require a high standard for a dying declaration and require that a declarant made the statement under a perception of immediate impending death and actually died.

The U.S. Supreme Court applied the common law understanding of a dying declaration. Dr. Charles A. Shepard was charged with the murder of his wife Zenana Shepard through the use of mercury poisoning. Zenana was first stricken with an illness on May 20 and two days later asked her nurse to go into the closet in the defendant's room and bring a bottle of whiskey from which she had drunk prior to her illness. Zenana found the smell and taste "were strange" and added that "Dr. Shepard has poisoned me." She subsequently passed away on June 15. The Court found that nothing in Zenana's condition "gives fair support" to the notion that her hope had been "lost." The statement to the nurse was "consistent with hope," and two weeks later she stated to her physician that "you will get me well, won't you?" This indicates that Zenana's statements were not "spoken with the conscientious of a swift and certain doom" (*Shepard v. United States*, 290 U.S. 96 [1933]). Would Zenana's statement be admissible as a dying declaration under Federal Rule 804(b)(2)?

Legal Equation

Statement under belief of impending death	=	The declarant must not actually die but must be unavailable.
	+	Civil cases and homicide prosecutions.
	+	Limited to the cause or circumstances of the declarant's death.
	+	Declarant must personally and actually believe that death is close and certain (at most several hours) and that death is inevitable.
	+	Declarant must possess firsthand knowledge of the facts, and suspicion is not sufficient.

9.10 YOU DECIDE

Henry Feltus was fatally wounded by a shotgun at roughly 3:15 p.m. and died roughly seventy-five minutes later. Wilson was convicted of first-degree murder and appealed his conviction. Feltus had been shot after exiting a restaurant with Wilson. Following a shotgun blast, the patrons saw Feltus stumble back into the restaurant, "holding his side with his blood . . . gushing out between his fingers, and his clothes were covered with blood from his chest to his feet . . . a large hole in right chest area." Feltus was asked who had shot him, and after a drink of brandy, he answered that "Stan had shot him." A Las Vegas police officer arrived, and when again asked who shot him, Feltus answered two or three times "Stan." The officer reported that Feltus was covered with blood, "gasping and thrashing around on the floor" with "large quantities of blood pouring from a wound in the chest." Would you admit Feltus's statement as a dying declaration? What if Feltus was told that he was not going to die and would "pull through"? See *Wilson v. State* (468 P.2d 346 [Nev. 1970]).

You can learn what the court decided by referring to the study site, **http://study.sagepub.com/lippmance.**

CRIMINAL EVIDENCE AND PUBLIC POLICY

In 2012, former police officer Drew Peterson was convicted of the first-degree murder of his third wife, Kathleen Savio. Peterson allegedly killed her to prevent her from filing for divorce and dividing the couple's estate and obtaining child custody. The prosecution because of the absence of physical evidence relied on "Drew's Law," a law specifically adopted by the state legislature in 2008 to permit the use of hearsay evidence in Peterson's prosecution. Peterson was convicted and sentenced to thirty-eight years in prison.

(Continued)

The law, 725 ILCS 5/115-10.6, creates an exception to the hearsay rule for a statement made by a witness who is the victim of a homicide. The proponent must meet the following three conditions for introducing the statement:

Murder. The witness is murdered.

Reliable. The statement must be reliable.

Justice. Justice must be served by relying on the exception.

Savio initially was thought to have slipped in the bathtub, and her death was ruled an accident. The disappearance of Peterson's fourth wife, Stacy Peterson, resulted in an exhumation of Savio's body and a determination that Savio had been the victim of wrongdoing.

Stacy and Drew began living together during Drew and Kathleen's divorce. Stacy's pastor and the divorce attorney that consulted with Stacy about a divorce from Drew both testified about statements made by Stacy to them about Drew. The pastor, for example, testified that Stacy told him that around the time of Kathleen's death Drew got out of bed and left the house and that she later discovered him stuffing women's clothing in the washing machine. She also testified that Drew coached her for several hours on how to lie to the police.

The defense tried to discredit the pastor through the testimony of the divorce attorney. He testified that Stacy asked him if she could "squeeze" more money out of Drew if she threatened to report to the police that Drew had killed Kathleen. The jurors, however, interpreted this testimony as evidence that Stacy was aware that Drew had killed his former wife. Peterson was convicted of murder and sentenced to thirty-eight years in prison.

Rule 804. Exceptions to the Rule Against Hearsay—When the Declarant Is Unavailable as a Witness

(b) The Exceptions. The following are not excluded by the rule against hearsay if the declarant is unavailable as a witness.

(2) *Statement Under the Belief of Impending Death.* In a prosecution for homicide or a civil case, a statement that the declarant, while believing the declarant's death to be imminent, made about its cause or circumstance.

[handwritten: people wouldn't make allegations about them self if they weren't true ≠ wouldn't say "I killed him"]

■ DECLARATION AGAINST INTEREST

Federal Rule 804(b)(3) establishes that a **declaration against interest** is an exception to the hearsay rule. It is easy to confuse admissions with declarations against interest because there are substantial similarities between the two rules (see Table 9.2).

A hearsay statement is admissible in evidence if the declarant either is a party to a case or is not a party to the case and is unavailable to testify. The statement when made must be against an important interest of the absent declarant, and a reasonable person in the same position would not have made a statement unless he or she believed it to be true.

This exception to the hearsay rule is based on the commonsense notion that an individual would not make a declaration against his or her own interest unless it was true.

The unavailability requirement is met if the declarant is absent and is unavailable to testify at the trial and his or her testimony could not be obtained by a deposition. The unavailability requirement means a declaration against interest in most cases will be directed at a nonparty to the case.

The individual whose declaration is being introduced at the time of the declaration is required to have possessed personal knowledge of the facts, and the statement may not be mere opinion, intuition, or conjecture. A declaration that "I ran a red light" is admissible; a declaration that "I guess I ran a red light" is inadmissible. The personal knowledge requirement is intended to ensure that the individual knows that the statement is untrue.

A declaration against interest may involve criminal liability for the declarant. The test as articulated in Federal Rule 804(b)(3) is whether the declarant at the time of the statement knew or must have known that the statement was so clearly contrary to his or her interest "that a reasonable person in the declarant's position would not have made the statement unless believing it to be true."

It often is not apparent whether a statement is against an individual's interest or in an individual's interest. Consider an individual accused of involvement in a murder who on hearing the accusation proclaimed that "I could not have been involved. I may be a bank robber and a thief, but I am not a killer."

The general view is that if an individual admitted involvement in the murder to a friend, this statement would be admissible at trial. An individual only may introduce the testimony of another individual admitting to the crime to demonstrate his or her own innocence if there are "corroborating circumstances that clearly indicate the trustworthiness of the statement." This is intended to prevent perjured statements by individuals denying the offense. Corroborating circumstances may include the fact the declarant's DNA or fingerprints were found at the crime scene and the testimony of multiple witnesses.

Table 9.2 ■ Comparison Between Declaration Against Interest and Admission by a Party Opponent

Declaration Against Interest	Admission by Party Opponent
Statement by party or nonparty	Statement required to be made by party
Declarant must be unavailable	Declarant may be available or unavailable
Declaration against interest when made	Statement need not be against interest when made
Statement of responsibility or guilt	Statement need not be a confession of guilt

---

Rule 804. Exceptions to the Rule Against Hearsay—When the Declarant Is Unavailable as a Witness

(a) **Criteria for Being Unavailable.** A declarant is considered to be unavailable as a witness . . .

(3) *Statement against Interest.* A statement that:

(A) a reasonable person in the declarant's position would have made only if the person believed it to be true because, when made, it was so contrary to the declarant's proprietary or pecuniary interest or had so great a tendency to invalidate the declarant's claim against someone else or to expose the declarant to civil or criminal liability; and

(B) is supported by corroborating circumstances that clearly indicate its trustworthiness, if it is offered in a criminal case as one that tends to expose the declarant to criminal liability.

■ STATEMENT OF PERSONAL OR FAMILY HISTORY

Federal Rule 804(b)(4) provides that when family relationships are at issue, a party may rely on hearsay, or a **statement of personal or family history**, to establish births, deaths, marriages, and adoption and other facts of personal and family history. In those instances in which the declarant is unavailable, a party may rely on statements by family members, entries in bibles or family journals, church records, or other hearsay evidence. Federal Rule 804(b)(4) requires that the declarant is related by blood or marriage to the family whose history is at issue or is "so intimately associated that the declarant's information likely is to be accurate." Most states, unlike the federal rule, require that the declaration was made before the controversy was transformed into a lawsuit.

■ STATEMENT OFFERED AGAINST A PARTY THAT WRONGFULLY CAUSED THE DECLARANT'S UNAVAILAILITY

Federal Rule 804(b)(6) states that an out-of-court statement offered against a party is admissible in evidence in those instances in which the party wrongfully prevents the declarant from being a witness at trial. The theory behind this rule is that a "wrongdoer" should not "benefit" by a wrongful act of "witness tampering." This includes acts such as bribing, threatening, intimidating, beating, or killing a witness. Federal Rule 804(b)(6) is based on the interest in fairness and equity at trial and applies to all witnesses regardless of whether they are central or marginal to a case. The Advisory Committee on Rules of Evidence notes that the rule is intended to "deal with abhorrent behavior which strikes the heart of the system of justice itself."

Federal Rule 804(b)(6) establishes the following requirements for what is known as **forfeiture by wrongdoing:**

Wrongfully. The party must have "wrongfully" caused or acquiesced in the witness's unavailability. The Advisory Committee notes that it is sufficient that the "wrongful" act is "improper," and it is not required to be a criminal act. This may include coercing, pressuring, or tricking a witness. Forfeiture by wrongdoing does not prohibit a party to a case from informing a witness of his or her legal alternatives such as the availability of a privilege.

Intent. The party must have intended to make the declarant unavailable.

Acquiesced. A party is not required to personally commit the wrongful act. Knowledge of a design to kill the witness and a failure to warn authorities has been held to be sufficient.

Unavailable. The party must have caused the declarant's unavailability.

Rule 804. Statement Offered Against a Party That Wrongfully Caused the Declarant's Unavailability

(b) The Exception. The following are not excluded by the rule against hearsay if the declarant is unavailable as a witness.

   (6) *Statement Offered Against a Party That Wrongfully Caused the Declarant's Unavailability.* A statement offered against a party that wrongfully caused—or acquiesced in wrongfully causing—the declarant's unavailability as a witness, and did so intending that result.

 9.11 YOU DECIDE

Robert Gray was convinced that his wife Wilma was attempting to kill him and filed criminal charges, alleging that Wilma had assaulted him with a club and with a knife and along with her "lover" Clarence Goode had threatened him with a 9-millimeter handgun. Goode left to live by himself in an apartment, and a warrant was issued for the arrest of Wilma and Goode. Shortly thereafter, Gray was found dead. Gray had a life insurance policy that provided for payment of the mortgage on the home he and Wilma had bought in Maryland with the excess going to Wilma. Following Gray's death, the life insurance company paid the remainder of the mortgage on the home. Wilma subsequently sold the home for a "significant profit." Wilma also was the beneficiary of Goode's life insurance policy, and Goode later was found dead in the trunk of his car. Wilma was convicted of fraud based on her receipt of insurance payments following the deaths of Robert and Goode. She contends that various statements of Robert were inadmissible under the doctrine of forfeiture by wrongdoing because she did not intend to procure Robert's unavailability as a witness at the trial. Are Robert's statements admissible under the doctrine of forfeiture by wrongdoing? See *United States v. Gray* (405 F.3d 227 [4th Cir. 2005]).

You can learn what the court decided by referring to the study site, **http://study.sagepub.com/lippmance.**

last resort

■ RESIDUAL EXCEPTION

Despite the numerous exceptions to the hearsay rule, the Advisory Committee on Rules of Evidence believed it would be "presumptuous to assume that all possible desirable exceptions to the hearsay rule have been catalogued and to pass the hearsay rule on to oncoming generations as a closed system." Judges have been reluctant to rely on the residual exception in Rule 807 because they share the view of the Advisory Committee that it should be used "very rarely, and only in exceptional circumstances." In other words, the residual exception should be viewed as a "last resort." There are various requirements that a judge is required to find before admitting evidence under the residual exception:

Existing rule. The statement must not be specifically covered by a hearsay exception in Rule 803 or 804.

Trustworthiness. The statement must have "circumstantial guarantees of trustworthiness" that are "equivalent" to those in existing exceptions. Courts consider the spontaneity of the statement, the lack of motive to fabricate, the context of the statement (e.g., made to a police officer), whether there is corroborating evidence, and the amount of time that has passed since the statement was made (*Idaho v. Wright*, 497 U.S. 805 [1990]).

Material fact. The statement must be relevant to a material fact in the case.

Probative. The hearsay must be "more probative of the information than other evidence that the proponent can obtain through reasonable efforts." The hearsay evidence will not be admitted into evidence in those instances in which the declarant is available or if the proponent can reasonably obtain equally probative evidence.

Interests of justice. The admission of the evidence will serve the purposes of the rules and the interests of justice. This is a broad standard that requires the court to evaluate the need for the evidence at trial.

Notice. The proponent must inform the opposing party of his or her intent to use the statement, the details of the statement, and the declarant's name and address.

There is disagreement on the **near-miss issue**. This arises when a statement narrowly misses admission under an existing exception. An example is an ancient document that is nineteen years old and fails to meet the requirement in Federal Rule 803(16) that a (ancient) document is twenty years old. The drafters of the rule likely had not anticipated that there would be such a "close call" on the admissibility of a document. On the other hand, Rule 807 specifically states that the residual exception is applicable to statements that are "not specifically covered by a hearsay exception in Rule 803 and 804," which would appear to prohibit admission of the nineteen-year-old document. The difficulty is that admission of the document would erode the specific requirements for admission of an ancient document that establishes twenty years as the threshold for the admission of a document. As a result, courts generally have rejected the near miss doctrine and require that a statement does not fall within an existing exception to the hearsay rule to be admitted under Rule 807.

9.12 YOU DECIDE

Hussein Osman Ahmed was charged with sexual assault based on his alleged abuse of his 3-year-old son, H.A., the son of his wife from a previous marriage. H.A. suffered from burns on his body, including his face, back, shoulder, abdomen, and sexual organ. A police officer took H.A. for an interview with a child social worker. H.A. did not respond to any of the interviewer's questions either in English or through a Somali interpreter. Because H.A. had spent most of his life with his maternal grandmother, F.B., the social worker arranged for another meeting on December 17, this time with F.B. present.

"F.B. testified that H.A. ran to her when he saw her in the lobby, before the interview. When she hugged him, H.A. told her in Somali that her hugs hurt him. When she asked who did this to him, H.A. responded that 'Abdirashiid' was the person who had hurt him. Abdirashiid is the familiar name" that Ahmed's in-laws use in interacting with him. The court declared H.A. incompetent to testify at trial although it "permitted F.B. to testify about the conversation she had with H.A. in the lobby . . . under the residual exception to the hearsay rule." Do you agree with the judge's decision? See *State v. Ahmed* (782 N.W.2d 253 [Minn. App. 2010]).

You can learn what the court decided by referring to the study site, **http://study.sagepub.com/lippmance.**

Rule 807. Residual Exception

(a) In General. Under the following circumstances, a hearsay statement is not excluded by the rule against hearsay even if the statement is not specifically covered by a hearsay exception in Rule 803 or 804:

    (1) the statement has equivalent circumstantial guarantees of trustworthiness;

    (2) it is offered as evidence of a material fact;

    (3) it is more probative on the point for which it is offered than any other evidence that the proponent can obtain through reasonable efforts; and

    (4) admitting it will best serve the purposes of these rules and their interests of justice.

(b) Notice. The statement is admissible only if, before the trial or hearing, the proponent gives an adverse party reasonable notice of the intent to offer the statement and its particulars, including the declarant's name and address, so that the party has a fair opportunity to meet it.

■ HEARSAY WITHIN HEARSAY

Federal Rule 805 provides that "**hearsay within hearsay**" is not excluded by the rule against hearsay if each part of the "combined statements conforms with an exception to the rule." This often is referred to as "double hearsay." April says to Jose that "Brittany was the shooter in the 'drive by' killing." Jose now tells a police officer that "Brittany was the shooter in the 'drive by' killing." Rule 805 requires that each statement must meet an exception to the hearsay rule. The most common situation in which the "hearsay within hearsay" rule arises is when a document that is hearsay contains statements by individuals that are also are hearsay. In this situation, both the document and the statement must constitute exceptions to the hearsay rule.

→ each must meet an exception.

■ CASE ANALYSIS

In *Grindle v. State*, a Mississippi court of appeals considered whether the victim's statement constituted a dying declaration.

Was the victim's statement admissible as a dying declaration?

Grindle v. State, KA-00006 (MS. App. 2013)

[Brandon Grindle was convicted of] deliberate-design murder. . . . On appeal, Grindle challenges the trial judge's decision that the shooting victim's nonverbal responses to a police officer's questions about who shot him, made immediately before his death, were admissible as dying declarations. He also claims the admission of these statements violated his Sixth Amendment confrontation right. . . .

[W]e find the trial judge did not abuse his discretion in admitting the victim's dying declaration. And since dying declarations have been accepted under common-law tradition since well before the founding and ratification of America's Constitution, we find applying this exception does not offend Grindle's Sixth Amendment confrontation rights. . . .

Charles Brown was walking down the street in front of his house when he was shot twice by the driver of a green Ford sport utility vehicle. When officers arrived, Brown was still conscious but bleeding heavily. Paramedics transported him to the hospital while officers remained at the scene to interview witnesses.

After interviewing several witnesses, officers determined there had been bad blood between Brown and Grindle. Brown's girlfriend, with whom he had a child, was also the mother of Grindle's daughter. And Grindle believed Brown was mistreating his young daughter. A month earlier, the two fathers had gotten into an argument during which Brown had purportedly pulled a gun on Grindle. But on the day of the shooting, it was Grindle who had a gun.

Although the actual pistol used to kill Brown was never recovered, two different witnesses testified that on the day of the shooting they saw Grindle riding around in a Ford SUV with a pistol. . . .

Two other witnesses who were in the vicinity of the shooting testified at trial. . . .

While a variety of witnesses implicated Grindle as the killer, Grindle primarily focuses his appeal on Officer Richard Browning, the responding officer who interviewed Brown in the emergency room. The victim, Brown, was intubated at this point and could not speak. But Officer Browning, who was familiar with Brown and Grindle from their prior run-in, testified that he was able to ask Brown a series of questions to which Brown responded by nodding his head affirmatively. The questions were aimed at identifying the shooter. According to Officer Browning, when he asked Brown if Grindle was the person who shot him, Brown emphatically nodded "yes." Shortly after this exchange, Brown died from his wounds. . . .

Officer Browning testified about his interaction with Brown in the emergency room. While doctors were trying to save Brown's life, Officer Browning asked Brown if he could hear him. When Brown nodded "yes," Officer Browning further inquired if Brown knew who shot him. Brown gave another affirmative nod. Officer Browning followed up by asking if it was the same person Brown had trouble with earlier—a reference to the altercation with Grindle a month earlier. Again, Brown nodded "yes." Officer Browning then asked if that person was "Grindle," to which Brown gave a final nod. At some point after this exchange, Brown began to decline rapidly and, within minutes, died.

Grindle's attorney cross-examined Officer Browning, honing in on Brown's condition at the time [of] the interview. . . . Throughout questioning, Officer Browning remained consistent that he believed Brown could understand him and was responding to his questions. . . .

The trial judge held that Brown's nodding, while nonverbal, met the criteria of a "dying declaration" and denied Grindle's motion to exclude Officer Brown's recitation of his questioning of Grindle. And though he ruled Officer Browning's testimony was admissible, the judge informed Grindle he was free to offer evidence challenging the credibility of Officer Browning's testimony at trial. . . .

Kayla Breland, the registered nurse who was in the emergency room while Brown was being treated, also testified in the State's case. Breland confirmed that Officer Browning was in the emergency room that evening. But she could not recall if any conversation took place, as she was busy with Brown's medical treatment. On cross-examination, Grindle's counsel questioned Breland about her responsibility for monitoring Brown's brain functioning th[r]ough observing his verbal communication, eye response, and movement. Breland's records showed she gave him a low Glasgow score when he arrived that decreased as the minutes passed. Breland testified that Brown's score meant he could not verbally communicate or control his bodily movements. But on redirect, Breland testified Brown "possibly could have" nodded his head in response to Officer Browning's questions. Grindle's counsel neither renewed her objection to Brown's dying declaration in light of Breland's testimony nor asked for any instruction limiting Officer Browning's testimony. . . .

[T]he Mississippi Supreme Court has found three general common-law requirements for a dying declaration—(1) that "[t]he wounded person is in extremis and dies after making the statement," (2) that "[t]he person realizes that he is mortally wounded," and (3) that "[h]e has no hope of recovery"—must still be met to admit a statement under belief of impending death under Rule 804(b)(2). . . .

When asked if Brown "was emphatic on knowing who shot him," Officer Browning responded, "Yes, sir." Officer Browning further explained that "between questions, [Brown] was completely—he was moving, but he wasn't trying to answer anything. The only time he tried to respond to yes or no is when I asked him a question, at which time he again nodded yes, repeatedly." From this, the judge held Brown's statement was admissible as a dying declaration. . . .

In light of the fact that we are unaware of any federal or state court that has held the admission of a dying declaration offends a defendant's constitutional right to confront his or her accuser, we too find the admission of Brown's dying declaration did not violate Grindle's Sixth Amendment right to confrontation.

CHAPTER SUMMARY

The general rule is that hearsay, which occurs when one person testifies in court about what another person stated outside of court, is inadmissible in court. Federal Rule 802 provides that "[h]earsay is not admissible except as provided by these [federal] rules or by other rules prescribed by the Supreme Court . . . or by act of Congress." Federal Rule 801(c) provides that "'Hearsay' means a statement that:

(1) the declarant does not make while testifying at the current trial or hearing; and

(2) a party offers in evidence to prove the truth of the matter asserted in the statement."

There are three components to the legal definition of hearsay:

1. A statement
2. A declarant
3. Offered in evidence to prove the truth of the matter asserted

Hearsay statements are subject to the requirements of the U.S. Constitution. The most important limitation is the Confrontation Clause of the Sixth Amendment. The Confrontation Clause provides that "in all criminal prosecutions, the accused shall enjoy the right . . . to be confronted with the witnesses against him." This clause extends to both federal and state prosecution. The Confrontation Clause permits the introduction of testimonial statements in those instances in which the declarant is unavailable and when, at an earlier time, he or she was subject to cross-examination by the accused. The Supreme Court also has recognized in addition to well-recognized hearsay exceptions that statements that are nontestimonial may be introduced at trial when the statements are made in response to an ongoing emergency and were not obtained for the purposes of gathering evidence for trial.

The Federal Rules list the hearsay exceptions in three separate rules. Rule 803 lists twenty-three exceptions that may be used whether or not the declarant is available to testify. Rule 804 lists six exceptions that may not be used unless the lawyer demonstrates to the judge that the declarant is unavailable as a witness. Rule 807 is a so-called residual or catch-all exception that provides for the recognition of other exceptions that are not specifically listed when there are "equivalent circumstantial guarantees of trustworthiness" to the exceptions recognized in the Federal Rules.

Two other exceptions to hearsay, out-of-court statements made by the defendant and prior inconsistent and prior consistent statements, are recognized by as many as ten states but are not included as an exception to hearsay under the Federal Rules of Evidence. Commentators often refer to these statements as exemptions from the hearsay rule because under the Federal Rule they are exempt from the rule on hearsay evidence.

CHAPTER REVIEW QUESTIONS

1. What is the definition of hearsay, and what is the reason for excluding hearsay evidence from trial?

2. Discuss the Supreme Court decisions addressing the relationship between the Confrontation Clause and hearsay evidence. Distinguish in your answer between testimonial and nontestimonial evidence.

3. What is the difference been an admission, adoptive admission, admission by an agent, and admission by a co-conspirator?

4. How do admissions differ from statements against interest?

5. Discuss the difference between a present sense impression and an excited utterance.

6. What is the difference between a then-existing mental, emotional, or physical condition and a statement made for medical treatment?

7. List the elements of the business records exception. When is the absence of a business record admissible in evidence?

8. Why is there a hearsay exception for public records?

9. Should there be a hearsay exception when a party wrongfully causes the absence of a witness?

10. What is the residual exception?

LEGAL TERMINOLOGY

admission by party-opponent
adoptive admission
business records
Confrontation Clause
declaration against interest
excited utterance
forfeiture by wrongdoing
former testimony

hearsay
hearsay within hearsay
identifications
medical treatment-diagnosis
near-miss issue
negative hearsay
present sense impression
prior consistent statements

public record
statement of personal or family
    history
statement under belief of impending
    death
then-existing mental, emotional,
    or physical condition
vital statistics

REFERENCE

Lilly, Graham C. 2006. *Principles of Evidence*, 4th ed. St. Paul, MN: West/Thomson.

Kerani Verma

CHAPTER 10

PRIVILEGES

May Lofton's spouse testify against him at trial?

Ronald Lofton, Sr. was charged by indictment with conspiracy possession with the intent to distribute cocaine, and use of the mail in committing, causing and facilitating an offense. Prior to trial, Lofton's wife moved to quash a subpoena requiring her to testify at Lofton's trial on the basis of her spousal testimonial privilege. . . .

The testimonial privilege, should the witness assert it, applies to all testimony against a defendant-spouse, including testimony on nonconfidential matters and matters which occurred prior to the marriage; the communications privilege, assertable by the defendant himself, applies only to communications made in confidence between the spouses during a valid marriage. . . .

Lofton alleged that his statements to his wife that, "The less you know the better off you are" and "Don't be so nosy," and that her knowledge whether she had seen Lofton use cocaine before and whether a package sent to their home containing cocaine was for him were privileged. (*United States v. Lofton* (957 F.2d 476 [7th Cir. 1992])

CHAPTER OUTLINE

Introduction
Attorney-Client Privilege
Clergy-Penitent Privilege
Physician-Patient Privilege
Psychotherapist-Patient Privilege
Husband-Wife Privilege

Government Privileges
News Media Privilege
Case Analysis
Chapter Summary
Chapter Review Questions
Legal Terminology

 TEST YOUR KNOWLEDGE

1. Can you explain testimonial privilege?

2. Do you know why the law of evidence provides for privileges?

3. Can you list exceptions to the attorney-client and clergy-penitent privileges?

4. Do you know who the "holder" of the spousal privilege is: the husband or the wife?

5. Are you aware of the purpose of the media privilege and what is covered by the media privilege?

6. Can you explain the executive privilege? Confidential informant privilege?

■ INTRODUCTION

A criminal trial and the determination of guilt or innocence depend to the extent possible on a full and accurate presentation of the facts. Witnesses are expected to truthfully and completely reveal what they observed, heard, and know about what occurred. We expect witnesses to state "the truth, the whole truth, and nothing but the truth." Some of the most persuasive and powerful testimony at a trial includes the statements made by the individual accused of the crime to a potential witness. The withholding of information impedes the ability of a jury to fairly evaluate the facts.

Certain confidential relationships are considered privileged and allow the holder of the privilege to avoid testifying regarding the content of what was said between the parties to the relationship in court. The individual who is holder of a **testimonial privilege** may waive the protection of the privilege or invoke the protection of the privilege and refuse to testify. The holder of the privilege also may prevent the other party to the privileged relationship from testifying. A holder of a privilege who is a defendant to a criminal case, for example, may prevent a member of the clergy or a doctor or lawyer with whom he or she has a privileged relationship from testifying at trial. The adverse lawyer may not comment in a negative fashion on the fact that an individual invoked a privilege to avoid testifying.

Privileges are criticized for inhibiting rather than encouraging the search for the truth. Once a privilege is invoked, a doctor, lawyer, or member of the clergy may be blocked from testifying by the defendant who holds the privilege and will not be subject to cross-examination, even if he or she has information that is crucial to the determination of a defendant's guilt. Of course, it is argued absent a privilege an individual may not have shared important information with his or her lawyer or doctor. Nonetheless, consider that the prosecutor cannot examine the defense lawyer as to whether the defendant admitted his or her guilt to the defense attorney.

Congress in formulating the Federal Rules of Evidence could not agree on which of thirteen proposed testimonial privileges should be recognized, and decided not to include proposed rules on privileges in the Federal Rules of Evidence. Rule 501 is the only rule that addresses privileges and leaves it to the courts to determine the relationships that are privileged in light of the "principles of the common law as they may be interpreted by the courts of the United States in the light of reason and experience."

Courts generally recognize the privileges that existed at common law. Other privileges result from legislative enactments. Congress expressed the intent to allow privileges to develop to meet the needs of society although some groups continue to be frustrated by the failure of courts to recognize new privileges. Journalists are concerned about the uneven protection accorded by the courts to what they view as their First Amendment constitutional right to withhold the names of sources and have called for Congress to pass a law protecting their ability to withhold the names of their confidential sources. As noted, in most states, privileges are a product of statutes passed by the state legislature, and not all states provide the same degree of protection for certain privileges. Only one-third of the states, for example, recognize an accountant-client privilege. The following are the primary privileges recognized by federal and state courts.

Attorney-client privilege

Clergy-penitent privilege

Physician-patient privilege

Psychotherapist-patient privilege

Husband-wife privilege

Government privileges

Executive privilege

State secrets privilege

Official information privilege

Confidential informant's privilege

Grand jury confidentiality

News media privilege

These privileges generally have certain common requirements.

Confidentiality. The <u>verbal</u> or <u>written</u> statements must be made or communicated in confidence.

Relationship. The relationship must fall within <u>one of the relationships required</u> for a conversation to be privileged.

[handwritten: must be in private → intended for conversation to be private]

Outside parties. The statements must <u>not be communicated or overheard</u> by other <u>nonessential individuals.</u>

Scope. Privileges protect the content of the communication between individuals.

Exceptions. Statements made in a confidential relationship only may be revealed if they fall within a recognized exception.

Waiver. The holder of the privilege <u>may waive</u> the privilege.

Deceased. Privileges generally <u>outlast the death</u> of one of the holders of the privilege. *[handwritten: → even if you die, can't tell.]*

Burden of proof. The burden of proof is <u>on the party claiming the privilege.</u>

[handwritten: → ex: Attorney client → client]

The recognized privileges are based on various policy considerations, not all of which are relevant to each and every privilege.

Social interest. Certain relationships are valued by society and merit protection. Examples are husband-wife and clergy-penitent privileges.

Effectiveness. Various relationships can function most effectively when individuals feel free to communicate and share information without fear that statements and documents will be revealed to outside parties. An example is the attorney-client privilege or psychotherapist-patient privilege.

Privacy. Privileges are based on the right to be "left alone" in certain important relationships such as marriage.

■ ATTORNEY-CLIENT PRIVILEGE

The **attorney-client privilege** was established in the early common law and is the oldest of privileges protecting the confidentiality of communications. The privilege recognizes the right of a client to prevent a lawyer with whom he or she has a professional relationship from disclosing communications between the two of them stemming from their professional relationship. Neither the client nor the lawyer may be compelled to testify about privileged information absent a waiver from the client. The privilege applies to both civil and criminal matters. (See Table 10.1.)

Table 10.1 ■ Scope of Attorney-Client Privilege
Confessions to a past crime
Consultation on whether a proposed business plan (e.g., tax deduction, investment scheme) is lawful
Asking a neighbor who is a licensed attorney for legal advice
Admission that individual has fraudulently concealed money

The Supreme Court recognized that "[t]he privilege promotes full and frank communication between attorneys and their clients and thereby promote[s] broader public interests in the observance of law and administration of justice" (*Upjohn Co. v. United States*, 449 U.S. 383 [1981]). As noted by the Supreme Court, there are good reasons for recognizing the attorney-client privilege.

Legal representation. There is a social interest in encouraging defendants to be represented by a lawyer at trial in order to mount an effective defense and to avoid the conviction of the innocent. Defendants are more likely to arrange for legal representation if their communications with a lawyer are confidential.

Effective representation. A lawyer cannot effectively represent a client unless he or she knows all the relevant information, and a client will not share this information unless guaranteed that the information will remain confidential.

Special relationship. The lawyer and client possess a relationship of trust, and requiring the lawyer to testify against his or her client is a violation of the lawyer's special obligation of loyalty to the client.

The attorney-client privilege is based on the following requirements.

Client. A client is an individual who communicates with a lawyer to obtain legal advice or representation.

Attorney. An attorney is an individual licensed to practice law. There is case law that the privilege attaches to an individual that the client reasonably believes is licensed to practice law. The attorney-client privilege extends to the lawyer's assistants.

Communication. Communication between the client and the attorney and from the attorney to the client is covered by the privilege. → even if Attorney decides not to represent

Confidentiality. Communications that are intended to be confidential are protected. → private

Scope. Communication between the client and the attorney regarding legal services to the client is protected. →

Payment. The attorney-client privilege is not dependent on payment of a fee. The client, even when a juvenile, is the holder of the privilege when the money is paid and the lawyer is hired by an outside party, such as a mother or father.

A client waives the privilege by authorizing disclosure of confidential materials.

Holder of the Privilege → If client isn't there, Attorney can invoke privilege if they want

The client is the holder of the attorney-client privilege. Congress considered, though failed to adopt, Rule 503 on "Lawyer-Client Privilege," which reads that a client "has a privilege to refuse to disclose and to prevent any other person from disclosing confidential communications made for the purpose of facilitating the rendition of professional legal services to the client."

The law presumes the client wants the attorney to claim the privilege when the lawyer receives a request for information covered by the privilege. The attorney is presumed to possess the ability to invoke the privilege on behalf of his or her client. Rule 503, which was not adopted, provides that the "lawyer may claim the privilege on behalf of the client. His [or her] authority to do so is presumed in the absence of evidence to the contrary." A lawyer may not waive the privilege absent the client's consent. Some states require a waiver to be made in writing. An attorney also may not invoke the privilege if waived by the client.

The privilege applies to communications made by any corporate official or employee to a lawyer who represents the corporation.

Scope of the Privilege

The attorney-client privilege applies to oral or written communications made for the purpose of professional legal services. The privilege bars the disclosure of privileged information and applies in all stages of litigation and in all other situations. The privilege attaches even if the individual does not retain the attorney or the attorney decides not to take the case. Physical evidence turned over to the attorney by the client, such as a firearm, is not privileged.

The lawyer-client privilege does not apply to business or personal advice between the client and a lawyer.

The privilege protects communications from being turned over during the pretrial and trial stages and in all other situations. The United States Supreme Court, in 1998, held that the attorney-client relationship continues following the death of the client. The only exception is when there is a dispute between individuals regarding inheritance under a will (*Swidler & Berlin v. United States*, 524 U.S. 399 [1998]).

The lawyer-client privilege applies to individuals assisting a lawyer in the provision of legal services. This encompasses legal assistants as well as non-lawyers such as clerical staff and experts. Statements made to the individuals assisting the lawyer for purposes of being communicated to the lawyer are protected.

The privilege is thought to be waived if the client consults the lawyer in the presence of a friend or another individual who is not covered by the privilege. However, the lawyer-client privilege is not waived if an unauthorized individual steals or finds confidential materials or overhears a confidential discussion between the lawyer and the client so long as the client has taken reasonable precautions to protect the communication.

In *People v. Urbano*, a California appeals court held the defendant had waived the attorney-client privilege regarding a statement that Raymond Guadalupe Urbano made to his attorney before his preliminary hearing that was loud enough to be overheard by the prosecutor. The court found that Urbano had no need to speak in a voice "loud enough for individuals in the audience to hear," as his attorney was sitting right next to him in the jury box, but nevertheless made his communication in a way that "clearly disclose[d] it to third persons." On the basis of those circumstances, the court ruled Urbano's jury box comment and gesture were not covered by the attorney-client privilege. Urbano had the ability to prevent his communication from being overheard by individuals in the courtroom. Urbano also made a statement to his defense attorney during the preliminary hearing that was loud enough to be heard by the prosecutor. The court held that the statement was protected by the attorney-client relationship because a defendant should be able to communicate with his or her attorney during the proceedings without fear that the statement will be used against him or her by the prosecution (*People v. Urbano*, 128 Cal. App. 4th 396 [2005]).

The attorney-client privilege does not cover an attorney's observations. This may involve wounds on a defendant's body, the defendant's mental statement, or observing an expert witness's destruction of evidence at the crime scene.

Exceptions

There are several exceptions to the confidential nature of attorney-client communications. Proposed Rule 503 recognized the **crime-fraud exception**. This exception provides that the privilege does not apply "[i]f the services of the lawyer were sought or obtained to enable or aid anyone to commit or plan to commit what the client knew or reasonably should have known to be a crime or fraud." In other words, the crime-fraud exception applies if the client asks for assistance to carry out a crime or asks for advice on carrying out a continuing or future crime. Communications between a lawyer and a client or between a lawyer and a third party regarding the destruction or concealment of evidence or perjured testimony are not privileged. A lawyer who cooperates in impeding a prosecution may have criminal liability as an accessory after the fact.

On the other hand, the attorney-client privilege prohibits the disclosure of past criminal activity (*United States v. Lentz*, 524 F.2d 501 [4th Cir. 2008]).

An attorney may not reveal that a client is committing perjury who takes the stand and denies his or her involvement in a crime. The attorney has an obligation to attempt to persuade the client to truthfully testify or to withdraw from the case. Some commentators advise the lawyer to tell the judge that the defendant will testify in narrative form and that he or she will not participate by questioning the defendant. This makes it clear to the judge that the lawyer is distancing him- or herself from the witness who is committing perjury.

A client waives the privilege by asserting the affirmative defense of "reliance on advice of counsel" or by calling his or her attorney as a witness. The advice of counsel defense involves a defendant's claim that he or she lacked a criminal intent because of reliance on a lawyer's opinion that an act was lawful.

A civil action for malpractice against the lawyer allows the lawyer to use confidential statements to defend him- or herself, and an attorney suing a client for the payment of fees may use confidential statements in seeking compensation. An attorney was permitted to testify as to his conversations with the defendant in a case in which the defendant alleged the lawyer provided ineffective assistance of counsel by advising the defendant to waive a jury trial and to plead guilty (*State v. Dominguez*, 2010 La. App. Lexis 1662 [2010]).

A lawyer may be compelled to reveal a client's name, the dates of consultation, and the amount and payment of a legal fee although a lawyer may not reveal the reasons the client sought legal advice. These areas are not covered by the attorney-client privilege because they do not involve the content of the communication between the parties. In *United States v. Cedeno*, the district court directed a defense attorney to reveal the amount he had been paid by the defendant and the name of the individual paying the fee. The court concluded that the information would be relevant in determining whether the defendant experienced sudden and unexplained wealth and whether other individuals thought to be involved in a drug conspiracy had paid the defendant's legal bills (*United States v. Cedeno*, 496 F.Supp. 2d 562 [E.D. Pa. 2007]).

Materials turned over to a lawyer typically fall within the attorney-client privilege.

The work product privilege is related though different from the attorney-client privilege. Work product applies to documents prepared in anticipation of litigation. The material is not part of the lawyer-client privilege because it is not a "communication" from the client. This material only may be discovered if the court finds that the adverse party has a "substantial need" for the material that cannot be obtained through other means. This is discussed later in the text. Documents that contain a lawyer's opinions, research, and legal opinions regarding litigation are absolutely immune from discovery.

10.1 YOU DECIDE

Arlen Slobodow and his wife Elsa Newman married in 1990, and thereafter they had two sons together, Lars and Herbie. In 1999, their marriage deteriorated, and the couple began divorce and custody proceedings, during which Newman was represented by Stephen Friedman. "On August 31, 2001, Newman met with Friedman in preparation for a custody hearing before Circuit Court Judge James Ryan. At one point Newman stated, "You know, I don't have to kill both children. I only need to kill Lars because I can save Herbie, and then Arlen [Slobodow] will go to jail and get what he deserves because he is a criminal, and I can at least save Herbie." Friedman protested that you "cannot involve me in a murder case" and you "need to convince me that you are just frustrated."

Friedman disclosed to Judge Louise Scrivener the statements made by Newman the previous Friday. After Judge Scrivener informed Judge James Ryan of Friedman's disclosure, Judge Ryan revealed the substance of Friedman's disclosure during the custody hearing on September 4, 2001. Newman was granted supervised visitation. The trial on the merits was postponed until December 7, 2001, and then again to January 28, 2002.

Prior to the trial on the merits, on January 7, 2002, Newman's friend Margery Landry entered Slobodow's house through an unlocked basement window carrying pornographic materials and a Smith and Wesson 9-mm handgun. In Slobodow's bedroom, she found him asleep in bed and fired two shots, wounding Slobodow. Landry planned to plant the pornographic materials in Slobodow's home as evidence that he had a sexual interest in young children. Later that morning, Montgomery County police arrested Landry at her home.

In January 2002, Newman was charged with conspiracy to commit first-degree murder of Slobodow and with conspiracy to commit assault in the first degree. The prosecution sought an order to compel Friedman to testify about Newman's August statement. Newman objected that Friedman's testimony about Newman's statement was barred by the attorney-client privilege. The prosecution contended Friedman may testify because Friedman's earlier statements to Judge Scrivener along with the crime-fraud exception resulted in a waiver of the attorney-client privilege. Is Friedman's testimony barred by the attorney-client privilege? See *Newman v. State* (384 Md. 285 [2004]).

You can learn what the court decided by referring to the study site, **http://study.sagepub.com/lippmance.**

10.2 YOU DECIDE

Thomas W. Blackmon was convicted by a jury of criminal mischief. He now appealed, claiming the trial court committed an error in permitting the prosecution to introduce evidence concerning a confidential conversation between Blackmon and his lawyer, Paul Canarsky.

During a recess in the trial, Blackmon and Canarsky engaged in a conversation that was partially overheard by Alaska State Trooper Lowden, who, at the time, was on duty safeguarding Blackmon. Trooper Lowden testified that Canarsky and Blackmon talked to one another in an area of the courtroom

(Continued)

(Continued)

about twenty-five feet away from Lowden. "He admitted that the conversation between Blackmon and Canarsky had the appearance of being private. Lowden further admitted that he was not invited to join the conversation, that Blackmon and Canarsky kept their backs turned toward him, and that both were whispering. Lowden stated that, of the entire conversation, he overheard only about eight or nine words."

Judge Stephen Cline allowed the prosecution to call Lowden as a witness to testify about the conversation he overheard. Judge Cline ruled that the conversation was not privileged, and that its probative value outweighed its prejudicial effect.

Was Blackmon and Canarsky's conversation protected by the attorney-client privilege? See *Blackmon v. State* (653 P.2d 669 [Alaska App. 1982]).

You can learn what the court decided by referring to the study site, **http://study.sagepub.com/lippmance.**

CRIMINAL EVIDENCE IN THE NEWS

In 1982, public defender Marc Miller was assigned to represent Edgar Hope who along with Alton Logan was charged with killing a security guard and wounding a second security guard during a robbery at a fast-food restaurant. Hope shared with Miller that he did not know Logan, that Logan was innocent, and that his co-perpetrator was Andrew Wilson, standing trial at the time for killing two police officers. Miller told Logan's lawyer that his client was innocent. Miller also told the public defenders representing Andrew Wilson, Dale Coventry, and W. Jamie Kunz that their clients had been involved in the McDonald's killings.

Coventry and Kunz questioned Wilson who admitted to being the shooter at the McDonald's robbery. The two lawyers knew that Wilson was truthful because ballistics tests connected a shotgun shell discovered at McDonald's with a weapon found at the beauty parlor where Wilson lived. The deceased police officers' firearms also were seized in the same location.

Coventry, Kunz, and Miller after consulting other lawyers and experts concluded they were barred by the attorney-client privilege from revealing that Logan was innocent. The three swore an affidavit that did not name Wilson although indicated that they had knowledge through privileged sources that Logan was innocent, which was placed in a sealed envelope and deposited in a locked box in Coventry's bedroom.

Logan avoided the death penalty and was sentenced to life imprisonment. Wilson when confronting capital punishment agreed that the lawyers could reveal Logan's innocence after his death. Wilson's death sentence, however, was reversed when it was discovered that his confession had been obtained as a result of police torture.

Both Wilson and Hope never came forward with the truth, and when confronted by Logan in prison, Wilson reportedly smiled and walked away.

Wilson ultimately passed away after twenty-six years in prison, and Coventry and Kunz finally produced an affidavit that resulted in the release of the 54-year-old Logan.

Kunz, when asked about remaining silent for all these years, responded, "If I had ratted him out . . . then I could feel guilty, then I could not live with myself. . . . I'm anguished and always have been over the sad injustice of Alton Logan's conviction. Should I do the right thing by Alton Logan and put my client's neck in the noose or not? It's clear where my responsibility lies and my responsibility lies with my client."

A Cook County, Illinois, judge issued a certificate of innocence to Logan, and the City of Chicago reached a $10.25 million settlement with Logan based on evidence that now-imprisoned Chicago police officer John Burge had concealed evidence implicating Wilson in the McDonald's homicide.

The ethical rules vary from state to state although several states provide that a lawyer may break a confidence to halt an execution although not to free an innocent inmate. Massachusetts seems to be unique in allowing lawyers to violate a privilege to prevent a "wrongful execution or incarceration of another." Most states consider that the attorney-client privilege is not waived by the death of a client. This is because the family still may be concerned about the deceased's reputation, civil liability, or retribution. There is the complicating factor of whether a lawyer has proof of a wrongful conviction other than the statement of his or her client. Should a lawyer violate the attorney-client privilege when he or she knows an innocent individual is imprisoned or imprisoned and sentenced to death?

■ CLERGY-PENITENT PRIVILEGE

State and federal courts all recognize the **clergy-penitent privilege**. The privilege reflects a respect for the human need to "disclose to a spiritual counselor, in total and absolute confidence, what are believed to be flawed acts or thoughts and to receive priestly consolation and guidance in return." As indicated in *Trammel v. United States*, the purpose of the clergy-penitent privilege is to allow individuals to confess and to find forgiveness for their sins and salvation without fear that their statements will be used against them in a criminal trial. Requiring clergy to testify against a penitent would conflict with their spiritual and moral responsibilities of clerics to the religious adherents to their faith. Another important consideration is that government interference with the religious function of clergy is contrary to the free exercise of religion (*Trammel v. United States*, 445 U.S. 40 [1980]).

The clergy-penitent privilege encompasses:

> *Communications* between a penitent and a member of the clergy; made in *confidence*; during *spiritual counseling*; to a member of the *clergy*.

Holder of the Privilege →person who is confessing

The proposed Federal Rule of Evidence 506 recognizing the clergy-penitent privilege provided that the privilege belongs to the communicant. The privilege in the proposed federal rule and in a number of states may be claimed on behalf of the communicant by a clergy member asked to testify because the role of the clergy is thought to constitute a sufficient safeguard that the clergy member is accurately representing the wishes of the communicant. In these jurisdictions, clergy may refuse to testify even when the communicant has waived the privilege if the disclosure would violate the clergy's sacred trust (*Waters v. O'Connor*, 103 P.3d 292 [Ariz. App. 2004]).

Definition of Clergy →

The proposed Federal Rule 506(a)(1) defines a "clergyman" as a minister, priest, rabbi, or "other similar functionary of a religious organization, or an individual reasonably believed to be by the person consulting him." The question remains whether clergy belonging to new religions or individuals who serve as "lay ministers" are able to claim benefit of the clergy-penitent privilege.

Scope of the Privilege

A communication is protected if made while seeking spiritual guidance. This is not limited to confessions and is interpreted as protecting all communications made to clergy while engaged in spiritual counseling. The line between privileged and non-privileged information can be difficult to discern and does not include marriage counseling or religious education sessions or casual conversations unrelated to religious counseling.

Confidentiality →must be in private

The communication is required to be confidential. The proposed federal rule requires that a communication is made "privately" and is not intended for "further disclosure." The presence of "multiple parties, unrelated by blood or marriage," may "defeat the condition that communications be made with a reasonable expectation of confidentiality in order for the privilege to attach." A counseling session involving a pastor and a group of neighbors seeking spiritual counseling in regard to racial violence in their neighborhood was held to be privileged (*In re Grand Jury Investigation*, 918 F.3d 374 [3d Cir. 1990]). A federal court held that the privilege was not applicable when an individual admitted his involvement in a murder to a priest during what the court described as a "heart-to-heart" talk rather than a "formal confession." The penitent also was found to have waived the privilege by disclosing the content of the conversation to three other individuals (*Morales v. Portuondo*, 154 F. Supp.2d 706 [S.D.N.Y. 2001]).

Exceptions

If clergy is told about child abuse—they have to tell.

There is no explicit crime-fraud exception because spiritual advice may be expected to include a clergy's dissuading of an individual from pursuing a course of criminal conduct. Various jurisdictions impose a duty on clergy to report child abuse (Ohio Rev. Stat. § 2151.421[A][1]).

Waiver

The privilege may be waived if not invoked by the penitent at trial or if the substance of the communication is conveyed to a third party. The privilege also is waived if the communicant testifies about the content of the communication at trial or if the penitent discloses a significant portion of the communication or authorizes another individual to disclose a significant portion of the communication.

10.3 YOU DECIDE

A federal grand jury conducted an investigation into the practice of some draft counselors of referring selective service registrants to dentists, psychiatrists, and doctors who were suspected of fabricating medical disabilities that would keep the registrant from being drafted to serve in Vietnam. A subpoena to testify before the grand jury was served on "Reverend Gordon Verplank, who is an ordained minister of the United Presbyterian Church and director of the McAlister Draft Counseling Center, which is supported by that Church. Verplank is also Chaplain of the Claremont Colleges, and in this capacity is officially responsible for all draft counseling services afforded by the Colleges." Reverend Verplank claims that the clergy-penitent privilege prohibits him from being asked about the substance of his counseling sessions with individuals confronting military service in Vietnam. Do you agree with Reverend Verplank? See *In Re Verplank* (329 F.Supp. 433 [Cal. Ct. App. 1971]).

You can learn what the court decided by referring to the study site, **http://study.sagepub.com/lippmance.**

important: privacy, doctor can't treat you properly unless you tell them everything. → you might not want other people to know ex: STD

■ PHYSICIAN-PATIENT PRIVILEGE

The **physician-patient privilege** was recognized in a 1928 New York statute and is not a product of the common law. Today, the physician-patient privilege is accepted by state courts although it is not recognized by federal courts. There are cases in which federal courts protect doctor-patient communications as part of the right to privacy. The basis of the privilege is that doctors require a free flow of information to provide adequate medical treatment. A doctor in prescribing medication needs to know whether an individual is a frequent user of illegal narcotics. A patient will feel more comfortable sharing this information if he or she is confident that his or her conversation will not be shared with law enforcement.

The requirements for the physician-patient privilege are similar to those for the attorney-client privilege:

Physician. The patient must have shared the information with a licensed physician. Most states also recognize the privilege if the patient reasonably believes the individual is licensed to practice medicine. The privilege includes MDs as well as medical professionals including osteopaths and chiropractors, and some states extend the privilege to dentists. The privilege in most states covers individuals working under the doctor's supervision. There is a separate privilege covering psychotherapists and their patients, which in some states is much broader than the physician-patient privilege.

Patient. The privilege covers an individual consulting a medical professional for diagnosis or treatment. A patient waives the privilege by testifying about the information he or she shared with the doctor.

Scope. The communication to the doctor is required to be made during medical diagnosis or treatment. This information includes the results of laboratory tests, X-rays, and laboratory tests performed for purposes of treatment. The privilege also covers advice provided to the patient by the doctor. Some states extend the doctor-patient privilege beyond communication between a patient and a doctor to include information obtained by the doctor in observing a patient's injuries. Medical examinations for purposes other than treatment, such as court-ordered examinations or examinations to qualify for insurance coverage, are not covered by the doctor-patient privilege.

Holder of privilege. The privilege belongs to the patient, and the patient may prevent a doctor from testifying. A doctor has the obligation to assert the privilege at trial if the patient is not present. A physician may be compelled to testify if the patient waives the privilege. The privilege likely will not apply if an outside, nonessential party is present during the conversation with the doctor. However, another privilege such as the spousal privilege may apply. The presence of medical staff does not result in a waiver of the privilege.

As with the attorney-client privilege, there are exceptions to the doctor-patient privilege. The most important are listed below:

Criminal plans. The physician-patient privilege does not cover information on how to conceal or carry out a crime. This may entail information on the lethal impact of various drugs, surgeries performed to conceal an individual's identity, and providing a drug addict with a prescription for drugs. Several states limit the privilege to civil cases and do not recognize the privilege in criminal cases. → how much of this is lethal? → not in criminal

Duty. State laws variously require the reporting to government authorities of sexually transmitted diseases, suspected child abuse, gunshot and knife wounds, severe burn injuries, injuries reasonably believed to be the product of domestic violence, and other suspicious activities. Some states establish a duty to report any and all criminal activity a patient discloses to a physician. This qualification of the privilege is based on the interest in public safety. We would want a school therapist who concludes a patient poses a potential threat to his or her fellow students to report this to police.

Incidental information. The doctor-patient privilege does not include incidental information such as the name, address, occupation, age, and date of treatment.

if you tell them you're going to kill

If it's ordered by the court, not confidential — assert

■ PSYCHOTHERAPIST-PATIENT PRIVILEGE

civil and criminal

In 1996, the U.S. Supreme Court in *Jaffee v. Redmond* recognized the **psychotherapist-patient privilege** as part of federal common law (*Jaffee v. Redmond*, 518 U.S. 1 [1996]). The Supreme Court stressed that effective therapy "depends upon an atmosphere of confidence and trust in which the patient is willing to make a frank and complete disclosure of facts, emotions, memories and fears" much of which, if disclosed, would result in "embarrassment or disgrace." There was a strong social interest in encouraging communication between therapists and patients to prevent patients from engaging in destructive behavior. → won't be comfortable talking unless they know its confidential

Scope. The privilege extends to communication with psychiatrists, psychologists, and social workers for the purpose of diagnosis or treatment of mental or emotional problems. A patient may refuse to reveal confidential communications between him- or herself and a psychotherapist made for the purpose of diagnosing or treating a mental or emotional condition. The patient also may prevent the therapist from testifying on these matters.

The psychotherapist-patient privilege extends to both civil and criminal cases. There is no privilege to prevent a therapist from testifying in a court-ordered mental examination. The privilege also is inapplicable when the patient has placed his or her mental condition in issue by offering an insanity defense.

A communication between a patient and a psychotherapist to qualify as privileged must be confidential. Individuals other than the doctor may be present if they are essential for the diagnosis or treatment.

Exceptions. A controversial question on which courts are divided is whether there should be a **dangerous patient exception** to the psychotherapist-patient privilege. On the one hand, society certainly wants to curb criminal behavior before it occurs. On the other hand, there is an interest in encouraging open communication between patients and therapists so as to treat patients' anti-social tendencies.

The Sixth Circuit Court of Appeals partially solved this problem by recognizing a "*duty to warn.*" A patient repeatedly reported a strong urge to kill his supervisor at work and described in detail how he would carry out the crime. The therapist contacted the supervisor who, in turn, contacted authorities who obtained the patient's records from his therapists. A court agreed with the patient that the psychiatric records were privileged and were inadmissible in any court proceeding.

If they say they are going to kill someone. They should tell/warn the person they are planning to kill

The Sixth Circuit Court of Appeals affirmed the trial court's decision but held that the therapist possessed a professional and legal duty to warn the supervisor (*United States v. Hayes*, 227 F.3d 578 [6th Cir. 2000]).

A patient waives the psychotherapist privilege if the patient's mental condition is "placed in issue." An example is an individual who relies on the insanity defense or the defense of diminished responsibility. In these instances, a prosecutor may examine the defendant's therapist regarding the defendant's mental condition. The privilege also does not apply to "incidental information," such as the fact an individual consulted a therapist, or to the date of the appointments. A therapist, for example, may testify that he or she has treated a specific patient.

■ HUSBAND-WIFE PRIVILEGE

The early common law prohibited the parties to a case from testifying on the grounds that an interested party would lack objectivity and would shade and misrepresent the facts. This same rationale provided the basis for the **husband-wife privilege**. This privilege involves two separate and distinct privileges (see also Table 10.2):

1. *Marital communications privilege.* Prohibits the revealing of confidential communications between spouses during marriage.

2. *Marital testimony privilege.* Prohibits the testimony of one spouse against the other spouse.

The philosophical basis for the husband-wife privilege is a respect for the sanctity of marriage and the interest in encouraging marital partners to share their innermost feelings and thoughts. Compelling one spouse to testify will interfere with the intimacy of the marital partners. There also is a general interest in respecting the two individuals' "zone of privacy."

Marital Communications Privilege

Scope. The privilege for confidential communication between husband and wife prohibits the use in court of statements made in confidence during marriage. The privilege applies if there is a legally recognized marriage under state law. There is no requirement that the individuals live together. Some states recognize common law marriage although states do not recognize the marital privilege for individuals who are living together.

Roughly half of the states provide that confidential conversations during marriage remain privileged following the end of the marriage. This means that the conversations between two individuals during marriage remain confidential following the death of one of the spouses or following divorce. A divorced spouse consequently may prevent his or her former spouse from testifying about their confidential communications.

The marital communication privilege encompasses all forms of communication between two spouses, including e-mails, tweets, letters, phone calls, and conversations. A number of states apply the confidential communication privilege to situations in which one spouse observed the actions of the other spouse. This may occur if one spouse observed the other spouse commit a theft.

Holder of privilege. Both spouses hold the privilege to refuse to disclose communications with the other and to prevent the other spouse from disclosing communications in court. In other words a spouse may not waive the privilege without the consent of the other spouse.

Scope. The marital communication privilege applies to both civil and criminal cases.

Waiver. A communication may not be privileged if overheard by other individuals, if the communications were read by other individuals, or if other individuals had access to the communication. There is an unusual twist. If only one spouse is responsible for disclosing communications to a third party, the waiver only applies to the spouse who discloses the communication. The other party still may claim the privilege to prevent the other spouse from disclosing the information or testifying in court.

Exceptions. One spouse may testify against the other spouse when there are charges of domestic violence, crimes of violence against children in the family, neglect or desertion of the family, bigamy, and crimes against the property of a spouse. Some states have an exception for situations in which both husband and wife plan or enter into a conspiracy to commit a crime.

spouse can refuse to testify against the other

Marital Testimony Privilege

The second prong of the husband-wife privilege provides that one spouse may refuse to testify against the other spouse.

Holder. States differ on the spouse who holds the privilege. In some states, the defendant holds the privilege and may prevent the other spouse from testifying against him or her. In other states and in the federal courts, the witness-spouse holds the privilege and may testify or refuse to testify. Several states recognize both spouses as holding the privilege. The privilege attaches on the date the parties marry one another. The privilege ends with the end of the marriage.

Scope. The husband-wife privilege applies to criminal cases, and either spouse may be compelled to testify in civil cases. The privilege attaches so long as the parties are married. Keep in mind that the privilege only is applicable to adverse testimony against the interests of a spouse and does not apply to testimony that is beneficial to a spouse.

Procedure. The lawyer who plans to invoke the privilege on behalf of a spouse notifies the trial court judge of his or her client's intent. A hearing is held in which the other side is allowed to challenge the potential witness's authority to invoke the husband-wife privilege. The judge either may recognize the spouse's privilege to refuse to testify or may order the witness-spouse to testify.

Exceptions. The exceptions are the same as for marital communications privilege. States generally will not recognize the privilege where two individuals married to prevent one or both individuals from testifying against the other spouse (*United States v. Apodaca*, 522 F.2d 568 [10th Cir. 1974]).

Table 10.2 ■ Marital Privileges	
Marital Testimony Privilege	**Marital Communications Privilege**
All testimony against a spouse	Confidential communications between Spouses
Applies to actions and observations	Only confidential communications
Spouses must be married	Spouses are not required to be married
Which spouse may assert differs	Either spouse may assert
Only in criminal cases	Civil and criminal cases
Applies to events before marriage	Does not apply to events before marriage
Does not survive end of marriage	Survives end of marriage
Various exceptions including spouse and children	Various exceptions including spouse and children

10.4 YOU DECIDE

Diana Arnold overheard her husband James making incriminating statements over the phone about burning down a house. The day following the fire, the defendant drove Diana by the burned house to view the damage. Diana and James subsequently separated and divorced. James objected to the trial court allowing his former wife to testify as to the substance of the phone conversation and to the defendant's driving by the burnt house. Alabama law provides that "[t]he husband and wife may testify either for or against each other in criminal cases, but shall not be compelled to do so." Was the trial court correct in allowing Diana to testify against James? See *Arnold v. State* (353 So.2d 523 [Ala. 1977]).

You can learn what the court decided by referring to the study site, **http://study.sagepub.com/lippmance.**

■ GOVERNMENT PRIVILEGES

There are five privileges that may be invoked by government officials: executive privilege, the state secrets privilege, the official information privilege, the confidential informant's privilege, and grand jury confidentiality.

Executive Privilege

The courts have recognized that the president of the United States has an **executive privilege** to protect confidential communications. The privilege generally is absolute in regard to military, diplomatic, or national security communication. Other types of communications are presumptively privileged and may be overridden by the need for specific information in a criminal trial. The privilege includes the president as well as the confidential communications of department and agency heads, such as the attorney general of the United States. State courts recognize an executive privilege for state governors.

The U.S. Supreme Court in *United States v. Nixon* in 1974 rejected President Richard Nixon's claim of an absolute executive privilege. At the request of a special prosecutor, a district court issued a subpoena directing President Nixon to hand over tape recordings and documents relating to his conversations with various advisers that were sought by the lawyers prosecuting former members of the executive branch.

Chief Justice Warren Burger recognized that executive privilege protected the public interest in open and objective debate in formulating presidential decision-making. This allowed views to be articulated privately that individuals may have been reluctant to articulate if they knew that the views would be made public. The Court balanced the "the importance of the general privilege of confidentiality of Presidential communications . . . against the inroads of such a privilege on the fair administration of criminal justice." In this instance, the Court held that "we cannot conclude that advisers will be moved to temper the candor of their remarks by the infrequent occasions of disclosure because of the possibility that such conversations will be called for in the context of a criminal prosecution."

Because this information often is sensitive, the trial court judge examines the information "*in camera*" (in chambers) to determine whether the information falls within the executive privilege. In the review, the attorney representing the president is to be present, and during the review, the judge is to provide the "high degree of respect due the President of the United States" (*United States v. Nixon*, 418 U.S. 683 [1974]). The government "must present evidence sufficient to support a reasonable belief that [*in camera*] review may yield evidence that establishes the exception's applicability" (*United States v. Zolin*, 491 U.S. 554 [1989]).

State Secrets Privilege

Federal Rule 509(b) provided for a government **state secrets privilege**. Rule 509(b) provides that "[t]he government has a privilege to refuse to give evidence and to prevent any person from giving evidence upon a showing of reasonable likelihood of danger that the evidence will disclose a secret of state or official information." Rule 509(c) requires that the chief officer of a government agency claim the privilege that is to be evaluated by the judge *in* *camera.* Confidential information covered by the state secrets privilege includes intelligence operations and defense, military, and diplomatic matters.

The U.S. Supreme Court first recognized the state secrets privilege in a suit for money by the estate of a deceased spy for espionage work on behalf of the Union Army during the Civil War (*Totten v. United States*, 92 U.S. 105 [1875]). The state secrets doctrine was most fully discussed in *United States v. Reynolds* in 1953 (*United States v. Reynolds*, 345 U.S. 1 [1953]). In *Reynolds*, a B-29 test aircraft crashed on a secret test mission. Surviving family members of civilian crew members sued for damages and in order to establish government liability asked for various documents relating to the crash. The U.S. Supreme Court upheld the Air Force's authority to withhold the documents under the state secrets privilege based on the fact the plane was equipped with secret electronic equipment.

The Tenth Circuit Court of Appeals more recently upheld the government's assertion of the state secrets doctrine in a damage claim against a private airline corporation allegedly involved in the secret and forced abduction and transportation of terrorism suspects to secret overseas detention centers (*Mohamed v. Jeppesen Dataplan, Inc.* 614 F.3d 1070 [D.C. Cir. 1983]).

Official Information Privilege

At common law, official governmental documents were privileged and were not required to be released if disclosure would be contrary to the public interest. An example was military plans and projects and diplomatic correspondence. The privilege was rarely invoked because individuals lacked the ability to sue the government absent the government's authorization.

One of the most important developments in United States democracy is the adoption of the federal Freedom of Information Act and state freedom of information acts that allow individuals to make a request for the release of government documents. The government's decision to refuse to release the documents may be challenged in court.

Various categories of information are exempt from the Freedom of Information Act. This **official information privilege** includes ongoing investigations, personnel records of government employees, and other information whose release would threaten national security.

Confidential Informant's Privilege

Law enforcement officers based on either state statutes or case law possess a limited **confidential informant privilege** to withhold the identities of confidential informants who assist the police in investigating and detecting criminal activities. This typically involves informants who reported the crime to the police or provided leads or whose information helped to establish probable cause to obtain an arrest warrant or a search warrant.

This type of informant differs from the informant involved in the crime or who observed the crime. The identity of an informant must be revealed where the informant's testimony is "material" to the defendant's guilt or innocence at trial. This may arise in those instances in which the informant directly participated in the crime or observed the defendant commit the crime. In these situations, the informant's testimony is directly relevant to establishing the defendant's guilt or innocence, and the informant's identity must be revealed. This duty to disclose the informant's identity to the defense is based on the defendant's right to confront the witnesses against him or her. A failure to reveal the informant's identity where the testimony is crucial to a fair trial for the defendant may result in the dismissal of the case against the accused.

Any doubt as to whether the informant is a material witness is to be resolved in favor of revealing the informant's identity. The defendant only is required to demonstrate a "reasonable possibility" that the informant's testimony may exonerate the accused (*Roviaro v. United States*, 353 U.S. 53 [1957]).

There are several public policy reasons for the confidential informant's privilege.

Crime investigation and detection. Information provided by citizens can assist the police in investigating and detecting crime.

Citizens' obligation. Citizens should feel an obligation to report crime to law enforcement officials.

Anonymity. The withholding of an informant's identity encourages individuals to cooperate with the police and protects individuals against retribution.

There is a strong public policy reason for revealing a confidential informant's identity when he or she directly participated in the crime and when he or she testifies against the defendant at trial.

Due process. The identity of the informant is crucial to the ability of the defendant to offer an effective defense and to confront his or her accusers.

Grand Jury Confidentiality

The federal government and a number of states rely on grand juries to criminally charge (indict) individuals. The Fifth Amendment to the United States Constitution requires the federal government to use grand juries to indict individuals for federal felonies.

Individuals serving on a grand jury are required to take an oath obligating them to keep the deliberations secret. Any individual who discloses the proceedings of a grand jury may be criminally punished for contempt of court. The government is the holder of privilege.

There are a number of reasons, listed below, for **grand jury confidentiality**:

Independence. The confidentiality of proceedings protects the independence and free deliberations of the grand jury.

Witnesses. The secrecy protects individuals required to testify before the grand jury and encourages witnesses to testify openly without fear of retribution.

Accused. Confidentiality helps ensure that individuals who may be indicted do not flee the jurisdiction to avoid impending criminal charges. The privacy of individuals who are not indicted is protected.

■ NEWS MEDIA PRIVILEGE

We depend on the media for information and to investigate and reveal wasteful, unethical, and criminal behavior by private individuals and public officials. The news media in the United States, in part, feels free to aggressively pursue stories because of the protection of the First Amendment. An important aspect of the ability of reporters to pursue stories is to promise "sources" that their identity will remain confidential and will not be revealed.

The common law did not recognize a **news media privilege** or what commonly is termed a **journalist shield law**. In *Branzburg v. Hayes*, the United States Supreme Court held that the First Amendment does not mandate recognition of a journalist's privilege to refuse to respond to a grand jury subpoena to reveal information relevant to a criminal prosecution. The Court stated that "we cannot seriously entertain the notion that the First Amendment protects a newsman's agreement to conceal the criminal conduct of his source, or evidence thereof, on the theory that it is better to write about crime than to do something about it." The Court further noted that the "crimes of news sources are no less reprehensible and threatening to the public interest when witnessed by a reporter than when they are not" (*Branzburg v. Hayes*, 408 U.S 665 [1972]). Four years later in *Zurcher v. Stanford Daily*, the Supreme Court held that the police seizure of material from the *Stanford Daily* student newspaper based on a probable cause warrant did not violate the newspaper's First Amendment rights. The Court stated that "nor are we convinced, any more than we were in *Branzburg v. Hayes*, that confidential sources will disappear and that the press will suppress news because of fears of warranted searches" (*Zurcher v. Stanford Daily*, 436 U.S. 547 [1978]).

The media privilege was the topic of a great deal of discussion when the District Columbia Court of Appeals ordered journalists to reveal the confidential sources and material to a grand jury relating to their revealing of the identity of CIA agent Valerie Plame. Although the decision led to revealing that the source of the leak was in the Office of the Vice President of the United States, the appellate court held that the Supreme Court in *Branzburg* "in no uncertain terms rejected the existence of such a privilege" (*In re Grand Jury Subpoena* [Judith Miller], 397 F.3d 964 [D.C. Cir. 2005]).

Most states provide for a qualified media privilege, and a number of federal courts have read *Branzburg* as providing a qualified media privilege. The laws do not distinguish the size or quality of news outlets and cover print as well as electronic media and, in the view of some judges, film. These statutes protect a journalist from testifying about, or responding to a *subpoena duces tecum* (subpoena to produce documents in court) with, material that has not been published or broadcast. Journalists under shield laws may refuse to testify and to withhold documents, transcripts, recordings of interviews, photographs, outtakes not used in a television story or film, and the identity of sources. Absent a privilege, a journalist can be required to testify before a grand jury or trial court, and a refusal to testify could result in the journalist being held in contempt of court.

A judge in response to a journalist who invokes the media privilege in most instances will conduct an *in camera* hearing to determine if the journalist may rely on his or her privilege. The judge typically will engage in a three-part test in determining whether to recognize the privilege. This entails asking whether the information is relevant, whether the information can be obtained by alternative means, and whether there is a compelling interest in the information. Because of the importance of preserving confidential sources, reporters often choose to be jailed for contempt of court rather than reveal their sources.

CRIMINAL EVIDENCE AND PUBLIC POLICY

A shield law is a law that provides protection to reporters against being compelled to disclose the names of confidential sources in state court. There is no federal shield law although the Obama administration has stated that it intends to push for Congress to adopt a federal shield law.

A shield law provides a privilege to reporters against being compelled by a subpoena or court order to testify or to turn over documents relating to a media story or to be compelled to reveal the name of a confidential source.

As noted in the textual discussion of the media privilege, in *Branzburg v. Hayes*, the Supreme Court held in a 5-4 decision that the media did not have a First Amendment right to withhold the name of confidential sources. The Court did provide that the government is required to "convincingly show a substantial relation between the information sought and a subject of overriding and compelling state interest." The states and the federal government were free to provide protections for journalists but were not required to provide protections.

Forty states and the District of Columbia have shield laws, and nine additional states provide some limited protections to journalists based on court decisions.

The primary debate involves whether there should be a federal shield law that will protect journalists reporting on national defense and security and diplomatic affairs. Journalists claim that confidential sources in national security agencies will not be willing to talk to journalists without an ironclad guarantee of anonymity and that a federal shield law is essential to protecting journalists reporting on national affairs. The free flow of information and an informed population is essential to democracy. Journalists argue that the media is cautious and responsible in their reporting and there is little risk of the press reporting material that they are cautious about or reporting on stories that may harm American security.

Individuals opposing shield laws contend that journalists should not be provided protections that are not available to other individuals. In particular, journalists should not be provided with protection for reporting on stories leaked from confidential government sources that may jeopardize the national security of the United States. The primary beneficiaries of a media shield are lawbreakers who are being protected by journalists. The difficulty in defining who is a journalist also may provide a shield for bloggers and websites looking to attract an audience by reporting sensationalistic material.

The debate over a shield law has been intensified by an estimated eight hundred subpoenas a year issued to journalists. As discussed above, in 2005, subpoenas were issued to several journalists asking that they turn over documents and testify about the source of a leak by a government official that unlawfully identified Valerie Plame, whose husband was a critic of the invasion of Iraq, as a CIA agent. *New York Times* journalist Judith Miller was held in contempt for her refusal to name her source and spent eighty-five days in jail before being released from her confidentiality agreement by her source. In 2011, the Department of Justice issued subpoenas, which later were withdrawn, in investigating the sources for Fox News reporter Mike Levine's reporting on the connection between young Somali-Americans and terrorist groups abroad. In 2013, Jana Winter, a Fox News reporter, was subpoenaed to testify about her sources in the Aurora, Colorado, movie theater shooting carried out by James Holmes. A young videographer, Josh Wolf, spent over 220 days in jail in 2006–2007 after being held in contempt for refusing to turn over his film recording individuals responsible for property damage during protests against international bankers in Seattle.

The issue became of even greater significance when a subpoena was issued to former *New York Times* reporter James Risen who, in 2006, refused to reveal the sources for his reporting on efforts to sabotage the Iranian nuclear program. The Fourth Circuit Court of Appeals overturned a federal district court decision and held that the First Amendment does not provide for a reporter's privilege. As a result, the court held that Risen had no right to refuse to testify. In his dissent, Judge Roger Gregory, appointed by George H. W. Bush,

(Continued)

protested that the Fourth Circuit Court had turned its back on the First Amendment, "one of our Constitution's most important and salutary contributions to human history. Our country's Founders established the First Amendment's guarantee of a free press as a recognition that a government unaccountable to public discourse renders that essential element of democracy—the vote—meaningless." The United States Supreme Court refused to review the Fourth Circuit Court decision. Risen when called to the stand to testify refused to answer questions that could reveal the name of his source.

Should there be a federal shield law for journalists? What about a journalist who is given access to a street gang and knows the identity of individuals responsible for a series of gang shootings and has information about the gang's involvement in drug trafficking and exoneration of store owners?

State shield laws only require a journalist to testify about his or her sources or to turn over information relevant to a criminal case when the party seeking disclosure has exhausted other alternatives and the information is essential to the prosecution of a crime. There is a strong presumption in favor of disclosure when the information could prevent death, kidnapping, substantial bodily harm, crimes against minors, terrorism, or breach of national security. Most policymakers want to limit protections to individuals who derive a substantial percentage of their income from journalism rather than extend protections to individuals such as bloggers who function as journalists but who are not professionally employed as journalists. Should the law recognize a media privilege?

■ CASE ANALYSIS

Trammel v. United States discussed the husband-wife spousal privilege.

Which spouse should hold the husband-wife privilege?

Trammel v. United States, 445 U.S. 40 (1980), Burger, J.

On March 10, 1976, petitioner Otis Trammel was indicted with two others, Edwin Lee Roberts and Joseph Freeman, for importing heroin into the United States from Thailand and the Philippine Islands and for conspiracy to import heroin. The indictment also named six unindicted co-conspirators, including petitioner's wife Elizabeth Ann Trammel.

According to the indictment, petitioner and his wife flew from the Philippines to California in August 1975, carrying with them a quantity of heroin. Freeman and Roberts assisted them in its distribution. Elizabeth Trammel then traveled to Thailand where she purchased another supply of the drug. On November 3, 1975, with four ounces of heroin on her person, she boarded a plane for the United States. During a routine customs search in Hawaii, she was searched, the heroin was discovered, and she was arrested. After discussions with Drug Enforcement Administration agents, she agreed to cooperate with the Government.

Prior to trial on this indictment, petitioner moved to sever his case from that of Roberts and Freeman. He advised the court that the Government intended to call his wife as an adverse witness and asserted his claim to a privilege to prevent her from testifying against him. At a hearing on the motion, Mrs. Trammel was called as a Government witness under a grant of use immunity. She

testified that she and petitioner were married in May 1975 and that they remained married. She explained that her cooperation with the Government was based on assurances that she would be given lenient treatment. She then described, in considerable detail, her role and that of her husband in the heroin distribution conspiracy.

After hearing this testimony, the District Court ruled that Mrs. Trammel could testify in support of the Government's case to any act she observed during the marriage and to any communication "made in the presence of a third person"; however, confidential communications between petitioner and his wife were held to be privileged and inadmissible. The motion to sever was denied.

At trial, Elizabeth Trammel testified within the limits of the court's pretrial ruling; her testimony, as the Government concedes, constituted virtually its entire case against petitioner. He was found guilty on both the substantive and conspiracy charges and sentenced to an indeterminate term of years pursuant to the Federal Youth Corrections Act.

The privilege claimed by petitioner has ancient roots. Writing in 1628, Lord Coke observed that "it hath been resolved by the Justices that a wife cannot be produced either against or for her husband." This spousal disqualification sprang from two canons of medieval jurisprudence: first, the rule that an accused was not permitted to testify in his own behalf because of his interest in the proceeding; second, the concept that husband and wife were one, and that since the woman had no recognized separate legal existence, the husband was that one. From those two now long-abandoned doctrines, it followed that what was inadmissible from the lips of the defendant-husband was also inadmissible from his wife.

Despite its medieval origins, this rule of spousal disqualification remained intact in most common-law jurisdictions well into the 19th century. Indeed, it was not until 1933, in *Funk v. United States* (290 U.S. 371), that this Court abolished the testimonial disqualification in the federal courts, so as to permit the spouse of a defendant to testify in the defendant's behalf. *Funk*, however, left undisturbed the rule that either spouse could prevent the other from giving adverse testimony.

The modern justification for this privilege against adverse spousal testimony is its perceived role in fostering the harmony and sanctity of the marriage relationship. Notwithstanding this benign purpose, the rule was sharply criticized.

In *Hawkins v. United States*, 358 U.S. 74 (1958), this Court considered the continued vitality of the privilege against adverse spousal testimony in the federal courts. *Hawkins*, then, left the federal privilege for adverse spousal testimony where it found it, continuing "a rule which bars the testimony of one spouse against the other unless both consent." Since 1958, when Hawkins was decided, support for the privilege against adverse spousal testimony has been eroded further. The trend in state law toward divesting the accused of the privilege to bar adverse spousal testimony has special relevance because the laws of marriage and domestic relations are concerns traditionally reserved to the states. Scholarly criticism of the *Hawkins* rule has also continued unabated.

Testimonial exclusionary rules and privileges contravene the fundamental principle that "'the public . . . has a right to every man's evidence.'" Here we must decide whether the privilege against adverse spousal testimony promotes sufficiently important interests to outweigh the need for probative evidence in the administration of criminal justice. It is essential to remember that the Hawkins privilege is not needed to protect information privately disclosed between husband and wife in the confidence of the marital relationship—once described by this Court as "the best solace of human existence." Those confidences are privileged under the independent rule protecting confidential marital communications. The *Hawkins* privilege is invoked, not to exclude private marital communications, but rather to exclude evidence of criminal acts and of communications made in the presence of third persons.

No other testimonial privilege sweeps so broadly. The privileges between clergy and penitent, attorney and client, and physician and patient limit protection to private communications. These privileges are rooted in the imperative need for confidence and trust. The clergy-penitent privilege recognizes the human need to disclose to a spiritual counselor, in total and absolute confidence, what are believed to be flawed acts or thoughts and to receive priestly consolation and guidance in return. The lawyer-client privilege rests on the need for the advocate and counselor to know all that relates to the client's reasons for seeking representation if the professional mission is to be carried out. Similarly, the physician must know all that a patient can articulate in order to identify and to treat disease; barriers to full disclosure would impair diagnosis and treatment.

The *Hawkins* rule stands in marked contrast to these three privileges. Its protection is not limited to confidential communications; rather, it permits an accused to exclude all adverse spousal testimony. As Jeremy Bentham observed more than a century and a half ago, such a privilege goes far beyond making "every man's house his castle," and permits a person to convert his house into "a den of thieves." It "secures, to every man, one safe and unquestionable and ever ready accomplice for every imaginable crime."

The ancient foundations for so sweeping a privilege have long since disappeared. Nowhere in the common-law world—indeed in any modern society—is a woman regarded as chattel or demeaned by denial of a separate legal identity and the dignity associated with recognition as a whole human being. Chip by chip, over the years, those archaic notions have been cast aside so that "no longer is the female destined solely for the home and the rearing of the family, and only the male for the marketplace and the world of ideas."

When one spouse is willing to testify against the other in a criminal proceeding—whatever the motivation—their relationship is almost certainly in disrepair; there is probably little in the way of marital harmony for the privilege to preserve. In these circumstances, a rule of evidence that permits an accused to prevent adverse spousal testimony seems far more likely to frustrate justice than to foster family peace. Indeed, there is reason to believe that vesting the privilege in the accused could actually undermine the marital relationship. For example, in a case such as this, the government is unlikely to offer a wife immunity and lenient treatment if it knows that her husband can prevent her from giving adverse testimony. If the government is dissuaded from making such an offer, the privilege can have the untoward effect of permitting one spouse to escape justice at the expense of the other. It hardly seems conducive to the preservation of the marital relation to place a wife in jeopardy solely by virtue of her husband's control over her testimony.

Accordingly, we conclude that the existing rule should be modified so that the witness-spouse alone has a privilege to refuse to testify adversely; the witness may be neither compelled to testify nor foreclosed from testifying. This modification—vesting the privilege in the witness-spouse—furthers the important public interest in marital harmony without unduly burdening legitimate law enforcement needs.

CHAPTER SUMMARY

Certain confidential relationships are considered privileged. The holder of the privilege is the individual who may invoke the protection of the privilege and avoid testifying, as well as preventing the other party to the privileged relationship from testifying. The holder of the privilege is not required to be a party to the litigation.

Courts generally recognize the privileges that existed at common law. Other privileges result from legislative enactments. Although Congress expressed an intent to allow privileges to develop to meet the demands of the times, some groups continue to be frustrated by the failure of courts to recognize new privileges.

In this chapter a number of privileges have been discussed.

Attorney-client privilege. A client may prevent a lawyer with whom he or she has a professional relationship from disclosing communications between the two of them stemming from their professional relationship. Neither the client nor the lawyer may be compelled to testify about privileged information absent a waiver from the client.

Clergy-penitent privilege. This privilege protects communications between a penitent and a member of the clergy, made in confidence, during spiritual counseling to a member of the clergy.

Physician-patient privilege. The privilege covers an individual consulting a medical professional for diagnosis or treatment.

Psychotherapist-patient privilege. The privilege extends to communication with psychiatrists, psychologists, and social workers for the purpose of diagnosis or treatment of mental or emotional problems.

Husband-wife privilege. The marital testimony privilege prohibits the testimony of one spouse against the other spouse. The marital communication privilege prohibits the revealing of confidential communications between spouses during marriage.

Executive privilege. Courts have recognized that the president of the United States has an executive privilege to protect confidential communications. The privilege generally is absolute in regards to military, diplomatic, or national security communication. Other types of communications are presumptively privileged and may be overridden by the need for specific information in a criminal trial. Executive privilege extends to the confidential communications of department and agency heads.

State secrets. The government has a privilege to refuse to provide evidence and to prevent any person from giving evidence based on a showing of a reasonable likelihood of a danger that the evidence will disclose a secret of state or official information. The government must demonstrate that the information, if disclosed, may threaten the national security of the United States.

Confidential police informant privilege. Law enforcement officers based on either state statutes or case law possess a limited confidential informant privilege to withhold the identities of confidential informants who assist the police in investigating and detecting criminal activities.

Grand jury privilege. Individuals serving on a grand jury are required to take an oath obligating them to keep the deliberations secret. Any individual who discloses the proceedings of a grand jury may be criminally punished for contempt of court.

News media privilege. This is a qualified privilege by journalists to withhold the names of confidential sources and information obtained in researching their stories. The privilege is recognized by most states but is not recognized by the federal government.

CHAPTER REVIEW QUESTIONS

1. What is the reason for testimonial privileges? Do privileges promote or interfere with the pursuit of truth at trial?

2. Discuss some of the common characteristics of most privileges.

3. Identify the central aspects of the attorney-client privilege, clergy-penitent privilege, and physician-patient privilege.

4. What are the two parts of the husband-wife privilege? Which spouse is the holder of the privilege?

5. What is the reason for executive privilege and for the state secrets privilege?

6. Why are grand jury deliberations secret?

7. Explain the confidential informant privilege and when the prosecution is required to disclose the identity of a confidential informant.

LEGAL TERMINOLOGY

attorney-client privilege

clergy-penitent privilege

confidential informant privilege

crime-fraud exception

dangerous patient exception

executive privilege

grand jury confidentiality

husband-wife privilege

journalist shield law

news media privilege

official information privilege

physician-patient privilege

psychotherapist-patient privilege

state secrets privilege

testimonial privilege

Visit the Student Study Site at **http://study.sagepub.com/lippmance** to access additional study tools, including mobile-friendly eFlashcards and Web quizzes as well as links to SAGE journal articles and hyperlinks for *Criminal Evidence* on the Web.

CHAPTER 11

THE EXCLUSIONARY RULE

Violation of 4th amendment search and siezure evidence cannot be admitted in trial.

Is the evidence that was seized by the police admissible in evidence?

A paper, claimed to be a warrant, was held up by one of the officers. [Miss Mapp] grabbed the "warrant" and placed it in her bosom. A struggle ensued in which the officers recovered the piece of paper and as a result of which they handcuffed appellant, because she had been "belligerent" in resisting their official rescue of the "warrant" from her person. Running roughshod over appellant, a policeman "grabbed" her, "twisted [her] hand," and she "yelled [and] pleaded with him" because "it was hurting." Appellant, in handcuffs, was then forcibly taken upstairs to her bedroom where the officers searched a dresser, a chest of drawers, a closet, and some suitcases. They also looked into a photo album and through personal papers belonging to the appellant. The search spread to the rest of the second floor, including the child's bedroom, the living room, the kitchen, and a dinette. The basement of the building and a trunk found therein were also searched. The obscene materials for possession of which she was ultimately convicted were discovered in the course of that widespread search.

At the trial no search warrant was produced by the prosecution, nor was the failure to produce one explained or accounted for. At best, "There is, in the record, considerable doubt as to whether there ever was any warrant for the search of defendant's home." (*Mapp v. Ohio*, 367 U.S. 643 [1961])

CHAPTER OUTLINE

Introduction
The Exclusionary Rule
Debating the Exclusionary Rule
Invoking the Exclusionary Rule
Exceptions to the Exclusionary Rule

Case Analysis
Chapter Summary
Chapter Review Questions
Legal Terminology

TEST YOUR KNOWLEDGE

1. Do you know the significance of *Weeks v. United States*, *Wolf v. Colorado*, *Elkins v. United States*, and *Mapp v. Ohio?*

2. Are you able to summarize the arguments for and against the exclusionary rule?

3. Can you describe the procedure for invoking the exclusionary rule and the significance of the standing doctrine?

4. Are you able to explain the exceptions of the exclusionary rule: collateral proceedings, attenuation, good faith, independent source, inevitable discovery, and impeachment?

■ INTRODUCTION

The text of the Fourth Amendment is silent on the consequences of an unreasonable search and seizure. Should the evidence be excluded from trial? What of imposing a penalty on the police officers or compensating the subject of the unlawful search?

Historically, federal agents and state police who carried out unconstitutional searches and seizures were subject to civil suits for the return of property or for damages, were criminally prosecuted, or were subjected to internal administrative discipline. These procedures had the advantage of focusing responsibility on the police officers who failed to follow the law. Critics of these remedies, however, argued that that civil actions, criminal prosecutions, and disciplinary procedures were ineffective in controlling police practices and that an alternative approach was required. Civil actions, for example, were expensive and rarely resulted in significant monetary awards for victims. Prosecutors were reluctant to bring criminal actions against the police, and law enforcement officials were equally hesitant to pursue administrative complaints against officers who may have carried out an unlawful search that led to a criminal conviction.

In 1914, in *Weeks v. United States*, the U.S. Supreme Court ruled that the Fourth Amendment required that evidence seized in an unlawful search was to be excluded from use as evidence in federal courts. In 1961, in *Mapp v. Ohio*, the U.S. Supreme Court sent shockwaves through the criminal justice system by extending the federal exclusionary rule to criminal trials in state and local courts. The Court explained that the exclusionary rule was required to deter the police from disregarding constitutional standards and to maintain the integrity of the judiciary by excluding unlawfully seized evidence from trials. The Supreme Court shortly thereafter held that the exclusionary rule was a judge-made remedy rather than a remedy that was guaranteed by the Fourth Amendment to the U.S. Constitution. The sole purpose of this judge-made exclusionary rule was to deter unreasonable searches and seizures.

The exclusionary rule has been one of the primary flashpoints in the debate over whether the American criminal justice system has gone too far in protecting criminal perpetrators while disregarding the interests of victims and society. Critics ask whether it makes sense to exclude reliable evidence from trial and thereby to permit criminal defendants to walk out the courthouse door without having to confront all the evidence against them.

In the first portion of this chapter, we trace the evolution of the exclusionary rule. Pay particular attention to development of the exclusionary rule following *Mapp v. Ohio*. Ask yourself whether the Supreme Court has unduly limited the exclusionary rule or has struck the proper balance. Keep in mind that the exclusionary rule applies to searches and seizures under the Fourth Amendment. Evidence also may be excluded from trial based on the violation of other constitutional amendments. Two examples are the suppression of confessions and the suppression of in-court identifications:

- *Interrogations and identifications and the Fifth, Sixth, and Fourteenth Amendments.* Coerced confessions and confessions obtained in violation of *Miranda v. Arizona*, as well as confessions extracted in violation of the Sixth Amendment, are excluded from the prosecutor's case-in-chief.
- *Sixth Amendment.* A failure to provide an attorney at a lineup following the initiation of criminal proceedings results in the exclusion at trial of evidence from the lineup.

It may strike you as unusual that so much time is spent discussing the exclusionary rule given that the exclusionary rule is infrequently applied by judges and appellate courts. This is due to the fact that the exclusionary rule raises important issues regarding the balance between the prosecution and the defense in the criminal justice system and poses the challenge of how to control and to provide a remedy for the violation of constitutional rights by the police. As you read this chapter, consider whether you favor the exclusionary rule. Are there better alternatives?

■ THE EXCLUSIONARY RULE

only federal court at first
now federal and state

As you have just read, the Supreme Court has extended the Fourth Amendment exclusionary rule to prosecutions in federal and state courts. The **exclusionary rule** provides that evidence that is obtained as a result of a violation of the Fourth Amendment prohibition on unreasonable searches and seizures is inadmissible in a criminal prosecution to establish a defendant's guilt. **Derivative evidence**, or evidence that is discovered as a result of the unlawfully seized items, is considered the **fruit of the poisonous tree** and also is excluded from evidence. For example, records of illegal drug transactions that are seized in the course of an unlawful search are excluded from evidence, because the records are the direct result of an illegal search. The confessions resulting from the interrogation of individuals whose names are listed as part of the drug transactions will be excluded from evidence as the fruit of the poisonous tree.

The exclusionary rule, in summary, excludes the following from trial:

- *Direct evidence.* Evidence that is directly derived from the unreasonable search.
- *Fruit of the poisonous tree.* Evidence that is derived from the evidence that is directly seized.

The exclusionary rule nevertheless remains controversial. Why the reluctance to exclude items that were unreasonably seized from evidence? The primary reason is that this might result in a guilty defendant being set free to rape, rob, and steal once again. What of the interests of victims and of society in the conviction of criminals? The next sections shed some light on why the Supreme Court embraced the exclusionary rule.

The Exclusionary Rule and Federal Courts

In *Weeks v. United States*, the Supreme Court held that evidence seized in the course of an unreasonable search that violates the Fourth Amendment is to be excluded from evidence in federal courts. The police arrested Fremont Weeks and searched his home without a warrant. They seized various personal papers that were turned over to the U.S. marshal. Later that same day, the police and U.S. marshal searched Weeks's home a second time and seized various lottery tickets and letters that were used to convict Weeks for the use of the mail to transport lottery tickets in violation of federal law. Justice William R. Day ruled that the introduction of this evidence against the defendant violated the Fourth Amendment to the U.S. Constitution. He stressed that if letters and documents that are unlawfully seized from a defendant are introduced into evidence against that defendant at trial, the Fourth Amendment "is of no value" and "might as well be stricken from the Constitution." The efforts to bring the guilty to the bar of justice, "praiseworthy as they are, are not to be aided by the sacrifice of those great principles established by years of endeavor and suffering which have resulted in their embodiment in the fundamental law of the land" (*Weeks v. United States*, 232 U.S. 383, 392 [1914]). The question remained whether this same remedy was available against state law enforcement officers.

The Exclusionary Rule and State Courts

In 1949, in *Wolf v. Colorado*, the U.S. Supreme Court held that the requirements of the Fourth Amendment were incorporated into the Fourteenth Amendment and were applicable to the states. Justice Felix Frankfurter wrote that the "security of one's privacy against arbitrary intrusion by the police—which is the core of the Fourth Amendment—is basic to a free society [and] is therefore implicit in the concept of ordered liberty" (*Wolf v. Colorado*, 338 U.S. 25, 27, 33 [1949]).

The Supreme Court, however, also ruled that states were not required to exclude from trial evidence obtained in violation of the Fourth and Fourteenth Amendments. The exclusionary rule, according to the opinion in *Wolf*, is not "an explicit requirement" of the Fourth Amendment and is a remedy created by the judiciary to maintain the integrity of the courtroom and to deter police disregard for the Fourth Amendment. In the words of Justice Frankfurter, "In a prosecution in a State court for a State crime, the Fourteenth Amendment does not forbid the admission of evidence obtained by an unreasonable search and seizure." The Court pointed to the fact that virtually none of the countries in the English-speaking world recognized the exclusionary rule and that thirty states rejected the *Weeks* doctrine, while only seventeen were in agreement with *Weeks*. There was nothing in the U.S. Constitution to prevent these thirty states from continuing to rely on civil, criminal, and administrative remedies rather than the exclusionary rule to deter the police from engaging in unreasonable searches and seizures. Judge Benjamin Cardozo summarized the point of view in the thirty states that rejected the exclusionary rule when he wrote in a New York Court of Appeals decision that the "criminal [should not] go free because the constable has blundered" (*People v. Defore*, 150 N.E. 585, 587 [1926]).

Three Supreme Court judges dissented, including Justice Frank Murphy, who strongly criticized his judicial brethren and wrote that he did not believe that the requirements of the Fourth Amendment should be determined by counting how many states or countries rely on the exclusionary rule. Justice Murphy warned that the decision in *Weeks*

> will do inestimable harm to the cause of fair police methods in our cities and states. It must have tragic effect upon public respect for our judiciary. For the Court now allows shabby business: lawlessness by officers of the law. (*Wolf v. Colorado*, 338 U.S. 25, 46 [1949])

The Supreme Court, despite its decision in *Wolf*, was not prepared to hold that the Due Process Clause of the U.S. Constitution permitted state courts to admit evidence obtained in a blatantly unreasonable fashion. In the case at issue in *Rochin v. California*, the police, suspecting that Richard Antonio Rochin had swallowed capsules containing illegal narcotics, directed a doctor to force a vomiting-inducing solution into Rochin's stomach. The police subsequently discovered two morphine tablets. The Supreme Court ruled that the police conduct "shocked the conscience and violated the Due Process Clause of the Fourteenth Amendment" and that the morphine tablets should have been excluded from evidence. The Court explained that

> [i]llegally breaking into the privacy of the petitioner, the struggle to open his mouth and remove what was there, [and] the forcible extraction of his stomach's contents . . . are methods too close to the rack and the screw to permit of constitutional differentiation. (*Rochin v. California*, 342 U.S. 165, 172 [1952])

The next important development following *Wolf* was a series of cases in which the Supreme Court limited the **silver platter doctrine**. This practice involved federal officials making an end run around the exclusionary rule by relying on evidence in federal prosecutions that had been seized by state officials in violation of the Fourth Amendment. The evidence was "served" by state law enforcement officers to federal prosecutors on a "silver platter." In 1960, the silver platter doctrine was ruled unconstitutional in *Elkins v. United States*. In *Elkins*, the Supreme Court proclaimed that the holding in *Wolf*—that the Fourteenth Amendment Due Process Clause prohibited unreasonable searches and seizures by state officials—marked the death knell for the silver platter doctrine:

> For sure no distinction can logically be drawn between evidence obtained in violation of the Fourth Amendment and that obtained in violation of the Fourteenth. The Constitution is flouted equally in either case. To the victim it matters not whether his constitutional right has been invaded by a federal agent or by a state officer. (*Elkins v. United States*, 364 U.S. 206, 215 [1960])

The Supreme Court now was ready to take the final step of extending the exclusionary rule to the states. What arguments persuaded the court to change course?

The Extension of the Exclusionary Rule to the State Courts

In 1961, in *Mapp v. Ohio*, the U.S. Supreme Court ruled that the Fourth Amendment right to privacy, which is applicable to the states through the Fourteenth Amendment Due Process Clause,

> is enforceable against [the states] by the same sanction of exclusion as is used against the Federal Government. Were it otherwise, then . . . the assurance against unreasonable searches and seizures would be "a form of words."

The Court observed that an increasing number of states had adopted the exclusionary rule after concluding that other remedies had proven ineffective in deterring unreasonable searches and seizures. The Supreme Court also stressed that the exclusionary rule ensured judicial integrity by ensuring that courts would not become accomplices to disobedience to the Constitution that judges were sworn to uphold. The three dissenting judges, however, objected that the Supreme Court was unjustifiably imposing the exclusionary rule on state criminal justice systems (*Mapp v. Ohio*, 367 U.S. 643 [1961]).

Mapp clearly stated that the exclusionary rule is "part and parcel" and is "an essential part" of the Fourth Amendment, which is to be applied in cases of unreasonable searches and seizures that violate the Fourth Amendment. In a series of decisions following *Mapp*, the Supreme Court retreated from this position and held that the exclusionary rule is not constitutionally required and is a judge-made remedy developed to deter police disregard for the Fourth Amendment. In 1974, in *United States v. Calandra*, the Supreme Court, in an often-quoted statement, proclaimed that the exclusionary rule is "a judicially created remedy designed to safeguard Fourth Amendment rights generally through its deterrent effect rather than a personal constitutional right of the party aggrieved" (*United States v. Calandra*, 414 U.S. 338, 347 [1974]).

Why is this significant? The view that the exclusionary rule is a judge-made remedy means that the doctrine is not an ironclad requirement of the Constitution that judges are compelled to apply in every circumstance.

■ DEBATING THE EXCLUSIONARY RULE

The Justification for the Exclusionary Rule

A great deal of ink has been spilled by authors debating the merits of the exclusionary rule. Four arguments traditionally are offered in support of the exclusionary rule.

Constitutional rights. The Fourth Amendment protects individuals against unreasonable searches and seizures, and this safeguard would be seriously weakened if evidence seized in an unreasonable search is used against an accused at trial. Justice Tom Clark observed in *Mapp v. Ohio* that the exclusionary rule is an "essential ingredient" of the Fourth Amendment and that a failure to recognize the constitutional status of the exclusionary rule is to "grant the right but in reality to withhold its privilege and enjoyment."

Deterrence. The exclusionary rule deters the police from disregarding constitutional procedures in future investigations. The Supreme Court noted in *Elkins v. United States* that the purpose of the exclusionary rule is to deter the police and to "compel respect for the constitutional guaranty in the only effectively available way . . . by removing the incentive to disregard it." The Court noted that the exclusionary "rule is calculated to prevent [future violations], not to repair [past violations]" (*Elkins v. United States*, 304 U.S. 206, 217 [1940]).

Judicial integrity. Judges are charged with interpreting and protecting the Constitution of the United States, and confidence in the rule of law is promoted by the fair and equal enforcement of the law. Courts, for this reason, must not be seen to be turning a blind eye to lawbreaking by government officials. This is what is referred to as the imperative of judicial integrity. Supreme Court Justice Louis Brandeis, dissenting in *Olmstead v. United States*, observed in an often-cited statement that

> the future of the government will be imperiled if it fails to observe the law scrupulously. Our Government is the potent, the omnipresent teacher. For good or for ill, it teaches the whole people by its example. Crime is contagious. If the Government becomes a lawbreaker, it breeds contempt for law; it invites every man to become

a law unto himself; it invites anarchy. To declare that in the administration of the criminal law the end justifies the means—to declare that the Government may commit crimes in order to secure the conviction of a private criminal—would bring terrible retribution. Against that pernicious doctrine this Court should resolutely set its face. (*Olmstead v. United States,* 277 U.S. 438, 468 [1928])

Social cost. The cost of excluding evidence has led police departments to stress the importance of *police professionalism* and to introduce training programs to ensure that law enforcement personnel follow Fourth Amendment procedures. The result is that a relatively small proportion of cases lead to the acquittal of defendants based on the exclusion of evidence. In those instances in which evidence is excluded and individuals are released, it is contended that it is better for society to bear this cost of governmental wrongdoing than to impose the cost on a defendant whose rights have been violated.

There are some equally strong arguments against the exclusionary rule. Examine the arguments presented in the next section and formulate your own opinion.

Arguments Against the Exclusionary Rule

There are a number of criticisms of the exclusionary rule. These criticisms taken together make the point that the exclusionary rule imposes a high cost on society in terms of the "loss" of evidence in criminal trials and thereby reduces rather than enhances respect for the criminal justice system.

Constitution. The Supreme Court has held that the exclusionary rule is a "judicially created remedy" that is intended to deter the police from engaging in unreasonable searches rather than a constitutionally required remedy that is "part and parcel" of the Fourth Amendment. This means that judges are free to limit or even abolish the exclusionary rule.

Deterrence. Former Chief Justice Warren Burger dismissed the notion that the exclusionary rule deters the police from violating Fourth Amendment rights as a "wistful dream." The police are concerned with gathering evidence and with making arrests and do not stop to analyze whether a search satisfies the ever-changing and complicated standards for searches and seizures established by the Supreme Court. The immediate impact of an unreasonable search is felt by the prosecutor who loses evidence rather than by the police officer. It may take several years and the exhaustion of appeals for the legality of a search to be finally decided (*Bivens v. Six Unknown Named Agents,* 403 U.S. 388 [1971]).

Judicial integrity. The exclusionary rule decreases respect for the judiciary by requiring courts to take the side of defendants rather than victims.

Truth seeking. The exclusionary rule undermines the purpose of a criminal trial, which is the determination of an individual's guilt or innocence based on available and reliable evidence.

Penalizing victims. The protection of criminal defendants undermines rather than promotes respect for the criminal justice system. This was articulated by the U.S. Supreme Court in *Irvine v. California.* The Court noted that "rejection of the evidence does nothing to punish the wrong-doing official, while it may, and likely will, release the wrong-doing defendant. It protects [the suspect] against whom incriminating evidence is discovered, but does nothing to protect innocent persons who are the victims of illegal but fruitless searches" (*Irvine v. California,* 347 U.S. 128, 136 [1954]).

Lack of flexibility. The exclusionary rule excludes evidence regardless of whether the police committed a technical violation of the law or engaged in a blatant and intentional violation of the Fourth Amendment. In both cases, the identical remedy is imposed: the exclusion of the evidence. As Chief Justice Burger observed, this equates the freeing of a tiger and a mouse in a schoolroom as equally serious offenses (*Bivens v. Six Unknown Named Agents,* 403 U.S. 388, 419 [1971]).

Limited application. The exclusionary rule has no impact on the police in those instances in which the police seize a gun or drugs in order to remove the contraband from the streets and have no intention of pursuing a criminal prosecution. In this instance, there is "no evidence to exclude" and "no penalty paid by the police." The reasonableness of the search and seizure also often does not come to the attention of the courts when a defendant plea bargains and enters a guilty plea in exchange for a lesser sentence or another consideration.

Alternative Remedies to the Exclusionary Rule

Critics of the exclusionary rule argue that deterrence may be more effectively achieved through various alternative procedures that do not require the exclusion of evidence from trial. Do you believe that any or all of the procedural mechanisms listed below will be more effective than the exclusionary rule in deterring unlawful Fourth Amendment searches?

Civil tort suits for damages against police officers who have engaged in unreasonable searches and seizures and the government: Civil actions against the police and state governments must overcome a number of difficult barriers to be successful. There also must be adequate monetary compensation provided to successful litigants to serve as an incentive for individuals to take the time and expense to file suit.

Criminal prosecution of the police for violation of civil liberties: Prosecutors may be reluctant to bring charges against police officers, particularly for relatively minor violations of the law.

Police administrative procedures subjecting officers to penalties that include demotions, fines, suspensions, and termination of employment: Police administrators may be hesitant to discipline officers and risk damaging morale, particularly when the evidence led to the arrest of dangerous criminals.

A civilian review board that examines cases of suspected abuse, which are referred to the board by defense lawyers and trial court judges: The panel would be composed of citizens, lawyers, judges, and police officials and would be authorized to impose penalties ranging from fines to termination from the police force. The police historically have been strongly opposed to outside review boards and complain that members of the board may not fully understand the demands and pressures of policing.

A judicial hearing conducted prior to the prosecution of the criminal charge: In the event that the judge concludes that a police officer carried out an unlawful search, the judge would be authorized to impose an appropriate penalty ranging from a fine or suspension to termination from the police force. A related proposal is to hold the hearing following the trial before the same judge and jury who heard the case. The judge would instruct the jury on the law, and they would decide whether the officer conducted an unlawful search. The judge then would impose an appropriate punishment. This approach saves the time and expense of gathering the facts. Critics point out that judges and juries will be influenced in their decision-making by whether the trial ended in a conviction.

As we shall see later in the chapter, the Supreme Court has responded to criticisms of the exclusionary rule by creating various exceptions. The next section of the text discusses the process that a defense lawyer follows when seeking to suppress evidence under the exclusionary rule.

■ INVOKING THE EXCLUSIONARY RULE

The first step in challenging the reasonableness of a search is filing a pretrial motion to suppress. Most states and the federal courts place the burden of proof on the defendant when the search or seizure is based on a warrant. The burden of proof is reversed and is placed on the government when the police act without a warrant. Why? A warrant has been issued by a judge based on evidence presented by the government that meets the probable cause standard. The presumption is that the evidence on which the warrant is based satisfies the probable cause standard, and the defendant is assigned the heavy burden of demonstrating that the warrant is deficient. The defendant must demonstrate a lack of probable cause by clear and convincing evidence. In the case of a warrantless search, the police are aware of the evidence that constitutes probable cause and are in the best position to demonstrate the legality of the search. The government also bears the burden of proving that a search was justified as an exception to the warrant requirement.

A decision by the trial judge to admit the evidence results in the evidence being introduced at trial. Following a conviction, the defense may appeal and raise the issue of whether the judge made the correct decision in admitting the evidence. In contrast, the prosecution in most states is required to act immediately if it wishes to appeal a decision not to admit evidence. Why? Because the defendant may be acquitted at trial. At this point, the prosecution is prevented from subjecting the defendant to the double jeopardy of an additional trial. The lengthy appeal process, of course, may persuade the prosecutor to take his or her chances at trial without the evidence.

A decision by a judge to admit evidence that was challenged by a defendant on a timely motion to suppress constitutes error when the judge's decision is held by an appellate court to have been based on an incorrect analysis of the law. This requires a reversal of the guilty verdict unless the judge's admission of the evidence is considered to be *harmless error*. The prosecution will want to preserve the guilty verdict and will argue on appeal that the trial judge's decision is correct and, in any event, constitutes harmless error. This requires that the prosecution establish beyond a reasonable doubt that there is no reasonable probability that the evidence influenced the outcome of the trial (*Chapman v. California*, 386 U.S. 18 [1967]).

A defendant who has exhausted his or her state court appeals and finds that the appellate courts have affirmed the ruling of the trial court judge can look to an additional avenue of relief by filing a writ of *habeas corpus* with a federal district court or by pursuing a similar remedy in the state court. *Habeas corpus* is a request to the court to require the government to bring an individual who is in custody before the court to determine the legality of his or her detention. Access to the federal courts requires an allegation that an individual's detention resulted from a violation of his or her constitutional rights before trial or during trial. A defendant in custody also may rely on federal *habeas corpus* in those instances in which new information comes to light that indicates that the conviction was based on a constitutional violation.

An application for *habeas corpus* is a noncriminal (civil) lawsuit in which the defendant (now called the petitioner or plaintiff) asks the court for a writ on the grounds that he or she is being unlawfully detained. The writ of *habeas corpus* (literally "you have the body") is an order issued by a judge to a government official (usually the warden of a correctional institution) who has the person in custody to bring the person to court and to explain why the individual is in detention. In the event that the court finds that the plaintiff was unlawfully convicted or is being held without justification, the judge will order the individual released from custody.

Standing

A defendant is required to have **standing** to challenge the introduction of evidence at trial. In other words, a defendant may be surprised to learn that he or she may not be eligible to contest the legality of a search. In 1969, in *Alderman v. United States*, the U.S. Supreme Court held that Willie Alderman did not have standing to suppress evidence obtained through an illegal wiretap of a co-defendant's telephone conversation. The Supreme Court explained that the extension of standing to individuals whose personal rights have not been violated would significantly increase the costs of the exclusionary rule (*Alderman v. United States*, 394 U.S. 165, 175 [1969]). The legal test to be applied for standing in the case of an alleged violation of the Fourth Amendment prohibition on unreasonable searches and seizures is whether the defendant has both a subjectively and an objectively reasonable expectation of privacy in the area that is subject to the search. The burden of proof typically is placed on the defendant. Below are some other examples of instances in which petitioners have lacked standing to suppress evidence.

Automobile passengers. A police officer stopped an automobile that he believed was fleeing the scene of a robbery. A search uncovered a box of rifle shells and a sawed-off shotgun under the front seat. The two petitioners were passengers, neither of whom owned the automobile. The Supreme Court ruled that the petitioners lacked an expectation of privacy in the glove compartment and under the seat and held that they lacked standing to suppress the evidence (*Rakas v. Illinois*, 439 U.S. 128 [1978]).

Overnight guests. The police entered a home without a warrant or consent looking for Robert Olson, an overnight guest, who was wanted for suspected involvement in a murder-robbery. Olson was found hiding in a closet. The Supreme Court held that an overnight guest such as Olson possessed a reasonable expectation of privacy in the home. The Court held that "to hold that an overnight guest has a legitimate expectation of privacy . . . merely recognizes the everyday expectations of privacy that we all share" (*Minnesota v. Olson*, 495 U.S. 91, 98 [1990]).

Possessory interest in items that are seized. The police directed Vanessa Cox to empty the contents of her purse. David Rawlings admitted that he owned a jar that was found in the purse containing 1,800 capsules of LSD. The Supreme

Court held that Rawlings's possession of the drugs did not provide standing to challenge the search and seizure and that he was required to possess an expectation of privacy in the "area of the search," that is, the purse. Rawlings had met Cox only a few days before the search and had never before placed any items in Cox's purse. The Supreme Court also found it significant that Rawlings had no right to exclude other individuals from access to the purse, and in fact other individuals had freely rummaged through the purse (*Rawlings v. Kentucky*, 448 U.S. 98 [1980]).

Commercial transactions. Wayne Thomas Carter and Melvin Johns traveled from Chicago to the Twin Cities to meet with Kimberly Thompson at her apartment. They had never before been in Thompson's apartment. The three of them spent two and a half hours bagging cocaine. A search of the apartment uncovered cocaine residue and plastic Baggies. The Supreme Court overturned the Minnesota Supreme Court's recognition of Carter and Johns's standing to seek to suppress the evidence seized in Thompson's apartment. The Court based its decision on the commercial nature of the relationship, the brief period of time the two had spent on the premises, and the lack of a previous connection between Carter, Johns, and Thompson (*Minnesota v. Carter*, 525 U.S. 83 [1998]).

The target of a police investigation. In *United States v. Payner*, the U.S. Supreme Court held that Jack Payner lacked standing to challenge the introduction of documents against him at trial that had been stolen by a private investigator from the briefcase of another individual as part of an Internal Revenue Service investigation of Payner (*United States v. Payner*, 447 U.S. 727 [1980]).

The standing doctrine is a method of limiting the "cost" of the exclusionary rule by restricting the number of individuals who are eligible to challenge the introduction of the evidence. The Supreme Court also has limited the cost of the exclusionary rule by creating a number of exceptions to its application.

CRIMINAL EVIDENCE AND PUBLIC POLICY

We have seen that the Supreme Court held in *Mapp v. Ohio* that the exclusionary rule is required under the Fourth Amendment to enforce the prohibition on unreasonable searches and seizures and to protect judicial integrity. A majority of the Supreme Court almost immediately retreated from this view and in a series of cases held that the exclusionary rule is a "judge-made" remedy that is not required by the Fourth Amendment. The Supreme Court has created a number of exceptions to the exclusionary rule. In most of these instances, the Court has determined that the application of the exclusionary rule is likely to have little deterrent impact and that the benefits of this modest amount of deterrence are outweighed by the costs of lost evidence and the possibility that a guilty defendant will walk out the courtroom door without a criminal conviction.

The Supreme Court no longer justifies the exclusionary rule on the grounds that the use of unlawfully seized evidence at trial undermines judicial integrity. After all, while it is true that the introduction of illegally seized evidence places judges in the position of endorsing a violation of the Constitution, there is the equally important concern that judges are assisting guilty defendants when they exclude reliable evidence from trial. Former Chief Justice Warren Burger, for instance, questioned whether the Supreme Court should continue to apply the exclusionary remedy when the result is "the release of countless guilty criminals" (*Bivens v. Six Unknown Named Agents*, 403 U.S. 383, 416 [1971]).

A number of social scientists have joined the debate over the exclusionary rule and have examined whether the exclusionary rule deters unconstitutional searches and seizures. Researchers concede that it is virtually impossible to answer the question of whether fewer illegal searches are carried out as a result of the exclusionary rule and have concluded that the data neither support nor refute the deterrent value of the exclusionary rule. Supreme Court Justice Harry Blackmun, after providing a detailed review of social science research in his opinion in *United States v. Janis*, concludes that "no empirical researcher, proponent or opponent of the [exclusionary] rule has yet been able to establish with any assurance whether the rule has a deterrent effect." The result according to Justice Blackmun is to call into question the argument that the exclusionary rule protects our Fourth Amendment rights (*United States v. Janis*, 428 U.S. 433, 450, n.22 [1976]).

We can only conclude that the benefits of the exclusionary rule in terms of deterring Fourth Amendment violations are uncertain. What of the costs? Does the exclusionary rule result in the exclusion of evidence that is required to convict defendants? Should we consider a less costly alternative? Thomas Davies (1983), in an important essay, reviews a number of studies and concludes that the "nonprosecution and/or nonconviction" of cases by the police, prosecutors, and judges based on the illegal seizure of evidence is "in the range of 0.6% to 2.35%" of all felony arrests. Davies concludes that while these "loss rates" are not "trivial," they do not amount to a "major impact" on the criminal justice system, "particularly in light of the fact that some of these charges likely would have been dropped or downgraded to misdemeanors or would not have resulted in prison sentences." In Davies's study of the California justice system, he finds that the highest percentage of cases lost due to the exclusionary rule involve drug charges (7.1 percent). In other areas, the exclusionary rule had almost no impact whatsoever.

Davies's findings are reinforced by Peter Nardulli (1983). Nardulli conducted a three-county study of 7,500 cases in three states. Motions to suppress physical evidence were filed in roughly 5 percent of cases, most of which involved narcotics or weapons violations. These motions were successful in only 0.56 percent of all cases, meaning that forty cases (0.56 percent) were lost as a result of the exclusionary rule. Nardulli observes that only eight of the forty cases involved crimes of violence and that some of the cases may not have resulted in convictions at trial in any event. The highest percentage of "lost cases" were for narcotics offenses. Nine of the forty defendants would have received less than one month in jail; fifteen would have received less than two months. Only one defendant could have expected a sentence of more than one year. Nardulli concedes that his study may not be representative of every jurisdiction, but that based on his data, the exclusionary rule has a "truly marginal effect on the criminal court system."

These data suggest that despite the heated debate and lengthy academic commentaries on the exclusionary rule, we are unable to draw a firm conclusion regarding the impact of the rule on the police. We also have seen that lawyers file motions to suppress physical evidence in a relatively small number of cases. In addition, few "criminals" escape punishment as a result of these motions to suppress physical evidence. This may indicate that the police may be adhering to legal standards or that defense lawyers simply do not believe that motions to suppress physical evidence will be successful in most instances. Critics may justifiably argue that even one "lost" case is too high a price to pay for the exclusionary rule. On the other hand, defenders of the exclusionary rule may credibly contend that the rule highlights the importance of police respect for the prohibition on unreasonable searches and seizures and that the rule serves to reinforce the commitment of the judicial branch to civil liberties.

■ EXCEPTIONS TO THE EXCLUSIONARY RULE

We have seen that in *Mapp v. Ohio* the Supreme Court held that the exclusionary rule was a constitutional rule that was intended to deter the police and to protect the integrity of the courts. The U.S. Supreme Court, in 1974, in *United States v. Calandra*, modified this holding and held that the exclusionary rule is a judge-made remedy that is designed to deter unreasonable searches and seizures.

Calandra was followed by a number of cases in which the Supreme Court recognized exceptions to the exclusionary rule. These exceptions are based on a determination in each instance that the modest amount of additional deterrence to be gained from excluding the evidence from trial is outweighed by the cost to society of excluding the evidence from trial. As you read this section, pay particular attention to the Supreme Court's employment of this balancing test. Is the court's analysis based on hard facts or on speculation? Should the Supreme Court have recognized these exceptions to the exclusionary rule? The next section of this chapter discusses the following exceptions:

- Collateral proceedings
- Attenuation
- Good faith exception
- Independent source
- Inevitable discovery rule
- Impeachment

Collateral Proceedings

The **collateral proceedings** exception permits the use of unlawfully seized evidence in proceedings that are not part of the formal trial (literally "off to the side" or "loosely related" to the trial). This includes bail hearings, preliminary hearings, grand jury proceedings, sentencing hearings, and *habeas corpus* review. What is the explanation for this exception? In most of these collateral proceedings, there is an interest in a full presentation of the facts. The application of the exclusionary rule would deny judges evidence that might prove useful in determining whether to charge a defendant with a criminal offense, in setting bail, or in sentencing a defendant. Balancing citizen protection against this is the fact that the Supreme Court has concluded that excluding the fruits of an unlawful search from these proceedings would have little additional impact in deterring police violations of the Fourth Amendment. The police already are deterred by the prospect that unlawfully seized evidence will not be available to establish a defendant's criminal guilt at trial, and little additional deterrence will be achieved by excluding the evidence from collateral proceedings.

The Supreme Court also has ruled that evidence seized in an unreasonable search is admissible in *various noncriminal proceedings*. This includes parole revocation hearings, immigration hearings, and tax and other administrative proceedings. Unlawfully seized evidence also is admissible in forfeiture hearings, which are quasi-criminal proceedings in which the Court determines whether property is connected to certain specified crimes and therefore should be forfeited to the government. In each of these instances, the Supreme Court weighed the additional deterrence that would result from the exclusion of evidence against the costs of excluding the evidence and held that the price paid by society in excluding the evidence far outweighs the modest benefits in terms of deterrence.

Attenuation

In the typical case, there is a direct causal connection between an unreasonable search and the seizure of evidence. The evidence is the product of an unlawful search and therefore is excluded from evidence. In other instances, however, the connection between the search and the seizure of the evidence is **attenuated** (weak), and the U.S. Supreme Court has held that the exclusionary rule does not apply. A weak connection between the unlawful search and the seizure of evidence also is referred to as *dissipating the taint* or as **purging the taint** of the illegality. As early as 1939, in *Nardone v. United States*, the Supreme Court recognized that evidence seized as a result of an illegal search may be admissible where the "connection [has] . . . become so attenuated as to dissipate the taint" (*Nardone v. United States*, 308 U.S. 338, 341 [1939]).

An example of attenuation is *United States v. Boone*. In *Boone*, Officer Phil Barney executed an unlawful search of a vehicle driven by defendant Judy Melinda Boone. The search led to the discovery of illegal narcotics, and as Barney stepped away from the car, defendants Boone and Gerard Anthony Greenfield sped away at an excessive speed. Barney followed in hot pursuit, and the defendants, facing imminent apprehension, threw narcotics out the window. The discarded narcotics were subsequently seized by the police. Should the drugs be excluded as the product of Officer Barney's unreasonable search and seizure? The Tenth Circuit Court of Appeals ruled that the suspects' tossing the drugs out the window was a voluntary act that broke the connection between the unlawful search and the discovery of the narcotics. As a result, the Tenth Circuit held that the drugs were admissible in evidence. The court observed that

> Officer Barney's initial illegal search did not cause the defendants to flee at a high rate of speed or to throw [the drugs] onto the highway. It would be nonsensical to hold that officer Barney had no right to collect the evidence of drug possession that defendants voluntarily discarded onto the highway. (*United States v. Boone*, 62 F.3d 323, 326 [10th Cir. 1995])

In *Brown v. Illinois*, the Supreme Court articulated three circumstances that determine whether there is an *attenuation of the taint* of an unlawful search (*Brown v. Illinois*, 422 U.S. 590, 603 [1975]). As you can see from these three factors, shown below, attenuation will be found when there is a significant passage of time between the initial illegality and the discovery of the evidence or where a number of factors intervene as well as in those instances in which the police mistakenly or unintentionally misinterpret the law.

In *Kaupp v. Texas*, the police without probable cause entered Robert Kaupp's bedroom at 3 a.m., handcuffed him, and took him to police headquarters. The police on the way to the police station drove Kaupp to the location where they discovered the victim's body. At the police station, Kaupp was interrogated and confronted with the confession of his co-confederate, and confessed. The Court in excluding Kaupp's confession from evidence held that "there is no indication . . . that any substantial time passed between Kaupp's removal from his home in handcuffs and his confession after only 10 or 15 minutes of interrogation. In the interim, he remained in his partially clothed state in the physical custody of a number of officers, some of whom, at least, were conscious that they lacked probable cause to arrest" (*Kaupp v. Texas*, 538 U.S. 628 [2003]).

Temporal proximity. A lengthy period of time attenuates the taint. In *United States v. Ceccolini*, the police illegally seized evidence that led them to a witness who testified for the prosecution at trial. The Supreme Court ruled that the four-month period between the initial illegality and the interrogation of the witness attenuated the taint and that the testimony was properly admitted at trial (*United States v. Ceccolini*, 435 U.S. 268 [1978]).

Intervening circumstances. Intervening events that weaken the connection between the unlawful search and the evidence that is seized may attenuate the initial taint. Independent and voluntary acts of individuals, for instance, may break the chain of causation. This is illustrated in *Boone* by the intervening events of the suspects' fleeing from the scene of the initial search and by their throwing the drugs out the window. In contrast, reading the *Miranda* warnings to a suspect and brief visits by friends and family have not been found to break the chain of causation of an illegal arrest.

Intentional violation. Judges resist finding attenuation where the police intentionally violate the law. A finding of attenuation would reward a conscious disregard of legal standards. In *Brown*, the police broke into the defendant's apartment, illegally arrested him at gunpoint without probable cause, and obtained a confession after reading him his *Miranda* rights. The Supreme Court stressed that the

> illegality here had a quality of purposefulness. The impropriety of the arrest was obvious. The manner in which Brown's arrest was effected gives the appearance of having been calculated to cause surprise, fright, and confusion. The deterrent purpose of the exclusionary rule would be well-served by excluding the subsequent confessions. (*Brown v. Illinois*, 322 U.S. 590, 592–595, 603–604 [1975])

Constitutional interest. In *Hudson v. Michigan*, the U.S. Supreme Court articulated a *constitutional interest* test for attenuation. The Court stated that evidence is admissible at trial when the police fail to follow a constitutional requirement under the Fourth Amendment that serves to alert an individual to the presence of the police and to protect an individual's privacy in the home rather than to protect an individual against unreasonable searches and seizures.

The Supreme Court in *Hudson* held that the requirement that the police knock and announce their presence and wait a reasonable period of time before executing a search warrant is intended to protect individuals against unannounced violations of the privacy of the home rather than to protect individuals against unreasonable searches and seizures. As a result, evidence seized following a failure to knock and announce should not be excluded from evidence. The Court stated that "even given a direct causal connection, the interest protected by the constitutional guarantee that has been violated would not be served by suppression of the evidence obtained" (*Hudson v. Michigan*, 547 U.S. 586 [2006]).

There is one last point to keep in mind: Courts are less inclined to find that a taint is attenuated in regard to a witness's testimony than in the case of physical evidence. Why? The cost of excluding a witness's testimony significantly harms the prosecution's case, and many witnesses undoubtedly would have voluntarily come forward and testified on behalf of the government after learning of the prosecution.

We now review the important and complicated 1963 case of *Wong Sun v. United States*. The U.S. Supreme Court in *Wong Sun* articulated the rule that has guided judicial decisions on attenuation: "whether, granting establishment of the primary illegality, the evidence by which instant objection is made has been come at by exploitation of that illegality or instead by means sufficiently distinguishable to be purged of the primary taint." This test asks whether the evidence was the direct result of an unlawful search and should be excluded from evidence or was so far removed from the unlawful search that it should be admitted into evidence (*Wong Sun v. United States*, 371 U.S. 471, 486 [1963]).

In the case at issue in *Wong Sun*, federal narcotic agents illegally arrested James Toy in the bedroom in the rear of his laundry. Toy, in turn, implicated Johnny Yee as a drug dealer; Yee was arrested, and several tubes of heroin were seized in his home. Yee, in turn, stated that he had obtained the drugs from Toy and "Sea Dog" Wong Sun. Wong Sun subsequently was arrested in the back room of his apartment by six officers. Yee, Toy, and Wong Sun all were charged with narcotics offenses, and Wong Sun was released on his own recognizance. Wong Sun later voluntarily returned, was interrogated, and provided statements to federal narcotics agents. The Supreme Court was asked to disentangle this knotty case and to rule on whether the narcotics and Wong Sun's confession were the fruits of the poisonous tree of what the defense alleged was Toy's illegal arrest.

Toy's statement. The Supreme Court ruled that the police lacked probable cause to enter Toy's laundry and to arrest him. The government argued that Toy's statement implicating Yee was an "act of free will" that purged the taint of the unlawful invasion. The Supreme Court, however, rejected the government's argument. Six or seven officers had broken down the door and followed Toy into the bedroom. He was immediately handcuffed and arrested. The Court held that "it is unreasonable to infer that Toy's response was sufficiently an act of free will to purge the primary taint of the unlawful invasion."

Seizure of narcotics from Yee. Was there a direct relationship between Toy's statement and the seizure of the narcotics from Yee? The Supreme Court held that the police would not have seized the narcotics absent Toy's statement and that the drugs had been detected through the "exploitation of that illegality" (i.e., the illegal arrest of Toy) and accordingly should be excluded from evidence.

Wong Sun's statement. Wong Sun's unsigned confession was not considered to be the fruit of the poisonous tree and was properly admitted into evidence at trial. Wong Sun was released on his own recognizance after his arraignment and returned voluntarily several days later to make the statement. The Supreme Court held that the connection between the arrest and the statement was "so attenuated as to dissipate the taint."

Miranda and Attenuation

Defendant Samuel Francis Patane was arrested outside his home and handcuffed. A federal agent had been informed that the defendant, a convicted felon, possessed a Glock pistol. The agent began giving the *Miranda* warning and was interrupted by the defendant who stated that he knew the rights. The defendant then informed the officer that "the Glock is in my bedroom on a shelf. The agent seized the pistol and the defendant was indicted and convicted for being a felon in possession of firearm in violation of federal law."

The government acknowledged on appeal that Patane had not been fully and effectively informed of his *Miranda* rights, and the Tenth Circuit Court of Appeals held that the pistol and the defendant's statement were both inadmissible into evidence. Justice Clarence Thomas, writing for the Court majority, held that a failure to provide the *Miranda* warnings does not violate a suspect's constitutional rights. Violations occur only "upon the admission of unwarned statements into evidence at trial." Justice Thomas further ruled that the introduction into evidence of the "nontestimonial fruit" of a voluntary statement, such as Patane's Glock, does not violate the Self-Incrimination Clause. The Self-Incrimination Clause prohibits compelling a defendant to be a "witness against himself." The term *witness*, according to Justice Thomas, restricts the right against self-incrimination to testimonial evidence. Nontestimonial evidence, such as a gun, is unable to "bear witness" against an accused.

Justice David Souter, with whom Justices John Paul Stevens and Ruth Bader Ginsburg joined in dissent, proclaimed that "in closing their eyes to the consequences of giving an evidentiary advantage to those who ignore *Miranda,* the majority adds an important inducement for interrogators to ignore the rule in that case." The dissenting judges argued that a failure to provide the *Miranda* warning raises a presumption that a confession is involuntary, and the confession as well as the fruits of the seizure of the evidence should be excluded from evidence. The dissenters concluded that the decision in *Patane* must be viewed as an "unjustifiable invitation to law enforcement to flaunt *Miranda* when there may be physical evidence to be gained" (*United States v. Patane*, 542 U.S. 630 [2004]).

How does *Patane* illustrate the attenuation doctrine? Do you agree with the decision? See *United States v. Patane* (542 U.S. 630 [2004]).

Good Faith Exception

In 1976, Supreme Court Justice Byron White, in dissenting in *Stone v. Powell*, argued that the exclusionary rule should not be applied where evidence is unlawfully seized by an officer acting in the "good faith belief" that his or her conduct complies with the Fourth Amendment and the officer has reasonable grounds for his or her belief. Justice White explained that a police officer who believes that he or she is acting lawfully will not be deterred by the prospect that unlawfully seized evidence will be excluded from evidence at trial. He concluded the only thing that is accomplished by withholding the evidence from the jury is interference with the "truth-finding function" of the trial. Briefly stated, the exclusionary rule under these circumstances provides little benefit while exacting a significant cost

(*Stone v. Powell*, 428 U.S. 465, 540 [1976]). In 1984, in *United States v. Leon*, the Supreme Court recognized the **good faith exception** to the exclusionary rule. In the last three decades, the Court has relied on the good faith exception to uphold the constitutionality of searches in five circumstances. In each of these cases, the police were found to have acted with an honest and objectively reasonable belief in the legality of the search.

- *Reliance on a warrant.* The police reasonably, but incorrectly, believed that the search warrant issued by the judge was based on probable cause (*United States v. Leon*).
- *Reliance on assurance by a judge that a warrant meets Fourth Amendment standards.* The police reasonably, but incorrectly, relied on the assurance of a judge that a warrant met the requirements of the Fourth Amendment (*Massachusetts v. Sheppard*).
- *Reliance on legislation.* The police reasonably relied on a statute that later was declared unconstitutional (*Illinois v. Krull*).
- *Reliance on data entered into a computer by a court employee.* A police officer reasonably relied on computer information that was incorrectly entered by a court employee (*Arizona v. Evans*).
- *Reliance on apparent authority of a third party to consent.* The police reasonably, but incorrectly, believed that an individual possessed the authority to consent to an entry of his or her home (*Illinois v. Rodriguez*).

Reliance on a warrant. In 1984, in *United States v. Leon* (468 U.S. 897), Justice White along with five other members of the Supreme Court recognized the good faith exception to the exclusionary rule. In the incident at issue in *Leon*, an informant alerted the police that he had witnessed a drug sale at a home in Burbank, California, five months previously. He reported that the suspects stored cash and narcotics in homes in Burbank. The police subsequently placed the residences and suspects under surveillance, and their observations appeared to corroborate the informant's information. They secured a warrant from a judge, searched the residences, seized drugs and a large amount of cash, and charged the defendants with conspiracy to possess and distribute cocaine as well as a variety of other criminal counts. A federal district court held a hearing and suppressed use of the narcotics as evidence. The judge ruled that the affidavit supporting the warrant failed to establish the informant's reliability and credibility and did not constitute probable cause.

The U.S. Supreme Court nevertheless held that the police had acted in objectively reasonable good faith reliance on the warrant and that application of the "extreme sanction of exclusion is inappropriate." The Court explained that "the marginal or nonexistent benefits produced by suppressing evidence obtained in objectively reasonable reliance on a subsequently invalidated search warrant cannot justify the substantial costs of exclusion."

What is the test for a good faith belief in the lawfulness of a search? In determining whether an officer acted in good faith, the Supreme Court instructed that courts should ask whether "a reasonably well trained officer would have known that the search was illegal" despite the warrant issued by a judge. The Court found that the police in *Leon* carried out a thorough and responsible investigation and obtained a warrant in good faith and, in the view of the Supreme Court, reasonably believed that their search of the homes was based on a warrant founded on probable cause.

Officers would not be acting in good faith, and suppression would be appropriate, in those instances in which

- the police clearly are aware or should be aware that the warrant lacks probable cause. This would arise in situations in which the police knew or should have known that the information in the affidavit was false or that the information did not meet the probable cause standard.
- the warrant is "fatally flawed." For instance, the warrant may not be specific in terms of the place to be searched or the items to be searched for.
- the judge issuing the warrant is not "neutral and detached" and acts as a "rubber stamp for the police" or as "an arm of the prosecution."

Reliance on assurance by a judge that a warrant meets Fourth Amendment standards. In the companion case of *Massachusetts v. Sheppard*, the Supreme Court affirmed that the exclusionary rule should not be applied in those cases in which the police act in good faith reliance on the assurance of a judge that a warrant, which later is determined by an appellate court to be defective, constitutes sufficient authority to carry out a search (*Massachusetts v. Sheppard*, 468 U.S. 981 [1984]).

The officers sought an arrest warrant for the search and seizure of items in Osborne Sheppard's residence linking him to a homicide. Detective Peter O'Malley was able to locate only a warrant form authorizing the seizure of a "controlled substance." The judge told the police that he would make the necessary changes to ensure that the warrant authorized a search for evidence of a murder. However, the judge did not modify that portion of the warrant that authorized a search for controlled substances and failed to incorporate the police officer's affidavit listing the items that the police were seeking in the home. As a result, the warrant authorized the police to seize unspecified controlled substances and did not authorize the seizure of various items that linked Sheppard to the homicide. As a result, the homicide evidence was suppressed by the trial court judge. The Supreme Court held that although the warrant clearly authorized a search for narcotics, a police officer should not be expected to "disbelieve a judge who has just advised him . . . that the warrant he possesses authorized him to conduct the search he requested."

Justices William Brennan and John Marshall objected in their dissent that the exclusionary rule was part of the protections included in the Fourth Amendment, and they called for a restoration of the principle recognized in *Weeks* that an individual whose privacy has been invaded in violation of the Fourth Amendment has a constitutional right to prevent the government from making use of any evidence obtained through illegal police conduct.

Reliance on legislation. The Supreme Court nevertheless continued to expand the application of the good faith exception. In 1987, in *Illinois v. Krull*, the Court held that evidence seized in objectively reasonable reliance on a statute later held to be unconstitutional was admissible at trial. The Court stated that "unless a statute is clearly unconstitutional, an officer cannot be expected to question the judgment of the legislature that passed the law" (*Illinois v. Krull*, 480 U.S. 340, 349–350 [1987]). The Court asked whether excluding the evidence from trial would deter the legislature from passing unconstitutional statutes in the future. The Supreme Court reasoned that legislatures are motivated by public opinion and politics and are relatively unconcerned about the fate of a statute in the courts. As a result, legislators are unlikely to be deterred from passing unconstitutional laws in the future by the court's exclusion of the evidence from trial. Balanced against this was the significant cost of excluding evidence that had been seized in good faith by the police.

Reliance on data entered into a computer by a court employee. In 1995, in *Arizona v. Evans*, the U.S. Supreme Court was asked to apply the good faith exception to an arrest executed by Phoenix police officer Bryan Sargent. Officer Sargent reasonably relied on information that he downloaded from the computer terminal in his squad car. The computer erroneously indicated that Isaac Evans, whom Officer Sargent had pulled over for driving the wrong way on a one-way street, was the subject of an outstanding misdemeanor arrest warrant. Evans was placed under arrest, and while he was being handcuffed, he dropped a marijuana cigarette. A search of Evans's automobile led to the seizure of a bag of marijuana that had been concealed under the front seat. It later was found that the arrest warrant had been quashed roughly seventeen days prior to his arrest. The Supreme Court noted that these types of errors occur on isolated occasions and that suppressing the evidence will not deter court clerks from making similar mistakes in the future (*Arizona v. Evans*, 514 U.S. 1 [1995]).

In *Herring v. United States* (555 U.S. 135 [2009]), the Supreme Court held that an officer acted in good faith when he reasonably believed that there was an outstanding arrest warrant, but that belief turned out to be wrong because of a negligent bookkeeping error by a police employee in another jurisdiction. The exclusionary rule in this situation did not prohibit the introduction into evidence of a gun and narcotics seized during a search incident to an arrest of the suspect.

Reliance on apparent authority of a third party to consent. In *Illinois v. Rodriguez* (this case appears in Chapter Fifteen under consent searches), Gail Fischer reported to the police that she had been the victim of domestic violence by Edward Rodriguez. She told the officers that he was at "our" apartment, where she had clothes and furniture. Fischer took the police over to the apartment. She let them in with her key, and they subsequently seized narcotics that they spotted in plain view and arrested Rodriguez. The contraband was suppressed on the grounds that Fischer lacked "common access and control for most purposes," which is the requirement for a third-party consent. Her name was not on the lease or mailbox, and she did not pay rent, only occasionally spent the night, and never entertained friends at the apartment. The Supreme Court reversed and held that the police "reasonably believed" that Fischer possessed authority to consent to a search of the apartment. See *Illinois v. Rodriguez* (497 U.S. 177 [1990]).

PHOTO 11.1

The police must conduct a vehicle search in accordance with the constitutional requirements established by Supreme Court decisions or risk the exclusion of the evidence that is seized.

Reliance on a precedent that is overturned. In *Davis v. United States* (564 U.S. ___ [2011]), the Supreme Court addressed whether the exclusionary rule applies to evidence that is seized by a police officer who conducts an "objectively reasonable" search based on a binding precedent that later is overruled. The police for almost thirty years in searching automobiles followed *New York v. Belton*, which held that as a contemporaneous incident of an arrest the police may search the passenger compartment of the automobile (*New York v. Belton*, 453 U.S. 454 [1981]). In 2009, in *Arizona v. Gant*, the Supreme Court modified *Belton* and held that a recent occupant's arrest is constitutional (1) if the arrestee is within reaching distance of the vehicle during the search or (2) if the police have reason to believe that the vehicle contains "evidence relevant to the crime of arrest" (*Arizona v. Gant*, 556 U.S. 332 [2009]).

In 2007, in *Davis*, police officers in Greenville, Alabama, conducted a routine traffic stop and arrested Stella Owens for driving while intoxicated and arrested the passenger, Willie Davis, for giving a false name to the police. The police handcuffed Owens and Davis and placed them in the back of separate patrol cars. The officers followed *Belton* and searched the passenger compartment of the vehicle and found a revolver inside the pocket of Davis's jacket.

Davis was indicted and convicted for possession of a firearm by a convicted felon. During Davis's appeal of his conviction, the Supreme Court decided *Gant*. Justice Samuel Alito, writing in a 7-2 decision, held that "[e]xcluding evidence in such cases does not deter police misconduct and imposes substantial social costs." The Court accordingly held "that when the police conduct a search in objectively reasonable reliance on binding appellate precedent, the exclusionary rule does not apply." Does *Davis* undermine the Fourth Amendment by recognizing that Davis's Fourth Amendment rights were violated while denying him a remedy under the exclusionary rule?

In summary, in each of the cases in which the Supreme Court recognized the good faith exception, the police reasonably believed that they were complying with the law. In both *Leon* and *Sheppard*, they acted in a diligent and responsible fashion based on warrants that later proved to be defective. In *Krull*, the police relied in good faith on a state statute that later was ruled to be unconstitutional, and the police officer in *Evans* acted on the basis of inaccurate computer information. The officers in *Davis* followed a binding precedent that was overturned by the Supreme Court while the case was on appeal.

11.1 YOU DECIDE

Baltimore police officers obtained and executed a warrant to search the person of Lawrence McWebb and the "premises known as 2036 Park Avenue third floor apartment." The police reasonably believed that there was only a single apartment on the third floor. This was based on information provided by a reliable informant, by visually examining the building, and by checking with the utility company. The third floor in fact was divided into two apartments, one occupied by McWebb and one occupied by Harold Garrison. Six Baltimore police officers executed the warrant; they encountered McWebb in the front of the building and used his key to enter the building. As they entered the vestibule on the third floor, they encountered Garrison. The doors to both apartments were open, and they could see into the interior of both McWebb's apartment to the left and Garrison's apartment to the right. It was only after entering Garrison's apartment and seizing heroin, cash, and drug paraphernalia that the police realized that the third floor contained two apartments and that they were searching the "wrong unit."

Was the search and seizure of Garrison's apartment lawful based on the police officers' reasonable belief that the third floor was one large unit? See *Maryland v. Garrison* (480 U.S. 79 [1987]).

You can learn what the court decided by referring to the study site, **http://study.sagepub.com/lippmance.**

Independent Source

We have seen that evidence that is directly obtained as a result of an unconstitutional search is excluded from evidence at trial. The **independent source doctrine** provides that evidence that is unlawfully seized nevertheless is admissible where the police are able to demonstrate that the evidence was *also* obtained through *independent* and *lawful* means. In *Silverthorne Lumber Company v. United States*, the U.S. Supreme Court held that facts obtained through a constitutional violation are not "inaccessible. If knowledge of them [also] is gained from an independent source they may be proved like any others, but the knowledge gained by the Government's own wrong cannot be used by it" (*Silverthorne Lumber Company v. United States*, 251 U.S. 385, 392 [1920]). Supreme Court Justice Antonin Scalia explained the independent source doctrine as follows: "Where an unlawful entry has given investigators knowledge of facts x and y [and z], but fact z [also] has been learned by other [lawful] means, fact z can be said to be admissible because [it is] derived from an 'independent source'" (*Murray v. United States*, 487 U.S. 533, 538 [1988]).

In 1984, in *Nix v. Williams*, the U.S. Supreme Court stated that

> the interest of society in deterring unlawful police conduct and the public interest in having juries receive all probative evidence of a crime are properly balanced by putting the police in the same, not a worse, position than they would have been had no police error or misconduct occurred. (*Nix v. Williams*, 467 U.S. 431, 444 [1984])

In other words, while the government is prohibited from using evidence obtained from the illegal search, this should not deprive the jury of hearing the same evidence so long as it can be demonstrated that the evidence also was obtained as a result of an independent and legal search.

The leading case on the independent source doctrine is *Murray v. United States*. In the case at issue in *Murray*, federal agents received information that a warehouse was being used for illegal drug activities. Law enforcement agents placed the warehouse under surveillance, developed probable cause, unlawfully entered the premises without a warrant, and observed bales of marijuana. The agents then left and applied for a warrant. The warrant application did not refer to the illegal entry or rely on information obtained during the illegal entry. The police then entered the warehouse with a warrant and seized the marijuana based on the information provided by the informant.

Justice Scalia observed that the agents' "lawful search appeared to be genuinely independent of the earlier tainted one." He remanded the case to clarify whether the two searches were truly independent and posed two questions to the lower court: whether the decision to seek a warrant was "prompted" by what they had seen during the initial entry, and whether information obtained during that entry was "presented to the Magistrate and affected his decision to issue the warrant." Can you explain why Justice Scalia wanted the appellate court judge to address these two questions?

Inevitable Discovery Rule

The **inevitable discovery rule** provides that evidence that is seized as the result of an unconstitutional search is admissible where the government can prove by the preponderance of the evidence that the evidence would have been inevitably discovered in the same condition in a lawful fashion. In *Nix v. Williams*, the Supreme Court explained that the independent source doctrine and the inevitable discovery rule both are based on the proposition that the police would have lawfully obtained the evidence had the police misconduct not taken place and that the government should not be punished by the exclusion of the evidence. In both instances, the government has not benefited by its wrongful behavior, and the defendant has not suffered any harm.

The inevitable discovery rule was first fully articulated by the Supreme Court in *Nix v. Williams*. In *Nix*, the defendant Robert Williams was interrogated by Officer Cletus Leaming in violation of Williams's Sixth Amendment right to counsel and subsequently led the police to the location of the body of his 10-year-old victim, Pamela Powers. The police called off their two-hundred-person search for Powers's body following Williams's promise to cooperate with the police. At the time, the Supreme Court observed that

> one search team was only two and one-half miles from where Williams soon guided Leaming and his party to the body. It is clear that the search parties were approaching the actual location of the body and we are satisfied that the volunteer search teams would have resumed the search had Williams not led the police to the body and the body inevitably would have been found [within an estimated three to five hours]. (*Nix v. Williams*, 467 U.S. 436, 448 [1984])

Justices Brennan and Marshall in dissent noted that the independent source doctrine was distinguished from the inevitable discovery rule by the fact that the evidence introduced at trial because of the independent source exception is in fact obtained by lawful means, while the evidence introduced at trial because of the inevitable discovery rule has not yet been discovered. The dissenters noted that the inevitable discovery exception "necessarily implicates a hypothetical finding that differs in kind from the factual finding that precedes application of the independent source rule." Justices Brennan and Marshall would require the government to satisfy a high standard of proof before admitting evidence under the inevitable discovery rule in order to "impress the fact finder with the importance of the decision and thereby reduce the risk that illegally obtained evidence will be admitted."

Michael Matthews - Police Images/Alamy

PHOTO 11.2

A frisk involves the pat-down of a suspect's outer clothing and is limited to the seizure of weapons and to immediately identifiable narcotics. An overly extensive search may result in the exclusion of any contraband that is seized from trial.

Courts have divided over whether a legal search must already have been under way at the time of the unlawful police behavior in order to establish that evidence inevitably would have been discovered. In *U.S. v. Pardue*, the First Circuit Court of Appeals determined that an officer had exceeded the scope of a *Terry* frisk, or a "pat down" of the outer clothing (see discussion of *Terry v. Ohio* in Chapter Thirteen), when he discovered two boxes of ammunition in Corey Pardue's backpack. The officer then arrested Pardue for misdemeanor domestic violence. The court held that the ammunition inevitably would have been discovered during a standard inventory search of the backpack at police headquarters. The question arises whether courts should extend inevitable discovery to searches that have not yet been initiated based on police testimony that such a search definitely would have been undertaken (*U.S. v. Pardue*, 385 F.3d 101 [1st Cir. 2004]).

11.2 YOU DECIDE

Police officers John Collins and Phillip Ratliff went to Lee Erwin Johnson's apartment in Detroit, Michigan, in response to a report that a young girl was being held against her will at Johnson's apartment. Angela Skinner, 14, answered the door and told the officers that Johnson was detaining her against her will and had locked her in the apartment behind an armored gate. The officers forcibly entered the apartment and cut the padlock from the door and freed Skinner.

Skinner told the police that the defendant had threatened to shoot her or her family if she attempted to leave and forced her to have sexual intercourse with him. Skinner reported that the defendant had guns in the apartment and showed the officers where the defendant stored his firearms. The officers seized three guns and ammunition from the defendant's closet. The Detroit police contacted the Federal Bureau of Alcohol, Tobacco, Firearms, and Explosives (ATF). ATF agents concluded that there was probable cause to believe that Johnson was a felon in possession of a firearm. The agents executed a search warrant for the defendant's apartment and failed to find any firearms, ammunition, documents, or narcotics. Johnson challenged the lawfulness of the officers' search of his apartment and the seizure of the firearms. The government argued that the firearms seized by Officers Collins and Ratliff inevitably would have been discovered by the ATF agents in executing the search warrant for Johnson's apartment. How would you rule? See *United States v. Johnson* (22 F.3d 674 [6th Cir. 1994]).

You can learn what the court decided by referring to the study site, **http://study.sagepub.com/lippmance.**

Impeachment

Evidence that is seized in an unlawful search may be used for the impeachment of a defendant who takes the stand. Impeachment is defined as an opposing lawyer's attack on a witness's *credibility* during cross-examination. Credibility means whether a witness is to be believed. For example, if a defendant charged with the possession of illegal child pornography states that he or she has never possessed child pornography, this statement may be challenged on cross-examination by introducing at trial child pornography that was unlawfully seized from his or her house. The jury is instructed that they may consider such evidence that is *inconsistent* with the defendant's testimony in evaluating the defendant's credibility. The judge also instructs the jury that it may not consider this evidence in evaluating whether the defendant is guilty of the possession of child pornography.

What is the reason for the impeachment exception to the exclusionary rule? The U.S. Supreme Court has reasoned that the jury is entitled to hear all the information that may assist in deciding the case and that a defendant should not be permitted to offer testimony that may be false (perjured) without being challenged.

The Supreme Court reasons that the police are deterred from unconstitutional conduct by the exclusion of unlawfully seized evidence from the prosecutor's case-in-chief. The fact that illegally obtained evidence may be used for impeachment purposes does not significantly limit the deterrent value of the exclusionary rule. All witnesses whose statements or actions are inconsistent leave their credibility open to question during cross-examination, and the fact that the evidence has been obtained in an illegal fashion should not prohibit its use at trial when the defendant takes the stand and "opens the door" to cross-examination. Keep in mind that the defendant is not required to testify in his or her own defense and that if the defendant does not take the stand, the jury will not hear the evidence.

The leading case on the impeachment exception is *Walder v. United States*. Sam Walder was charged with the sale of illegal narcotics. Two years earlier, he had been indicted for purchasing narcotics, but the indictment was dismissed after the narcotics had been suppressed as the fruit of an illegal search. Two witnesses testified at Walder's trial that they had purchased narcotics from Walder. Walder took the stand and testified on direct questioning that he had never sold, given, or transmitted narcotics to anyone. On cross-examination, Walder repeated that he had never "purchased, sold or sent" narcotics, and he denied that the government had ever seized narcotics from his home. A police officer then took the stand and testified that narcotics had been seized in an earlier unlawful search of Walder's home (*Walder v. United States*, 347 U.S. 62 [1954]).

The U.S. Supreme Court, in affirming the use of unlawfully seized evidence for impeachment purposes, held that

> it is one thing to say that the Government cannot make any affirmative use of evidence unlawfully obtained. It is quite another to say that the defendant can turn the illegal method by which evidence was obtained to his advantage and provide himself with a shield against the contradiction of his untruths.

The majority stressed that the defendant was free to deny the charges when he took the stand. In this case, however, the defendant offered a "sweeping claim" that he had never trafficked in or possessed narcotics.

In *Walder*, the defendant's statement on *direct testimony* led to the prosecutor's introduction of the fact that drugs were uncovered in the earlier search. In *United States v. Havens*, the Supreme Court held that a statement by a defendant on *cross-examination* was subject to impeachment. The Supreme Court rejected the court of appeals ruling that only a defendant's statements on direct testimony were subject to impeachment by the fruits of an illegal search. The Court proclaimed that

> it is essential to the proper functioning of the adversary system that when a defendant takes the stand, the government be permitted proper and effective cross-examination in an attempt to elicit the truth. The defendant's obligation to testify truthfully is fully binding . . . when . . . cross-examined. (*United States v. Havens*, 446 U.S. 620, 622–626 [1980])

Justices Brennan and Marshall, in dissent, were critical of the Supreme Court majority's "disregard" of their obligation to enforce the Bill of Rights as a "bulwark of our national unity." They asked whether the Court would be prepared to

> acquiesce in torture . . . if it demonstrably advanced the factfinding process. . . . [T]he Constitution does not countenance police misbehavior, even in the pursuit of truth. The processes of our judicial system may not be fueled by the illegalities of government authorities. (*United States v. Havens*, 446 U.S. 633–634 [1980])

Defendants also may be impeached by confessions that were unlawfully obtained by the police in violation of *Miranda*.

Inconsistent statements. In *Harris v. New York*, the Supreme Court held that a defendant's testimony denying that he had sold narcotics may be impeached on cross-examination by the prosecutor through the use of the defendant's confession that had been suppressed by the judge. The Supreme Court explained that *Miranda* cannot be "perverted into a shield" that permits a defendant to "use perjury" without the "risk of confrontation with prior inconsistent utterances" (*Harris v. New York*, 401 U.S. 222, 226 [1971]). In 2009, the Supreme Court held in *Kansas v. Ventris* that confessions obtained by a jailhouse informant in violation of the Sixth Amendment also could be used to impeach a defendant's testimony at trial (*Kansas v. Ventris*, __ U.S. __ [2009]).

Defense witnesses. In *James v. Illinois*, the Supreme Court refused to extend the impeachment exception to include the impeachment of defense witnesses by statements unlawfully obtained from the defendant. Why? The interest in "discouraging or disclosing perjured testimony" by defense witnesses is outweighed by the fact that the police would have an added incentive to disregard legal rules knowing that defense witnesses as well as the defendant himself or herself would be subject to impeachment. Defendants also would be reluctant to call defense witnesses knowing that the witnesses may be subject to impeachment, effectively limiting their ability to mount a defense. Defense witnesses, in turn, would be reluctant to testify, knowing that they may be impeached and possibly charged with perjury (*James v. Illinois*, 493 U.S. 307, 317, 319 [1990]).

In this chapter, we have seen that the exclusionary rule is based on the proposition that the rule deters police disregard of the Fourth Amendment. The exceptions to the exclusionary rule such as good faith are justified on the grounds that excluding the evidence would not greatly contribute to deterrence. The concluding section asks whether the empirical evidence supports the argument that the exclusionary rule deters the police. We also examine the contention that the exclusionary rule results in the guilty escaping punishment.

Legal Equation

Exceptions to the Exclusionary Rule

Collateral proceedings	=	Permit the use of unlawfully seized evidence in proceedings that are not part of the formal trial. This evidence also may be introduced in noncriminal proceedings.
Attenuation	=	Whether the evidence has been seized as a result of a Fourth Amendment violation or by means sufficiently distinguishable to be purged of the primary taint.
Good faith	=	Police acted in an honest and objectively reasonable belief in the legality of the search.
Independent discovery	=	Evidence that is unlawfully seized is admissible where the evidence also was obtained through independent and lawful means.
Inevitable discovery	=	Evidence that is seized as the result of an unconstitutional search is admissible where the government can prove by the preponderance of the evidence that this evidence would inevitably have been discovered in a lawful fashion.
Impeachment	=	Evidence that is seized in an unlawful search may be used on cross-examination to challenge the credibility of a defendant who takes the stand.
Impeachment and confessions	=	A defendant's testimony may be impeached on cross-examination through the use of an unlawful confession (a prior inconsistent statement).

CRIMINAL EVIDENCE IN THE NEWS

Detective Jason Arbeeny was convicted in 2011 of official misconduct for falsifying police arrest records in drug cases. Arbeeny was accused of planting a small bag of crack cocaine on two innocent individuals in 2007. He allegedly approached the individuals' automobile and placed crack in the automobile and exclaimed, "Look what I found." Prosecutors presented evidence that there was rampant corruption in the drug units in which Detective Arbeeny worked. Former detective Stephen Anderson testified that the officers in these units frequently planted drugs on suspects.

The case against Detective Arbeeny was part of a larger pattern of corruption in which several narcotics officers in Brooklyn were caught mishandling drugs, leading to the dismissal of hundreds of potentially compromised drug cases. New York City reached financial settlements with individuals victimized by wrongful arrests and convictions.

State Supreme Court Justice Gustin L. Reichbach in announcing the verdict criticized the New York Police for a widespread culture of corruption in drug units. Justice Reichbach announced that "I thought I was not naïve," he said. "But even this court was shocked, not only by the seeming pervasive scope of misconduct but even more distressingly by the seeming casualness by which such conduct is employed." Justice Reichbach described the drug units as possessing a "cowboy culture" in which drugs seized as evidence were regularly stolen by officers who sold them on the street, traded them in return for sexual favors, used the drugs to falsify arrests, and planted them on innocent individuals to turn them into informants.

In 2012, Justice Reichbach sentenced Arbeeny to five years' probation and three hundred hours of community service and called his behavior a "reprehensible abuse of trust and authority" and the "corruption of the entire criminal justice system."

■ CASE ANALYSIS

In *Herring v. United States*, the U.S. Supreme Court decided the admissibility of contraband seized during a search incident to an arrest was based in good faith on an error in the police data, which erroneously indicated that there was an outstanding warrant for Bennie Dean Herring's arrest.

Herring v. United States, 555 U.S. 135 (2009), Roberts, J.

On July 7, 2004, Investigator Mark Anderson learned that Bennie Dean Herring had driven to the Coffee County Sheriff's Department to retrieve something from his impounded truck. Herring was no stranger to law enforcement, and Anderson asked the county's warrant clerk, Sandy Pope, to check for any outstanding warrants for Herring's arrest. When she found none, Anderson asked Pope to check with Sharon Morgan, her counterpart in neighboring Dale County. After checking Dale County's computer database, Morgan replied that there was an active arrest warrant for Herring's failure to appear on a felony charge. Pope relayed the information to Anderson and asked Morgan to fax over a copy of the warrant as confirmation. Anderson and a deputy followed Herring as he left the impound lot, pulled him over, and arrested him. A search incident to the arrest revealed methamphetamine in Herring's pocket and a pistol (which as a felon he could not possess) in his vehicle.

There had, however, been a mistake about the warrant. The Dale County sheriff's computer records are supposed to correspond to actual arrest warrants, which the office also maintains. But when Morgan went to the files to retrieve the actual warrant to fax to Pope, Morgan was unable to find it. She called a court clerk and learned that the warrant had been recalled five months earlier. Normally when a warrant is recalled, the court clerk's office or a judge's chambers calls Morgan, who enters the information in the sheriff's computer database and disposes of the physical copy. For whatever reason, the information about the recall of the warrant for Herring did not appear in the database. Morgan immediately called Pope to alert her to the mix-up, and Pope contacted Anderson over a secure radio. This all unfolded in ten to fifteen minutes, but Herring had already been arrested and found with the gun and drugs, just a few hundred yards from the sheriff's office.

Herring was indicted in the District Court for the Middle District of Alabama for illegally possessing the gun and drug violations. He moved to suppress the evidence on the ground that his initial arrest had been illegal, because the warrant had been rescinded. The magistrate judge recommended denying the motion, because the arresting officers had acted in a good faith belief that the warrant was still outstanding. Thus, even if there were a violation, there was "no reason to believe that application of the exclusionary rule here would deter the occurrence of any future mistakes." The Court of Appeals for the Eleventh Circuit affirmed.

The Fourth Amendment protects "the right of the people to be secure in their persons, houses, papers, and effects, against unreasonable searches and seizures," but it "contains no provision expressly precluding the use of evidence obtained in violation of its commands." Nonetheless, our decisions establish an exclusionary rule that, when applicable, forbids the use of improperly obtained evidence at trial. We have stated that this judicially created rule is "designed to safeguard rights generally through its deterrent effect."

The fact that a violation occurred—that is, that a search or arrest was unreasonable—does not necessarily mean that the exclusionary rule applies. Indeed, exclusion "has always been our last resort, not our first impulse," and our precedents establish important principles that constrain application of the exclusionary rule.

First, the exclusionary rule is not an individual right and applies only where it "result[s] in appreciable deterrence." We have repeatedly rejected the argument that exclusion is a necessary consequence of a violation. Instead we have focused on the efficacy of the rule in deterring violations in the future.

In addition, the benefits of deterrence must outweigh the costs. "We have never suggested that the exclusionary rule must apply in every circumstance in which it might provide marginal deterrence." "To the extent that application of the exclusionary rule could provide some incremental deterrent, that possible benefit must be weighed against [its] substantial social costs." The principal cost of applying the rule is, of course, letting guilty and possibly dangerous defendants go free—something that "offends basic concepts of the criminal justice system." "The rule's costly toll upon truth-seeking and law enforcement objectives presents a high obstacle for those urging [its] application."

These principles are reflected in the holding of *Leon*: When police act under a warrant that is invalid for lack of probable cause, the exclusionary rule does not apply if the police acted "in objectively reasonable reliance" on the subsequently invalidated search warrant. We (perhaps confusingly) called this objectively reasonable reliance "good faith." In a companion case, *Massachusetts v. Sheppard*, we held that the exclusionary rule did not apply when a warrant was invalid because a judge forgot to make "clerical corrections" to it.

Shortly thereafter, in *Krull*, we extended these holdings to warrantless administrative searches performed in good faith reliance on a statute later declared unconstitutional. Finally, in *Evans*, we applied this good faith rule to police who reasonably relied on mistaken information in a court's database that an arrest warrant was outstanding. We held that a mistake made by a judicial employee could not give rise to exclusion for three reasons: The exclusionary rule was crafted to curb police rather than judicial misconduct, court employees were unlikely to try to subvert the Fourth Amendment, and "most important, there [was] no basis for believing that application of the exclusionary rule in [those] circumstances" would have any significant effect in deterring the errors. *Evans* left unresolved "whether the evidence should be suppressed if police personnel were responsible for the error," an issue not argued by the State in that case, but one that we now confront.

(Continued)

[T]he abuses that gave rise to the exclusionary rule featured intentional conduct that was patently unconstitutional. In *Mapp v. Ohio*, which extended the exclusionary rule to the states, officers forced open a door to Ms. Mapp's house, kept her lawyer from entering, brandished what the court concluded was a false warrant, and then forced her into handcuffs and canvassed the house for obscenity. "The situation in *Mapp*" featured a "flagrant or deliberate violation of rights." . . . [S]ince *Leon*, we have never applied the rule to exclude evidence obtained in violation of the Fourth Amendment, where the police conduct was no more intentional or culpable than this.

To trigger the exclusionary rule, police conduct must be sufficiently deliberate that exclusion can meaningfully deter it and sufficiently culpable that such deterrence is worth the price paid by the justice system. As laid out in our cases, the exclusionary rule serves to deter deliberate, reckless, or grossly negligent conduct or in some circumstances recurring or systemic negligence. The error in this case does not rise to that level. The pertinent analysis of deterrence and culpability is objective, not an "inquiry into the subjective awareness of arresting officers." We have already held that "our good-faith inquiry is confined to the objectively ascertainable question whether a reasonably well trained officer would have known that the search was illegal" in light of "all of the circumstances." . . . We do not suggest that all recordkeeping errors by the police are immune from the exclusionary rule. In this case, however, the conduct at issue was not so objectively culpable as to require exclusion. In *Leon* we held that "the marginal or nonexistent benefits produced by suppressing evidence obtained in objectively reasonable reliance on a subsequently invalidated search warrant cannot justify the substantial costs of exclusion." The same is true when evidence is obtained in objectively reasonable reliance on a subsequently recalled warrant.

If the police have been shown to be reckless in maintaining a warrant system, or to have knowingly made false entries to lay the groundwork for future false arrests, exclusion would certainly be justified under our cases should such misconduct cause a violation. . . . In a case where systemic errors were demonstrated, it might be reckless for officers to rely on an unreliable warrant system. . . . But there is no evidence that errors in Dale County's system are routine or widespread. Officer Anderson testified that he had never had reason to question information about a Dale County warrant, and both Sandy Pope and Sharon Morgan testified that they could remember no similar miscommunication ever happening on their watch. That is even less error than in the database at issue in *Evans*, where we also found reliance on the database to be objectively reasonable. . . . [T]he Eleventh Circuit was correct to affirm the denial of the motion to suppress.

Petitioner's claim that police negligence automatically triggers suppression cannot be squared with the principles underlying the exclusionary rule as they have been explained in our cases. In light of our repeated holdings that the deterrent effect of suppression must be substantial and outweigh any harm to the justice system, we conclude that when police mistakes are the result of negligence such as that described here, rather than systemic error or reckless disregard of constitutional requirements, any marginal deterrence does not "pay its way." In such a case, the criminal should not "go free because the constable has blundered." The judgment of the Court of Appeals for the Eleventh Circuit is affirmed.

CHAPTER SUMMARY

In 1914, in *Weeks v. United States*, the U.S. Supreme Court ruled that evidence seized in violation of the Fourth Amendment is to be excluded from evidence in federal prosecutions. Thirty-five years later, in *Wolf v. Colorado*, the Court held that the requirements of the Fourth Amendment are incorporated into the Fourteenth Amendment and are applicable to proceedings in state and local courts. In 1961, in *Mapp v. Ohio*, the Supreme Court held that the Fourth Amendment exclusionary rule also applied to prosecutions in state courts. The Court explained that the exclusionary rule is "part and parcel" of the Fourth Amendment, provides a deterrent to police disregard for the Fourth Amendment, and protects the integrity of the judicial process by excluding tainted evidence from trial. These twin goals, according to the majority of the justices on the Court at that time, could not be accomplished through civil remedies, criminal prosecution, or disciplinary proceedings. Subsequently, in a series of judgments, the Court shifted its position and ruled that the exclusionary rule is a "judge-made" remedy that is not required by the Fourth Amendment, whose sole purpose is to deter unreasonable searches and seizures.

The typical avenue for challenging the reasonableness of a search and seizure is the filing of a pretrial motion to suppress. Most states and the federal courts place the burden of proof on the defendant when the search or seizure is based on a warrant. The burden is reversed and is placed on the government when the police act without a warrant. The legal test to be applied for standing to file a motion to suppress an alleged violation of the Fourth Amendment prohibition on unreasonable searches and seizures is whether an individual has a subjective and reasonable expectation of privacy in the area that was searched. The burden of proof for demonstrating standing customarily is placed on the defendant.

The Supreme Court has created a number of exceptions to the exclusionary rule in those instances in which the Court has concluded that the limited deterrent value of excluding the evidence is outweighed by the costs of excluding the evidence from the trial. In other words, in these cases, the Court found that there was "too much pain for too little gain." These exceptions are as follows:

- *Collateral proceedings.* The evidence is admissible in criminal proceedings that are not part of the formal trial as well as in certain civil proceedings.
- *Attenuation.* There is a weak connection between the unlawful search and the seizure of the evidence.
- *Good faith.* The police acted in an objectively reasonable fashion in seizing the evidence.
- *Independent source.* The evidence was also discovered through lawful means that are separate and distinct from the unlawful seizure of the evidence.
- *Inevitable discovery.* The evidence eventually would have been lawfully discovered.
- *Impeachment.* Unlawfully seized items may be introduced on cross-examination to attack the defendant's credibility.

CHAPTER REVIEW QUESTIONS

1. Trace the development of the exclusionary rule from Weeks to Mapp.
2. State the arguments for and against the exclusionary rule? What alternatives have been proposed?
3. What are the steps in filing a motion to suppress evidence?
4. Who has standing to file a motion to suppress?
5. List and discuss the exceptions to the exclusionary rule.

LEGAL TERMINOLOGY

attenuated

collateral proceedings

derivative evidence

exclusionary rule

fruit of the poisonous tree

good faith exception

independent source doctrine

inevitable discovery rule

purging the taint

silver platter doctrine

standing

REFERENCES

Davies, Thomas A. 1983. "A Hard Look at What We Know (and Still Need to Learn) About the 'Social Costs' of the Exclusionary Rule: The NIJ Study and Other Studies of 'Lost Arrests.'" *American Bar Foundation Research Journal* 8 (Summer): 611–690.

Nardulli, Peter. 1983. "The Societal Cost of the Exclusionary Rule: An Empirical Assessment." *American Bar Foundation Research Journal* 8 (Summer): 585–609.

Visit the Student Study Site at **http://study.sagepub.com/lippmance** to access additional study tools, including mobile-friendly eFlashcards and Web quizzes as well as links to SAGE journal articles and hyperlinks for *Criminal Evidence* on the Web.

CHAPTER 12

SEARCHES AND SEIZURES AND PRIVACY

[Handwritten annotations: Why search + seize? • looking for evidence • looking for instruments there illegally (guns or drugs). 4th Amendment only limits searches of government]

Did the police require a warrant to search Greenwood's garbage?

On April 6, 1984, [Police Officer Jenny] Stracner asked the neighborhood's regular trash collector to pick up the plastic garbage bags that [Billy] Greenwood had left on the curb in front of his house and to turn the bags over to her without mixing their contents with garbage from other houses. The trash collector cleaned his truck bin of other refuse, collected the garbage bags from the street in front of Greenwood's house, and turned the bags over to Stracner. The officer searched through the rubbish and found items indicative of narcotics use. She recited the information that she had gleaned from the trash search in an affidavit in support of a warrant to search Greenwood's home.

Police officers encountered both respondents at the house later that day when they arrived to execute the warrant. The police discovered quantities of cocaine and hashish during their search of the house. Respondents were arrested on felony narcotics charges. (*California v. Greenwood*, 486 U.S. 35 [1988])

CHAPTER OUTLINE

Introduction
The Historical Background of the Fourth Amendment
Searches
Informants and Electronic Eavesdropping
Plain View
Expectation of Privacy
Open Fields
Curtilage and Aerial Surveillance

Technology and Searches and Seizures
Public Places and Private Businesses
Abandoned Property
Seizures of Persons
Case Analysis
Chapter Summary
Chapter Review Questions
Legal Terminology

TEST YOUR KNOWLEDGE

1. Do you know the Fourth Amendment protections and the historical background of the Fourth Amendment?

2. Are you able to state the significance of *Katz v. United States* in the development of the Fourth Amendment?

3. Do you know why there is no constitutionally protected expectation of privacy in conversations with an informant or undercover officer even when conducted in the home?

268 ■ Criminal Evidence

4. Can you identify the requirements for a plain view search?

5. Are you able to distinguish between curtilage and open fields and the factors to consider in determining whether an area is curtilage or open fields? Compare the expectation of privacy for curtilage with the expectation of privacy for open fields.

6. Do you know whether curtilage has an expectation of privacy from aerial surveillance?

7. Are you able to explain the expectation of privacy that attaches to public places, businesses, and abandoned property?

8. Do you know the difference between "show of authority" seizures and physical seizures, and encounters?

■ INTRODUCTION

In this chapter, we begin our discussion of Fourth Amendment searches and seizures. The primary purpose of searches and seizures is to collect items that will assist law enforcement in the investigation of unlawful activity. These searches and seizures may involve various types of evidence (*Warden v. Hayden*, 387 U.S. 294 [1967]):

- *Instrumentalities of crime.* Items used to carry out a crime, such as firearms.
- *Fruits of a crime.* Money stolen from a bank, jewelry taken from a home, a wallet taken during a robbery, or computers stolen from a store. → watch, rings, car, TVs
- *Contraband.* Unlawful drugs and other prohibited substances. → bombs
- *Evidence of criminal activity.* Clothes with gunpowder stains, bloody clothes, or DNA traces that link a suspect to a crime.
- *Incriminating statements.* Statements overheard during electronic surveillance. → not statements made to the police → over heard or people talking (calls recorded in prison).

The Fourth Amendment to the U.S. Constitution addresses searches and seizures and reads as follows:

> The right of the people to be secure in their persons, houses, papers, and effects, against unreasonable searches and seizures, shall not be violated, and no Warrants shall issue, but upon probable cause, supported by Oath or affirmation, and particularly describing the place to be searched, and the persons or things to be seized.

The Fourth Amendment is directed at searches and seizures by the government and does not restrict searches and seizures by private individuals. The amendment protects individuals against "unreasonable" governmental searches and seizures in four constitutionally protected areas: → your wife takes all your drugs and gives to police. Fine] Private school searching locker—fine.

- *Persons.* This protects individuals against unreasonable detentions and unreasonable searches of their persons.
- *Houses.* Homes encompass all residences, dwellings attached to the residence, and areas immediately surrounding the home as well as areas of commercial businesses that are not open to the public.
- *Papers.* Letters, diaries, and business records are protected.
- *Effects.* Effects include personal possessions such as automobiles, clothing, and firearms.

The Fourth Amendment tells the police that they may **search** for and seize evidence of unlawful activity involving a person, house, paper, or effect so long as these searches and seizures follow the dictates of the Fourth Amendment. As we shall see in the next few chapters, the U.S. Supreme Court has devoted well over one hundred cases and thousands of pages to interpreting the requirements of the fifty-three words that compose the Fourth Amendment. In undertaking this task, the Supreme Court has struggled to balance the social interest in conducting searches and seizures to investigate unlawful activity against the interest of individuals in being free from governmental interference in their personal lives.

In this chapter, we define and discuss Fourth Amendment searches and seizures of individuals. Why is this important to consider? As technology advances, the Supreme Court undoubtedly will be asked to determine whether various types of intrusions constitute Fourth Amendment searches and seizures that require the police to obtain a warrant based on **probable cause** from a magistrate or judge, or whether the intrusions do not constitute Fourth Amendment searches and seizures and may be undertaken by the police without the approval of a judicial official. Consider whether the police should be required to obtain a warrant before directing individuals to donate DNA samples; prior to monitoring e-mail activity, search engines, or cell phones; or before examining databases that contain personal information.

We first turn our attention to the definition of searches and then discuss the definition of seizures of individuals. Ask yourself whether you agree with the Supreme Court decisions discussed in this chapter. Pay particular attention to the Court's effort to balance the need for the police to investigate crime against the protection of the individual interest in privacy.

general warrant-could go in and out as they wanted

■ THE HISTORICAL BACKGROUND OF THE FOURTH AMENDMENT

The Fourth Amendment was included in the Bill of Rights to protect individuals against the types of far-reaching searches and seizures conducted by British authorities in the American colonies. A particular source of anger was the use of **general warrants** and **writs of assistance** to search homes, businesses, and warehouses for goods that had been smuggled into the country to avoid paying the exorbitant customs duties imposed by the British. Searches also were used to seize able-bodied young men who were forced into the Royal Navy.

The general warrant was issued by a judge or government official and authorized searches anywhere, at any time, and for anything. The writ of assistance was a form of general warrant that authorized an official of the English Crown to compel police officers and citizens to assist in a search. These documents, once authorized, were legally effective for the life of the sovereign and did not expire until six months following the sovereign's death.

In 1761, in the *Writs of Assistance* case, sixty-three Boston merchants unsuccessfully challenged the legal authority of the Massachusetts Superior Court to issue writs of assistance. The superior court found that the English Parliament had granted Massachusetts colonial judges the authority to issue writs of assistance. Attorney James Otis in a celebrated argument proclaimed that the writ was a practice as "destructive of English liberty and the fundamental principles of law, that ever was found in an English law-book." He went on to note that "one of the most essential branches of English liberty is the freedom of one's house. A man's house is his castle. This writ, if it should be declared legal, would totally annihilate this privilege."

A number of the colonial state legislatures responded by prohibiting general warrants. The Virginia Declaration of Rights in 1776 proclaimed that "general warrants are grievous and oppressive, and ought not to be granted." Both English and American colonial courts slowly began to declare "illegal and void" search warrants that authorized "all persons and places throughout the world to be searched" and insisted that local magistrates issue warrants only when there was probable cause that contraband was located in a "particular place or places" (*Frisbie v. Butler*, Kirby 213 [Conn. 1787]).

The Fourth Amendment reflected the tenor of the times and was intended to abolish general warrants and writs of assistance by prohibiting "unreasonable" searches and seizures and providing that "no warrants shall issue, but upon probable cause, supported by oath or affirmation, and particularly describing the place to be searched and the person or things to be seized." In other words, a warrant requires the government to present evidence to a magistrate or judge that shows probable cause that evidence or contraband is located in a specific location at a particular time. A general warrant would be unreasonable under this standard.

The Supreme Court, while expressing a preference that searches be conducted based on a warrant founded on probable cause, has recognized that it is "reasonable" in various instances for the police to conduct a search and make a seizure without a warrant. Examples are "special needs" searches that are intended to protect the public safety rather than to collect evidence of a crime. These searches to do not greatly intrude on an individual's privacy while they protect the public safety. They include searches at airports or at the border between the United States and Mexico or the United States and Canada.

■ SEARCHES

Expectation of Privacy

In *Boyd v. United States* (116 U.S. 616 [1886]), the U.S. Supreme Court adopted a **property rights** or **trespassory approach** to the Fourth Amendment. The property rights theory protected individuals against physical intrusions or trespasses against their persons, houses, papers, and effects.

- *Physical intrusions.* For an intrusion to occur, there must be an actual <u>physical entry into the home or physical examination of an individual or his or her papers or possessions</u>.
- *Scope of protection.* Persons, houses, papers, and effects are protected.

Justice Hugo Black captured the essence of the property rights approach when he proclaimed that the Fourth Amendment was "aimed directly at the abhorrent practice of breaking in, ransacking and searching homes and other buildings and seizing people's personal belongings without warrants issued by magistrates" (*Katz v. United States*, 389 U.S. 347, 367 [1967]).

The famous 1928 case of *Olmstead v. United States* starkly presents the limitations of the property rights approach. Roy Olmstead was convicted of conspiracy to unlawfully import, possess, and sell liquor. The central evidence that was relied on at trial was gathered through warrantless wiretaps of the office and home phones of Olmstead and his co-conspirators. The U.S. Supreme Court, by a 5-4 vote, rejected Olmstead's contention that the close to eight hundred pages of notes gathered from the wiretaps had been obtained in violation of his Fourth Amendment rights.

The majority decision rested on two conclusions. First, the conversations that were heard by federal agents were transmitted across telephone wires and did not involve the search and seizure of a "physical object." Second, the wiretaps were attached to phone lines outside the home and did not involve a physical intrusion into the home. The Supreme Court reasoned that the language of the Fourth Amendment "cannot be extended or expanded to include the telephone wires reaching to the whole world from the defendant's home or office. The intervening wires are not part of his house or office any more than are the highways along which they are stretched."

In what was to prove an important dissent, Justice Louis Brandeis argued that the Fourth Amendment must be interpreted in light of changing circumstances. He argued that "the makers of our Constitution . . . conferred, as against the Government, the right to be let alone—the most comprehensive of rights and the right most valued by civilized men" and so "every unjustifiable intrusion . . . upon the privacy of the individual, whatever the means employed, must be deemed a violation of the Fourth Amendment" (*Olmstead v. United States*, 277 U.S. 438, 465, 478 [1928]). In 1942, in *Goldman v. United States*, the Supreme Court followed the precedent established in *Olmstead* and affirmed that the installation of a detectaphone on the outside wall of an adjoining office for purposes of monitoring a conversation did not violate the Fourth Amendment (*Goldman v. United States*, 316 U.S. 129 [1942]).

In 1967, in *Katz v. United States*, the Supreme Court adopted Justice Brandeis's viewpoint and overruled *Olmstead*. In *Katz*, the Supreme Court rejected the trespassory approach and adopted an **expectation of privacy** test for the application of the Fourth Amendment. The FBI, acting without a search warrant, had attached microphones to the outside of a clear glass enclosed telephone booth and recorded Charles Katz's placing of interstate gambling bets and receipt of wagering information. The Supreme Court rejected the "trespass doctrine as no longer controlling" and held that the Fourth Amendment "protects people, not places. What a person knowingly exposes to the public . . . is not a subject of Fourth Amendment protection. . . . But what he seeks to preserve as private, even in an area accessible to the public, may be constitutionally protected." In this instance, the government was determined to have violated the privacy of the telephone booth on which Katz justifiably relied. The fact that the government did not seize a "material object" or "penetrate the wall of the booth" did not remove the search from Fourth Amendment protection (*Katz v. United States*, 389 U.S. 347, 351 [1967]).

Justice John Marshall Harlan in his concurring opinion in *Katz* established a <u>two-part test</u> for a Fourth Amendment expectation of privacy that has been followed by the U.S. Supreme Court.

Test:
- <u>*Subjective.*</u> An individual exhibits a personal expectation of privacy. *believe they have privacy*
- <u>*Objective.*</u> Society recognizes this expectation as reasonable.—*Judge must agree (reasonable person)*

Katz v. US

whatever you tell other people— you assume the risk others will tell some one else. → NEVER know who you're talking to

Justice Harlan illustrated the test by noting that people retain an expectation of privacy in the home, while they do not retain an expectation of privacy in their public words or public actions.

In 2007, the Sixth Circuit Court of Appeals in *Warshak v. United States* considered whether Steven Warshak possessed an expectation of privacy in the content of his personal e-mail account. Warshak and his company, Berkeley Premium Nutraceuticals, were the subject of a criminal investigation involving mail and wire fraud, money laundering, and other federal offenses. The U.S. government obtained a court order directing Internet service provider (ISP) NuVox Communications to give government agents information involving Warshak's e-mail account. This included "'[t]he contents of wire or electronic communications (not in electronic storage unless greater than 181 days old) that were placed or stored in directories or files owned or controlled' by Warshak; and . . . '[a]ll Log files and backup tapes.'"

The Sixth Circuit Court of Appeals held that while Warshak assumed the risk that the recipient of a communication will reveal the contents of e-mails, Warshak maintained an expectation of privacy in regard to his ISP. The ISP was not expected to "access the e-mails in the normal course of business," and Warshak maintained an expectation of privacy in the content of these communications. Otherwise, phone conversations would

> never be protected, merely because the telephone company can access them; letters would never be protected, by virtue of the Postal Service's ability to access them; the contents of shared safe deposit boxes or storage lockers would never be protected, by virtue of the bank or storage company's ability to access them.

"Compelled disclosure of subscriber information and related records" are "records of the service provider as well, and may likely be accessed by . . . employees in the normal course of their employment," and access to these records "likely creates no Fourth Amendment problems." However, there is a heightened expectation of privacy in regard to the contents of e-mail communications that society considers reasonable.

E-mail is an "ever-increasing mode of private communication, and protecting shared communications through this medium is as important to Fourth Amendment principles today as protecting telephone conversations has been in the past." The ISP's right to access e-mails under the user agreement is reserved for "extraordinary circumstances." The outcome may be different where a user agreement calls for regular auditing, inspection, or monitoring of e-mails. The fact that e-mails may be scanned for pornography or a virus was not considered by the Sixth Circuit Court of Appeals to "invade an individual's content-based privacy interest in the e-mails and has little bearing on his expectation of privacy in the content." This is analogous to the Post Office screening packages for drugs or explosives, which does not expose the content of written communications (*Warshak v. United States*, No. 06-00357 [S.D. Ohio, 2007]).

12.1 YOU DECIDE

Plainclothes Los Angeles Police Officer Richard Aldahl and two other plainclothes officers observed defendant Leroy Triggs enter a men's room in Arroyo Seco Park. Ten minutes later, David Crockett was observed entering the same men's room. The three officers entered a plumbing access area between the men's room and women's room that provided a vantage point to observe activity in the restrooms. Officer Aldahl was able to position himself in such a fashion that he was able look through vents down into the doorless toilet stalls. He spotted Triggs and Crockett engaged in unlawful oral copulation. Triggs was convicted and placed on probation under the condition that he serve thirty days in the county jail. Officer Aldahl testified at trial that he had entered the plumbing access area roughly fifty times in the past to observe activity in the men's room. Did Triggs possess a reasonable expectation of privacy? Was this an unlawful, warrantless search under the Fourth Amendment? What if there were doors on the stalls that the suspects had closed? See *People v. Triggs* (506 P.2d 232 [Cal. 1973]).

You can learn what the court decided by referring to the study site, **http://study.sagepub.com/lippmance.**

Expectation of privacy	=	Exhibit an actual (subjective) expectation of privacy
	+	the expectation is one that society is prepared to recognize as reasonable.
Expectation unreasonable	=	What persons knowingly expose to the public, even in their own home or office (what they seek to preserve as private, even in an area accessible to the public, may be constitutionally protected)
	+	information turned over to a third party (assumption of the risk).

■ INFORMANTS AND ELECTRONIC EAVESDROPPING

In *Katz*, the government electronically monitored a conversation without the consent of either of the participants. The Supreme Court recognized that Katz had a subjective as well as a reasonable expectation of privacy in the content of his phone calls and held that a reasonable search under the Fourth Amendment required that the government obtain a warrant based on probable cause. The U.S. Supreme Court has taken a different approach to the so-called false friend cases in which a suspect talks to an individual without knowing that he or she is an undercover government agent or informant. In a second type of false friend scenario, the agent or informant is wired and the conversation is recorded or directly transmitted to the police at a remote location. The Supreme Court has held in both situations that the suspect has no reasonable expectation of privacy under the Fourth Amendment that has been violated. He or she *assumes the risk* that the conversation may not remain confidential and will be communicated to the police (Dressler and Michaels 2006: 84–88).

In *Hoffa v. United States*, Edward Partin, a local Teamsters official and government informant, visited the hotel room of Teamsters national president Jimmy Hoffa, who was standing trial for union-related corruption. Partin reportedly overheard conversations in which Hoffa conspired to bribe jurors; Partin later testified as the government's central witness at Hoffa's prosecution for jury tampering. The Supreme Court held that although the hotel room was a "constitutionally protected area," Hoffa was

> not relying on the security of the hotel room; he was relying upon his misplaced confidence that Partin would not reveal his wrongdoing. [Nothing in the] Fourth Amendment protects a wrongdoer's misplaced belief that a person to whom he voluntarily confides his wrongdoing will not reveal it. (*Hoffa v. United States*, 385 U.S. 293, 302–303 [1996])

Would it make a difference that an informant was wired with an electronic device that recorded the conversation? In *United States v. White*, the informant was wired with a radio transmitter that relayed the conversation to government agents. The Supreme Court continued to follow a "risk analysis" and held that

> if the conduct and revelations of an agent operating without electronic equipment do not invade the defendant's constitutionally justifiable expectations of privacy, neither does a simultaneous recording of the same conversations made . . . from transmissions received from the agent to whom the defendant is talking and whose trustworthiness the defendant necessarily risks. (*United States v. White*, 401 U.S. 745, 751 [1971])

In summary, we *assume the risk* that the person with whom we are communicating may be working as a government agent or informant. There is no constitutionally protected expectation of privacy in conversations that we engage in with other individuals. It makes no difference whether the other individual is an informant or a government agent who

- immediately reports the contents of the conversation to the police and writes down his or her conversation,
- records the conversation using electronic equipment, or
- transmits the conversation to police officers who are monitoring the conversation.

[handwritten top margin: party on Main St. w/ window open. cop sees bong in window while driving by, they can come in and take it]

Justice Harlan, in his dissent in *United States v. White*, complained that the Supreme Court's embrace of risk analysis and warrantless surveillance of conversations threatened the trust and security that makes people comfortable with freely talking to one another.

Do you agree with the Supreme Court that James A. White assumed the risk that his conversation would be directly transmitted to law enforcement authorities? Should the Court distinguish between conversations in the home and conversations in public? In the next sections, we briefly review the requirements for a plain view search and seizure and discuss the relationship between plain view and the expectation of privacy in the areas surrounding the home and in the home.

[handwritten: if police are lawfully where they are and they see something they can take it and arrest you]

■ PLAIN VIEW

Plain view is an exception to the Fourth Amendment warrant requirement; it allows the police to seize an item without a search warrant under two conditions:

- *Legally situated.* The police officer is lawfully positioned: he or she "has a right to be where he or she is situated."
- *Probable cause.* The police officer has probable cause to believe that the object is evidence of criminal activity. The probable cause must be immediately apparent upon observing the item.

We will be discussing plain view searches in greater detail in Chapter Fifteen. At the moment, it is sufficient that you understand that an officer who sees an unlawful object or object connected to unlawful activity may seize the object without a warrant. The individual, by exposing the object to "plain view," has lost his or her expectation of privacy with respect to the item. The police, for example, may lawfully stop an individual for a traffic violation and spot and seize drugs or an open bottle of alcohol in plain view on the back seat. An officer searching a house for drugs may encounter and seize unlawful child pornography.

In *Arizona v. Hicks*, the police responded to a gunshot and entered a rundown apartment without a warrant. The officers saw a brand-new stereo unit; one of the officers moved the unit, read the serial numbers, and called headquarters, which confirmed that the stereo had been stolen. The Supreme Court agreed with Hicks that this was not a plain view search. The officers were "lawfully situated," but it was not "immediately apparent" that the stereo was stolen, because the officer was forced to move the unit and to call headquarters to determine whether it had been stolen (*Arizona v. Hicks*, 480 U.S. 321 [1987]). The Supreme Court also has recognized a "plain feel" doctrine when an officer patting down a suspect concludes that he or she has encountered narcotics, and other courts have recognized a "plain smell" doctrine when an officer smells narcotics or alcohol in an automobile. In 2008, a Virginia Court of Appeals noted that an *[handwritten: → weed, alcohol, meth]*

[handwritten right margin: apparent that it's weapon or drugs can take]

individual, after all, has no privacy interest in his odors. He cannot broadcast an unusual odor (particularly one associated with illegal drugs) and reasonably expect everyone he comes into contact with, including police officers, to take no notice of it. [We therefore agree with the accepted view that] there is no "reasonable expectation of privacy" from lawfully positioned agents "with inquisitive nostrils." (*Bunch v. Commonwealth*, 658 S.E.2d 724 [Va. App. 2008])

Courts also have recognized a "plain hearing" doctrine in those instances in which individuals have no reasonable expectation of privacy and their conversation are heard by a law enforcement officer (*United States v. Ceballos*, 385 F.3d 1120 [7th Cir. 2004]).

The next section on open fields and curtilage provides a good example of how the police rely on plain view. We then explore whether the police may rely on technology to enhance their ability to conduct plain view searches and seizures.

[handwritten: Home = highest level of privacy/protection]

■ EXPECTATION OF PRIVACY

The U.S. Supreme Court has divided the home and the land surrounding the home into three separate categories with differing degrees of expectation of privacy and Fourth Amendment protection:

Home → curtilage → public property
privacy – – – – – – – – – no privacy

- *Open fields.* This includes land distant from the home, which the police may enter without probable cause or a warrant.
- *Home.* The physical structure of the dwelling-house is accorded full and complete protection under the Fourth Amendment, and to enter it, the police in most instances require a search warrant founded on probable cause.
- *Curtilage.* The area immediately surrounding the home is considered part of the dwelling-house. Curtilage has no expectation of privacy from aerial surveillance.

There are three other categories of property that we will discuss in this chapter. Each lacks an expectation of privacy under the Fourth Amendment:

- *Public property.* This land is generally open to the public, and a warrant is not required for the police to seize property.
- *Commercial property.* The police may enter and seize items without a warrant from stores and businesses that are open to the public. A warrant is required to enter those areas reserved for employees.
- *Abandoned property.* Property that is intentionally abandoned has no expectation of privacy and may be seized by the police without a warrant.

■ OPEN FIELDS

In *Oliver v. United States*, the Kentucky State Police investigated reports that Richard Thornton and Ray E. Oliver were raising marijuana on Oliver's farm. The police drove past Oliver's house to a locked gate with a "No Trespassing" sign, followed a path around one side of the fence, and walked down the path until they discovered a field of marijuana over a mile from Oliver's home. "No Trespassing" signs were posted along the path, and the marijuana field was surrounded by woods, fences, and embankments and was not visible from any location accessible to the public. The U.S. Supreme Court held that the Fourth Amendment protection of "persons, houses, places and effects" from unreasonable searches and seizures is not intended to protect open fields. Open fields consequently possess no expectation of privacy, and the Kentucky police acted reasonably in entering and seizing the marijuana without a search warrant.

The Supreme Court explained that there are good reasons why **open fields** are not provided with Fourth Amendment protection and lack an expectation of privacy (*Oliver v. United States*, 466 U.S. 170 [1984]):

- *Purpose.* The Fourth Amendment is intended to protect "intimate" activities. There is no interest in protecting the type of activities that typically take place in open fields, such as the cultivation of crops.
- *Access.* Open fields are more accessible to the public than are houses or offices and are easily monitored from aircraft.

The Supreme Court also held that Oliver did not have an expectation of privacy in the open field despite the warnings to trespassers and efforts to conceal the marijuana plants. The Court explained that declaring that open fields lacked an expectation of privacy despite the "No Trespassing" signs avoided placing the police in the position of having to decide on a case-by-case basis whether a particular open field merited Fourth Amendment protection.

Curtilage is the area immediately surrounding the home. Curtilage, in contrast to open fields, is the site of the "intimate activity" associated with the "sanctity of a man's [or woman's] home and the privacies of life" and therefore is considered part of the home itself. The Supreme Court noted that people use their decks, porches, and backyards to barbecue, socialize, and engage in recreation and other activities that are closely identified with the enjoyment of the home.

As a practical matter, how can a police officer distinguish curtilage from open fields? In *Dunn v. United States*, the Supreme Court listed four factors that are to be considered (*United States v. Dunn*, 480 U.S. 294 [1987]):

- *Distance.* Whether the area is distant or close to the area of the home.
- *Enclosure.* Whether the area is within an enclosure surrounding the home. — *Fence*

- *Function.* Whether the area is used for activities that normally are part of the home activities. → used for BBQ
- *Protection.* Whether an effort is made to protect the area from observation. → huge fence

These are general guidelines. The essential question is whether the area is "so intimately tied to the house itself" that it should be accorded Fourth Amendment protection. One federal judge accurately described the division between curtilage and open fields as an "imaginary boundary line between privacy and accessibility to the public" (*United States v. Redmon*, 138 F.3d 1109, 1112 [7th Cir. 1998]).

In *Dunn*, the U.S. Supreme Court held that a barn was part of open fields rather than the curtilage and that the federal officer who discovered a crystal meth laboratory did not require a search warrant to look into the barn. The barn was outside the fence surrounding the home and was fifty yards from the fence and sixty yards from the house, and Ronald Dunn had not taken sufficient steps to protect the inside of the barn from observation. Aerial photographs and chemical odors from the barn indicated that it was not being used for intimate activities associated with the home.

A number of state supreme courts, including those of Mississippi, Montana, New York, Tennessee, Vermont, and Washington, have interpreted their state constitutions to provide protection for open fields in those instances in which signs and fencing indicate that an individual possesses an expectation of privacy. These state courts have explained that the central question is whether an individual's expectation of privacy is reasonable rather than whether the land is separate and apart from the home or curtilage or whether the land is used for "intimate activities" associated with the home.

Which approach do you believe makes more sense? Does it make sense that individuals lack a reasonable expectation of privacy in land that they own?

must be @ lawfully regulated height ⟩ *drone → questionable*

■ CURTILAGE AND AERIAL SURVEILLANCE

Curtilage is viewed as part of the home and has a high expectation of privacy. The general rule is that a warrant is required for a search of the home and the curtilage. However, in this section, we shall see that the curtilage does not receive the same degree of protection as the home itself. The U.S. Supreme Court held, in the two cases discussed below, that the warrantless, aerial surveillance of the curtilage does not violate an individual's expectation of privacy.

In *California v. Ciraolo*, the police received information from an informant that Dante Carlo Ciraolo was growing marijuana in his backyard. Ciraolo had surrounded his yard with a six-foot outer fence and a ten-foot inner fence that prevented the police from investigating the tip. The police refused to be discouraged; two trained narcotics investigators flew a plane within navigable airspace at one thousand feet, observed marijuana plants in Ciraolo's backyard, took a photograph, obtained a search warrant, and seized the plants. Ciraolo claimed that the police had violated his reasonable expectation of privacy.

The U.S. Supreme Court held that in an age in which air travel is "routine," it is unreasonable for Ciraolo to expect that his marijuana plants are constitutionally protected from plain view observation with the naked eye from an altitude of one thousand feet. Ciraolo did not possess a reasonable expectation of privacy, and the police officers were not required to obtain a warrant to conduct aerial surveillance (*California v. Ciraolo*, 476 U.S. 207, 215 [1986]).

The Supreme Court's holding in *Ciraolo* was relied on as precedent by the Supreme Court in *Florida v. Riley*. The police were unable to verify an informant's tip from the street that Michael A. Riley was growing marijuana in the greenhouse ten to twenty feet behind his mobile home. Two of the four sides of the greenhouse were enclosed, and the top of the greenhouse was partially covered by corrugated roofing panels. An officer circled over the greenhouse in a helicopter flying at four hundred feet and was able to see through a slit in the roof and through the open sides of the greenhouse; he identified what he believed were marijuana plants. The officer obtained a warrant, and a search of the greenhouse resulted in the seizure of marijuana plants. The Supreme Court stressed that the helicopter was flying at a legal altitude, and the Court found "nothing" to "suggest that helicopters flying at 400 feet are sufficiently rare in this country to lend substance to respondent's claim that he reasonably anticipated that his greenhouse would not be subject to observation from that altitude" (*Florida v. Riley*, 488 U.S. 445, 452 [1989]).

Dow Chemical Company v. United States is a third case involving aerial surveillance. Although it involved an industrial plant, the case is significant for its discussion of visual enhancement technology. In *Dow*, the Environmental Protection Agency relied on aerial surveillance using a standard precision aerial camera to determine whether Dow's two-thousand-acre chemical plant was in compliance with governmental regulations. The Supreme Court held that the "mere fact that human vision is enhanced somewhat, at least to the degree here, does not give rise to constitutional problems." In other words, the camera only clarified what was already visible to the naked eye. Keep in mind that the Supreme Court noted that Dow's plant fell somewhere in between open fields and curtilage and did not deserve the same expectation of privacy as the home (*Dow Chemical Company v. United States*, 476 U.S. 227, 238–239 [1986]).

In summary, the Supreme Court held that despite the fact that curtilage is part of the home and despite efforts to insulate the curtilage from plain view, the curtilage has no expectation of privacy from aerial surveillance, even, it appears, as in *Dow*, where the surveillance is assisted by technology. Do you agree with the Supreme Court's judgments on aerial surveillance? Could Ciraolo and Riley reasonably have anticipated that their curtilage would be subject to aerial surveillance? Would a ruling that warrantless aerial surveillance of the curtilage violates individuals' Fourth Amendment rights handcuff the police? Keep in mind that although aerial surveillance may result in the detection of contraband, the police still require a warrant to enter the curtilage and seize the contraband or other evidence.

In *State v. Bryant*, the Vermont Supreme Court held that aerial surveillance of the cartilage violates an individual's reasonable expectation of privacy under the Vermont Constitution (*State v. Bryant*, 950 A.2d 467 [Vt. 2008]).

> *heat/thermal imaging—can't do without search warrant* => *need warrant for heat*

TECHNOLOGY AND SEARCHES AND SEIZURES

Search warrants and arrest warrants generally are required to enter into the home, which has the highest expectation of privacy. In *Kyllo v. United States*, the U.S. Supreme Court confronted the question of whether the police may employ a thermal-imaging device without a warrant to measure the heat emanating from a home. The theory behind the use of thermal imaging is that an unusually high degree of warmth provides probable cause that heat lamps are being used inside the home to grow marijuana.

As we have seen, the Supreme Court has upheld the employment of recording devices, aerial overflights, and photographic technology to enhance surveillance. In the decades to come, we are likely to see new and even more powerful technological techniques of criminal investigation. The Supreme Court has adopted two general rules in regard to police reliance on technology:

- *Plain view.* Technology may be used without a search warrant to enhance observation of an area or object already in plain view (open fields, curtilage).

- *Home.* The physical structure of the home possesses a high expectation of privacy. Technology may not be used without a warrant founded on probable cause to engage in the surveillance of the interior of the home in order to detect activity that otherwise would not be revealed without physically entering the home.

An example of the use of technology to enhance surveillance of an object in plain view is *Texas v. Brown*. In *Brown*, the Supreme Court ruled that the use of a flashlight to "illuminate a darkened area" in the interior of an automobile does not constitute a Fourth Amendment search (*Texas v. Brown*, 460 U.S. 730 [1983]). In another example, the Supreme Court upheld the use of a beeper installed in a five-gallon drum of chloroform to track the movements of an automobile driven by a suspect in an illegal narcotics ring. The Court reasoned that the defendant's movements on the public roadways also were being tracked through aerial surveillance and that the beeper revealed no information that was not already available to the general public or to the police. The Supreme Court observed that "nothing in the Fourth Amendment prohibit[s] the police from augmenting the sensory faculties bestowed upon them at birth with such enhancement as science and technology afforded them in this case" (*United States v. Knotts*, 460 U.S. 276 [1983]) (Rule 1).

On the other hand, the Supreme Court drew the line at continuing to electronically monitor a beeper in a can of ether once the can was taken into a home. The purpose was to verify that the can remained inside a home thought to be the site of an illegal narcotics laboratory while the police obtained a search warrant. The Court reasoned that the government may not physically enter the home (without a warrant) to ensure that the ether is inside, and the result is the same where the government secretly "employs an electronic device to obtain information that it could not have obtained by observation from outside the . . . house" (*United States v. Karo*, 468 U.S. 705 [1984]) (Rule 2).

GPS device – installing a device you NEED a warrant.

In 2001, in *Kyllo v. United States*, the U.S. Supreme Court was asked to rule on whether the warrantless use of a thermal-imaging device to measure infrared radiation that emanates from a house constitutes a search. The scan from the device, when combined with other information, provided probable cause to support a warrant to search Danny Lee Kyllo's home, and the search resulted in the seizure of more than one hundred marijuana plants. Justice Antonin Scalia held that the Fourth Amendment draws "'a firm line at the entrance to the house.' . . . Where, as here, the Government uses a device that is not in general public use, to explore details of the home that would previously have been unknowable without physical intrusion, the surveillance is a 'search' and is presumptively unreasonable without a warrant" (*Kyllo v. United States*, 533 U.S. 27 [2001]).

In 2012 in *United States v. Jones*, the U.S. Supreme Court addressed the constitutionality of the warrantless attachment of a global positioning system (GPS) tracking device to Antoine Jones's car for the purpose of monitoring the movement of his vehicle on a public street. Jones claimed that his reasonable expectation of privacy had been violated by the warrantless twenty-eight-day surveillance of his movements.

Justice Scalia writing in a 5-4 decision held that the government's physical trespass and installation of a GPS device on Jones's vehicle for the purpose of obtaining information constituted a "search." He concluded that the government had "improperly physically intruded on a constitutionally protected area by affixing the GPS to Jones'[s] vehicle." Justice Scalia wrote that "[w]e have no doubt that such a physical intrusion would have been considered a 'search' within the meaning of the Fourth Amendment when it was adopted." As a result, Justice Scalia observed that there was no need to resolve whether Jones's expectation of privacy had been violated.

A four-judge concurring opinion written by Justice Samuel Alito relied on a privacy-based approach. Justice Alito concluded that "the use of long term GPS monitoring in investigations of most offenses impinges on expectations of privacy." In the case of narcotics crimes, "society's expectation has been that law enforcement agents and others would not—and indeed, in the main, simply could not—secretly monitor and catalogue every single movement of an individual's car for a very long period." He noted that there may be "extraordinary offenses" justifying reliance on long-term tracking (*United States v. Jones*, 565 U.S. ___ [2012]).

CRIMINAL EVIDENCE AND PUBLIC POLICY

Law enforcement increasingly is employing dogs to detect whether narcotics and explosives are being carried into subways, airports, and train stations. Dogs also are used to detect prohibited foods, plants, and fruits that are brought into the United States and to uncover land mines in war zones; it is even claimed that some dogs are able to detect cancer in patients. Dogs are currently employed at over seventy-three ports of entry into the United States and are described as much more efficient than humans in detecting contraband in vehicles and large shipping containers.

You might have wondered whether the Fourth Amendment permits the use of dogs to "search" for contraband. In 1983 in *United States v. Place* (462 U.S. 696), Drug Enforcement Administration officers at Miami International Airport tipped off agents at New York's LaGuardia Airport that their suspicions had been aroused by passenger Raymond Place. Agents in New York monitored Place's movements at LaGuardia and also found his behavior suspicious. The agents approached Place and informed him that they suspected that he was carrying narcotics. Place refused to consent to a search of his baggage, and the agents removed the bags to John F. Kennedy International Airport where a trained narcotics dog indicated that one of the bags contained unlawful narcotics. Based on the dog's reaction, a federal magistrate issued a search warrant, and the agents discovered 1,125 grams of cocaine in the bag. Place appealed and argued that the dog sniff constituted an unlawful, warrantless search of his luggage and that the resulting search warrant had been based on evidence that had been obtained in an unconstitutional search of his bag.

The U.S. Supreme Court held that a canine sniff is "one of a kind." The Court was aware of no other investigative procedure that is so "limited" both in the manner in which the information is obtained and in the "content" of the information revealed. The sniff discloses only the presence or absence of narcotics and does not require agents to search through a suspect's belongings. The Supreme Court accordingly ruled that the exposure of luggage to a trained narcotics dog does not constitute a "search" within the meaning of the Fourth Amendment. Subsequently, in 2005, in *Illinois v. Caballes*, the Supreme Court held that the use of a narcotics dog during a lawful traffic stop does not infringe on the driver's Fourth Amendment rights (543 U.S. 405).

In summary, *Place* and *Caballes* stand for the proposition that law enforcement personnel are not required to obtain a warrant based on probable cause to use dogs to search containers, automobiles, and other property, because dog sniffs are not a Fourth Amendment search. Federal and state courts remain divided over whether dogs may be lawfully employed without a warrant to search persons.

Law enforcement as a result is relatively free to employ trained narcotics and bomb sniffing dogs. The Transportation Security Administration is spending roughly $2.7 million to train and certify roughly thirty German Shepherds, Belgian Malinois, and Labrador Retrievers and their handlers for explosive detection in the nation's subways. Dogs' noses have been estimated to be between one hundred and ten thousand times more sensitive than the human nose, depending on the scent. They are able to detect small amounts of certain substances and are able to single out a specific substance even when it is surrounded by other odors.

Despite the deserved praise and regard for our canine friends, some law enforcement officers have noted that dogs are not quite as effective as we might want to believe. In his dissent in *Caballes*, Justice David Souter noted that the "infallible" dog is largely a "legal fiction." He noted that errors by handlers and dogs combined to create a rate of false positives in artificial testing situations of between 12.5 and 60 percent. The most comprehensive study of the accuracy of dogs was undertaken in the Australian state of New South Wales, where Sydney is located. A study of the use of trained narcotics dogs over a two-year period by the New South Wales Ombudsman found that drug dogs are accurate between 25 and 30 percent of the time. Only slightly more than 1 percent of the "positive sniffs" resulted in the seizure of a significant amount of marijuana ("one in every 526 positive sniffs"). In most instances, the police uncovered a small amount of drugs to be used for personal use. The Ombudsman concluded that there is "little evidence" to support the argument that drug detection dogs "deter drug use, reduce drug-related crime or increase perceptions of public safety. Further, criticisms of the cost-effectiveness of general drug detection operations appear well-founded." In other words, most people stopped in New South Wales either were completely innocent or possessed only small amounts of drugs.

The Supreme Court responded to these criticisms in *Florida v. Harris* in 2013. Aldo conducted a "free air sniff" and alerted the officer whose search of the car led to the seizure of a chemical precursor for methamphetamine (pseudoephedrine pills) in the car on which the dog was not trained. On another occasion, the dog falsely indicated the same automobile contained narcotics. The U.S. Supreme Court held that a dog's reliability should be evaluated based on evidence of a dog's satisfactory performance in a certification program conducted by a bona fide organization or by the dog's performance on a training program in a controlled setting. The Court noted that the dog's actual field performance may be given some weight although the Court stressed that an officer may not be aware that the dog failed to find narcotics in the car and a "false alert" may be accurate because the drugs were either removed from the car or too well hidden to be located (*Florida v. Harris*, 568 U.S. ___ [2013]). The Court also avoided answering whether a dog may be used to search a home without a warrant by holding that the police were not legally entitled to enter a defendant's porch with a trained narcotics dog who indicated there were narcotics in the home (*Florida v. Jardines*, 569 U.S. ___ [2013]).

There are several explanations as to why dogs may not be as useful as we have been led to believe:

Training. There are instances in which trainers have falsely represented the capacity of dogs that they have sold to governmental agencies. Dogs also typically are trained for specific chemicals and are unable to detect other compounds. There are some explosives that are so unstable and so likely to ignite that dogs cannot be trained to detect them.

Effectiveness. Dogs may indicate the presence of a chemical when an individual is not actually in possession of a prohibited substance but has indirectly come in contact with a narcotic or explosive. In their desire to please their handler and to receive a reward, dogs may respond to a smell that is similar to one that they have been trained to detect. Dogs function at a high level in a quiet and contained environment. They can become distracted and confused by noise and people.

Fatigue. Dogs are no different from other creatures. They are likely to grow bored and tired and typically are in need of rest after thirty minutes of intense work.

The Russians claim to have overcome the weakness of existing breeds by creating the Sulimov, which is a combination of reindeer herding hound, fox terrier, and spitz dog. Forty Sulimovs are currently employed in Russian airports, and it is claimed that these dogs are able to detect twelve different chemical components that are used in explosives.

In the coming years, efforts likely will be made to replace dogs with a new generation of more accurate technology. We nevertheless likely will see continuing efforts to harness the unique abilities of animals to counter crime. Some researchers have claimed that nonstinging wasps encapsulated in a plastic container and connected to a laptop computer have proven to be easily trained and highly accurate.

> fine in public places, businesses → need warrant to go into the

■ PUBLIC PLACES AND PRIVATE BUSINESSES back — employee only places.

The police may seize items that they observe in public places, streets, parks, and monuments. Public places also include private businesses that are open to the public. A search warrant is required for the police to enter portions of a business that are not open to the public, such as employee-only work areas and employee offices. In *Maryland v. Macon*, a nonuniformed police detective entered a store and paid for a magazine. He later returned and arrested the clerk for distributing obscene material. The U.S. Supreme Court held that the officer's entering the bookstore and examining the material that was "intentionally exposed to all who frequent the place of business did not infringe a legitimate expectation of privacy and hence did not constitute a search within the meaning of the Fourth Amendment" (*Maryland v. Macon*, 472 U.S. 463, 469 [1985]).

throw gun on roof while running → you have abandoned that property. → throwing things out of the car while the police are chasing you.

■ ABANDONED PROPERTY

Abandoned property is the last type of property that we will discuss. Abandoned property is property that an individual intends to abandon and physically abandons. An individual has no expectation of privacy in abandoned property, and the property has no Fourth Amendment protection. As a result, the police are not required to obtain a warrant to examine and take control of the property. Property typically does not carry a sign indicating that it is abandoned. Judges rely on the totality of the circumstances and consider where the property is found, the condition of the property, and the type of property along with other factors. For example, an old and worn-out suitcase found in a Dumpster clearly has been abandoned. A different conclusion might be reached if the bag is a new and very expensive leather purse that reportedly has been stolen.

In most instances, the question whether property is abandoned is straightforward. In *Hester v. United States*, Charlie Hester fled from government revenue agents and dropped a jug and a jar, and an agent later uncovered a bottle; all three containers held unlawfully manufactured moonshine whiskey. The Supreme Court ruled that the containers had been abandoned and lacked an expectation of privacy and that there had been no Fourth Amendment seizure (*Hester v. United States*, 265 U.S. 57, 58 [1924]). In *Abel v. United States*, the petitioner was found to have voluntarily abandoned items that he left behind in the trash can of his hotel room, and the Supreme Court held that there was "nothing unlawful in the Government's appropriation of such abandoned property" (*Abel v. United States*, 362 U.S. 217, 241 [1960]).

In another case, *California v. Greenwood*, the U.S. Supreme Court was asked to decide whether the petitioners retained an expectation of privacy in sealed garbage bags that a local ordinance required to be placed on the side

PHOTO 12.1

The Supreme Court has held that individuals have no expectation of privacy in trash and the police may search garbage without a warrant founded on probable cause.

AP Photo/Tony Dejak

of the road outside of the curtilage. The police received information that Billy Greenwood was linked to drug trafficking and asked the regular trash collector to pick up the garbage bags that Greenwood had left on the curb in front of his house and to turn the contents over to the police. On two occasions, the police recovered narcotics paraphernalia from Greenwood's garbage; these provided the basis to obtain search warrants for the home, and the search resulted in the seizure of unlawful narcotics. The petitioners moved to suppress the introduction of the narcotics at trial based on the fact that they retained an expectation of privacy in the trash. They argued that their expectation was that the garbage collector would pick up and mingle the trash with other garbage and deposit the debris in the garbage dump. It was not anticipated that the trash would be turned over to the police and examined.

totality of circumstance:
- where was it found
- condition of property
- what is it?

Garbage reveals the most intimate aspects of an individual's life, and most people do not expect that it will be examined by the police. On the other hand, garbage that is left at the curb arguably has been abandoned and may be examined by anyone who happens to walk down the street. Consider whether the police should be required to obtain a search warrant to search and seize material from the trash. The Supreme Court held that the defendant had no expectation of privacy in the garbage that he had left on the side of the road to be picked up by the trash collection company. In addition to turning the garbage over to a third party, the Court noted that garbage left on the side of the road is "readily accessible to animals, children, scavengers, snoops, and other members of the public" (*California v. Greenwood*, 486 U.S. 35 [1988]). The supreme courts of Hawaii, New Hampshire, New Jersey, Vermont, and Washington all have interpreted their state constitutions to provide an expectation of privacy in garbage.

garbage on curb → not yours

garbage in can in garage - still yours

12.2 YOU DECIDE

Alan Scott was suspected by the Internal Revenue Service (IRS) of involvement in a plan to defraud the government through the filing of false income tax returns. IRS agents seized garbage bags from the front of Scott's home. They discovered various shredded documents. The agents methodically reconstructed the documents, which provided the probable cause required to obtain a search warrant. The warrant resulted in the search and seizure of additional documents that formed the basis of a forty-seven-count indictment. Scott moved to suppress the reconstructed documents. As a judge, how would you rule in this case? See *United States v. Scott* (975 F.2d 927 [1st Cir. 1992]).

You can learn what the court decided by referring to the study site, **http://study.sagepub.com/lippmance.**

12.3 YOU DECIDE

The Saint Paul, Minnesota, police observed suspicious activity by Benjamin Carter at the storage units he rented at Secure Mini Storage. A drug-detection dog conducted a "sniff" outside Carter's storage units within a fenced self-storage facility. The dog entered with the permission of the facility's management and indicated that a controlled substance was stored within one of the units. The Saint Paul police obtained a warrant for Carter's storage unit and home. The warrant application alleged that Carter and his brother were gang members with prior arrests for drugs and unlawful possession of a firearm.

The police executed the warrants and seized cocaine at Carter's home and two firearms, ammunition, and a nylon bag containing a stocking cap at the storage unit. Carter was charged with illegal possession of a firearm and filed a motion to suppress the firearm seized from the storage locker.

The Minnesota Supreme Court addressed whether a warrantless "dog sniff" outside a storage facility is a search within the meaning of the Fourth Amendment. What is your view? See *State v. Carter* (697 N.W.2d 199 [Minn. 2005]).

You can learn what the court decided by referring to the study site, **http://study.sagepub.com/lippmance.**

Table 12.1 ■ Expectations of Privacy and Police Fourth Amendment Searches	
Expectation of Privacy/Search	**No Expectation of Privacy/No Search**
Electronic surveillance of a phone conversation	Eavesdropping on a conversation
Opening luggage	Entry onto farmland
Entering a home	Aerial surveillance of a backyard
Opening and reading a private diary	Examination of trash in a Dumpster

CRIMINAL EVIDENCE IN THE NEWS

Michael Robertson, 31 years of age, was arrested in Massachusetts under a "Peeping Tom" law for taking photos under the skirt of a woman. Robertson contended that his "upskirt" photos of women on the subway in 2010 did not violate the state statute.

(Continued)

(Continued)

In 2013, the Massachusetts Supreme Judicial Court in *Commonwealth v. Robertson* held that the law only applied to people photographed unknowingly who are either "nude or partially nude" in locations like dressing rooms where individuals possess a reasonable expectation of privacy. "Partially nude" according to the Massachusetts Supreme Judicial Court means a person who is "partially clothed but who has one or more of the private parts of body exposed in plain view at the time that the . . . defendant secretly photographed her." A female passenger on the subway "who is wearing a skirt, dress, or the like covering these parts of her body is not a person who is 'partially nude,' no matter what is or is not underneath the skirt by way of underwear or other clothing."

The Massachusetts Supreme Judicial Court also reasoned that because the photographs were taken on a "public transit system operating in a public place" that "uses cameras," the two alleged victims . . . were not in a place and circumstance where they reasonably would or could have had an expectation of privacy."

Following the court's decision, the Massachusetts legislature passed a law stating that anyone who "photographs, videotapes or electronically surveils" another person's sexual or intimate parts without consent is guilty of a misdemeanor carrying two-and-a-half years in jail and a $5,000 fine. Photographing a child under 18 is a felony carrying a maximum penalty of five years in prison and a $10,000 fine. Distribution of such photos is punishable by a maximum penalty of ten years in prison and a $10,000 fine.

Arizona, Illinois, Washington, and Hawaii have laws specifically penalizing "upskirt" photos. The Video Voyeurism Prevention Act of 2004 (18 U.S.C. § 1801) criminalizes "upskirt" photos on federal property. The law punishes an individual who "has the intent to capture an image of a private area of an individual without their consent, and knowingly does so under circumstances in which the individual has a reasonable expectation of privacy, shall be fined under this title or imprisoned not more than one year, or both."

■ SEIZURES OF PERSONS

The drafters of the U.S. Constitution were concerned with protecting persons as well as their houses, papers, and effects from unreasonable searches and seizures. A Fourth Amendment seizure occurs when a law enforcement officer detains an individual and restricts his or her freedom of movement. You may want to consult Table 12.2 as you read this section to help you understand the material.

Table 12.2 The Fourth Amendment and Searches and Seizures of Persons

Standard of Justification	Requirements	Scope of Search
Probable cause	Reasonable person would conclude that individual has committed a crime	Full body search for weapons/evidence
Reasonable suspicion	Reasonable person would believe that a crime has been or is about to be committed	Frisk for weapons
Encounter	No justification required	None/may ask for consent

The U.S. Constitution is intended to promote individual freedom and limits that freedom only to the extent required to protect the safety and security of society. Fourth Amendment seizures follow a simple formula that we will develop in detail in the next few chapters. The greater the interference with an individual's freedom, the greater the factual burden that must be satisfied by the police to justify the stop. An arrest of an individual that may result in the person's being taken into custody, and the accompanying search incident to an arrest for weapons or contraband, requires probable cause. In contrast, a brief investigative stop of an individual may be based on the less demanding standard of reasonable suspicion and permits only the protective frisk of an individual's outer clothing for weapons.

The Supreme Court has recognized a third category of police–citizen interactions that law professors refer to as **encounters**. These are non-coercive and voluntary contacts between the police and citizens that are not regulated by the Fourth Amendment. The Court has observed that not all street contacts between citizens and the police constitute a seizure. There are any number of casual interactions on the street, in a park, or in a restaurant that do not restrain an individual's freedom of movement. The Supreme Court has stressed that the police should be free to carry out investigations by briefly questioning individuals in public about suspected criminal activity. In *United States v. Mendenhall*, the Court observed that "characterizing every street encounter between a citizen and the police as a 'seizure' . . . would impose wholly unrealistic restrictions upon a wide variety of legitimate law enforcement practices" (*United States v. Mendenhall*, 446 U.S. 544, 554 [1980]).

Courts analyze the totality of the circumstances to distinguish a **seizure** from an encounter. The distinction at times can be unclear. Consider whether Sylvia Mendenhall's interaction with federal agents was a seizure or an encounter. In *United States v. Mendenhall*, two federal drug agents approached Mendenhall in the concourse of the airport in Detroit. They identified themselves and asked to examine her driver's license and airline ticket. The ticket was issued in the name of "Annette Ford." The agents noticed that Mendenhall appeared "shaken" and "nervous" and had difficulty speaking. The agents returned Mendenhall's identification and ticket, and she agreed to accompany them to an office fifty feet from where they were standing. Once inside the office, she consented to a body search, which resulted in the seizure of heroin.

The Supreme Court held that this was not a Fourth Amendment seizure. As a result, the officers were not required to establish either probable cause (as would be required if they were to arrest her) or reasonable suspicion (as would be required to stop and frisk her) to justify their decision to approach Mendenhall. Mendenhall had not been seized

> simply by reason of the fact that the agents approached her, asked her if she would show them her ticket and identification and posed a few questions. Otherwise inoffensive contact between a member of the public and the police cannot, as a matter of law, amount to a seizure of that person.

Examples of circumstances that might indicate a seizure would be the

> threatening presence of several officers, the display of a weapon by an officer, some physical touching . . . or the use of language or tone of voice indicating that compliance might be compelled.

The fact that the agents returned Mendenhall's identification and ticket before asking her to accompany them to the office likely was a central consideration in the Supreme Court's analysis.

The lesson is that the police must remain aware of the distinction between seizures and encounters. Note that the federal agents had no firm facts to justify approaching Mendenhall and that if the Supreme Court had ruled that their interaction with Mendenhall constituted a seizure, this would have meant that she had been unlawfully detained, and the drugs would have been inadmissible as the "fruit" of her illegal seizure (*United States v. Mendenhall*, 446 U.S. 544, 553 [1980]).

The recognition that not every contact between a police officer and a citizen is a seizure is consistent with the recommendation of the American Law Institute's *Model Code of Pre-Arraignment Procedure*, which in Section 110.1 provides that a law enforcement officer may request an individual to voluntarily

> respond to questions, to appear at a police station, or to comply with any other reasonable request . . . [and that c]ompliance with the request . . . shall not be regarded as involuntary or coerced solely on the ground that such a request was made by a law enforcement officer.

When is an individual seized under the Fourth Amendment? There are two types of seizures: a **physical seizure** of a suspect, and a **show of authority seizure** in which police officers restrain individuals through the display of official authority without the use of actual physical force. Remember that a seizure requires a showing of either probable cause or reasonable suspicion.

- *Physical seizures.* A law enforcement officer intentionally takes physical hold of a suspect with the intent to prevent the individual from leaving. →not free to leave
- *Show of authority seizures.* Law enforcement officers demonstrate their authority by directing an individual to halt, displaying their weapons, blocking the suspect's movement, or other conduct that would lead a reasonable person not to feel free to leave or otherwise to terminate the encounter. The suspect must actually submit to the demonstration of authority.
→show weapons and say "stop"—— if you run and get away you're not seized

In summary, an individual is seized once he or she is physically restrained or once a law enforcement officer acts in a way that would result in a reasonable person not feeling free to leave or to terminate the encounter. In the latter case, the individual must actually submit to the officer's demonstration of authority. As noted, the distinction between a seizure and an encounter is not always crystal clear. Consider the following cases in which the Supreme Court has held that there was no Fourth Amendment seizure.

Factory sweeps. Immigration and Naturalization Service agents carrying walkie-talkies entered a plant, blocked the exits, and asked workers questions regarding their legal status. The sweep lasted between one and two hours. The Supreme Court noted that the workers were free to move around the plant and that their freedom of movement was restricted by their voluntary commitment to their job rather than by the federal agents (*Immigration and Naturalization Service v. Delgado*, 466 U.S. 210 [1984]).

Bus sweeps. Two sheriff's deputies, one of whom was openly armed, boarded a crowded interstate bus during a stop to pick up passengers and approached Terrance Bostick, who was sitting in the back of the bus. The agents asked Bostick a few questions and requested permission to search his luggage. They did not threaten him or display their weapons. Bostick consented, and the search revealed illegal narcotics. The Supreme Court held that the question, in light of the totality of the circumstances, was whether a reasonable (innocent) person would feel free to decline the officer's request or otherwise terminate the encounter (*Florida v. Bostick*, 501 U.S. 429 [1991]). See also *United States v. Drayton* (536 U.S. 194 [2002]).

Vehicle surveillance. Four officers in a squad car observed a man exit his automobile and approach Michael Chesternut. Chesternut appeared surprised to see the squad car and fled. The officers accelerated and drove alongside Chesternut for a short distance. The officers observed Chesternut discard four packages; one of the officers discovered that these contained unlawful narcotics. The officers did not activate the siren or flashers on their squad car, display weapons, or block Chesternut's movements. The Supreme Court held that Chesternut could not have reasonably concluded that the officers' "mere presence was so intimidating that the particular police conduct as a whole and within the setting of all of the surrounding circumstances" had "in some way restrained his liberty so that he was not free to leave" (*Michigan v. Chesternut*, 486 U.S. 567 [1988]).

California v. Hodari established the legal test for a Fourth Amendment show of force seizure. Four or five juveniles fled as they saw an unmarked police car approach. Officer Jerry Pertoso gave chase, and Hodari D. claimed that he did not see Pertoso until "he saw Officer Pertoso running towards him." Hodari immediately tossed away what appeared to be a small rock of crack cocaine and was tackled, handcuffed, and arrested. Hodari claimed that Officer Pertoso engaged in an unreasonable seizure (lacking reasonable suspicion or probable cause) when he confronted Hodari and that the narcotics should be excluded from evidence as the fruit of the unlawful seizure. The government, on the other hand, argued that Hodari abandoned the drugs and that this provided probable cause to tackle and to seize (arrest) Hodari. In other words, the government's theory was that it was only when Hodari was tackled that he was seized by the officer.

The United States Supreme Court held that Hodari was not seized until physically subdued by Officer Pertoso. "Assuming that Pertoso's pursuit in the present case constituted a show of authority enjoining Hodari to halt, because Hodari did not comply with that injunction, he was not seized until he was tackled. The cocaine abandoned while he was running was in this case not the fruit of a seizure, and his motion to exclude evidence of it was properly denied" (*California v. Hodari*, 499 U.S. 821 [1999]).

12.4 YOU DECIDE

Four Buffalo, New York, police officers were patrolling in an unmarked car on June 11, 2002, in search of Kenneth Foster-Brown, who was wanted for dealing drugs. All four officers had encountered Foster-Brown in the past. He was described as an African American male who was five feet, eight inches tall and who weighed 145 pounds. Defendant Swazine Swindle also is an African American and is six feet, one inch tall and at the time weighed 215 pounds.

The officers observed a black Pontiac Bonneville, a type of car that Foster-Brown had previously been seen "near," but had never been known to drive. The officers observed the automobile halting in front of a known drug house that Foster-Brown had frequented in the past. The officers watched an African American male exit the Bonneville, enter the house, leave a short time later, and drive away. The officers were uncertain whether the driver was Foster-Brown.

In fact, the man in the Bonneville was Swindle. The officers followed in their car, and within a minute activated their police lights and ordered Swindle to pull over. Swindle disregarded the order to stop and kept driving. While being pursued, Swindle violated two traffic laws by crossing a double yellow lane divider and driving the wrong way on a one-way street. Swindle also threw a plastic bag out of the car window. The bag was found to contain thirty-three smaller bags of crack cocaine. Swindle eventually pulled over and then fled on foot. The police apprehended him and placed him under arrest. He was charged with unlawful possession of a controlled substance.

At what point was Swindle seized? Why is it significant when Swindle was seized? See *United States v. Swindle* (407 F.3d 562 [2nd Cir. 2005]).

You can learn what the court decided by referring to the study site, **http://study.sagepub.com/lippmance.**

12.5 YOU DECIDE

Police Officers Nowell and Ashe responded to dispatcher's report that an informant had observed an individual with a gun at 1009 West Seventh Street in Wilmington, Delaware. The officers saw three women and two men on the porch at the address on West Seventh Street. Officer Ashe approached and positioned herself eight to ten feet from the residence while Officer Nowell approached the home. Ashe took the precaution of ordering the individuals on the porch to place their hands over their heads. They all complied with the exception of Christopher Waterman who kept his hands in his jacket pocket. Ashe and Nowell drew their weapons and repeatedly ordered the defendant to put his hands in the air. Waterman did not respond and unsuccessfully tried to open the front door. The door suddenly opened, and Waterman entered the residence.

The police followed Waterman into the residence and seized a firearm and narcotics. A federal district court held that the police officers did not have reasonable suspicion to seize the five individuals on the porch and that the seizure of the contraband in the home had resulted from an unlawful search and seizure.

The Third Circuit Court of Appeals was asked to decide whether Waterman had been seized by the police officers. How should the Court of Appeals rule based on the precedent in *California v. Hodari*? Would the firearm and narcotics be admissible if Waterman had not been seized on the porch? See *United States v. Waterman* (569 F.3d 144 [3rd Cir. 2009]).

You can learn what the court decided by referring to the study site, **http://study.sagepub.com/lippmance.**

■ CASE ANALYSIS

In *Florida v. Riley*, the Supreme Court decided whether aerial surveillance of the curtilage violates an individual's right to privacy under the Fourth Amendment.

Did Riley have a reasonable expectation of privacy to be free from aerial surveillance?

Florida v. Riley, 488 U.S. 445 (1989), White, J.

Respondent [Michael A.] Riley lived in a mobile home located on five acres of rural property. A greenhouse was located 10 to 20 feet behind the mobile home. Two sides of the greenhouse were enclosed. The other two sides were not enclosed but the contents of the greenhouse were obscured from view from surrounding property by trees, shrubs, and the mobile home. The greenhouse

(Continued)

was covered by corrugated roofing panels, some translucent and some opaque. At the time relevant to this case, two of the panels, amounting to approximately 10% of the roof area, were missing. A wire fence surrounded the mobile home and the greenhouse, and the property was posted with a "DO NOT ENTER" sign.

This case originated with an anonymous tip to the Pasco County Sheriff's office that marijuana was being grown on respondent's property. When an investigating officer discovered that he could not see the contents of the greenhouse from the road, he circled twice over respondent's property in a helicopter at the height of 400 feet. With his naked eye, he was able to see through the openings in the roof and one or more of the open sides of the greenhouse and to identify what he thought was marijuana growing in the structure. A warrant was obtained based on these observations, and the ensuing search revealed marijuana growing in the greenhouse. Respondent was charged with possession of marijuana under Florida law. The trial court granted his motion to suppress; the Florida Court of Appeals reversed but certified the case to the Florida Supreme Court, which quashed the decision of the Court of Appeals and reinstated the trial court's suppression order. . . .

We arrive at the same conclusion in the present case. In this case, as in *Ciraolo*, the property surveyed was within the curtilage of respondent's home. Riley no doubt intended and expected that his greenhouse would not be open to public inspection, and the precautions he took protected against ground-level observation. Because the sides and roof of his greenhouse were left partially open, however, what was growing in the greenhouse was subject to viewing from the air. Under the holding in *Ciraolo*, Riley could not reasonably have expected the contents of his greenhouse to be immune from examination by an officer seated in a fixed-wing aircraft flying in navigable airspace at an altitude of 1,000 feet or, as the Florida Supreme Court seemed to recognize, at an altitude of 500 feet, the lower limit of the navigable airspace for such an aircraft. Here, the inspection was made from a helicopter, but as

is the case with fixed-wing planes, "private and commercial flight [by helicopter] in the public airways is routine" in this country, and there is no indication that such flights are unheard of in Pasco County, Florida. Riley could not reasonably have expected that his greenhouse was protected from public or official observation from a helicopter had it been flying within the navigable airspace for fixed-wing aircraft.

Nor on the facts before us, does it make a difference for Fourth Amendment purposes that the helicopter was flying at 400 feet when the officer saw what was growing in the greenhouse through the partially open roof and sides of the structure. We would have a different case if flying at that altitude had been contrary to law or regulation. But helicopters are not bound by the lower limits of the navigable airspace allowed to other aircraft. Any member of the public could legally have been flying over Riley's property in a helicopter at the altitude of 400 feet and could have observed Riley's greenhouse. The police officer did no more. This is not to say that an inspection of the curtilage of a house from an aircraft will always pass muster under the Fourth Amendment simply because the plane is within the navigable airspace specified by law. But it is of obvious importance that the helicopter in this case was not violating the law, and there is nothing in the record or before us to suggest that helicopters flying at 400 feet are sufficiently rare in this country to lend substance to respondent's claim that he reasonably anticipated that his greenhouse would not be subject to observation from that altitude. Neither is there any intimation here that the helicopter interfered with respondent's normal use of the greenhouse or of other parts of the curtilage. As far as this record reveals, no intimate details connected with the use of the home or curtilage were observed, and there was no undue noise, and no wind, dust, or threat of injury. In these circumstances, there was no violation of the Fourth Amendment.

The judgment of the Florida Supreme Court is accordingly reversed.

CHAPTER SUMMARY

The Fourth Amendment was intended to protect individuals against the type of dragnet searches and seizures that were carried out by British colonial authorities through the use of general warrants and writs of assistance. The Fourth Amendment effectively abolishes general warrants and writs of assistance by prohibiting unreasonable searches and seizures and by providing that no warrant shall issue but upon probable cause, particularly describing the place to be searched and the person or things to be seized. The Supreme Court, while expressing a preference for warrants, has recognized that it is reasonable in certain limited circumstances for the police to conduct warrantless searches.

The Supreme Court initially adopted a property rights or trespassory approach to the Fourth Amendment. This protected individuals against physical intrusions or trespasses into their persons, houses, papers, and effects. In 1967, in *Katz v. United States*, the Supreme Court rejected a property rights or trespassory approach and adopted a privacy test for application of the Fourth Amendment. Justice Harlan in his important concurring opinion in *Katz* established the test for an expectation of privacy. The question is whether an individual exhibits a personal (subjective) expectation of privacy and whether society (objectively) recognizes this expectation as reasonable. An individual is considered to lack a reasonable expectation of privacy in those instances in which he or she turns information over to a third party or where an object or area is accessible to the public.

Commentators question whether the privacy-based approach has increased Fourth Amendment protections. For example, an individual "assumes the risk" that conversations with a government informant in and outside of the home will be overheard or recorded or transmitted to law enforcement authorities. Plain view permits the police to seize items in open fields and to conduct aerial surveillance of curtilage. There also is no expectation of privacy in public areas, in commercial businesses open to the public, or in abandoned objects and trash.

The Supreme Court did draw a firm line of protection at the home in *Kyllo v. United States*. The Court held that the government may not employ heat-sensing technology to obtain information regarding the interior of the home that could not otherwise have been obtained without physical intrusion into the dwelling.

Fourth Amendment seizures of individuals must be based on factual grounds that constitute either probable cause or reasonable suspicion. A seizure may be accomplished by a physical restraint by a show of authority. The show of authority must lead a reasonable person to believe that he or she is not free to leave or to refuse to cooperate, and the individual must actually submit to police authority. The Supreme Court has recognized that not every interaction between the police and citizens constitutes a seizure. The police may engage in informal contacts or encounters without being required to meet the probable cause or reasonable suspicion standard. This provides the police with the flexibility to engage in criminal investigations without being required to satisfy the probable cause or reasonable suspicion requirements of the Fourth Amendment. The line between an encounter and a seizure at times may be difficult to determine. The police run the risk that an encounter will be viewed by a court as constituting a seizure and that any evidence that is uncovered will be excluded on the grounds that the police unreasonably detained a suspect.

In summary, in this chapter we reviewed the requirements for a Fourth Amendment search and a Fourth Amendment seizure. The Supreme Court has struck a balance in Fourth Amendment searches and seizures between the need for the police to detect and investigate crime and individuals' expectation of privacy. Individuals have full Fourth Amendment protection in those areas, such as the home, that have an expectation of privacy that society views as reasonable. On the other hand, areas and objects in plain view do not enjoy an expectation of privacy, and the police are not required to obtain a warrant. These areas generally are accessible to the public or in the case of information or objects have been turned over to a third party. The Supreme Court requires the police to justify seizures on either probable cause or reasonable suspicion. The police, however, may engage in encounters and may question suspects so long as the suspect feels free to leave or to decline to cooperate with the police.

In the next three chapters, we discuss the requirements for a reasonable search and seizure under the Fourth Amendment. Chapter Thirteen covers reasonable suspicion "stops and frisks," Chapter Fourteen discusses probable cause and arrests, and Chapter Fifteen addresses searches and seizures of property.

CHAPTER REVIEW QUESTIONS

1. How did the use of general warrants and writs of assistance by British colonial authorities influence the drafting of the text of the Fourth Amendment?

2. Distinguish the property rights or trespassory approach to the Fourth Amendment from the expectation of privacy approach. Which in theory provides individuals with greater protection?

3. What is the legal test for the expectation of privacy established in *Katz v. United States*?

4. Define plain view "searches" and seizures. Describe the relationship between plain view and expectation of privacy.

5. Discuss the expectation of privacy in relation to pen registers, the electronic monitoring of conversations, and trash.

6. Distinguish open fields from curtilage. Why is this significant?

7. What is the importance of the Supreme Court judgment in *Kyllo v. United States*?

8. Describe the difference between physical seizures and show of authority seizures.

9. How do seizures differ from encounters? Why is this distinction significant?

10. What is the holding in *Hodari*?

LEGAL TERMINOLOGY

abandoned property

curtilage

encounters

expectation of privacy

general warrants

open fields

physical seizure

plain view

probable cause

property rights approach

search

seizure

show of authority seizure

trespassory approach

writs of assistance

REFERENCE

Dressler, Joshua, and Alan C. Michaels. 2006. *Understanding Criminal Procedure: Investigation*, vol. 1, 4th ed. New York: LexisNexis.

Visit the Student Study Site at **http://study.sagepub.com/lippmance** to access additional study tools, including mobile-friendly eFlashcards and Web quizzes as well as links to SAGE journal articles and hyperlinks for *Criminal Evidence* on the Web.

(handwritten notes)

reasonable suspicion
- what you need to search - not arrest
★seeing people casing a store ★
· Terry v. Ohio

STOP AND FRISK

Was the seizure of Weaver's bags lawful?

[Carl] Hicks testified that he took the following factors into consideration when he decided to detain [Arthur T.] Weaver's bags: (1) that Weaver got off a direct flight from Los Angeles, a source city for drugs; (2) that he was a roughly dressed young black male who might be a member of a Los Angeles street gang that had been bringing narcotics into the Kansas City area; (3) that he moved rapidly from the airplane toward a taxicab; (4) that he had two carry-on bags and no checked luggage; (5) that he had no identification on his person; (6) that he did not have a copy of his ticket; (7) that he appeared very nervous when he talked to Hicks; (8) and that he made no mention of visiting his mother until the last second before he tried to leave the consensual interview. (*United States v. Weaver*, 966 F.2d 301 [8th Cir. 1992])

CHAPTER OUTLINE

Introduction
Reasonable Suspicion
Informants and Hearsay
Drug Courier Profiles
Race and Reasonable Suspicion
The Scope and Duration of *Terry* Stops

Stop-and-Identify Statutes
Frisks
Case Analysis
Chapter Summary
Chapter Review Questions
Legal Terminology

TEST YOUR KNOWLEDGE

1. Do you know the basis for stops and frisks in the text of the Fourth Amendment?

2. Can you state the difference between investigative *Terry* stops and arrests?

3. Are you able to state the definition of reasonable suspicion and the various factors that the police consider in determining whether there is reasonable suspicion?

4. Do you know the circumstances under which an informant's tip constitutes reasonable suspicion?

5. Can you state the role of drug courier profiles in reasonable suspicion stops?

(Continued)

(Continued)

6. Do you know the significance of "race" in the police determinations of reasonable suspicion?

7. Can you discuss *Terry* stops and the movement of suspects, the length of seizures, and the intrusiveness of the methods used to investigate suspected criminal activity?

8. Can you state the circumstances in which the police may require drivers as well as the passengers in a vehicle they detain on a reasonable suspicion traffic stop to exit an automobile and the circumstances under which the police may frisk the driver and passengers?

9. Can you define the circumstances under which the police may frisk a suspect and the scope of a *Terry* frisk?

10. Do you know when the police who stop a vehicle on reasonable suspicion may search the passenger compartment of an automobile?

11. Do you know the legal test for the seizure of narcotics in *Minnesota v. Dickerson*?

■ INTRODUCTION

The text of the Fourth Amendment appears to indicate that a seizure and search of an individual must be based on a warrant founded on probable cause. In 1968, in *Terry v. Ohio*, the U.S. Supreme Court confronted the issue of whether individuals may be lawfully stopped and frisked under the Fourth Amendment based on reasonable suspicion. The practice of stopping, interrogating, and frisking individuals without probable cause had been part of the arsenal of local and state law enforcement officers for decades. Reliance on this tactic increased in the late 1960s in reaction to demonstrations over civil rights, the Vietnam War, protests against conditions on college campuses, a rising crime rate, and violent confrontations between police and various self-proclaimed radical groups. States like New York passed statutes explicitly authorizing the police to "stop any person" who is reasonably suspected of engaging or being about to engage in criminal activity and to carry out a search to protect "life or limb" (N.Y. Code Crim. Proc. 180-a [1964]). In 1967, the Presidential Commission on Law Enforcement and Administration of Justice recommended that in view of the rising crime rate, the state legislatures of the fifty states should provide the police with the clear authority to stop, frisk, and question individuals on a standard of less than probable cause. Civil libertarians objected that in the past, seizures of individuals on less than probable cause had been employed to harass the homeless, minorities, and political activists.

Law enforcement authorities responded that it would be unreasonable to tell the officer on the beat that he or she is prohibited from stopping an individual who the officer suspects is engaged in criminal activity or about to commit a crime or who the officer suspects has recently completed a crime. On the other hand, Justice William Douglas warned that abandoning the probable cause standard was a step down a "totalitarian path" and that the "hydraulic pressure" of events would lead to the evaporation of civil liberties.

The Supreme Court in the past had resisted efforts to weaken Fourth Amendment protections and had held that a "reasonable search" under the Fourth Amendment required a warrant founded on probable cause or on probable cause in those instances in which time did not permit the police to obtain a warrant (*Henry v. United States*, 361 U.S. 98 [1959]). *Terry v. Ohio* broke new ground and employed a balancing test to establish that brief investigative stops of individuals may be based on reasonable suspicion. The Court explained that field interrogations are essential for investigating and detecting street crimes. These stops are distinguished from custodial arrests by their narrow investigative purpose and limited intrusion on individual liberty and therefore may be based on the lesser standard of reasonable suspicion rather than probable cause. *Terry* took the additional step of holding that an officer is entitled to conduct a frisk to protect himself or herself in those instances in which he or she possesses reasonable grounds to believe that a suspect is armed and presently dangerous. The central holding of *Terry* is summarized below:

- *Reasonable suspicion and warrant clauses.* The Fourth Amendment prohibition against "unreasonable searches and seizures" and the Fourth Amendment provision that no warrants shall issue but upon probable cause should no longer be interpreted to mean that searches not based on a warrant founded on probable cause are unreasonable and unlawful under the Fourth Amendment. The Reasonableness Clause authorizes the police to conduct investigative stops and frisks based on reasonable suspicion.

- *Balancing.* The *Terry* reasonable suspicion standard for stops and frisks is based on balancing the interest in swift action by an officer on the beat to detect, investigate, and prevent crime against the slight intrusion on the privacy of the individual citizen.

In this chapter, we cover the following topics in reviewing the law of stop and frisk:

- *Reasonable suspicion.* Individuals may be seized (stopped) based on reasonable suspicion.
- *Informants and hearsay.* The police may rely on informants and hearsay to reach a conclusion that there is reasonable suspicion to stop an individual.
- *Race and reasonable suspicion.* A stop may not be based solely on race, ethnicity, or religion. These characteristics may constitute one factor that, along with other factors, constitutes reasonable suspicion.
- *The scope and duration of a* Terry *stop. Terry* stops are limited in the permissible movement of a suspect and in duration and purpose.
- *Automobiles and* Terry *stops.* The police may direct the driver and passengers to exit an automobile during an investigative stop.
- *Frisks.* The police may conduct a frisk of a suspect's outer clothing for weapons. This has been extended to passenger compartments and to frisks for drugs.

[handwritten: would endanger people if they waited for probable cause to approach/stop someone]

■ REASONABLE SUSPICION

The Balancing Test

Terry v. Ohio was the first case in which the Supreme Court approved a search and seizure of an individual in a criminal case under the Fourth Amendment based on reasonable suspicion. Chief Justice Earl Warren writing for the majority in *Terry* held that a police officer may in "appropriate circumstances" approach a suspect to investigate possible criminal behavior despite the fact that the officer does not have probable cause to make an arrest. The standard for these investigative stops is **reasonable suspicion**.

The reasonable suspicion standard was derived by *balancing* the need for swift action by an officer to investigate and to detect crime against the modest intrusion on individual privacy. The Supreme Court reasoned that requiring an officer to wait until he or she has developed probable cause would place society at risk. A suspect's interest in

■ ■ ■ ■ ■ ■ ■ ■ ■ ■

PHOTO 13.1

Terry v. Ohio authorizes the police to seize individuals based on reasonable suspicion and to conduct a frisk of the outer clothing for weapons.

William F. Campbell/Contributor/Getty Images

being free from unreasonable searches and seizures is adequately protected by requiring that the facts relied on by the police officer are to be judged against the objective standard of whether the facts available to the officer at the moment of the seizure "warrant a man of reasonable caution in the belief that the action taken was appropriate." As we shall see in the next section, Justice Warren applied this reasonable suspicion test to determine the lawfulness of the **stop and frisk** of the suspects in *Terry*.

Reasonable Suspicion and Terry v. Ohio

Plainclothes detective Martin McFadden, a thirty-nine-year veteran of the Cleveland, Ohio, police department, observed Richard Chilton and John W. Terry standing on the corner of the downtown streets of Huron Road and Euclid Avenue. The men took turns walking southwest on Huron, looking in a store window, and then returning to the street corner. Each of the men repeated this routine roughly five or six times. At one point, they were joined by a third man, Carl Katz. Katz then left and walked west on Euclid Avenue. He thereafter was joined by Chilton and Terry. At this point, McFadden confronted the three men and asked their names. The men "mumbled something," and McFadden patted down the outside of their clothing and discovered a revolver in Terry's pocket and a revolver in the outer pocket of Chilton's overcoat. McFadden later explained that he had concluded that the three men were "casing a job, a stick-up."

Justice Warren stressed that McFadden observed the three men engage in a "series of acts," each of which may have been "innocent in itself, but which taken together warranted further investigation." He noted that "[i]t would have been poor police work indeed for an officer of thirty years' experience in the detection of thievery from stores in the same neighborhood to have failed to investigate this behavior."

We all likely would agree that McFadden reasonably concluded that although the three men were acting legally, they may have been planning a crime. However, we might get a different result by changing the facts. For instance, we might ask how many times Chilton and Terry would have to walk past the store to arouse reasonable suspicion. The case does not discuss whether McFadden took the race or appearance of the men into consideration. Would McFadden's decision be less persuasive had he approached a group of well-dressed businessmen or individuals who he knew lived in the neighborhood?

The Reasonable Suspicion Determination

The Supreme Court provided guidance in *Terry* for the methodology to use in determining reasonable suspicion in future cases. Keep in mind that each situation confronting the police is different and that the facts that give rise to reasonable suspicion cannot be "reduced to a neat set of legal rules." The determination of reasonable suspicion is a **case-by-case determination**. – diff each time

Articulable suspicion. A police officer, in justifying an intrusion, must present *specific and articulable facts* that, together with rational inferences drawn from those facts, reasonably suggest that an individual has committed a crime or is about to commit a crime. This is termed **articulable suspicion**. → something clearly about to happen or from informant.

Objective standard. The facts are to be judged in accordance with a *reasonable person* standard and not based on what the officer (subjectively) believed. Police officers may not rely on a hunch, generalization, or stereotype. This would open the door to discrimination and to the evaporation of individuals' right to be free from unreasonable searches and seizures under the Fourth Amendment.

Experience and expertise. The facts are to be interpreted in light of an *officer's experience and training*. McFadden was a thirty-nine-year veteran of the police and was aware that the store that the three men were "casing" had been the target of recent robberies.

Informants. As discussed later in the chapter, reasonable suspicion may be based on information from a reliable informant or on information from an anonymous **informant** who provides information that is corroborated (found to be correct) by law enforcement officers (*Alabama v. White*, 496 U.S. 325 [1990]).

Totality of the circumstances. The entire factual situation is to be taken into account in determining whether there is reasonable suspicion. Courts consider factors such as whether the suspect is calm or nervous, whether the suspect is observed in a high-crime area, the time of day, the number of arrests for a particular type of crime made in the vicinity by the officer in the past, the suspect's willingness to cooperate with the police, and whether the suspect's pattern of behavior suggests that he or she may be engaged in criminal conduct. The evidence "must be seen and weighed not in terms of library analysis by scholars, but as understood by those versed in the field of law enforcement" (*United States v. Cortez*, 449 U.S. 411, 418 [1981]).

Probabilities. Reasonable suspicion is based on probabilities rather than certainties. The Supreme Court, in *United States v. Arvizu*, observed that while each of the factors relied on by the police officer viewed individually "undoubtedly [were] susceptible to innocent explanation . . . [t]aken together . . . they sufficed to form a particularized and objective basis for . . . stopping the vehicle, making the stop reasonable within the meaning of the Fourth Amendment" (*United States v. Arvizu*, 534 U.S. 266, 277–278 [2002]).

Particularized suspicion. The "detaining officer must have a particularized and objective basis for suspecting the particular person stopped of criminal activity" (*United States v. Cortez*, 449 U.S. 411 [1981]).

Probable cause and reasonable suspicion. The Supreme Court has clarified that probable cause means "a fair probability that contraband or evidence of a crime will be found." The reasonable suspicion standard, in contrast, is "less demanding" than probable cause and requires "at least a minimal level of objective justification for making the stop. . . . The officer must be able to articulate more than . . . unparticularized suspicion or [a] 'hunch' of criminal activity" (*Illinois v. Wardlow*, 528 U.S. 119 [2000]).

[handwritten: → totality of circumstances test]

Facts Constituting Reasonable Suspicion

Judges have found reasonable suspicion to justify a *Terry* stop in a variety of situations. This determination often is like a "puzzle" in which the officer connects a number of innocent acts together to determine whether there is reasonable suspicion to justify a Fourth Amendment seizure. Reasonable suspicion requires an evaluation of the totality of circumstances. This contrasts to a finding of probable cause to arrest an individual in which an officer directly observes an individual robbing a bank or committing an assault and battery. The Supreme Court has recognized that "articulating what reasonable suspicion means is not possible." It is a "fluid concept" that must be evaluated in a "particular context" (*Ornelas v. United States*, 517 U.S. 690, 694 [1996]). The following are some of the factors that in combination with other factors have been held to constitute reasonable suspicion:

[handwritten: → must know the crime he is committing or about to commit]

- *Criminal activity.* Acts that may indicate criminal activity such as casing a store as in *Terry* or an exchange of money on the street. *[handwritten: → can't be walking down street looking funny]*
- *Time.* Acts that take place at a time of day in which criminal activity is likely to occur. This may involve loading an unmarked van at a warehouse late at night. *[handwritten: → if they give you reasonable answer that should be it]*
- *Location.* A high-crime area or an area that is characterized by a particular type of criminal conduct.
- *Criminal record.* Police officer awareness of the individual's arrest record or record of criminal involvement.
- *Evasion.* Fleeing from or evading the police.
- *Noncooperation.* Noncooperation when approached or questioned.
- *Nervous.* Acting nervous during the encounter with police.
- *Experience.* Police officer's experience in making arrests for the type of activity.

[handwritten: look @ these while studying]

Consider some cases in which courts found that the police possessed reasonable suspicion to stop a suspect. Can you identify the factors that the police relied on in finding reasonable suspicion?

- The suspect smelled strongly of the illegal narcotic PCP, the suspect appeared nervous, the area was widely known for heavy drug trafficking, and the officers knew that drug traffickers would hide PCP in or near apartment complex Dumpsters. One of the officers had made eighty-five PCP-related arrests in the apartment complex (*U.S. v. Foster*, 376 F.3d 577 [6th Cir. 2004]).

- An officer observed an illegally parked vehicle, and an individual emerged from a restaurant, glanced at the officer, hurried to the vehicle, and started to drive away. After being stopped by the police officer for a parking violation, the driver gave the officer an expired as well as a valid driver's license. The suspect was sweating and nervous and evasive when asked direct questions. Although it was late April, the driver wore a thick down coat with a hole in the inseam that the officer concluded could be used to conceal drugs. In addition, feathers were falling out of a hole in the coat's lining that the officer believed might be designed to hide a weapon. A frisk revealed a weapon and narcotics (*State v. DeValle*, 2006 Conn. Super. LEXIS 484 [Super. Ct. Conn. 2006]).

- Uniformed officers John Prilla and Ronald Absten were in a convenience store. Prilla remarked that a customer appeared to be carrying a firearm in the right front pocket of his three-quarter-length leather jacket. Absten then made his own assessment based on Bureau of Alcohol, Tobacco, Firearms and Explosives training on identifying armed individuals and types of firearms. He detected the outline of a small handgun in the defendant's right pocket and observed that the pocket hung lower than its opposite pocket, indicating that it contained a weighty object. The defendant was described as carrying the gun in a manner that differed from individuals who are accustomed to possessing a licensed firearm. The suspect also looked nervously over his shoulder at the officers and continually placed his hand on his pocket. Absten had made arrests of individuals in the past who carried illegal firearms in their jackets or pants. The defendant exited the store, and the officers directed him to raise his hands above his head and to place them on his head. The officers then conducted a frisk and discovered a firearm (*Commonwealth v. Stevenson*, 894 A.2d 759 [Sup. Ct. Pa. 2006]).

- Border patrol agent Rudy Sanchez was patrolling the Texas–Mexico border and stopped a vehicle that he suspected to be, and, in fact, was, carrying illegal immigrants. Sanchez, who was an experienced agent, observed Guadalupe Quintana-Garcia driving the type of SUV with tinted windows that was favored by smugglers. Quintana-Garcia was speeding and noticeably slowed his automobile when he spotted Sanchez's patrol car. This particular highway was favored by smugglers because there was no permanent checkpoint. Sanchez was particularly alert because smugglers had learned to cross the border in the early afternoon when there were fewer agents deployed. Quintana-Garcia's vehicle carried Mexican license plates and had entered the United States in an area that was primarily frequented by domestic American drivers (*United States v. Quintana-Garcia*, 343 F.3d 1266 [10th Cir. 2003]).

- William "Sam" Wardlow's unprovoked flight on the approach of the last squad car in a four-car caravan was held to constitute reasonable suspicion. A frisk resulted in the seizure of a .38-caliber handgun. "Headlong flight—wherever it occurs—is the consummate act of evasion: It is not necessarily indicative of wrongdoing, but it is certainly suggestive of such" (*Illinois v. Wardlow*, 528 U.S. 119 [2000]).

Some critics contend that *Terry* has provided the police with too much discretion to stop individuals and that, as a result, a significant number of innocent individuals are seized by the police. In the alternative, you might take the position that *Terry* stops rarely inconvenience the relatively small number of individuals who are detained and that the police should be accorded an even greater degree of authority to detain individuals (*Brown v. Texas*, 443 U.S. 47 [1979]).

Legal Equation

Fourth Amendment seizure of the person based on reasonableness	=	The police officer, in justifying the intrusion, must present specific and articulable facts that, together with rational inferences drawn from those facts, reasonably suggest that an individual has committed a crime or is about to commit a crime (objective test)	+	Facts are to be considered based on the totality of the circumstances
		+ Facts evaluated in light of the officer's experience.		

13.1 YOU DECIDE

Adam Orlando Jaquez pled guilty to unlawful possession of a firearm by a convicted felon. Abilene, Texas, police officer Jennifer Holderead was on patrol when she received a radio call that gunshots had been fired in the area of 10th and Pine Streets, a high-crime area. The dispatcher reported that the shots had been fired from a "red vehicle." Holderead stated that she stopped Jaquez because he was driving a red car, in the general vicinity of the incident reported fifteen minutes earlier, late at night, in the vicinity of an area known for its high crime rate. Did Holderead have reasonable suspicion to seize Jaquez? See *United States v. Jaquez* (421 F.3d 338 [5th Cir. 2005]).

You can learn what the court decided by referring to the study site, **http://study.sagepub.com/lippmance.**

13.2 YOU DECIDE

Omaha police officer Paul Hasiak saw a person later identified as Fonta M. Jones walking across a church parking lot wearing a long-sleeved hooded sweatshirt and "clutching the front area of his pocket with his right hand." Jones watched as the marked police cruiser drove past him. The officers drove around the block and again saw Jones, still walking with his right hand clutching his front hoodie pocket. Officer Hasiak stopped and frisked Jones. Hasiak seized a 9-mm handgun in the front hoodie pocket and a loaded magazine in Jones's back right pocket.

Hasiak testified that, in his four years as a cruiser officer, he stopped ten other people walking in this manner, and each of them was carrying a firearm. Officer John Supeh, Hasiak's "street survival" trainer at the Omaha Police Training Academy, testified that holding one's hand against the body is "considered a protective arm movement" to secure a weapon, an action which "would lead to what we consider a stop and frisk." Hasiak's belief that there was reasonable suspicion also was supported by additional facts: (1) that Jones was walking in a high-crime precinct in a neighborhood considered to be a violent "hot spot" in that precinct; (2) that it was sunny and 68 degrees and Jones by wearing a long-sleeved sweatshirt "was obviously hiding something he did not want the world, and the cruiser officers, to see"; and (3) that Jones "continually watched the officers [as the cruiser drove by] as if concerned that they would stop him." Did Hasiak have reasonable suspicion to stop and frisk Jones? See *United States v. Jones* (606 F.3d 984 [8th Cir. 2010]).

You can learn what the court decided by referring to the study site, **http://study.sagepub.com/lippmance.**

[handwritten: annon informant → police must prove, make sure they are right.
ex: anon says x, y and z is about to happen.
police must watch that x, y and z happen before they go in.]

■ INFORMANTS AND HEARSAY

Reasonable suspicion may be based on a police officer's direct observations or on information from an informant, victim, eyewitness, or police bulletin. Information that is obtained in this "secondhand fashion," rather than through a police officer's direct observation, is a *hearsay report*. The classic example is a bloody victim who flags down a squad car and describes the identity of his or her attacker. In other circumstances, the police understandably may have less confidence in hearsay information. Consider a police officer who is informed by an anonymous phone caller that there is an individual wearing a baseball cap selling narcotics on a street corner across from an elementary school. Would it make a difference if the caller stated that the alleged "drug dealer" is armed?

In *Adams v. Williams*, Sergeant John Connolly was on patrol in a high-crime area of Bridgeport, Connecticut. Sergeant Connolly was approached by an individual "known to Connolly who reported that an individual in a nearby vehicle possessed narcotics and was carrying a gun at his waist." Connolly tapped on the window of the automobile and requested that Robert Williams, the driver, open the door of the vehicle. Williams reacted by rolling

[handwritten: → what is there basis of knowledge]

down the window, and Connolly immediately reached into the car and removed a loaded revolver from Williams's waist (*Adams v. Williams*, 407 U.S. 143, 144–145 [1972]).

The U.S. Supreme Court confronted the question of whether reasonable suspicion may be based on the hearsay report of an informant. The Court held that the informant's tip possessed sufficient "*indicia of reliability*" to justify Connolly's acting on it. The informant was known to the officer and had provided information in the past. The informant also came forward personally to provide information that was immediately verifiable at the scene. This was particularly important because Connecticut law provided that it was a crime to make a "false complaint."

The Supreme Court stressed that Connolly properly relied on a *credible informant* and that the police also may justifiably rely on information provided by the victim of a street crime. However, "[s]ome tips, completely lacking in indicia of reliability, would either warrant no police response or require further investigation before a forcible stop of a suspect would be authorized." The Court cautioned that while the informant's unverified tip in *Williams* would have been insufficient to establish probable cause for a narcotics arrest or search warrant, the information carried enough indicia of reliability to justify the officer's investigative stop of Williams.

The Supreme Court observed in *Adams v. Williams* that the informant's tip was "stronger" than "an anonymous telephone tip." This raises the question of whether the police may rely on an **anonymous tip**. This was the precise issue that confronted the court in *Alabama v. White*. Corporal B. H. Davis of the Montgomery, Alabama, police received an anonymous phone call stating that Vanessa White would be leaving 235-C Lynwood Terrace Apartments in a brown Plymouth station wagon with the right tail light lens broken, that she would be going to Dobey's Motel, and that she would be in possession of roughly an ounce of cocaine inside a brown attaché case. Corporals Davis and P. A. Reynolds immediately placed Lynwood Terrace under surveillance and observed White leave the 235 building without a briefcase and enter a station wagon. They followed White as she headed toward Dobey's Motel and pulled her over before she reached her destination. The officers seized a locked brown attaché case that was in the automobile, received consent to open the case, and found marijuana. Did the police have reasonable suspicion to stop White (*Alabama v. White*, 496 U.S. 325, 327 [1990])?

The Supreme Court observed in *White* that *Adams v. Williams* established that reasonable suspicion is a "less demanding standard than probable cause" and may be based on less complete and less reliable information than is required for probable cause. The Supreme Court applied a totality-of-the-circumstances test that stressed two critical considerations: first, is the informant reliable (trustworthy), and second, what is the "basis of [his or her] knowledge"? In this instance, the police knew nothing about the informant, and there was no basis to determine whether the anonymous tip satisfied either of these considerations.

The Supreme Court nevertheless ruled that the police possessed reasonable suspicion to stop White based on their corroboration of the facts provided by the informant. On the one hand, the police were unable to verify the name of the woman leaving the building, the apartment from which she left, or whether she was carrying a brown attaché case. On the other hand, the informant made a number of accurate predictions. This included the building from which the defendant left, the general time of departure, the type of automobile, and the driver's apparent destination. The Court, in particular, stressed that "because only a small number of people are generally privy to an individual's itinerary, it is reasonable for police to believe that a person with access to such information is likely to also have access to reliable information about that individual's illegal activities." The Supreme Court held that although this is a "close case," under the totality of the circumstances, the anonymous tip, as corroborated by the police, exhibited sufficient indicia of reliability.

Justices John Paul Stevens, William Brennan, and John Marshall objected that an anonymous neighbor with a grudge could have provided the information relied on by the police. An unethical police officer also could fabricate the existence of an anonymous informant and falsely claim that he or she was able to corroborate the informant's account. The decision, in the view of the dissenting judges, undermines and "makes a mockery" of the protections accorded to individuals under the Fourth Amendment. Would you have voted with the majority or with the dissenting judges? Do you believe that courts should approve police reliance on informants whose identity and background is unknown to the police?

In summary, the Supreme Court in *Adams v. Williams* and in *Alabama v. White* established that a police officer under certain circumstances may rely on an informant's tip to establish reasonable suspicion.

- *Reliability.* The judge asks whether the informant is known to the officer and considers whether the informant has been accurate in the past. The court will consider whether there is a statute that makes it a crime to make a false complaint and whether the informant personally approached the police.

- *Basis of knowledge.* The judge also asks how the informant has obtained the information. An informant with firsthand knowledge of criminal activity should be able to provide detailed information.

- *Police corroboration.* A tip that lacks these two indicia of reliability may be relied on where corroborated in essential details by the police. Most important is the informant's ability to predict a suspect's future conduct.

- *Totality of the circumstances.* The judge strikes a balance. The less reliable the informant, the more a court may insist that the informant is in the position to provide detailed information. A tip that is thought to lack the indicia of reliability may be strengthened by police corroboration, by the fact that the informant came forward personally, and by a criminal statute that punishes intentionally "false criminal reports."

In 1984, in *United States v. Hensley*, the Supreme Court decided an additional case that approved of police reliance on hearsay. The Court held that Kentucky police were justified in stopping an individual based on a "wanted bulletin" issued by police in Ohio so long as the officers issuing the bulletin themselves possessed facts supporting a *Terry* stop. Relying on a "wanted bulletin" is similar to basing a stop on hearsay information from an informant (*United States v. Hensley*, 469 U.S. 221 [1985]).

Chief Justice John Roberts and Justice Antonin Scalia dissented from the Court's decision not to review a decision of the Virginia Supreme Court in *Virginia v. Harris* (denial of *certiorari*). In *Harris*, a Virginia police officer relied on an anonymous tip that Joseph A. Moses Harris was driving while intoxicated. The tip described Harris, his automobile, and the direction he was traveling in "considerable detail." Harris when pulled over by the officer reeked of alcohol, his speech was slurred, and he failed a field sobriety test. The Virginia court found that this was an unreasonable search and seizure because the police officer relied on an anonymous informant and did not independently verify that Harris was driving while inebriated.

Justice Roberts observed that the "imminence" of the danger posed by drunk drivers exceeds the danger in other types of cases. The effect of the Virginia Supreme Court's ruling in the view of Justice Roberts will be to give drunk drivers "one free swerve" before they may be lawfully pulled over by a police officer. It will be difficult for an officer to explain to the family of the victim killed by the swerve that while the police had a tip that the driver was driving while inebriated the officer was powerless to pull the driver over for a brief check (*Virginia v. Harris*, 558 U.S. ___ [2009]). In 2014, the Supreme Court adopted Justice Roberts's view in *Navarette v. California*.

In *Florida v. J. L.* (529 U.S. 266 [2000]), the Supreme Court held that the police were not justified in seizing a suspect based on an anonymous tip that a suspect reportedly was in possession of a firearm. What if the police receive an anonymous tip that an individual on a street corner is about to ignite a terrorist bomb in the downtown area of a major city? Are the police required to passively wait to determine whether there is an explosion?

Legal Equation

| The police reliance on an informant's tip | = | Reliability of the informant | + | Basis of the informant's knowledge |
| | + | Police corroboration of the essential details where indicia of reliability are lacking | + | Totality of the circumstances. |

13.3 YOU DECIDE

California Highway Patrol Officer Julian Irigoyen received a police dispatch based on an anonymous tip that reported that a driver who possibly may be intoxicated was "weaving all over the roadway." The vehicle was described as a 1980s model blue van traveling northbound on Highway 99 at Airport Drive, north of Bakersfield. Officer Irigoyen was headed southbound three to four miles north of that location, with only one entry/exit ramp between his position and the reported location of

(Continued)

happens @ wilmington train station

■ DRUG COURIER PROFILES

Law enforcement officers have developed profiles to assist in detecting and investigating criminal conduct. An officer relying on a profile compares an individual's actions to the behavior pattern in the profile. A match between an individual's pattern of activity and the profile is thought to provide reasonable suspicion.

Profiles typically are based on an analysis of the behavior of individuals who have been arrested in the past for crimes such as air hijacking and illegal immigration. The first profiles were developed to detect trafficking in illegal narcotics. Primary credit is given to Drug Enforcement Administration (DEA) agent Paul J. Markonni in Atlanta. He identified seven primary characteristics and four secondary characteristics that comprise the "Markonni drug courier profile" (*United States v. Elmore*, 595 F.2d 1036, 1039 [5th Cir. 1979]).

The seven primary characteristics of the Markonni drug profile are (1) arriving from or departing to an identified source city; (2) carrying little or no luggage or large quantities of empty suitcases; (3) having an unusual itinerary, such as a rapid turnaround time for a very lengthy airplane trip; (4) using an alias; (5) carrying an unusually large amount of currency; (6) purchasing airline tickets with small denominations of currency; and (7) displaying unusual nervousness. The secondary characteristics are (1) almost exclusively using public transportation, particularly taxicabs, in departing from the airport; (2) immediately making a telephone call after deplaning; (3) leaving a false or fictitious call-back telephone number with the airline; and (4) excessively frequent travel to source or distribution cities. → *Philly, Miami, New York → all of them are source cities*

The difficulty, of course, is that innocent individuals may display several of these characteristics. Some critics complain that the focus on source or distribution cities tends to single out certain ethnic and racial minorities. On the other hand, profiles merely recognize that we rely on past experience to make judgments on a daily basis. In the case of drug courier profiles, there is an indication that the profiles are reasonably accurate. Data from the Detroit Airport, cited by Justice Lewis Powell Jr. in a 1980 Supreme Court decision, indicate that during a period of eighteen months, DEA agents relying on a drug courier profile searched 141 persons in ninety-six encounters, and a controlled substance was discovered in seventy-seven of those encounters, leading to the arrest of 122 persons (*United States v. Mendenhall*, 446 U.S. 544, 562 [1980]).

Courts have avoided weighing in on the debate over the accuracy of profiles and generally do not give particular weight to the claim that an individual fits a "profile." Judges, instead, ask whether the combination of the factors identified in the profile constitutes reasonable suspicion. In some instances, courts have found reasonable suspicion where law enforcement agents have supplemented the profile with additional observations.

The U.S. Supreme Court in *Reid v. Georgia* held that law enforcement officers in seizing and questioning Reid improperly relied on a **drug courier profile** (*Reid v. Georgia*, 448 U.S. 438, 440–441 [1980]).

The U.S. Supreme Court considered whether the DEA agent had reasonable grounds to suspect Reid of wrongdoing. The Court considered that Reid arrived in Atlanta from the known drug distribution center of Fort Lauderdale in the early morning, a time when law enforcement at the airport is understaffed. The DEA agent also relied on the facts that Reid and his companion apparently attempted to conceal the fact that they were traveling together and that they carried all their belongings in shoulder bags. The Supreme Court ruled that only the observation that Reid preceded his companion and occasionally looked backward focused on Reid's "particular conduct." The DEA agent's conclusion that they were concealing that they were traveling together was little more than a "hunch" and was not a substantial enough basis to justify a *Terry* stop. The other factors "describe a very large category of presumably innocent travelers, who would be subject to virtually random seizures were the Court to conclude as little foundation as there was . . . could justify a seizure." Are you troubled by the fact that the Supreme Court substituted its judgment for the accurate conclusion of trained law enforcement agents that the totality of the circumstances indicated that Reid was engaged in drug smuggling?

In *Florida v. Royer*, the Supreme Court found reasonable suspicion where the police went beyond the drug profile and learned that Mark Royer was traveling under an assumed name. Royer was observed in Miami International Airport by plainclothes narcotics detectives. The detectives concluded that Royer fit the drug courier profile in that he was traveling from a major drug distribution city and had purchased a one-way ticket to New York in cash with small bills. The police discovered after approaching Royer that his plane ticket was issued to a name that did not match the name on his driver's license. He also appeared to be nervous when conversing with the detectives (*Florida v. Royer*, 460 U.S. 491, 493–494 [1983]). The Supreme Court held that "when the officers discovered that Royer was traveling under an assumed name, this fact, and the facts already known to the officers . . . were adequate grounds for suspecting Royer of carrying drugs and for temporarily detaining him . . . while they attempted to verify or dispel their suspicions."

As you can see, the determination of whether an officer possesses reasonable suspicion is more of an art than a science. In *Royer*, the Supreme Court held that Royer's use of an assumed name when combined with a combination of factors provided law enforcement officers with reasonable suspicion to stop Royer. In contrast, in *Reid*, the police officer could not point to specific acts that indicated the suspect may have been engaged in illegal activity. The Supreme Court determined that most of the factors relied on by the officer were characteristic of a large number of innocent individuals and that the totality of circumstances listed in the profile did not provide law enforcement officers with reasonable suspicion to stop Reid.

Three points emerge concerning reliance on profiles:

- *Reasonable suspicion.* Courts will examine profiles to determine whether the factors constitute reasonable suspicion.

- *Suspect's conduct.* Reasonable suspicion must be based on evidence of an individual's specific action or actions, which in combination with other factors indicate that criminal conduct may be afoot.

- *Nonsuspicious conduct.* A pattern of conduct that is innocent or characteristic of a large number of individuals may contribute to a finding of reasonable suspicion based on the totality of the circumstances. These facts alone are not sufficient to constitute reasonable suspicion.

Legal Equation

| Seizure of a person based on a profile | = | Courts will not automatically find reasonable suspicion based on a profile | + | Suspect's action or actions are characteristic of an individual engaged in illegal activity |
| | | + Totality of the circumstances. | | |

■ RACE AND REASONABLE SUSPICION

The claim is made that the police and law enforcement officials engage in **racial profiling** or stopping individuals because of their race, ethnicity, gender, or other characteristic rather than because of their actions. This practice would be contrary to the Fifth and Fourteenth Amendments to the U.S. Constitution, which entitle individuals to equal protection of the law and make it unlawful to discriminate against individuals based on their race, ethnicity, gender, or religion. But may a police officer consider race along with an individual's conduct in determining reasonable suspicion? At present, there is an ongoing debate over whether it is lawful to consider an individual's ethnicity or religion in determining whether there is reasonable suspicion that an individual is engaged in terrorism.

Consider *Brown v. City of Oneonta*. Shortly before 2:00 A.M., a male broke into a house outside Oneonta, New York, and attacked a 77-year-old woman with a knife. The victim was not able to identify her assailant but, during the struggle, saw his hand and forearm and reported that he was an African American. She told the police that he cut his hand with the knife during the scuffle and that he must have been young because of the speed with which he crossed the room. The police proceeded to contact African American male students at the nearby State University of New York College at Oneonta. They failed to find the burglar and initiated a sweep in which they stopped and questioned every African American on the streets of Oneonta and inspected their hands for knife wounds. In justifying this tactic, the police stressed that Oneonta had a small African American population. Do you believe that the police acted in a constitutional fashion (*Brown v. City of Oneonta*, 221 F.3d 329 [2d Cir. 1999])?

There are a number of general points to keep in mind concerning whether the police may consider race in initiating a *Terry* stop:

Sole factor. An individual may not be stopped when the only reason for his or her seizure is his or her race, ethnicity, gender, religion, or other descriptive characteristic. In *United States v. Jones*, an anonymous caller reported to a police dispatcher at 1:13 A.M. that several African American males were drinking at a certain intersection and causing a disturbance. Officer Claude Hart did not find anyone on the corner and, as he was driving out of the neighborhood, encountered and stopped four African American males driving into the area, one of whom subsequently was arrested for drug possession. The Fourth Circuit Court of Appeals concluded that Officer Hart had stopped the men because of their race and that this did not constitute reasonable suspicion to detain the four African American men (*United States v. Jones*, 242 F.3d 215, 218 [4th Cir. 2001]).

Incongruity. An individual may not be stopped based on the fact that he or she "does not belong in a neighborhood." The Washington Supreme Court noted "racial incongruity . . . should never constitute a finding of reasonable suspicion of criminal behavior. Distinctions between citizens solely because of their ancestry are odious to a free people whose institutions are grounded upon the doctrine of equality" (*State v. Barber*, 823 P.2d 1068 [Wash. 1992]).

Identifications. Race may be considered as a factor in determining whether there is reasonable suspicion. The police, for example, may stop an individual who fits the description of a suspect where the totality of the circumstances leads the police to reasonably believe that the individual is the offender. In *United States v. Bautista*, the Ninth Circuit Court of Appeals noted that "[r]ace or color alone is not a sufficient basis for making an investigatory stop. However, race can be a relevant factor." The police in *Bautista* stopped two Hispanic suspects who were the only "people in sight who matched the description of the robbers" as either Iranian or Hispanic. The suspects also were encountered on a likely escape route one-half mile from the bank and a few blocks from the suspected getaway car. The defendants' light and dry clothes were suspicious given that there had been a steady rain (*United States v. Bautista*, 684 F.2d 1286, 1289 [9th Cir. 1982]).

Profiles. Race, ethnicity, or some other description may be considered as one of several factors in a profile. In *United States v. Weaver*, DEA agent Carl Hicks and two local detectives saw Arthur T. Weaver exit a plane from Los Angeles. Hicks focused on Weaver because he was "aware that a number of young roughly dressed black males from street gangs in Los Angeles frequently brought cocaine into Kansas City . . . and that walking quickly towards a taxicab was a common characteristic of narcotics couriers at the airport." Weaver also did not check his luggage, appeared nervous, and did not have any identification or a copy of his ticket. The Eighth Circuit Court of Appeals ruled that a stop based solely on race would be unconstitutional. However, in this case, race was "coupled with other factors." The appellate court stressed that Hicks had knowledge, based upon his own experience and intelligence reports, that "young male members of black Los Angeles gangs were flooding the Kansas City area with cocaine" (*United States v. Weaver*, 966 F.2d 391, 394 [8th Cir. 1992]).

13.4 YOU DECIDE

Officer David Mathison was an eighteen-month veteran of the Saint Paul, Minnesota, Police Department. He was working with the vice unit when he spotted Stephen D. Uber, a Caucasian, at 2:15 a.m. Mathison once again saw Uber's pickup truck at 2:45 a.m. Mathison radioed in the license plate number and learned that the vehicle was registered to a person in Mounds View, Minnesota, a predominantly Caucasian suburb. After checking the registration of the automobile, Mathison made a decision to stop Uber because he thought that Uber was "engaging in suspicious criminal activity relative to prostitution." Mathison stated that he did not observe Uber drive in an erratic or unlawful fashion and did not observe Uber circle the block, stop, or pick up anyone. Mathison testified that the Summit–University area is a "mixed neighborhood" well known for prostitution and that Uber demonstrated various characteristics that typify a person looking for prostitutes. These characteristics include there being one person in a car, late at night, which is observed in the area on multiple occasions in a short period of time, stops frequently, and may pick up a passenger. In addition, Uber had an out-of-the-area address. Was this a lawful Terry stop? See *City of St. Paul v. Uber* (450 N.W.2d 623 [Minn. App. 1990]).

You can learn what the court decided by referring to the study site, **http://study.sagepub.com/lippmance.**

CRIMINAL EVIDENCE AND PUBLIC POLICY

Judge Shira Scheindlin held that New York City's stop-and-frisk policy was unconstitutional, in violation of the Fourth Amendment and Equal Protection Clause of the U.S. Constitution. Judge Scheindlin appointed a federal monitor to supervise a reform of the New York City policy of stop and frisk, including the use of body-worn cameras for officers in some precincts, community consultation on the use of stop and frisk, and a modification in training.

Judge Scheindlin concluded that although NYPD policy formally prohibited racial profiling, the police practiced a policy of conducting stops in a "racially discriminatory manner." Between January 2004 and the middle of 2012, roughly 4.4 million stops were recorded by the police. Eighty-three percent of the stops involved African Americans (52 percent) or Hispanics (31 percent), although these two groups constitute somewhat more than 50 percent of New York City residents. In 2011, over 40 percent of stops targeted African American and Latino males between the ages of 14 and 24, a demographic group that comprises 4.7 percent of the New York City population.

Then mayor Michael Bloomberg and the police defended the stop-and-frisk policy based on the fact that young minority men commit a disproportionate percentage of crime. Judge Scheindlin noted that this argument might be valid if the "people stopped were criminals." However, she pointed out that the data indicate that 88 percent of individuals stopped are "overwhelmingly innocent" and their seizure results in neither an arrest (6 percent of detainees) nor a summons (6 percent of detainees) to appear in court for a minor violation of the law. Judge Scheindlin wrote, "It is impermissible to subject all members of a racially defined group to heightened police enforcement because some members of that group are criminals." There also was little evidence that the *Terry* stops resulted in the seizure of weapons.

Judge Scheindlin went on to note that roughly half of all individuals detained are frisked, although only 1.5 percent of frisks lead to the seizure of weapons. Weapons were seized in 1 percent of stops involving African Americans, 1.1 percent of stops involving Hispanics,

(Continued)

and 1.4 percent of stops involving whites. Contraband other than a weapon was seized in 1.8 percent of stops involving African Americans, 1.7 percent of stops involving Hispanics, and 2.3 percent involving whites. Once stopped, African Americans and Hispanics were treated differently than whites. African Americans were 14 percent more likely and Hispanics 9 percent more likely than whites to be subjected to physical force during a stop.

Judge Scheindlin concluded the focus on African American and Hispanic young people for investigative stops was based at least "in part" on the fact they were viewed as the "right people." She pointed to police supervisors lecturing officers to stop "the right people, the right time, the right location," which she concluded, based on the testimony of high-ranking police officials, was a code for targeting African American and Hispanic young people.

Judge Scheindlin noted that police reports indicated that minority youth were detained based on broad categories of behavior such as "furtive movement" or a "suspicious bulge" in their pocket. Furtive movements might encompass being "fidgety, changing directions, walking in a certain way, grabbing at a pocket or looking over one's shoulder." Eleven percent of African Americans and 9.6 percent of Hispanics were stopped based on a "suspicious bulge" as compared to 4.6 percent of whites. In most instances, the bulge turned out to be a wallet or cell phone. Judge Scheindlin stressed that a wallet or cell phone does not justify a stop, nor does the presence of a wallet or cell phone entitle the officer to continue to conduct a search.

Judge Scheindlin noted there was no reason to believe this behavior was disproportionately characteristic of minority males. She observed that if the NYPD mistakenly believed this type of behavior constitutes reasonable suspicion, it should come as no surprise that so many stops yield so little evidence of criminal activity.

In other instances, individuals aged 14 to 21 were stopped because they allegedly fit the profile of the individuals responsible for committing crimes. Individuals falling into this category were stopped even if they were not acting in a suspicious fashion or did not fit the description of the perpetrator or a crime.

Judge Scheindlin stressed that the Equal Protection Clause does not authorize treating similarly situated members of different racial groups differently based on racial disparities in crime data. The result was that minorities were being detained based on a lesser standard of reasonable suspicion than was being used to detain whites.

Judge Scheindlin cited the seizure of Cornelio McDonald, who was walking down the street in Queens late at night. He was stopped based on the fact two African American males had committed robberies and a burglary in the vicinity. "In other words, because two black males committed crimes in Queens, all black males . . . were subject to heightened police attention."

Judge Scheindlin noted that the larger impact of this policy was to make individuals fearful of walking down the street, distrustful of the police, and afraid to venture into white areas of the city.

Despite the awareness of government and police officials that the stop-and-frisk policy was being carried out in an unlawful and racially discriminatory fashion, Judge Scheindlin concluded these individuals were indifferent to the discriminatory application of stop and frisk. Police officers were pressured to increase the number of stops and frisks regardless of whether the stops were justified, and as a result, the number of stops increased sevenfold between 2002 and 2011 (97,000 stops in 2002 to 686,000 in 2011).

Judge Scheindlin concluded that New York City's highest officials "have willfully ignored overwhelming proof that the policy of targeting 'the right people' is racially discriminatory and . . . violates the United States Constitution."

A 2012 *New York Times* poll revealed that New Yorkers were fairly equally divided on whether stop and frisk was an acceptable method to make New York City safe. Fifty-five percent of white voters believed stop and frisk made New York safer while 39 percent of white voters did not believe the policy made New York safer; 35 percent of African American voters believed stop and frisk made New York safer while 56 percent believed stop and frisk had not made New York safer; and 48 percent of Hispanics agreed that stop and frisk had made New York City safer. Do you believe young people of color are singled out for *Terry* stops and frisks? Should stop and frisk be abolished?

Controversy once again erupted over police tactics in December 2014 when a Staten Island grand jury failed to indict an officer for the chokehold death of Eric Garner, a 29-year-old African American arrested for the unlawful misdemeanor sale of cigarettes.

who are you and why are you here?

THE SCOPE AND DURATION OF *TERRY* STOPS

A *Terry* stop and frisk is a limited intrusion to investigate and to detect crime. You recall that because *Terry* seizures are for a narrow purpose and involve a limited restraint on freedom, the police are required to satisfy a lesser standard of proof (reasonable suspicion) than is required for an arrest (probable cause). It is a basic constitutional principle that law enforcement officials may interfere with your freedom and privacy only to the extent required to accomplish their purpose. As the Supreme Court observed, *Terry* stops "warrant a limited intrusion on the personal security of the suspect. . . . [A]n investigative detention must be temporary and last no longer than is necessary to effectuate the purpose of the stop" (*Florida v. Royer*, 460 U.S. 491, 500 [1983]). As a result, a *Terry* stop may be challenged as unlawful when a suspect is treated as if he or she is being subjected to a probable cause arrest rather than to a reasonable suspicion stop. This inquiry typically focuses on three areas:

- *Movement.* A *Terry* stop does not permit the involuntary and significant movement of a suspect unless required by reasons of safety and security. You cannot be involuntarily transported to police headquarters.
- *Length of detention.* A *Terry* stop must be for a limited duration. You cannot be subjected to a lengthy detention or interrogation. →good answers should end the stop.
- *Intrusiveness.* The police are to employ the "least intrusive" methods reasonably available to them to investigate suspected criminal activity under the circumstances and to interfere as little as possible with an individual's freedom. A suspect ordinarily may not be detained by force, handcuffed, or locked in a patrol car.

In other words, the justification for the stop (e.g., *Terry*) defines the scope (limited movement and intrusiveness) and duration (limited time) of the stop. A probable cause stop, in contrast, permits an arrest that may result in the jailing of an individual for an extended period while awaiting trial. *The question is whether the Terry stop is being conducted in an unreasonable fashion and whether any evidence that is seized is the product of this unlawful seizure.*

Movement

The Supreme Court has held that a *Terry* stop permits only the modest movement of a suspect for the purpose of protecting the safety and security of a suspect or the police.

Terry stops have been held to be unlawful in those instances in which individuals have been removed to a police-dominated location or police headquarters and subjected to treatment resembling a probable cause arrest.

You may recall that we previously discussed *Florida v. Royer* in which two plainclothes detectives stopped Royer in Miami International Airport after determining that he fit a drug courier profile. The U.S. Supreme Court observed that the detectives had impermissibly moved Royer forty feet to an office where Royer consented to a search of his two suitcases that the police had retrieved from the airline. The Supreme Court rejected the agents' explanation that Royer had been moved to the office in order to question him in a more secure location. The purpose, in the view of the Court, was to isolate Royer and to gain his consent to a search of his luggage. Royer, as "a practical matter," was under arrest, and "[w]hat had begun as a consensual inquiry in a public place had escalated into an investigatory procedure in a police interrogation room, where the police, unsatisfied with previous explanations, sought to confirm their suspicions" (*Florida v. Royer,* 460 U.S. 491, 502 [1983]).

The U.S. Supreme Court also has condemned removing individuals subjected to *Terry* stops to police headquarters for questioning. For example, in *Dunaway v. New York,* the police detained Dunaway, who they suspected had killed an individual during an attempted robbery, and took him to police headquarters for questioning. He was not formally arrested or charged and confessed to the crime. The Supreme Court held that this type of lengthy and involuntary detention could be justified only by a probable cause arrest and that the police in *Dunaway* had gone far beyond the "narrowly defined intrusions" permitted under *Terry* (*Dunaway v. New York*, 442 U.S. 200 [1979]). In *Kaupp v. Texas*, 17-year-old Robert Kaupp was awakened at three in the morning by several police officers who suspected that Kaupp had been involved in a homicide. Dressed only in his underwear, Kaupp was handcuffed, placed in a patrol car, driven to the scene of the crime, and then taken to police headquarters and questioned. The Supreme Court held that Kaupp's removal and detention were "'in important respects indistinguishable from a traditional arrest' and therefore required probable cause or judicial authorization to be legal" (*Kaupp v. Texas*, 538 U.S. 626, 631 [2003]).

Length of Detention

We have seen that *Terry* stops are brief seizures whose purpose is to detect and to investigate suspected criminal conduct. The U.S. Supreme Court accordingly has held that *Terry* detentions are required to be limited in duration and do not permit the type of lengthy detentions that are characteristic of probable cause custodial arrests. The Supreme Court noted that the length of a detention is an "important factor in determining whether the seizure is so minimally intrusive as to be justifiable on reasonable suspicion" (*United States v. Place*, 462 U.S. 696, 709 [1983]).

In *United States v. Sharpe*, DEA agent Luther Cooke was on patrol near the North Carolina coast, a known center of drug activity. Cooke observed a blue pickup truck driving in tandem with a blue Pontiac Bonneville. Cooke suspected that the vehicles were transporting narcotics and followed the vehicles for roughly twenty miles before radioing state police for assistance. Cooke was joined by a squad car driven by Officer Kenneth Thrasher. Cooke pulled the Pontiac over based on reasonable suspicion. The pickup continued down the highway roughly one-half mile before being pulled over by State Trooper Thrasher. Thrasher radioed Cooke, who arrived twenty minutes later. Cooke opened the back doors of the truck, discovered marijuana, and arrested Donald Davis Savage. Cooke then returned to the Pontiac and arrested both occupants of the vehicle, William Harris Sharpe and Savage. Thirty to forty minutes had passed between Cooke's initial stop of the Pontiac and the arrest of Sharpe and Savage (*United States v. Sharpe*, 470 U.S. 675, 677–680 [1984]).

The issue before the Supreme Court was whether Savage had been detained for too lengthy a period under a *Terry* stop and whether Savage's detention therefore constituted the "functional equivalent" of a formal arrest. The Supreme Court held that Cooke acted in a "diligent and reasonable manner" and that there was no "unnecessary delay" in investigating Savage. The Court declined to establish a time limit on *Terry* seizures and held that a twenty-minute stop is not "unreasonable when the police have acted diligently and a suspect's actions contribute to the added delay about which he complains."

Sharpe suggests that the permissible time of a *Terry* detention is measured by whether the police carried out a criminal investigation "that was reasonably likely to confirm or dispel their suspicions" in a reasonable fashion without unreasonable delay. The twenty-minute period should not be thought of as a "bright-line" limit on *Terry* stops. A good example of an overly lengthy seizure is provided in *United States v. Place*. In *Place*, DEA agents detained Raymond Place for ninety minutes at LaGuardia Airport in New York while they waited for the arrival of a drug dog to examine Place's luggage. The Supreme Court observed that the police had caused this delay by failing to arrange for a drug dog to be present when Place's plane arrived at LaGuardia.

The Court declined to adopt any outside limit on a *Terry* stop but ruled that the ninety-minute period made the seizure unreasonable (*United States v. Place*, 462 U.S. 696, 709 [1983]).

On the other hand, in *United States v. Montoya de Hernandez*, the Supreme Court upheld the reasonableness of the twenty-four-hour seizure of Rosa Elvira Montoya de Hernandez at an international border. Customs agents suspected that Montoya de Hernandez had swallowed narcotics-filled balloons that she was smuggling into the United States. Montoya de Hernandez refused an X-ray, and the Court ruled that customs agents had no alternative other than to wait until she discharged the balloons in a bowel movement. The Supreme Court observed that the defendant's detention was "long, uncomfortable, indeed, humiliating; but both its length and its discomfort resulted solely from the method by which she chose to smuggle illicit drugs into this country. . . . [T]he customs officers were not required by the Fourth Amendment to pass respondent and her 88 cocaine-filled balloons into the interior. Her detention for the period of time necessary to either verify or dispel the suspicion was not unreasonable" (*United States v. Montoya de Hernandez*, 473 U.S. 531, 544 [1985]).

In summary, the Supreme Court has adopted a flexible approach to the length of *Terry* detentions and asks whether the length of the stop is reasonable under the totality of the circumstances. The Court examines whether the police acted in a diligent and responsible fashion in discharging their responsibilities and, in the case of lengthy detentions, examines whether the suspect contributed to the length of the detention. This approach differs from Section 110.2 of the American Law Institute's *Model Penal Code of Pre-Arraignment Procedure,* in which a group of respected lawyers, professors, and judges stated that a *Terry* stop may last "for such period as it is reasonably necessary . . . but in no case for more than twenty minutes." Does it make sense to tell the police that after twenty minutes, they are required to release a criminal suspect? On the other hand, we want to guard against the police employing *Terry* stops to engage in lengthy investigations, interrogations, or various forensic tests.

Intrusiveness

The Supreme Court also examines whether the investigative techniques employed by the police during a *Terry* stop violate an individual's privacy to a greater extent than is reasonable under the circumstances.

As you recall, in *Florida v. Royer*, the detectives at the airport detained Royer and moved him against his will to a room where he agreed to a search of his luggage. The Supreme Court held that nothing was achieved by moving Royer to the office that could not have been accomplished by questioning him in the airport concourse where he was first detained. The Court suggested that the police could have achieved the same results in a "more expeditious way" by relying on trained drug dogs. In the event that the search by the dogs "proved negative, Royer would have been free to go much earlier and with less likelihood of missing his flight" (*Florida v. Royer*, 460 U.S. 491, 502 [1983]).

Courts have approved intrusive techniques of detention during *Terry* stops when the police reasonably believe that they are confronting potentially violent suspects and must take precautions for their safety. In determining whether the police have carried out the *Terry* stop and frisk in a reasonable fashion, courts inquire whether the investigative methods employed were the *least intrusive means reasonably available to verify or dispel the officer's suspicion in a short period of time*. In those instances in which a suspect threatens an officer's safety and the police resort to physical force, to displaying a weapon, or to detaining an individual in a squad car, courts examine whether these tactics were necessary under the circumstances.

Judges in these instances consider a number of factors (*United States v. Seelye*, 815 F.2d 48 [8th Cir. 1987]):

- The number of officers and number of suspects
- The nature of the crime and whether there is reason to believe that the suspect is armed
- The need for immediate action for the officer to protect himself or herself
- Threatening behavior by the suspect
- The opportunity for the police to make the stop in a less intrusive fashion

In a drug case, the Minnesota Supreme Court held that the police had acted in a reasonable fashion to protect themselves.

- The police stopped an SUV with several occupants late at night. The officers had received information that the occupants might be armed and that the vehicle might contain a large cache of illegal drugs. The Minnesota Supreme Court held that it was reasonable to approach the SUV with "weapons drawn, removing the occupants from the Blazer, frisking them placing them in the back seat of squad cars and even handcuffing them briefly until it was determined that they were not armed" (*State v. Munson*, 594 N.W.2d 128, 137 [Minn. 1999]).

The Ninth Circuit Court of Appeals found that the police had acted reasonably in investigating a burglary.

- In *United States v. Gallegos*, Francisco Gallegos was stopped by the police who suspected that he was the suspect they were seeking for attempting to burglarize his daughter's home. He was stopped several miles from the burglary and, like the burglar, was Hispanic and was wearing a red shirt. Thee police removed Gallegos from his truck, handcuffed him, and placed him in the back of the squad car without asking for his identification. They drove Gallegos to the nearby crime scene where they found out from a neighbor that he was not the victim's father. The police returned Gallegos to his truck, and he was released within an hour of having been detained. The Ninth Circuit Court of Appeals concluded that the police had acted in a objectively reasonable fashion in diligently pursuing the investigation. The court stressed that there is "more than one way" to investigate a crime. The police selected a reasonable approach to determining immediately whether Gallegos was the burglar (*Gallegos v. City of Los Angeles*, 308 F.3d 987 [9th Cir. 2002]).

In another drug case, a federal court of appeals ruled that DEA agents had gone beyond the permissible limits of a *Terry* stop and acted as if they were executing a probable cause arrest rather than a reasonable suspicion stop.

- A car containing two suspected drug dealers was stopped by four DEA agents waiving firearms, and the occupants were handcuffed, placed in the backseats of separate DEA vehicles, transported to a nearby parking lot, read their *Miranda* rights, and questioned by the police. The court of appeals ruled that the police had gone beyond the measures required for their safety by transporting the suspects to another location and questioning them (*United States v. Lopez-Arias*, 344 F.3d 623, 628 [6th Cir. 2003]).

The Supreme Court held that the detention and interrogation of an individual detained on reasonable suspicion for a period of four days violated the Fourth Amendment (*Davis v. Mississippi*, 394 U.S. 721 [1969]).

In *Hayes v. Florida* (470 U.S. 811 [1985]), the Supreme Court stressed that the "line is crossed when the police, without probable cause or warrant, forcibly remove a person from his home or other place . . . and transport him to the police station, where he is detained, although briefly for investigative purposes." The Court significantly observed that "[n]one of the foregoing implies that a brief detention in the field for the purpose of fingerprinting, where there is only reasonable suspicion not amounting to probable cause, is necessarily impermissible under the Fourth Amendment. . . . There is . . . support . . . for the view that the Fourth Amendment would permit seizures for the purpose of fingerprinting, if there is reasonable suspicion that the suspect has committed a criminal act, if there is a reasonable basis for believing that fingerprinting will establish or negate the suspect's connection with that crime, and if the procedure is carried out with dispatch" (*Hayes v. Florida*, 470 U.S. 811 [1985]).

In reaction to the decision in *Hayes*, several states, including Arizona, Idaho, Indiana, Iowa, Nebraska, and Utah, passed statutes providing for the limited detention of suspects for fingerprinting and other identification procedures when a judge finds that there is probable cause that a crime has been committed and that there are reasonable grounds to believe that a suspect committed the offense. See *People v. Madson* (638 P.2d 18 [Colo. 1981]).

Can you see why the Fourth Circuit Court of Appeals ruled that police acted in an overly intrusive fashion in the case summarized below?

- The suspect entered into a store that was closed, triggered the burglar alarm, and was detained by the police for suspected breaking and entering. The suspect began to walk away and was handcuffed, had his legs kicked apart, was thrown against a wall, and was locked in the patrol car until the owner arrived. The Fourth Circuit Court of Appeals concluded that his freedom was improperly "curtailed to a degree associated with formal arrest" (*Park v. Shiflett*, 250 F.3d 843 [4th Cir. 2001]).

■ STOP-AND-IDENTIFY STATUTES

In *Hiibel v. Sixth Judicial District* (542 U.S. 177 [2004]), the Supreme Court addressed the constitutionality of **stop-and-identify statutes** that require individuals to present identification during a *Terry* stop. A deputy sheriff was dispatched to investigate an incident of an attack by a man on a woman and encountered Larry Dudley Hiibel standing next to a truck containing a woman. The officer explained he was investigating a fight and observed that Hiibel appeared to be intoxicated. The officer asked Hiibel if he had "any identification on [him]," which the Court interpreted as a request to produce a driver's license or some other form of written identification. Hiibel refused to present identification after being asked several times and was arrested on the misdemeanor of obstructing a police officer in discharging a legal duty. In this instance, the suspect impeded the officer in carrying out Nevada law, which specifies that an individual who is detained "shall identify himself, but may not be compelled to answer any other inquiry of any peace officer."

The Supreme Court held that the ability to stop a suspect and ask questions or check identification during a reasonable suspicion stop "promotes the strong government interest in solving crimes and bringing offenders to justice." An officer may ask an individual to identify him- or herself, briefly question the individual, or briefly detain the individual to obtain additional information. "A brief stop of a suspicious individual, in order to determine his identity or to maintain the status quo momentarily while obtaining more information, may be most reasonable in light of the facts known to the officer at the time."

The Court explained that the requirement that an individual identify himself or herself serves important governmental interests. Knowledge of an individual's identity may alert an officer that a suspect is wanted for another offense or has a record of violence or mental disorder. Learning a suspect's identity may help clear a suspect and allow the officer to focus his or her attention on other individuals. Identity may be of particular significance in a domestic dispute in which officers need to be aware of whom they are dealing with in order to determine the danger to themselves and to the potential victim.

The Court concluded that a request for identity "has an immediate relation to the purpose, rationale, and practical demands of a *Terry* stop." The threat of criminal punishment helps ensure that the suspect complies with the request for identity. At the same time, the Nevada statute does not lengthen the duration or intrusiveness of the stop.

Legal Equation

A *Terry* stop may not be carried out in an unreasonable fashion.

Movement	=	A *Terry* stop does not permit the involuntary and significant movement of a suspect unless required by reasons of safety and security.
Length of detention	=	A *Terry* stop is for a limited duration. A stop longer than twenty minutes is not unreasonable if the police have acted diligently or a suspect's actions have contributed to the added delay.
Intrusiveness	=	The investigative techniques should be the least intrusive means reasonably available to verify or dispel the officer's suspicion in a short period of time.

Automobiles and Terry Stops

May law enforcement officers require the driver as well as the passengers in a vehicle that they detain on a traffic stop to exit the automobile? On one hand, this seems to interfere with the liberty of individuals without reasonable suspicion that they pose a danger. On the other hand, an officer should not be required to run the risk that a motorist or passenger has a firearm and to place the officer's life in jeopardy.

In *Pennsylvania v. Mimms*, the Supreme Court ruled that the "legitimate and weighty" interest in protecting the safety of a police officer outweighed the "de minimis" (minor) intrusion on the liberty of the citizen and justified requiring a driver to exit an automobile (*Pennsylvania v. Mimms*, 434 U.S. 106, 108–111 [1977]). In *Maryland v. Wilson*, the Supreme Court extended the ruling in *Mimms* and held that an officer may require a *passenger* to leave a car (*Maryland v. Wilson*, 519 U.S. 408 [1997]).

The dissenting justices in *Wilson* viewed the judgment as an unwarranted extension of *Terry* and argued that a passenger should be ordered out of the automobile only where the officer reasonably believes that the passenger poses a threat. The dissenters argued that approving the automatic removal of an individual from a car imposes a burden on thousands of innocent citizens who may be "offended, embarrassed, and sometimes provoked" by "arbitrary official commands."

In 2009, the Supreme Court issued an opinion in *Arizona v. Johnson*. In *Johnson*, three members of the Arizona police gang task force pulled over an automobile after a license plate check revealed that the vehicle's registration had been suspended. The stop took place in a neighborhood frequented by the Crips street gang. Officer Maria Trevizo observed that Lemon Montrea Johnson, the passenger in the backseat, was wearing a bandanna that symbolized membership in the Crips, had a police scanner, and told Trevizo that he lived in an area that was a known home of the Crips street gang. Johnson also admitted that he had served time in prison for burglary and had been released roughly a year ago. Trevizo asked Johnson to exit the vehicle and fearing for her safety patted him down and seized a handgun. The U.S. Supreme Court held that the driver as well as passengers in an automobile are "effectively seized" when the vehicle is "pulled over for investigation of a traffic violation." The temporary seizure of the driver and passengers "ordinarily continues, and remains reasonable for the duration of the stop." The Court went on to hold that an officer is free to interrogate and investigate criminal activity on the part of passengers that is unrelated to the purpose of the traffic stop so long as this investigation does not "measurably extend the duration of the stop." The officer also may frisk a passenger or driver when there are reasonable grounds to believe that the passenger or driver is armed and presently dangerous (*Arizona v. Johnson*, 555 U.S. 323 [2009]).

Three state supreme courts have refused to follow the U.S. Supreme Court and have held that the police require reasonable suspicion to order a driver out of an automobile. These state supreme courts have reasoned that their state constitutions provide individuals with greater protections against searches and seizures than the Fourth Amendment to the U.S. Constitution. For instance, the Massachusetts Supreme Court ruled in *Commonwealth v. Gonsalves* that the state constitution requires that a police officer in a "routine traffic stop . . . have a reasonable belief that the officer's safety, or the safety of others, is in danger before ordering a driver out of a motor vehicle." The Massachusetts court noted that state courts under a federal system must be "strong and independent repositories of authority in order to protect the rights of their citizens" (*Commonwealth v. Gonsalves*, 711 N.E.2d 108, 111, 115 [1999]).

CRIMINAL EVIDENCE IN THE NEWS

On the evening of February 4, 1999, four plainclothes officers in New York's specially organized Street Crimes Unit were patrolling the Bronx in an unmarked police car in search of a serial rapist. Officers Sean Carroll, Edward McMellon, Kenneth Boss, and Richard Murphy spotted 22-year-old Amadou Diallo at roughly 12:45 A.M. The officers concluded that Diallo fit the description of the serial rapist. The ensuing confrontation resulted in the fatal shooting of Diallo and in the criminal prosecution and ultimate acquittal of four officers.

Diallo was born in Liberia, West Africa. His father was a businessman, and the family had lived in a number of countries, including Togo, Guinea, Thailand, and Singapore. Amadou possessed a love of reading, music, and dancing and was an avid fan of basketball star Michael Jordan. He attended a string of private schools abroad and, in 1996, immigrated to New York City to pursue his "American dream" of education in computer technology. Amadou initially was employed as a delivery man and then worked six days a week as a street peddler selling gloves, socks, and videotapes. He was a devout Muslim who sent his earnings home to his parents while continuing to foster his educational ambitions. Amadou was returning from getting something to eat when he encountered the police officers.

Officer Carroll would later testify that his attention was drawn to Diallo's suspicious behavior, hiding in the shadows of a vestibule and periodically darting out of the darkness to look up and down the block. Carroll and McMellon testified that they approached Diallo in order to question him, and when they identified themselves as police officers, Diallo fled into the dimly lit vestibule. The officers gave chase. Carroll testified that he did not want Diallo to get inside the building and risk that Diallo would take a resident hostage. Both Carroll and McMellon saw Diallo reach into his pocket with his right hand while opening the door with his left hand. As Diallo turned toward the officers, Carroll cried "gun, he's got a gun," and both officers fired their weapons in what they described as self-defense. McMellon fell off the step leading to the vestibule, and Carroll thought that his partner had been shot. Boss and Murphy saw Diallo standing in the vestibule amid the gunfire and testified that they thought that Diallo was aiming a weapon at them as they rushed to the defense of their fellow officers. Boss testified that "I think, oh my God, I'm going to die. I start firing. . . . I was in the line of fire." Murphy added that "I had this empty feeling, this sick feeling in my stomach that I was going to be hit. I pulled the trigger, jumping out of the way."

The officers fired a total of forty-one shots, hitting Diallo nineteen times. Professor James Fyfe, an expert on police procedures, testified that the officers had followed New York City Police Department (NYPD) procedures and had acted properly. Diallo had disregarded an order to halt and had run into the vestibule, and at this point, the police had an obligation to protect the residents of the building.

The trial was moved to Albany, New York, to avoid the taint of pretrial publicity. The prosecution argued that the police had improperly escalated the confrontation and that Diallo was unarmed and apparently was reaching for his wallet. The only other object in his possession was his keys. The prosecution stressed that standing in the vestibule of your home and looking up and down the street is not suspicious behavior and under no circumstances merits the police use of deadly force.

A prosecution expert testified that an analysis of the bullet wounds indicated that Diallo almost immediately had been knocked to the ground and that the officers nevertheless continued firing, allegedly intentionally killing Diallo or killing him with depraved indifference as to whether he lived or died. The defense contended that Diallo had remained standing throughout the police assault. An eyewitness contradicted this version and testified that she heard someone shout "gun" and that Diallo had been shot while on the ground.

The jury deliberated for twenty-three hours over a three-day period before acquitting all four officers of second-degree murder, reckless endangerment, and various lesser included offenses. Large demonstrations against police brutality in New York City led to the arrest of 1,700 individuals. Diallo's parents filed a civil suit against the officers for gross negligence and wrongful death and other civil rights violations, which was settled for $3 million.

Diallo's death became a source of criticism for individuals who objected to the stop-and-frisk policies of the NYPD, and thousands of people turned out for his funeral. In June 2000, Bruce Springsteen found himself in the middle of this controversy when he wrote and performed the song "American Skin," in which he addressed the Diallo shooting with the powerful lyrics, "You can get killed just for living in your American skin / 41 shots / 41 shots / 41 shots." Patrick Lynch, president of the Patrolmen's Benevolent Association, wrote a letter to his members calling for a boycott of Springsteen's concerts. Lynch's letter stated, "I consider it an outrage that [Springsteen] would be trying to fatten his wallet by reopening the wounds of this tragic case at a time when police officers and community members are in a healing period."

The officers who shot Diallo were members of the elite Street Crimes Unit created to rid New York of illegal handguns. The city was flooded with these guns, and the rate of serious crimes and homicides seemed to be escalating out of control. The tactic of the Street Crimes Unit was to conduct widespread stops and frisks in order to confiscate handguns and to deter individuals from carrying firearms. The 138 officers were known as the "commandos" of the New York police, and their motto was "We Own the Night." The unit's productivity was measured by firearms and drug seizures, and its tactic was to swarm a suspect, often with guns drawn. The plainclothes officers in the Street Crimes Unit were given a great deal of credit for radically shrinking crime statistics.

FBI statistics over the past seven years indicate that roughly four hundred individuals are killed each year in police use of deadly force. An average of ninety-six of the victims are African American, 18 percent of whom are under 21 years of age. In terms of Caucasian victims, 8.7 percent are under 21 years of age.

[handwritten: → cant pat unless you have a reasonable belief that the person is armed]

- FRISKS *[handwritten: @ Terry stop person cannot ALWAYS be patted down]*

The Terry Standard

The Supreme Court in *Terry v. Ohio* recognized that American criminals have a "long tradition of armed violence" and that a number of law enforcement officers are killed and wounded every year in the "line of duty." Most of these fatalities and injuries are inflicted at fairly close range with guns and knives. The Court accordingly ruled that where "nothing in the initial stages of the encounter serves to dispel [an officer's] reasonable fear for his own or others' safety, he is entitled for the protection of himself and others in the area to conduct a carefully limited search of the outer clothing of such persons in an attempt to discover weapons which might be used to assault him." You should keep the following several points in mind:

Weapons. The Supreme Court explained that this carefully limited **frisk** is intended to protect the officer and others in the vicinity and that it must therefore be "confined to an intrusion reasonably designed to discover guns, knives, clubs or other hidden instruments for assault of the police officer."

Reasonableness. The officer need not be absolutely certain that the individual is armed and presently dangerous. The test is whether a reasonably prudent man or woman under the circumstances would believe that his or her safety or the safety of others is at risk. Reasonableness is to be determined based on the facts as interpreted in light of the officer's experience. This is an objective test. An officer may not base a frisk on the officer's subjective fear or apprehension or hunch. The opposite also is true. An officer who lacks fear that a suspect is armed and presently dangerous may conduct a frisk so long as an objective person would believe that the frisk is required.

Scope. The frisk must be directed at the discovery of guns, knives, and other weapons. The officer may reach inside the clothing only when he or she feels an object that is reasonably believed to be a weapon (*Minnesota v. Dickerson*, which is discussed below, later extended this rule to narcotics). An officer may remove a container or package and open it if the officer reasonably believes that it may contain a weapon.

Dispel. The frisk does not automatically follow from the stop. A suspect is to be afforded the opportunity to dispel the officer's fear that the suspect is armed and presently dangerous.

The key fact is whether the suspect is reasonably believed to pose a threat. Courts have upheld frisks based on a combination of factors:

- A bulge in the suspect's pocket
- A suspect's reaching into his or her pocket
- The suspect's movements

- The officer's knowledge that the suspect has been involved in violent activity
- The type of criminal activity
- The suspect's presence in a high-crime neighborhood, particularly late at night
- An individual's being with another individual who is arrested by the police for a serious offense

A cooperative suspect who immediately offers a credible explanation and does not appear to pose a threat may *dispel* (eliminate) an officer's reasonable fear that the suspect is armed and presently dangerous. Despite the fact that the frisk does not automatically follow from the stop, it should be noted that a number of courts have approved "automatic" frisks in the cases of suspected drug trafficking on the grounds that drugs, gangs, and guns are closely connected to one another (see *United States v. Garcia*, 459 F.3d 1059 [10th Cir. 2006]).

On the same day that the Supreme Court decided *Terry*, the Court held in *Sibron v. New York* that the fact that a suspect had been observed talking to known narcotics addicts for a number of hours did not give "rise to reasonable fear of life and limb on the part of the police officer." The Court also ruled that, assuming that there were adequate grounds to search Nelson Sibron for weapons, the officer had gone beyond the limits of a *Terry* frisk when he immediately thrust his hand into Sibron's pocket and removed heroin rather than first frisking Sibron's outer clothing and then removing weapons (*Sibron v. New York*, 392 U.S. 40, 63–65 [1968]).

In *Adams v. Williams*, as discussed above, an officer responding to an informant's tip approached a narcotics dealer sitting in his car at 2:15 in the morning. The suspect rolled down his window rather than comply with a request to exit his automobile, and Sergeant Connolly immediately responded by removing a pistol from the suspect's waist, which was precisely where the informant stated that it was located. The Supreme Court held that Connolly had acted to protect himself from an imminent harm and ruled that he had undertaken a "limited intrusion designed to insure his safety" (*Adams v. Williams*, 407 U.S. 143, 147–148 [1972]).

Terry *Searches of Passengers in Automobiles*

As you may recall in *Arizona v. Johnson*, Officer Trevizo was held to have lawfully directed Johnson to exit the backseat of a vehicle that had been stopped by three officers assigned to the Arizona police gang task force. Trevizo suspected that Johnson was a member of the Crips street gang and wanted to question him to gather intelligence about the gang's activities.

Trevizo, based on her observations and on Johnson's answers to her questions, suspected that Johnson was carrying a weapon. She frisked him and discovered a firearm at his waist. The Supreme Court held that the interest in *officer safety* outweighed the slight intrusion into individual privacy in this situation. The Court noted that a passenger has the same motivation as the driver to use violence to prevent the officers from detecting criminal activity unrelated to the reason for the traffic stop. "Trevizo . . . was not constitutionally required to give Johnson an opportunity to depart the scene after he exited the vehicle without first ensuring that in so doing she was not permitting a dangerous person to get behind her" (*Arizona v. Johnson*, 555 U.S. 323 [2009]).

Terry *Searches of Automobiles*

In 1983, in *Michigan v. Long*, the U.S. Supreme Court extended *Terry* frisks to the passenger compartment of automobiles when police officers possess a reasonable fear for their safety. Deputies Lewis and Howell observed a car swerve into a ditch in rural Michigan. The officers stopped to investigate and were met by David Long at the rear of the car. The door on the driver's side of the vehicle was left open. Long, who one of the officers testified "appeared to be under the influence of something," failed to respond to a request to produce his registration and turned and began walking toward the open door of the vehicle. The officers followed Long and spotted a hunting knife on the floorboard of the driver's side of the car. Deputy Howell shined his flashlight into the car, noticed something protruding from under the armrest on the front seat, lifted the armrest, and discovered marijuana (*Michigan v. Long*, 463 U.S. 1032, 1035 [1983]).

How can this search of Long's automobile be justified as a limited *Terry* frisk for weapons? The Supreme Court upheld Deputy Howell's search and explained that the search of the passenger compartment of an automobile is justified in those instances in which an officer possesses a reasonable belief that the suspect is potentially dangerous and may gain immediate control of weapons. The Court stressed that the search must be limited to those areas in which a "weapon may be placed or hidden." In this case, there was the possibility that Long might have broken away from the police and gained access to a weapon. In the event that Long was not arrested, he might have grabbed a weapon after reentering his car. Are you persuaded that Long posed a threat to the officers? Should the Court have required the police to demonstrate that the search was the only alternative available to protect themselves? How would the Supreme Court have ruled in the event that the automobile was locked?

We also should note the Supreme Court decision in *Maryland v. Buie*. In *Buie,* the police relied on an arrest warrant to arrest Jerome Edward Buie in his home for armed robbery. The Court cited *Michigan v. Long* to uphold the right of the police to carry out a protective sweep of a home where there is reasonable suspicion that the sweep is necessary to locate individuals who may pose a threat to the safety and security of the police officers. Buie's co-conspirator had yet to be found, and the police could reasonably have concluded that he was hiding in the basement (*Maryland v. Buie*, 494 U.S. 325, 327–331 [1990]).

Terry *Searches for Illegal Narcotics*

In 1993, in *Minnesota v. Dickerson*, the U.S. Supreme Court upheld the right of a police officer conducting a frisk to seize illegal narcotics. The officer must have immediate probable cause to believe that the items he or she encounters are illegal narcotics.

The Supreme Court explained that a pat down in which a law enforcement officer feels an object that he or she has probable cause to believe is an illegal narcotic is analogous to a plain-view search. The Court explained that the plain-view doctrine permits a law enforcement officer to seize contraband that he or she views during the course of a lawful search. An illustration of plain view is a police officer who while searching a home for drugs encounters and seizes an illegal assault rifle. The "plain-feel" doctrine is based on an officer's touch rather than visual examination. This permits a police officer to seize an object that the officer's physical examination indicates is contraband.

The Supreme Court in *Dickerson* held that "[i]f a police officer lawfully pats down a suspect's outer clothing and feels an object whose contour or mass makes its identity immediately apparent, there has been no invasion of the suspect's privacy beyond that already authorized by the officer's search for weapons; if the object is contraband, its warrantless seizure would be justified by the same practical considerations that inhere in the plain-view context" (*Minnesota v. Dickerson*, 508 U.S. 366, 375 [1993]). Keep in mind that a major limitation on the seizure of illegal narcotics under the **plain-feel doctrine** is that it must be "immediately apparent" (probable cause) to the officer that he or she is feeling illegal narcotics.

Legal Equation		
A *Terry* frisk	=	Where nothing in the initial stages of the encounter serves to dispel an officer's reasonable fear for his or her own or others' safety
	+	The officer is entitled for the protection of himself or herself and others in the area to conduct a carefully limited search of the outer clothing of such persons
	+	In an attempt to discover weapons that might be used to assault him.
A *Terry* search of the passenger compartment of an automobile	=	The search of the passenger compartment of an automobile is justified in those instances in which an officer possesses a reasonable belief that the suspect is dangerous and may gain immediate control of weapons
	+	The search must be limited to those areas in which a weapon may be placed or hidden in those cases in which the police possess articulable and objectively reasonable belief that the suspect is potentially dangerous.
A *Terry* frisk and the seizure of drugs	=	A police officer who lawfully pats down a suspect's outer clothing
	+	Feels an object whose contour or mass makes its identity as illegal narcotics immediately apparent.

13.5 YOU DECIDE

Officer B. C. Davis of the Portsmouth Redevelopment and Housing Authority Police approached Darrio L. Cost who was sitting in the passenger seat of a car parked in a lot reserved for residents of the complex. Davis observed Cost reach across his body toward his left front pants pocket. Davis did not respond when asked what he was reaching for in his pocket. Davis told Cost to "get away from" his pocket, but Cost once again reached toward his pocket.

Davis directed Cost to exit the auto and "immediately frisked Cost's left front pants pocket. Davis . . . felt numerous capsules inside." Davis removed a plastic bag containing twenty capsules of heroin. He testified that he had been a police officer for four and half years and "knew" that the capsules were heroin based on his "training and experience." Are the heroin capsules admissible at trial? See *Cost v. Commonwealth* (657 S.E. 2nd 505 [Va. 2008]).

You can learn what the court decided by referring to the study site, **http://study.sagepub.com/lippmance.**

13.6 YOU DECIDE

The Beloit, Wisconsin, police received an anonymous telephone tip that four or five African American males were selling drugs to motorists at a specific intersection. Two officers arrived at the location within thirty minutes and saw a Ford with three black males seated on the hood of the car. One of the officers approached Lamardus D. Ford and smelled marijuana. The officer ordered Ford off the car, placed Ford's hands on the hood, and began patting him down. The officer testified that the frisk was routine practice because he was investigating possible drug activity, he had smelled marijuana, and it was his routine practice to conduct frisks during street encounters for safety reasons. During the pat down, the officer felt a large square wad of soft material in Ford's front pants pocket. Ford was asked what it was and replied that it was money. Ford became "jumpy" whenever the officer's hands approached the front of Ford's waist, and Ford even grabbed the officer's hand as it

approached that area. Because Ford was not cooperative, the officer took Ford in a "full nelson" hold to his squad car, where he placed Ford's hands behind his back and handcuffed him. The officer then resumed the pat down. Ford was still jumpy whenever the officer approached the waistband of his boxer shorts, which were visible above Ford's jeans. The officer testified that it is common practice for people to put guns and other contraband down the front of their shorts. The officer asked if he could look inside Ford's shorts. Ford took a step back. The officer responded by pulling out the waistband about one and one-half inches and shined a flashlight into Ford's underwear. The officer discovered plastic bags of marijuana between Ford's thigh and the genitals. The officer removed the bags of marijuana and arrested Ford for possession of a controlled substance. Were the narcotics legally seized by the officer? See *State v. Ford* (565 N.W.2d 286 [Ct. App. Wis. 1997]).

You can learn what the court decided by referring to the study site, **http://study.sagepub.com/lippmance.**

■ CASE ANALYSIS

In *State v. Wardlow*, the Supreme Court decided whether unprovoked flight in an area characterized by "heavy narcotics trafficking" constitutes reasonable suspicion.

Did Wardlow's fleeing from the police constitute reasonable suspicion?

Illinois v. Wardlow, 528 U.S. 119 (2000), Rehnquist, C.J.

Facts

On September 9, 1995, Officers Nolan and Harvey were working as uniformed officers in the special operations section of the

Chicago Police Department. The officers were driving the last car of a four-car caravan converging on an area known for heavy narcotics trafficking in order to investigate drug transactions. The officers were traveling together because they expected to find a crowd of people in the area, including lookouts and customers.

As the caravan passed 4035 West Van Buren, Officer Nolan observed respondent Wardlow standing next to the building holding an opaque bag. Respondent looked in the direction of the officers and fled. Nolan and Harvey turned their car southbound, watched him as he ran through the gangway and an alley, and eventually cornered him on the street. Nolan then exited his car and stopped respondent. He immediately conducted a protective pat-down search for weapons because in his experience it was common for there to be weapons in the near vicinity of narcotics transactions. During the frisk, Officer Nolan squeezed the bag respondent was carrying and felt a heavy, hard object similar to the shape of a gun. The officer then opened the bag and discovered a .38-caliber handgun with five live rounds of ammunition. The officers arrested Wardlow.

The Illinois trial court denied respondent's motion to suppress, finding the gun was recovered during a lawful stop and frisk. Following a . . . bench trial, Wardlow was convicted of unlawful use of a weapon by a felon. The Illinois Appellate Court reversed Wardlow's conviction, concluding that the gun should have been suppressed because Officer Nolan did not have reasonable suspicion sufficient to justify an investigative stop pursuant to *Terry v. Ohio*. . . . The Illinois Supreme Court agreed. . . .

The state courts have differed on whether unprovoked flight is sufficient grounds to constitute reasonable suspicion. This case, involving a brief encounter between a citizen and a police officer on a public street, is governed by the analysis we first applied in *Terry.* We granted certiorari solely on the question of whether the initial stop was supported by reasonable suspicion. Therefore, we express no opinion as to the lawfulness of the frisk independently of the stop.

Nolan and Harvey were among eight officers in a four-car caravan that was converging on an area known for heavy narcotics trafficking, and the officers anticipated encountering a large number of people in the area, including drug customers and individuals serving as lookouts. It was in this context that Officer Nolan decided to investigate Wardlow after observing him flee. An individual's presence in an area of expected criminal activity, standing alone, is not enough to support a reasonable, particularized suspicion that the person is committing a crime. But officers are not required to ignore the relevant characteristics of a location in determining whether the circumstances are sufficiently suspicious to warrant further investigation. Accordingly, we have previously noted the fact that the stop occurred in a "high crime area" among the relevant contextual considerations in a *Terry* analysis.

In this case, moreover, it was not merely respondent's presence in an area of heavy narcotics trafficking that aroused the officers' suspicion but his unprovoked flight upon noticing the police. Our cases have also recognized that nervous, evasive behavior is a pertinent factor in determining reasonable suspicion. Headlong flight—wherever it occurs—is the consummate act of evasion: It is not necessarily indicative of wrongdoing, but it is certainly suggestive of such. In reviewing the propriety of an officer's conduct, courts do not have available empirical studies dealing with inferences drawn from suspicious behavior, and we cannot reasonably demand scientific certainty from judges or law enforcement officers where none exists. Thus, the determination of reasonable suspicion must be based on commonsense judgments and inferences about human behavior. We conclude Officer Nolan was justified in suspecting that Wardlow was involved in criminal activity and, therefore, in investigating further.

When an officer, without reasonable suspicion or probable cause, approaches an individual, the individual has a right to ignore the police and go about his business. And any "refusal to cooperate, without more, does not furnish the minimal level of objective justification needed for a detention or seizure." But unprovoked flight is simply not a mere refusal to cooperate. Flight, by its very nature, is not "going about one's business"; in fact, it is just the opposite. Allowing officers confronted with such flight to stop the fugitive and investigate further is quite consistent with the individual's right to go about his business or to stay put and remain silent in the face of police questioning.

Respondent . . . also argue[s] that there are innocent reasons for flight from police and that, therefore, flight is not necessarily indicative of ongoing criminal activity. This fact is undoubtedly true, but does not establish a violation of the Fourth Amendment. Even in *Terry,* the conduct justifying the stop was ambiguous and susceptible of an innocent explanation. The officer observed two individuals pacing back and forth in front of a store, peering into the window and periodically conferring. All of this conduct was by itself lawful, but it also suggested that the individuals were casing the store for a planned robbery. *Terry* recognized that the officers could detain the individuals to resolve the ambiguity. In allowing such detentions, *Terry* accepts the risk that officers may stop innocent people. . . . The *Terry* stop is a far more minimal intrusion, simply allowing the officer to briefly investigate further. If the officer does not learn facts rising to the level of probable cause, the individual must be allowed to go on his way. But in this case the officers found respondent in possession of a handgun, and arrested him for violation of an Illinois firearms statute. No question of the propriety of the arrest itself is before us.

The judgment of the Supreme Court of Illinois is reversed, and the cause is remanded for further proceedings not inconsistent with this opinion.

CHAPTER SUMMARY

In *Terry v. Ohio*, Chief Justice Earl Warren stressed that a police officer may in "appropriate circumstances" approach and seize an individual to investigate possible criminal behavior despite the fact that the officer does not have probable cause to make an arrest. The question asked by a judge in reviewing a police officer's decision to stop an individual is "whether the facts available to the officer at the moment of the intrusion warrant a man or woman of reasonable caution in the belief" that there is reasonable suspicion that a crime has occurred, is under way, or is about to occur.

The Supreme Court stressed that reasonable suspicion is a "less demanding standard than probable cause" and may be based on less complete and less reliable information. In determining whether there is reasonable suspicion, the "totality of the circumstances" is to be taken into account. Judges consider a number of factors, including whether there is a pattern of conduct indicative of criminal activity, the time of day, whether the events occur in a high-crime area, the police officer's knowledge that a suspect has an arrest record or criminal background, flight or evasion or nervousness of the suspect, and the officer's experience in making arrests for this type of activity. The facts are to be interpreted in light of an officer's experience and training. Reasonable suspicion is based on probabilities rather than certainties, and in putting together the pieces of the puzzle that constitute reasonable suspicion, innocent people inevitably may be mistakenly stopped and searched.

Reasonable suspicion also may be based on an informant's tip. An informant is required to be known to the police and to have proven reliable in the past. The court also will ask how the informant has obtained the information. An informant with firsthand knowledge of criminal activity should be able to provide detailed information.

A tip that lacks these indicia of reliability may be relied on where corroborated in essential details by the police. Most important is the informant's demonstrated ability to have predicted a suspect's pattern of activity. The judge strikes a balance. The less reliable the informant, the more a court may insist that the informant is in the position to provide detailed information. A tip that is thought to initially lack the indicia of reliability may be strengthened by police corroboration and by the fact that the informant came forward personally and by a criminal statute that punishes intentionally "false criminal reports."

Law enforcement has developed profiles to detect terrorists, drug couriers, and other offenders. Courts generally do not give particular weight to the claim that an individual fits a "profile" and, instead, ask whether the combination of the factors identified in the profile constitutes reasonable suspicion. In many instances, courts have found reasonable suspicion where law enforcement agents have supplemented the profile with additional observations.

An individual may not be lawfully stopped by the police when the sole reason for his or her seizure is race, ethnicity, gender, religion, or other descriptive characteristic. An individual also may not be stopped based on the fact that he or she "does not belong in a neighborhood." Race, ethnicity, or some other physical characteristic, however, may be considered as one of several factors in a finding of reasonable suspicion.

The Supreme Court has stressed that a *Terry* stop and frisk is a limited intrusion to investigate and to detect crime. Law enforcement officials may interfere with your freedom and privacy only to the extent required to accomplish their purpose. A *Terry* stop is open to constitutional challenge when a suspect is treated as if he or she has been subjected to a probable cause arrest rather than to a reasonable suspicion stop. This inquiry typically focuses on three areas: movement, length of detention, and intrusiveness.

The Supreme Court has introduced some modest flexibility into *Terry* in the case of traffic stops. In *Pennsylvania v. Mimms*, the Supreme Court held that the "legitimate and weighty" interest in protecting the safety of a police officer outweighs the "de minimis" (trivial) intrusion on the liberty of the citizen involved in requiring a driver to leave an automobile. In *Maryland v. Wilson*, the Supreme Court extended the ruling in *Mimms* and held that an officer may require a passenger or passengers to exit a car. Several state supreme courts, however, have rejected the U.S. Supreme Court's rulings and require that law enforcement officers possess reasonable suspicion before directing individuals to vacate a motor vehicle. The Supreme Court also has held that an officer is free to interrogate and investigate criminal activity on the part of passengers that is unrelated to the purpose of the traffic stop so long as this investigation does not "measurably extend the duration of the stop."

The second prong of the judgment in *Terry* addresses the nature and scope of a *Terry* frisk. The Supreme Court in *Terry v. Ohio* recognized that American criminals have a "long tradition of armed violence" and that a number of law enforcement officers are killed and wounded every year in the line of duty. Most of these fatalities and injuries are inflicted at fairly close range with guns and knives. The Court accordingly ruled that where "nothing in the initial stages of the encounter serves to dispel [an officer's] reasonable fear for his own or others' safety, he is entitled for the protection of himself and others in the area to conduct a carefully limited search of the outer clothing of such persons in an attempt to discover weapons which might be used to assault him." The frisk is not automatic. The suspect must be provided with the opportunity to dispel the officer's reasonable fear for his own or others' safety and security.

The driver and a passenger in an automobile detained by the police may be frisked based on reasonable suspicion. In *Michigan v. Long*, the Supreme Court extended *Terry* frisks to the passenger compartment of automobiles. The Court stressed that the search must be limited to those areas in which a "weapon may be placed or hidden" and to those instances in which the police "possess [an] articulable and objectively reasonable belief that the suspect is potentially dangerous and may gain immediate control of weapons." *Minnesota v. Dickerson* affirmed the limited right of a police officer conducting a frisk to seize illegal narcotics. The officer under the "plain-feel" doctrine must have probable cause to believe that the object that he or she encounters is an illegal narcotic.

In summary, in *Terry v. Ohio*, the Supreme Court explicitly balanced the interest in investigating and detecting crime against the intrusion into individual privacy and held that individuals may be subjected to limited seizures based on reasonable suspicion. The Court further ruled that officers may conduct frisks to protect themselves. The Court attempted to ensure that these police–citizen interactions would be perceived as fair and neutral by requiring that an officer base his or her decision-making on objective facts interpreted in light of his or her experience. This balancing test has been employed by the Court in addressing areas ranging from the removal of the occupants of automobiles to the searches of passenger compartments and intrusions to seize narcotics. *Terry* stops and frisks are based on probabilities and predictions and on occasion may result in interference with the liberty of innocents. We have traded a measure of liberty for safety and security. Do you agree that the appropriate balance has been struck by the Supreme Court in regard to stop and frisk?

CHAPTER REVIEW QUESTIONS

1. What is the constitutional basis for the police practice of stop and frisk?

2. Summarize the decision in *Terry v. Ohio*.

3. Discuss the role of reasonableness, objectivity, experience, expertise, probability, and the totality of the circumstances in the determination of reasonable suspicion.

4. What are some of the factors that a police officer may consider in determining whether there is reasonable suspicion to stop an individual?

5. What is the standard adopted by courts to determine whether the police were justified in relying on an informant's tip to determine reasonable suspicion?

6. How are profiles developed? Do courts give particular weight to profiles in determining reasonable suspicion?

7. Under what circumstances may race be considered in determining reasonable suspicion? Is racial profiling ever justified?

8. Discuss the scope and duration of a *Terry* stop in regard to the permissible movement of a suspect, the length of the detention, and the intrusiveness of the stop.

9. What is the legal standard for a *Terry* frisk?

10. May a police officer order a driver or a passenger to exit an automobile? Under what circumstances may an officer frisk a driver or passenger who has exited a vehicle?

11. Discuss the extension of *Terry* frisks to automobile passenger compartments and to drugs.

12. Write a one-page essay for police officers summarizing the law of stops and frisks.

LEGAL TERMINOLOGY

anonymous tip
articulable suspicion
case-by-case determination
drug courier profile

frisk
informant
plain-feel doctrine
racial profiling

reasonable suspicion
stop and frisk
stop-and-identify statutes

14

PROBABLE CAUSE AND ARRESTS

Did the police have probable cause to arrest Draper?

On the morning of September 8, Marsh and a Denver police officer went to the Denver Union Station and kept watch over all incoming trains from Chicago, but they did not see anyone fitting the description that Hereford [a government informant] had given. Repeating the process on the morning of September 9, they saw a person, having the exact physical attributes and wearing the precise clothing described by Hereford, alight from an incoming Chicago train and start walking "fast" toward the exit. He was carrying a tan zipper bag in his right hand and the left was thrust in his raincoat pocket. Marsh, accompanied by the police officer, overtook, stopped, and arrested him. They then searched him and found the two "envelopes containing heroin" clutched in his left hand in his raincoat pocket, and found the syringe in the tan zipper bag. Marsh then took him (petitioner) into custody. (*Draper v. United States*, 358 U.S. 307 [1959])

CHAPTER OUTLINE

Introduction
Arrests
Probable Cause
Reasonableness and Arrests
Probable Cause, Warrants, and the Courts

Arrests and Warrants
Case Analysis
Chapter Summary
Chapter Review Questions
Legal Terminology

TEST YOUR KNOWLEDGE

1. Do you know the definition of probable cause and the type of facts that the police may rely on in determining probable cause?

2. Can you distinguish between the *Aguilar-Spinelli* test for evaluating whether the police may rely on an informant and the totality-of-the-circumstances test?

3. Are you able to describe the process for obtaining an arrest warrant?

4. Do you know when an arrest warrant is required for felony arrests and for misdemeanor arrests in public and in the home?

5. Can you define exigent circumstances?

6. Are you able to describe circumstances under which the police may rely on deadly force and may rely on non-deadly force?

7. Do you know the law on misdemeanors, citations, and arrests?

■ INTRODUCTION

An arrest is reasonable under the Fourth Amendment when two conditions are satisfied:

- The arrest must be based on *probable cause.* Probable cause may be based on *direct observations* or on *hearsay.*
- The arrest is carried out in a *reasonable fashion.*

Carrying out an arrest in a reasonable fashion involves various requirements that will be discussed in this chapter:

- *Determination of probable cause.* An arrest warrant must be issued by a judge or magistrate. A warrantless arrest must be found by a judge or magistrate to have been based on probable cause.
- *Warrants.* An *arrest warrant* is not required to arrest individuals in most instances. Absent consent or exigent circumstances, arrests in the home require a warrant.
- *Physical force.* The police may employ *reasonable force* to seize a suspect.
- *Arrests and citations.* Individuals are subject to *arrest* for both felonies and misdemeanors. There is no requirement that a citation be issued to an individual who has committed a misdemeanor in the presence of an officer.

As you read the chapter, consider how the probable cause standard and the requirement that arrests be carried out in a reasonable fashion balance the individual right to privacy with the responsibility of the police to enforce the law and to arrest individuals.

■ ARRESTS

An **arrest** under the Fourth Amendment occurs when an individual is lawfully taken into custody. An arrest is more intrusive than an investigative stop and frisk in several respects:

- *Place.* An investigative stop typically involves a brief detention on the street or in a public location. In contrast, an individual who is arrested is detained at the police station or in jail.
- *Time.* An investigative stop may last only as long as required to complete the investigation, while an arrest may result in detention for several hours or several days or, in some cases, even longer.
- *Documentation.* A stop and frisk is not recorded as part of an individual's criminal history. An arrest is entered into an individual's criminal record.
- *Searches.* An investigative stop may be accompanied by a brief interrogation and frisk. A custodial arrest may lead to a full search and to an inventory of an individual's possessions at the police station and to an extended interrogation.
- *Criminal consequences.* A stop and frisk results in a brief investigative stop. A custodial arrest may lead to a criminal indictment, trial, and criminal punishment.

How do you know that you have been arrested rather than stopped for a *Terry* investigation? An officer may directly tell you that "you are under arrest." This is a *formal arrest.* A *de facto arrest* occurs when an officer does not directly tell you that you are under arrest but, based on the totality of the circumstances, a reasonable person would conclude that he or she is under arrest. An individual under this objective test would know that he or she is detained when handcuffed, restrained by force or the threat of force, or involuntarily taken to the police station. There are three characteristics of an arrest to keep in mind:

- *Lawful authority.* The officer is acting in his or her official capacity as a law enforcement official. Restraint by a private person is kidnapping.

- *Detention.* An officer may restrain an individual through a formal statement ("you are under arrest") or through actions that constitute a de facto arrest.
- *Reasonable person.* A reasonable person, based on the objective circumstances, would believe that he or she is under arrest.

■ PROBABLE CAUSE

As you recall, a stop and frisk is a brief investigative stop and requires reasonable suspicion. An arrest, as we have seen, is more intrusive than a stop and frisk, and courts have held that under the Fourth Amendment reasonableness standard, an arrest requires probable cause. Officers possess probable cause for an arrest where the facts and circumstances within their knowledge and of which they have reasonably trustworthy information are sufficient to warrant a person of reasonable caution in the belief that an offense has been or is being committed. Stated somewhat more simply, probable cause requires that a police officer objectively conclude, based on reasonably reliable facts, that a crime has been committed and that the person being arrested has committed the crime (*Carroll v. United States*, 267 U.S. 132, 162 [1925]).

■ ■ ■ ■ ■ ■ ■ ■ ■ ■

PHOTO 14.1

The police may arrest an individual where there is probable cause to believe that the individual has committed or is committing a felony or where the police observe a misdemeanor and are authorized to arrest the individual for the misdemeanor.

AP Photo/Grand Rapids Press, Chris Clark

The Supreme Court has stressed on a number of occasions that probable cause is based on "common sense" and on a "practical evaluation of the totality of the facts" and that probable cause cannot be reduced to a set of rules or to a mathematical formula. It is a matter of "probabilities" rather than "certainties." In an effort to clarify the degree of proof that is required for probable cause, the Supreme Court has observed that probable cause is more than reasonable suspicion and less than the beyond-a-reasonable-doubt standard required for a criminal conviction. In making this objective determination, judges recognize that law enforcement officers may possess a special expertise based on their experience on the streets. In *United States v. Ortiz*, the U.S. Supreme Court observed that border patrol officers are entitled to rely on their experience in combating illegal immigration in making a probable cause determination (*United States v. Ortiz*, 422 U.S. 891 [1975]).

The central point is that probable cause is based on facts, and an officer may not rely solely on intuition, opinion, or a hunch. You can think of probable cause to arrest an individual as more than 50 percent likelihood that the particular individual committed a crime.

The U.S. Supreme Court explained that the probable cause standard strikes a balance between the responsibility of law enforcement to investigate crimes and to apprehend offenders and the interest of citizens in protecting their privacy. The Court noted in *Brinegar* that "[r]equiring more would unduly hamper law enforcement. To allow less would be to leave law-abiding citizens at the mercy of the officer's whim or caprice" (*Brinegar v. United States*, 338 U.S. 160, 176 [1949]).

In the next sections, we will see that the police may rely on their five senses to establish probable cause. An officer also may rely on hearsay or facts reported by informants to the police officer that the officer does not directly observe himself or herself.

Direct Observations

A police officer may rely on his or her five senses in developing probable cause to arrest an individual. This means that the officer may develop probable cause through sight, sound, smell, touch, and taste. In some instances, the officer may directly observe a crime. In other instances, an officer must piece together a factual jigsaw puzzle. An officer may *hear* a gunshot, *observe* an individual flee, *stop and frisk* the individual, *seize* an unlawful firearm, and *arrest* the individual based on *probable cause*. The police may rely on various types of observations in making a probable cause determination:

- *Direct observations.* An officer may directly *observe* an individual engage in criminal conduct or conduct characteristic of an individual who is about to commit a crime or who has committed a crime.
- *Statements.* The police may *hear* a suspect make an incriminating remark or confess to a crime.
- *Seize evidence.* The police may *collect and analyze* scientific evidence that indicates that a suspect was involved in a crime. This includes DNA, blood, fingerprints, and hair samples.
- *Smell.* A police officer may *smell* narcotics or alcohol.

United States v. Humphries illustrates how the police rely on various "senses" in developing probable cause to make an arrest. The officers were patrolling in an area known for drug trafficking and observed a group of men gathered on the street. As the officers pulled their marked squad car onto the block, they saw the defendant pat his waist, an act that the officers interpreted as the defendant's ensuring that his firearm was readily accessible. As the officers approached the men, the officers smelled marijuana, and the defendant began to quickly walk away. The officers followed the suspect and smelled an even stronger aroma of marijuana as they closed within five or ten feet. The defendant disregarded the officer's order to halt and went into a house where he was arrested. Can you identify the facts that the Fourth Circuit Court of Appeals found constituted probable cause (*United States v. Humphries*, 372 F.3d 653 [4th Cir. 2004])?

The Supreme Court's 1968 judgment in *Peters v. United States* also illustrates how visually observable factors can combine to constitute probable cause. Police officer Samuel Lasky heard noises outside the door of his apartment that suggested that someone was trying to enter his apartment. He peered out and saw two men tiptoeing down the hallway whom he had never seen before in the twelve years he had lived in the building. Lasky entered the hallway, and the men fled and were apprehended by Lasky in the stairwell. John Peters was unable to explain why he was in the building, and Lasky searched him and found burglar tools. The U.S. Supreme Court concluded that although Lasky did not actually see the two men attempt to jimmy the lock, it is "difficult to conceive of stronger grounds for an arrest, short of actual eyewitness observation of criminal activity" (*Peters v. United States*, 392 U.S. 40, 66 [1968]).

What if an officer strongly believes there is probable cause but lacks objective facts? In *Beck v. Ohio*, a police officer stopped William Beck's automobile and searched Beck based on the fact that the officer recognized Beck and knew that on three previous occasions he had been arrested and convicted of gambling offenses. The Supreme Court held that the officer's knowledge of Beck's background did not constitute probable cause to arrest Beck for unlawful gambling. The Court stressed that an arrest could not be justified based on such "scant evidence" and that if "these facts constituted probable cause," "anyone with a previous criminal record could be arrested at will." The officer's subjective good faith belief is not in and of itself sufficient to constitute probable cause. "If subjective good faith alone were the test, the protections of the Fourth Amendment would evaporate, and the people would not be 'secure in their persons, houses, papers, and effects'" (*Beck v. Ohio*, 379 U.S. 89, 94, 97 [1964]).

Hearsay

Probable cause also may be based on hearsay or secondhand information that is communicated to the police (hearsay, you may recall from Chapter Nine, is commonly defined as information that is derived not from the personal knowledge of the witness but from the repetition of what he or she has heard others say). This information may come from eyewitnesses, crime victims, police officers, or informants. Informants typically are individuals who themselves are involved in criminal activity and who cooperate with the police by providing information. The problem with hearsay is that it is difficult to determine whether secondhand information is truthful and accurate. This is because the police officer who appears before the judge did not actually witness the events himself or herself and is reporting the observations of another person. Judges in criminal trials, for this reason, strictly limit the introduction of hearsay evidence. The police do not have the luxury of deciding whether to rely on hearsay. Law enforcement officers must react immediately to reports of crime and would be criticized for failing to investigate a citizen's complaint that an armed and dangerous individual is in a school parking lot.

In determining whether hearsay provides probable cause, courts follow several simple rules. First, eyewitnesses and victims along with police officers are considered reliable, and their reports are accepted as accurate. Second, informants are presumed to be unreliable, and as a result, the information provided by informants must satisfy strict standards before a judge or magistrate finds that the information constitutes probable cause. The approach of courts to informants is summarized below:

informants = usually bad → doing it for many diff reasons.

- *Citizen-informants*. Eyewitnesses and victims are presumed reliable, and their reports may constitute probable cause. These individuals do not have a motive to distort the truth, and their credibility is enhanced by the fact that they often are interviewed immediately after observing a crime or being victimized by a crime (*Commonwealth v. Carey*, 554 N.E.2d 1199, 1203 [Mass. 1990]).

- *Police*. The reports of law enforcement officers are considered credible and may constitute probable cause (*United States v. Ventresca*, 380 U.S. 102 [1965]).

- *Informants.* Courts are reluctant to find that the reports of informants constitute probable cause. Informants may have a self-interest in the prosecution of the individuals named in their reports. They may hope that their cooperation and assistance lead to a plea bargain or other benefits. The U.S. Supreme Court accordingly has adopted special requirements that are discussed below for evaluating whether an informant's report constitutes probable cause (*Jones v. United States*, 266 F.2d 924 [D.C. Ct. App. 1959]).

The U.S. Supreme Court has devoted a significant amount of time to the question of informants. An example is *McCray v. Illinois*. In *McCray*, Chicago police arrested George McCray based on a tip from a police informant that McCray "was selling narcotics and had narcotics on his person and that he could be found in the vicinity of 47th and Calumet at this particular time." The officers drove the informant to the designated intersection, and the informant pointed to McCray walking at a fast pace between two buildings. Officer Charles Jackson testified that the informant had assisted in the arrest of drug dealers in the past and that the informant had told him that McCray had supplied him with narcotics over the course of the past year. The U.S. Supreme Court concluded that the police possessed probable cause to arrest McCray based on the informant's report that he was in possession of narcotics.

The Court went on to hold that the prosecution is not required to disclose an informant's identity at a probable cause hearing before a judge or even at a trial in which a defendant's guilt or innocence is at stake. Disclosure would discourage informants from assisting the police. The judge has the discretion to require that the government produce an informant to testify in those instances in which the judge questions the informant's existence or in which the judge is persuaded that the defendant must be given the opportunity to cross-examine the informant to establish the defendant's innocence. For example, federal courts have held that the **informant privilege** does not protect an informant from testifying in those cases in which the defendant is charged with selling narcotics to the informant and there are no other prosecution witnesses who observed the sale (*McCray v. Illinois*, 386 U.S. 300 [1967]).

└ privilege not to testify

The Aguilar-Spinelli Test

The traditional approach for evaluating whether the police may rely on an informant's report to establish probable cause is the so-called **Aguilar-Spinelli test**. In 1983, in *Illinois v. Gates*, the U.S. Supreme Court modified this test and adopted a "totality-of-the-circumstances" analysis. Several states nonetheless continue to follow the *Aguilar-Spinelli* approach. The standard that must be met for an informant's tip to constitute probable cause is the same whether the police are relying on an informant to obtain an arrest warrant or to obtain a search warrant (*Illinois v. Gates*, 462 U.S. 213 [1983]).

In *Aguilar v. Texas*, two police officers obtained a warrant from a local justice of the peace. The officers submitted a sworn statement, an **affidavit**, to the justice of the peace, which recounted that they had received "reliable information from a credible person" that Nick Alford Aguilar was engaged in the unlawful sale of narcotics and that the officers "believe that heroin, marijuana, barbituates [*sic*] and other narcotics and narcotic paraphernalia are being kept" at Aguilar's home. A search of Aguilar's home based on the warrant led to the discovery of heroin, and Aguilar was sentenced to twenty years in prison. The U.S. Supreme Court held that the warrant relied on by the police was based on "mere conclusions" and did not provide probable cause to search Aguilar's home. Justice Arthur Goldberg, writing for the majority, held that probable cause may be based on the hearsay report of an informant so long as the *veracity prong* and the *basis-of-knowledge prong* are satisfied by the information in the affidavit. Justice Goldberg stressed that these two requirements are "commonsense conditions" for relying on "secondhand information" (*Aguilar v. Texas*, 378 U.S. 108 [1964]). The two prongs are explained below:

Veracity prong. The police officer is required to demonstrate that he or she has good reason to believe that the informant's information is accurate. How is this accomplished? An informant's credibility is established by highlighting that the informant has provided accurate information in the past. In *McCray v. Illinois*, the informant had provided the police with accurate information that had led to narcotics arrests fifteen or sixteen times over the past year. Trustworthiness also may be established by an informant who exposes himself or herself to criminal liability by admitting involvement in illegal activity. In *United States v. Harris*, the informant reported that he had purchased unlawfully produced alcohol from the suspect over the past two years. The U.S. Supreme Court held that this was a sufficient indicator of credibility to support a finding of probable cause. Justice Warren Burger explained that people "do not lightly admit a crime" and "place critical evidence in the hands of the police" and "place themselves at risk of criminal prosecution" (*United States v. Harris*, 403 U.S. 573, 583–584 [1971]).

Basis-of-knowledge prong. The police officer must indicate how the informant obtained knowledge of the criminal activity. Did the informant witness a narcotics sale or purchase narcotics, or is the informant relying on a hearsay report from a friend? The U.S. Supreme Court held that in some instances, detailed information provided to the police may be sufficient because this detail could have been obtained only by someone who witnessed the criminal activity. In *Draper v. United States*, the Supreme Court held that the accurate detail provided by the informant James A. Hereford justified the inference that Hereford obtained the information regarding James Alonzo Draper's possession of three ounces of heroin in a reliable fashion. The Supreme Court pointed to the fact that the information Hereford provided federal narcotic agent John W. Marsh accurately reported the date that Draper's train from Chicago would arrive in Denver and accurately described Draper's "exact physical attributes . . . [and] precise clothing" and the fact that he was carrying a "tan zipper bag" and typically walked at a rapid pace (*Draper v. United States*, 358 U.S. 307 [1959]).

The Supreme Court followed this two-prong test in *Spinelli v. United States* in holding that the informant's tip relied on by the police did not constitute probable cause. The Court stressed that both conditions established in *Aguilar* must be satisfied to constitute probable cause. William Spinelli was convicted of traveling to Saint Louis, Missouri, from an adjacent Illinois suburb with the intention of conducting gambling activity. He alleged that the affidavit on which the arrest warrant was based did not constitute probable cause. The affidavit contained a report from an anonymous informant along with the results of an FBI investigation that corroborated the informant's tip. The affidavit contained the following four allegations (*Spinelli v. United States*, 393 U.S. 410 [1969]):

- The FBI had monitored Spinelli's movements for five days, and on four occasions, he crossed a bridge leading from Illinois to Saint Louis and entered an apartment house.
- An FBI investigation revealed that the apartment contained two telephones.

- Spinelli was known to law enforcement agents and to the informant as a bookmaker and gambler.
- The FBI had been informed by a confidential and reliable informant that Spinelli was accepting wagers and disseminating wagering information through two telephones.

The Supreme Court concluded that the affidavit did not satisfy the two-prong test established in *Aguilar*. First, there was no information supporting the past accuracy of the informant and the veracity prong. What of the basis-of-knowledge prong? The tip does not indicate how the FBI's source obtained the information. It is not "alleged that the informant personally observed Spinelli at work or that he had ever placed a bet with him." In other words, there was not enough detail for the magistrate to conclude that the informant was relying on "something more substantial than a casual rumor." The fact that Spinelli had two telephones was not the type of detailed information that indicates that the informant obtained the information in a reliable fashion. There is nothing unusual about an apartment with two separate telephone lines. The allegation that Spinelli was a "known" gambler and an associate of gamblers is an "unilluminating assertion of suspicion that is entitled to no weight in appraising the magistrate's decision." The Supreme Court in *Spinelli* stressed that the informant's tip may have proved significant had the FBI provided *corroborating information* that more fully supported the informant's tip. For example, the FBI could have bolstered the tip by reporting that there was a significant amount of activity at the apartment or that there was an unusual number of phone calls being made from the two phones. *Spinelli* teaches us that an informant's tip that lacks detail may be enhanced by a police investigation that supplements the information in the tip.

In summary, the *Aguilar-Spinelli* test provides that information obtained from an informant must satisfy both the veracity prong and the basis-of-knowledge prong in order to constitute probable cause. The Supreme Court characterizes this as a "commonsense approach" because these are the two factors that most of us would consider when we decide to rely on information that is provided by another person. Do you believe that the Supreme Court is correct in holding that because the tip in *Spinelli* did not meet the two-prong test, the affidavit did not constitute probable cause?

Legal Equation

Aguilar-Spinelli test = Veracity prong (informant has provided accurate information or admission of own criminal conduct) + Basis-of-knowledge prong (how informant obtained information or detailed information)
+ Independent corroboration to bolster a tip lacking in detail.

not all states follow Illinois v. Gates

Totality of the Circumstances

Justice Hugo Black was a strong dissenting critic of the *Aguilar-Spinelli* test. Justice Black complained that "[n]othing in our Constitution . . . requires that the facts be established with that degree of certainty and with such elaborate specificity before a policeman can be authorized by a disinterested magistrate" to conduct an arrest or search based on probable cause. This exacting standard threatened to "'make it increasingly easy for criminals to operate.'" In 1983, in *Illinois v. Gates*, the U.S. Supreme Court adopted Justice Black's point of view and abandoned the *Aguilar-Spinelli* test in favor of a "totality-of-the-circumstances" approach (*Illinois v. Gates*, 462 U.S. 213 [1983]).

In *Gates*, the Bloomingdale, Illinois, Police Department received an anonymous handwritten letter by mail. The letter alleged that two of the town's residents, Sue and Lance Gates, were engaged in selling narcotics. The letter reported that the unlawful enterprise involved Sue's driving their automobile to Florida, where she would leave the car to be loaded with drugs. Sue would fly back after dropping the car off in Florida. Lance would then fly down and drive the car back to Bloomingdale. The letter stated that Sue was driving down to Florida on May 3, 1978, and that when Lance drove the auto back to Bloomingdale the trunk would be loaded with over $100,000 in unlawful narcotics. The letter also stated that the couple had drugs stored in their basement valued at $100,000.

The police verified the Gateses' address and that Lance was scheduled to fly to Florida on May 5. In West Palm Beach, Lance was observed taking a taxi to a motel where Sue was registered. The next morning, Sue and Lance were seen driving their automobile on an interstate used by travelers to the Chicago area. These facts were incorporated into an affidavit, and a judge issued a search warrant for the Gateses' residence and for their automobile. Twenty-two hours after leaving Florida, Lance and Sue returned home. The police seized the automobile and discovered 350 pounds of marijuana in the trunk. A search of the Gateses' home led to the seizure of marijuana, weapons, and other contraband.

The U.S. Supreme Court found that the informant's letter did not satisfy the *Aguilar-Spinelli* two-prong test. The letter provided "virtually nothing from which one might conclude that its author is either honest or his information reliable; likewise, the letter gives absolutely no indication of the basis for the writer's predictions regarding the Gates[es]' criminal activities." The Supreme Court majority, however, held that the letter satisfied the probable cause standard. The Court explained that the veracity and basis-of-knowledge prongs are not independent requirements; both of them must be established. The two prongs are best thought of as "relevant considerations" in evaluating whether a tip satisfies probable cause. In other words, looking at the "totality of the circumstances," the Court concluded that there was probable cause to issue a search warrant. Three aspects of the tip discussed below are important in understanding the Court's conclusion that there is a "substantial basis" to conclude that there was probable cause to search the Gateses' home and car:

Future action. The Supreme Court was impressed by the fact that the tip contained a range of details including the suspects' "future actions" and that these facts were corroborated by law enforcement.

Type of information. The tip was consistent with law enforcement's knowledge of drug dealing. Florida is a center of drug activity, and the Gateses' predicted pattern of behavior is typical of drug traffickers. An informant with access to this type of detailed information in the view of the Supreme Court likely had "access to reliable information of the Gates[es]' alleged illegal activities," perhaps from the Gateses themselves.

Corroboration. Confidence in the accuracy of the information provided by the informant was bolstered by the fact that the police corroborated a significant number of the details.

The Supreme Court recognized that the tip in *Gates* was not completely accurate and that some of the information could have been based on rumor or speculation. The Court, however, stressed that probable cause requires only a "fair probability that the writer of the anonymous letter had obtained his entire story either from the Gates or someone they trusted. And corroboration of major portions of the letter's predictions provides just this probability."

Why did the Supreme Court adopt the totality-of-the-circumstances test? The Court likely concluded that anonymous tips from informants may not always easily satisfy both prongs of the *Aguilar-Spinelli* test. The entire process simply had become much too technical and demanding. Justices William Brennan and John Marshall dissented and warned that the totality-of-the-circumstances test left judicial officials with no guidance for determining whether informants' tips constituted probable cause and that, as a result, magistrates were likely to "rubber-stamp" requests from the police. This threatened to "obliterate one of the most fundamental distinctions between our form of government, where officers are under the law, and the police-state, where they are the law."

Several state supreme courts have held that their state constitutions provide greater protection in regard to the use of informants than the U.S. Constitution and have rejected the totality-of-the-circumstances approach. Courts in Alaska, California, Massachusetts, New York, Oregon, Tennessee, Vermont, and Washington have reasoned that *Aguilar-Spinelli* provides definite standards that provide a check on the police, which is lacking under the test established in *Gates* (*People v. Campa*, 686 P.2d 634 [Cal. 1984]; *State v. Jackson*, 688 P.2d 136 [Wash. 1984]).

 14.1 YOU DECIDE

Whiskey was stolen from a storage facility in Chicago. The next day, two FBI agents were in the area investigating the theft. They saw John Patrick Henry and Albert Rudolph Pierotti leave a tavern and get into an automobile. The agents had been given information of an "undisclosed nature" from Pierotti's employer suggesting that Pierotti was involved with interstate shipments. The tip did not

(Continued)

■ REASONABLENESS AND ARRESTS

The Fourth Amendment, as we have seen, requires that arrests be based on probable cause. An arrest also must be carried out in a reasonable fashion. The remainder of the chapter discusses six points regarding the reasonableness requirement:

- *Warrants.* There are strict requirements for the issuance of warrants.
- *Arrests and warrants.* Arrests, under some circumstances, require arrest warrants.
- *Arrests in the home.* Arrest warrants are required for arrests in the home.
- *Exigent circumstances.* There is an exigent-circumstances exception to the warrant requirement for arrests in the home.
- *Arrests and force.* Officers may use reasonable force in making arrests.
- *Misdemeanors, citations, and arrests.* States and localities may authorize arrests for misdemeanors.

■ PROBABLE CAUSE, WARRANTS, AND THE COURTS

The Supreme Court has expressed a preference for arrests to be based on arrest warrants. An **arrest warrant** is issued by a judge, magistrate, or other judicial official acting as a representative of the government and establishes that there is probable cause to arrest a particular individual or individuals. Why this preference for warrants? To obtain a warrant, the police appear before a neutral and detached judge or magistrate and are required to satisfy the judge or magistrate that there is probable cause to arrest an individual. As the Supreme Court observed in *Aguilar v. Texas*, "the informed and deliberate determinations of magistrates empowered to issue warrants . . . are to be preferred over the hurried action of officers . . . who happen to make arrests." The thinking is that an arrest can be an intrusive and demeaning experience and that the liberties of citizens are best protected when the police appear before a public official and are required to present evidence that there is probable cause to make an arrest (*Aguilar v. Texas*, 378 U.S. 108, 111 [1964]).

The Fourth Amendment requires that "no Warrants shall issue but upon probable cause, supported by Oath or affirmation." There are several important constitutional requirements for issuing a warrant under the Fourth Amendment:

Probable cause. There must be a demonstration by the police that there is a "fair probability" that a crime has been committed and that the person named in the warrant committed the crime.

Neutral officials. Probable cause must be established before a neutral and detached official who reviews the request. This typically is a judge or magistrate although the Supreme Court approved the issuance of a misdemeanor warrant by a non-lawyer court clerk who was part of the judicial branch of government. A non-lawyer must have the ability to determine probable cause.

Warrants and affidavits. The warrant must specify with "particularity" the name of the person to be arrested, the time and place of the offense, and the specific crime with which the individual is charged. This must be supported by an affidavit (statement), which typically is sworn under oath by a police officer (**affiant**) who swears to the specific facts and circumstances set forth in the affidavit that constitute the probable cause on which the warrant is based.

Judicial official. A judge or magistrate determines whether there is probable cause to issue a warrant. The warrant process is not an adversarial procedure and usually involves a police officer who presents the warrant and the affidavit to a magistrate or judge. Article 41 of the Federal Rules of Criminal Procedure authorizes officers to phone or radio in a warrant request to a federal magistrate who is authorized to issue the warrant over the phone.

As outlined below, a defendant may challenge the legality of an arrest based on the contention that the warrant was not based on probable cause or that proper procedures were not followed in issuing the warrant.

Probable cause. A warrant may be attacked on the grounds that it was not based on probable cause. An example is the challenge to the warrants in *Aguilar* and *Spinelli*.

Affidavit. The warrant may be overturned on the grounds that the probable cause is based on a knowingly false statement by the affiant (*Franks v. Delaware*, 483 U.S. 154 [1978]).

Procedural irregularity. A warrant may be overturned based on improper procedures. Warrants must be issued by a judge, a magistrate, or, in the case of minor misdemeanors, another qualified member of the judicial branch of government. The U.S. Supreme Court has held that a warrant issued by a prosecutor or police officer does not adequately protect the rights of individuals and is invalid (*Coolidge v. New Hampshire*, 403 U.S. 443 [1971]). In *Connally v. Georgia*, the U.S. Supreme Court held that the warrant procedure violated the Fourth Amendment where the warrant had been issued by an unsalaried justice of the peace who received $5 for each warrant he issued and no payment for warrants that he refused to issue (*Connally v. Georgia*, 429 U.S. 245 [1977]).

What about post-arrest challenges to warrantless arrests? The probable cause required for a warrantless arrest must meet the same standard as the probable cause required for an arrest based on a warrant. In *Gerstein v. Pugh*, the Supreme Court held that a police officer's "on-the-scene" assessment of probable cause provides legal justification for the arrest of an individual suspected of a crime. Once the suspect is in custody, the "reasons that justify dispensing with the magistrate's neutral judgment [of probable cause] evaporate." At this point, the Supreme Court ruled that the Fourth Amendment requires that the individual who is experiencing an extended loss of his or her liberty is entitled to a *Gerstein* hearing to determine whether a "reasonable person would believe that the suspect committed the offense" (*Gerstein v. Pugh*, 420 U.S. 103 [1975]). In *County of Riverside v. McLaughlin*, the U.S. Supreme Court held that the Fourth Amendment requires that the *Gerstein* probable cause hearing be conducted within forty-eight hours of an arrest. The hearing may be delayed only by an emergency or other pressing circumstance (*County of Riverside v. McLaughlin*, 500 U.S. 44 [1991]).

■ ARRESTS AND WARRANTS

Despite the U.S. Supreme Court's preference for warrants, most arrests take place without warrants. In *United States v. Watson*, the U.S. Supreme Court recognized that under some circumstances, warrants may slow the enforcement of the law. In *Watson*, the Court upheld the warrantless arrest by federal postal inspectors of Henry Ogle Watson for possession of stolen credit cards based on an informant's tip. The inspectors relied on a federal statute that authorizes postal inspectors to carry out warrantless arrests for felonies. Watson challenged the warrantless arrest and subsequent search that uncovered the credit cards as a violation of the Fourth Amendment. The Supreme Court held that *warrantless arrests in public* of individuals based on probable cause that they have committed a felony is consistent with the historic practice of the common law as well as with state statutes and state constitutions and therefore is reasonable under the Fourth Amendment. The warrantless arrest of individuals is permissible even when the officers could have obtained a warrant. The U.S. Supreme Court concluded by declaring that it "declined to transform the judicial preference for warrants into a constitutional requirement" when the state and federal governments historically had authorized warrantless public arrests on probable cause (*United States v. Watson*, 423 U.S. 411, 423–424 [1976]).

The Supreme Court has taken a somewhat different approach to arrests for misdemeanors. In *Atwater v. City of Lago Vista*, the Supreme Court answered the question whether it is *constitutionally permissible* for the police to carry out a warrantless arrest for a misdemeanor. Justice David Souter found that the common law and historic practice of the federal government and fifty states for two centuries establish that an arrest for a misdemeanor may be carried out without a warrant only when the offense is "*committed in the officer's presence*" (*Atwater v. City of Lago Vista*, 532 U.S. 318, 327–345 [2001]). The requirement that a misdemeanor take place in an officer's presence has been interpreted to mean that the officer must actually perceive the commission of the misdemeanor with one of the five senses of sight, hearing, touch, taste, or smell, or the individual must admit the crime to the officer. The officer also must carry out the arrest as promptly as possible. The "in-presence standard" is strictly interpreted to require that the officer actually witness every element of the offense. A California court of appeals held that an officer did not satisfy the in-presence standard when he did not actually see a juvenile ingesting paint fumes. The appellate court noted that the "mere fact that Alonzo had paint on his face and an odor of paint and had dropped the sock saturated with paint only shows that at sometime in the past Alonzo had undoubtedly been sniffing, but the time of any sniffing is not established. . . . While the officer may have had reasonable cause to believe that Alonzo had violated penal section 381 [prohibiting ingesting the fumes of paint and other substances] the officer did not have reasonable cause to believe that that misdemeanor took place in his presence" (*People v. Alonzo*, 151 Cal. Rptr. 192, 196 [Cal. App. 1978]).

Atwater establishes that the police may arrest an individual without a warrant for misdemeanors committed in an officer's presence. What about misdemeanors committed outside an officer's presence? A number of lower appellate courts have questioned whether the Fourth Amendment requires warrants for arrests for misdemeanors committed outside an officer's presence. Several state legislatures accordingly have authorized warrantless arrests for various misdemeanors including domestic violence, shoplifting, drunken driving, and violations of hunting and fishing regulations despite the fact that the officer may not have actually witnessed the offense. We shall be returning to *Atwater* later in the chapter when we discuss arrests and citations.

In summary, we have seen that although there is a preference for arrest warrants, arrests for felonies and for misdemeanors may be carried out without warrants. The next sections discuss the warrant requirement and arrests in the home.

- *Arrests in the home.* An arrest warrant is required.
- *Exigent circumstances.* Warrants are not required for arrests in the home when there are exigent circumstances.

Legal Equation

| Felony arrests in public | = | Warrant not required for arrests in public. |
| Misdemeanor arrests | = | Warrant not required where crime is committed in officer's presence. |

need warrant before coming into home

Arrests in the Home

United States v. Watson, as you recall, held that an arrest warrant is not required to arrest an individual for a felony in public. *Watson* left open the question whether a warrant is required to arrest an individual in his or her home. *Payton v. New York* answered this question and held that (1) absent consent or exigent circumstances, (2) an arrest warrant founded on probable cause is required to arrest individuals in the home (3) when there is "reason to believe that the suspect is within" (*Payton v. New York*, 445 U.S. 573, 602–603 [1980]).

The U.S. Supreme Court stressed that the unjustified "physical entry into the home is the chief evil at which the Fourth Amendment is directed" and that the Fourth Amendment draws a firm line of protection at the entrance to an individual's house. The requirement that the arrests in the home must be based on an arrest warrant protects an individual's privacy in the home from searches that are not based on probable cause.

The entry into the home of a "third party" to arrest a suspect requires a search warrant, and an arrest warrant is insufficient. The Supreme Court has held that the purpose of a warrant is to allow a neutral judicial officer to assess whether the police have probable cause to carry out an arrest or conduct a search. The Court stressed that while both warrants require a probable cause determination, they protect different interests. An arrest warrant protects individuals from unreasonable seizures. A search warrant, in contrast, is based on probable cause that the object of a search is located in a specific location and therefore protects an individual's interest in the privacy of his or her dwelling and possessions from an unjustified intrusion by the police. The burden placed on the police by the search warrant requirement is outweighed by the right of presumptively innocent people to be secure in their homes from unjustified forcible intrusions. The Supreme Court expressed the concern that permitting the police to search the homes of "third parties" based on an arrest warrant would give the police the freedom to search the homes of a suspect's friends, relatives, and acquaintances. See *Steagald v. United States* (451 U.S. 204 [1981]).

You may be interested in learning whether an arrest warrant is required when arresting individuals for felonies in some of the scenarios sketched below:

Doorways. A number of courts have held that a defendant who is arrested when he or she opens the door is arrested in his or her home and that a warrant is required. Other courts have ruled that so long as the police remain outside the dwelling when executing the arrest of an individual who is inside the home, the arrest occurs in public, and an arrest warrant is not required (*United States v. Berkowitz*, 927 F.2d 1376 [7th Cir. 1991]). Courts differ on whether an individual who exits his or her residence in response to an order by the police and who then is arrested is considered to have been arrested in the home without a warrant (*United States v. Al-Azzawy*, 784 F.2d 890 [9th Cir. 1985]).

Common hallways. An arrest that is made in the hallway outside the defendant's apartment does not require a warrant (*United States v. Holland*, 755 F.2d 253 [2d Cir. 1985]).

Hotels. An arrest warrant is required to apprehend an individual in a hotel or motel room that he or she has rented (*United States v. Morales*, 737 F.2d 761 [8th Cir. 1984]).

In summary, the Supreme Court held in *Payton v. New York* that if there is sufficient evidence of a citizen's participation in a felony to convince a judicial officer that his or her arrest is justified, it is constitutionally reasonable to require the individual to "open his [or her] doors to the officers of the law" who are armed with an arrest warrant.

Exigent Circumstances

In *Payton v. New York*, the Supreme Court held that arrests inside the home without an arrest warrant are presumptively unreasonable absent **exigent circumstances** or consent. The Court in *Payton* did not define or discuss exigent circumstances. *Exigent* means an urgent need to take action. In *Mincey v. Arizona*, the U.S. Supreme Court pronounced that warrants "are generally required . . . unless the 'exigencies of the situation' make the needs of law enforcement so compelling that the warrantless search is objectively reasonable under the Fourth Amendment" (*Mincey v. Arizona*, 437 U.S. 385, 393–394 [1978]). In *Warden v. Hayden*, the police arrived at Bennie Jo Hayden's residence within minutes after having been informed that Hayden, who the police had probable cause to believe had just robbed the office of a taxicab company, had fled into his home. The U.S. Supreme Court in affirming the legality of the police officers' warrantless entry into Hayden's home noted that "the exigencies of the situation made that course imperative." The Fourth Amendment "does not require police officers to delay in the course of an investigation [if] to do so would gravely endanger their lives or the lives of others. Speed here was essential" (*Warden v. Hayden*, 387 U.S. 294, 298–299 [1967]). The Supreme Court has recognized various emergencies that qualify as exigent circumstances that permit the police to enter a home without a warrant when they have probable cause to justify the entry. The following situations have been held to constitute exigent circumstances:

⌐ risk to safety

└ *Hot pursuit.* The police are in pursuit of a suspect. In *United States v. Santana*, "Mom" Santana fled inside her house when the police attempted to arrest her for drug possession. The police pursued her and executed a warrantless arrest within her house. The U.S. Supreme Court held that the police were in hot pursuit and that the narcotics would have been destroyed had the police waited to obtain a warrant. The Court explained that a suspect "may not defeat an arrest which has been set in motion in a public place" by retreating into the home (*United States v. Santana*, 427 U.S. 38, 43 [1976]).

Public safety. The police believe that the public safety is endangered. In *Michigan v. Tyler*, the U.S. Supreme Court approved of the warrantless entry to fight a fire. A "burning building clearly presents an exigency of sufficient proportions to render a warrantless entry 'reasonable.' Indeed, it would defy reason to suppose that firemen must secure a warrant or consent before entering a burning structure to put out the blaze" (*Michigan v. Tyler*, 436 U.S. 499, 509 [1978]).

Destruction of evidence. A failure to act will result in the destruction of evidence. In *Ker v. California,* police officers had probable cause to believe that they observed George Douglas Ker purchase narcotics and that he was dealing drugs from his apartment. Fearing that Ker was aware that they were following him, the officers hurried to his apartment, obtained the key from the landlord, seized narcotics, and subsequently arrested Ker. The Supreme Court held that "suspects have no constitutional right to destroy or dispose of evidence, and no basic constitutional guarantees are violated because an officer succeeds in getting to a place where he is entitled to be more quickly than he would had he complied" with the warrant process (*Ker v. California,* 374 U.S. 23, 39 [1963]). In *Missouri v. McNeely*, the Supreme Court held that in "drunk-driving investigations, the natural dissipation of alcohol in the bloodstream does not constitute an exigency in every case sufficient to justify conducting a blood test without a warrant" (*Missouri v. McNeely*, 569 U.S. ___ (2013).

Flight. The suspect may flee the jurisdiction. Federal officers entered a hotel room and arrested Richard Sumpter, a major drug trafficker who was supervising the delivery from California to Detroit of a significant quantity of narcotics. Sumpter dropped his cellular phone on the floor when the federal agents entered his hotel room, and the phone line remained open during the arrest. The officers feared that the individual on the other end of the line had learned of the arrest and would either flee or destroy evidence. As a consequence, the police immediately entered a nearby hotel room and arrested Charles Crehore, a drug courier who worked for Sumpter. The Sixth Circuit Court of Appeals held that "[i]t was not unreasonable for officers to believe Sumpter's companions, who had not yet been arrested, would have been alerted of the arrests through the open phone line, and imminently would have destroyed the evidence or fled the hotel" (*United States v. Gaitan-Acevedo*, 148 F.3d 577 [6th Cir. 1998]).

In the frequently cited case of *United States v. Rubin*, the Third Circuit Court of Appeals indicated that the crucial question in determining whether there are exigent circumstances is whether the police have probable cause to believe that they must act immediately and that they do not have time to secure a warrant (*United States v. Rubin*, 474 F.2d 262 [3d Cir. 1973]). A court's consideration of a claim of exigent circumstances is based on an analysis of the facts that confronted the police at the time of the entry. There is an appreciation that the police must act on the "spur of the moment."

The police, by relying on exigent circumstances, risk that a judge may find that the police mistakenly concluded that there were exigent circumstances justifying entry into the home without an arrest warrant. In *Minnesota v. Olson*, the police apprehended one of two men thought to be responsible for the robbery and murder of a service station attendant. The police shortly thereafter located Robert Olson, the driver of the getaway car, in an upstairs apartment where he was staying as the guest of two women. The police entered the apartment without a warrant and arrested Olson, who subsequently confessed. The U.S. Supreme Court agreed with the Minnesota Supreme Court that the police had unlawfully arrested Olson in the apartment without a warrant. The Court stressed that Olson likely was unarmed because the police had recovered the murder weapon and knew that the two women with the suspect were not in danger and that three or four Minneapolis police squads had surrounded the apartment. The Supreme Court concluded that under the circumstances, there was little likelihood that Olson would have been able to flee and that the police had sufficient time to obtain a warrant (*Minnesota v. Olson*, 495 U.S. 91 [1990]).

In *Welsh v. Wisconsin*, Edward G. Welsh drove his car off the road and walked away on foot in what witnesses indicated appeared to be an inebriated condition. The police arrived soon thereafter and arrested Welsh in his home without an arrest warrant. The Court noted that the first offense in Wisconsin for driving while intoxicated was a non-criminal civil forfeiture. There was no hot pursuit or threat to public safety. Although the defendant's blood-alcohol level may have dissipated had the police not immediately detained Welsh, the Court held that the offense was not sufficiently severe to justify entry into the home based on exigent circumstances (*Welsh v. Wisconsin*, 466 U.S. 740 [1984]).

In 2009 in *Brigham City v. Stuart*, four police officers responded to a call complaining about a loud party. They arrived at the residence at roughly 3:00 A.M. and heard "shouting," "crashing," and "thumping" and entered the backyard. They looked through a screen door and windows and observed four adults attempting to restrain a juvenile. The juvenile broke free and hit one of the adults in the face and drew blood. The other adults pressed the juvenile against a refrigerator with such force that the unit moved across the floor. One of the officers opened the screen door and announced the presence of the police. The men were so involved in the physical confrontation that they did not hear the announcement. The officer then entered the kitchen and again cried out, and the men abandoned the struggle.

The Supreme Court held that "one exigency obviating the requirement of a warrant is the need to assist persons who are seriously injured or threatened with such injury. 'The need to protect or preserve life or avoid serious injury is justification for what would be otherwise illegal absent an exigency or emergency.'" In other words, the **emergency-aid doctrine** authorizes the warrantless entry into a home to provide emergency assistance to an injured occupant or to protect an occupant from imminent harm.

The test is whether the circumstances viewed objectively justify the warrantless entry to render emergency assistance. The fact that the police may have possessed the subjective motivation to make an arrest rather than to render assistance is not relevant to this analysis.

A second important aspect of the decision in *Brigham City* is the Supreme Court's holding that the criminal conduct was sufficiently serious to justify the warrantless entry into the home. The Supreme Court noted that *Welsh* involved an entry to arrest an individual for driving while intoxicated. The only emergency that confronted the officers in *Welsh* was the need to preserve evidence of the suspect's blood-alcohol content. In contrast, the officers in *Brigham City* "were confronted with ongoing violence occurring within the home. *Welsh* did not address such a situation." The Supreme Court concluded that the police possessed an "objectively reasonable basis" for believing that the injured adult might be in need of assistance and that the violence was likely to escalate. "Nothing in the Fourth Amendment required [the police] to wait until another blow rendered someone 'unconscious' or 'semi-conscious' or worse before entering" (see *Brigham City v. Stuart*, 547 U.S. 398 [2006]). In *Michigan v. Fisher*, the Supreme Court affirmed that the test for exigent circumstances "is not what [the police officer] believed, but whether there was 'an objectively reasonable basis for believing' that medical assistance was needed, or persons were in danger" (*Michigan v. Fisher*, 558 U.S. 45 [2009]). In *Ryburn v. Huff*, the police went to the home of high school student Vincent Huff who was alleged to have threatened to "shoot up the school." There was no answer when the officers knocked on the door and they called the home phone. The officers reached Mrs. Huff on her cell phone, and she hung up in the middle of their conversation.

Several minutes later, Mrs. Huff and Vincent walked out of the house. Officer Edmundo Zepeda told Vincent that he and the other officers were there to discuss the threats. Vincent responded, "I can't believe you're here for that." Sergeant Darin Ryburn asked Mrs. Huff if they could talk inside the house and she refused without knowing the topic of the officer's visit. "In Sergeant Ryburn's experience as a juvenile bureau sergeant, it was 'extremely unusual' for a parent to decline an officer's request to interview a juvenile inside."

Sergeant Ryburn asked her if there were any guns in the house. Mrs. Huff responded by "immediately turn[ing] around and r[unning] into the house." Sergeant Ryburn, who was "scared because [he] didn't know what was in that house" and had "seen too many officers killed," entered the house behind her. Vincent entered the house behind Sergeant Ryburn, and Officer Zepeda entered after Vincent. They explained that they were concerned about "officer safety" and did not want Sergeant Ryburn to enter the house alone. The two remaining officers, "who had been standing out of earshot while Sergeant Ryburn and Officer Zepeda talked to Vincent and Mrs. Huff, entered the house last, on the assumption that Mrs. Huff had given Sergeant Ryburn and Officer Zepeda permission to enter." The officers determined that the allegations against Vincent were unfounded. A civil suit was filed against the officers for their warrantless entry into the Huffs' home.

The Supreme Court held that the police reasonably feared for their own safety and for the safety of individuals inside the home. Exigent circumstances are to be evaluated based on the totality of the circumstances. Courts should be hesitant to "second-guess" the police response to evolving situations. Officers often are forced to make split-second decisions, and their decisions are to be judged based on the circumstances that confronted them at the time rather with 20/20 hindsight. The police confronted a situation that was "tense, uncertain, and rapidly evolving" (*Ryburn v. Huff*, 565 U.S. __ [2012]).

Exigent circumstances **=** Probable cause **+** Hot pursuit, public safety, destruction of evidence, flight, or emergency assistance.

14.2 YOU DECIDE

Manchester, New Hampshire, police responded to a reported robbery. Witnesses reported to the police that a white male, 25 to 30 years old, roughly six feet tall and weighing two hundred pounds, wearing a New England Patriots jacket and a green hooded sweatshirt, entered the store, went behind the counter, and stabbed the clerk at least three times before leaving with cash from the register. The police found a key ring containing a key to a Kia automobile, which the police concluded belonged to the suspect, Scott Robinson. Officers found a Kia nearby, and after relaying the license plate to dispatch, police learned that the car belonged to the defendant, that he lived eight blocks from the store, and that he had a prior robbery conviction. At that point, officers were sent to the defendant's apartment building.

Four officers were dispatched to the defendant's apartment and could see and hear movement inside the apartment. There also were wet footprints in the hallway leading to the defendant's door.

The officers knocked on the defendant's door and announced their presence but received no response. They then spoke to a neighbor and asked her if the defendant lived in that apartment. After officers brought her down to a police cruiser and showed her a picture of the defendant on a computer, she confirmed that he lived there. Upon returning to the defendant's door, police heard a female voice say something to the effect of "you're such an idiot," and again knocked and announced their presence.

The defendant's girlfriend, Kimberly Dunn, opened the door and two officers stepped into the apartment and opened a closed closet to ensure nobody was hiding inside. Upon opening the closet, the officers saw a Patriots jacket and a green hooded sweatshirt.

Dunn then told the officers that the defendant was in the bedroom with a knife to his chest. The officers went to the bedroom, found the defendant, arrested him, and took him out of the apartment. The officers secured the premises and applied for a search warrant. Were the police officers justified in entering Robinson's apartment based on exigent circumstances? Exigent circumstances exist where police face a compelling need for immediate official action and a risk that the delay inherent in obtaining a warrant will present a substantial threat of imminent danger to life or public safety or create a likelihood that evidence will be destroyed. See *State v. Robinson* (973 A.2d 277 [N.H. 2009]).

You can learn what the court decided by referring to the study site, **http://study.sagepub.com/lippmance.**

> *cannot* shoot you when you run.

Deadly Force and Arrests → can only use deadly force when ⎰ -officer @ risk
-safety of others @ risk
-seriousness of the offence they are running from.

We have seen that the Fourth Amendment requires probable cause to make an arrest and requires that an arrest be carried out in a reasonable fashion. The U.S. Supreme Court has balanced the interest in individual privacy against the interest in enforcing the criminal law to determine when a warrant is required to arrest an individual. The Court also has employed a balancing test to determine (1) when it is reasonable for the police to use physical force in making an arrest and (2) how much force is reasonable for the police to use under the circumstances.

There are few areas as controversial as the employment of deadly force by police officers who are attempting to apprehend a fleeing suspect. This, in effect, imposes a fatal punishment without trial. The police up until the fourteenth century possessed the right to employ deadly force against an individual who the officer reasonably believed had committed a felony. This was the case even in those circumstances in which a felon could have been apprehended without the use of deadly force. The authorization of deadly force was based on the notion that felons were a lawless element whose lives could be taken in order to safeguard the public. This presumption was strengthened by the fact that felons were subject to capital punishment and to the forfeiture of property. Felons were considered to have forfeited their right to life, and the police were merely imposing the punishment that awaited offenders in any event. In contrast, only reasonable force could be applied to apprehend a **misdemeanant**. Misdemeanors were punished by a modest fine or brief imprisonment and were not considered to pose a threat to the community. As a consequence, it was considered inhumane for the police to employ deadly force against individuals responsible for minor violations of the law.

The arming of the police and the **fleeing-felon rule** were reluctantly embraced by the American public, which, while distrustful of governmental power, remained fearful of crime. The common law fleeing-felon rule authorizes the police to use deadly force to apprehend a felon who is fleeing from the police. Some state legislatures attempted to moderate the fleeing-felon rule by adopting the standard that a police officer who reasonably believed that deadly force was required to apprehend a suspect would be held criminally liable in the event that he or she was shown to have been mistaken.

The judiciary began to seriously reconsider the application of the fleeing-felon rule in the 1980s. Only a small number of felonies remained punishable by death, and offenses in areas such as white-collar crime posed no direct danger to the public. The rule permitting the employment of deadly force against fleeing felons also developed prior to arming the police with firearms in the mid-nineteenth century. Deadly force under the fleeing-felon rule traditionally was employed at close range and rarely was invoked to apprehend a felon who escaped an officer's immediate control. An additional problematic aspect of the fleeing-felon rule was the authorization for private citizens to employ deadly force although private citizens in most states risked criminal liability in the event that they were proven to have been incorrect.

The growing recognition that criminal suspects retained various constitutional rights also introduced a concern with balancing the interests of suspects against the interests of the police and society. In 1986, the U.S. Supreme Court reviewed the fleeing-felon rule in *Tennessee v. Garner*. The case was brought under a federal civil rights statute by the family of the deceased who were seeking monetary damages for deprivation of the "rights . . . secured by the Constitution" (42 U.S.C. § 1983 [see the "Case Analysis" feature at the end of this chapter]). The Supreme Court, in an important statement, dismissed Tennessee's contention that so long as the police possess probable cause, the Fourth Amendment has "nothing to say about how that seizure is made." The Court in *Garner* balanced the intrusion on a suspect's privacy interest against the need for the seizure and held that probable cause to seize a suspect did not justify the employment of deadly force in every instance. On the other hand, "[w]here the officer has probable cause to believe that the suspect poses a threat of serious physical harm, either to the officer or to others, it is not constitutionally unreasonable to prevent escape by using deadly force" (*Tennessee v. Garner*, 471 U.S. 1 [1985]).

We may question whether it is fair to place the fate of a police officer who is charged with the unlawful employment of deadly force in the hands of a judge or jury who may not fully appreciate the pressures confronting an officer who is required to make a split-second decision. On the other hand, some commentators argue that the law is ineffective in controlling the police use of deadly force because the utilization of deadly force in many instances occurs in situations in which there are few witnesses and that the judge and jury typically must rely on the well-rehearsed testimony of the police. Do you think the standard established in *Garner* strikes a fair balance between the interests of the suspect and the interests of society in apprehending felons?

Legal Equation

Deadly force in an arrest	= Fleeing felon	+ Law enforcement officer and civilian acting under officer's direction
	+ No substantial risk of injury to innocents	+ Probable cause that felony involves use or threatened use of deadly force or substantial risk of death or serious injury to police or to the public if apprehension is delayed
	+ Substantial risk of death or serious injury to police or to the public if apprehension is delayed.	

question = was use of force reasonable
- type of offense — resisting arrest?
- immediate threat?

Non-Deadly Force

What about police use of non-deadly force? In *Graham v. Connor*, the Supreme Court held that claims of excessive non-deadly force as well as claims of excessive deadly force are to be analyzed under the Fourth Amendment reasonableness standard. The question is whether the use of force to seize an individual is objectively reasonable under the totality of the circumstances (*Graham v. Connor*, 490 U.S. 386 [1989]).

PHOTO 14.2

Police officers may secure individuals placed under arrest to protect themselves and the public, prevent individuals from fleeing, and guard against the destruction of evidence.

was the force justified?

REUTERS/Lucy Nicholson

Police Officer Connor observed Delthorne Graham rushing out of a convenience store. Graham later related that he was suffering a diabetic reaction and was in need of orange juice to counteract the reaction. He explained that he was deterred by the long line in the store from purchasing orange juice, hurriedly left the store, and asked his friend William Berry to drive him to a friend's house. The officer grew suspicious and pulled Graham and William Berry over for investigation. Berry explained to the officer that Graham was suffering from a "sugar reaction." The police arriving at the scene were convinced that Graham was drunk and questioned whether he was suffering from a diabetic reaction. The situation escalated and culminated in four officers' throwing Graham headfirst into the squad car.

The U.S. Supreme Court held that cases in which the police are alleged to have employed non-deadly excessive force during an arrest, investigative stop, or other seizure are to be analyzed under the Fourth Amendment objective reasonableness standard. The Court stated that the question is whether the police officer's actions are "objectively reasonable in light of the facts and circumstances." The relevant factors to be considered are the seriousness of the offense, the immediacy of the threat posed by the suspect, and whether the suspect is resisting arrest or attempting to escape. In evaluating the officer's response, courts must consider the circumstances confronting the police at the time rather than analyze the situation with the benefit of "20/20 vision of hindsight." The fact that an officer personally believes that non-deadly force is required to seize a suspect is not the determining factor. The question is whether the force is justified under the objective circumstances that confront the officer (*Graham v. Connor*, 490 U.S. 386 [1989]).

CRIMINAL EVIDENCE AND PUBLIC POLICY

In 2007, in *Scott v. Harris* (550 U.S. 372 [2007]), a Georgia county deputy clocked Victor Harris's vehicle traveling at seventy-three miles per hour on a road with a fifty-five-mile-per-hour speed limit. Deputy Timothy Scott turned on his flashing lights indicating that Harris should stop. Harris, instead, accelerated, and the deputy initiated a high-speed chase. The two sped down two-lane roads at speeds exceeding eighty-five miles per hour. Deputy Scott heard the radio communication and joined the pursuit. In the middle of the chase, Scott pulled into a parking lot, and Harris was nearly boxed in by several police vehicles. Harris evaded the trap by making a sharp right turn, colliding with Scott's police car, exiting the parking lot, and speeding down the highway. Scott's squad car was the lead police chase vehicle. Six minutes and nearly ten miles following the beginning of the chase, Scott decided to disable Harris's automobile and was given radio authorization to employ a "Precision Intervention Technique" maneuver, which causes the fleeing vehicle to spin to a stop. Scott, instead, applied his push bumper to the rear of Harris's vehicle. Harris lost control of his automobile, which left the roadway, ran down an embankment, overturned, and crashed. Harris was seriously injured and was left a quadriplegic. Harris filed a suit under 42 U.S.C. § 1983 seeking civil damages for Deputy Scott's use of what Harris alleged was excessive force and an unreasonable seizure under the Fourth Amendment.

The U.S. Supreme Court determined that the videotape indicated that Harris's vehicle sped down narrow two-lane roads at "shockingly fast" speeds. This was a "Hollywood-style car chase of the most frightening sort, placing police officers and innocent bystanders alike at great risk of serious injury." Scott conceded that his decision to ram Harris's vehicle constituted a Fourth Amendment seizure, which the Supreme Court defined as the "governmental termination of freedom of movement through means intentionally applied."

The Supreme Court held that the claim that Scott employed excessive force in making a seizure is properly analyzed under the Fourth Amendment's "objective reasonableness" standard. The questions are whether Scott's actions are reasonable and whether they constitute deadly force.

In determining reasonableness, the Court balances the nature and quality of the intrusion on an individual's Fourth Amendment interests against the importance of the governmental interests justifying the intrusion. Thus, "in judging whether Scott's actions were reasonable, we must consider the risk of bodily harm that Scott's actions posed to [Harris] in light of the threat to the public that Scott was trying to eliminate." The Court concluded that Harris "posed an actual and imminent threat to the lives of any pedestrians who might have been present, to other civilian motorists, and to the officers involved in the chase." On the other hand, Scott's actions also "posed a high likelihood of serious injury or death" to Harris—"though not the near certainty of death posed by, say, shooting a fleeing felon in the back of the head."

The Supreme Court placed particular weight on the number of innocent lives that Harris intentionally placed at risk by engaging in a reckless high-speed police chase. Under the circumstances, the Court had "little difficulty in concluding it was reasonable for Scott to take the action that he did."

The Supreme Court rejected the contention that the reasonable course of action was for Scott to abandon the pursuit with the expectation that Harris would no longer fear apprehension and would reduce the speed of his vehicle. "Whereas Scott's action—ramming respondent off the road—was certain to eliminate the risk that respondent posed to the public, ceasing pursuit was not." Harris was equally as likely to have responded to the abandonment of the pursuit by continuing to drive in a reckless fashion as by slowing down. He might have concluded that the police abandonment was a trick and that they planned to intercept his vehicle at a later time. Requiring the police to abandon a pursuit whenever a motorist drives so recklessly that he or she places other people's lives in danger would lead "[e]very fleeing motorist [to] know that escape is within his [or her] grasp, if only he [or she] accelerates to 90 miles per hour, crosses the double-yellow line a few times, and runs a few red lights." The Court, instead, established a "more sensible rule: *A police officer's attempt to terminate a dangerous high-speed car chase that threatens the lives of innocent bystanders does not violate the Fourth Amendment, even when it places the fleeing motorist at risk of serious injury or death.*"

In summary, Harris posed a "substantial and immediate risk of serious physical injury to others." Scott's attempt to terminate the chase by forcing Harris off the road was reasonable. The Court cautioned that the facts of a high-speed chase may lead to a different result under different circumstances: "A high-speed chase in a desert in Nevada is, after all, quite different from one that travels through the heart of Las Vegas."

Justice John Paul Stevens, in dissent, argues that the videotape indicated that Harris's flight did not pose a risk to the public and that, under the circumstances, the employment of deadly force was unreasonable. He asked what would have happened if the police had decided to abandon the chase. Justice Stevens contends that there is no basis for concluding that an individual will continue to flee once the police call off a pursuit. The police in any event had recorded Harris's license number and could have apprehended him at a later date. Even if Harris would have eluded capture had Officer Scott abandoned the pursuit, "the use of deadly force in this case was no more appropriate than the use of a deadly weapon against a fleeing felon in *Tennessee v. Garner*." Justice Stevens proposed an alternative test to the standard adopted by the majority of the Court. This test establishes a preference for the police to abandon pursuits rather than engage in high-speed automobile pursuits. "When the immediate danger to the public created by the pursuit is greater than the immediate or potential danger to the public should the suspect remain at large, then the pursuit should be discontinued or terminated. . . . [P]ursuits should usually be discontinued when the violator's identity has been established to the point that later apprehension can be accomplished without danger to the public."

In 2014, in *Plumhoff v. Rickard*, the Supreme Court held that the police had acted reasonably in firing fifteen shots and killing a fleeing driver who after crashing into a police cruiser continued to make an effort to flee from the police. Donald "Rickard's outrageously reckless driving posed a grave public safety risk. . . . Under the circumstances at the moment when the shots were fired, all that a reasonable police officer could have concluded was that Rickard was intent on resuming his flight and that, if he was allowed to do so, he would once again pose a deadly threat for others on the road" (*Plumhoff v. Rickard*, 572 U.S. ___ [2014]).

High-speed pursuits are the leading cause of police deaths and various departments have abandoned the practice. What is your view?

Misdemeanor Arrests and Citations

An arrest, as previously noted, results in a considerable restriction on an individual's liberty. As Justice Lewis Powell noted in *United States v. Robinson*, a custodial arrest is a "significant intrusion of state power" that severely restricts an individual's freedom and may prove to be humiliating and degrading. Professor Malcolm Feeley captured this in the title of his book *The Process Is the Punishment* (1992). An individual who is arrested is taken into police custody and may be searched along with the passenger compartment of his or her automobile. The arrestee then can expect to be taken to the police station or to jail. Suspects now enter into a legal process in which they are booked, photographed, fingerprinted, and subjected to an inventory of their possessions. They may be held for as long as forty-eight hours before they must be formally charged with a criminal offense.

An issue of continuing debate is whether a person under arrest for a minor misdemeanor traffic offense or other minor misdemeanors may be subject to a custodial arrest. The alternative course is for the officer to issue a **citation**. An individual who receives a citation from a police officer is not taken into custody so long as he or she is able to present reliable identification and agrees to appear in court at a later date.

There are good reasons for issuing citations rather than arresting individuals for minor misdemeanors. The argument is that it is unreasonable to subject individuals to the indignity and inconvenience of an arrest for a minor offense. An arrest also consumes the time and energy of the police and of the criminal justice system. Civil libertarians argue that permitting arrests for minor crimes invites the police to profile minorities and to arrest people pretextually for minor offenses who the police suspect are engaged in more serious offenses. The strong case for issuing citations accounts for Justice Potter Stewart's observation in *Gustafson v. Florida* that a "persuasive claim might have been made . . . that the custodial arrest of the petitioner for a minor traffic offense violated [the petitioner's] rights" (*Gustafson v. Florida*, 414 U.S. 260, 266–267 [1973]).

On the other hand, the police understandably do not want to be burdened with the responsibility of distinguishing between offenses that permit an arrest and offenses that require a citation. What standard would we use to distinguish offenses deserving of an arrest from offenses that merit the issuance of a citation in any event? Society benefits when the police are able to arrest and to search and question misdemeanants who very well may be involved in other types of criminal activity. In *People v. Pendleton,* an Illinois appellate court held that the police had properly arrested James Pendleton for a failure to display a front license plate and for a failure to produce a valid driver's license. This ruling took on particular significance because as a result of the arrest, the police discovered that Pendleton was a suspect in a rape prosecution, and he subsequently was identified by the victim in a lineup (*People v. Pendleton*, 433 N.E.2d 1076 [Ill. App. 1982]).

How should the balance be struck between these considerations? In 2001, in *Atwater v. City of Lago Vista*, the Supreme Court was asked to decide whether the Fourth Amendment reasonableness standard permits the police to arrest individuals for a minor criminal offense committed in the officer's presence. In other words, did the Fourth Amendment require the police to issue citations for minor misdemeanors, or could the police continue to arrest violators? Was the same rule to be followed in the case of every misdemeanor?

Gail Atwater was driving her pickup truck with her two young children in the front seat. None of the three was wearing a seat belt. Officer Barton Turek stopped, arrested, and handcuffed Atwater and drove her to the police station. At the station, Atwater was booked, forced to remove and turn her possessions over to the police, photographed, and detained in a jail cell for one hour before being released on a $310 bond. She later pled guilty to a misdemeanor and paid a $50 fine (*Atwater v. City of Lago Vista*, 532 U.S. 318, 323–324 [2001]).

Texas law authorized Officer Turek to arrest Atwater or to issue a citation. Atwater asked the U.S. Supreme Court to hold that the Reasonableness Clause of the Fourth Amendment prohibits a custodial arrest for an offense that is not punishable by jail when there is no immediate need for detention. Justice Souter conceded that he would have ruled for Atwater if he was required to consider only the facts in her case. Justice Souter, however, held that the police should not be placed in the position of having to distinguish in the heat of the moment between offenses that permit an arrest and offenses that require a citation. For example, this might require the police to determine whether an offense carries a "jail sentence" or a "fine" or to determine whether an arrest is required because the suspect might flee or posed a threat to the police or to the public. The Supreme Court accordingly adopted a "bright-line" rule and held that "[i]f an officer has probable cause to believe that an individual has committed even a very minor criminal offense in his presence, he may without violating the Fourth Amendment arrest the offender."

Justice Sandra Day O'Connor, in her dissenting opinion, argued that it is unreasonable to permit the police to arrest an individual for a misdemeanor in every instance. She proposed that when there is probable cause to believe that a fine-only offense has been committed, the police should issue a citation unless there are facts that "reasonably warrant" a full custodial arrest.

Atwater is significant for allowing states to continue to give police officers the choice whether to arrest individuals for minor misdemeanor offenses. Several state supreme courts have held that their constitutions provide greater protection than the Fourth Amendment and have upheld statutes providing that absent "special circumstances," the police are required to issue citations rather than arrest individuals for misdemeanors. The Supreme Court of Montana, in the frequently cited case of *Montana v. Bauer*, explained that it is unreasonable for a police officer to undertake a custodial arrest and detention for a misdemeanor "in the absence of special circumstances such as a concern for the safety of the offender or the public." The Montana court held that a person stopped for a "non-jailable offense such as . . . a seatbelt infraction should not be subjected to the indignity of an arrest and a police station detention when a simple non-intrusive notice to appear . . . will serve the interests of law enforcement" (*Montana v. Bauer*, 36 P.3d 892 [Mont. 2001]). The Ohio Supreme Court issued a similar ruling in the case of an arrest for jaywalking (*State v. Brown*, 792 N.E.2d 175 [Ohio 2003]). The Nevada Supreme Court, in following these precedents, noted that issuing citations conserves police resources and limits the arbitrary arrest and harassment of minority groups (*State v. Bayard*, 71 P.3d 498 [Nev. 2003]).

CRIMINAL EVIDENCE IN THE NEWS

Following the police killing of Michael Brown, the African American residents of Ferguson, Missouri, took to the streets to protest the killing and other grievances against the criminal justice system. Commentators noted that a major source of dissatisfaction and frustration was the discriminatory enforcement of the law.

Statistics indicate that African Americans are pulled over in Ferguson and in adjoining communities by the police at a greater rate than their white neighbors.

In Ferguson, 86 percent of vehicle stops involved an African American driver although African Americans comprise 67 percent of the 21,000 residents. African Americans, according to a report by the public interest group Arch City Defenders, "are almost twice as likely as whites to be searched (12.1 percent versus 6.9 percent) and twice as likely to be arrested (10.4 percent versus 5.2 percent)." The report also notes that searches of African Americans result in the seizure of contraband 21.7 percent of the time; contraband is seized from Caucasian drivers 34.0 percent of the time.

Saint Louis County has ninety small jurisdictions, each with its own city government, and eighty-six have their own court system. In Maplewood, Missouri, a 2013 report by the state attorney general found that African American motorists were searched or arrested during traffic stops at twice the rate of white motorists. Searches of whites and blacks were equally as likely to lead to the seizure of contraband. In the city of Hazelwood, African Americans were twice as likely as whites to be searched during a traffic stop and roughly three times as likely to be arrested. Yet searches of whites were one and a half times more likely to result in the seizure of contraband.

A number of neighboring towns rely on fines to support as much as 35 percent of their local governmental budget. In Ferguson, traffic fines account for roughly 8 percent of the city budget, and 20 percent of the budget is derived from fines. Revenues from traffic fines have increased 44 percent since 2011. A warrant is issued for a person who fails to appear in court on his or her court date to pay his or her fine. This results in the suspension of the person's license and an increase in the fine. An individual who is stopped by the police with an outstanding warrant also will accumulate towing fees and incarceration fees. In Ferguson, there is an average of three warrants for each Ferguson household. Local lawyers estimate that a $90 fee for a broken taillight in the end may result in an individual owing $1,000. An individual who is pulled over also may be arrested for what lawyers call a "poverty offense," a failure to have auto insurance or have current automobile registration.

Cynics assert that the police pull over African Americans to find individuals with outstanding warrants with accumulated fees that can generate revenue for the city.

Individuals in Ferguson have a difficult time paying the fines and invariably find themselves in jail. In Saint Louis County, which contains Ferguson, the unemployment rate for African Americans is 10 percent higher than for whites, and one in five individuals lives below the poverty line. Many individuals are faced with the choice of paying their rent or paying a traffic fine. An individual with outstanding warrants in several towns who is pulled over for a traffic stop in North Saint Louis Country will be sent from one jail to the next jail ("making the rounds"). At each stop, he or she will need to raise bail money before being released. Once released, individuals

(Continued)

(Continued)

complain that in many cases their fines and other charges are not discharged, and they still owe the money. Because many jurisdictions, to save money, only have court dates once or twice a week or once every two weeks, an individual may be in jail waiting to appear before a judge. During this period, he or she may miss work, job interviews, or school and must find child care.

A public interest group of lawyers asserts that the doors to the courtroom in Ferguson are locked after the beginning of court, resulting in individuals who are late being charged an additional fine for missing their court date. The courtroom also is closed to individuals other than defendants and lawyers. The number of traffic tickets issued by Ferguson police has increased in the past few years at a slow though steady rate. Traffic tickets are seen by informed observers as contributing to the tension between African American residents and the town's police force, which at the time of Brown's shooting was comprised solely of white officers.

In response to protests by Ferguson residents, the City Council announced a number of reforms including capping how much of the city revenue can be derived from fines, abolishing fines for individuals with outstanding warrants who do not appear for court, limiting administrative fees imposed for towing and impounding vehicles, and renegotiating the amount of money owed by individuals in fines. These reforms do not address the traffic policies in adjacent cities.

14.3 YOU DECIDE

The Washington, D.C., Metropolitan Area Transit Authority (WMATA) was receiving complaints about "bad behavior" by students using the Metrorail. In response, the WMATA embarked on an undercover operation to enforce a "zero-tolerance" policy regarding violations of various ordinances, including a law that makes it unlawful to eat or drink in a Metrorail station. Adults who violate the ordinance typically receive a citation subjecting them to a fine of between $10 and $50.

District of Columbia law does not provide for citations to be issued to individuals under 18 for non-traffic offenses. A criminal offense under District of Columbia law, such as eating in a Metrorail station, constitutes a juvenile "delinquent act." A minor who has committed a delinquent act may be

taken into custody. On October 23, 2000, 12-year-old Ansche Hedgepeth and a classmate entered a Metrorail station. Ansche removed and ate a French fry from the takeout bag that she was holding. Ansche was detained by a plainclothes Metro Transit Police officer who proceeded to arrest her for eating in the station. The officer handcuffed Ansche, and her backpack was searched and shoelaces removed. Ansche was taken to the District of Columbia Juvenile Processing Center, where she was fingerprinted and processed. Three hours later, Ansche was released to the custody of her mother. Was the arrest of Ansche lawful under *Atwater v. City of Lago Vista*? See *Hedgepeth v. Metropolitan Area Transit Authority* (386 F.3d 1148 [D.C. App. 2004]).

You can learn what the court decided by referring to the study site, **http://study.sagepub.com/lippmance.**

■ CASE ANALYSIS

In *Tennessee v. Garner*, the Supreme Court decided whether it is reasonable for a police officer to use deadly force to seize a "fleeing felon."

Was the officer justified in using deadly force to apprehend the suspect?

Tennessee v. Garner, 471 U.S. 1 (1985), White, J.

This case requires us to determine the constitutionality of the use of deadly force to prevent the escape of an apparently unarmed suspected felon. . . .

At about 10:45 P.M. on October 3, 1974, Memphis Police Officers Elton Hymon and Leslie Wright were dispatched to answer a "prowler inside call." Upon arriving at the scene, they saw a woman standing on her porch and gesturing toward the adjacent house. She told them she had heard glass breaking and that "they" or "someone" was breaking in next door. While Wright radioed the dispatcher to say that they were on the scene, Hymon went behind the house. He heard a door slam and saw someone run across the backyard. The fleeing suspect, who was appellee-respondent's decedent, Edward Garner, stopped at a six-feet-high chain link fence at the edge of the yard. With the aid of a flashlight, Hymon was able to see Garner's face and hands. He saw no sign of a weapon, and, though not certain, was "reasonably sure" and "figured" that Garner was unarmed. He thought Garner was 17 or 18 years old and about 5'5" or 5'7" tall. [In fact, Garner, an eighth grader, was 15. He was 5'4" tall and weighed around 100 or 110 pounds.] While Garner was crouched at the base of the fence, Hymon called out "police, halt" and took a few steps toward him. Garner then began to climb over the fence. Convinced that if Garner made it over the fence, he would elude capture, Hymon shot him. The bullet hit Garner in the back of the head. Garner was taken by ambulance to a hospital, where he died on the operating table. Ten dollars and a purse taken from the house were found on his body. . . .

Garner had rummaged through one room in the house, in which, in the words of the owner, "[all] the stuff was out on the floors, all the drawers was pulled out, and stuff was scattered all over." The owner testified that his valuables were untouched but that, in addition to the purse and the ten dollars, one of his wife's rings was missing. The ring was not recovered. . . .

In using deadly force to prevent the escape, Hymon was acting under the authority of a Tennessee statute and pursuant to Police Department policy. The statute provides that "[if], after notice of the intention to arrest the defendant, he either flee or forcibly resist, the officer may use all the necessary means to effect the arrest." Tenn. Code Ann. section 40-7-108 (1982). The Department policy was slightly more restrictive than the statute but still allowed the use of deadly force in cases of burglary. Although the statute does not say so explicitly, Tennessee law forbids the use of deadly force in the arrest of a misdemeanant. The incident was reviewed by the Memphis Police Firearm's Review Board and presented to a grand jury. Neither took any action. . . .

Garner's father then brought this action in the Federal District Court for the Western District of Tennessee, seeking damages under 42 U.S.C. § 1983 for asserted violations of Garner's constitutional rights. . . . After a three-day bench trial, the district court entered judgment for all defendants. . . . [I]t . . . concluded that Hymon's actions were authorized by the Tennessee statute, which in turn was constitutional. Hymon had employed the only reasonable and practicable means of preventing Garner's escape. Garner had "recklessly and heedlessly attempted to vault over the fence to escape, thereby assuming the risk of being fired upon." The court of appeals reversed. . . .

Whenever an officer restrains the freedom of a person to walk away, he has seized that person. . . . There can be no question

that apprehension by the use of deadly force is a seizure subject to the reasonableness requirement of the Fourth Amendment. A police officer may arrest a person if he has probable cause to believe that person committed a crime. . . . Petitioners and appellant argue that if this requirement is satisfied, the Fourth Amendment has nothing to say about how that seizure is made. This submission ignores the many cases in which this Court, by balancing the extent of the intrusion against the need for it, has examined the reasonableness of the manner in which a search or seizure is conducted. . . .

The same balancing process . . . demonstrates that, notwithstanding probable cause to seize a suspect, an officer may not always do so by killing him. The intrusiveness of a seizure by means of deadly force is unmatched. The suspect's fundamental interest in his own life need not be elaborated upon. The use of deadly force also frustrates the interest of the individual, and of society, in judicial determination of guilt and punishment. Against these interests are ranged governmental interests in effective law enforcement. It is argued that overall violence will be reduced by encouraging the peaceful submission of suspects who know that they may be shot if they flee. Effectiveness in making arrests requires the resort to deadly force, or at least the meaningful threat thereof. "Being able to arrest such individuals is a condition precedent to the state's entire system of law enforcement." . . .

Without in any way disparaging the importance of these goals, we are not convinced that the use of deadly force is a sufficiently productive means of accomplishing them to justify the killing of nonviolent suspects. . . . [W]hile the meaningful threat of deadly force might be thought to lead to the arrest of more live suspects by discouraging escape attempts, the presently available evidence does not support this thesis. The fact is that a majority of police departments in this country have forbidden the use of deadly force against nonviolent suspects. If those charged with the enforcement of the criminal law have abjured the use of deadly force in arresting nondangerous felons, there is a substantial basis for doubting that the use of such force is an essential attribute of the arrest power in all felony cases. . . . Petitioners and appellant have not persuaded us that shooting nondangerous fleeing suspects is so vital as to outweigh the suspect's interest in his own life. [The use of punishment to discourage flight has been largely ignored. The Memphis City Code punishes escape with a $50 fine.]

The use of deadly force to prevent the escape of all felony suspects, whatever the circumstances, is constitutionally unreasonable. It is not better that all felony suspects die than that they escape. Where the suspect poses no immediate threat to the officer and no threat to others, the harm resulting from failing to apprehend him does not justify the use of deadly force to do so. It is no doubt unfortunate when a suspect who is in sight escapes, but the fact that the police arrive a little late or are a little slower afoot does not always justify killing the suspect. A police officer may not seize an unarmed, nondangerous suspect by shooting

(Continued)

him dead. The Tennessee statute is unconstitutional insofar as it authorizes the use of deadly force against such fleeing suspects. . . .

It is not, however, unconstitutional on its face. Where the officer has probable cause to believe that the suspect poses a threat of serious physical harm, either to the officer or to others, it is not constitutionally unreasonable to prevent escape by using deadly force. Thus, if the suspect threatens the officer with a weapon or there is probable cause to believe that he has committed a crime involving the infliction or threatened infliction of serious physical harm, deadly force may be used if necessary to prevent escape, and if, where feasible, some warning has been given. As applied in such circumstances, the Tennessee statute would pass constitutional muster. . . .

Officer Hymon could not reasonably have believed that Garner—young, slight, and unarmed—posed any threat. Indeed, Hymon never attempted to justify his actions on any basis other than the need to prevent an escape. . . . The fact that Garner was a suspected burglar could not, without regard to the other circumstances, automatically justify the use of deadly force. Hymon did not have probable cause to believe that Garner, whom he correctly believed to be unarmed, posed any physical danger to himself or others. . . .

While we agree that burglary is a serious crime, we cannot agree that it is so dangerous as automatically to justify the use of deadly force. The FBI classifies burglary as a "property" rather than a "violent" crime. Although the armed burglar would present a different situation, the fact that an unarmed suspect has broken into a dwelling at night does not automatically mean he is physically dangerous. This case demonstrates as much. Statistics demonstrate that burglaries only rarely involve physical violence. During the ten-year period from 1973 to 1982, only 3.8 percent of all burglaries involved violent crime. . . .

We hold that the statute is invalid insofar as it purported to give Hymon the authority to act as he did. . . .

Dissenting, O'Connor, J., joined by Burger, C.J. and Rehnquist

According to recent Department of Justice statistics, "[three-fifths] of all rapes in the home, three-fifths of all home robberies, and about a third of home aggravated and simple assaults are committed by burglars." During the period 1973–1982, 2.8 million such violent crimes were committed in the course of burglaries. . . . I cannot accept the majority's creation of a constitutional right to flight for burglary suspects seeking to avoid capture at the scene of the crime.

CHAPTER SUMMARY

An arrest satisfies the reasonableness requirement of the Fourth Amendment when the seizure is supported by probable cause and the arrest is executed or carried out in a reasonable fashion.

The first requirement is probable cause. Police officers have probable cause where "the facts and circumstances within their knowledge and of which they had reasonably trustworthy information are sufficient in themselves to warrant a man of reasonable caution in the belief that an offense has been or is being committed." The Supreme Court, in an effort to clarify this standard, has explained that probable cause is more than reasonable suspicion and less than the beyond-a-reasonable-doubt standard required for a criminal conviction. This test balances the responsibility of law enforcement to investigate crimes and to apprehend offenders with the protection of individual privacy.

Probable cause to arrest an individual may be developed through an officer's five senses: sight, sound, smell, touch, and taste. Probable cause also may be based on hearsay, or "secondhand" information from victims, eyewitnesses, police officers, and informants. Courts are particularly cautious in accepting the accuracy of tips from informants. The Supreme Court initially relied on the *Aguilar-Spinelli* two-prong test for informants. The affidavit under this test must establish both the informant's veracity and the informant's basis of knowledge. These requirements proved difficult to satisfy, and in 1983, in *Illinois v. Gates*, the Supreme Court adopted a totality-of-the-circumstances test. The veracity and basis-of-knowledge prongs under *Gates* are described as relevant considerations in determining whether there is probable cause rather than as separate considerations.

The second requirement is that the arrest must be carried out in a reasonable fashion. The Fourth Amendment provides that "no Warrant shall issue but upon probable cause, supported by Oath or affirmation." The central element that is important in the warrant process is that probable cause must be established in a non-adversarial hearing before a neutral and objective magistrate capable of determining probable cause. The warrant must with "particularity" specify the person to be arrested, the time and place of the offense, and the specific statutory violation. This must be supported by an affidavit swearing to the facts on which the probable cause is based. In *Gerstein v. Pugh*, the U.S. Supreme Court held that a police officer's on-the-scene assessment of probable cause provides legal justification for the arrest of an individual. Once the suspect is taken into custody, the Fourth Amendment requires that a *Gerstein* hearing determine whether a "reasonable person would believe that the suspect committed the offense."

The Supreme Court has expressed a preference for warrants. In *United States v. Watson*, the U.S. Supreme Court nevertheless upheld the warrantless arrest of individuals in public based on probable cause that they had committed a felony. This was permissible even when the officers could have obtained a warrant. The law as to misdemeanors is somewhat different. In *Atwater v. City of Lago Vista*, the U.S. Supreme Court held that the common law and the historic practice of the federal government and the fifty states establish that it is constitutionally permissible under the Fourth Amendment to arrest an individual without a warrant for a misdemeanor when the offense is committed in an officer's presence.

Watson left open the question whether a warrant is required to arrest an individual in his or her home. In *Payton v. New York*, the U.S. Supreme Court held that an arrest warrant founded on probable cause is required to arrest an individual in his or her home when there is "reason to believe that a suspect is within." The Court reasoned that the unreasonable physical entry into the home is the "chief evil at which the Fourth Amendment is directed." There is an exigent-circumstances exception to the warrant requirement in those instances in which the police have probable cause that they are in hot pursuit of a suspect, that there is a threat to public safety, or that there is probable cause that evidence may be destroyed or that a suspect may flee. The Supreme Court recently recognized the exigent circumstance of "emergency aid" as an additional exception to the Fourth Amendment warrant requirement.

In 1985, in *Tennessee v. Garner*, the Supreme Court held that the police may resort to deadly force to apprehend a fleeing felon under the Fourth Amendment where the officer has probable cause to believe that the suspect threatens the officer with a weapon or where there is probable cause to believe that he or she has committed a crime involving the infliction or threatened infliction of serious physical harm. The officer, where feasible, should issue a warning. Four years later, in *Graham v. Connor*, the U.S. Supreme Court held that the exercise of non-deadly force also is to be analyzed under the Fourth Amendment reasonableness standard. In evaluating the officer's response, courts must evaluate the circumstances confronting the police at the time rather than consider the situation with "20/20 hindsight." The relevant facts and circumstances include the severity of the crime, whether the suspect posed an immediate threat to the officers, and whether the suspect was actively resisting or evading arrest.

CHAPTER REVIEW QUESTIONS

1. Compare and contrast reasonable suspicion and probable cause.

2. Define probable cause and explain the meaning of probable cause in your own words.

3. How does the probable cause standard for arrests balance the privacy interests of the individual against the societal interest in criminal investigation and the apprehension of offenders?

4. Discuss how a police officer's use of his or her "five senses" may constitute probable cause.

5. Compare and contrast the *Aguilar-Spinelli* test with the totality-of-the-circumstances test in *Illinois v. Gates*.

6. How does *Draper v. United States* illustrate the determination of probable cause?

7. Describe the process of issuing a warrant. What information must appear on the face of the warrant? Discuss the purpose of a *Gerstein* hearing.

8. When do arrests for felonies and arrests for misdemeanors require warrants?

9. Compare *Watson v. United States* with *Payton v. New York*.

10. What are exigent circumstances? Discuss the justifications for exigent circumstances.

11. Discuss the significance of *Tennessee v. Garner* and *Graham v. Connor*.

12. What is the difference between an arrest and receiving a citation for a misdemeanor? Explain the Supreme Court's holding in *Atwater v. City of Lago Vista*.

LEGAL TERMINOLOGY

affiant

affidavit

Aguilar-Spinelli test

arrest

arrest warrant

citation

emergency-aid doctrine

exigent circumstances

fleeing-felon rule

informant privilege

misdemeanant

REFERENCE

Feeley, Malcolm M. 1992. *The Process Is the Punishment: Handling Cases in a Lower Criminal Court.* New York: Russell Sage Foundation.

Visit the Student Study Site at **http://study.sagepub.com/lippmance** to access additional study tools, including mobile-friendly eFlashcards and Web quizzes as well as links to SAGE journal articles and hyperlinks for *Criminal Evidence* on the Web.

CHAPTER

SEARCHES AND SEIZURES OF PROPERTY

Were the police legally justified in breaking down the door to Richards's hotel room?

Officer Pharo knocked on [Steiney] Richards's door and, responding to the query from inside the room, stated that he was a maintenance man. With the chain still on the door, Richards cracked it open. Although there is some dispute as to what occurred next, Richards acknowledges that when he opened the door he saw the man in uniform standing behind Officer Pharo. He quickly slammed the door closed and, after waiting two or three seconds, the officers began kicking and ramming the door to gain entry to the locked room. At trial, the officers testified that they identified themselves as police while they were kicking the door in. When they finally did break into the room, the officers caught Richards trying to escape through the window. They also found cash and cocaine hidden in plastic bags above the bathroom ceiling tiles. (*Richards v. Wisconsin*, 520 U.S. 385 [1997])

CHAPTER OUTLINE

Introduction
Search Warrants
Warrantless Searches
Consent Searches
Probable Cause Searches of Motor Vehicles

Other Warrantless Searches
Case Analysis
Chapter Summary
Chapter Review Questions
Legal Terminology

 TEST YOUR KNOWLEDGE

1. Can you describe the process for obtaining a search warrant and the information that is required to be included in a valid search warrant?

2. Do you understand the knock and announce rule and circumstances in which the police are not required to knock and announce?

3. Are you able to explain the scope of a search incident to an arrest of an individual and the circumstances in which the police are justified in searching an automobile based on a search incident to an arrest?

(Continued)

(Continued)

4. Do you know the definition of a pretext arrest and the constitutionality of pretext arrests under the Fourth Amendment?

5. Can you explain the legal standard for a valid consent search, the standard for determining the scope of a consent search, and the legal test for determining whether an individual withdrew consent?

6. Are you able to explain the law on third-party consent?

7. Can you describe the automobile exception to the Fourth Amendment?

8. Do you know the requirements for inventory searches?

9. Do you know the purpose of administrative inspections and whether these searches require a warrant based on probable cause?

10. Can you define and list examples of special-needs searches?

■ INTRODUCTION

The Fourth Amendment's Reasonableness Clause prohibits "unreasonable searches and seizures," and its Warrant Clause proclaims that "no warrants shall issue, but upon probable cause, supported by oath or affirmation, and particularly describing the place to be searched, and the person or things to be seized."

Historically, the U.S. Supreme Court has expressed a preference for searches to be conducted with warrants based on probable cause issued by a magistrate or by a judge. The Court has reasoned that the question of whether there is probable cause to justify a search is best answered by a "neutral and detached magistrate" rather than by a police officer "engaged in the often competitive enterprise of ferreting out crime" (*Johnson v. United States*, 333 U.S. 10, 14 [1948]).

In this chapter, we briefly look at search warrants and at the "knock and announce" rule. The remainder of the chapter is devoted to reviewing warrantless searches. These exceptions to the warrant requirement enable the police to act immediately to detect and investigate crime without the need to obtain a search warrant from a magistrate or judge (*Harris v. United States*, 331 U.S. 145, 162 [1947]). We review several types of warrantless searches:

- Searches incident to an arrest of a person
- Searches incident to an arrest of a person in a motor vehicle or of a recent occupant of a motor vehicle
- Consent searches
- Probable cause searches of automobiles
- Probable cause searches of containers in automobiles
- Other warrantless searches
- Inventories

In reading this chapter, keep in mind that the Supreme Court once again is engaged in the balancing of interests. In addressing the issue of searches and seizures, the Court is balancing the need to conduct searches to investigate crimes and to seize evidence of crimes against the interest in individual privacy. The warrant process has the benefit of ensuring that a magistrate or judge determines whether the police possess probable cause to search. This provides protection for the privacy of individuals. On the other hand, requiring the police to obtain a warrant before undertaking every search may endanger the police and public, interfere with the investigation and prevention of crime, and prove unreasonably time-consuming. In reading this chapter, consider whether the Supreme Court has struck the proper balance in defining the situations in which police are authorized to conduct warrantless searches. We first turn our attention to search warrants.

PHOTO 15.1

A search warrant specifies
what the police are looking
for and where the item may
be found in the home.

AP Photo/Damian Dovarganes

■ SEARCH WARRANTS

We discussed the arrest warrant process in Chapter Fourteen. Virtually the same process is involved in obtaining a **search warrant**. Table 15.1 lists some important points to keep in mind in regard to search warrants. This topic can be extremely complex, and you may want to read more on your own. Keep in mind that a warrant must be based on probable cause. The facts supporting probable cause appear in the sworn affidavit submitted by the police officer applying for the search warrant. Most important is the particularity requirement. The warrant must set forth the specific address to be searched and the objects that are the subject of the search. These objects define the scope of the search. The police may search wherever these objects are likely to be found. Some important points regarding the warrant process for telephones and for eavesdropping and for electronic devices are summarized in Table 15.2.

The first topic discussed in this chapter is the "knock and announce" rule that the police are required to follow in executing a search and seizure in a home or residence.

If at residence - give you opportunity to come to door before they come in.

Knock and Announce — *protect your property and privacy. and police*

In 1603, in *Semayne's Case*, the English common law courts pronounced that a sheriff in serving an arrest warrant or a search warrant is required to announce his or her presence and purpose for entering a home and wait to be admitted by the occupant. The English court qualified the **knock and announce** rule and held that if a homeowner refuses to open his or her door to the King's representative, the sheriff is entitled to break down the door to the home (*Semayne's Case*, 77 Eng. Rep. 194–195 [K.B. 1603]). The common law knock and announce rule was incorporated into the constitutions of the original American states. In 1995, in *Wilson v. Arkansas*, Supreme Court Justice Clarence Thomas held that a reasonable search and seizure under the Fourth Amendment requires that the police follow the long-standing common law principle of knock and announce. Justice Thomas explained that the knock and announce rule is an acknowledgment of the special status of the home as an individual's "castle," which merits heightened protections against governmental intrusions. Three explanations typically are offered for the knock and announce rule (*Wilson v. Arkansas*, 514 U.S. 927 [1995]).

- *Violence.* Knock and announce protects against individuals mistakenly believing that their home is being burglarized and acting in self-defense against the "intruders."

→ shoot police

no knock warrant = to protect evidence and police *→ diff in each state*
— not in DE.

flush evidence

Table 15.1 ■ Search Warrants

1. Neutral and detached judicial official. —no interest in outcome

   Warrants should be issued by an objective magistrate or judge or individual with the ability to determine probable cause. In *Coolidge v. New Hampshire*, the Supreme Court held that a warrant issued by the attorney general of New Hampshire was invalid. The attorney general was the chief law enforcement officer of the state and was engaged in investigating the murder that was the subject of the search warrant and in preparing the prosecution (*Coolidge v. New Hampshire*, 403 U.S. 443 [1971]).

2. Affidavit.

   The warrant must be supported by a sworn affidavit that details the facts and circumstances supporting the warrant.

3. Probable cause.

   The affidavit should establish that a crime has been committed and that there are objects relating to the criminal offense in a particular location. The objects should be described with specificity.

4. Anticipatory warrants. —get warrant in the future ? •show enough predicting evidence

   In *United States v. Grubbs*, the U.S. Supreme Court upheld the reasonableness of anticipatory search warrants. These warrants are based on probable cause that an object not yet at a location will have arrived at the time that the warrant is served. Jeffrey Grubbs had ordered a videotape of unlawful child pornography from an undercover postal inspector, and the warrant specified that the search was to be carried out following the arrival of the package (*United States v. Grubbs*, 547 U.S. 90 [2006]).

   ex: plane coming in will have weed on it

5. Property and persons subject to search or seizure.

   The Federal Rules of Criminal Procedure, in Article 41(c), state that warrants may be issued for evidence of a crime; contraband, fruits of crime, and other illegally possessed items; property designed or intended for use in committing a crime; or a person to be arrested or a person who is to be lawfully restrained.

6. The particularity of the location to be searched. —show where and what they want

   The warrant must identify the place to be searched with a "reasonable particularity" that removes "any uncertainty" about the premises that are to be searched. The test is whether the description is sufficient "to enable an officer to locate and to identify the premises with reasonable effort and whether there is any reasonable probability another premise may be mistakenly searched that is not the one intended to be searched under the search warrant" (*United States v. Prout*, 526 F.2d 380, 387–388 [5th Cir. 1978]). This typically requires a street address and, where relevant, an apartment number. The police are not required to be technically accurate in every detail. An accurate physical description of the structure and the surrounding area likely will be determined to be reasonable. The police are required to make reasonable efforts to describe the premises and are not required to achieve the impossible.

   In *Maryland v. Garrison*, a search was conducted based on a warrant that authorized the search of the third floor of 2036 Park Avenue. Following the search, the police discovered that there were two apartments rather than a single apartment on the third floor and that they had seized unlawful narcotics from the "wrong" unit. The Supreme Court nonetheless affirmed the constitutionality of the search and explained that the police had taken a number of steps before applying for the warrant to determine the layout of the building. The Court held that the constitutionality of the police conduct must be evaluated "in light of the information available to them [the police] at the time they acted. [Facts] that emerge after the warrant is issued have no bearing on whether or not a warrant was validly issued" (*Maryland v. Garrison*, 480 U.S. 79, 85 [1987]).

7. Particularity of things to be seized.

   The warrant must describe with particularity the "things" to be seized. In *Marron v. United States*, the Supreme Court explained that this is intended to inform the police of the objects that are to be seized, to ensure that the police do not conduct a general or dragnet search throughout the entire home, and to ensure that "nothing is left to the discretion of the officers executing the warrant" (*Marron v. United States*, 275 U.S. 192 [1927]). A warrant that authorized the police to seize jewelry rather than the specific items that a store listed as stolen was held to be invalid (*United States v. Blakeney*, 942 F.2d 1010, 1027 [6th Cir. 1991]). A warrant that authorized the seizure in a warehouse of stolen cartons of women's clothing was invalid, because the warrant did not provide identifying information that distinguished stolen cartons from boxes of legally purchased clothing (*United States v. Fuccillo*, 808 F.2d 173, 176–177 [1st Cir. 1987]). In *Groh v. Ramirez*, the failure to particularly describe the items to be seized in the warrant resulted in the U.S. Supreme Court holding that the warrant was "obviously deficient" and that the resultant search and seizure were unconstitutional (*Groh v. Ramirez*, 540 U.S. 551 [2004]).

8. Staleness. *— 10 days to execute warrant.*

A search must be carried out while the evidence is likely to be located at a designated location. This depends on various factors, including the nature of the criminal activity. Drugs are bought and sold relatively quickly, and it would be unreasonable to delay the search. Rule 41(2)(A)(ii) of the Federal Rules of Criminal Procedure requires that all searches must be carried out within ten days. State rules differ on the required time in which a search is to be conducted.

9. Time of day. *during day (6am – 10pm in DE)*

Most states and the federal government require that search warrants are to be executed during the day absent "reasonable cause" to conduct the search at night. This is because searches at night are more intrusive of personal privacy and increase the likelihood of a violent confrontation.

10. Scope of the search.

The area that may be searched is defined by the objects that are the subject of the search. The Supreme Court observed in *United States v. Ross* that the search "generally extends to the entire area in which the object of the search may be found and is not limited by the possibility that separate acts of entry or opening may be required to complete the search." In other words, a warrant for a firearm "provides authority to open closets, chests, drawers, and containers in which the weapon may be found." The police are to remain on the premises as long as it is reasonably necessary to search for the objects of the search and are to avoid unnecessary damage to property (*United States v. Ross*, 456 U.S. 798, 820–821 [1982]).

- *Privacy.* The occupants of the home are able to prepare for the entry of the police and avoid embarrassment.
- *Destruction of property.* The police are voluntarily admitted into the home and are not forced to knock down the door and destroy property.

The U.S. Supreme Court followed the common law in cautioning that knock and announce is not a strict requirement and is not required where it interferes with the enforcement of the criminal law. In *Wilson v. Arkansas*, the Supreme Court listed three situations in which knock and announce is not required and in which it is "reasonable" for the police to break down the door to the home.

- *Physical violence.* There is a threat of physical violence.
- *Prison escape.* A prisoner escapes and flees into the home.
- *Destruction of evidence.* There is reason to believe that evidence will be destroyed.

The police are not required to knock and announce when they gain entrance through a trick and misrepresent their identity, and some courts hold that knock and announce is not required where there is an open door.

The Supreme Court judgment in *Wilson* raises a number of questions that the Court addressed in later cases. May the police simply disregard the knock and announce requirement in the case of searches for narcotics because of the risk that the drugs will be destroyed and because of the risk that the drug traffickers will be armed and dangerous? What is the standard that the police must satisfy before they can disregard the knock and announce requirement and forcibly enter a home? How long must police officers wait at the door after knocking and announcing their presence before deciding to forcibly enter a home?

Table 15.2 ■ Electronic Surveillance

Title III of the Omnibus Crime Control and Safe Streets Act of 1968. The requirements for a warrant for telephones and eavesdropping on "oral communication" are set forth in Title III of the Omnibus Crime Control and Safe Streets Act of 1968, 18 U.S.C. §§ 2510–2520. States may employ electronic surveillance by passing implementing legislation. Only twenty-eight states have passed such statutes.

Electronic Communications Privacy Act of 1986 (ECPA). Title I of this act amended Title III of the 1968 omnibus act to provide protection for electronic communications, including cellular telephones, computer-to-computer transmissions, and electronic mail systems. The ECPA also provides protection for "stored wire and electronic communication," such as voice mail, and for information held by an Internet service provider. Some protections are provided in regard to pen registers, which allow the government to determine the phone numbers a suspect calls and those numbers from which he or she receives calls. A law enforcement official must demonstrate to a judge that the "information likely to be obtained by such installation and use is relevant to an ongoing criminal investigation."

Communications Assistance for Law Enforcement Act of 1994 (CALEA). Telephone companies are required to design their digital equipment to facilitate government monitoring of these lines.

Uniting and Strengthening America by Providing Appropriate Tools Required to Intercept and Obstruct Terrorism Act of 2001 (USA PATRIOT Act). This act provided various investigative tools to combat terrorism. These searches generally are carried out under the Foreign Intelligence and Surveillance Act of 1978 (FISA).

Applications for warrants. A judge who is asked to issue a warrant for wiretapping, eavesdropping, or electronic surveillance must determine whether such action is justified based on whether the facts submitted by the applicant satisfy all of the following conditions:

1. There is probable cause to believe that an individual is committing, has committed, or is about to commit a particular offense that may be the subject of electronic surveillance.
2. There is probable cause to believe that particular communications concerning that offense will be obtained through such interception.
3. Normal investigative procedures have been tried or have failed or reasonably appear unlikely to succeed if tried or will prove too dangerous.
4. There is probable cause to believe that the facilities from which, or the place where, the wire, oral, or electronic communications are to be intercepted are being used, or are about to be used, in connection with the commission of the offense, or are commonly used by the person who is the subject of surveillance.

Warrant contents. Each order authorizing the interception of any wire, oral, or electronic communication under Title III must include

1. the identity of the applicant;
2. the identity of the agency authorized to intercept the communication;
3. details of the offense;
4. a particular description of the type of communications to be intercepted and of the types of "facilities" to be used in intercepting the communication;
5. the identity of the individual whose conversation is to be intercepted;
6. the time period of the surveillance. In the event that the surveillance will not automatically terminate when the described communication has been first obtained, facts are to be presented establishing probable cause to believe that additional communications of the same type will occur in the future. The *minimization* requirement provides that wire, oral, or electronic communications shall not be intercepted for any period longer than is necessary to achieve the object of the authorization and, in any event, shall not be approved for longer than thirty days. This period may be extended an additional thirty days;

[handwritten: If police are running to door, person in window see police and run, don't need to knock]

In *Richards v. Wisconsin*, introduced at the beginning of this chapter, the U.S. Supreme Court answered the first and second questions posed above. In *Richards*, the police obtained a warrant to search Steiney Richards's motel room for drugs and drug paraphernalia. An officer dressed as a maintenance man knocked on the door. Richards cracked open the door, observed a uniformed officer, and, realizing that the police were at the door, slammed it shut. The police waited two or three seconds and then kicked and rammed the door open, entered, and seized drugs and drug paraphernalia. Richards sought to suppress the evidence on the grounds that the police failed to knock and announce their presence prior to breaking down the door (*Richards v. Wisconsin*, 520 U.S. 385, 388–389 [1997]).

In *Richards*, the Wisconsin Supreme Court upheld the search of Richards's motel room and ruled that because drug crimes always create danger and the risk of destruction of evidence, the police may enter without knocking and announcing their presence. The U.S. Supreme Court rejected the Wisconsin court's blanket exception for narcotics offenses for two reasons:

- *Overly broad.* There is no necessity to disregard the knock and announce requirement in every instance of a search for narcotics. For example, the individuals involved in the drug trade may not be in the home at the time that the police serve the warrant.
- *Other crimes.* The reasons for a "no knock" entry and search for drug crimes may be applied to a number of other offenses, such as bank robbery. Creating a blanket exception will lead to additional exceptions and to the eventual disappearance of the knock and announce rule.

As for the second question, what is the standard for determining whether the police may dispense with the knock and announce requirement? Justice John Paul Stevens held that the reasonableness of a no knock search is based on a determination that the "facts and circumstances of the particular entry justified dispensing with the knock and announce requirement" at the "time that the police entered the hotel room." The Supreme Court held that to justify a no knock entry, the police must have reasonable suspicion that knocking and announcing their presence would be dangerous or futile (serve no purpose) or inhibit the effective investigation of crime by allowing for the destruction of evidence. The Court stated that reasonable suspicion as opposed to probable cause "strikes the right balance." The reasonable suspicion standard was easily satisfied by the fact that Richards knew after opening the door that the police were outside. At this point, it was reasonable for the police to forcibly enter Richards's motel room given the "disposable nature of the drugs." In *United States v. Ramirez*, the Supreme Court upheld a failure to knock and announce and the breaking of a window, because the police had reasonable suspicion that announcing their presence might be dangerous to the police and to individuals in the home (*United States v. Ramirez*, 523 U.S. 65, 71 [1998]). Do you agree with critics that the exceptions to the knock and announce rule established by the Supreme Court's decision in *Richards* are so broad that they enable the police to disregard the rule in a significant number of criminal investigations?

In 2003, in *United States v. Banks*, the Supreme Court answered the third question and considered how long the police must wait before breaking down the door after knocking and announcing their presence. Too brief a waiting period would make the knock and announce requirement meaningless, while too lengthy a period would risk the destruction of evidence, allow a suspect's escape, or enable individuals inside the home to arm themselves and endanger the police. In *Banks*, the Las Vegas Police and FBI obtained a warrant to search Lashawn Banks's home for cocaine. The officers loudly announced "police search warrant" and rapped loudly on the door. There was no response, and after waiting fifteen to twenty seconds, the officers broke open the front door with a battering ram. Banks emerged from the shower as the police entered his home. The officers seized weapons, crack cocaine, and other evidence of drug dealing (*United States v. Banks*, 540 U.S. 31, 33 [2003]).

The Supreme Court stated that in the absence of exigent circumstances, the police may forcibly enter a home when the occupant's "failure to admit [the police] fairly suggested a refusal to let them in." This period generally depends on the "size of the establishment." In *Banks*, the Court rejected the argument that the officers had failed to wait a sufficient amount of time before breaking down the door. The test is not how long it would take the suspect to reach the front door, but the time required

> to get rid of the cocaine, which a prudent dealer will keep near a commode or kitchen sink. . . . And 15 to 20 seconds does not seem an unrealistic guess about the time that someone would need to rid his quarters of cocaine.

The officers served the warrant during the day at a time when individuals would have been up and around and able to quickly dispose of the narcotics.

The Court held that a reasonable time to wait before breaking down a door varies with the circumstances and the police should not damage property absent real suspicion that a failure to act will interfere with the enforcement of the criminal law. The time required for the inhabitants of a home to destroy evidence depends on the nature of the evidence. The Court explained that if the police were seeking a bulky piano, "they may be able to spend more time to make sure they really need the battering ram."

Legal Equation

Knock and announce	=	Police must announce their presence in executing a warrant.
No knock and announce	=	The police have a reasonable suspicion that knocking and announcing their presence, under the particular circumstances, would be dangerous or futile, or that it would inhibit the effective investigation of the crime by, for example, allowing the destruction of evidence.
Time before forcibly entering the home	=	Time varies with the circumstances, and the police should not damage property absent reasonable suspicion that a failure to act will interfere with the enforcement of the criminal law.
Time required for the inhabitants of a home to destroy evidence	=	Period depends on the nature of the evidence.

⚖ 15.1 YOU DECIDE

The Denver Police Department's SWAT team along with FBI agents stormed into defendant George Stewart's residence and seized cocaine and marijuana. The defendant appealed the trial court's dismissal of his motion to suppress. The affidavit accompanying the search warrant noted that "drug dealers usually keep records, receipts, cash and contraband at their residences, and maintain the names of associates." Drug dealers also "commonly possess and carry a firearm during the sale and distribution of cocaine and/or controlled substances."

The affidavit stated that an undercover agent on two occasions purchased narcotics from Wiley McClain in Stewart's home. There was no effort to knock and to announce the presence of law enforcement. The SWAT team used a two-man steel battering ram to break down the front door and threw a full-charge stun grenade into the living room, where it detonated with an explosion and a flash. The three occupants were blinded and disoriented for five or ten seconds. None of the three were armed, although a semiautomatic pistol was seized in an upstairs room. The search led to the discovery of considerable amounts of cocaine, crack cocaine, marijuana, and drug-related paraphernalia and over $10,000 in cash, and a loaded .45-caliber semiautomatic pistol was found in an upstairs bedroom.

There was no testimony that undercover agents had seen a firearm, although several months before the entry, the police had been told by a private investigator that an informant had told him that Stewart had been seen with a gun. The police knew that the defendant was "a Jamaican and that some Jamaican drug dealers fortified their houses and most were armed."

Was the entry into Stewart's home lawful? See *United States v. Stewart* (867 F.2d 581 [10th Cir. 1989]).

You can learn what the court decided by referring to the study site, **http://study.sagepub.com/lippmance.**

CRIMINAL EVIDENCE AND PUBLIC POLICY

In December 2013, Henry Magee, fearing his trailer house in Texas was being robbed, grabbed a pistol and killed a SWAT team member serving a no knock warrant. In February 2014, a grand jury in Burleson County refused to indict Magee for murder.

The warrant had been issued by a judge who had been convinced by an informant that McGee was cultivating marijuana and had a stockpile of firearms. Deputy Adam Sowders who was killed by McGee during the raid reportedly told the judge that providing advance warning would be "dangerous, futile, or would inhibit effective investigation."

In a case in Los Angeles County, the deputies claimed that as they entered a home they were confronted by an 80-year-old man with a shotgun. The evidence later indicated that the decedent, Eugene Mallory, was likely armed and in bed at the time he was killed. The deputy's command to "drop the gun" was issued after Mallory had been shot six times. Mallory was a retired engineer who was hard of hearing and likely never understood what was going on when the deputies entered his house. The raid had been initiated after an officer erroneously determined that the home was the site of illegal narcotics manufacturing based on the "strong odor of chemicals" he concluded was emanating from the home.

Ogden, Utah, members of a local multi-jurisdiction police unit dressed in black and armed with assault weapons burst into a home in the evening shouting "Police! Search warrant!"

A video of the incident shows a man appearing in a hallway holding a shiny tube that the police thought was a sword but in fact was a golf club. Three shots were fired and killed 45-year-old Todd Blair. The officers involved were found to have acted properly because this was a "split-second decision" and they "acted according to [their] training."

The number of "no-knock searches" conducted every year has grown from two to three thousand in the 1980s to seventy to eighty thousand today. Critics assert that "no knock" warrants are being issued in cases in which there is no need for these surprise entries and that the surprise entry of armed officers into a home can precipitate a violent response by fearful homeowners. They also point out that the police may be relying on inaccurate information supplied by a police informant and that the homeowner poses little threat to the police. The courts also are criticized for issuing no knock warrants based on flimsy grounds such as that the resident of the home is a gun owner.

The dilemma is that judges do not want to jeopardize the police by refusing to issue a no knock warrant and the police are understandably reluctant to risk a "knock and announce" search that will endanger their lives. The police want to send a message that they will resort to deadly force to protect themselves and that individuals are advised to peacefully surrender rather than to challenge the police. On the other hand, commentators point to a number of no knock raids in which the police have been shot and even killed by surprised homeowners.

Radley Balko is a journalist who has campaigned against the reliance on "no-knock raids." He claims to have documented at least fifty cases in which civilians were needlessly killed during no knock raids. These include Kathryn Johnston, a 92-year-old woman killed by an Atlanta narcotics team relying on a bad tip in 2006; Alberto Sepulveda, an 11-year-old shot by a California SWAT officer during a drug raid; and Eurie Stamps, killed in a 2011 raid in Framingham, Massachusetts, when an officer's gun mistakenly discharged. Police also have been wounded or killed in raids. Should the no knock raids be more closely limited by the police and judiciary?

need warrant to search your phone

■ WARRANTLESS SEARCHES

The next section of the chapter discusses warrantless searches. The interest in conducting these searches without warrants is considered to outweigh individuals' privacy interests. As you read about warrantless searches, pay attention to the U.S. Supreme Court's explanation for holding that these warrantless searches are reasonable.

if you're arrested, you're getting searched.

Searches Incident to an Arrest → *for officer safety* *search you are area in immediate control. - any where you can reach*

In 1969, in *Chimel v. California*, the U.S. Supreme Court defined the scope (extent) of a **search incident to an arrest**. Ted Chimel was arrested in his home for the burglary of a coin shop. The police proceeded to search the entire house and the garage and seized coins and medals. Chimel claimed that this wide-ranging search could not be justified as a search incident to an arrest. See *Chimel v. California* (395 U.S. 752, 754 [1969]).

The Supreme Court held that when an individual is arrested, it is reasonable for an officer to search the person arrested. This warrantless search has three purposes:

- *Safety.* To seize weapons that may harm the officer.
- *Resist arrest.* To seize weapons that may be used to resist arrest or to flee.
- *Evidence.* To prevent the destruction or concealment of evidence.

Once again, the U.S. Supreme Court strikes a balance. The scope of a search incident to an arrest is carefully limited to achieve these three purposes. A police officer may search the person and the area of his or her immediate control for weapons, evidence, or contraband (unlawful objects). Immediate control includes those areas from which an individual may obtain a weapon or destroy contraband. The Supreme Court observed that a gun on a table or in a drawer in front of an individual who is arrested may prove as dangerous to the arresting officer as a firearm concealed in the clothing of the individual who is arrested. The area of immediate control commonly is referred to as the **grab area** or lunging area. The Court held that Chimel was properly arrested, and while the police properly searched Chimel and the area within his immediate control, there is no justification for the police to search rooms other than the room in which the arrest occurred or to search through all the desk drawers or other closed or concealed containers in the room itself. As a result, the Court determined that the coins and medals had been unlawfully seized by the police.

In thinking about *Chimel*, consider why the Supreme Court ruled that a search incident to an arrest is limited to the arrestee and to his or her area of immediate control and why the Court did not extend searches incident to an arrest to a broader area or to the entire house. Following *Chimel*, we will look at the requirement that a search must be contemporaneous with the arrest.

In 2014 in *Riley v. California*, reprinted at the end of this chapter, David Riley was stopped by the police for driving with expired registration tags, and the officer subsequently learned Riley was driving with a suspended license. He also was arrested for possession of the two handguns found under the hood of the car.

An examination of his cell phone seized by the police as a search incident to the arrest led to evidence that Riley was affiliated with the "Bloods" street gang. Information uncovered on Riley's phone led to Riley being charged, in connection with an earlier shooting, with firing at an occupied vehicle, assault with a semiautomatic firearm, and attempted murder. The state alleged that Riley had committed those crimes for the benefit of a criminal street gang, a charge carrying an enhanced sentence. Riley moved to suppress the information obtained on his phone on the grounds that the police were required to obtain a warrant. In 2014, in the companion case of *United States v. Wurie*, Brima Wurie moved to suppress the call log information obtained from his flip phone, which allowed the police to obtain a warrant to search the apartment where he stored narcotics.

Chief Justice Roberts held in *Riley* that the examination of a cell phone implicates privacy concerns far beyond those involved in the search of an ordinary object. A cell phone is different from other personal items in quantity and quality. The smartphone may contain a vast amount of personal information; it is a mini-computer, camera, calendar, telephone, video player, watch, tape recorder, diary, television, map, and library.

As for quality, an analysis of a phone may reveal "the sum of an individual's private life" including photographs, purchases, bank statements, prescriptions, and communications. Justice John G. Roberts noted that "[i]t is no exaggeration to say that many of the more than 90% of American adults who own a cell phone keep on their person a digital record of nearly every aspect of their lives—from the mundane to the intimate. Allowing the police to scrutinize such records on a routine basis is quite different from allowing them to search a personal item or two in the occasional case."

The police accordingly may examine the cell phone to ensure that it does not pose a physical threat and may decide to seize the phone and obtain a search warrant to examine the contents of the phone. The chief justice recognized that there may be situations such as probable cause that the suspect is in the process of contacting accomplices in which the police need to seize and examine a phone.

Modern cell phones are not just another technological convenience. With all they contain and all they may reveal, they hold for many Americans "the privacies of life." The fact that technology now allows an individual to carry such information in his or her hand does not make the information any less worthy of the protection for which the Founders fought. Our answer to the question of what police must do before searching a cell phone seized incident to an arrest is accordingly simple—get a warrant.

15.2 YOU DECIDE

Detectives Michael Bland and John Centrella were engaged in the undercover investigation of narcotics trafficking in the District of Columbia. An informant assisted them in arranging to purchase two kilograms of cocaine from Judah Lyons, who had flown in from Colorado. Lyons was staying in a local hotel. Centrella and Bland purchased cocaine from Lyons, and immediately thereafter, they were joined by four police officers, who arrested and handcuffed Lyons. Lyons was seated on a chair close to the door of the room. One of the police officers systematically searched the room. The officer located an overcoat that Lyons had been wearing earlier in the day in an open closet that was several yards from Lyons. The officer noticed that one side of the coat was unusually heavy, reached into the pocket, and discovered a loaded revolver. From a suitcase at the foot of the bed, the officer seized a shoulder holster, two "speed loaders," ammunition, and financial records. The police did not have a search warrant.

Was the seizure of the weapon in the coat a search incident to an arrest? See *United States v. Lyons* (706 F.2d 321 [Ct. App. D.C., 1983]).

You can learn what the court decided by referring to the study site, **http://study.sagepub.com/lippmance.**

15.3 YOU DECIDE

Acting on an informant's tip that John August Paulino was in possession of narcotics that he carried in his buttocks, Baltimore County Police seized Paulino. A police officer testified that:

Mr. Paulino was removed from the vehicle and laid on the ground, his pants were already pretty much down around his—below his butt, because I guess that's the fad, these guys like wearing their pants down real low, so it was just a matter of lifting up his shorts, and—and between his butt cheeks the drugs were—I believe one of the detectives actually put on a pair of gloves and just spread his cheeks apart a little bit and it was right there.

The court found that "in this instance, the police did not only lift up Paulino's shorts, but also the officers manipulated his buttocks to allow for a better view of his anal cavity." The narcotics only were visible after Officer Latchaw spread Paulino's "buttocks cheeks." The officer's search of Paulino was witnessed by his fellow officers.

Paulino was charged with possession with intent to distribute cocaine and with possession of cocaine. He contended that the search was unreasonable and that a visual body cavity search went beyond a permissible search incident to arrest. In examining the reasonableness of a search incident to an arrest, courts are required to consider "the scope of the particular intrusion, the manner in which it is conducted, the justification for initiating it, and the place in which it is conducted." What is your view? See *Paulino v. State* (924 A.2d 308 [Md. 2007]).

You can learn what the court decided by referring to the study site, **http://study.sagepub.com/lippmance.**

at the time of the arrest or very soon after

Searches Incident to an Arrest and the Contemporaneous Requirement

A search incident to an arrest is required to be **contemporaneous** with the arrest. This means that the search must be undertaken "immediately before the arrest, at the same time as the arrest or immediately after the arrest" (*Rawlings v. Kentucky*, 448 U.S. 98, 111 [1980]). What is the reason for this requirement? It would make no sense to delay the search and give a suspect the opportunity to destroy evidence or to use a weapon against an officer. The Supreme Court accordingly has held that a search that is "remote in time and place" fails to meet the "test of reasonableness under the Fourth Amendment."

In the arrest at issue in *Preston v. United States*, three individuals sitting in a car at 3:00 A.M. in the business district of Newport, Kentucky, were arrested for vagrancy. The car was driven to the police station and searched, resulting in the seizure of two pistols. A second search led to the discovery of objects that clearly were meant to be used during a robbery. One of the detainees admitted that the men planned to rob a bank. The U.S. Supreme Court held that the justifications for searches incident to an arrest "are absent where a search is remote in time or place from the arrest. Once an accused is under arrest and in custody, then a search made at another place without a warrant is simply not incident to an arrest." The Court noted that at the time the car was searched, there was "no danger that any of the men arrested could have used any weapons in the car or could have destroyed any evidence of the crime" (*Preston v. United States*, 376 U.S. 384, 367–368 [1964]). The Supreme Court has upheld the reasonableness of a search incident to an arrest where the police had probable cause to arrest and the arrest followed "quickly on the heels" of the search (*Rawlings v. Kentucky*, 448 U.S. 98, 111 [1980]).

United States v. Edwards is viewed as a significant exception to the contemporaneous requirement. In *Edwards,* the U.S. Supreme Court upheld the warrantless search and seizure of paint chips from Eugene Edwards's clothing ten hours after he arrived at the jail as a "normal incident of an arrest." The Court held that the "effects" in Edwards's "immediate possession" may be searched "on the spot at the time of arrest" or "later when the accused arrives at the place of detention, if need be." See *United States v. Edwards* (415 U.S. 800 [1974]).

An example of an application of *Edwards* is *Curd v. City Court of Judsonia.* In *Curd*, the Eighth Circuit Court of Appeals held that searches of the person and articles "immediately associated with the person of the arrestee" are measured by a "flexible constitutional time clock" and may be searched either at "the time of arrest or when the accused arrives at the place of detention." The court noted that a purse, like a wallet, is an object "immediately associated" with the person and accordingly held that the "search of [Shirley] Curd's purse at the station house fifteen minutes after her arrest fell well within the constitutionally acceptable time zone for searches of persons and objects 'immediately associated' with them incident to arrest." Courts have not yet fully defined those objects that are "immediately associated with the person" of an arrestee. See *Curd v. City Court of Judsonia* (141 F.3d 839, 844 [8th Cir. 1998]).

[handwritten: Arizona v. Gant → cannot search car if you have been removed from the car. — you cannot get any weapons if you arent in the car anymore]

Searches of the Area of Immediate Control and Automobiles

[handwritten left margin: not a search incident to arrest ↑]

In 1981, in *New York v. Belton*, the U.S. Supreme Court defined the scope of a search incident to an arrest of an individual in an automobile. Agent Douglas Nicot pulled a vehicle over for speeding on the New York State Thruway. Officer Nicot smelled burnt marijuana and saw an envelope marked "Supergold" (a brand of marijuana) on the floor of the car. He ordered the driver and passengers out of the automobile and placed them under arrest. Officer Nicot then searched the passenger compartment and found a black leather jacket belonging to Roger Belton, the driver. Nicot unzipped one of the pockets and discovered cocaine, and Belton subsequently was charged with criminal possession of a controlled substance. The question before the Supreme Court was the lawfulness of the seizure of cocaine (*New York v. Belton*, 453 U.S. 454, 455–456 [1981]).

Justice Potter Stewart applied the precedent in *Chimel* and held that articles within the passenger compartment as a rule are within the area in which an individual might "reach in order to grab a weapon or evidentiary item." The Court accordingly held that when officers make lawful custodial arrests of individuals in automobiles, they may as a "contemporaneous incident of that arrest search the passenger compartment of that automobile." Containers within the passenger compartment also are within the grasp of the arrestee and may be searched. The jacket was inside the passenger compartment of the car, and the court held that it was properly searched as an object "within the arrestee's immediate control."

In the incident at issue in *Thornton v. United States*, Officer Deion Nichols determined that the license tags on Marcus Thornton's automobile had been issued to another vehicle. Thornton drove into a parking lot, and as Thornton exited his vehicle, he was detained by Nichols. Thornton admitted that he was in possession of marijuana and cocaine and was placed under arrest, handcuffed, and secured in the backseat of the patrol car. Nichols then proceeded to search the passenger compartment of Thornton's automobile and discovered a handgun. Thornton sought to suppress the handgun as evidence, contending that the precedent in *Belton* was not applicable, because it is limited to situations in which the suspect is first encountered while inside the passenger compartment of an automobile. The U.S. Supreme Court dismissed this argument and held that *Belton* applies to "recent occupants" who have exited an automobile. "Once an officer determines that there is probable cause to make an arrest, it is reasonable to allow officers to ensure their safety and to preserve evidence by searching the entire passenger compartment" (*Thornton v. United States*, 541 U.S. 615 [2004]).

Justices Antonin Scalia, Ruth Bader Ginsburg, John Paul Stevens, and Stephen Breyer dissented from the Supreme Court's ruling in *Thornton*. Scalia and Ginsburg questioned the reasonableness of searching the passenger compartment of an automobile, because there was little risk that an arrestee like Thornton, once handcuffed and placed in a squad car, could gain access to his or her vehicle and seize a weapon. Justice Scalia would limit searches incident to an arrest to "situations in which the car might contain evidence relevant to the crime for which he was arrested."

In *Arizona v. Gant*, the U.S. Supreme Court significantly modified the bright-line rule established in *Belton*. Justice Stevens in his plurality opinion held that

Belton does not authorize a vehicle search incident to a recent occupant's arrest after the arrestee has been secured and cannot access the interior of the vehicle. . . . We also conclude that circumstances unique to the automobile context justify a search incident to arrest when it is reasonable to believe that evidence of the offense of arrest might be found in the vehicle. (*Arizona v. Gant*, 556 U.S. 332 [2009])

15.4 YOU DECIDE

Pete Agapito Chavez was a suspect in a carjacking and in a home invasion robbery. Three officers encountered Chavez outside his apartment. Officer Anthony Desimone asked Chavez to stop so they could talk. Chavez walked away from the officer and got into his automobile.

Desimone walked behind the back of the auto to write down the license plate number. Officers Jose Lopez and Jose Martinez approached the driver's window of the car.

Chavez started the car and began edging the car back. Desimone was about three feet behind the rear of the car when Lopez told Chavez to stop and Chavez responded "F--- you. I ain't stopping." Lopez once again directed Chavez to stop, and Chavez continued to back toward Desimone. Lopez unholstered his gun and directed Chavez to put the car in park.

Lopez told Chavez, "Don't reach for anything." Chavez reached for a backpack in the backseat of the car and brought it to the front seat. Lopez was concerned that Chavez was reaching for a weapon. Both Lopez and Martinez drew their weapons, and Lopez told Chavez to keep his hands away from the backpack and to place them where he could see them.

Lopez then told Chavez to step out of the vehicle. Chavez again reached to the back of the car and grabbed a black jacket

from the backseat. Chavez exited the vehicle. Lopez asked him to turn around and put his hands behind his head. Chavez turned around and started running north out of the apartment complex. He turned and threw a "roundhouse punch with his right hand to Lopez's cheek." Lopez and Martinez testified that prior to Chavez striking Lopez there was no basis for arrest. Lopez, Desimone, and Martinez chased after Chavez.

Martinez returned to the vehicle and removed the backpack from the car and searched it. He found a semiautomatic Beretta handgun and $4,000 in cash. Martinez testified that he did not believe he would find any evidence relating to Chavez's striking of Lopez in the car. The search was directed at finding evidence relating to one of the robberies.

Defendant Chavez was taken into custody approximately twenty to twenty-five minutes after Martinez found the gun. He was charged with battery on a peace officer; resisting, delaying, or obstructing a peace officer in the performance of his duty; and possession of a concealed weapon within a car. Was Officer Martinez's search of the automobile and seizure of the Beretta handgun and $4,000 in cash admissible in evidence under *Arizona v. Gant*? See *United States v. Chavez* (No. 2:09-cr-033fcd [E. Dist. Cal. 2009]).

You can learn what the court decided by referring to the study site, **http://study.sagepub.com/lippmance.**

Misdemeanors and Searches Incident to an Arrest

May the police conduct a search incident to an arrest for a minor misdemeanor such as driving without a seat belt, as in the *Atwater* case (that we discussed in Chapter Fourteen)? Gail Atwater was not likely to be armed, and there was no evidence linked to the crime that might have been destroyed. The rule is that any arrest permits a search incident to an arrest of the individual who is placed under arrest. In other words, there is no requirement that the officer reasonably believe that the suspect is armed or dangerous or that the offense for which the suspect is arrested is associated with the possession of weapons or that there is a risk that evidence may be concealed or destroyed.

In the incident at issue in *United States v. Robinson*, Officer Richard Jencks stopped Willie Robinson for operating a motor vehicle after Robinson's driver's license had been revoked. Jencks arrested Robinson and then conducted a search incident to the arrest; during the search, Jencks discovered a crumpled cigarette package that contained heroin. Robinson contended that the search of his person was unlawful, because there was no indication that Jencks believed that there was evidence associated with the offense of driving without a license that might be destroyed. The defense attorney challenged the legality of the search on the grounds that Jencks would have been adequately protected by a *Terry* frisk and that a frisk would have the added advantage of minimally intruding on Robinson's privacy. The U.S. Supreme Court upheld the constitutionality of the search and explained that

> it is the . . . custodial arrest which gives rise to the authority to search, it is of no moment that Jencks did not indicate any subjective fear of [Robinson] or that he did not himself suspect that [Robinson] was armed. (*United States v. Robinson*, 414 U.S. 218, 235 [1973])

In the companion case of *Gustafson v. Florida,* the Supreme Court upheld the lawfulness of an officer's arrest and full search of James Gustafson for driving without a license. The Supreme Court noted that Florida law provides a police officer with discretion to arrest the suspect or to issue a citation. The Court relied on the precedent established in *Robinson* and noted that the fact of the arrest provided a justification to search Gustafson despite the facts that the officer did not fear that Gustafson was armed and that there was no basis for believing that the officer would uncover incriminating evidence (*Gustafson v. Florida*, 414 U.S. 260 [1973]).

The Supreme Court decisions in *Robinson* and *Gustafson* establish a **bright-line rule**. The fact of an arrest authorizes a search incident to an arrest regardless of the offense for which a suspect is arrested. Why did the Supreme Court adopt this bright-line approach?

- *Judicial review.* The courts do not have the time and resources to review the reasonableness of every search incident to an arrest conducted by the police that may be challenged by a defendant. Each situation involves a complicated factual determination.
- *Safety.* Searches incident to an arrest protect the safety of officers. A frisk does not fully safeguard the police.
- *Evidence.* Searches incident to an arrest may result in the seizure of evidence of other crimes.
- *Privacy.* A search is a modest intrusion on an individual who, once having been subjected to an arrest, already has lost a degree of personal privacy.

In *Knowles v. Iowa*, an officer pulled over Patrick Knowles for speeding. The arresting officer under Iowa law is provided with the discretion to issue a citation or to arrest an individual stopped for speeding and in either instance to conduct a search incident to an arrest. The officer issued Knowles a citation and carried out a search of the automobile that resulted in the seizure of a bag of marijuana and a "pot pipe." The U.S. Supreme Court held that the interest in officer safety may authorize an officer to order individuals out of a car and if necessary to conduct a *Terry* frisk for weapons to protect him- or herself. The Court also held that it was unreasonable to search the automobile to preserve evidence because once the officer had issued the citation there was nothing relating to the stop to be found in the automobile. As for destroying evidence of other crimes, "the possibility that an officer would stumble onto evidence wholly unrelated to the speeding seems remote" (*Knowles v. Iowa*, 525 U.S. 113 [1986]).

[handwritten annotation: — cop sees you walk out of Grottos and try to get in your car— cops follow you to try and stop you for traffic violations then DUI → fine to do]

Pretext Arrests and Searches Incident to an Arrest

In *United States v. Robinson*, discussed in the previous section, Officer Jencks pulled Robinson over based on a prior investigation that indicated that Robinson was driving with a revoked driver's license. A pat-down led to the seizure of heroin. Robinson alleged that Jencks was aware that Robinson had two prior drug arrests and had used the traffic stop as a **pretext arrest** to enable Jencks to search for unlawful narcotics. The Supreme Court did not address Robinson's contention that Jencks had engaged in a pretext arrest and in a footnote merely observed that Robinson had been "lawfully arrested for an offense." Justice John Marshall, however, insisted in his dissent that "an arrest may not be used as a pretext for a search for evidence" (*United States v. Robinson*, 414 U.S. 218, 220, 248 [1963]).

Thirty-three years later, in *Whren v. United States* (517 U.S. 806 [1996]), the U.S. Supreme Court provided an answer to the questions of whether a defendant may raise the defense that his or her seizure is the product of a pretext arrest and whether any items seized pursuant to the resulting search should be excluded from evidence. In the case at issue in *Whren*, Michael Whren and James Brown were stopped in Brown's truck for three traffic violations in a "high drug area" in Washington, D.C., by plainclothes vice officers. On approaching the truck, the officers observed two bags of crack cocaine in the truck, and they arrested both Whren and Brown. The two arrestees conceded that there was probable cause to stop them. However, they alleged that the traffic stop was a pretext to investigate their suspected narcotics activity. They also suggested that they had been singled out because they were African Americans. Whren and Brown pointed out that police regulations stated that plainclothes vice officers were to make traffic arrests only in situations posing a threat to public safety.

The Supreme Court held that a police officer may arrest the driver of an automobile based on probable cause that the driver is violating the law and may then conduct a search incident to an arrest. An officer's subjective motivations "play no part in Fourth Amendment analysis" and do not make otherwise lawful conduct "illegal or unconstitutional." The Court stressed that the U.S. Constitution prohibits selective enforcement of the law based on considerations such as race. But the basis for objecting to the intentionally discriminatory application of the laws is the Equal Protection Clause rather than the Fourth Amendment.

Legal Equation

Search incident to an arrest = Arrest

+ Contemporaneous with arrest

+ Search of person and area of immediate control (automobile passenger compartment)

+ Officer's motive not considered.

CRIMINAL EVIDENCE IN THE NEWS

In 1996, in *Washington v. Lambert*, the Ninth Circuit Court of Appeals reluctantly concluded that "neither society nor our enforcement of the law is yet 'color-blind'" (*Washington v. Lambert*, 98 F.3d 1181, 1187–1188 [9th Cir. 1996]). The racially biased enforcement of the law by the police is thought to be exemplified by the policy of singling out African American and Hispanic drivers for minor traffic offenses. This practice of racial profiling is commonly referred to as "driving while black" and in the case of Hispanics "driving while brown [DWB]." See *United States v. Jones* (242 F.3d 215 [4th Cir. 2001]).

It is alleged that stopping individuals for DWB singles out members of minority groups for stops and arrests for relatively minor traffic violations as a pretext for questioning individuals and for searching their persons and vehicles for narcotics, drugs, and evidence of criminal activity. In this practice of stopping individuals for DWB, the police arrest and search minorities for offenses that they generally overlook when committed by individuals who are not members of minority groups.

What is the evidence? Studies made during the 1990s in Maryland, New Jersey, Illinois, Ohio, and other states document the disproportionate stop, arrest, and search of African American drivers by the police. In Maryland, a lawsuit brought by the American Civil Liberties Union against the Maryland State Police was settled when an internal police memo was discovered that advised troopers to be alert to the fact that drug dealers are "predominantly" African American. The memo provided evidence of a policy of encouraging the stop and search of African Americans by the Maryland State Police. The settlement required Maryland to turn data over to the plaintiffs regarding police stops and searches on Interstate 95 north of Baltimore.

An analysis of drivers on Interstate 95 by Temple University professor John Lamberth concluded that over 90 percent of drivers on Interstate 95 north of Baltimore disregard speed laws and, as a result, may be justifiably stopped by the police. Roughly three-quarters of these drivers who were breaking the law were found to be Caucasian, and roughly 17 percent were African American. These data, according to Lamberth, are difficult to reconcile with the fact that between January 1995 and September 1996, the Maryland State Police reported searching 823 motorists on Interstate 95. Six hundred, or 72.9 percent, of the individuals who were searched were African Americans, while 19.7 percent of the individuals who were searched were Caucasian. Lamberth reports that the disparity between these figures is "statistically vast," and the possibility that this result occurred "by chance" is "infinitesimally small." He concludes that the data indicate "without question a racially discriminatory impact on blacks and other minority motorists from state police behavior along I-95" (Lamberth 1998: C-1).

An Illinois Department of Transportation Study of all traffic stops in 2010 found that white drivers who were stopped received a ticket 55 percent of the time and that minority motorists who were stopped received tickets 63 percent of the time. Roughly 1 percent of traffic stops involved a consent search. Minority drivers were twice as likely to be subjected to a consent search. Ninety-five percent of drivers who were asked gave their consent to the search of their automobile. Police discovered contraband in 25 percent of the searches of the vehicles of white motorists as opposed to 19 percent of the searches of the vehicles of minority motorists. The Illinois American Civil

(Continued)

Liberties Union alleged that it's clear that the police "suspect drivers of color to be engaged in transporting contraband more frequently than they suspect white drivers. But in fact they're wrong more of the time with minority drivers than they are with white drivers."

In June 1999, President Bill Clinton directed federal agencies to collect data on the race and ethnicity of drivers stopped or searched. In February 2001, President George W. Bush condemned racial profiling as "wrong" and pledged to "end" racial profiling in America. Twenty states presently have laws addressing racial profiling. Some merely mandate training programs, while others call for the voluntary collection of data by local police departments. In 2001, Texas passed a strong Racial Profiling Data Collection Law that requires Texas law enforcement agencies that are engaged in traffic and pedestrian stops to collect "race data" on stops and searches. In the first phase of this program, agencies are required to collect data on stops that result in a ticket or arrest. In the second phase, a locality is provided the option to mount cameras on their squad cars or to submit data on every traffic stop and pedestrian stop. A majority of departments in Texas have responded by installing cameras on their squad cars.

Experts have concluded that in addition to strong reporting requirements, there are various steps that should be taken to limit racial profiling. These include the training of police officers, the recruitment of a diverse police force, the denial of federal funds to departments that engage in racial profiling, and the establishment of local hotlines for victims to report racially motivated pretext stops and searches.

In articles written in 2001, 2002, and 2005, Heather MacDonald of the Manhattan Institute challenges the notion that minority drivers are discriminated against by the police and points out that a 2002 survey of eighty thousand adults by the Bureau of Justice Statistics found that an identical proportion of African Americans, Hispanics, and Caucasians report being stopped by the police (9 percent). According to MacDonald, "These results demolish the claim that minorities are disproportionately subject to 'pretextual' stops." The difference between the three groups, according to the survey, lies in the fact that 10.2 percent of African Americans, 11.4 percent of Hispanics, and 3.3 percent of Caucasians report that they were subjected to a search following a stop. A second difference is that 2.4 percent of Hispanics, 2.7 percent of African Americans, and 0.8 percent of Caucasian drivers claimed that force had been threatened or used against them (e.g., pushing, grabbing, or hitting).

MacDonald contends that the differences in the percentages of individuals in various groups who report being subject to a search and who report having been subject to the application of force is explained by the fact that African Americans and Hispanics are "far more likely to be arrested following a stop." MacDonald concludes that the higher arrest rates for African Americans and Hispanics are due to the fact that these drivers are more likely to have outstanding arrest warrants that turn up when the police run a computer search, more likely to be violating the traffic laws when stopped, or more likely to challenge police officers and provoke a confrontation. MacDonald writes that "these higher arrest rates in turn naturally result in higher search rates. . . . Moreover, the higher crime rates among blacks and Hispanics mean a greater likelihood that evidence of a crime, such as weapons or drugs, may be in plain view, thereby triggering an arrest and a search." *hey*

MacDonald argues that the allegation that the police engage in racial profiling in enforcing traffic laws is based on "junk science." She concludes that the accusation that the police enforce the law in a racially discriminatory fashion damages police–community relations and leads the police to avoid enforcing the law out of a fear that they will be accused of racial profiling. Do you believe that there are police officers who single individuals out for arrest based on race or gender or other factors? Should the police be required to record the race of each individual operating a motor vehicle whom they stop or arrest or search?

limiting scope of search

waiver of your right to privacy

■ CONSENT SEARCHES – *has to be voluntary*   *hello*

In *Schneckloth v. Bustamonte* (412 U.S. 218 [1973]), the U.S. Supreme Court held that a **consent search** is a reasonable Fourth Amendment search. An individual who consents to a search waives his or her right to privacy under the Fourth Amendment. This provides legal authorization for the police to conduct a search even in those instances in which the police do not have a legal basis to conduct a search of a person or of a container, home, or automobile. The Supreme Court noted that consent searches are part of the standard investigatory technique of law enforcement agencies and that consent in many instances may be the only means of obtaining important and reliable evidence.

Schneckloth held that the legal test for a consent search is that the consent must be voluntary and may not be the result of duress or coercion, express or implied. Voluntariness is to be determined by the totality of the circumstances, and the fact that an individual is aware of the right to refuse consent is one factor to be taken into consideration. The Supreme Court noted that this "voluntary test" balances the need for the police to conduct consent searches against the need to ensure that consent is freely given and is not the result of duress or coercion. The Court candidly conceded in *Schneckloth* that informing individuals of the right to refuse consent runs the risk of individuals refusing consent and might interfere with police investigations. The judges also observed that individuals benefit from consent searches, because these searches permit the police to quickly determine guilt or innocence and enable innocent individuals to avoid being the target of a criminal investigation or arrest.

The burden of proof is on the prosecution to establish voluntariness by a preponderance of the evidence (51 percent). There is no single factor that determines voluntariness. In evaluating the totality of the circumstances, courts consider various factors to be significant. The question to ask is whether the totality of the circumstances indicates that the defendant voluntarily consented to the search. Some of the factors typically considered by courts in evaluating voluntariness are listed below (*United States v. Gonzalez-Basulto*, 898 F.2d 1011 [5th Cir. 1990]):

- *Coercive police procedures.* Whether there is police psychological pressure or a police-dominated atmosphere that may coerce an individual into consenting to a search against his or her will.
- *Requests for consent.* Whether there are a number of requests for consent before the individual agrees to the consent. The more requests that are made, the less likely it is that there is voluntary consent.
- *Custody.* Whether the individual is in custody or physically restrained or handcuffed when he or she is requested to consent to a search. An individual who voluntarily turns himself or herself in to the police is more likely to have voluntarily cooperated with the police and to have freely consented to a search. A suspect who proposes on his or her own initiative that the police conduct a search also is less likely to have been coerced into a waiver.
- *Awareness of the right to refuse.* Whether an individual is informed of his or her right to refuse consent.
- *Experience in the criminal justice system.* An individual who has experience in the criminal justice system is less likely to be tricked or coerced into a waiver.
- *Consent to search form.* Many police departments provide individuals with a form to sign that indicates that they consent to the search. Did the defendant sign or refuse to sign the consent form? A refusal to sign a form is not considered controlling in those instances in which a defendant verbally agrees to a consent search. The fact that a defendant signed a form that clearly indicated that the defendant possessed the right to refuse consent is strong evidence that the consent was voluntary.
- *Miranda warning.* Individuals in custody who are read the *Miranda* warnings are informed that they are not required to submit to police interrogation, and in many cases when asked to consent to a search they also are informed that any objects seized during a consent search may be used against them. An individual who receives a warning is less likely to have been coerced into a waiver.
- *Seizure of contraband.* Defendants in several cases have argued that their consent could not have been voluntary because the police found incriminating evidence in the course of the consent search. Courts, however, generally have held that the fact that the object of the search is well hidden may indicate that the individual consented because he or she did not expect that it would be discovered.

The U.S. Supreme Court next addressed arrests and consent searches in *Ohio v. Robinette*. Robert D. Robinette was clocked at almost twenty-five miles over the speed limit. Deputy Roger Newsome examined Robinette's driver's license, and a check of the computerized records indicated that Robinette had no previous traffic violations. Newsome then asked Robinette to exit his vehicle, turned on his mounted video camera, issued a verbal warning to Robinette, and returned Robinette's license. Newsome then asked, "One question before you get gone; are you carrying . . . any weapons of any kind, drugs, anything like that [in your car]?" Robinette consented to a search of his motor vehicle, and Newsome seized illegal narcotics that were in the auto. Newsome had used this same technique for searching automobiles 786 times in a one-year period. Robinette claimed that Newsome had unlawfully detained him after processing the driving offense and that he had been held without probable cause and that the consent search therefore was the product of an unconstitutional seizure. Robinette argued that he should have been told by Newsome that he was free to leave following the return of Robinette's license. The Supreme Court noted that in *Schneckloth* it had held that it would be "impractical to impose on the normal consent search the detailed requirements of an effective warning . . . [and] so too would it be unrealistic to require police officers to always inform detainees that they are free to go before a consent to search may be deemed voluntary." The Court in *Robinette* held that the question is whether a motorist would feel free to leave and that whether an individual would feel free to leave is a question of fact. In this instance, Robinette's license had been returned, and a reasonable person would feel free to leave (*Ohio v. Robinette*, 519 U.S. 33 [1996]). Do you agree that Robinette should have been aware that he was free to leave?

United States v. Gonzalez-Basulto (98 F.2d 1011 [5th Cir. 1991]) nicely illustrates how a court weighs and balances the totality of the circumstances. Edilberto Gonzalez and Jose Rodriguez-Minozo were stopped at an immigration checkpoint. Gonzalez, who claimed to be hauling oranges, was asked whether he would consent to opening the trailer attached to his truck for inspection and replied, "No problem." A drug-sniffing dog discovered cocaine in the trailer. The Fifth Circuit Court of Appeals held that Gonzalez's consent was voluntary. The agents did not display weapons or threaten Gonzalez in any fashion. He readily cooperated with the search and was not placed under arrest until the cocaine was discovered. Gonzalez was not well educated, but he clearly understood the federal agent's request. He responded to the request by stating "no problem" and unlocked and opened the trailer doors. The agent admitted that he did not inform Gonzalez of his right to refuse to consent and merely asked for permission to search the trailer. Gonzalez, according to the court, nevertheless appeared to understand the request and did not appear confused. The Fifth Circuit Court of Appeals noted that Gonzalez may well have consented because he believed that the drugs would not be found. The cocaine was well concealed in boxes, and there was limited crawl space in the trailer.

Consider some of the situations in which courts have held that the defendants did not voluntarily consent to a search. These cases illustrate that in determining the voluntariness of a consent, judges engage in a detailed analysis of the facts:

- *Lack of consent.* Two juveniles walked past a squad car. The police officer had previously arrested one of the young men for burglary and possession of LSD. The young man "spread his hands out" and proclaimed "I'm clean this time." The officer searched the young man and seized marijuana and amphetamines. The Massachusetts Supreme Court held that the defendant had not consented to the search. A consent must be "unequivocal and specific" (*Commonwealth v. McGrath*, 310 N.E.2d 601 [Mass. 1974]).

- *Mental disability.* Clarence Tye lived next door to the victim of a fatal stabbing. A police investigator and a police photographer approached Tye on his porch and, seeing blood on Tye's clothes, requested that Tye give the officer his shoes. The blood on the shoes was traced to the victim. The Georgia Supreme Court held that Tye had not freely consented to the search. Tye had a low IQ and a predisposition to comply with requests from authority figures. The pressure on Tye to consent was increased by the fact that the interview took place next to an ongoing crime scene investigation at a time when a large number of officers were searching the neighborhood (*State v. Tye*, 580 S.E.2d 528 [Ga. 2003]).

- *Threats to obtain a warrant.* The police received an anonymous tip lacking in reliability that two occupants of a hotel room were armed and were selling narcotics. Three armed police officers knocked on the door and asked 17-year-old Kane Searcy for consent to search the room. Twenty-year-old Ruth Anne McMorran also was in the room. One officer testified that he "invaded Searcy's space to control the situation," and Searcy then consented to the search. The police informed Searcy that he was not required to consent, and Searcy then changed his mind. The officers next stated that they would remain in the room, while a third officer obtained a search warrant. (The police had no intention of seeking a warrant, and this was a trick.) McMorran responded by consenting to the search, and the police searched for and seized narcotics. The Nevada Supreme Court held that based on the "totality of the circumstances," the consent was involuntary (*McMorran v. Nevada*, 46 P.2d 81 [Nev. 2002]).

- *False claims of a warrant.* Four Caucasian law enforcement officers went to the home of 66-year-old Hattie Leath. She met the officers at the front door, and the officers told her that they had a warrant to search the house. Leath responded, "Go ahead." The police discovered a rifle in the kitchen that was introduced in the murder trial of Leath's grandson. The U.S. Supreme Court held that Leath's consent was invalid. The prosecution never presented a warrant in court and justified the search on the grounds of consent. The claim of a warrant "announces, in effect that the occupant has no right to resist the search. The situation is instinct [sic] with coercion. . . . Where there is coercion there cannot be consent" (*Bumper v. North Carolina*, 391 U.S. 543 [1968]).

- *Coercion.* Ralph Hatley was arrested for selling narcotics. The police threatened to take his child into custody unless he consented to a search of his automobiles. Hatley consented, and the police seized eight ounces of cocaine. The Ninth Circuit Court of Appeals held that the officers' "manifestly improper behavior rendered defective the signed consent form" (*United States v. Hatley*, 15 F.3d 856 [9th Cir. 1993]).

- *Trickery.* The police received a tip from an unnamed informant that narcotics were being sold at an apartment. Two patrolmen knocked on the door and stated that they were investigating a gas leak. The door to the apartment was opened, and the police saw a clear plastic bag containing marijuana and arrested the occupants. The court held that the police misrepresentation prevented the residents from making a fair assessment of whether to consent (*People v. Jefferson*, 350 N.Y.S.2d 3 [N.Y. S. Ct. 1973]).

The Arkansas and Washington State supreme courts have held that the protections in their state constitutions provide greater privacy protection to individuals than is provided by the Fourth Amendment to the U.S. Constitution. They have ruled that their constitutions indicate that in conducting consent searches in the home, the police are required to inform individuals of their right to refuse consent. (Hence, these are called "knock and talk" searches.) These courts have explained that the "knowing and voluntary" standard is an important safeguard for individuals' expectation of privacy in the home (*State v. Ferrier*, 960 P.2d 927 [Wash. 1998]). Most courts approve of **knock and talk searches** on the grounds that the police by knocking on an individual's door are doing no more than any citizen might do and are not violating a resident's expectation of privacy. These searches only have been held unconstitutional when the police pressure a resident by drawing their weapons or threatening or coercing the resident, or when the police enter into an area of the home with an expectation of privacy without a warrant (*United States v. Thomas*, 430 F.3d 274 [6th Cir. 2005]).

15.5 YOU DECIDE

Shelby County Sheriff's Department officers were told by an informant that a fugitive they were interested in was at a Memphis, Tennessee, address. Pursuant to this tip, officers went to the home of James Ivy, who admitted them. On entering the home, an officer found a small quantity of cocaine, and other officers then were summoned. The officers obtained Ivy's consent to search the house. In a bedroom, they found and seized crack cocaine in a dresser drawer and over $15,000 in cash in a nightstand. They seized a set of scales in another bedroom, and in the kitchen they found several guns in a drawer and a cooking tube with cocaine residue.

The Sixth Circuit Court of Appeals found that Ivy refused to sign the form for roughly ninety minutes before consenting to sign it. Ivy asked what would occur in the event that he refused to consent to a search. Sergeant Jackie Setliff told him that a "search warrant would be sought; that all adults in the house (including Tina Jones) would be arrested and that, since there would be no adults to take care of the child who was also in the house, the child would be taken to the Department of Human Services for care." The police handcuffed Jones to the kitchen table, took Jones's child from her, and only returned the child after Ivy signed the consent form.

Was this a voluntary consent search? See *United States v. Ivy* (165 F.3d 397 [6th Cir. 1998]).

*You can learn what the court decided by referring to the study site, **http://study.sagepub.com/lippmance**.*

The Scope of a Consent Search

How broad is a consent search? May an officer search an entire automobile or home? The U.S. Supreme Court provided a partial answer in *Florida v. Jimeno*. Officer Frank Trujillo overheard Enio Jimeno negotiating what appeared to be a drug transaction, followed Jimeno's car, and pulled Jimeno over for making an illegal turn. Officer Trujillo informed Jimeno that he had grounds to believe that Jimeno was transporting narcotics and asked for permission to search Jimeno's automobile. Jimeno stated that he had nothing to hide and gave Trujillo permission to search the car. Trujillo spotted and opened a brown paper bag on the floorboard and found a kilogram of cocaine in it. Jimeno challenged the search on the grounds that he had not consented to Trujillo opening containers in the auto (*Florida v. Jimeno*, 500 U.S. 248 [1990]).

The Supreme Court held that the standard for "measuring the scope of a suspect's consent under the Fourth Amendment is that of 'objective' reasonableness—what would the typical reasonable person have understood by the exchange between the officer and the suspect?" The Court recognized that Jimeno may not have intended to consent to a search of the brown paper bag, but concluded that it was reasonable for Trujillo to conclude that Jimeno's consent to a search of the automobile for unlawful narcotics included authorization to open bags and containers. In other words, Trujillo reasonably concluded that Jimeno's consent to a search of his automobile for narcotics included consent to open bags and containers.

A search that goes beyond the scope of the consent is unlawful. In the case at issue in *United States v. Dichiarinte*, Anthony Dichiarinte was arrested for the sale of narcotics. In response to a question of whether he had narcotics in his home, Dichiarinte responded that "I have never seen narcotics. You guys come over to the house and look, you are welcome to." As the search progressed, one of the agents began to examine and seize various financial records that later proved important in convicting Dichiarinte for evading federal taxes by failing to disclose his drug-related income. The Seventh Circuit Court of Appeals stated that a "consent search is reasonable only if kept within the bounds of the actual consent. . . . The defendant's consent sets the parameters of the agents' conduct at that which would reasonably be necessary to determine whether he had narcotics in his home." In this instance, federal agents read through Dichiarinte's private papers, and this "constituted a greater intrusion into a defendant's privacy than he had authorized" (*United States v. Dichiarinte*, 445 F.2d 126, 131 [7th Cir. 1971]).

In *Dichiarinte*, the agents went beyond the scope of Dichiarinte's consent. The reasonable scope of a suspect's consent, however, in some cases is not completely clear. In the incident at issue in *United States v. Rodney*, Dylan Rodney was approached by a plainclothes police officer, Detective Vance Beard, in a Washington, D.C., bus station and asked if he was carrying drugs. Rodney denied carrying drugs, and when asked for his consent to a body search, he replied "sure" and raised his hands above his head. Detective Beard "placed his hands on Rodney's ankles and, in one sweeping motion, ran them up through the inside of Rodney's legs. As he passed over the crotch area, Beard felt small, rock-like objects." Rodney was placed under arrest, and Beard unzipped Rodney's pants and seized cocaine.

The United States Court of Appeals for the District of Columbia relied on *Jimeno* and held that "a request to conduct a body search for drugs reasonably includes a request to conduct some search of [the crotch] area." Indeed, Detective Beard testified that narcotics are seized from the crotch area in roughly 75 percent of the cases involving body searches for drugs (*United States v. Rodney*, 956 F.2d 295 [D.C. Cir. 1992]). The court in *Rodney* did indicate that a separate consent would be required to search an individual's body cavities. Other courts have held that separate consent should be required to conduct a search of an individual's genital area. The Eleventh Circuit Court of Appeals, in *United States v. Blake*, held that "it cannot be said that a reasonable individual would understand that a search of one's person would entail [an] officer touching his or her genitals" (*United States v. Blake*, 888 F.2d 795, 800–801 [11th Cir. 1989]). What is your view?

In summary, the Supreme Court has held that consent should be interpreted in accordance with objective reasonableness—what a reasonable person would understand is the extent of the individual's consent. Another challenge confronting the Supreme Court in regard to consent search is the question of whether an individual may withdraw his or her consent.

> *if they found something before withdraw - you're stuck*

Withdrawal of Consent → *you can take it away*

In *Dichiarinte*, Dichiarinte saw the federal agents going through his papers and complained to the agents that he had consented to a search for narcotics and had not consented to a search of his personal financial records. The question is whether the federal agents would have been required to stop the entire search had Dichiarinte withdrawn his consent to the search of his home. The rule is that an individual can withdraw his or her consent or limit the scope of the consent search at any time. Keep in mind that a withdrawal of consent does not affect the items already seized by the police. As noted in *United States v. Lattimore*, "a consent to search is not irrevocable, and thus if a person effectively revokes . . . consent prior to the time that the search is complete, the police may not thereafter search in reliance upon the earlier consent" (*United States v. Lattimore*, 87 F.3d 647, 651 [4th Cir. 1996]).

In general, courts require a clear, unambiguous, and unequivocal act or statement of withdrawal of consent. Individuals who verbally consent and then refuse to sign a consent form are sending a mixed message, and courts have held that such individuals have not unequivocally withdrawn their consent (*United States v. Thompson*, 876 F.2d 1381, 1384 [8th Cir. 1989]). In the incident at issue in *United States v. Fuentes*, federal narcotics agents stopped Juan

Carlos Fuentes, whom the police suspected of drug activity, as he boarded a flight. Fuentes was observed continually fingering a lump in his right front pants pocket that appeared to be roughly the size of a split softball. Fuentes consented to a search despite the fact that he was informed that he had the right to refuse consent. The officer reached inside Fuentes's right front pocket and felt "a thick rubbery bulge" that the officer believed to be a package of cocaine. As the officer reached into Fuentes's pocket and asked "What's this," Fuentes shouted "No, wait." He tried to push one officer away with one arm and pull his other arm free of the second officer. The Ninth Circuit Court of Appeals affirmed the district court judge's decision that Fuentes had revoked his consent before the officer pulled the cocaine out of Fuentes's pocket and before the officer concluded that it was cocaine.

At what point would the court have determined that it was too late for Fuentes to have withdrawn his consent? See *United States v. Fuentes* (105 F.3d 487, 489 [9th Cir. 1997]).

[handwritten: roommate can give consent to the apartment but not your bedroom if door is closed — police can look inside but can't go in unless they see something inside.]

Third-Party Consent

The last issue regarding consent searches is the complicated area of third-party consent. As you read In *Schneckloth v. Bustamonte*, the Court did not address how Joe Alcala could have the authority to consent to a police search of his brother's auto. Who in addition to the owner may consent to a search of an automobile? What about a passenger or an individual who has borrowed the car? May consent be given by the mechanic who is repairing the vehicle or by the tow truck driver who is hauling the car to the service station? What of the garage attendant where the automobile is parked? May a car thief who has stolen the car consent to a search of the car? As you can see, the issue of **third-party consent** is more complicated than you might have imagined, and the U.S. Supreme Court has attempted to clarify the requirements of consent searches in several decisions.

In *Frazier v. Cupp*, the Supreme Court held that Martin Frazier, by leaving his duffel bag at his cousin Jerry Lee Rawls's home and allowing Rawls to jointly use the bag, had "assumed the risk that Rawls would allow someone else [the police] to look inside." Under these circumstances, there was no doubt that Rawls as a joint user of the bag had authority to consent to the search (*Frazier v. Cupp*, 394 U.S. 731, 740 [1969]).

In 1990, in *Illinois v. Rodriguez* (497 U.S. 177 ([1990]), the Supreme Court established the legal standard for third-party consent searches. An individual may consent who possesses *common authority* over the premises to be searched. A consent also is valid in those instances in which the police reasonably rely on consent from an individual who, in fact, lacks common authority. In brief, as outlined below, the police may rely on individuals exercising *actual authority* as well as *apparent authority*:

[handwritten: living w/ someone else - person gives them consent]

- *Common authority third-party consent.* This requires "mutual use of the property by persons having joint access or control for most purposes." The important point is not ownership. Think about this as frequent and free use of the property. A roommate may consent to a search of all areas of a house that he or she shares with the other co-inhabitants. The roommate would not be in a position to consent to a search of his or her co-inhabitants' individual bedrooms.

- *Apparent authority third-party consent.* In this instance, police officers reasonably (but mistakenly) believe that a person has common authority. For example, the police may mistakenly but reasonably conclude, based on a roommate's statements, that he or she shares use of an automobile parked in the driveway with the owner and shares possession of a key to the car. *[handwritten: → you (cops) think the person who gives consent is the roommate]*

Keep in mind that there are some relationships in which courts have held that individuals do not have common authority as a matter of law and that it is unreasonable for the police to rely on third-party consent. The approach of courts to various relationships is outlined in Table 15.3.

In reading *Illinois v. Rodriguez*, Gail Fischer reported that she had been beaten by Edward Rodriguez earlier in the day. She consented to drive to Rodriguez's apartment where he was asleep and unlock the door with her key. On several occasions, Fischer referred to "our apartment" where she kept furniture and clothes. The police entered the unit and seized drug paraphernalia and cocaine.

The Supreme Court found that Fischer lacked "common authority" over the unit. She had moved from the apartment, her name was not on the lease or mailbox, she did not contribute to the rent or entertain guests there, she did not enter the apartment when Rodriguez was not there, and she moved most of her personal belongings out of the unit. The Court, however, held that the police had reasonably relied on Fischer's representation of her apparent

Table 15.3 Authority for Third-Party Consent

Relationship	Authority to Consent
Wife–Husband	Either spouse may consent to a search of the home other than those areas under the exclusive control of the other spouse.
Parent–Child	A parent may consent to a search of those areas under the control of a juvenile, such as the juvenile's bedroom. A juvenile may not consent to a search of the home.
Motel Clerk	A motel clerk may not consent to the search of a room that has been rented out.
Landlord–Tenant	A landlord may not consent to the search of a tenant's apartment.
Employer–Employee	An employer may give consent to a search of all areas other than those with a high expectation of privacy, such as a locked desk drawer in an office.
Garage Manager–Customer	An individual who parks his or her car in a garage and leaves the key with the attendant assumes the risk that consent will be given to search the car.
Roommates	Roommates may consent to searches of areas that they share with one another.

authority over the apartment. The question is "would the facts available to the officer at the moment warrant a man of reasonable caution in the belief that the consenting party had authority over the premises? If not, then warrantless entry without further inquiry is unlawful, unless authority actually exists. But if so, the search is valid."

Third-Party Consent and Co-Occupants

In *United States v. Matlock*, the U.S. Supreme Court held that a co-occupant of a house has the right to consent to a search. William Earl Matlock was arrested in the front yard of a house that he lived in along with Gayle Graff, her 3-year-old son, her mother, and various members of Graff's extended family. Gayle consented to a search of the bedroom that she "jointly occupied" with Matlock, and the police discovered cash in a diaper bag. The Court upheld the search on the grounds that Gayle exercised "common authority" over the bedroom. Matlock had "assumed the risk" that Gayle might permit the search of the areas that they shared in the home (*United States v. Matlock*, 415 U.S. 164, 171 [1974]).

What would have been the judgment of the U.S. Supreme Court if Matlock had refused consent and Graff had disagreed and had given consent? In 2006, in *Georgia v. Randolph*, the U.S. Supreme Court addressed the issue of whether the police may rely on the consent of one spouse to search a home when the other spouse refuses to consent.

Respondent Scott Randolph and his wife, Janet, separated in late May 2001, when she left the marital residence in Americus, Georgia, and went to stay with her parents in Canada, taking their son and some belongings. In July, she returned to the Americus house with the child, though the record does not reveal whether her object was reconciliation or retrieval of remaining possessions.

She complained one morning following a domestic dispute that Scott had taken her child, and when the police arrived at the Randolphs' home, she reported that her husband was a cocaine user. Shortly after the police arrived, Scott returned and explained he had taken their son to a neighbor's because he feared his wife would take the child out of the country once again. Janet reported that there were "items of drug evidence" in the bedroom, and despite Scott's objections, Janet led the officer to Scott's bedroom where the officer seized cocaine. The police obtained a warrant and returned to the home and seized additional evidence of drug use.

Scott moved to suppress the evidence of the consent search.

The U.S. Supreme Court held that it was unreasonable for the police to rely on the consent of one co-tenant when a present co-tenant objected to their entry. "In sum, there is no common understanding that one cotenant generally has a right or authority to prevail over the express wishes of another, whether the issue is the color of the curtains or invitations to outsiders. . . . Since the co-tenant wishing to open the door to a third party has no recognized authority in law or social practice to prevail over a present and objecting co-tenant, his disputed invitation, without more, gives a police officer no better claim to reasonableness in entering than the officer would have in the absence of any consent at all."

The Court further held that the police may not remove a co-tenant to prevent him or her from objecting to their entry although they also are not required to seek out a co-tenant to determine whether he or she approves or objects to the search of the home. This would impose a burden on the police and prevent them from responding rapidly to information they receive while on patrol (*Georgia v. Randolph*, 547 U.S. 103 [2006]).

In *Fernandez v. California*, police officers heard screaming and fighting from an apartment.

> The officers knocked on the door of the apartment unit from which the screams had been heard. Roxanne Rojas answered the door. She was holding a baby and appeared to be crying. Her face was red, and she had a large bump on her nose. The officers also saw blood on her shirt and hand from what appeared to be a fresh injury. Rojas told the police that she had been in a fight. Officer [Joseph] Cirrito asked if anyone else was in the apartment, and Rojas said that her 4-year-old son was the only other person present.
>
> After Officer Cirrito asked Rojas to step out of the apartment so that he could conduct a protective sweep, petitioner [Walter Fernandez] appeared at the door wearing only boxer shorts. Apparently agitated, petitioner stepped forward and said, "You don't have any right to come in here. I know my rights." Suspecting that petitioner had assaulted Rojas, the officers removed him from the apartment and then placed him under arrest. [Abel] Lopez identified petitioner as his initial attacker, and petitioner was taken to the police station for booking.

Roughly one hour following Fernandez's arrest, Detective Kelly Clark returned and received oral and written consent from Rojas to search the apartment where the police found gang paraphernalia, a butterfly knife, clothing worn by the suspect in a robbery, and ammunition and a sawed-off shotgun. The Supreme Court held that *Randolph* was limited to a situation in which the objecting spouse was physically present.

The Court clarified that the police had a reasonable basis to arrest and to remove Fernandez from the home because of his domestic assault on Rojas. "We . . . hold that an occupant who is absent due to a lawful detention or arrest stands in the same shoes as an occupant who is absent for any other reason." The Court explained that its holding was consistent with social expectations. An individual may be reluctant to enter a home when the objecting tenant is present but is much more likely to enter when the objector is absent (*Fernandez v. California*, __ U.S. __ [2014]).

15.6 YOU DECIDE

Police were called to the home of Patricia and Kevin Henderson to investigate a report of domestic abuse. The police met Patricia standing on the front lawn. She reported that her husband, Kevin, had choked her and thrown her out of the house. She stated that Kevin had weapons in the house and had a history of drug and gun arrests. The police used a key provided by the Hendersons' teenage son to enter the home and encountered Kevin inside. He ordered them out, and then was arrested for domestic battery and taken to jail.

Patricia at the request of the police immediately signed a consent-to-search form and led the police on a search of the home that uncovered several firearms, crack cocaine, and items associated with narcotics trafficking. Kevin was indicted on federal weapon and drug charges. He argued that the search was unreasonable under the Fourth Amendment based on the Supreme Court's decision in *Georgia v. Randolph*. Do you agree with Kevin? See *United States v. Henderson* (536 F.3d 76 [7th Cir. 2008]).

You can learn what the court decided by referring to the study site, **http://study.sagepub.com/lippmance.**

Legal Equation

Consent search	= Voluntary based on totality of circumstances	+	Not a product of duress or coercion
	+ Knowledge of right to refuse is one factor to be considered	+	Scope of search based on reasonable person standard
	+ May limit scope of search	+	May withdraw consent with clear statement.
Third-party consent by common authority	= Consent on the authority of an individual who has "mutual use of the property" and "joint access or control for most purposes."		
Third-party consent by apparent authority	= Consent on the authority of an individual who police officers reasonably (but mistakenly) believe has common authority.		
Co-tenant	= Tenant may consent unless an objecting co-tenant is physically present.		

☆ If they think there is something in the car – search it ⟩ because cars can easily get away
☆ bag in the car – search

■ PROBABLE CAUSE SEARCHES OF MOTOR VEHICLES

We have seen that a search incident to an arrest may permit the search of the passenger compartment of a motor vehicle. The police also may conduct a consent search of a car. There is a third type of warrantless search of an automobile. The **automobile exception** to the Fourth Amendment permits the police to conduct warrantless searches of automobiles where there is probable cause to believe that the vehicle contains contraband or evidence related to criminal activity. The U.S. Supreme Court first established the automobile exception in 1925 in *Carroll v. United States*. Defendants George Carroll and John Kiro were convicted for unlawfully transporting sixty-eight quarts of alcohol in violation of the National Prohibition Act. They challenged the search of their automobile and the seizure of the bottles of alcohol on the grounds that the federal agents had not obtained a search warrant.

The U.S. Supreme Court observed that the Fourth Amendment freedom from unreasonable searches and seizures historically had been interpreted to distinguish between a search of a dwelling, house, or other structure, which in most instances requires a warrant founded on probable cause, and the search of a ship, motorboat, wagon, or automobile, which may be searched on probable cause without a warrant. The Court explained that it is not "practicable" to require the police to obtain a search warrant for motor vehicles, because the mobility of the automobile might result in the vehicle disappearing down the highway by the time the federal agents obtained a warrant (*Carroll v. United States*, 267 U.S. 132, 153 [1925]). As the U.S. Supreme Court observed in *Chambers v. Maroney*, "The car is movable, the occupants are alerted, and the car's contents may never be found again if a warrant must be obtained. Hence an immediate search is constitutionally permissible" (*Chambers v. Maroney*, 399 U.S. 42, 51 [1970]).

The explanation in *Carroll* that the mobility of automobiles makes it impractical to require that the police obtain a warrant to search a motor vehicle does not fit each and every situation. Consider a case in which the police stop, seize, and immobilize a motor vehicle and transport the car to the police station. The police, once having taken the automobile into custody, could easily obtain a warrant. In *Texas v. White* (423 U.S. 67 [1975]), the Supreme Court nevertheless affirmed that

> when police officers have probable cause to believe that there is contraband inside an automobile that has been stopped on the road, the officers may conduct a warrantless search of the vehicle, even after it has been impounded and is in police custody. . . . The justification to conduct such a warrantless search does not vanish once the car has been immobilized. (*Michigan v. Thomas*, 458 U.S. 259, 261 [1958])

In 1985, in *California v. Carney*, the U.S. Supreme Court held that the automobile exception to the Fourth Amendment warrant requirement is based on the mobility of the vehicle as well as on the vehicle's reduced expectation of privacy. In the events at issue in *Carney*, federal narcotics agents conducted a warrantless search of a motor home parked in a public lot in downtown San Diego. The agents observed marijuana, plastic bags, and a scale used in weighing drugs. A search of the vehicle at the police station led to the seizure of additional marijuana. The

Supreme Court explained that while "ready mobility alone" is the original justification for the automobile exception, warrantless searches also are based on the reduced expectation of privacy in an automobile.

> When a vehicle is being used on the highways, or if it is readily capable of such use and is found stationary in a place not regularly used for residential purposes, . . . the two justifications for the vehicle exception come into play. (*California v. Carney*, 471 U.S. 386, 388, 399 [1985])

The two justifications for the warrantless search of motor vehicles are summarized below:

- *Mobility.* The motor vehicle is "obviously readily mobile by the turn of a switch key, if [it is] not actually [already] moving."
- *Regulation.* There is a reduced expectation of privacy in a motor vehicle, because the vehicle is subject to a range of "police regulation inapplicable to a fixed dwelling." This includes a license to drive, vehicle registration, and safety and environmental regulations. The Supreme Court in other cases has held that motor vehicles have a reduced expectation of privacy based on the facts that vehicles travel on public highways, the exterior and interior of autos is easily observable by a plain view search, and individuals rarely store personal belongings in their cars.

The Supreme Court in *Carney* rejected the argument that the fact that a motor home is "capable of functioning as a home" provides the vehicle with a heightened degree of privacy that requires the police to obtain a search warrant. The Court reasoned that the motor home in *Carney* was readily mobile and was clearly being used as a mode of transport. The Supreme Court indicated that a warrant might be required where a motor home is "situated in a way or place that objectively indicates that it is being used as a residence."

Probable Cause Searches of Containers in Automobiles

The U.S. Supreme Court has held that individuals retain a reasonable expectation of privacy in enclosed containers. A container is defined as "any object capable of holding another object" (*New York v. Belton*, 453 U.S. 454, 460 [1981]). Containers include luggage, book bags, knapsacks, boxes, and paper bags. In *United States v. Chadwick*, the U.S. Supreme Court held that federal agents should have obtained a warrant before opening a footlocker that they had probable cause to believe contained unlawful narcotics. The Court explained that a warrant is required to open the footlocker, because, in contrast to automobiles, the content of luggage is not "open to public view . . . [and] subject to regular inspections and official scrutiny on a continuing basis. Unlike an automobile, whose primary function is transportation, luggage is intended as a repository of personal effects" (*United States v. Chadwick*, 433 U.S. 1, 13 [1977]). Keep in mind that there is some precedent for the view that there are containers that "communicate their contents by their appearance" and therefore lack a significant expectation of privacy and may be opened without a warrant (e.g., a guitar case) (*Texas v. Brown*, 460 U.S. 730 [1983]).

The Supreme Court has struggled with the question of whether a warrant is required to open containers encountered during the search of an automobile. Clearly, a warrant is required to open luggage that is seized outside of an automobile. Does it make sense for luggage to lose its reasonable expectation of privacy because it is inside an automobile? The Supreme Court's internal debate over this question has taken a number of twists and turns. The judges now have settled on the sensible rule that a container inside the automobile may be searched without a warrant when there is probable cause to believe that the container houses the object of the search.

Consider the following two scenarios involving containers:

- *Probable cause limited to container.* The police have probable cause to believe that there is contraband or criminal evidence inside a container that is within an automobile. For example, the police observe a drug courier place a backpack containing unlawful narcotics in his or her automobile. The police have probable cause to seize and to search the backpack and do not require a search warrant. Their search is limited to the backpack.
- *Probable cause extends to the vehicle.* The police have probable cause to believe that there are narcotics somewhere within a motor vehicle. They therefore may search the entire vehicle for narcotics and open, without a warrant, any containers that may house the narcotics.

In *California v. Acevedo*, the police possessed probable cause to believe that a paper bag that Charles Steven Acevedo carried to his automobile contained marijuana. He placed the bag in the trunk of his automobile and drove away. The police stopped the vehicle, opened the trunk, and removed the marijuana from the bag. The Supreme Court held that "if probable cause justifies the search of a lawfully stopped vehicle, it justifies the search of every part of the vehicle and its contents that may conceal the object of the search." The police had probable cause to believe that the paper bag in the automobile's trunk contained marijuana. They therefore were entitled to conduct a warrantless search of the paper bag. On the other hand, the

> facts in the record reveal that the police did not have probable cause to believe that contraband was hidden in any other part of the automobile and a search of the entire vehicle would have been without probable cause and unreasonable under the Fourth Amendment.

Do you believe that it makes sense to hold that the expectation of privacy in a container depends on whether it is inside or outside the automobile? (*California v. Acevedo*, 500 U.S. 565, 570, 580 [1991]).

In *Wyoming v. Houghton*, a police officer stopped David Young, the driver of an automobile, for speeding and driving with a faulty brake light. The officer, while questioning Young, saw a hypodermic syringe in Young's shirt pocket, and Young stated that he used the syringe to take drugs. In conducting the search of Young's automobile, the officer opened a purse that female passenger Sandra Houghton stated belonged to her. The police in the purse found drug paraphernalia and a syringe with sixty cubic centimeters of methamphetamine. Houghton argued that probable cause to search the automobile only extended to items owned by Young.

The Supreme Court reaffirmed that if there is probable cause to search a vehicle for narcotics the police may search every container in the vehicle that may contain narcotics. The authority of the police to search the automobile is not limited by the ownership of a container. A "passenger exception" would lead to a driver denying ownership of a container in the car or storing drugs in a bag owned by a passenger. In some instances, the passenger may not be present to claim ownership of the container, causing the police to be forced to delay their search (*Wyoming v. Houghton*, 526 U.S.295 [1999]).

Legal Equation

Probable cause searches of automobile	=	Warrant not required	+	Warrant not required for containers
	+	May search wherever the item being sought may be located.		

■ OTHER WARRANTLESS SEARCHES

We previously discussed three other warrantless searches:

- *Plain view.* Most law school texts categorize plain view as a warrantless search. An officer who is legally situated may seize an object that he or she has probable cause to believe constitutes evidence of criminal behavior (*Arizona v. Hicks*, 480 U.S. 321 [1987]).

- *Frisks.* The police may conduct a frisk of an individual subjected to a reasonable suspicion stop who fails to dispel an officer's reasonable fear that the individual is armed and presently dangerous (*Terry v. Ohio*, 392 U.S. 1 [1968]).

- *Exigent circumstances.* The police may enter a dwelling without a warrant to prevent the destruction of evidence or in hot pursuit of a fleeing suspect or in response to a threat to the public safety. The scope of a warrantless exigent-circumstances search is defined by the object of the search. A search that goes beyond this limited purpose requires a search warrant. The U.S. Supreme Court also has upheld the warrantless seizure of evidence from an individual's person or immediate possession when there is an imminent threat that it may be destroyed. In *Cupp v. Murphy*, the Court held that it was reasonable for the police to scrape an individual's fingernails without a warrant when there was a threat that the individual would destroy evidence relevant to a homicide investigation (*Cupp v. Murphy*, 412 U.S. 291 [1973]).

[handwritten: when car is towed- inventory of car things is taken- not criminal search. If something is found- warrant]

Inventories *[handwritten: protect evidence and police → can't blame police for stealing anything]*

We have seen that automobiles are subject to warrantless searches incident to an arrest and to warrantless probable cause searches. Automobiles also may be inventoried.

In an **inventory**, the police record on an inventory form all of the *possessions and clothes* that are with an arrestee at the time he or she is detained. This includes the objects inside an automobile that is impounded. Objects that typically are inventoried include jewelry, cash, keys, credit cards, and various forms of identification. An inventory is a reasonable administrative procedure under the Fourth Amendment; it is intended to achieve four principal purposes. Keep in mind that an inventory is not undertaken to investigate criminal activity.

- *False claims.* Deter false claims of theft by the police.
- *Property.* Protect property against theft by the police.
- *Safety.* Prevent arrestees from injuring themselves or others using belts, knives, firearms, or other instrumentalities that are smuggled into the jail lockup.
- *Identification.* Confirm or ascertain an individual's identity.

Law school textbooks typically refer to inventories as *inventory searches*, because any unlawful objects that are seized during an inventory may be used against the arrestee. The U.S. Supreme Court has held that the governmental interest in conducting an inventory far outweighs the intrusion on an individual's privacy that is involved in the inventory. The individual already has been arrested, and the inventory does not involve a significant additional intrusion on his or her privacy. The Supreme Court has noted that inventories at the station house allow the police to intrude on individuals' privacy in a way that would be "impractical or embarrassingly intrusive" on the street, such as requiring individuals to turn their clothes over to the police. There are several important aspects of inventories to keep in mind:

- *Uniformity.* An inventory search must be a *standardized* or uniform procedure. This means that there are fixed guidelines, and all individuals and objects are treated alike. These guidelines establish matters such as whether suitcases are to be opened and the contents inventoried or whether suitcases are to be sealed rather than opened. The police are to follow a routine procedure in every arrest situation. In other words, the "minister's picnic basket and grandma's knitting bag are opened and inventoried right along with the biker's tool box and the gypsy's satchel" (*State v. Shamblin*, 763 P.2d 425, 428 [Ut. Ct. App. 1988]).
- *Probable cause.* There is no requirement that the police have probable cause in order to inventory an object or to open and inventory the contents of a container.
- *Reasonable procedures.* The Supreme Court will not second-guess the inventory procedure adopted by a police department as long as the procedure is reasonably designed to protect the police against false allegations of theft, ensure safety, and protect a detainee's property.
- *Criminal investigation.* An inventory search is unlawful and invalid where it is intended to investigate a crime rather than to inventory an individual's possessions.

The U.S. Supreme Court has approved inventory searches in three separate cases:

- *Shoulder bag.* In *Illinois v. Lafayette*, the Court upheld the seizure of amphetamines found in Ralph Lafayette's shoulder bag during an inventory at the police station (*Illinois v. Lafayette*, 462 U.S. 640 [1983]).

- *Automobile.* In *South Dakota v. Opperman*, the Court affirmed the legality of the warrantless inventory of the contents of Opperman's automobile, which had been towed to the police impound lot (*South Dakota v. Opperman,* 428 U.S. 364 [1976]).
- *Containers.* Steven Lee Bertine was arrested for driving while under the influence of alcohol and taken into custody. In *Colorado v. Bertine*, the police were held to have lawfully inventoried the contents of his backpack, which was found to contain narcotics, cocaine paraphernalia, and cash (*Colorado v. Bertine*, 479 U.S. 367 [1987]).

In *Florida v. Wells*, the Supreme Court held that a Florida state police officer had improperly inventoried a locked suitcase in an impounded vehicle, because the Florida Highway Patrol had no established policy and left the decision regarding the objects to be inventoried to the individual officer (*Florida v. Wells*, 495 U.S. 1 [1990]). Inventory searches also have been held to be unlawful where an officer "clearly had an investigatory purpose" (*United States v. Monclavo-Cruz*, 662 F.2d 1285, 1289 [9th Cir. 1980]).

Inventories often are categorized as "special-needs" searches, because they are undertaken for an administrative purpose and not to investigate a criminal offense. The next section in the text discusses other special-needs searches.

Legal Equation

Inventory	=	Record objects in arrestee's possession and in an impounded automobile	+	As soon as reasonable after reaching police station
	+	Standardized procedure.		

agency regulations · fire code

Administrative Inspections

Searches of homes and businesses are carried out by government administrative agencies as well as by the police. Agencies undertake these **administrative inspections** to ensure that individuals and businesses are conforming to a broad range of agency regulations. This includes complying with health regulations by restaurants, adhering to fire codes by bars and clubs, maintaining records by gun dealers, protecting worker safety in factories, and ensuring that apartments and homes satisfy housing codes. Another example is the U.S. Citizenship and Immigration Services' monitoring of businesses to determine whether they are employing undocumented workers. These searches typically are carried out by administrative investigators, although the police at times may be involved. A violation of an administrative requirement may result in both a civil fine and a criminal conviction. Criminal liability also may result when the administrative violation violates a separate criminal statute. For example, a business may be fined for failing to obey environmental regulations regarding water pollution. The corporation's chemical pollution of the water supply also may violate a separate criminal statute and result in penal punishment.

In the frequently cited case of *Camara v. Municipal Court*, the U.S. Supreme Court held unconstitutional a San Francisco ordinance that authorized fire, health, housing, and other inspectors to enter private residences without a warrant based on probable cause. The Court held that administrative inspections are regulated by the Fourth and Fourteenth Amendments and observed that the failure to require a warrant would leave individuals without protection against administrative intrusions (*Camara v. Municipal Court*, 387 U.S. 523, 534 [1967]).

Camara refused to permit a housing inspector to enter his home without a warrant on three occasions and was subject to a fine and imprisonment. The Court held that administrative inspections for housing code violations are entirely reasonable under the Fourth Amendment. Society, for example, has an interest in ensuring that fire escapes, fire alarms, and sprinkler systems are operating properly that clearly outweighs the limited inconvenience caused by an administrative inspection to a resident or to residents of a building.

The Supreme Court noted that it is virtually impossible to require an agency to establish probable cause that a particular building has a specific defect. Safety hazards such as faulty wiring or a defective elevator often are not even apparent to occupants. The Supreme Court accordingly ruled that it is entirely reasonable to base an administrative warrant to search a house or apartment on a *modified probable cause* standard. This may entail an "area warrant" that authorizes the search of every building of a particular age or design or the search of all homes in an area of the city. A warrant is not required in those instances in which an individual consents to the administrative search.

In *See v. City of Seattle*, the Supreme Court considered whether a "routine, periodic citywide canvass" to determine whether *commercial buildings* are in compliance with the city fire code may be conducted without a warrant. The owner of a warehouse refused access to a city inspector and was fined $100. The Supreme Court applied the precedent in *Camara* and held that the "businessman, like the occupant of a residence, has a constitutional right to go about his business free from unreasonable official entries upon his private commercial property. The businessman, too, has that right placed in jeopardy if the decision to enter and inspect for violation of regulatory laws can be made and enforced by the inspector in the field without official authority evidenced by a warrant." The Supreme Court also recognized that there is a significant governmental interest in conducting the commercial inspection and held that an inspector may obtain a warrant to search a commercial enterprise on the same modified probable cause standard that applies to residences. The inspector is required to demonstrate only that the business is the type of structure that is subject to inspection (*See v. City of Seattle*, 387 U.S. 541, 543 [1967]).

In 1987, the Supreme Court, in *New York v. Burger*, affirmed the reasonableness of a warrantless search by the police of an automobile junkyard under the **closely regulated business** exception. In *Burger*, the police arrived unannounced at Joseph Burger's automobile junkyard and found that Burger did not have the required license to operate the junkyard or maintain the required records of automobiles and vehicle parts. The officers then carried out an inspection and discovered various stolen vehicles and vehicle parts. Burger was arrested and charged with five counts of possession of stolen property and one count of operating without a license (*New York v. Burger*, 482 U.S. 691 [1987]).

The Supreme Court held that automobile junkyards historically have been subject to numerous administrative regulations and obligations and qualified as closely regulated businesses. Warrantless searches without probable cause of automobile junkyards are justified by the substantial government interest in assisting the police in tracing stolen goods and in deterring "auto dismantlers" from purchasing and selling stolen vehicles and vehicle parts. Burger was aware that his business was subject to periodic inspections, and despite the fact that the police were not required to obtain a warrant, his privacy interest in his heavily regulated business was adequately protected by the New York law that provided that inspections are to be conducted during business hours and are to be limited to an examination of business records and of vehicles and vehicle parts.

The closely regulated business exception has been extended to authorize the warrantless inspection of liquor and gun dealers, the mining industry, racetracks, chemical and nuclear power plants, and railroads. Note that evidence of a crime that is discovered in plain view during an administrative search may be seized by the police. In the event that the police decide to launch a criminal investigation, they must obtain a criminal warrant based on probable cause and can no longer rely on an administrative warrant (*Michigan v. Clifford*, 464 U.S. 287 [1984]).

In the next section of this chapter, we turn our attention to the reasonableness of special-needs searches.

Legal Equation

Administrative inspections	= Conducted primarily by administrative agencies	+ Enforce administrative regulations
	+ A reasonableness test in which a significant governmental interest in carrying out administrative searches outweighs the limited intrusion into individuals' privacy	+ Consent or a warrant based on a modified probable cause standard.
Closely regulated business exception	= Heavily regulated and a history of regulation	+ Substantial state interest in enforcing the regulation
	+ Warrantless entry without probable cause or reasonable suspicion; the statute is an adequate substitute for a warrant in protecting individuals' privacy.	

[handwritten annotation:] ✳no probable cause needed✳

[handwritten annotation:] racetrack, casino, gun store, liquor store, junkyards

Special-Needs Searches — *[handwritten:]* airport search

Special-needs searches do not serve the ordinary needs of law enforcement and are intended to promote the safety and welfare of individuals and of the public. They are not intended to gather evidence of a crime. The reasonableness of these searches is determined by balancing the interests of the government against the privacy rights of the individual, and these searches generally do not require a warrant or probable cause.

The courts employ a two-step analysis in a special-needs search.

The first step is to establish that the search is directed at a special need "beyond the special needs of law enforcement." In other words, the search is not being carried out to investigate a crime.

The second step is to evaluate the reasonableness of the search. The Court asks whether the government interest at stake outweighs the individual privacy interest. In those instances in which the probable cause and/or warrant requirement interferes with the government's achievement of the special need, courts have held that it is reasonable to conduct the search based on the "lesser standard" of reasonable suspicion or without any articulable suspicion whatsoever.

for safety and welfare of public - not investigating crime

- *Border searches*. Brief and non-intrusive routine searches at the U.S. border may be conducted without reasonable suspicion or probable cause. Non-routine searches require reasonable suspicion.

- *Automobile checkpoints*. Automobiles may be briefly stopped at fixed checkpoints in the interests of highway safety.

- *Airport screening of passengers*. Airline passengers and their belongings and baggage may be searched without reasonable suspicion.

- *Workplace drug testing*. Employees who are on the job during a railroad accident or whose jobs involve dangers that pose a threat to the public may be required to submit to suspicionless drug testing.

- *School drug testing and searches*. Drug tests of certain students may be carried out in the schools without reasonable suspicion. Physical searches of students' purses and possessions require reasonable suspicion.

- *Probationers and parolees*. Individuals under the supervision of state authorities have a diminished expectation of privacy and generally may be searched based on reasonable suspicion.

- *Prisoners*. Prisoners lack an expectation of privacy in their cells, and their cells may be searched without reasonable suspicion. Inmates who have had contact with individuals from outside the institution may be reasonably subjected to body-cavity searches.

Legal Equation

Special-needs searches	=	A special need beyond the ordinary requirements of law enforcement
	+	Balancing the governmental interest against the privacy interest of the individual to determine the reasonableness of the search (may be based on reasonable suspicion or no articulable suspicion).

■ CASE ANALYSIS

In *Riley v. California*, the Supreme Court decided whether the police as part of a search incident to an arrest may search a smartphone.

May the police search a smartphone as part of a search incident to an arrest?

Riley v. California, __ U.S. __ (2014), Roberts, J.

In the first case, petitioner David Riley was stopped by a police officer for driving with expired registration tags. In the course of the stop, the officer also learned that Riley's license had been suspended. The officer impounded Riley's car, pursuant to department policy, and another officer conducted an inventory search of the car. Riley was arrested for possession of concealed and loaded firearms when that search turned up two handguns under the car's hood. An officer searched Riley incident to the arrest and found items associated with the "Bloods" street gang. He also seized a cell phone from Riley's pants pocket. According to Riley's uncontradicted assertion, the phone was a "smart phone," a cell phone with a broad range of other functions based on advanced computing capability, large storage capacity, and Internet connectivity. The officer accessed information on the phone and noticed that some words (presumably in text messages or a contacts list) were preceded by the letters "CK"—a label that, he believed, stood for "Crip Killers," a slang term for members of the Bloods gang.

At the police station about two hours after the arrest, a detective specializing in gangs further examined the contents of the phone. The detective testified that he "went through" Riley's phone "looking for evidence, because . . . gang members will often video themselves with guns or take pictures of themselves with the guns." Although there was "a lot of stuff" on the phone, particular files that "caught [the detective's] eye" included videos of young men sparring while someone yelled encouragement using the moniker "Blood." The police also found photographs of Riley standing in front of a car they suspected had been involved in a shooting a few weeks earlier.

Riley was ultimately charged, in connection with that earlier shooting, with firing at an occupied vehicle, assault with a semiautomatic firearm, and attempted murder. The State alleged that Riley had committed those crimes for the benefit of a criminal street gang, an aggravating factor that carries an enhanced sentence. Prior to trial, Riley moved to suppress all evidence that the police had obtained from his cell phone. He contended that the searches of his phone violated the Fourth Amendment, because they had been performed without a warrant and were not otherwise justified by exigent circumstances. The trial court rejected that argument. At Riley's trial, police officers testified about the photographs and videos found on the phone, and some of the photographs were admitted into evidence. Riley was convicted on all three counts and received an enhanced sentence of 15 years to life in prison.

The California Court of Appeal affirmed. The California Supreme Court denied Riley's petition for review.

Digital data stored on a cell phone cannot itself be used as a weapon to harm an arresting officer or to effectuate the arrestee's escape. Law enforcement officers remain free to examine the physical aspects of a phone to ensure that it will not be used as a weapon—say, to determine whether there is a razor blade hidden between the phone and its case. Once an officer has secured a phone and eliminated any potential physical threats, however, data on the phone can endanger no one. . . . To the extent dangers to arresting officers may be implicated in a particular way in a particular case, they are better addressed through consideration of case-specific exceptions to the warrant requirement, such as the one for exigent circumstances

The United States asserts that a search of all data stored on a cell phone is "materially indistinguishable" from searches of . . . physical items. That is like saying a ride on horseback is materially indistinguishable from a flight to the moon. Both are ways of getting from point A to point B, but little else justifies lumping them together. Modern cell phones, as a category, implicate

privacy concerns far beyond those implicated by the search of a cigarette pack, a wallet, or a purse. A conclusion that inspecting the contents of an arrestee's pockets works no substantial additional intrusion on privacy beyond the arrest itself may make sense as applied to physical items, but any extension of that reasoning to digital data has to rest on its own bottom.

Cell phones differ in both a quantitative and a qualitative sense from other objects that might be kept on an arrestee's person. The term "cell phone" is itself misleading shorthand; many of these devices are in fact minicomputers that also happen to have the capacity to be used as a telephone. They could just as easily be called cameras, video players, rolodexes, calendars, tape recorders, libraries, diaries, albums, televisions, maps, or newspapers.

One of the most notable distinguishing features of modern cell phones is their immense storage capacity. Before cell phones, a search of a person was limited by physical realities and tended as a general matter to constitute only a narrow intrusion on privacy. Most people cannot lug around every piece of mail they have received for the past several months, every picture they have taken, or every book or article they have read—nor would they have any reason to attempt to do so. And if they did, they would have to drag behind them a trunk. . . .

But the possible intrusion on privacy is not physically limited in the same way when it comes to cell phones. The current top-selling smart phone has a standard capacity of 16 gigabytes (and is available with up to 64 gigabytes). Sixteen gigabytes translates to millions of pages of text, thousands of pictures, or hundreds of videos. Cell phones couple that capacity with the ability to store many different types of information: Even the most basic phones that sell for less than $20 might hold photographs, picture messages, text messages, Internet browsing history, a calendar, a thousand-entry phone book, and so on. We expect that the gulf between physical practicability and digital capacity will only continue to widen in the future.

The storage capacity of cell phones has several interrelated consequences for privacy. First, a cell phone collects in one place many distinct types of information—an address, a note, a prescription, a bank statement, a video—that reveal much more in combination than any isolated record. Second, a cell phone's capacity allows even just one type of information to convey far more than previously possible. The sum of an individual's private life can be reconstructed through a thousand photographs labeled with dates, locations, and descriptions; the same cannot be said of a photograph or two of loved ones tucked into a wallet. Third, the data on a phone can date back to the purchase of the phone, or even earlier. A person might carry in his pocket a slip of paper reminding him to call Mr. Jones; he would not carry a record of all his communications with Mr. Jones for the past several months, as would routinely be kept on a phone.

Finally, there is an element of pervasiveness that characterizes cell phones but not physical records. Prior to the digital age, people did not typically carry a cache of sensitive personal information with them as they went about their day.

(Continued)

(Continued)

Now it is the person who is not carrying a cell phone, with all that it contains, who is the exception. According to one poll, nearly three-quarters of smartphone users report being within five feet of their phones most of the time, with 12% admitting that they even use their phones in the shower. A decade ago police officers searching an arrestee might have occasionally stumbled across a highly personal item such as a diary. But those discoveries were likely to be few and far between. Today, by contrast, it is no exaggeration to say that many of the more than 90% of American adults who own a cell phone keep on their person a digital record of nearly every aspect of their lives—from the mundane to the intimate.

Allowing the police to scrutinize such records on a routine basis is quite different from allowing them to search a personal item or two in the occasional case.

Although the data stored on a cell phone is distinguished from physical records by quantity alone, certain types of data are also qualitatively different. An Internet search and browsing history, for example, can be found on an Internet-enabled phone and could reveal an individual's private interests or concerns—perhaps a search for certain symptoms of disease, coupled with frequent visits to WebMD. Data on a cell phone can also reveal where a person has been. Historic location information is a standard feature on many smartphones and can reconstruct someone's specific movements down to the minute, not only around town but also within a particular building. . . .

Mobile application software on a cell phone, or "apps," offer a range of tools for managing detailed information about all aspects of a person's life. There are apps for Democratic Party news and Republican Party news; apps for alcohol, drug, and gambling addictions; apps for sharing prayer requests; apps for tracking pregnancy symptoms; apps for planning your budget; apps for every conceivable hobby or pastime; apps for improving your romantic life. There are popular apps for buying or selling just about anything, and the records of such transactions may be accessible on the phone indefinitely. There are over a million apps available in each of the two major app stores; the phrase "there's an app for that" is now part of the popular lexicon. The average smart phone user has installed 33 apps, which together can form a revealing montage of the user's life.

In 1926, Learned Hand observed . . . that it is "a totally different thing to search a man's pockets and use against him what they contain, from ransacking his house for everything which may incriminate him." If his pockets contain a cell phone, however, that is no longer true. Indeed, a cell phone search would typically expose to the government far *more* than the most exhaustive search of a house: A phone not only contains in digital form many sensitive records previously found in the home; it also contains a broad array of private information never found in a home in any form—unless the phone is.

To further complicate the scope of the privacy interests at stake, the data a user views on many modern cell phones may not in fact be stored on the device itself. Treating a cell phone as a container whose contents may be searched incident to an arrest is a bit strained as an initial matter. But the analogy crumbles entirely when a cell phone is used to access data located elsewhere, at the tap of a screen. That is what cell phones, with increasing frequency, are designed to do by taking advantage of "cloud computing." Cloud computing is the capacity of Internet-connected devices to display data stored on remote servers rather than on the device itself. Cell phone users often may not know whether particular information is stored on the device or in the cloud, and it generally makes little difference. Moreover, the same type of data may be stored locally on the device for one user and in the cloud for another.

The United States concedes that the search incident to arrest exception may not be stretched to cover a search of files accessed remotely—that is, a search of files stored in the cloud. Such a search would be like finding a key in a suspect's pocket and arguing that it allowed law enforcement to unlock and search a house. But officers searching a phone's data would not typically know whether the information they are viewing was stored locally at the time of the arrest or has been pulled from the cloud.

We cannot deny that our decision today will have an impact on the ability of law enforcement to combat crime. Cell phones have become important tools in facilitating coordination and communication among members of criminal enterprises, and can provide valuable incriminating information about dangerous criminals. Privacy comes at a cost.

Our holding, of course, is not that the information on a cell phone is immune from search; it is instead that a warrant is generally required before such a search, even when a cell phone is seized incident to arrest. Our cases have historically recognized that the warrant requirement is "an important working part of our machinery of government," not merely "an inconvenience to be somehow 'weighed' against the claims of police efficiency." Recent technological advances similar to those discussed here have, in addition, made the process of obtaining a warrant itself more efficient. . . .

Moreover, even though the search incident to arrest exception does not apply to cell phones, other case-specific exceptions may still justify a warrantless search of a particular phone. "One well-recognized exception applies when 'the exigencies of the situation' make the needs of law enforcement so compelling that [a] warrantless search is objectively reasonable under the Fourth Amendment." Such exigencies could include the need to prevent the imminent destruction of evidence in individual cases, to pursue a fleeing suspect, and to assist persons who are seriously injured or are threatened with imminent injury. . . . In light of the availability of the exigent circumstances exception, there is no reason to believe that law enforcement officers will not be able to address some of the more extreme hypotheticals that have been suggested: a suspect texting an accomplice who, it is feared, is preparing to detonate a bomb, or a child abductor who may have information about the child's location on his cell phone. The defendants here recognize—indeed, they stress—that such fact-specific threats may justify a warrantless search of cell phone data. The critical point is that, unlike the search incident to arrest exception, the exigent circumstances exception requires a court to examine whether an emergency justified a warrantless search in each particular case. . . .

Modern cell phones are not just another technological convenience. With all they contain and all they may reveal, they hold for many Americans "the privacies of life," The fact that technology now allows an individual to carry such information in his hand does not make the information any less worthy of the protection for which the Founders fought. Our answer to the question of what police must do before searching a cell phone seized incident to an arrest is accordingly simple—get a warrant.

CHAPTER SUMMARY

The U.S. Supreme Court has held that there is a preference under the Fourth Amendment for searches to be based on warrants founded on probable cause. In the view of the Court, the rights of citizens are more fully protected when the existence of probable cause is determined by a judge rather than by a police officer acting under the pressures of the moment. A magistrate or judge must find that an affidavit provides probable cause to issue a search warrant. The warrant must "particularly" describe the object of the search and the address where there is probable cause to believe that the object is located. The search may extend to any place in a home or structure where the object "may be found." The police are required to knock and announce their presence in executing a warrant. The knock and announce requirement may be disregarded when the facts and circumstances justify an immediate entry. In such cases, the proper balance between the need of the police to investigate crime and the personal privacy of the individual is struck where there is reasonable suspicion that an announcement of the police presence would be dangerous or futile or inhibit the effective investigation of a crime by allowing for the destruction of evidence.

Despite the preference for warrants, the U.S. Supreme Court has recognized the reasonableness under the Fourth Amendment of a number of warrantless searches. Warrantless searches incident to an arrest are reasonable under the Fourth Amendment when an individual is arrested for a felony or even for a minor misdemeanor. Contemporaneous with the arrest, the police may conduct a search for weapons or contraband on the individual's person and in the area under his or her immediate control. This protects the officer and prevents the destruction of evidence. In *Arizona v. Gant*, the Supreme Court held that a search incident to an arrest permits the contemporaneous search of the passenger compartment of an automobile and any containers within the passenger compartment. A search of an automobile incident to an arrest may be undertaken when the

arrestee is within reaching distance of the passenger compartment at the time of the search or it is reasonable to believe the vehicle contains evidence of the offense of arrest. When these justifications are absent, a search of an arrestee's vehicle will be unreasonable unless police obtain a warrant or show that another exception to the warrant requirement applies. (*Arizona v. Gant*, 556 U.S. 332 [2009])

A court will not examine the motivation of an officer who executes an arrest. The only question is whether there is probable cause. A "pretext arrest" accordingly does not constitute a defense to an arrest under the Fourth Amendment. An individual may challenge a pretext arrest as a violation of the Equal Protection Clause of the Fifth and Fourteenth Amendments.

A consent search also is reasonable under the Fourth Amendment. The standard is whether the consent is voluntary and is not the product of duress or coercion, express or implied. The prosecution possesses a heavy burden to establish that a consent is voluntary based on the totality of the circumstances. The scope of a consent search is based on what a reasonable person would understand by the exchange between the individual and the police officer. An individual may limit the scope of his or her consent and may withdraw consent by a clear, unambiguous, and unequivocal statement. The Supreme Court has recognized the reasonableness of a third party's consent when an individual possesses common authority or apparent authority. The Court also has held that there is "no recognized authority in law or social practice" for a third party to consent to a search when a co-occupant is present and refuses to consent.

The automobile exception to the Fourth Amendment warrant requirement permits the police to search a motor vehicle without a warrant. The search may extend to any part of the automobile or container within the automobile where the object of the search may be located. In Chapter Fourteen, we discussed other warrantless searches: plain view, frisks pursuant to reasonable suspicion stops, and exigent circumstances.

An inventory of an automobile and of a suspect's possessions may be conducted as soon as is reasonable after reaching the station house. An inventory is considered a special-needs search, because it is an administrative procedure that is not intended to investigate a crime.

Administrative inspections to enforce administrative requirements involving health, safety, fire, and other matters require warrants based on a modified probable cause standard. Special-needs searches do not serve the ordinary needs of law enforcement and are intended to promote the safety and welfare of individuals and of the public. The reasonableness of these searches is determined by balancing the interests of the government against the privacy rights of the individual, and these searches generally do not require a warrant or probable cause.

CHAPTER REVIEW QUESTIONS

1. Discuss search warrants and the particularity requirement.

2. Define the knock and announce rule. When are the police justified in not adhering to the knock and announce requirement?

3. Discuss the purpose of a search incident to an arrest. Compare and contrast searches incident to arrest with frisks.

4. What is the scope (extent) of a search incident to an arrest? Why is there a contemporaneous requirement for searches incident to an arrest?

5. Define the scope of a police search when they arrest the driver of an automobile on the highway. How does *Thornton* expand the holding in *Belton*?

6. Elaborate on pretext arrests and whether pretext arrests constitute a defense under the Fourth Amendment.

7. What is the legal standard for a consent search?

8. Define the scope of a consent search. May an individual withdraw his or her consent?

9. What is the scope of a probable cause search of an automobile?

10. Discuss the requirements for a third-party consent search.

11. Under what circumstances may the police search a container in an automobile without a warrant? Does it matter whether the container is owned by the driver or by a passenger? Is a warrant required when the same container is searched when it is outside the motor vehicle?

12. When may the police conduct an inventory? What are the requirements for an inventory search?

13. Explain why administrative inspections are based on a modified probable cause standard.

14. What are the requirements for a special-needs search? What are some examples of special-needs searches?

LEGAL TERMINOLOGY

administrative inspections

automobile exception

bright-line rule

closely regulated business

consent search

contemporaneous

grab area

inventory

knock and announce

knock and talk searches

pretext arrest

search incident to an arrest

search warrant

special-needs searches

third-party consent

REFERENCES

Lamberth, John. 1998. "Driving While Black: A Statistician Proves That Prejudice Still Rules the Road." *Washington Post*, August 16.

MacDonald, Heather. 2001. "The Myth of Racial Profiling." *City Journal*, Spring. http://www.city-journal.org/html/11_2_the_myth.html (accessed December 10, 2014).

———. 2002. "The Racial Profiling Myth Debunked." *City Journal*, Spring. http://www.city-journal.org/html/12_2_the_racial_profiling.html (accessed December 10, 2014).

———. 2005. "Reporting While Wrong." *National Review*, September 26. http://www.manhattan-institute.org/html/miarticle.htm?id=4596 (accessed December 10, 2014).

CHAPTER 16

INTERROGATIONS AND CONFESSIONS

Did the police constitutionally obtain the defendant's confession to murder?

Dr. Jeffrey Metzner, a psychiatrist employed by the state hospital, testified that respondent was suffering from chronic schizophrenia and was in a psychotic state at least as of August 17, 1983, the day before he confessed. Metzner's interviews with respondent revealed that respondent was following the "voice of God." This voice instructed respondent to withdraw money from the bank, to buy an airplane ticket, and to fly from Boston to Denver. When respondent arrived from Boston, God's voice became stronger and told respondent either to confess to the killing or to commit suicide. Reluctantly following the command of the voices, respondent approached Officer [Patrick] Anderson and confessed.

Dr. Metzner testified that, in his expert opinion, respondent was experiencing "command hallucinations." This condition interfered with respondent's "volitional abilities; that is, his ability to make free and rational choices." (*Colorado v. Connelly*, 479 U.S. 157 [1986])

CHAPTER OUTLINE

Introduction
Due Process
The Right Against Self-Incrimination
Miranda v. Arizona
Sixth Amendment Right to Counsel: Police Interrogations

Case Analysis
Chapter Summary
Chapter Review Questions
Legal Terminology

TEST YOUR KNOWLEDGE

1. Do you know the role of confessions in the criminal investigation process, the potential challenges and problems presented by confessions, and the explanations for false confessions?

2. Are you able to discuss the protections provided by the Fifth Amendment right against self-incrimination and what is protected by the Fifth Amendment and what is not protected?

3. Can you explain how *Miranda v. Arizona* protects the Fifth Amendment rights of individuals in police custody?

(Continued)

4. Do you know the factors to be considered in determining whether an individual is subjected to custodial interrogation?

5. Can you explain the public safety exception?

6. Can you explain how the *Miranda* rights are to be read and the requirements for invoking the *Miranda* rights?

7. Do you know the test for the waiver of the *Miranda* rights? Explain explicit and implicit waiver.

8. Can you define "question first and warn later"?

9. Do you know the legal tests for a waiver following invocation of the *Miranda* rights?

10. Can you describe the test for interrogation?

11. Do you know the Sixth Amendment protections provided to defendants in police custody?

■ INTRODUCTION

Interrogations

The writings of the late professor Fred Inbau of Northwestern University continue to have a significant influence on the tactics and strategy of police interrogations. Professor Inbau argued throughout his career that detective novels, films, and television had misled the public into believing that the police solve most crimes by relying on scientific evidence or eyewitness testimony. He pointed out that in a significant number of cases, this type of evidence is unavailable and that the police are forced to rely on **confessions**.

Professor Inbau illustrates the importance of confessions by pointing to the hypothetical example of discovering the dead body of a female who appears to have been the victim of a criminal assault. There is no indication of a forced entry into her home, and the police investigation fails to yield DNA, fingerprints, clothing fibers, or witnesses. Law enforcement officers question everyone who may have had a motive to kill the victim, including the victim's angry former husband and her brother-in-law, who has accumulated large gambling debts and owes the victim money. The brother-in-law eventually tires under skillful police questioning and confesses. This example, according to Inbau, illustrates three important points concerning the importance of confessions (Inbau 1961):

- Many criminal cases can be solved only through confessions or through information obtained from other individuals.

- Suspects often will not admit their guilt unless subjected to lengthy interrogations by the police.

- Successful police questioning requires sophisticated interrogation techniques that may be considered trickery or manipulative in ordinary police interactions with the public.

Inbau's argument is nicely echoed by Supreme Court Justice Antonin Scalia's remark that "even if I were to concede that an honest confession is a foolish mistake, I would welcome rather than reject it; a rule that foolish mistakes do not count would leave most offenders not only unconvicted but undetected" (*Minnick v. Mississippi*, 498 U.S. 146, 166–167 [1990]). It often is overlooked that in addition to speeding the conviction and punishment of the guilty, confessions can help exonerate the innocent without subjecting these individuals to the time and expense of a lengthy criminal investigation and trial. There also is the practical consideration that the **admission** of criminal guilt is an important step in an offender's acceptance of responsibility and commitment to rehabilitation.

There are no reliable data that clearly establish the percentage of cases in which interrogations play a central role in establishing a defendant's guilt. We can only note that jurors credit confessions with a great deal of importance in the determination of a defendant's guilt or innocence. In summary, confessions play an important role in the criminal justice process for several reasons:

- *Crime detection.* Confessions help the police solve crimes where there is an absence of scientific evidence and witnesses.
- *Accountability.* Acknowledging guilt is a significant step toward rehabilitation.
- *Efficiency.* Confessions facilitate both criminal convictions of the guilty and exoneration of the innocent.

Confessions also present potential challenges and problems for the criminal justice system:

- *Abuse.* The police may be tempted to employ physical abuse and psychological coercion to extract confessions. Abusive conduct is encouraged by the practice of incommunicado police interrogation—the carrying out of interrogations in police stations without the presence of defense lawyers or judicial supervision.
- *Fair procedures.* A reliance on pretrial confessions to establish a suspect's guilt is contrary to the principle that guilt is to be established beyond a reasonable doubt through the adversarial process in a courtroom.
- *Reliability.* There is the danger that a conviction will be based on a false confession.
- *Inequality.* Uneducated and disadvantaged suspects and individuals lacking self-confidence may be particularly vulnerable to manipulation and trickery. On the other hand, the wealthy and educated are more likely to possess the self-confidence and understanding to refuse to talk to the police and are more likely to be able to afford a lawyer.

The threat of **false confessions** and convictions has been of particular concern. This calls into question the adequacy of the protections that are made available to defendants in the criminal justice process and is pointed to by critics as illustrating the lack of fairness in the criminal justice process.

Three Constitutional Limitations on Police Interrogations

The judiciary has relied on three constitutional provisions to ensure that confessions are the product of fair procedures:

Fourteenth Amendment Due Process Clause. As we have seen, there is a danger that the pressures of the interrogation process may lead to false confessions. The poor, uneducated, and mentally challenged are particularly vulnerable to trickery and manipulation. Former Supreme Court justice Arthur Goldberg observed that history teaches that "a system of criminal law enforcement which comes to depend on the 'confession' will, in the long run, be less reliable and more subject to abuses than a system which depends on extrinsic evidence independently secured through skillful investigation" (*Escobedo v. Illinois*, 378 U.S. 478, 488–489 [1964]).

In the 1930s, the Supreme Court began to rely on the Fourteenth Amendment Due Process Clause to ensure that confessions obtained by state law enforcement officials were voluntary and were not the product of psychological or physical abuse. The Due Process Clause provides that "[n]o state shall . . . deprive any person of life, liberty, or property without due process of law" and continues to be employed by courts to ensure that confessions are voluntary. An **involuntary confession** violates an individual's *liberty* to make a voluntary choice whether to confess and ultimately may lead to imprisonment and to a loss of liberty.

Fifth Amendment Self-Incrimination Clause. In the American *accusatorial system* of criminal procedure, the burden is on the prosecution to establish guilt beyond a reasonable doubt at trial, and the defendant may not be compelled to testify against himself or herself. This is distinguished from an *inquisitorial system* of criminal procedure in which the defendant does not enjoy the privilege against self-incrimination and must answer questions posed by the judge, who typically interrogates witnesses. The drafters of the U.S. Constitution were familiar with the English **Star Chamber**, a special court established by the English king in the fifteenth century that was charged with prosecuting and punishing political and religious dissidents. This inquisitorial tribunal employed torture and abuse to extract confessions and was authorized to hand out any punishment short of death. The reign of terror was effectively ended by Puritan John Lilburne who, in 1637, defied the chamber's order that he confess to spreading dissident religious views. Lilburne was fined, pilloried, whipped, and imprisoned in leg irons in solitary confinement. Parliament ordered his release in 1640, and the House of Lords subsequently vacated Lilburne's sentence, noting that it was "'illegal . . . unjust . . . [and] against the liberty of the subject and law of the land'" (Levy 1968: 272–291).

The right against self-incrimination was viewed as sufficiently important that eight of the original American states included provisions that no one may be "compelled to give witness against himself," and the right against self-incrimination subsequently was included in the Fifth Amendment to the U.S. Constitution.

In 1966, in *Miranda v. Arizona*, the U.S. Supreme Court concluded that the inherently coercive environment of **incommunicado interrogation** overwhelmed individuals' ability to assert their right against self-incrimination. The Supreme Court responded by interpreting the Self-Incrimination Clause requirement that "[n]o person . . . shall be compelled in any criminal case to be a witness against himself" to require the police to read individuals the *Miranda* rights prior to police interrogation (*Miranda v. Arizona*, 384 U.S. 436 [1966]).

The Supreme Court later held that the Sixth Amendment right to counsel protects individuals subjected to interrogation following the "initiation of proceedings against them."

Sixth Amendment right to counsel. The U.S. Supreme Court supplemented the *Miranda* judgment in a series of cases that held that once the government has taken formal steps to prosecute an individual, he or she possesses a Sixth Amendment right to counsel. At this point, it is clear that the government is determined to prosecute, and the Supreme Court ruled that the police are prohibited by the Sixth Amendment from circumventing the trial process and establishing a suspect's guilt through extrajudicial interrogation. The Court explained that the right to an attorney cannot be limited to the trial itself because the denial of access to a lawyer at this early stage of the prosecutorial process may seal the defendant's fate and reduce the trial into a "mere formality" (*Brewer v. Williams*, 430 U.S. 387, 398 [1977]).

Your goal in this chapter should be to learn the strengths and weaknesses and differences between the three constitutional approaches to interrogations. Pay attention to the judiciary's effort to strike a balance between the need for confessions and the rights of suspects. Consider whether the pendulum has swung too far toward law enforcement or the protection of defendants or whether a proper balance has been struck. One final point: Keep three terms in mind as you read this chapter. The text, at times, uses these terms interchangeably, but they have distinct meanings:

Admission. An individual admits a fact that tends to establish guilt, such as his or her presence at the shooting scene. An admission when combined with other facts may lead to a criminal conviction.

Confession. An individual acknowledges the commission of a crime in response to police questioning or may voluntarily approach the police and admit to the crime.

Statement. In an oral or written declaration to the police, an individual may assert his or her innocence.

■ DUE PROCESS

The Voluntariness Test

Between 1936 and 1966, the U.S. Supreme Court held over thirty confessions obtained by state and local police unconstitutional and inadmissible at trial under the **Fourteenth Amendment due process voluntariness test**.

The *voluntariness test* can be traced to the English common law. Eighteenth-century English common law judges declared that confessions were inadmissible into evidence if they had been extracted through the threat or application of force, through a false promise not to prosecute, or through a promise of lenient treatment. Confessions obtained by a threat or promise of favorable treatment were thought to be unreliable and might result in the conviction of innocent individuals. There was no easy method to determine whether a confession was true or false, and English courts employed the shorthand test of asking whether the defendant's **statement** was voluntary or involuntary (*Rex v. Warickshall*, 168 Eng. Rep. 234, 235 [K.B. 1783]).

Voluntariness

The Supreme Court has held that to be admissible into evidence, a confession must have been made freely, voluntarily, and without compulsion or inducement of any sort. A confession violates due process and is excluded from evidence that involves the following:

Coercion. The police or government officials subject the defendant to physical or psychological coercion.

Will to resist. The coercion overcomes the will of an individual to resist.

How do courts determine whether there was coercion and whether the coercion overcame a defendant's will to resist? The determination as to whether a confession is involuntary is based on the totality of the circumstances surrounding a confession (*Haynes v. Washington*, 373 U.S. 503, 533–534 [1963]). The prosecution bears the burden of establishing voluntariness by a "preponderance of the evidence" (*Lego v. Twomey*, 404 U.S. 477 [1972]). In evaluating the totality of the circumstances, courts consider a number of factors:

- *Physical abuse.* Physical abuse and threats of abuse by the police or angry crowds.
- *Psychological abuse and manipulation.* Threats, rewards, or trickery inducing a suspect to confess.
- *Interrogation.* The length, time, and place of questioning and the number of police officers involved.
- *Attorney.* A refusal to permit a suspect to consult with an attorney, friends, or family.
- *Defendant.* The age, education, and mental and emotional development of the defendant.
- *Procedural regularity.* A failure by the police to follow proper legal procedures, including the *Miranda* warning.
- *Necessity.* The police are provided greater flexibility in interrogation when attempting to solve a crime or exonerate a defendant than when they already possess evidence of a defendant's guilt.

Spano v. New York illustrates the totality-of-the-circumstances approach to determining whether a confession is voluntary or involuntary. In *Spano*, the U.S. Supreme Court held that the defendant's "will was overborne by official pressure, fatigue and sympathy falsely aroused." The Court's conclusion was based on a number of factors (*Spano v. New York*, 360 U.S. 315, 323 [1959]):

- *Psychological abuse.* The police employed a childhood friend to play on the defendant's sympathy.
- *Interrogation.* The defendant was questioned for eight hours at night by fourteen officers, and his confession was written down by a skilled and aggressive prosecutor.
- *Attorney.* The police disregarded the defendant's refusal to speak on the advice of counsel and ignored his request to contact his lawyer.
- *Defendant.* The defendant was 25 years of age and never before had been subjected to custodial arrest or to police interrogation. He had not completed high school and had a psychological disability.
- *Procedural regularity.* The police failed to immediately bring the defendant before a judge and instead subjected him to interrogation.
- *Necessity.* The police already possessed eyewitnesses to the shooting and were engaged in securing the evidence required to convict the defendant rather than in identifying the individual responsible for the crime.

The Due Process Test Today

Keep in mind as you continue to read this chapter that an involuntary confession violates due process of law and is inadmissible into evidence, even in those instances in which a defendant may have been read his or her *Miranda* rights. Two recent cases illustrate the U.S. Supreme Court's continuing reliance on the due process voluntariness test:

Mincey v. Arizona. Rufus Mincey, while in intensive care in the hospital, was interrogated by a police detective who informed him that he was under arrest for murder. Mincey's requests for a lawyer were disregarded, and the detective continued the interrogation. The suspect was unable to talk because of a tube in his mouth and responded by writing down his answers. The Supreme Court determined that Mincey was "weakened by pain and shock, isolated from family, friends, and legal counsel, and barely conscious, and his will was simply overborne" and that his confession had been obtained in violation of due process of law. The Court stressed that an involuntary confession may not be used at trial for any purpose whatsoever (*Mincey v. Arizona*, 437 U.S. 385, 401–402 [1978]).

Arizona v. Fulminante. Oreste Fulminante was incarcerated on federal firearms charges and established a friendship with Anthony Sarivola, a paid federal informant who was serving a sixty-day sentence for extortion and posing as an organized crime figure. Sarivola was instructed to obtain information regarding Fulminante's possible involvement in the murder of his young daughter. Sarivola offered to protect Fulminante from the other inmates who allegedly disliked "child killers" on the condition that Fulminante tell him what happened to his daughter. Fulminante admitted sexually assaulting and shooting his daughter in the head. Sarivola later testified at Fulminante's murder trial. The Supreme Court examined the totality of circumstances and concluded that the confession was involuntary. The Court reasoned that Fulminante was a child murderer whose fear of physical retaliation led him to confide in Sarivola. Fulminante, according to the Court, felt particularly susceptible to physical retaliation because he possessed a slight build and, while previously incarcerated, could not cope with the pressures of imprisonment and in the past had been admitted to a psychiatric institution (*Arizona v. Fulminante*, 499 U.S. 279 [1991]).

In *Colorado v. Connelly*, Francis Connelly approached a unformed officer in downtown Denver and without prompting stated he had murdered someone and wanted to talk about the killing. Connelly was read his *Miranda* rights and stated he had been a patient in several mental hospitals and he wanted to talk to Officer Patrick Anderson because his conscience had been bothering him. The defendant was read his *Miranda* rights by a second officer and in response stated he had come all the way from Boston to confess to the murder of Mary Ann Junta, a young girl whom he had killed in Denver. A search of police records revealed that the body of a female had been discovered in the area where Connelly stated the killing occurred (*Colorado v. Connelly*, 479 U.S. 157 [1986]).

The defendant, after being incarcerated, became increasingly disoriented, began giving confused answers, and stated "voices" directed him to come to Denver and that he had followed the voices in confessing. A psychiatric examination determined that Connelly was a chronic schizophrenic and was in a psychotic state at the time he confessed. After Connelly arrived in Boston, the voices became stronger and told him to confess to the killing or commit suicide. The defendant was suffering from command hallucinations that interfered with his ability to make free and rational choices.

The Colorado Supreme Court excluded Connelly's confession on the grounds that it was involuntary. The U.S. Supreme Court reversed the Colorado court on the grounds that Connelly had failed to demonstrate that his confession was the product of government coercion.

> The difficulty with the approach of the Supreme Court of Colorado is that it fails to recognize the essential link between coercive activity of the State, on the one hand, and a resulting confession by a defendant, on the other. . . . The most outrageous behavior by a private party seeking to secure evidence against a defendant does not make that evidence inadmissible under the Due Process Clause. . . . The purpose of excluding evidence seized in violation of the Constitution is to substantially deter future violations of the Constitution. . . . A statement rendered by one in the condition of respondent might be proved to be quite unreliable, but this is a matter to be governed by the evidentiary laws of the forum.

Legal Equation

Due process voluntariness test	=	Confession is made freely, voluntarily, and without compulsion or inducement.
Confession is inadmissable	=	Police or government officials subject an individual to physical or psychological coercion
	+	Coercion overcomes the will of an individual to resist as determined by a totality of the circumstances.

■ THE RIGHT AGAINST SELF-INCRIMINATION

The Self-Incrimination Clause of the Fifth Amendment to the U.S. Constitution provides that "[n]o person . . . shall be compelled in any criminal case to be a witness against himself." This constitutional right was extended to the states in *Malloy v. Hogan* in which the U.S. Supreme Court held that the Fifth Amendment's prohibition on compulsory self-incrimination is incorporated into the Fourteenth Amendment and is applicable against the states. Justice William Brennan observed that the state and federal governments are "constitutionally compelled to establish guilt by evidence independently and freely secured, and may not, by coercion prove a charge against an accused out of his own mouth" (*Malloy v. Hogan*, 378 U.S. 1, 6 [1964]).

In other words, *you do not have to answer questions that may tend to incriminate you, and your failure to respond cannot be used against you in a criminal proceeding.* Why do we have a right that works to the advantage of guilty individuals by allowing them to withhold evidence from prosecuting authorities? This right was a reaction to procedures in religious courts and in the politically repressive Star Chamber in sixteenth-century England. These tribunals placed the burden on individuals to answer questions and to prove that they were not heretics or political dissidents. Justice Arthur Goldberg provided several reasons for the right against self-incrimination, a right that he stated "reflects many of our fundamental values and most noble aspirations" (*Murphy v. Waterfront Commission*, 378 U.S. 52, 55 [1964]). In considering these points, ask yourself whether we should have a right against self-incrimination:

- *Cruel trilemma.* Individuals should not be compelled to choose between "self-accusation, perjury or contempt." The law, in other words, should not place an individual in the position of making the unhappy choice of admitting guilt, denying guilt and facing a perjury charge for false testimony, or refusing to speak and being held in contempt of court for failing to cooperate with the judicial process.
- *Coercion.* There is a fear that coercion and force will be used to compel individuals to incriminate themselves.
- *Adversarial system.* We have an *adversarial* rather than *inquisitorial* legal system. The accused is not required to establish his or her innocence; the state has the burden of proving guilt beyond a reasonable doubt.
- *Privacy.* An individual should not be forced to disclose information to the government.

Information is *incriminating* if there is a "substantial" and "real" threat that the information may lead to a criminal charge or establish a link in the chain of evidence that may result in a criminal prosecution. The U.S. Supreme Court recently dismissed a defendant's challenge to a "stop-and-identify" statute on the grounds that the defendant did not possess "any articulated real and appreciable fear that his name would be used to incriminate him, or that it 'would furnish a link in the chain of evidence needed to prosecute' him. . . . Answer[ing] a request to disclose a name is likely to be so insignificant . . . as to be incriminating only in unusual circumstances" (*Hiibel v. Sixth Judicial Court*, 542 U.S. 177 [2004]).

The second point to remember is that the privilege against self-incrimination is violated when the incriminating information is used against an individual in a legal proceeding. In *Chavez v. Martinez*, the defendant was shot by a police officer and was questioned by the officer while he was in intense pain in a hospital. Ben Chavez admitted during the interrogation that he had taken the officer's pistol from his holster and pointed the weapon at him. Chavez filed a civil action for damages against the officer for violating his right against self-incrimination. The Supreme Court ruled that Oliverio Martinez was never made a "witness" against himself because his statements were never admitted as testimony against him in a criminal case. Nor was he ever placed under oath and exposed to "the cruel trilemma of self-accusation, perjury or contempt" (*Chavez v. Martinez*, 538 U.S. 760 [2003]).

The third point is that the requirement that you may not be *compelled* to be a witness against yourself is satisfied when you are *required* to answer questions asked by the government. In *Hoffman v. United States*, the Supreme Court upheld the right of an organized crime figure to refuse to answer questions regarding his employment and associates before a grand jury investigating frauds perpetrated against the government. The Supreme Court observed that the "immediate and potential evils of compulsory self-disclosure transcend any difficulties that the exercise of the privilege may impose on society in the detection and prosecution of crime" (*Hoffman v. United States*, 341 U.S. 479, 485 [1951]). On the other hand, there is no compulsion when a driver arrested for drunk driving is *offered the choice* of either submitting to a simple and relatively painless blood alcohol test or having his or her refusal to do so used against him or her in court (*South Dakota v. Neville*, 459 U.S. 553 [1983]).

Finally, the prohibition against being compelled to be a witness against oneself is limited to testimonial evidence, or evidence that is communicative in character. What does this mean? The Supreme Court explained the testimonial or communicative requirement in *Doe v. United States*. The Court stated that the government is prohibited from compelling you to make a factual statement, forcing you to disclose information that connects you to a criminal offense, or requiring you to share your private thoughts or beliefs with the government.

The Supreme Court has noted that the privilege against self-incrimination encompasses trial testimony, oral confessions to the police, and personal documents. On the other hand, there is no privilege against self-incrimination where the government compels you to provide **nontestimonial evidence**. Judges have held that nontestimonial evidence includes voice and handwriting exemplars, fingerprints, participation in a lineup, the police requiring you to try on clothes or to walk in a straight line, hair and urine samples, the withdrawing of blood, the examination of scars and tattoos, and the taking of photos. This evidence may be used against you in a criminal proceeding, and your failure to cooperate in these procedures may be introduced at trial to establish your guilt. You also will be held in contempt of court if you refuse to provide this type of physical or nontestimonial evidence (*Doe v. United States*, 487 U.S. 201 [1988]).

In the case of *Schmerber v. California*, Armando Schmerber was convicted of driving an automobile while under the influence of alcohol. At the direction of the police, a blood sample was withdrawn from Schmerber's body by a physician at the hospital. The chemical analysis of this sample revealed "a percent by weight of alcohol in his blood at the time of the offense which indicated intoxication, and the report of this analysis was admitted in evidence at the trial" (*Schmerber v. California*, 384 U.S. 757 [1966]).

Both federal and state courts have usually held that it offers no protection against compulsion to submit to fingerprinting, photographing, or measurements; to write or speak for identification; to appear in court; to stand; to assume a stance; to walk; or to make a particular gesture. The distinction that has emerged, often expressed in different ways, is that the privilege is a bar against compelling "communications" or "testimony," but that compulsion which makes a suspect or accused the source of "real or physical evidence" does not violate it.

You no doubt have a puzzled look on your face because the line between testimonial or communicative and nontestimonial or physical evidence does not appear to be crystal clear. You are correct. Consider *Pennsylvania v. Muniz*. Inocencio Muniz was arrested for driving while intoxicated. He was taken to a "booking center," and his subsequent interrogation by the police was recorded. Muniz was first asked his name, address, height, weight, eye color, date of birth, and current age. His response was slow and slurred. These questions asked for routine information and were not incriminating. The police officer then asked Muniz whether he knew the date of his sixth birthday. Muniz replied, "No, I don't."

Was Muniz's answer to the sixth-birthday question admissible in evidence? The Supreme Court held in a 5-4 ruling that this question called for a *testimonial response* that violated Muniz's right against self-incrimination and that his response was inadmissible in evidence. The question confronted Muniz with the unhappy situation of choosing either self-incrimination or perjury. Muniz, according to Justice Brennan, either could admit that he did not know the date of his sixth birthday or could answer untruthfully and report a date of birth that he knew was inaccurate. His answer in either case would indicate that Muniz's mental state was impaired by alcohol. The Supreme Court majority reasoned that either alternative would be the equivalent of Muniz's admitting that he was too intoxicated to answer the question accurately.

Eight justices also held for different reasons that Muniz's slurred speech in answering the booking questions was admissible to establish that he was inebriated. Four of these justices explained that Muniz's slurred speech was nontestimonial and demonstrated Muniz's lack of "muscular coordination" in forming his words and that this related to Muniz's physical act of speaking rather than to the words that he was speaking. As a result, the slurred speech was nontestimonial rather than testimonial evidence, did not violate Muniz's right against self-incrimination, and was properly introduced into evidence. Is this distinction persuasive? (*Pennsylvania v. Muniz*, 496 U.S. 582 [1990]).

Legal Equation

Privilege against self-incrimination	=	Compulsion
	+	Criminal case
	+	Witness against yourself
	+	Reveal testimonial evidence.

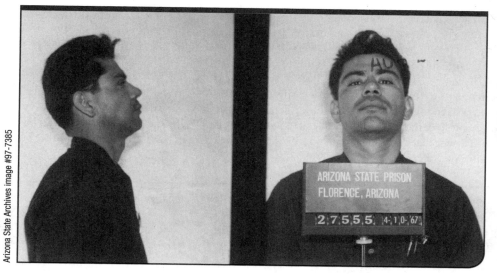

PHOTO 16.1

Ernest Miranda was the principal defendant in the famous case of *Miranda v. Arizona* that established the *Miranda* rule for interrogation.

■ *MIRANDA V. ARIZONA*

In 1966, in *Miranda v. Arizona*, a five-judge majority of the U.S. Supreme Court held that the prosecution may not use statements stemming from the custodial interrogation absent procedural safeguards to protect a defendant's Fifth Amendment privilege against self-incrimination. The Court majority concluded that absent a three-part *Miranda* warning, the "inherently coercive" pressures of police interrogation had been proven to overwhelm individuals' capacity to exercise their right against self-incrimination, and no confession given under these conditions "can truly be the product of a suspect's free choice" (*Miranda v. Arizona*, 384 U.S. 436 [1966]).

What were these coercive pressures? According to the Court, individuals held in detention were isolated from friends, family, and lawyers in unfamiliar surroundings and were subject to sophisticated psychological tactics, manipulation, and trickery designed to wear down their resistance. The Court pointed to police manuals instructing officers to engage in tactics such as displaying confidence in a suspect's guilt, minimizing the seriousness of the offense, wearing down individuals through continuous interrogation, and using the "Mutt and Jeff" strategy in which one officer berates a suspect and the other gains the suspect's trust by playing the part of his or her protector. The "false lineup" involves placing a suspect in a lineup and using fictitious witnesses to identify the suspect as the perpetrator. In another scenario, fictitious witnesses identify the defendant as the perpetrator of a previously undisclosed serious crime, and the defendant panics and confesses to the offense under investigation.

Miranda extended the Fifth Amendment privilege against self-incrimination to police-orchestrated interrogations committed prior to trial. The Court held that if a person in custody is to be subjected to interrogation, he or she must be informed in clear and unequivocal terms of each of the following rights:

Silence. He or she has the right to remain silent. The government may not use an individual's decision to remain silent against him or her.

Consequences of waiver. The warning of the right to remain silent must be accompanied by the explanation that anything said can and will be used against the individual in court.

Counsel. Because the circumstances surrounding in-custody interrogation can operate very quickly to overhear the will of an individual made aware of his or her privilege by interrogators, the warning that the individual has the right to consult with a lawyer prior to interrogation and to have counsel present during questioning is indispensable to the protection of the Fifth Amendment privilege.

Appointed counsel. The individual should be warned not only that he or she has the right to consult with an attorney, but also that if he or she is indigent, a lawyer will be appointed to represent him or her. Without this additional warning, the warning of the right to consult with counsel would often be understood as meaning only that he or she can consult with a lawyer if he or she has one or has the funds to obtain one.

The warnings are a prerequisite to the interrogation of a suspect. An individual may not be interrogated if the suspect indicates he or she wants to invoke his or her right to silence or right to consult with an attorney. A heavy burden rests on the government to demonstrate that a suspect knowingly, voluntarily, and intelligently waived his or her rights. There is no requirement that the police stop an individual who enters a police station and states that he or she wishes to confess voluntarily to a crime.

16.1 YOU DECIDE

Robert L. Brown was charged in a Louisiana court with unlawful possession of heroin. He was convicted and sentenced to ten years in prison. Brown was apprehended when he unsuccessfully attempted to flee from a police raid of a drug house. He was advised that he had a right to speak or remain silent, that anything he said might be used against him, and that he had a right to counsel. During the reading of the *Miranda* warnings, Brown proclaimed, "I know all that." Brown then confessed that he used narcotics and, in fact, had injected earlier in the day.

A federal district court pointed out that Brown was not told that he had the right to have an attorney present if he decided to make a statement and that he was not told that a lawyer would be appointed to represent him in the event that he lacked funds. One of the arresting officers also testified that he did not afford the defendant "any opportunity to procure a lawyer." Did Brown's statement that "I know all that" constitute a waiver of Brown's right to receive the full *Miranda* warnings? Cite language from the *Miranda* decision in support of your answer. See *Brown v. Heyd* (277 F. Supp. 899 [D.C.E.D. La. 1967]).

You can learn what the court decided by referring to the study site, **http://study.sagepub.com/lippmance.**

Legal Equation

Fifth Amendment privilege against self-incrimination and police interrogation	=	The prosecution may not use inculpatory or exculpatory statements stemming from custodial interrogation of the defendant unless it demonstrates use of procedural safeguards effective to secure privilege against self-incrimination
	+	Custodial interrogation is questioning initiated by law enforcement officers after an individual has been taken into custody or deprived of his or her freedom of action in a significant way
	+	Prior to any questions, the suspect must be clearly and unequivocally informed that he or she has the right to remain silent, that any statement he or she makes may be used as evidence against him or her, and that he or she has the right to the presence of an attorney, appointed or retained
	+	The *Miranda* decision also provides that the defendant may voluntarily, knowingly, and intelligently waive any or all of these rights; the fact that a defendant answers some questions does not prohibit a defendant from invoking his or her right to silence or to a lawyer
	+	A heavy burden rests on the prosecution to prove that a defendant waived his or her right against self-incrimination and/or the right to a lawyer; silence does not constitute a waiver, and a defendant who invokes his or her right to silence is not subject to additional interrogation
	+	A defendant who invokes his or her right to a lawyer may not be questioned outside the presence of the attorney
	+	A prosecutor may not penalize a defendant's invocation of his or her right against self-incrimination by commenting on the invocation of this right at trial
	+	Statements in violation of *Miranda* may not be introduced into evidence.

Miranda *and the Constitution*

Miranda, as we have seen, supplemented the due process voluntariness test by requiring that the police read suspects subjected to custodial interrogation the *Miranda* warnings. The decision in *Miranda* sparked a wave of criticism, and in 1968, the U.S. Congress took the aggressive step of passing legislation that required federal judges to apply the voluntariness test. The Omnibus Crime Control and Safe Streets Act provided that a confession shall be admissible as evidence in federal court if it is "voluntarily given." The act listed a number of factors that judges were to consider in determining whether a confession was voluntary.

In 2000, in *Dickerson v. United States*, Chief Justice William Rehnquist, who himself had been a constant critic of *Miranda*, held that *Miranda* was a "constitutional decision" that is required by the Fifth Amendment to ensure that detainees are able to exercise their right against self-incrimination in the inherently coercive atmosphere of custodial interrogation. This is an important statement because laws passed by Congress are required to conform to the U.S. Constitution, in this instance, the Fifth Amendment. Congress accordingly lacked authority to instruct the judiciary to disregard the requirements of *Miranda* and to rely solely on the voluntariness test. Justice Rehnquist also stressed that *Miranda* has become "embedded in routine police practice to the point where the warnings have become part of our national culture" (*Dickerson v. United States*, 530 U.S. 428 [2000]). We now examine the central elements of the *Miranda* rule:

- Custodial interrogation
- The public safety exception
- The *Miranda* warnings
- Invoking the *Miranda* rights
- Waiver
- Interrogation

The chapter concludes by discussing the Sixth Amendment right to counsel.

In reading this chapter, you will see that although the Supreme Court affirmed the constitutional status of the *Miranda* decision, the requirements of *Miranda* are constantly being adjusted in an effort to balance *Miranda*'s protection of suspects against society's interest in obtaining confessions. As you progress through the chapter, ask yourself whether the *Miranda* warnings provide adequate protection for defendants. In the alternative, does *Miranda* handcuff the police? In addition, consider whether the *Miranda* rules are too complex to be easily absorbed by police, lawyers, and judges. We start by examining custodial interrogation.

CRIMINAL EVIDENCE AND PUBLIC POLICY

Individuals isolated in interrogation rooms have been known to make false confessions, even in instances in which the police did not pressure or manipulate suspects and treated suspects in a balanced and respectful fashion.

On April 19, 1989, a 28-year-old jogger was viciously attacked and raped in Central Park in New York City. Five African American and Latino teenagers ranging in age from 14 to 16 who had been arrested for muggings in the park that night confessed and the following year were convicted in two separate trials. Four of the five made videotaped statements with parents or relatives present. Typical was one young man's description that "Raymond had her arms, and Steve had her legs. He spread it out. And Antron got on top, took her panties off." A second confessed that "I grabbed one arm, some other kid grabbed one arm, and we grabbed her legs and stuff. Then we all took turns getting on her, getting on top of her." One suspect went so far as to reenact how he pulled off her running pants.

The young men claimed in court that they had been pressured into the confessions. The jurors at the two trials nevertheless convicted the defendants. The massive publicity surrounding the case may have influenced the jurors to overlook the inconsistencies in the defendants' accounts and to disregard the fact that only a few hairs on one of the defendants linked the juveniles to the rape. In 2002, Matias Reyes, who was serving over thirty years for murder and four rapes, confessed to the Central Park rape, and his DNA was found to match that of the perpetrator. On December 19, 2002, the convictions of the five men were overturned.

(Continued)

(Continued)

How is this possible? A number of factors in the Central Park jogger case combined to create the danger of a false confession:

- **Police bias.** The police were under intense pressure to solve the crime and quickly concluded that the suspects must be guilty and focused on obtaining confessions.
- **Age and intelligence.** Several of the young suspects may have been tricked into confessing. Two had IQs below 90 and may have failed to understand the meaning of a confession.
- **Misleading remarks and false evidence.** Some of the young men claimed that they had been told that they would be permitted to go home if they confessed. One suspect reportedly was told that his fingerprints had been found at the crime scene, another was informed that the others had implicated him, and others were told that hairs linked one of the young men to the crime.
- **Lengthy interrogations.** The young men confessed after being interrogated for more than twenty-eight hours.

How frequent are false confessions? Professors Steve Drizen and Richard Leo (2004) documented 125 proven false confessions between 1971 and 2002. The good news is that the criminal justice system responded by detecting two-thirds of these confessions prior to trial. On the other hand, forty-four of the defendants were sentenced to at least ten years in prison, and nine of these defendants were sentenced to death. This is not an overwhelming number of false convictions, but even a small number of false convictions are "too many." Psychologists tell us that there are three types of false confessors:

- **Voluntary false confessors.** Suspects provide false confessions out of a desire for publicity or because they feel guilty about a past crime or are mentally challenged.
- **Compliant false confessors.** Suspects confess in order to obtain a benefit such as the avoidance of abuse or mistreatment or to receive favorable consideration at sentencing. This might range from a lighter sentence to imprisonment in an institution nearby to an offender's family.
- **Internalized false confessors.** Suspects accept the police version of the facts or fail a lie detector test and come to believe that they actually committed the crime.

False confessions are a small percentage of all confessions obtained by the police. These confessions, however, may result in conviction of the innocent and undermine respect for the entire criminal justice system. Many legal scholars advocate the taping of interrogations to provide a record of what transpired in the interrogation room and to guard against psychologically and physically coercive interrogations. The FBI and various states, by statute or court decision, require taping of at least some serious felony cases. This has been required by the supreme courts of Alaska, Minnesota, and New Jersey and for certain offenses by the state legislatures of Illinois, Maine, New Mexico, Texas, and Wisconsin and by the District of Columbia. In 2004, the American Bar Association also endorsed the audio or video recording of interrogations. Australia, Canada, and England provide for the taping of confessions. At last count, 450 local police departments also require the videotaping of interrogations.

Custodial Interrogation

The *Miranda* warnings are triggered when an individual is in custody and interrogated. The *Miranda* decision defines **custodial interrogation** as "questioning initiated by law enforcement officers after a person has been taken into custody or otherwise deprived of his [or her] freedom of action in any significant way." In *Beckwith v. United States*, the Supreme Court clarified that a *focus* by law enforcement on an individual is not sufficient to require the reading of the *Miranda* rights. In *Beckwith*, two Internal Revenue Service (IRS) agents interviewed the defendant for three hours in a private home; the conversation was described by one of the agents as "friendly" and "relaxed." The Supreme Court held that being the focus of an investigation does not involve the inherently coercive pressures that *Miranda* described as inherent in incommunicado custodial interrogation (*Beckwith v. United States*, 425 U.S. 341 [1976]).

What, then, is meant by custodial interrogation? *Miranda* stated that it is not considered custody and the *Miranda* warnings are not required when the police engage in general questioning at a crime scene or other general investigative questioning of potential witnesses. The *Miranda* warnings also need not be given to an individual who voluntarily enters a police station and wishes to confess to a crime or to a person who voluntarily calls the police to offer a confession or another statement. On the other hand, the *Miranda* warnings are required when an individual is subjected to a custodial arrest and to interrogation. At this point, an individual is under the control of the police and likely will be subjected to incommunicado interrogation in an isolated and unfamiliar environment.

The challenge is to determine at what point, short of being informed that he or she is under custodial arrest, an individual is exposed to pressures that are the "functional equivalent of custodial arrest" and the *Miranda* rights must be read. What if you are walking home and are stopped by the police late at night and they ask what you are doing in the neighborhood? This has important consequences for law enforcement. Requiring *Miranda* warnings whenever an officer comes in contact with a citizen would impede questioning. This might make sense because every citizen interaction with an officer is somewhat intimidating and coercive. On the other hand, requiring a clearly coercive environment before the *Miranda* warnings are required would limit the *Miranda* warnings to a narrow set of circumstances. How does the Supreme Court resolve these considerations? At what point short of a custodial arrest are the *Miranda* warnings required?

The Supreme Court adopted an "objective test" for custodial interrogation that requires judges to evaluate the totality of the circumstances. In *Stansbury v. California*, the Supreme Court held that "the initial determination of custody depends on the objective circumstances of the interrogation, not on the subjective views harbored by either the interrogating officers or the person being questioned" (*Stansbury v. California*, 511 U.S. 318, 323 [1994]).

Custodial interrogation is not based solely on the seriousness of the crime for which you have been stopped and questioned or based simply on the location of the interrogation. Custody is based on whether, in the totality of the circumstances, a reasonable person would believe that he or she is subjected to formal arrest or to police custody to a degree associated with a formal arrest (i.e., the functional equivalent of formal arrest).

Courts typically *ask whether a reasonable person would feel free to leave*. In evaluating the totality of circumstances, judges consider a number of factors. Remember, no single factor is crucial in determining whether a reasonable person would believe that he or she is subject to custodial interrogation (not free to leave). The factors to be considered include the following:

- The number of police officers
- Whether the officer tells the individual that he or she is free to leave or not free to leave
- The length and intensity of the questioning
- Whether the officer employs physical force to restrain the individual
- Whether the stop is in public or in private
- The location of the interrogation
- Whether a reasonable person would believe that the stop would be brief or whether the stop would result in a custodial arrest
- Whether the individual is in familiar or unfamiliar surroundings
- Whether the suspect is permitted to leave following the interrogation

The totality-of-the-circumstances test means that custody is determined on a case-by-case basis. Consider the Supreme Court decisions in the following cases:

Home. In *Orozco v. Texas*, the Supreme Court held that the defendant was subjected to custodial interrogation when four police officers entered his bedroom at 4:00 A.M. to interrogate him regarding a shooting (*Orozco v. Texas*, 394 U.S. 324 [1969]).

Parole interview. Marshall Murphy, a probationer, agreed to meet his probation officer regarding his "treatment plan" and, during the meeting, admitted that he had committed a rape and murder. The Supreme Court found that Murphy was familiar both with the surroundings and with his probation officer and that he was not physically restrained and could have left at any time. The possibility that terminating the meeting would lead to revocation of probation, in the view of the Court, was not comparable to the pressure on a criminal suspect who is not free to walk away from interrogation by the police (*Minnesota v. Murphy*, 465 U.S. 420 [1984]).

Police station. In *Oregon v. Mathiason*, Carl Mathiason, a parolee, voluntarily appeared at the police station at the request of an officer. Mathiason confessed after the officer stated that he believed that the suspect was involved in a recent burglary, falsely told Mathiason that his fingerprints had been discovered at the scene of the crime, and explained that truthfulness would possibly be considered in mitigation at sentencing. The Supreme Court determined that there was no custodial interrogation because the defendant voluntarily came to the station house, was informed that he was not under arrest, and left following the interview (*Oregon v. Mathiason*, 429 U.S. 492 [1977]).

Prison. In *Howes v. Fields*, the Supreme Court held that whether the questioning of an inmate who is "removed from the general prison population" and interrogated about "events that occurred outside the prison" is custodial depends on the totality of circumstances. The Court stressed that there was no "categorical rule" that the interrogation of an inmate "always" is custodial. The objective circumstances of the interrogation were consistent with an interrogation environment in which a reasonable person would "have felt free to terminate the interview and leave." Randall Lee Fields was escorted by a corrections officer to a conference room where he was questioned for between five and seven hours by two sheriff's deputies about his alleged sexual molestation of a 12-year-old boy. Fields was informed that he could leave and return to his cell at any time, was not physically restrained or threatened, and was interrogated in a well-lit conference room and offered food and water, and the door was occasionally left open. An inmate does not suffer the fear and anxiety of an individual who is arrested and feels isolated and alone in an alien environment, will not be persuaded to confess to obtain his or her release, and is aware that his interrogators do not have the authority to prolong his or her detention (*Howes v. Fields*, 565 U.S. ___ [2012]).

Traffic stop. In *Berkemer v. McCarty*, McCarty was stopped by Highway Patrol Officer Williams who observed McCarty weaving in and out of a lane. Williams observed that McCarty experienced difficulty with his balance when he exited the vehicle and concluded that he would charge him with a traffic arrest and take him into custody. McCarty was unable to successfully complete a field sobriety test and in response to questions admitted that he had consumed several beers and marijuana. McCarty was taken into custody without being read his *Miranda* rights and made several additional incriminating statements. McCarty was subsequently convicted of the first-degree misdemeanor of operating a motor vehicle while under the influence of drugs or alcohol. McCarty appealed and argued that he was in custody when pulled over by Officer Williams and should have been read his *Miranda* rights.

The Supreme Court rejected the argument that the *Miranda* warnings are required only for felonies. The Court nonetheless ruled that McCarty was not in custody when initially required to pull over, ruling that a traffic stop normally does not exert pressures that significantly impair an individual's exercise of his or her Fifth Amendment right against self-incrimination. Traffic stops presumably are brief and public and typically are not police dominated. The Supreme Court also held that between the initial stop and the custodial arrest, McCarty was not subject to constraints "comparable" to formal arrest. During this relatively short period, Williams did not communicate his intent to arrest McCarty, and his unarticulated plan was considered to have little relevance to the question of custody. The relevant inquiry in determining whether an individual is in custody is how a reasonable person in the suspect's situation would understand his or her situation. Would a reasonable person feel free to leave (not in custody), or would a reasonable person feel that his or her freedom of movement was restricted (custody)? In this case, a single police officer asked a limited number of questions and requested that McCarty perform a field sobriety test. The Supreme Court held that McCarty was not subjected to the "functional equivalent of formal arrest" (*Berkemer v. McCarty*, 468 U.S. 420 [1984]).

In *Yarborough v. Alvarado*, Michael Alvarado's parents responded to a police request to bring their 18-year-old son to the police station. Alvarado's parents waited in the lobby while he was interviewed by Officer Cheryl Comstock. Comstock assured Alvarado's parents that the interview was not going to be "long." Comstock did not give Alvarado the *Miranda* warnings, and Alvarado when interrogated admitted helping Paul Soto steal a truck and stated that he had helped conceal the murder weapon following Soto's killing of the driver. Comstock throughout the two-hour interview focused on Soto's crimes rather than on Alvarado's role in the killing, and Alvarado was not threatened with arrest or prosecution. At the end of the interview, Comstock twice asked Alvarado if he needed to take a bathroom break. Following the interview, Alvarado was released to return home with his parents.

The Supreme Court recognized that although this was a "close case" the state court had acted reasonably in deciding that Alvarado had not been subjected to custodial interrogation. The Court held that whether Alvarado "would have felt that he was at liberty to terminate the interrogation and leave" was to be evaluated based on an objective test and that an individual's age and inexperience was not to be considered. In dissent, Justice Stephen Breyer and three other justices argued that Alvarado's age was "relevant" to determining whether a "reasonable person in Alvarado's position [would] have felt free to get up and walk out of the . . . station house." According to the dissenting judges, it was not persuasive to evaluate Alvarado on the same standard as a "middle-aged gentleman, well-versed in police practices" (*Yarborough v. Alvarado*, 541 U.S. 652 [2004]).

In 2011, in *J.D.B. v. North Carolina*, the U.S. Supreme Court reversed course and held that the age of a juvenile subjected to police questioning is "relevant to the custody analysis" of *Miranda v. Arizona*. The Court stressed that "it is beyond dispute that children will often feel bound to submit to police questioning when an adult in the same circumstances would feel free to leave." The Court held that that "so long as the child's age was known to the officer at the time of police questioning, or would have been objectively apparent to a reasonable officer, its inclusion in the custody analysis is consistent with the objective nature" of the test for custodial interrogation (*J.D.B. v. North Carolina*, __ U.S. __ [2011].

In *Illinois v. Perkins*, the Supreme Court held that an individual interrogated by an inmate working as an informant does not constitute custodial interrogation and that as a result the *Miranda* rights need not be read to the inmate. The reason is that the inmate is not confronted with the coercion of police interrogation (*Illinois v. Perkins*, 496 U.S. 292 [1990]).

Legal Equation

Custody	=	Custodial arrest or functional equivalent of custodial arrest.
Functional equivalent of custodial arrest	=	A reasonable person
	+	Considering the totality of the circumstances
	+	Would believe that he or she is in police custody to a degree associated with a formal arrest (is not free to leave).

16.2 YOU DECIDE

In early 2007, agents from the Department of Homeland Security Immigration and Customs Enforcement (ICE) discovered that an individual in Illinois was using the username "neodmoney" to send and receive images of child pornography. Upon further investigation, they learned that the username was associated with an address in Hanover Park where Richard Ahrens, Dale Ahrens (Richard's brother), Daniel Littledale, and Cynthia Littledale resided.

Agents Demetrius Flowers and Timothy Morris were met by campus police officers when they arrived at the College of DuPage. The officers were in uniform and carried holstered weapons, and the agents wore blue jeans and T-shirts, one of which read "Special Agent."

A uniformed officer asked Littledale to leave his classroom. The federal agents met with Littledale in the hallway and asked if he would agree to talk to them in a private office at the campus police station. Littledale consented. During the walk to the police station, the agents did not draw weapons or handcuff or physically restrain Littledale or search his backpack.

The agents reportedly spoke in a monotone and testified that Littledale appeared calm.

The private office contained a desk, a computer, and other personal items; it was not an interrogation room or an interview room. The police officers waited in the hallway during the interrogation.

Agent Flowers informed Littledale that he was not under arrest and that he was not in any trouble and told Littledale that ICE agents were executing a search warrant at his home. Littledale agreed to speak to the agents. "Approximately twenty-five minutes later, Littledale admitted that he had viewed child pornography on the computer, that he had been sending and receiving child pornography for about five or six years, and that his username was 'neodmoney' and his password was 'blackrose.'" Agent Flowers then read Littledale his *Miranda* rights and prepared a statement that Littledale signed. Littledale then confessed once again, adding that his mother had caught him looking at child pornography in the past. See *United States v. Littledale* (652 F.3d 698 [7th Cir. 2011]).

You can learn what the court decided by referring to the study site, **http://study.sagepub.com/lippmance.**

The Public Safety Exception

In *New York v. Quarles*, the U.S. Supreme Court recognized a **public safety exception** to *Miranda*. This exception permits the police to ask questions reasonably prompted by a concern with public safety without first advising a suspect of his or her *Miranda* rights. The Supreme Court explained that a reasonable concern with the safety of the police or the public outweighs the interest in protecting a suspect's right against self-incrimination. This "narrow exception" requires that questions be directed at public safety rather than guilt or innocence. Coerced and involuntary statements are not admissible under the public safety rule. Reliance on the public safety exception requires that the following steps be satisfied (*New York v. Quarles*, 467 U.S. 649 [1984]):

- *Reasonableness.* There must be a reasonable need to protect the police or the public. The exception does not depend on the officer's subjective motivation.
- *Threat.* There must be a reasonable belief that the threat is immediate.
- *Questions.* Questions must be prompted by a reasonable concern for public safety and must be directed at public safety rather than guilt or innocence.
- *Coercion.* The statements may not be the product of police compulsion that overcomes the suspect's will to resist.

New York v. Quarles broadly defines public safety and offers no clear guidance to lower court judges and the police. A police officer who concludes that there is a threat to public safety and who fails to administer the *Miranda* warnings may find that the trial judge disagrees and orders the confession excluded from evidence. The lack of a clear definition of public safety also runs the risk that courts will broadly interpret the public safety exception. In *United States v. Reyes*, the police arrested a narcotics dealer who an informant reported might be armed. Ramon Reyes, when asked by the arresting officer whether he had "anything in his pocket that could harm the officer," responded that he had a gun. The officer removed the firearm and repeated the question. Reyes stated that there were drugs in his car. The federal court of appeals ruled that the officer's question was directed at public safety and that the drugs were properly admitted into evidence at Reyes's trial, but the court warned of the "inherent risk that the public safety exception might be distorted into a general rule" that individuals arrested on narcotics charges could be questioned in every instance prior to reading the *Miranda* rights (*United States v. Reyes*, 353 F.3d 148, 155 [2d Cir. 2003]).

Legal Equation

Public safety exception	=	A reasonable need to protect the police or the public
	+	A reasonable belief that the threat is immediate
	+	Questions must be prompted by a reasonable concern for public safety and directed at public safety rather than guilt or innocence
	+	The statements may not be the product of police compulsion that overcomes the suspect's will to resist.

 ## 16.3 YOU DECIDE

Richard Carrillo was arrested for selling narcotics and was transported to a detention facility. Before beginning to search Carrillo and prior to reading Carrillo his *Miranda* rights, Officer Weeks asked Carrillo "if he had any drugs or needles on his person." Carrillo responded, "No, I don't use drugs, I sell them." Weeks asked no additional questions. Is Carrillo's response admissible under the public safety exception? See *United States v. Carrillo* (16 F.3d 1046 [9th Cir. 1994]).

You can learn what the court decided by referring to the study site, **http://study.sagepub.com/lippmance.**

16.4 YOU DECIDE

John Wayne Dean and his wife kidnapped Ellen Slater, the daughter of a wealthy family, and demanded a ransom. Throughout the negotiation, there was no indication whether the young woman was dead or alive or how she was being treated. Four days following the abduction, FBI agents staked out the "drop location." Agent Krahling spotted Dean in the woods, armed with a pistol. Krahling pointed a shotgun at Dean and ordered him to throw down his gun. He then drew his pistol and ordered Dean to lie on the ground. Krahling proceeded to handcuff Dean and holstered his service revolver. In response to a question from Krahling, Dean then revealed where Ellen was being held, and she subsequently was rescued. Does the public safety exception extend to the protection of a single member of the public? See *People v. Dean* (114 Cal. Rptr. 555 [Cal. App. 1974]).

You can learn what the court decided by referring to the study site, **http://study.sagepub.com/lippmance.**

The Miranda Warnings

The three-part **Miranda warnings** inform suspects of their Fifth Amendment rights and the consequences of waiving these rights. These warnings require that the police inform individuals of the right to remain silent, that anything they say may be used against them, and of their right to an attorney, retained or appointed. The *Miranda* judgment specifies that the rights are to be recited in "clear and unequivocal terms" and that a suspect should be "clearly informed" of his or her rights. At this point, you might want to review the Supreme Court's explanation as to why the police are required to read *Miranda* rights to suspects.

These rights may be communicated to a suspect verbally, or a suspect may be asked to read the rights for himself or herself. In practice, the police typically employ both approaches. How should the rights be read to a suspect? As a judge, you might take the position that the rights must be read as set forth in the *Miranda* decision. On the other hand, you might take the position that a suspect's rights can be effectively communicated without using the precise language of the *Miranda* judgment. This would be a practical recognition that an officer in the field may not have access to a *Miranda* card or may inadvertently depart from the required warnings. What are the costs and benefits of these alternative approaches?

The Supreme Court has provided broad guidance to the police on how to recite the *Miranda* warnings. *Miranda is a flexible formula. The test is whether the warnings viewed in their totality convey the essential information to the suspect.*

In 1981, in *California v. Prysock*, Police Sergeant Byrd told the suspect, Randall Prysock, that he had "the right to talk to a lawyer before you are questioned, have him present with you while you are being questioned, and all during the questioning." Prysock then was informed that as a juvenile, he had the right to have his "parents present, which they are." Sergeant Byrd completed the warnings on Randall's right to a lawyer by advising Randall that "you have the right to have a lawyer appointed to represent you at no cost to yourself." Mrs. Prysock stated that she "didn't understand," inquired if her son "could still have an attorney at a later time if he gave a statement now without one," and agreed that Randall would talk to the sergeant (*California v. Prysock*, 453 U.S. 355, 356, 357 [1981]).

The outcome of this case centered on the meaning of the term *represent*. Does this mean that a lawyer would be appointed to represent Randall at trial while Randall would have to pay for an attorney before that time? Did Sergeant Byrd contribute to the confusion by giving two separate warnings regarding the right to a lawyer and using the term *represent* rather than the term *consult*, which is the term used in the *Miranda* decision? The U.S. Supreme Court majority ruled that the "rigidity" of *Miranda* does not extend to the precise formulation of the warnings given a criminal defendant. The judges noted that the *Miranda* judgment indicates that "no talismanic incantation" was required to satisfy its strictures. Three dissenting judges argued that Sergeant Byrd's warnings did not adequately inform Randall of his rights and that "a lawyer appointed to represent you" could reasonably have been understood by Mrs. Prysock to refer to a lawyer at trial.

If *Miranda* is not a *talismanic incantation*, how much flexibility is permitted? At what point are the rights so inadequately and incoherently read that a suspect is not fully and effectively informed of his or her rights? In

Duckworth v. Eagan, the defendant was arrested for an attempted murder and was informed that he had the right to the advice and presence of a lawyer, "even if you cannot afford to hire one." Gary Eagan then was told that "we have no way of giving you a lawyer, but one will be appointed for you, if you wish, if and when you go to court." The police officer then stated that Eagan had the right to answer or not to answer questions and that he had "the right to stop answering at any time until you've talked to a lawyer." The Supreme Court pointed out that the "if and when language" merely provided the defendant with the additional information that in Indiana, lawyers are appointed at the defendant's initial appearance in court and that, if he requested an appointed attorney, the police would not question him until a lawyer was present (*Duckworth v. Eagan*, 492 U.S. 195 [1989]).

The Supreme Court stressed that the warnings in their totality satisfied *Miranda* and, most important, that Eagan was informed of his immediate right to a lawyer and right to refuse to answer questions until a lawyer was present. The test was whether the warnings *reasonably conveyed the Miranda rights*. The Supreme Court majority stressed that judges should not closely examine every word of the *Miranda* warnings as if "construing a will or defining the terms of an easement." The four dissenting judges observed that the "if and when you go to court" language would reasonably lead a suspect to believe that a lawyer would not be appointed until "some indeterminate time in the future after questioning." Justice John Marshall noted that an unsophisticated suspect might be understandably confused and decide to talk to the police in an "effort to extricate himself from his predicament."

In both *Prysock* and *Duckworth*, the warnings in their totality were held to satisfy the requirements of *Miranda*. On the other hand, warnings that judges have considered to fail to provide the essential information required by the *Miranda* rights or which judges have concluded are misleading have been held to be inadequate.

In 2010, in *Florida v. Powell*, the Supreme Court revisited the question whether a *Miranda* warning "clearly informed" a suspect of his or her rights. Kevin Powell was arrested in connection with a robbery. The Tampa, Florida, police before asking Powell any questions informed him that "[i]f you cannot afford to hire a lawyer, one will be appointed for you without cost and before any questioning. You have the right to use any of these rights at any time you want during this interview." Powell waived his rights and admitted that as a felon he was in unlawful possession of a firearm when arrested. He contended that the *Miranda* warning was deficient because he was not explicitly informed of the right to the presence of a lawyer throughout his interrogation. The warning instead indicated that Powell only could consult with a lawyer before the interrogation (*Florida v. Powell*, 559 U.S. 50 [2010]).

The Court held that "although the warnings were not the clearest possible formulation of [the] right to counsel advisement, they were sufficiently comprehensive and comprehensible when given a common sense reading." Powell was informed that he could consult with a lawyer before the interrogation started and that he could exercise the right to consult with a lawyer at "any time . . . during the interview."

The Supreme Court noted that while "no precise formulation" of the *Miranda* warnings was required, the standard FBI warnings were "admirably informative." The FBI warnings inform suspects that they have the right to talk to a lawyer before questioning and also inform suspects of the right to have a lawyer present during questioning.

Justices Stevens and Breyer in their dissent argued that the warnings in *Powell* "entirely failed" to inform Powell of the right to have a lawyer present during questioning. According to the dissenters, the case marked "the first time the Court has approved a warning which, if given its natural reading, entirely omitted an essential element of a suspect's rights."

The Supreme Court also has been reluctant to require the police to expand the *Miranda* warnings beyond the three-part warning required in the *Miranda* judgment. In *Colorado v. Spring*, John Leroy Spring waived his rights, presumably thinking that he would be interrogated by federal agents on an illegal gun charge, and then was surprised with a question regarding a homicide. The Supreme Court held that Spring's admission that he had "shot [a] guy once" was admissible. The Court explained that Spring had been read his *Miranda* rights and that it was neither trickery nor deception for the police to fail to inform him of the topic of interrogation (*Colorado v. Spring*, 479 U.S. 546 [1987]). Another case, *Moran v. Burbine*, asks whether the police are required to go beyond the warnings required in the *Miranda* judgment and inform a suspect of the availability of an attorney.

In *Moran v. Burbine*, Brian Burbine was arrested for a burglary. The police had received a tip from a confidential informant about the identity of an individual responsible for a murder and discovered the address and nickname of the alleged murderer fit Burbine.

A public defender called the police headquarters and was told that the police would not be interrogating Burbine or putting him in a lineup and that they were through with Burbine for the night, and she was not told that he was a suspect in a murder. Roughly an hour later, Burbine was interrogated on three occasions and in each instance waived his rights after receiving the *Miranda* warning and confessed to the murder.

Burbine appealed on the grounds that he should have been told that a lawyer was available to assist him. The Supreme Court held that "how the police treat an attorney" has "no relevance" to "the degree of compulsion experienced by the defendant during interrogation." In addition, the Court held that it was not prepared to "adopt a rule requiring that the police inform a suspect of an attorney's efforts to reach him. . . . A rule requiring the police to inform the suspect of an attorney's efforts to contact him would contribute to the protection of the Fifth Amendment privilege only incidentally if at all" (*Moran v. Burbine*, 476 U.S. 412 [1986]). Several state supreme courts have rejected the Supreme Court's reasoning in *Burbine* and have held that their state constitutions require the police to inform a defendant of an attorney's immediate availability (*People v. McCauley*, 163 Ill.2d 414 [1994]).

Legal Equation

Three-part *Miranda* warnings	=	Reasonably convey rights
	+	*Miranda* is a flexible formula. The test is whether the warnings viewed in their totality convey the essential information to the suspect. The *Miranda* warnings are not a talismanic incantation.

Invoking the Miranda *Rights*

Following the reading of the *Miranda* rights, a defendant may assert his or her right to a lawyer or right to silence or may waive both of these rights. Is it sufficient that a defendant indicates that he or she "might" want a lawyer or "probably" should remain silent? Are the police required to ask the defendant to clarify his or her intent?

In *Davis v. United States*, Davis, a member of the Navy, was suspected of murdering another sailor and, when interviewed by the Naval Criminal Investigative Service, initially waived his *Miranda* rights. An hour and a half into the interview, Davis blurted out that "maybe I should talk to a lawyer." One of the agents later testified at trial that they made it clear that they "weren't going to pursue the matter unless we have it clarified is he asking for a lawyer or is he just making a comment about a lawyer." Davis replied, "No, I'm not asking for a lawyer," and then added, "No, I don't want a lawyer." Following a break in the interrogation, the investigators again read Davis his *Miranda* rights, and the interview continued for an additional hour. At this point, Davis asserted, "I think I want a lawyer before I say anything," and the investigators stopped their interrogation (*Davis v. United States*, 512 U.S. 452 [1994]).

Did Davis invoke his right to an attorney when he remarked that "maybe" he should talk to a lawyer? Was he then impermissibly persuaded to continue the interrogation as a result of the investigators' request for clarification? The U.S. Supreme Court held that an individual intending to assert his or her right to have counsel present must articulate this "sufficiently clearly that a reasonable police officer in the circumstances would understand the statement to be a request for an attorney." A rule that required the police to cease questioning following an ambiguous statement by the accused would transform *Miranda* into a "wholly irrational obstacle to interrogations."

In other words, the investigators were free to continue interrogating Davis following his ambiguous statement as to whether he "should talk to a lawyer." They were not required to clarify his intent. In fact, in an effort to clarify a suspect's statement, the police might be accused of influencing the suspect to waive his or her right to an attorney. For example, in *Hart v. A.G.*, a police officer was asked by the suspect about the pros and cons of hiring a lawyer. The Eleventh Circuit Court of Appeals ruled that an officer had discouraged the suspect from invoking his right to an attorney when the officer stated that "I'm going to want to ask you questions and he's [the lawyer] going to tell you can't answer me," but I am telling you that "honesty wouldn't hurt" (*Hart v. A.G.*, 323 F.3d 884 [11th Cir. 2003]).

Justice David Souter, writing on behalf of four concurring judges in *Davis*, observed that the Court's ruling in *Davis* would impose a special hardship on the poor and uneducated and on women and minorities. These individuals were particularly likely to feel overwhelmed by the interrogation process and would find it difficult to assert themselves. Justice Souter accordingly favored requiring the police to clarify ambiguous statements that might "reasonably be understood" as expressing a desire for the protection of a lawyer.

In another important ruling, the Supreme Court held in *Fare v. Michael C.* that the right to a lawyer did not encompass a juvenile's request to talk to his probation officer and that the juvenile's confession was properly admitted at his murder trial. The Supreme Court explained that lawyers, rather than probation officers, clergy, or friends, are trained and equipped to protect a suspect's right against self-incrimination (*Fare v. Michael C.*, 442 U.S. 707 [1979]).

In 2010, in *Berghuis v. Thompkins*, the U.S. Supreme Court clarified the standard for invoking the right to counsel. The Court held that an accused who wants to invoke his or her right to silence is required "to do so unambiguously." The justices reasoned that the police should not be required to "read a suspect's mind" and guess as to whether a suspect is invoking his or her right to silence. Van Chester Thompkins was largely silent for two hours and forty-five minutes before making incriminating statements. The Court held that his statement was admissible because he "did not say that he wanted to remain silent or that he did not want to talk with the police." Had he made either of these . . . statements, he would have invoked his "right to cut off questioning." Should the Court have required the police to try to clarify a suspect's intent? See *Berghuis v. Thompkins* (560 U.S. 370 [2010]).

In 2013, in *Salinas v. Texas*, Genovevo Salinas was asked to come to the police station to clear himself as a suspect in a murder case. The defendant when he arrived at the police station was not in custody and was free to leave. He was asked and answered a number of questions. He then was asked whether the shotgun in his home would match the shells recovered at the murder scene. He did not answer and instead "looked down at the floor, shuffled his feet, bit his bottom lip, and clenched his hands in his lap." After a few moments of silence, he answered other questions.

The prosecutor in his closing argument at trial used the defendant's silence when asked about the shotgun as evidence of Salinas's guilt. The Court held that it would have been a "simple matter" for Salinas to say that "he was not answering the officer's question on Fifth Amendment grounds. Because he failed to do so, the prosecution's use of his noncustodial silence did not violate the Fifth Amendment" (*Salinas v. Texas*, __ U.S. __ [2013]).

Legal Equation

Invocation of *Miranda* rights	=	Sufficiently clear that a reasonable police officer would understand that the suspect is asserting a right to a lawyer or to silence.

Waiver

A suspect, of course, may choose to waive his or her *Miranda* right to silence or right to an attorney. The Supreme Court stressed in *Miranda* that the government is required to meet a "heavy burden" in demonstrating that a suspect voluntarily, knowingly, and intelligently waived his or her rights. The *Miranda* judgment stated that a waiver requires an express statement and may not be presumed from the fact that an accused remains silent following the warnings.

What do we mean by a **voluntary, knowing, and intelligent waiver**? In *Moran v. Burbine*, the Supreme Court explained that a waiver inquiry involves a three-step process (475 U.S. 412, 421 [1985]).

Voluntary. The right must be voluntarily relinquished, it must be the product of a free and deliberate choice, and it may not be caused by intimidation, coercion, or deception. *I am doing this because I want to; the police did not make me waive my rights.*

Knowing and intelligent. The waiver must be made with a full awareness both of the nature of the right being abandoned and of the consequences of the decision to abandon the right. A suspect must possess sufficient mental competence to understand the rights and the significance of a waiver. *I know what the Miranda rights mean and what may happen to me if I talk.*

Totality of the circumstances. The determination whether the waiver is voluntary, knowing, and intelligent is based on the totality of the circumstances surrounding the interrogation. *We cannot read your mind, but we can see from the entire situation that the police did not pressure you into waiving your rights, and you seemed to know what you were doing.*

The prosecution is required to establish a *knowing, voluntary, and intelligent waiver* by a *preponderance of the evidence* (51 percent). The Supreme Court explained in *Colorado v. Connelly* that holding the prosecution to this relatively modest burden of proof is sufficient to deter illegal behavior on the part of the police (*Colorado v. Connelly*, 479 U.S. 157, 169 [1986]).

Voluntary

The *Miranda* decision noted that evidence that an accused was threatened, tricked, or cajoled (pressured) into a waiver is sufficient to establish that a suspect did not voluntarily waive his or her rights. A waiver also will not be recognized if obtained under coercive circumstances, such as a lengthy interrogation or a lengthy incarceration prior to the confession.

The Supreme Court has equated the test for voluntariness under *Miranda* with the due process voluntariness ("but for") test. In *Oregon v. Elstad*, the Supreme Court dismissed the defendant's claim that his confession was involuntary and explained that the defendant had not alleged "coercion of a confession by physical violence or other deliberate means calculated to break the suspect's will" (*Oregon v. Elstad*, 470 U.S. 298, 312 [1985]).

As you recall, in *Colorado v. Connelly*, the Supreme Court ruled that a defendant's confession that was the product of a mental disability was not involuntary for the purposes of *Miranda*. An involuntary confession requires an "*essential link between coercive activity of the State, on the one hand, and a resulting confession by a defendant on the other.*" In determining whether a confession is involuntary, a court will evaluate the impact of the police interrogation techniques in light of the totality of the circumstances. The factors to be considered include the following:

- *Offender.* The age, education, background, and other characteristics of the accused.
- *Conditions of interrogation.* The length of the interrogation or the length of the suspect's detention prior to the reading of the *Miranda* rights.
- *Interrogation techniques.* Whether there was the threat or use of coercion, duress, or violence.
- *Motivation.* Whether the suspect had a reason to confess such as a desire for a reduced sentence that was not related to the actions of the police.

The question always is whether the totality of circumstances caused the defendant to involuntarily confess. Was his or her will overborne by the totality of the circumstances? See *Colorado v. Connelly* (479 U.S. 157, 166 [1986]).

Knowing and Intelligent

We have seen that a suspect is required to understand the meaning of the *Miranda* rights as well as the consequences of a waiver. Once having read the *Miranda* warnings, may an officer assume that a suspect fully comprehends his or her rights? What if an individual clearly does not understand the rights?

In *Tague v. Louisiana*, the arresting officer testified that he read Tague the *Miranda* warnings, but the officer "could not presently remember what those rights were . . . could not recall whether he asked [Tague] whether he understood the rights as read to him, and 'couldn't say yes or no' whether he rendered any tests to determine whether [Tague] was literate or otherwise capable of understanding his rights." The U.S. Supreme Court concluded that Louisiana had failed to satisfy the heavy burden of establishing that Tague knowingly and intelligently waived his rights before confessing. In other words, a police officer may not automatically assume that an individual knowingly and intelligently waived his or her rights (*Tague v. Louisiana*, 444 U.S. 469 [1980]).

What factors are relevant in determining whether a suspect's waiver of *Miranda* is knowing and intelligent? In *Fare v. Michael C.*, introduced earlier in the chapter, the Supreme Court indicated that this is based on the *totality of the circumstances*. Michael was 16 and a half years of age and the Supreme Court indicated that the proper approach is to inquire into a "juvenile's age, experience, education, background, and intelligence and into whether he [or she] has the capacity to understand the warnings given him [or her], the nature of his [or her] Fifth Amendment rights, and the consequences of waiving those rights." The Court stressed that the police were careful to ensure that Michael C. understood his rights and that he clearly indicated a desire to waive them. In addition, there was nothing in Michael's background to indicate that he lacked the capacity to understand his rights. He was a 16-and-a-half-year-old juvenile who had significant experience in the criminal justice system, including a history of multiple arrests, internment in a youth camp, and having been on probation for several years. There also was no indication that he lacked the intelligence to understand the *Miranda* rights (*Fare v. Michael C.*, 442 U.S. 707, 725–727 [1979]). Judges also examine a defendant's behavior during interrogation. In *United States v. Gaddy*, the Eleventh Circuit Court of Appeals noted that despite the defendant's addiction to drugs and his mental illness, he was of above-average intelligence, had been involved with the criminal justice system on several occasions in the past, and did not exhibit "'scattered' thinking, 'panicky' behavior,'" severe depression, or anxiety during his interrogation and that his waiver was knowing and voluntary (*United States v. Gaddy*, 894 F.2d 1307, 1312 [11th Cir. 1990]).

We have already seen in *Colorado v. Spring* and in *Moran v. Burbine* that the Supreme Court has resisted requiring the police to incorporate additional information into the *Miranda* warnings, such as informing defendants of the topic of interrogation or of the availability of an attorney. The Court has stressed that the U.S. Constitution does not require that an individual be informed of all information that might prove useful in arriving at his or her decision, such as the strength of the prosecution's case. The Supreme Court also has recognized that absent this information, a decision to talk might be voluntary but not necessarily the best course to follow (*Colorado v. Spring*, 479 U.S. 564, 577 [1987]). In other words, a voluntary, knowing, and intelligent waiver is not necessarily a wise waiver.

Express and Implied Waiver

A waiver, as we have seen, must be voluntary, knowing, and intelligent. *Miranda* indicated that an "express statement" that the individual is willing to make a statement and does not want an attorney followed closely by a statement constitutes a waiver and that a waiver will not be presumed from silence or "from the fact that a confession was in fact eventually obtained." Have courts continued to require a clear and affirmative statement? Must a defendant sign a waiver form?

A mentally competent defendant who affirmatively waives his or her rights clearly meets the **express waiver** standard. However, the issue of waiver is not always this clear. Consider *North Carolina v. Butler*. William Thomas Butler was convicted of kidnapping, armed robbery, and felonious assault stemming from the robbery of a service station and the shooting of the attendant. He was arrested and fully advised of his rights. Butler thereafter was taken to the FBI office, and after determining that he had an eleventh-grade education and was able to read, he was given a written *Miranda* warning form to review. Butler stated that he understood his rights and refused to sign the waiver of his right to silence and right to a lawyer at the bottom of the page. The FBI agents assured him that he was not required to speak or to sign the form and asked whether Butler was willing to talk to them. He replied that he would talk to the agents but would not sign the rights waiver form and then proceeded to make incriminating statements. An FBI agent testified at trial that Butler had said "nothing" when advised of his rights and attempted neither to request an attorney nor to halt the interrogation (*North Carolina v. Butler*, 441 U.S. 369 [1979]).

The U.S. Supreme Court ruled that the prosecution's burden is "great, but that . . . in some cases, a waiver can be clearly inferred from the actions and words of the person interrogated." In these instances, the prosecution is required to establish that although there was no affirmative waiver, the suspect nevertheless understood his or her rights and engaged in a "course of conduct indicating waiver." This is an **implied waiver**. Do you believe that Butler fully understood that he was waiving his *Miranda* rights? A similar issue arose in *Connecticut v. Barrett*. William Barrett was arrested for sexual assault and indicated that he would not provide a written statement without his lawyer but that he was happy to talk to the police. Was Barrett's confession admissible?

Berghuis v. Thompkins (discussed above) is the latest case discussing an implicit waiver of the *Miranda* rights. Thompkins was suspected of involvement in a shooting. At the beginning of the interrogation, Detective Christopher Helgert presented Thompkins with a form containing the *Miranda* rights. Helgert asked Thompkins to read the fifth warning out loud to determine whether he could read. The right read as follows:

> You have the right to decide at any time before or during questioning to use your right to remain silent and your right to talk with a lawyer while you are being questioned.

Thompkins then read the *Miranda* warnings on the form aloud and refused to sign the form. Helgert and another officer then began the interrogation, and at no point during the questioning did Thompkins express that he wanted to "remain silent, that he did not want to talk with the police, or that he wanted an attorney," and he was "'[l]argely' silent during the interrogation, which lasted three hours." Thompkins gave a few limited verbal responses such as "yeah," "no," and "I don't know" and in some instances nodded his head. He declined an offer of a peppermint and complained that the small chair was "hard."

Roughly two hours and forty-five minutes into the interrogation, Helgert asked, "Do you believe in God?" Thompkins looked at Helgert and responded "Yes," and his eyes "well[ed] up with tears." Helgert then asked,

"[D]o you pray to [G]od to forgive you for shooting that boy down?" Thompkins stated "Yes" and turned his head away. Thompkins refused to make a written confession, and the interrogation ended roughly fifteen minutes later.

Thompkins claimed that he did not knowingly and voluntarily waive his *Miranda* rights. The Supreme Court affirmed that a waiver may be either explicit or implicit. An implicit waiver is established where the prosecution "shows that a *Miranda* warning was given and that it was understood by the accused and [in such circumstances] an accused's uncoerced statement establishes an implicit waiver of the right to remain silent."

The Court concluded that Thompkins knowingly and voluntarily waived his right to silence.

Received and read his rights. Thompkins read his rights, and there is no evidence indicating that he did not understand his rights.

Course of conduct. Thompkins's answer to the question about praying to God for forgiveness was "sufficient to show a course of conduct indicating waiver."

Uncoerced. There is no evidence indicating Thompkins's statement was coerced by threats or sleep or food deprivation, or that an interrogation of this length is "inherently coercive."

The *Berghuis* decision seemingly lessens the "heavy burden" on the prosecution to establish a defendant's waiver of his or her *Miranda* rights. A defendant is not required to explicitly waive his or her rights. A waiver will be "presumed" when an individual acts in a "manner inconsistent" with the invocation of his or her rights.

Legal Equation

Waiver = Voluntary, knowing, and intelligent
+ An affirmative statement (express waiver) or totality of the circumstances (implied waiver).

Waiver: Question First and Warn Later

In *Oregon v. Elstad*, introduced above, the police visited the home of 18-year-old Michael James Elstad, briefly and casually interrogated him regarding a burglary, and obtained a voluntary incriminating statement. The officers then arrested Elstad and, at police headquarters, read Elstad his *Miranda* rights and obtained a detailed confession. The U.S. Supreme Court had no difficulty in ruling that the first confession was inadmissible because the officers had failed to read Elstad his *Miranda* rights. What of the second confession? Elstad clearly must have believed that there was little reason not to continue talking to the police after having already "let the cat out of the bag" concerning his guilt. It would seem only fair to require the police to inform Elstad that in considering whether to invoke his *Miranda* rights, he should be aware that his first confession was inadmissible.

The U.S. Supreme Court held that the unlawful character of Elstad's first voluntary confession did not automatically taint his second voluntary confession and ruled that a "suspect who has once responded to unwarned yet uncoercive questioning is not thereby disabled from waiving his rights and confessing after he has been given the requisite *Miranda* warnings." The Supreme Court found that the *Miranda* warnings cured the taint of the initial confession and that warning a suspect that his or her first confession was inadmissible was neither "practicable nor constitutionally necessary." The police, according to the majority, were sufficiently deterred from failing to give the *Miranda* warning by excluding the first confession. Justices Brennan and Marshall in dissent criticized what they viewed as the Supreme Court's growing impatience with constitutional rights and condemned their fellow justices for increasingly viewing civil liberties as impediments to combating crimes (*Oregon v. Elstad*, 470 U.S. 298, 312 [1985]).

Following *Elstad*, a number of police departments adopted a policy of interrogating suspects in "successive, unwarned and warned phases." The Supreme Court reacted to this tactic in *Missouri v. Seibert* by reconsidering the judgment in *Elstad*. Patrice Seibert's 12-year-old son, Jonathan, had cerebral palsy and died in his sleep. Fearing charges of neglect because of the bedsores on Jonathan's body, Seibert entered into a plan with her sons and some of their friends to incinerate Jonathan's body in the family's mobile home. They intentionally left Donald Rector, a mentally challenged teenager who lived with the Seiberts, in the home to give the impression that he was looking after Jonathan at the time of the fire.

Five days later, Seibert was arrested at the hospital where Donald was being treated for burns. She was taken to the police station and left alone in the interrogation room for fifteen to twenty minutes. Officer Richard Hanrahan then followed orders and neglected to give Seibert the *Miranda* warnings prior to the thirty- to forty-minute interrogation. Seibert ultimately confessed to her crime and was given a twenty-minute break. Officer Hanrahan then turned on the tape recorder, indicated that they should continue their conversation, and gave Seibert the *Miranda* warnings, and Seibert waived her rights. Hanrahan initiated the questioning by confronting Seibert with her prewarning statements, and she immediately admitted that the plan was for Donald "to die in his sleep" (*Missouri v. Seibert*, 542 U.S. 600 [2004]).

The Supreme Court stated that the issue when the police **question first and warn later** is whether "it would be reasonable to find that in these circumstances the warnings could function 'effectively'" to advise the suspect that he or she "had a real choice about giving an admissible statement." In other words, when a suspect is warned that "anything you say may be used against you," will he or she understand that the first confession is inadmissible and cannot be introduced into evidence to establish his or her guilt and that the defendant may find that it is in his or her self-interest to invoke the right to silence or the right to an attorney?

The Supreme Court pointed out that in *Elstad* one of the arresting officers likely was confused as to whether the suspect was in custodial interrogation and committed the "oversight" of casually remarking that he believed that Elstad was involved in the burglary. Elstad then confirmed that he was at the crime scene. The living-room conversation in *Elstad* was corrected at the police station when another officer read Elstad the *Miranda* warnings before undertaking a systematic interrogation. The Supreme Court noted that a reasonable person would view the stationhouse interrogation by a separate police officer as "a markedly different experience from the short conversation at home."

In *Seibert*, the plurality of the Supreme Court concluded that the facts challenge the "efficacy of the *Miranda* warnings to the point that a reasonable person in the suspect's shoes would not have understood them to convey a message that she retained a choice about continuing to talk." In contrast to the casual, inadvertent, and brief questioning in *Elstad*, the facts in *Seibert* reveal a police strategy intended to undermine the *Miranda* warnings. Both the unwarned interrogation and the warned interrogation took place in the stationhouse and were conducted by the same officer. The first interrogation was systematic and exhaustive and conducted with psychological skill, and the officer did nothing to inform Seibert that the first confession could not be used against her. Officer Hanrahan gave the impression that the second interrogation was a continuation of the earlier questioning when he noted that he had been talking to Seibert about "what happened."

Legal Equation

Confession resulting from a "question first and warn later" interrogation	=	Reasonable to find that in these circumstances, the warnings could function effectively to advise the suspect that he or she had a real choice about giving an admissible statement
	+	Relevant facts and circumstances of the interrogation.

16.5 YOU DECIDE

Alexander Texidor was arrested by federal authorities for the unlawful purchase of firearms and agreed to provide the FBI with information concerning other individuals involved in the illicit trade in firearms. This led to the arrest of Luis Gonzalez-Lauzan Sr. on January 8, 2002. On January 28, 2002, Texidor was murdered, and Gonzalez-Lauzan Sr. and his son, Luis Gonzalez-Lauzan Jr., and two other individuals were indicted for the murder in September 2002. Gonzalez-Lauzan Jr.

was in prison on unrelated charges prior to the indictment when he was questioned by state and federal authorities in the interview room of the courthouse regarding Texidor's murder. The three officers made a decision not to administer the *Miranda* warnings and spent between two and a half and three hours talking to Gonzalez-Lauzan Jr. The officers explained that they were working on a murder investigation and believed that Gonzalez-Lauzan Jr. was involved. The officers instructed Gonzalez-Lauzan Jr. that "we are not asking you any questions. We don't want you to say anything. We just have something to say to you and we ask that you listen to it so that you can understand where we are coming from." The officers described the evidence linking Gonzalez-Lauzan Jr. to the killing in detail and instructed him several times merely to listen when he occasionally interjected and denied involvement. After roughly two and a half hours, Gonzalez-Lauzan Jr. interrupted and exclaimed that "okay, you got me." Gonzalez-Lauzan Jr. was then immediately read his *Miranda* rights and signed a form agreeing to waive his rights. He admitted that he instructed the co-conspirators to teach Texidor a lesson, that he had provided the murder weapon, and that he had been present at the killing. Is Gonzalez-Lauzan Jr.'s confession admissible? See *United States v. Gonzalez-Lauzan Jr.* (437 F.3d 1128 [11th Cir. 2006]). See also *Hairston v. United States* (905 A.2d 765 [D.C. 2006]).

You can learn what the court decided by referring to the study site, **http://study.sagepub.com/lippmance.**

Waiver Following Invocation of the Miranda Rights

Once an individual invokes his or her *Miranda* rights, are the police prohibited from questioning him or her again? On one hand, the police clearly are obligated to respect a suspect's desire to invoke his or her *Miranda* rights. On the other hand, the police may desire to confront a suspect with new evidence or to question a suspect concerning an unrelated offense. How does the Supreme Court balance these competing interests?

The Supreme Court has established one legal test in those instances in which a defendant invokes his or her right to silence and another legal test in those instances in which a defendant invokes his or her right to an attorney. In this section, we describe the two legal tests and explain the reason for the Court's reliance on separate tests. We first turn to the approach employed when a suspect invokes his or her right to silence.

In *Michigan v. Mosley*, Richard Bert Mosley was arrested in connection with two robberies. He was read his *Miranda* rights and invoked his right to silence, and the robbery detective ceased questioning. The detective then took Mosley to the cell block. Two hours later, Mosley was moved to the homicide bureau for questioning about "an unrelated holdup murder." He once again was advised of his rights and this time waived them and made an incriminating statement. Mosley later appealed that his second interrogation for murder was unlawful and pointed out that *Miranda* clearly stated that if an individual indicates at any time that he wishes to remain silent, the interrogation must cease. Did this mean that the police interrogation of Mosley for the homicide was a violation of his right against self-incrimination? See *Michigan v. Mosley* (423 U.S. 96 [1975]).

The U.S. Supreme Court ruled that the Detroit police acted in lawful fashion. The legal test for whether a statement obtained after a person in custody decides to remain silent depends on whether his or her right to silence was **scrupulously honored**. What does this mean?

- The police immediately ceased questioning.
- The police suspended interrogation for a significant period.
- The police provided a fresh set of *Miranda* warnings.
- The second interrogation focused on a crime different in *time, nature, and place.*

The Supreme Court stressed that the critical consideration is whether the police respected Mosley's "right to cut off questioning." This was not a situation in which the police failed to honor a decision to terminate questioning by refusing to discontinue the interrogation or by engaging in repeated efforts to wear down Mosley's resistance and pressure him to change his mind.

The dissent pointed out that Mosley initially did not want to talk about the robberies and argued that the police had taken advantage of the coercive environment of Mosley's incommunicado detention to extract a confession to an unrelated criminal offense.

The scrupulously honored test is subject to several criticisms. Clearly, the police were aware when they arrested Mosley that he possibly was involved in a killing, and the Court's holding invites the police to subject a defendant to a series of interrogations when they have evidence of the defendant's involvement in multiple crimes. What did the Supreme Court mean when it required that the second interrogation address a crime different in time, nature, and place? What about a bank robber who flees in a car and hits a pedestrian? Are the bank robbery and auto accident different in time, nature, and place?

An example of the application of *Mosley* is *United States v. Tyler*. Willie Tyler was arrested for the murder of a government informant and, after being read his *Miranda* rights, invoked his right to silence. He was taken to a small room in the police barracks in which a timeline of the murder investigation and crime scene photographs were pasted to the wall. After several hours, Detective Ronald Egolf entered the room and engaged Tyler in a general discussion on his family, education, and hunting and, after roughly an hour, directed Tyler to "tell the truth." Tyler allegedly started to cry, Egolf again warned him of his *Miranda* rights, and Tyler confessed to involvement in the murder. The Third Circuit Court of Appeals held that Tyler's interrogation was inconsistent with "scrupulously honoring Tyler's assertion of silence." Can you explain the court's decision? See *United States v. Tyler* (164 F.3d 150, 155 [3d Cir. 1998]).

The Supreme Court, in *Edwards v. Arizona*, established a separate **initiation** test for determining whether a defendant who invokes his or her right to an attorney may be once again interrogated. Under what circumstances would a waiver and subsequent confession be considered voluntary, knowing, and intelligent? The facts in *Edwards* are remarkably similar to the facts in *Mosley*. Robert Edwards was arrested for burglary, robbery, and murder and then waived his rights, agreed to talk, and later asserted his right to counsel. The next morning, two detectives approached Edwards and again read him his *Miranda* rights. Edwards agreed to talk to the police and confessed.

The confession obtained by the detectives to a crime to which Edwards earlier had invoked his right to counsel clearly would be inadmissible under the *Mosley* test. The U.S. Supreme Court, however, explained that a new test was required because an individual who invokes his or her right to counsel clearly lacks confidence in his or her ability to withstand the pressures of interrogation and desires the help of a lawyer. The Court held that Edwards "is not subject to further interrogation by the authorities until counsel has been made available to him, unless the accused himself *initiates* further communication, exchanges or conversations with the police." A confession obtained in the absence of counsel is presumed to be involuntary (*Edwards v. Arizona*, 451 U.S. 477, 484–485 [1981]).

In *Arizona v. Roberson*, the Supreme Court extended *Edwards*, which prohibits reinterrogation about the same crime, to prohibit the police from reinterrogating a suspect about a *different crime*. Justice John Paul Stevens explained that a suspect who requests a lawyer clearly believes that he or she is in need of legal assistance regardless of whether interrogated about the same offense or a different offense. Stevens reasoned that such a suspect who is again approached by the police will find it difficult to overcome the pressures of custodial interrogation and again assert his or her right to a lawyer. Justice Anthony Kennedy, in dissent, pointed out that the *Edwards-Roberson* rule will prevent the police from interrogating suspects based on newly discovered evidence or offenses (*Arizona v. Roberson*, 486 U.S. 675 [1988]).

Some of the difficulties with the initiation test are illustrated by *United States v. Green*. In *Green*, a defendant was arrested on a drug charge, was read his *Miranda* rights, invoked his right to an attorney, and pled guilty. Three months later, the police obtained an arrest warrant charging the defendant with an unrelated homicide that had taken place six months before he had been arrested on the drug charge. The defendant subsequently was interrogated on the homicide and, after being advised of his *Miranda* rights, confessed. Despite the fact that five months had passed between the time that the defendant invoked his right to counsel and the time that he confessed to the murder, the District of Columbia Court of Appeals ruled that a strict interpretation of the *Edwards* rule dictated that the confession should be suppressed (*United States v. Green*, 592 A.2d 985 [D.C. App. 1991]). The U.S. Supreme Court was in the process of considering this case when the defendant died, and as a result, no ruling was issued. How would you resolve the dilemma confronting the judge in *Green*?

In 2010, the Supreme Court addressed the prohibition on interrogation of a suspect who has invoked his or her right to counsel in *Maryland v. Shatzer*. In August 2003, Michael Blaine Shatzer was incarcerated in Maryland for child sexual abuse. A detective interviewed Shatzer in 2003 about another allegation of child abuse against his son, and Shatzer invoked his right to a lawyer and the investigation was dropped (*Maryland v. Shatzer*, 559 U.S. 98 [2010]).

Thirty months later, additional information developed that supported the allegation of child abuse. In March 2006, a second detective, Paul Hoover, interviewed Shatzer in a second correctional institution to which he had been transferred. Hoover explained that he wanted to question Shatzer about the alleged abuse of his son and read Shatzer the *Miranda* rights and obtained a written waiver. Shatzer admitted to masturbating in front of his son from a distance of less than three feet. He agreed to take a polygraph examination, and after being read the *Miranda* rights, Shatzer failed the test. He was visibly upset, started to cry, and incriminated himself by saying that "I didn't force him. I didn't force him." Shatzer requested an attorney, and Hoover ended the interrogation.

Edwards protects a suspect who has invoked the right to a lawyer from being coerced or badgered into waiving his or her right to a lawyer, and Shatzer's confession would have been thrown out under the *Edwards* rule. The Supreme Court, however, avoided this harsh result by establishing a **break in custody rule** that regulates police interrogation of suspects who have invoked their right to counsel under *Edwards*. The Court noted that when a suspect is released from pretrial custody and "has returned to his normal life for some time . . . there is little reason to think that his change of heart regarding interrogation without counsel has been coerced." The suspect is no longer isolated and has been able to seek advice from a lawyer, family, and friends. His or her change of heart likely is a result of a calculation of his or her self-interest rather than a result of police coercion.

The Supreme Court held that where a suspect has been released from custody for fourteen days the police may once again approach a suspect. This provides time for the suspect to consult with friends and lawyers. The fourteen-day waiting period insulates a suspect against police continually attempting to interrogate and to wear a suspect down. Shatzer, though incarcerated, was not under pressure to talk to the police. He was in medium-security institutions and had access to a law library, exercise, and adult education, and was able to send and receive letters and to receive visitors.

The next issue confronting the U.S. Supreme Court was clarifying what the Court meant in *Edwards* when it wrote that a suspect is not subject to interrogation until a lawyer has been "made available to him." In *Minnick v. Mississippi*, Mississippi argued that once a defendant requests and meets with an attorney, "counsel has been made available to him." Following this meeting, Mississippi argued that the police are free to interrogate a suspect without a lawyer being present. The Supreme Court, however, held that a "fair reading of *Edwards* . . . demonstrates that we have interpreted the rule to bar police-initiated interrogation unless the accused has counsel with him at the time of questioning. . . . When counsel is requested, interrogation must cease, and officials may not reinitiate interrogation without counsel present, whether or not the accused has consulted with his attorney" (*Minnick v. Mississippi*, 498 U.S. 146, 150 [1990]).

In summary, keep three points in mind when it comes to a suspect's invocation of the *Miranda* rights and waiver of the *Miranda* rights:

- *Invocation of counsel.* We saw in *Davis* and in *Thompkins* that the invocation of a right to counsel and the right to silence requires a *clear and unambiguous* statement.
- *Scrupulously honored. Mosley* taught us that the waiver of the right to silence following the assertion of this right is considered voluntary in those instances in which the police *scrupulously honored* the suspect's rights.
- *Initiation.* A waiver of the invocation of the right to an attorney following the assertion of this right is considered voluntary in those instances in which the defendant *initiates* contact with the police.

What do we mean by *initiation*? Must there be a clear and affirmative statement of waiver? The U.S. Supreme Court provided an answer to this question in *Oregon v. Bradshaw*. In considering *Bradshaw*, pay attention to the legal test for waiver of the right to a lawyer. The Supreme Court ruled that James Edward Bradshaw's question to a police officer, "Well, what is going to happen to me now?" constituted initiation and a waiver of Bradshaw's previous request for a lawyer. The Court reasoned that "[a]lthough ambiguous, the respondent's question in this case as to what was going to happen to him evinced a willingness and a desire for a generalized discussion about the investigation; it was not merely a necessary inquiry arising out of the incidents of the custodial relationship." Did Bradshaw intend to waive his right to an attorney? Ask yourself whether the law has made it difficult or easy for the police to obtain a waiver from an individual who has previously invoked his or her right to an attorney.

Waiver following invocation of right to silence	=	(Scrupulously honor rights) Immediately cease interrogation	+	Suspend questioning for a significant period of time
	+	Fresh set of *Miranda* warnings	+	Interrogation on crime different in time, nature, and place.
Waiver following invocation of right to an attorney	=	Initiate contact with the police.		

16.6 YOU DECIDE

Defendant Wayne Montgomery was convicted of possession of a sawed-off shotgun and three firearms. Montgomery asserted his right to an attorney. The federal agents then proceeded to photograph and fingerprint Montgomery. The following conversation then occurred.

Montgomery:	Am I being charged with each gun?
Agent Sherman:	You will probably be charged with two counts.
Montgomery:	Did all of the guns fire?
Agent Sherman:	Yes. Why do you want to know?
Montgomery:	The sawed-off was in pieces [in a duffel bag].
Agent Sherman:	That is right, but it only took a minute to put together.

Montgomery:	Ya, but it was missing a spring.
Agent Sherman:	Well, the State Police fired the gun and it worked. Did you have any problem firing the gun?
Montgomery:	I could not get it to work.

Montgomery then indicated that he did not want to talk anymore about the firearms, and the conversation ended. His attorney unsuccessfully sought to suppress this statement, and it was introduced into evidence at trial as evidence that the defendant knowingly possessed the firearms. Did Montgomery initiate the conversation with Agent Sherman and waive his right to an attorney? See *United States v. Montgomery* (714 F.2d 201 [1st Cir. 1983]).

You can learn what the court decided by referring to the study site, **http://study.sagepub.com/lippmance.**

CRIMINAL EVIDENCE IN THE NEWS

In 2006, the United Nations Committee against Torture called for an impartial national investigation of alleged "police brutality and torture in Chicago, about which nothing has been done for a long time." The report was issued by ten independent international experts charged with monitoring compliance with the international Convention against Torture and Other Cruel, Inhuman or Degrading Treatment or Punishment (1984).

This echoed a 1990 report by the international human rights organization Amnesty International that called for an investigation into ongoing allegations of torture of individuals subjected to police interrogation in Chicago.

It is alleged that between 1973 and 1991, at least sixty-six individuals were tortured by Chicago Police Commander Jon Burge and by the officers under his supervision in the Area 2 police headquarters in Chicago. Burge and his fellow officers are accused of beating suspects, shocking them with electric wires and cattle prods, suffocating them using plastic bags, and jamming guns against their heads or in their mouths in order to extract confessions. The credibility of this charge is bolstered by a report by the Chicago Police Department's Office of Professional Standards (OPS), which, in 1990, listed the names of fifty alleged victims of police torture. The report determined that physical abuse "did occur and . . . it was systematic. . . . [T]he type of abuse . . . was not limited to the usual beatings, but went into such areas as psychological techniques and planned torture." The OPS investigation also concluded that members of the police command were aware of the "systematic abuse" and either participated in the activity or failed to intervene to bring it to an end.

The case that first brought these charges to public attention involved Andrew Wilson, convicted of killing two police officers. Wilson ultimately won a civil judgment against the City of Chicago, which admitted that Wilson had been tortured and that Burge and others had acted in an "outrageous manner and utilized methods far beyond those . . . permitted and expected by the Police Department." Lawyers for the city also conceded that Burge and others had tortured another suspect nine days earlier. This led to Burge's termination in 1993 and to the suspension of two detectives. It later was revealed that Chicago had spent more than $30 million in legal fees defending Burge and the police under his command against charges of torture.

There is no question that some of the individuals who were apparently tortured by Burge and his men, in fact, were guilty. Some innocent individuals, however, were convicted. In January 2003, Illinois Governor George Ryan granted four death row inmates pardons after concluding that their confessions had been obtained by Burge and his unit through torture.

The claims of torture have received support from a number of state and federal courts. In 1999, Federal District Court Judge Milton Shadur wrote that it is "now common knowledge that . . . Jon Burge and . . . officers working under him regularly engaged in the physical abuse and torture of prisoners to extract confessions . . . beatings and other means of torture occurred as an established practice, not just on an isolated basis" (*United States ex rel. Maxwell v. Gilmore*, 37 F.2d 1078 [N.D. Ill. 1999] [Memorandum and order]).

Federal District Court Judge Diane Wood, in *Hinton v. Uchtman* (2005), wrote that the defendant's torture allegations were "reminiscent of the news reports of 2004 concerning the notorious Abu Ghraib facility in Iraq." She observed that this type of conduct "imposes a huge cost on society: it creates distrust of the police generally, despite the fact that most police officers would abhor such tactics, and it creates a cloud over even the valid convictions in which the problem officers played a role" (*Hinton v. Uchtman*, 395 F.3d 810, 833 [7th Cir. 2005]).

There is no doubt that the systematic use of torture has called into question the credibility of criminal convictions in Chicago. In 2006, two special prosecutors issued a three-hundred-page report discussing 148 cases of alleged torture in Chicago. The report concluded that Burge and a dozen police officers abused suspects and that at least three former prosecutors failed to inquire into the condition of suspects. The same pattern of indifference was displayed by high-level police and prosecutorial officials in Chicago. The prosecution of individuals accused of torture, according to the report, likely is barred by the statute of limitations.

United States prosecutor Patrick Fitzgerald charged Burge with perjury and with obstruction of justice for having allegedly committed perjury by denying torture in a civil case in federal court. He was convicted in June 2011 and sentenced to four and a half years in prison. The key witness was former Chicago Police Department detective Michael McDermott, who corroborated the testimony of five individuals who claimed to have been tortured by Burge and his "Midnight Gang." Fitzgerald following the verdict stated that it was "important to send a message that this sort of thing" will not be tolerated in the criminal justice system.

Interrogation

You should have it firmly fixed in your mind that a defendant may not be interrogated by the police prior to the reading of the *Miranda* warnings. Following the reading of the *Miranda* rights, there also are firm limits on police **interrogation**. As we have seen, once a suspect invokes either the right to silence or the right to an attorney, he or she is not subject to interrogation. The police must *scrupulously honor* the right to silence and may interrogate a suspect only about a crime different in time, nature, and place after suspending interrogation for a period of time and issuing a fresh set of *Miranda* warnings. A suspect who invokes his or her right to an attorney may be interrogated only in the event that the suspect initiates contact with the police.

What is the definition of *police interrogation*? Does this mean that the police are prohibited from conversing with the suspect? Can the police let a suspect know that they found several hundred pounds of cocaine in his or her house or inform the suspect of the progress of the investigation or of the fact that a co-conspirator confessed?

In *Rhode Island v. Innis*, the U.S. Supreme Court defined *interrogation*. The Court explained that interrogation involves either **express questioning** or the **functional equivalent of express questioning**:

- *Express questioning.* Questions directed to a suspect by the police.
- *Functional equivalent.* Words or actions on the part of the police (other than those normally attendant to arrest and custody) that the police should know are reasonably likely to elicit an incriminating response from the suspect.

Express questioning entails a direct question. The test for the functional equivalent of questioning is whether the police should know that a practice is likely to elicit an incriminating statement from a suspect. The police are required to put themselves in the shoes of the suspect and ask themselves whether a statement or practice is likely to lead the suspect to incriminate himself or herself. For example, the police should anticipate that an appeal to religion may lead a suspect who is a member of the clergy to incriminate himself or herself.

In *Innis*, Thomas J. Innis was taken into custody as a suspect in the murder of a taxicab driver. Two police officers carried on a conversation in the squad car in Innis's presence about their fear that a physically challenged child at a nearby school would find the shotgun used in the murder and hurt him- or herself. Innis immediately waived his right to an attorney and directed the officers to the location of the shotgun. The Supreme Court held that there is nothing in the trial court record to suggest that the officers "should have known that their conversation was reasonably likely to elicit an incriminating response from the respondent." The officers were unaware that Innis "was peculiarly susceptible to an appeal to his conscience concerning the safety of handicapped children. Nor is there anything in the record to suggest that the police knew that the respondent was unusually disoriented or upset at the time of his arrest" (*Rhode Island v. Innis*, 446 U.S. 291 [1980]).

16.7 YOU DECIDE

Leeander Jerome Blake and Terrance Tolbert robbed and killed Staughan Lee Griffin and carjacked his automobile. Tolbert was arrested and implicated Blake. Blake was arrested and read his *Miranda* rights and invoked his right to an attorney and was jailed.

Thirty-five minutes later, Detective William Johns returned to Blake's cell to give Blake a statement of the charges. Maryland law requires that defendants receive a statement of the charges against them. Johns was accompanied by Officer Curtis Reese. Johns told Blake, "[I]t's very serious, this is your copy, you need to read it over." The statement contained a description of each charge as well as the maximum penalty for each offense. The maximum penalty listed for the first-degree murder charge was "DEATH." The death penalty is indeed the maximum penalty that can be imposed in Maryland for first-degree murder although Blake himself could not have received the death penalty because he was 17 years old on the night of the murder. The factual summary on which the charges were based included an accusation by Tolbert that Blake was the one who shot Griffin and drove Griffin's vehicle from the scene.

As Johns began to leave, Reese said in a loud and confrontational voice, "I bet you want to talk now, huh?"

Detective Johns loudly stated to Reese, "[N]o he doesn't want to talk to us, you can't say anything to him, he asked for a lawyer."

Roughly one half-hour after Johns had spoken to Blake, Johns returned to the cell block to deliver Blake some clothing that had been delivered for him. Blake asked, "I can still talk to you?" Johns replied, "Are you saying you want to talk to me now?" Blake said "[Y]es," and Johns told him he would have to reread Blake his *Miranda* rights before they could talk. Blake walked back to the interview room, where he was re-Mirandized. Blake provided a full account of the robbery, murder, and carjacking.

At the end of the interview, Detective Johns asked if Blake would agree to a polygraph exam, and Blake said he would. The polygraph administrator told Blake that he appeared to have been deceptive, and Blake then admitted that on the day of the murder, he knew Tolbert had a gun. He also admitted that they were looking for someone to carjack, and that Blake initially noticed Griffin and pointed him out to Tolbert. Was Blake improperly interrogated by the Annapolis, Maryland, police officers under *Rhode Island v. Innis*? In the alternative, did Blake initiate the contact with the police under *Bradshaw*? See *United States v. Blake* (571 F.3d 331 [4th Cir. 2009]).

You can learn what the court decided by referring to the study site, **http://study.sagepub.com/lippmance.**

■ SIXTH AMENDMENT RIGHT TO COUNSEL: POLICE INTERROGATIONS

The Sixth Amendment provides for the right to a speedy and public trial before an impartial jury with the right to obtain witnesses and to confront your accusers. The amendment further guarantees that an individual shall "have the assistance of counsel for his defense." The right to an attorney is crucial; without the skill and expertise of a lawyer, an individual may find himself or herself unable to meaningfully contest his or her guilt at trial. The U.S. Supreme Court, in a series of cases, extended the Sixth Amendment right to counsel beyond the criminal trial to provide protections to individuals subjected to interrogation in the post-indictment phases of the criminal justice process. Keep two points in mind as we explore the Sixth Amendment right to counsel.

The Sixth Amendment right supplements the due process voluntariness and Fifth Amendment *Miranda* protections. The Sixth Amendment automatically attaches following the initiation of criminal proceedings. At this point, guilt or innocence is to be determined in a court of law.

The Sixth Amendment protection ensures that the criminal justice process functions in a fair fashion. In contrast, the due process voluntariness test protects individuals against involuntary confessions, and *Miranda* is intended to safeguard the right against self-incrimination.

In 2008, in *Rothgery v. Gillespie County*, the U.S. Supreme Court clarified that the Sixth Amendment right attaches at a criminal defendant's "initial appearance before a judicial officer," where he or she learns the charge against him, a probable cause determination is made, and bail is set restricting the defendant's liberty (*Rothgery v. Gillespie County*, 554 U.S. 191 [2008]). At this point, an individual's status has shifted from that of a criminal suspect to that of a criminally accused. As the Supreme Court observed in *Moran v. Burbine*, the Sixth Amendment's "intended function is not to wrap a protective cloak around the attorney–client relationship for its own sake. . . . [By] its very terms, [the Sixth Amendment] becomes applicable only when the government's role shifts from investigation to accusation. . . . [I]t is only then that the assistance of one versed in the intricacies of law is needed to assure the prosecution's case encounters the 'crucible of meaningful adversarial testing'" (*Moran v. Burbine*, 475 U.S. 412, 430 [1986]).

The philosophy underlying the Sixth Amendment protection from involuntary interrogation is that individuals against whom criminal proceedings have been initiated are entitled to have their guilt or innocence determined in a court of law before a judge and jury and that this process should not be short-circuited by permitting the police to elicit incriminating information from an individual in the absence of his or her lawyer.

Massiah v. United States provided the foundation for the development of the Sixth Amendment right to counsel. Winston Massiah was indicted for federal narcotics violations, retained a lawyer, pled guilty, and was released on bail. Massiah's co-defendant, Jesse Colson, agreed to cooperate with the government and engaged Massiah in a conversation in Colson's car, which was equipped with a radio transmitter. A government agent overheard Massiah make several incriminating remarks. The Supreme Court ruled that although Massiah had made a voluntary admission, his statement was obtained in violation of Massiah's Sixth Amendment right to counsel. Justice Stewart explained that at a time when Massiah was entitled to have his guilt adjudicated in a courtroom presided over by a judge, Massiah had been subjected to police-orchestrated extrajudicial interrogation in the absence of counsel. This denied Massiah a range of rights, including the opportunity to cross-examine the witnesses against him. In summary, Massiah had been denied his right to counsel "where there was used against him at his trial evidence of his own incriminating words, which federal agents had deliberately elicited from him after he had been indicted and in the absence of counsel" (*Massiah v. United States*, 377 U.S. 201, 204 [1964]).

The Supreme Court did not return to the **Sixth Amendment protection against the deliberate eliciting of a confession** until *Brewer v. Williams* in 1977. Robert Williams had been arraigned for the murder of a 10-year-old child and was being transported to Des Moines, Iowa. The deeply religious, former mental patient confessed after one of the officers gave an emotional speech on the importance of providing the young woman with a "Christian burial." The Supreme Court concluded that Detective Cletus Leaming "deliberately and designedly set out to elicit information from Williams just as surely as and perhaps more effectively than if he had formally interrogated him." Detective Leaming was fully aware that Williams was represented by an attorney, and the Supreme Court stressed that in such circumstances, a heavy burden rests on the government to establish that Williams intentionally relinquished or abandoned his Sixth Amendment right to counsel. The Supreme Court concluded that Williams's Sixth Amendment rights had been violated and held that his confession had been improperly admitted into evidence. *Brewer* is important for extending the Sixth Amendment and Fourteenth Amendment right to a lawyer by holding that a person is "entitled to the help of a lawyer at or after the time that judicial proceedings have been initiated against him—'whether by way of formal charge, preliminary hearing, indictment, information or arraignment'" (*Brewer v. Williams*, 430 U.S. 398 [1977]).

The main importance of the Sixth Amendment is in providing defendants protection against interrogation by government informants. In 1980, in *United States v. Henry*, the Supreme Court held that the Sixth Amendment provided protections to prison inmates facing trial against unknowing interrogations by undercover government agents. The Court held that the government had contravened Henry's Sixth Amendment right when the FBI instructed Nichols, a paid government informant, to gather information on Henry's involvement in a bank robbery. Nichols was directed to engage Henry in discussions but not to directly question Henry about the crime. The Supreme Court nevertheless concluded that the informant was not a passive listener. He had engaged Henry in conversation and succeeded in eliciting a confession. Justice Warren Burger noted that even if the government officials did not intend for the informant to take active steps to obtain a confession, the government must have anticipated that it had created a situation that was likely to "induce Henry to make incriminating statements without the assistance of counsel." Consider how the decision in *Henry* differs from the U.S. Supreme Court decision in the *Miranda* case of *Illinois v. Perkins* (*United States v. Henry*, 447 U.S. 264, 272–273 [1980]).

Six years later, in *Kuhlmann v. Wilson*, the Supreme Court seemingly reversed course and ruled that the government did not violate Wilson's Sixth Amendment rights. An informant was instructed not to ask questions concerning Wilson's pending murder and robbery prosecution and was advised to "keep his ears open" and to pay attention to any unsolicited admissions of guilt. The informant reportedly listened to Wilson's spontaneous statements of guilt and testified against Wilson at trial. The Supreme Court stressed that the Sixth Amendment is not violated when the government through "luck or happenstance" obtains incriminating statements from the accused after the right to counsel has attached. The defendant must demonstrate that the police and the informant did not merely listen but took some action that was "designed deliberately to elicit incriminating remarks" (*Kuhlmann v. Wilson*, 477 U.S. 436, 459 [1986]).

In summary, the Sixth Amendment right to counsel applies under certain conditions:

- *Judicial proceedings.* The Sixth Amendment applies to both federal and state government agents at or after the time that judicial proceedings have been initiated against an accused—whether by way of formal charge, preliminary hearing, indictment, information, or arraignment.
- *Deliberately elicited.* The government may not intentionally elicit information. This prohibits the use of informants to directly interrogate suspects as well as the creation of a situation likely to induce a defendant to make incriminating statements concerning a pending charge without the assistance of counsel.
- *Waiver.* The police may initiate contact with an individual whose Sixth Amendment right to counsel has attached following a preliminary hearing, and the individual is free to talk to the police. The suspect must voluntarily, knowingly, and intelligently relinquish his or her right to counsel prior to his or her interrogation.

You likely are fairly confused at this point. The important point is that once proceedings have been initiated against a suspect and the suspect has requested or retained a lawyer, the police are prohibited from interrogating the suspect outside the presence of a lawyer. This is intended to ensure that innocence or guilt is established at trial rather than through police questioning. Now that you understand the Sixth Amendment right to counsel, you might ask yourself why we need this protection. Why is *Miranda* not sufficient?

Legal Equation

Sixth Amendment right to counsel at interrogation	=	The Sixth Amendment applies at the time that judicial proceedings have been initiated against an accused—whether by way of formal charge, preliminary hearing, indictment, information, or arraignment
	+	The accused must have requested or arranged for legal representation
	+	The government may not deliberately elicit information absent a waiver
	+	The suspect must voluntarily, knowingly, and intelligently relinquish his or her right to an attorney.

■ CASE ANALYSIS

In *Moran v. Burbine*, the U.S. Supreme Court decided whether the police under *Miranda* were required to inform a suspect that a lawyer informed the police that he or she was available to assist the defendant.

Moran v. Burbine, 475 U.S. 412 (1986), O'Connor, J.

On the morning of March 3, 1977, Mary Jo Hickey was found unconscious in a factory parking lot in Providence, Rhode Island. Suffering from injuries to her skull apparently inflicted by a metal pipe found at the scene, she was rushed to a nearby hospital. Three weeks later, she died from her wounds.

Several months after her death, the Cranston, Rhode Island, police arrested respondent and two others in connection with a local burglary. Shortly before the arrest, Detective Ferranti of the Cranston police force had learned from a confidential informant that the man responsible for Ms. Hickey's death lived at a certain address and went by the name of "Butch." Upon discovering that respondent lived at that address and was known by that name, Detective Ferranti informed respondent of his *Miranda* rights. When respondent refused to execute a written waiver, Detective Ferranti spoke separately with the two other suspects arrested on the breaking and entering charge and obtained statements further implicating respondent in Ms. Hickey's murder. At approximately 6 P.M., Detective Ferranti telephoned the police in Providence to convey the information he had uncovered. An hour later, three officers from that department arrived at the Cranston headquarters for the purpose of questioning respondent about the murder.

That same evening, at about 7:45 P.M., respondent's sister telephoned the public defender's office to obtain legal assistance for her brother. Her sole concern was the breaking and entering charge, as she was unaware that respondent was then under suspicion for murder. She asked for Richard Casparian, who had been scheduled to meet with respondent earlier that afternoon to discuss another charge unrelated to either the break-in or the murder. As soon as the conversation ended, the attorney who took the call attempted to reach Mr. Casparian. When those efforts were unsuccessful, she telephoned Allegra Munson, another assistant public defender, and told her about respondent's arrest and his sister's subsequent request that the office represent him.

At 8:15 P.M., Ms. Munson telephoned the Cranston police station and asked that her call be transferred to the detective division. A male voice responded with the word "Detectives." Ms. Munson identified herself and asked if Brian Burbine was being held; the person responded affirmatively. Ms. Munson explained to the person that Burbine was represented by attorney Casparian who was not available; she further stated that she would act as Burbine's legal counsel in the event that the police intended to place him in a lineup or question him. The unidentified person told Ms. Munson that the police would not be questioning Burbine or putting him in a lineup and that they were through with him for the night. Ms. Munson was not informed that the Providence police were at the Cranston police station or that Burbine was a suspect in Mary's murder. At all relevant times, respondent was unaware of his sister's efforts to retain counsel and of the fact and contents of Ms. Munson's telephone conversation.

Less than an hour later, the police brought respondent to an interrogation room and conducted the first of a series of interviews concerning the murder. Prior to each session, respondent was informed of his *Miranda* rights, and on three separate occasions, he signed a written form acknowledging that he understood his right to the presence of an attorney and explicitly indicating that he "[did] not want an attorney called or appointed for [him]" before he gave a statement. Uncontradicted evidence at the suppression hearing indicated that at least twice during the course of the evening, respondent was left in a room where he had access to a telephone, which he apparently declined to use. Eventually, respondent signed three written statements fully admitting to the murder.

Prior to trial, respondent moved to suppress the statements. The court denied the motion, finding that respondent had received the *Miranda* warnings and had "knowingly, intelligently, and voluntarily waived his privilege against self-incrimination [and] his right to counsel." The jury found respondent guilty of murder in the first degree, and he appealed to the Supreme Court of Rhode Island. A divided court rejected his contention that the Fifth and Fourteenth Amendments to the Constitution required the suppression of the inculpatory statements and affirmed the conviction.

The record amply supports the state-court findings that the police administered the required warnings, sought to assure that respondent understood his rights, and obtained an express written waiver prior to eliciting each of the three statements. Nor does respondent contest the Rhode Island courts' determination that he at no point requested the presence of a lawyer. He contends instead that the confessions must be suppressed because the police's failure to inform him of the attorney's telephone call deprived him of information essential to his ability to knowingly waive his Fifth Amendment rights. In the alternative, he suggests that to fully protect the Fifth Amendment values served by *Miranda*, we should extend that decision to condemn the conduct of the Providence police. . . .

The purpose of the *Miranda* warnings . . . is to dissipate the compulsion inherent in custodial interrogation and, in so doing, guard against abridgment of the suspect's Fifth Amendment rights. Clearly, a rule that focuses on how the police treat an attorney—conduct that has no relevance at all to the degree of compulsion experienced by the defendant during interrogation— would ignore both *Miranda*'s mission and its only source of legitimacy.

Nor are we prepared to adopt a rule requiring that the police inform a suspect of an attorney's efforts to reach him. While such a rule might add marginally to *Miranda*'s goal of dispelling the compulsion inherent in custodial interrogation, overriding practical considerations counsel against its adoption. As we have stressed on numerous occasions, "[one] of the principal advantages" of *Miranda* is the ease and clarity of its application. . . .

We have little doubt that the approach urged by respondent . . . would have the inevitable consequence of muddying *Miranda*'s otherwise relatively clear waters. The legal questions it would spawn are legion: To what extent should the police be held accountable for knowing that the accused has counsel? Is it enough that someone in the station house knows, or must the interrogating officer himself know of counsel's efforts to contact the suspect? Do counsel's efforts to talk to the suspect concerning one criminal investigation trigger the obligation to inform the defendant before interrogation may proceed on a wholly separate matter? . . .

The position urged by respondent would upset this carefully drawn approach in a manner that is both unnecessary for the protection of the Fifth Amendment privilege and injurious to legitimate law enforcement. Because, as *Miranda* holds, full comprehension of the rights to remain silent and request an attorney are sufficient to dispel whatever coercion is inherent in the interrogation process, a rule requiring the police to inform the suspect of an attorney's efforts to contact him would contribute to the protection of the Fifth Amendment privilege only incidentally, if at all. This minimal benefit, however, would come at a substantial cost to society's legitimate and substantial interest in securing admissions of guilt. Indeed, the very premise of the court of appeals was not that awareness of Ms. Munson's phone call would have dissipated the coercion of the interrogation room, but that it might have convinced respondent not to speak at all. Because neither the letter nor purposes of *Miranda* require this additional handicap on otherwise permissible investigatory efforts, we are unwilling to expand the *Miranda* rules to require the police to keep the suspect abreast of the status of his legal representation. . . .

CHAPTER SUMMARY

Confessions are essential in the investigation and detection of crime. The procedural standards governing confessions are based on the following:

- *Due Process Clause* of the Fourteenth Amendment
- *Fifth Amendment* right against self-incrimination
- *Sixth Amendment* right to counsel

The three constitutional approaches to confessions are summarized below:

Due process. The due process voluntariness test requires that a confession be the result of a free and voluntary choice and not be the product of compulsion. Courts decide whether a confession is voluntary by analyzing the totality of the circumstances. This test is criticized for failing to provide law enforcement officials with clear standards to guide their decisions and is difficult for courts to apply.

Miranda. The Fifth Amendment provided the basis for *Miranda v. Arizona* (1966). *Miranda* established that individuals subjected to custodial interrogation are to be informed that anything they say may be used against them and that they have the right to silence and the right to an attorney, appointed or retained. The *Miranda* warning is intended to provide individuals with the necessary information to resist the inherent pressures of custodial interrogation. There are a number of central components of the *Miranda* rule.

Custodial interrogation. Miranda is triggered by *custodial interrogation.* This is the *threshold determination* and occurs when there is a custodial arrest or the functional equivalent of a custodial arrest. In determining whether there is the functional equivalent of custodial interrogation, judges ask whether a reasonable person, based on the totality of the circumstances, would believe that the individual is in police custody to a degree associated with a formal arrest. Courts typically ask whether a reasonable person would feel free to leave. In *J.D.B. v. North Carolina*, the Supreme Court held that a juvenile's age should be considered in determining whether he or she was subjected to custodial interrogation.

Public safety. In *New York v. Quarles*, the U.S. Supreme Court recognized a *public safety exception* to *Miranda*. This exception permits the police to ask questions reasonably prompted by a reasonable concern with public safety without first advising a suspect of his or her *Miranda* rights. The Supreme Court concluded that a reasonable concern with the safety of the police or the public outweighs the interest in protecting the suspect's right against self-incrimination.

Miranda warning. The *three-part Miranda warning* is essential for informing suspects of their rights and of the consequences of waiving their rights. The *Miranda* judgment states that the warnings are to be recited in "clear and unequivocal terms" and that a suspect is to be "clearly informed" of his or her rights. The Supreme Court has provided broad guidance to the police on how to recite the *Miranda* rights. *Miranda* is a flexible formula. The test is whether the warnings viewed in their totality convey the essential information to the suspect.

Invocation of rights. Following the reading of the *Miranda* rights, a defendant has the opportunity to *assert his or her right to a lawyer or right to silence or to waive these rights.* In *Davis v. United States* (1994), the Supreme Court held that an individual is required to "articulate his desire to have counsel present . . . sufficiently clearly that a reasonable police officer in the circumstances would understand the statement to be a request for an attorney." The Court reasoned that a rule that required the police to cease questioning following an ambiguous statement by the accused would transform *Miranda* into a "wholly irrational obstacle to interrogations." In *Berghuis v. Thompkins*, the Supreme Court held that a defendant is required to invoke the right to silence in an unambiguous fashion.

Voluntary waiver. The Supreme Court stressed in *Miranda* that the government is required to meet a "heavy burden" in demonstrating that a suspect voluntarily, knowingly, and intelligently waived his or her rights. The *Miranda* decision noted that any evidence that an accused was threatened, tricked, or cajoled into a waiver is sufficient to demonstrate that a suspect did not *voluntarily waive* his or her rights. A waiver also will not be upheld if obtained under coercive circumstances such as a lengthy interrogation or a lengthy incarceration prior to a confession.

Knowing and intelligent waiver. We have seen that an individual must understand the *Miranda* rights as well as the consequences of waiving them. *Tague v. Louisiana* held that a police officer may not automatically conclude that an individual *knowingly and intelligently* waived his or her rights. What factors are relevant in determining whether a waiver of *Miranda* is knowing and intelligent? In *Fare v. Michael C.*, the Supreme Court indicated that the question whether a waiver is knowing and intelligent is determined on a case-by-case basis by the totality of the circumstances. In *Fare*, this analysis considered the "juvenile's age, experience, education, background, and intelligence and whether he has the capacity to understand the warnings given him . . . and the consequences of waiving those rights." Courts also will examine whether the defendant acted in a calm and rational fashion or in an emotional and incoherent manner. The Supreme Court stressed that the Constitution does not require that an individual should be informed of all the information that might prove useful in arriving at a decision whether to waive his or her rights, such as the strength of the prosecution's case.

Express and implied waiver. A waiver, as we have seen, must be voluntary, knowing, and intelligent. *Miranda* indicated that an "express statement that the individual is willing to make a statement and does not want an attorney followed closely by a statement could constitute a waiver." A waiver will not be presumed from an accused's silence. The Supreme Court has recognized implied as well as explicit waivers and ruled that "in some cases, a waiver can be clearly inferred from the actions and words of the person interrogated." In these instances, the prosecution is required to establish that although there was no affirmative waiver, the suspect engaged in a "'course of conduct indicating waiver.'"

Question first and warn later. The U.S. Supreme Court was next asked to address whether a waiver is valid that is obtained through a *question first and warn later* tactic. In *Missouri v. Seibert*, the Supreme Court stated that the issue when the police question first and warn later is whether "it would be reasonable to find that in these circumstances the warnings could function 'effectively' to advise the suspect that he or she had a real choice about giving an admissible statement." In other words, when a suspect is warned that "anything you say may be used against you," will he or she understand that despite the initial confession, he or she need not speak to the police? The Supreme Court suggested in a footnote that this might require that the police inform a suspect that the first confession is inadmissible in evidence.

Interrogation following invocation of the Miranda *rights.* Once individuals invoke their *Miranda* rights, the Supreme Court has recognized that they still may be subjected to interrogations. The Court ruled that the admissibility of statements obtained after a person in custody had decided to remain silent depends on whether his or her right to silence had been *scrupulously honored.* The Court, in *Edwards v. Arizona,* established a separate *initiation test* for determining whether a defendant who invokes his or her right to an attorney may be once again interrogated. Initiation does not require a direct waiver of an individual's right to a lawyer. *Maryland v. Shatzer* limited *Edwards* by permitting the interrogation of a suspect who has invoked his or her right to counsel after having been released from custody for fourteen days. In *Oregon v. Bradshaw,* the Supreme Court held that the initiation standard is satisfied by a generalized discussion regarding the criminal investigation.

Interrogation. In *Rhode Island v. Innis,* the Supreme Court defined *interrogation.* The Court explained that interrogation entails *express questioning* or the *functional equivalent of direct questioning.* The test for the functional equivalent of direct questioning is whether the police should know that their words or actions are likely to elicit an incriminating statement from a suspect.

Sixth Amendment. In 1966, in *Massiah v. United States,* the U.S. Supreme Court proclaimed that following the initiation of criminal proceedings, individuals enjoy a *Sixth Amendment right to counsel* that protects them from the government's deliberately eliciting incriminating statements. The Sixth Amendment was not again applied to protect individuals from interrogation in the pretrial phase of the criminal justice process until 1977 when the Supreme Court applied the Sixth Amendment in *Brewer v. Williams. Brewer* was followed by a number of decisions that further defined the Sixth Amendment right to counsel.

As noted above, the Sixth Amendment provides protections to individuals *confronting formal criminal proceedings.* At this point, an individual's status has shifted from that of a criminal suspect to a criminally accused. The philosophy underlying the Sixth Amendment protection is that an individual against whom criminal proceedings have been initiated is entitled to have his or her guilt or innocence determined in a court of law before a judge and jury and that this process should not be short-circuited by permitting the police to elicit incriminating information from a defendant in the absence of his or her attorney or a waiver of the defendant's Sixth Amendment right.

In reviewing this chapter, be certain that you understand the three constitutional approaches to interrogations and the points in the criminal justice process in which each applies:

- *Fourteenth Amendment due process voluntariness test* prohibits involuntary confessions and applies at all stages of the criminal justice process. You always have this protection.

- *Fifth Amendment* Miranda *rights* provide protections during custodial interrogation. You only have this protection during custodial interrogation.

- *Sixth Amendment right to counsel* applies after the initiation of formal proceedings against an accused following a request or hiring of a lawyer. You have this protection once your status shifts from criminal suspect to criminal defendant.

CHAPTER REVIEW QUESTIONS

1. Why are confessions important tools in criminal investigation?

2. What are some of the dangers of relying on confessions to obtain criminal convictions?

3. Can you identify some of the reasons that suspects make false confessions?

4. Write a one-page response to the following quote. Supreme Court Justice Felix Frankfurter famously remarked, in regard to the due process test, that it is "impossible . . . to . . . precisely . . . delimit the power of interrogation allowed to state law enforcement officers in obtaining confessions. No single litmus-paper test . . . has . . . evolved" (*Culombe v. Connecticut,* 367 U.S. 568, 601–602 [1961]).

5. Summarize the holding in *Escobedo v. Illinois.* How did this set the stage for the Supreme Court's decision in *Miranda v. Arizona?*

6. Why was the right against self-incrimination included in the U.S. Constitution? Distinguish between testimonial and nontestimonial evidence.

7. What is the holding of the U.S. Supreme Court in *Miranda v. Arizona?* Explain how this decision is intended to counter the pressures inherent in incommunicado interrogation.

8. What is the test for custodial interrogation? Discuss the public safety exception.

9. How should the *Miranda* rights be read to a suspect?

10. Give an example of a statement that satisfies the legal test for invoking the right to a lawyer under *Miranda.* Provide an example of a statement that would not satisfy the standard for invoking the right to a lawyer under *Miranda.*

11. Distinguish between a voluntary and an involuntary waiver. What factors does a court consider in determining whether a waiver is knowing and intelligent? What is the difference between an express and an implied waiver?

12. Why is it important whether an individual is considered to be subject to custodial interrogation? List the factors that a court evaluates in determining whether a suspect is subjected to custodial interrogation.

13. What is the legal test for determining whether the police can interrogate a suspect who has invoked his or her right to silence? What is the legal test for determining whether the police can interrogate a suspect who has invoked his or her right to a lawyer?

14. What is the legal test determining whether an individual has initiated contact with the police?

15. Define *interrogation* as articulated by the U.S. Supreme Court. Distinguish between direct questioning and the functional equivalent of direct questioning. Why would it be helpful for the police to understand the concept of interrogation under *Miranda*?

16. How does the Sixth Amendment right to counsel protect individuals from interrogation by the police?

17. Does *Miranda* handcuff the ability of the police to rely on confessions, or does it favor the police?

18. Write a brief essay illustrating how the U.S. Supreme Court's decisions on police interrogation have balanced the interests of the suspect and the interests of society.

LEGAL TERMINOLOGY

break in the custody rule

confessions

custodial interrogation

express questioning

express waiver

false confession

Fourteenth Amendment due process
voluntariness test

functional equivalent of express questioning

implied waiver

incommunicado interrogation

initiation

interrogation

involuntary confessions

Miranda warnings

nontestimonial evidence

public safety exception

question first and warn later

scrupulously honor

Sixth Amendment protection against the
deliberate eliciting of a confession

Star Chamber

statements

voluntary, knowing, and intelligent waiver

REFERENCES

Drizen, Steven A., and Richard A. Leo. 2004. "The Problem of False Confessions in the Post-DNA World." *North Carolina Law Review* 82: 891–1007.

Inbau, Fred E. 1961. "Police Interrogation: A Practical Necessity." *Journal of Criminal Law, Criminology & Police Science* 1: 16–19.

Levy, Leonard W. 1968. *The Origins of the Fifth Amendment*. New York: Oxford University Press.

CHAPTER 17

EYEWITNESS IDENTIFICATIONS

Was the police officer's identification of the suspect reliable?

Jimmy D. Glover drove to headquarters where he described the [narcotics] seller to [Officers] D'Onofrio and Gaffey. Glover at that time did not know the identity of the seller. He described him as being "a colored man, approximately five feet eleven inches tall, dark complexion, black hair, short Afro style, and having high cheekbones, and of heavy build. He was wearing at the time blue pants and a plaid shirt." D'Onofrio, suspecting from this description that respondent might be the seller, obtained a photograph of respondent from the Records Division of the Hartford Police Department. He left it at Glover's office. D'Onofrio was not acquainted with respondent personally but did know him by sight and had seen him "[s]everal times." Glover, when alone, viewed the photograph for the first time upon his return to headquarters on May 7; he identified the person shown as the one from whom he had purchased the narcotics. (*Manson v. Brathwaite*, 432 U.S. 98 [1977])

CHAPTER OUTLINE

Introduction
The Psychology of Identifications
The Sixth Amendment and Eyewitness Identifications
The Sixth Amendment and Critical Stages of Criminal Prosecution
The Sixth Amendment and Prearraignment Identifications
The Sixth Amendment and Photographic Displays
The Due Process Test

Suggestiveness, Reliability, and the Totality of the
    Circumstances
The Requirement of Police Involvement
Case Analysis
Chapter Summary
Chapter Review Questions
Legal Terminology

TEST YOUR KNOWLEDGE

1. Do you know the three stages of eyewitness identification and the threats to the accuracy of eyewitness identification at each stage?

2. Can you explain the *Wade-Gilbert* rule?

3. Are you able to describe the difference between the right to counsel at pre-indictment lineups and the right to counsel at post-indictment lineups?

4. Do you know whether individuals have the right to counsel for photographic displays?

5. Can you describe the due process test for identifications?

6. Do you understand the significance of police involvement in suggestive identifications?

■ INTRODUCTION

You are confronted by a gun-waving assailant wearing a baseball hat in the early evening. She demands your wallet, and when you hesitate, she threatens you with a knife. You nervously hand over your wallet and, still shaking, call the police. The officer asks you to describe the robber. Would you be able to provide an accurate description of her height, weight, face structure, and voice? As you read this, you likely are already forming a vision of the robber in your mind.

The police move quickly to solve the crime and, the next day, arrange for you to view an individual whom they have arrested for another armed robbery on the same day. The police want to determine whether this is the person who robbed you. They likely will make use of one of three forms of **eyewitness identification**:

1. *Lineups.* Victims or eyewitnesses view a group of individuals, typically six in number. They then are asked to identify the perpetrator from this "six pack." **Fillers**, **foils**, or **distractors** are people innocent of the particular offense who are recruited by the police to participate in the lineup. The police ask the victim or eyewitness, "Did any of these individuals commit the crime?"

2. *Showups.* The police may stage a **confrontation** between the victim or eyewitness and a single suspect. The police ask the victim or eyewitness, "Is this the man or woman who committed the crime?"

3. *Photographic identifications.* The victim or eyewitness is asked to determine whether the perpetrator is pictured in any of the photographs. In most cases, the photo array is composed of at least six photographs that are similar in size and shape. The police ask the victim or eyewitness, "Is the individual who committed the crime pictured in any of the photos?"

These various types of identifications serve several functions in the criminal investigative process:

- *Identification.* Identifications may narrow the range of individuals under investigation.
- *Exoneration.* Identifications may eliminate suspects from the investigation.
- *Criminal charge.* Identifications may lead to charging an individual with a crime.
- *Confidence in indictment and conviction.* Identifications supplement the other evidence at trial and increase confidence that the defendant was properly indicted, prosecuted, and convicted.

Returning to our armed robbery case, your eyewitness identification of the perpetrator may lead to her being charged with a felony. At trial, when you take the stand, you likely will be asked whether you identified an individual as the robber at a lineup or showup or in a photographic identification. Your positive response will support the credibility of your **in-court identification** when you testify that the individual whom you earlier identified as the robber is the defendant sitting at the defense table. There is little doubt that your testimony will have a powerful influence on the jury when they consider the defendant's guilt or innocence.

In this chapter, we will see that the U.S. Supreme Court has held that identification procedures must comply with the Sixth Amendment and with the Fifth and Fourteenth Amendments to the U.S. Constitution. These constitutional standards are intended to ensure fair procedures that will prevent innocent individuals from being misidentified as the perpetrators of a crime.

Sixth Amendment. The Sixth Amendment provides, in part, that "[i]n all criminal prosecutions, the accused shall . . . have the assistance of counsel for his defense." The U.S. Supreme Court has held that an individual has the right to an attorney during lineups and showups that are conducted following the initiation of adversary criminal proceedings (whether by way of formal charge, preliminary hearing, indictment, information, or arraignment). There is no right to an attorney for photographic identifications. The defendant may file a motion to exclude the lineup identification from trial by demonstrating that the "government denied my right to an attorney."

Due process. Both the Fifth and Fourteenth Amendments provide that an individual shall not be "deprived of life, liberty, or property without due process of law." Due process entitles individuals to reliable identification procedures prior to the initiation of criminal proceedings and throughout the criminal justice process. The results of identifications that run the risk of misidentifying innocent individuals are to be excluded from evidence at trial. The defendant has the burden of demonstrating that "yes, I was identified, but the procedure was so unfair that there is a substantial likelihood that I might have been misidentified." The prosecution may respond by establishing that the results of the identification are reliable or accurate.

You may recall from our discussion of interrogations in Chapter Sixteen that identification procedures do not violate the right against self-incrimination and that a suspect does not possess a Fifth Amendment right to refuse to participate. The Fifth Amendment protects individuals against being required to disclose information or what is termed *testimonial evidence*. This, as we have seen, involves words that communicate guilt. Identification procedures entail the display of an individual's physical characteristics, and scientific tests require the taking of physical material from the human body. The government may obtain a court order to compel a suspect's participation, and a refusal to cooperate may result in an individual's being held in contempt of court. A failure to participate also may be used as evidence of guilt at trial. In other words, you can be required to appear in a police lineup, to submit to a photograph, or to give a voice exemplar, fingerprint, or handwriting sample.

In this chapter, we first briefly explore the *three stages of eyewitness identification* and the threats to the accuracy of identifications. These three stages are as follows:

1. *Perception.* You view the crime.

2. *Memory.* You remember what happened.

3. *Identification.* You recall what happened and identify the perpetrator.

As you read this material, ask yourself whether we can completely eliminate the possibility of error or misidentifications. You also should consider whether this is "much ado about nothing." How important are eyewitness identifications in the determination of guilt and innocence? Following our overview of the psychology of

PHOTO 17.1

Eyewitnesses may be asked to identify the perpetrator from a physical lineup.

Rich Legg/Getty Images

identifications, we will outline some suggested procedures to ensure accurate identifications. The bulk of the chapter discusses the two constitutional tests for identifications:

- *Sixth Amendment* right to counsel
- *Fifth and Fourteenth Amendment* protection of due process of law

As you read this chapter, pay particular attention to the balance that is struck by the U.S. Supreme Court between the right of the individual to be protected against suggestive identification procedures and the societal interest in investigating crime and in identifying the perpetrators of crime. We certainly want to prosecute and to convict criminals. At the same time, these procedures must be viewed as fair and should not be so biased that we run the risk that innocent individuals will be prosecuted or convicted.

■ THE PSYCHOLOGY OF IDENTIFICATIONS

Witness identifications are a complex process with the possibility for misidentification of the perpetrator and wrongful convictions.

Perception

It may surprise you to learn that misidentification is the primary cause of false convictions. In other words, even under the best of conditions, there is the possibility that your faulty memory will lead you to select an innocent individual as your attacker. As early as 1932, Edwin Borchard studied sixty-five cases of wrongful convictions and found that twenty-nine of the individuals were convicted as a result of faulty eyewitness identifications. In eight of these cases, the wrongfully convicted person and the guilty criminal "bore not the slightest resemblance to each other," while in twelve other instances, the "resemblance, while fair, was still not at all close. In only two cases can the resemblance be called striking." In 1996, a National Institute of Justice study of twenty-eight wrongfully convicted individuals concluded that in the majority of the cases, the most "compelling evidence" was eyewitness testimony, which clearly was "wrong." In 2005, a study of 340 incarcerated individuals who later were exonerated determined that the "most common cause" of wrongful convictions is eyewitness misidentification. At least one misidentification was involved in 64 percent of the false convictions and in 90 percent of the false convictions for rape.

Why does the identification of the perpetrator of a crime involve such a high degree of error? Psychologists previously thought that our minds were like video cameras that recorded every experience. We now are more sophisticated and realize that most crime victims are frightened and overwhelmed and are unable to accurately observe or recount the offender's age, dress, weight, height, facial features, voice, and other distinguishing characteristics. Psychologists identify three sets of factors that explain misidentifications:

Crime factors. Your ability to perceive what occurred may be limited when the crime is committed relatively quickly. The victim may explain to the police that "it happened so rapidly that I did not even know what hit me."

Victim factors. You may be too nervous to focus on the perpetrator or may find that you primarily concentrate on the weapon or on the offender's hat, clothes, shoes, voice, or physical build and overlook other factors. There also is a tendency to perceive "what we expect to see." Our biases, prejudices, and fears may lead us to identify a perpetrator as a member of a certain race, ethnic group, or religion. We simply are unaccustomed to paying close attention to the people we encounter. Individuals often are able to offer only a general description. We all have experienced the phenomenon of drawing a blank when asked to describe someone and have been able to recount only that he or she "was tall or short," "big and bulky," or "small and slim."

Offender factors. Studies indicate that people are unable to accurately identify the features of individuals of a different race. We all have heard victims report that an attacker was Asian, Latino, Caucasian, or African American and draw a blank concerning the perpetrator's features. This difficulty is compounded by a range of factors such as the facts that the perpetrator may hide his or her features under a hat, that the crime occurred at night, or that there are multiple offenders.

Memory

The second step is to store our *perception* in our *memory*. Memory is our personal diary of what happened. However, unlike a written diary, memories fade and change with the passage of time. We particularly want to forget painful events, and few of us can claim the capacity to remember the type of small details that may be crucial in a criminal case. Would you be able to recall an assailant's eye color, hair texture, and face style or shape? In addition, the power of suggestion can lead us to unconsciously change our memory. We know that witnesses who view an individual in a photo array are likely to select the same individual in a lineup because they are drawn to a "familiar face." In the case of Dale Brison, discussed in the National Institute of Justice study, a Pennsylvania court observed that the victim was unable to describe her assailant to the police and may have selected Brison "merely because she remembered seeing him in the neighborhood." Another example of the modification of memory through the power of suggestion occurred in 2003 during the pursuit of the "Beltway snipers," who were responsible for killing ten people in the Washington, D.C., area. The media reported that a white van was at the scene of one of the initial shootings. Witnesses to other shootings all subsequently reported that they had spotted a white van. The police were surprised to find that the two killers were arrested while driving a blue Chevrolet Caprice and had never driven a white van.

Identifications

Assuming that you overcome the challenges of perception and memory, the third step is *identification*, or retrieval. Identification, like perception and memory, involves threats to accuracy.

Selection. Identification is like a multiple-choice test. Victims and eyewitnesses first mentally compare one person to another. They then typically select the individual in the lineup or photo display who most closely resembles their memory of the perpetrator, even in those instances in which none of the individuals seems to fit the witnesses' memory of the perpetrator.

Suggestiveness. The police examiner conducting the lineup or photo array may unintentionally or intentionally influence a witness's identification. This may occur as a result of the examiner's tone of voice, nod of approval, or body language.

Closure. A victim may become tired and exhausted and identify an individual as the perpetrator in order to "move on with his or her life."

These factors combine to create a risk of misidentification. The Innocence Project at Cardozo Law School in New York analyzed eighty-two cases of misidentification. Forty-five percent involved a photo display, 37 percent a physical lineup, and 20 percent a one-person showup. Studies indicate that following an identification, a witness typically develops increasing confidence in his or her selection. This self-assurance, in turn, leads jurors to unquestioningly trust the accuracy of the victim's courtroom identification of the offender. We next outline several steps that might improve the accuracy of identifications.

The suggested procedures sketched in this section of the text are intended to strengthen the constitutional protections accorded to defendants during criminal identifications. We next examine these two constitutional safeguards:

- *Right to an attorney.* The Sixth Amendment right to an attorney at lineups and showups applies once adversary proceedings have been initiated against the accused.
- *Due process.* The Fifth and Fourteenth Amendments' due process guarantee of reliable procedures applies at every stage of the criminal process.

■ THE SIXTH AMENDMENT AND EYEWITNESS IDENTIFICATIONS

In 1967, the U.S. Supreme Court announced in *United States v. Wade* that the existing system in which suspects are unrepresented by a lawyer at lineups and showups violated the Sixth Amendment right to counsel (*United States v.*

Wade, 388 U.S. 218 [1967]). The holding in *Wade* was affirmed and clarified by the Supreme Court in another case decided on the same day (*Gilbert v. California*, 388 U.S. 263 [1967]]). The **Wade-Gilbert rule** provides as follows:

Right to a lawyer. A suspect has a constitutional right to a lawyer at all post-indictment lineups and confrontations.

Lineup results at trial. Absent the presence of a lawyer, or a suspect's waiver of a lawyer, at a post-indictment lineup or showup, the results may not be introduced by the prosecutor at trial.

In-court identification. A prosecutor may not ask a witness for an in-court identification of the defendant unless the prosecutor establishes by clear and convincing evidence that the in-court identification is not the product of an identification at which the suspect was denied a lawyer in violation of the Sixth Amendment.

In the next sections, we outline the *Wade* decision. The first step is to explore why the Supreme Court ruled that Wade had the right to a lawyer at his post-indictment identification.

■ THE SIXTH AMENDMENT AND CRITICAL STAGES OF CRIMINAL PROSECUTION

The U.S. Supreme Court held that Billy Joe Wade was entitled to the "guiding hand of counsel" at the lineup. The Supreme Court majority explained that the Sixth Amendment right to an attorney applies at **critical stages of a criminal proceeding**. *Critical stages* are those procedures following the initiation of criminal proceedings at which a failure to provide the defendant a lawyer may prevent him or her from obtaining a fair trial. The lineup according to the majority of the Court is a critical stage because the pretrial lineup may "well settle the accused's fate and reduce the trial itself to a mere formality" (*Wade*, 388 U.S. at 224).

Why is a lineup "critical"? We know that a victim or eyewitness who identifies an individual as the perpetrator in a lineup is likely to identify the same person as the offender when testifying at trial. These courtroom identifications tend to heavily influence jurors. A mistaken identification in a lineup or showup as a result may contribute to the conviction of an innocent individual. A lawyer at the lineup or showup provides a defendant with two levels of protection:

1. *Protection at the identification.* A lawyer's observation of a lineup provides an incentive for the police to ensure that the identification process is fair and reliable and is not suggestive.

2. *Protection at the trial.* The lawyer at trial is able to point out to the jury that the lineup was unfair and argue that the jury should question the accuracy of the identification.

In the next section, we examine some of the practices that the Supreme Court in *Wade* described as being used in lineups that made it important to provide suspects the protection of a lawyer.

Legal Equation

A lineup or showup is a critical stage of criminal prosecution	=	Critical stages are those procedures following the initiation of criminal proceedings at which a failure to provide the defendant a lawyer may prevent him or her from obtaining a fair trial
	+	The lineup is a critical stage because the pretrial lineup may "settle the accused's fate and reduce the trial itself to a mere formality."

The Threat of Suggestive Lineups

The Supreme Court in *Wade* pointed to "numerous instances of **suggestive procedures**" to illustrate why defendants require the assistance of an attorney at a pretrial lineup or showup. The Court observed that the police typically believe that they have arrested the perpetrator of the crime and often unintentionally or intentionally communicate this to the victim or eyewitnesses. The Court highlighted several common practices:

- Everyone in the lineup other than the suspect is known to the victim.
- The suspect is the only person in the lineup whose physical appearance and dress match the description of the perpetrator.
- The individuals in the lineup are asked to try on an item of clothing that fits only the suspect.
- The police point out the suspected perpetrator to the victim prior to the lineup.
- The victim is asked to identify whether an individual in a jail cell is the suspected perpetrator.

We next examine how the presence of defense lawyers can ensure fair and reliable identification procedures.

The Role of the Defense Attorney

Remember that the failure to provide a defendant with a lawyer at a lineup or showup during a critical stage results in the exclusion at trial of the results of the confrontation. Individuals should be informed of their right to the presence and advice of an attorney of their choice and that a lawyer will be appointed at no expense in the event that they cannot afford legal representation. A defendant may knowingly, voluntarily, and intelligently waive his or her right to a lawyer.

A lawyer's role is to observe the lineup and to take note of how the police conduct the lineup. The lawyer's presence provides an incentive for the police to ensure fair procedures. The U.S. Supreme Court explained that an attorney serves an important purpose because suspects are likely to be nervous and lack the training to detect improper influences and may be distracted by other individuals in the lineup and by the commotion and bright lights. There is disagreement among commentators, but most agree that the attorney should not object to or correct police procedures. The lawyer will have the opportunity to question the fairness and accuracy of the lineup on cross-examination at trial.

Law enforcement officers are required to notify the lawyer in advance of the lineup to ensure his or her presence. In the event that the lawyer is unavailable, the lineup should be postponed or a substitute attorney appointed, or the suspect should be asked whether he or she is willing to waive representation by a lawyer. The next section discusses the consequences of failing to provide legal representation to a defendant at a post-indictment lineup or showup.

Tainted Lineups and Courtroom Identifications

As you recall, the Supreme Court held in *Wade* and in *Gilbert* that a failure to provide a defendant with a lawyer results in the exclusion of the results of a post-indictment identification from trial. The Supreme Court explained that "[o]nly a per se [automatic] exclusionary rule" can ensure that law enforcement authorities will "respect the accused's constitutional right to the presence of his counsel at the critical lineup" (*Gilbert*, 388 U.S. at 272).

What is the impact of a failure to provide an attorney on courtroom identifications? In *Gilbert*, the Supreme Court held that a witness may still identify the offender where the prosecution establishes by clear and convincing evidence that the in-court identification is based on observations that are not derived from the lineup. The test to be applied is "[w]hether, granting establishment of the primary illegality, the evidence to which instant objection is made has been come at by exploitation of that illegality or instead by means sufficiently distinguishable to be purged of the primary taint." Application of this test requires the weighing and balancing of various factors. A judge is likely to permit a courtroom identification by a witness who had a clear view of the crime, whose description of the offender matched the individual he or she selected at the lineup, and for whom a short period elapsed between the identification and the crime. Several factors for judges to consider were identified in *Gilbert*:

- The witness's opportunity to observe the offender during the criminal act
- The extent of the similarity between the pre-lineup description of the offender and the physical appearance of the individual identified in the lineup
- The identification or failure to identify the defendant in a photographic array or at the lineup
- Whether there was a brief or lengthy period between the criminal act and the lineup identification

Inadmissibility of pretrial identification of suspect	=	Critical stage of the criminal process	+	A failure to provide a defendant with a lawyer

+ Per se inadmissibility of the identification by the prosecutor at trial.

Admissibility of in-court identification where an attorney was not provided at a lineup or showup	=	The prosecution should be provided with the opportunity to establish by clear and convincing evidence that the in-court identification is based on observations of the suspect that are independent of the lineup

+ The test to be applied is "[w]hether, granting establishment of the primary illegality, the evidence to which instant objection is made has been come at by exploitation of that illegality or instead by means sufficiently distinguishable to be purged of the primary taint"

+ Application of this test requires the weighing and balancing of various factors.

■ THE SIXTH AMENDMENT AND PREARRAIGNMENT IDENTIFICATIONS

In *Kirby v. Illinois*, the U.S. Supreme Court held that a **showup** following arrest but before the initiation of adversary criminal proceedings (whether by way of formal charge, preliminary hearing, indictment, information, or arraignment) is not a critical stage of criminal prosecution at which the suspect is entitled to counsel (*Kirby v. Illinois*, 406 U.S. 682 [1972]).

Willie Shard reported to the Chicago police that two men had robbed him of his wallet containing traveler's checks and a Social Security card. The next day, two officers stopped Thomas Kirby and Ralph Bean, and when asked for identification, the two men produced three traveler's checks, a Social Security card, and other documents bearing the name Willie Shard. Kirby and Bean were arrested and taken to the police station where Shard positively identified them as the robbers. Six weeks later, Kirby and Bean were indicted for the robbery of Willie Shard. Shard testified that he had identified the two men at the police station, and he then identified them in the courtroom. Both Kirby and Bean were convicted and appealed on the grounds that they had been denied a lawyer at the showup.

The U.S. Supreme Court held that the defendants were not entitled to legal representation at the showup following their arrest. The Court explained that the Sixth Amendment right to counsel attaches following the commencement of criminal proceedings, which is the "starting point of our whole system of adversary criminal justice." The Supreme Court offered two reasons for the right to a lawyer attaching following the initiation of criminal proceedings:

1. *Efficiency.* During the investigative stage, the police should not be required to slow their investigation and to delay lineups and showups until the defendant hires a lawyer.

2. *Prosecution.* The initiation of criminal proceedings by the filing of a formal charge indicates that the government has decided to prosecute the accused, and it is at this point that the accused is in need of legal protection, advice, and assistance.

Justices William Brennan, William O. Douglas, and John Marshall, dissenting from the majority, argued that suspects should receive the assistance of a lawyer at all stages of the criminal justice process. Five years following *Kirby*, in *Moore v. Illinois*, the Supreme Court once again confronted the question at what point a suspect should be entitled to the assistance of an attorney.

In *Moore*, the victim was raped at knifepoint in her bedroom. She was able to view James R. Moore's face for ten to fifteen seconds and provided the police with a description of the rapist along with a notebook that the assailant left behind. The police showed the victim two groups of photographs. She selected thirty suspects who resembled her attacker from the first group of two hundred photos. The victim then selected two or three individuals from a second group of ten photographs. Defendant Moore was among this group. The police also found a letter in the notebook left behind by the perpetrator written by a woman with whom Moore had been staying (*Moore v. Illinois*, 434 U.S. 220, 222 [1977]).

Six days following the sexual assault, Moore was arrested for the crime, and the next morning, he appeared at a preliminary hearing to determine whether he should be bound over to a grand jury. Moore appeared before the judge and was charged with rape and deviate sexual behavior. The victim was asked by the judge whether she saw her assailant in the courtroom, and she pointed at Moore.

The victim testified at trial that she had identified Moore as her assailant in the preliminary hearing. She then proceeded to identify the defendant in the courtroom as the man who had raped her. Moore was convicted of rape, deviate sexual behavior, burglary, and robbery.

The Supreme Court had little difficulty in holding that Moore's Sixth Amendment rights were violated by his identification without legal representation at the preliminary hearing. The Supreme Court observed that it was difficult to conceive of a more suggestive identification. The victim viewed her assailant for only ten to fifteen seconds and later was asked to make an identification "after she was told she was going to view the suspect, after she was told his name and heard it called as he was led before the bench, and after she heard the prosecutor recite the evidence believed to implicate the petitioner."

Why is the identification of Moore excluded from evidence while the identification of Kirby is admissible in evidence? An identification that is obtained prior to the initiation of a formal criminal prosecution (*Kirby*) is just as likely to influence the jury or to run the risk of misidentification as an identification that is obtained following the initiation of a formal criminal prosecution (*Moore*). On the other hand, providing a suspect an attorney prior to the initiation of criminal proceedings may prove burdensome to the police who require the flexibility and freedom to utilize lineups and confrontations as an investigative tool without being required to wait for the arrival of a lawyer. As noted in *Kirby*, the Court did not want to "import into a routine police investigation an absolute constitutional guarantee historically and rationally applicable only after the onset of formal prosecutorial proceedings." As we shall see later in this chapter, a defendant subjected to a suggestive confrontation prior to the initiation of adversary proceedings always has a remedy under the Due Process Clause of the U.S. Constitution.

In 1981, the California Supreme Court, in *People v. Bustamonte*, ruled that Article I, Section 15 of the California Constitution, which provides a defendant "the assistance of counsel," guarantees a lawyer at lineup. The California Supreme Court held that a pretrial lineup is a "critical stage in the prosecution of a criminal case." It is at this point that many innocent individuals are at risk of being swept up into the criminal justice system. The court characterized the rule in *Kirby* as "wholly unrealistic." The *Kirby* rule "removes the protective effects of counsel's presence precisely when the danger of convicting an innocent defendant upon a mistaken identification is greatest." The California Supreme Court observed that the police can circumvent *Wade* and *Gilbert* by simply delaying a formal indictment and then conducting a lineup at which a lawyer is not required. Extending the right to counsel to pre-indictment lineups may burden the police and delay lineups, but this is not a sufficiently significant obstacle to justify denying suspects the protection of a lawyer. See *People v. Bustamonte* (634 P.2d 927 [Cal. 1981]). Alaska, Pennsylvania, and several other states have endorsed the view of California that in "balancing the need for prompt investigation against a suspect's right to fair procedures . . . a suspect who is in custody is entitled to have counsel present at a pre-indictment lineup unless exigent circumstances exist so that providing counsel would unduly interfere with prompt and purposeful investigation." See *Blue v. State* (558 P.2d 636 [Alaska 1977]).

In the next section, we explore whether defendants have a Sixth Amendment right to a lawyer during a photographic identification.

Legal Equation

Preindictment lineups and right to an attorney	=	A showup or lineup after arrest but before the initiation of adversary criminal proceedings (whether by way of formal charge, preliminary hearing, indictment, information, or arraignment) is not a critical stage of criminal prosecution at which the accused is entitled to counsel.

■ THE SIXTH AMENDMENT AND PHOTOGRAPHIC DISPLAYS

In *United States v. Wade*, the U.S. Supreme Court held that an individual had no right to a lawyer to observe the taking of fingerprints, hair and blood samples, and other tests that relied on standard scientific techniques and procedures. The Court reasoned that the defense attorney and defense experts could easily examine the test results and procedures following the test and effectively cross-examine the police laboratory technicians at trial.

What about photographic identifications? **Photographic displays**, or **non-corporeal identifications**, pose a particular challenge. On one hand, the defense attorney typically is informed of the results of an identification and is able to examine the photographs to detect whether the suspect's photo was larger, more colorful, or distinguished in any fashion from the other photos. On the other hand, unless a lawyer is present, there is no way of knowing what occurred during the identification.

In 1973, in *United States v. Ash*, the U.S. Supreme Court held that a post-indictment photographic display is not a "critical stage" of the prosecution and that the Sixth Amendment does not entitle the accused to the presence of a lawyer (*United States v. Ash*, 413 U.S. 300 [1973]).

Almost three years after being arrested for armed robbery and two years following their indictment, Charles Ash and John Bailey were brought to trial. On the eve of the trial, the prosecutor used an array of five color photographs to confirm that the eyewitnesses would be able to make in-court identifications. Three of the four witnesses selected the picture of Ash. None of the witnesses selected the photo of Bailey.

At trial, the three eyewitnesses who were in the bank at the time of the robbery identified Ash as the gunman but cautioned that they were uncertain of their identifications. None of the eyewitnesses made an in-court identification of Bailey. The fourth eyewitness who had seen the robbers remove their masks made positive in-court identifications of both Ash and Bailey. Ash was convicted and sentenced to a prison term of between eighty months and twelve years. Bailey was acquitted.

Ash claimed that he had been denied the right to counsel at the photo display, which constituted a "critical stage" of the criminal process. How could Ash's lawyer effectively challenge the fairness of the photographic display on cross-examination when he did not observe the identification?

The U.S. Supreme Court held that there was much less need for a lawyer at a photographic display than at a lineup. A lawyer must be present at a lineup to observe any bias and suggestiveness and to effectively cross-examine the police at trial. In contrast, in a photographic display, the accused is not present and has no need for a lawyer's assistance. The defense attorney is able to guard against suggestiveness by inspecting the size and format of the photographs and then has the opportunity to point out any bias to the jury.

Justices Brennan, Douglas, and Marshall challenged the reasoning of the majority, noting that a defense lawyer's access to a photo display cannot capture gestures, facial expressions, inflections, or comments by the police that may have intentionally or unintentionally influenced a witness. The dissenters argued that a fair trial could be guaranteed only by providing for the right to a lawyer at both a **corporeal identification** and a non-corporeal photographic display.

Justice Brennan pointed out that the fact that a witness identified a suspect in a photographic display is as potentially harmful to a defendant at trial as the fact that a witness identified a suspect at a lineup. He observed that there is "something ironic about the court's conclusion today that a pretrial lineup identification is a 'critical stage' of the prosecution because counsel's presence can help to compensate for the accused's deficiencies as an observer, but that a pretrial photographic identification is not a 'critical stage' . . . because the accused is not able to observe it at all. [T]here simply is no meaningful difference . . . between corporeal and photographic identifications."

The Supreme Court's ruling in *Ash* that a lawyer is not required at photo arrays, according to some commentators, has led the police to rely on photographic identifications rather than physical lineups. Do you agree with the Supreme Court's conclusion that "[w]e are not persuaded that the risks inherent in the use of photographic displays are so pernicious that an extraordinary system of safeguards is required"?

The Pennsylvania Supreme Court and several other state courts have interpreted their constitution as requiring the presence of a lawyer during a post-arrest photo array. There is no requirement of a lawyer prior to an arrest (*Commonwealth v. Ferguson*, 475 A.2d 810 [Pa. Super. Ct. 1984]).

Photo display and Sixth Amendment right to counsel	=	The right to a lawyer historically is limited to a "trial-like adversary confrontation" in which a suspect is physically present and is being examined by governmental authorities
	+	These post-indictment confrontations are considered critical only when the presence of a lawyer is necessary to protect the defendant and to guarantee the defendant a fair trial
	+	In a photographic display, the accused is not present, and therefore, there is no need for the lawyer to assist him or her. The photographic array can be re-created by the defense attorney prior to trial.

■ THE DUE PROCESS TEST

We have seen that suspects involved in lineups and showups following the initiation of criminal proceedings are entitled to representation by a lawyer. The dissenting judges pointed out that this left suspects in lineups or showups conducted prior to the initiation of criminal proceedings and in photo displays with little protection against suggestive identification procedures.

On the same day that the Supreme Court decided *Wade* and *Gilbert,* the Court responded in *Stovall v. Denno* (388 U.S. 293 [1967]) to the concerns of the dissenting judges and held that suspects during the pre-indictment phase are protected by the Due Process Clauses of the Fifth and Fourteenth Amendments against identification procedures that create a likelihood that an innocent individual will be misidentified and deprived of life (the death penalty) or liberty (prison) without due process of law (unfairly).

The due process test applies throughout the criminal justice process. In other words, the due process test applies to lineups, showups, and photographic displays, whether pre-indictment or post-indictment. The next section examines the Fifth and Fourteenth Amendment due process test as explained in 1977 by the Supreme Court in *Manson v. Brathwaite* (432 U.S. 98 [1977]).

■ SUGGESTIVENESS, RELIABILITY, AND THE TOTALITY OF THE CIRCUMSTANCES

In *Manson*, introduced at the beginning of this chapter, Glover, a police undercover agent, and Henry Alton Brown, a police informant, went to an apartment in Hartford, Connecticut, to purchase narcotics from "Dickie Boy" Cicero. They knocked, and the door was opened twelve to eighteen inches. Glover observed a man and a woman, asked for "two things" of narcotics, and handed the man two $10 bills. The door closed, and when the door reopened, the man handed Glover two glassine bags. Glover stood within two feet of "the seller" and observed his face. Glover immediately drove to police headquarters where he described the seller to Officer D'Onofrio, who concluded that the description fit Nowell Brathwaite. D'Onofrio then obtained a photo of Brathwaite that he left for Glover. Two days following the sale, Glover identified the photo as the individual who sold him narcotics, and Brathwaite accordingly was arrested and, eight months later, was brought to trial for the possession and sale of heroin. Glover testified that there was no doubt that the photograph pictured the man whom he had seen at the apartment and proceeded to make an in-court identification of Brathwaite. The jury rejected Brathwaite's alibi defense and convicted him of two counts of selling an illegal narcotic (*Manson v. Brathwaite*, 432 U.S. 98, 101–103 [1977]).

Brathwaite argued that Glover's testimony regarding his identification of Brathwaite in the photograph should have been excluded from evidence on the grounds that the identification was so suggestive that it created an unreasonable risk that Glover would make a false identification and select Brathwaite as the individual who had sold him drugs. After all, why was Glover not given the pictures of various individuals from which to choose rather than a single photograph? There also was a significant possibility that Glover was influenced by D'Onofrio's conclusion that Glover's description fit Brathwaite.

The U.S. Supreme Court recognized that Brathwaite was correct in arguing that the single photo identification was so suggestive that it ran an unreasonable risk that Glover would select Brathwaite as the individual who sold him drugs. This procedure also was unnecessary because D'Onofrio easily could have compiled an array of several photographs. The Court nevertheless rejected Brathwaite's argument that testimony regarding the identification process should have been automatically excluded from evidence (per se exclusion). The adoption of such an inflexible rule inevitably would "frustrate" rather than "promote" justice. The fact that a procedure was suggestive did not mean that the identification was inaccurate and should be automatically excluded from evidence. The Supreme Court adopted a "totality-of-the-circumstances" test to the admission of identifications under the due process test. There are four steps involved in determining whether to admit identification evidence under this test.

First, the defendant must establish by a preponderance of the evidence (51 percent) that the procedure was suggestive:

- *Suggestive.* The defendant must establish that the identification was impermissibly suggestive by a preponderance of the evidence.

Second, the obligation shifts to the prosecution to demonstrate that the procedure nevertheless is reliable, meaning that the result can be trusted:

- *Reliable.* The prosecution must demonstrate that the identification is reliable, meaning that the identification can be trusted.

Reliability is the central question in determining whether an identification violates due process of law. Reliability is determined by a totality of the circumstances considering various factors relating to the witness's observation of the offender. Third, the judge examines the following six factors to determine the reliability of the identification:

- *Perception.* Opportunity to view the offender at the time of the crime.
- *Concentration.* Ability to focus on the offender's appearance.
- *Accuracy.* Accuracy of the description of the suspect following the crime.
- *Certainty.* Certainty in the identification of the defendant.
- *Time.* Length of time that elapsed between the crime and the identification.
- *Other evidence.* Additional evidence that the defendant was involved in the crime.

These factors tell us that we should have confidence in the identification of an offender by a victim or eyewitness who closely observed an offender for a lengthy period of time. On the other hand, we may question the identification of an offender by a victim or eyewitness who did not have the opportunity to clearly view the offender.

Fourth, these factors are to be weighed against the fact that the witness may be influenced by the suggestiveness of the identification. *The court must determine whether, based on the totality of the circumstances, the suggestive procedures create a "very substantial likelihood of irreparable misidentification."* In other words, did the identification result from the observation of the suspect at the scene of the crime, or did the identification result from the suggestive identification? The judge must now rule whether the identification is admissible or inadmissible:

- *Admissible.* The witness may testify at trial that he or she identified the defendant prior to the trial if the judge determines, based on the totality of the circumstances, that there is no substantial likelihood of irreparable misidentification.

- *Inadmissible.* The witness may not testify at trial that he or she identified the defendant prior to the trial if, based on the totality of the circumstances, there is a substantial likelihood of irreparable misidentification.

The Supreme Court in *Brathwaite* held that Glover's identification of Brathwaite was reliable and was not the product of the suggestiveness of the photograph. Glover was a trained observer who stood within two feet of Glover for two to three minutes. He provided D'Onofrio an accurate description within several minutes of having purchased narcotics and viewed the photograph two days later. At trial, Glover indicated that there is "no question whatsoever" concerning the accuracy of his identification. The Supreme Court concluded that "[t]hese indicators of Glover's ability to make an accurate identification are hardly outweighed by the corrupting effect of the challenged identification itself. Although identifications arising from single-photograph displays may be viewed in general with suspicion, . . . [in this case] Glover examined the photograph alone, [and] there was no coercive pressure to make an identification arising from the presence of another. The identification was made in circumstances allowing care and reflection."

Neil v. Biggers is an example of the Supreme Court's application of the totality-of-the-circumstances approach to a one-person showup. The victim was grabbed from behind in her kitchen by an assailant and then taken at knifepoint to the woods where she was raped. The entire incident lasted between fifteen and thirty minutes. The victim testified that she was able to see the perpetrator's face, which was illuminated by the light from the bedroom and by the full moon. As a result, she was able to provide the police with a general description of the assailant's age, height, complexion, skin texture, hair, and high-pitched voice (*Neil v. Biggers,* 409 U.S. 188 [1972]).

Over the course of the next seven months, the victim viewed lineups, showups, and thirty or forty photographs, none of which she believed included her assailant. The police then asked the victim to come to the police station to view a detainee. Two detectives walked the suspect past the victim, and at the victim's request, Archie Biggers was directed to say, "Shut up or I'll kill you." The victim testified that she had "no doubt" that Biggers was her assailant.

The Supreme Court concluded that the victim's identification was reliable. She spent a significant amount of time with her assailant, was able to view his face, and provided a fairly complete description following the rape. As a nurse, she was accustomed to viewing people's physical characteristics and had an "unusual opportunity to observe and identify her assailant." The victim had viewed a number of individuals before singling out her assailant. The Court concluded that the victim's identification undoubtedly was reliable and more than likely was not influenced by the suggestiveness of the lineup. In addition, there was a compelling reason for accepting the identification because there "are rarely witnesses to a rape other than the victim, who often has a limited opportunity of observation."

Legal Equation

Due process test whether identification is conducive to irreparable mistaken identification	=	Unnecessarily suggestive identification procedures
	+	Reliability of identification
	+	Totality of the circumstances.

The Due Process Test and Suggestiveness

Single-person showups and due process. In *Stovall v. Denno*, as noted earlier, the Supreme Court analyzed the totality of the circumstances and affirmed the reliability of a single-person showup. Mrs. Behrendt, the victim of a brutal stabbing, identified her assailant and the killer of her husband from her hospital bed after having undergone an emergency surgery the previous day. Theodore Stovall was brought into the victim's hospital room while handcuffed to one of five police officers. He was the only African American in the room. Behrendt testified at trial that she identified Stovall as the perpetrator when he was presented to her, and she then proceeded to make an in-court identification. The defendant was convicted and sentenced to death, and appealed on the grounds that the victim's identification in the hospital room under suggestive circumstances violated due process of law.

The Supreme Court observed in *Stovall* that single-person showups have been "widely condemned" and observed that the confrontation in the hospital room was "unnecessarily suggestive and conducive to irreparable mistaken identification." The showup in this particular case, however, was not in violation of due process because the victim was the only person who could "exonerate Stovall." The hospital staff was uncertain how long Mrs. Behrendt might live, and the police wanted to learn as quickly as possible whether they had apprehended the correct suspect. The police, "[f]aced with the responsibility of identifying the attacker, with the need for immediate action and with the knowledge that Mrs. Behrendt could not visit the jail . . . followed the only feasible procedure and took Stovall to the hospital room. Under the circumstances, the usual police station line-up . . . was out of the question." See *Stovall v. Denno* (388 U.S. 293 [1967]).

The Supreme Court in *Stovall* held that due process is to be determined in light of the totality of the circumstances. Under this test, the suggestiveness of the identification was balanced against the fact that Mrs. Behrendt was able to see her assailant during the attack and was balanced against Mrs. Behrendt's severe medical condition. The police also needed to act quickly to determine whether the killer was still at large. Do you agree with the Supreme Court that the identification satisfied the demands of due process?

The Supreme Court in both *Biggers* and *Stovall* criticized single-person showups as suggestive but recognized that, at times, this procedure is unavoidable. Single-person showups typically are conducted by the police in three instances:

- *Crime scene.* The police may apprehend a suspect immediately following a crime and present the suspect to the victim or to an eyewitness for identification. Showups that have been conducted immediately following a crime generally have been found to be reliable. The resort to this extraordinary procedure is justified by the need to protect the public against an offender who threatens the community.

- *Courthouse.* A victim or eyewitness may observe a suspect during an arraignment before a judge or inadvertently encounter the suspect in the courthouse. Courts will examine the impact of this encounter on the reliability of a witness's courtroom identification.

- *Emergency.* The police may face an emergency in which they are unable to rely on a lineup or photographic identification. Identifications under these circumstances are considered necessary to preserve identification evidence that otherwise may be lost. Courts balance the opportunity of the eyewitness or victim to view the crime against the suggestiveness of the identification and the risk of losing evidence.

Lineups and due process. *Foster v. California* is an example of an identification tainted by "impermissible suggestiveness." Foster and Grice were prosecuted for the armed robbery of a Western Union office in violation of the California Penal Code. The only witness was Joseph David, the late-night manager of the Western Union office. David was called to the police station following Foster's arrest. There were three men in the lineup. Foster was close to six feet in height. The other men were short, and Foster was the only individual in the lineup who wore a leather jacket similar to the one worn by the robber. David "thought" that Foster was the robber but was not certain. He then asked to speak to Foster, and the two sat across from one another in an office. Following this meeting, David told the police that he remained uncertain as to whether Foster was the robber. A week later, the police arranged for a second five-person lineup; Foster was the only person who appeared in both lineups. David now was convinced that Foster was the robber and identified him as the offender.

The U.S. Supreme Court had little difficulty in reaching the conclusion based on the totality of the circumstances that the identification procedures were "unnecessarily suggestive and conducive to irreparable mistaken identification." Justice Abe Fortas concluded that *Foster* presents a "compelling example of unfair lineup procedures." First, Foster stood out from the other two men in the first lineup based on his height and his leather jacket. The police then resorted to a one-to-one confrontation. After failing to obtain an identification, another lineup was conducted, and Foster was the only individual who appeared in both the first and the second lineups. This finally yielded a definite identification. The "suggestive elements . . . made it all but inevitable that David would identify petitioner whether or not he was in fact 'the man.'" In effect, the police repeatedly said to the witness, "This is the man." The "pretrial confrontations" were "clearly so arranged as to make the resulting identifications virtually inevitable." Can you explain why the identifications in *Manson* and *Biggers* were considered reliable and the identification in *Foster* was considered unreliable? See *Foster v. California* (394 U.S. 440, 441–444 [1969]).

Photographic identifications and due process. In 1968, in *Simmons v. United States,* the U.S. Supreme Court relied on the due process test to determine the admissibility of an in-court identification.

Three men robbed a savings and loan association in Chicago. Two of the men remained in the bank for roughly five minutes. The police were able to link the automobile used in the robbery to Andrews, Simmons, and Garrett. The police obtained six photos of Andrews and Simmons from Andrews's sister. These two individuals in most instances were pictured in a group along with various other individuals. A day following the robbery, the photos were separately shown to the five bank employees. Each witness identified Simmons as one of the robbers. A week or two later, three of the witnesses identified photographs of Garrett as the other robber; the other two stated that they did not have a clear view of the second robber. None identified Andrews. Simmons, Garrett, and Andrews were subsequently indicted. The FBI later showed the employees a series of photos, and they once again were able to identify Simmons.

The government did not introduce the results of the photographic identification at trial and relied solely on the in-court identifications by the five bank employees. Each identified Simmons as one of the robbers at trial, and three identified Garrett. Simmons and Andrews subsequently were convicted of armed robbery. Andrews's conviction was reversed on appeal.

Simmons argued that the pretrial photographic identifications were unnecessarily suggestive and conducive to misidentification at trial, that the use of the photographs denied him due process of law, and that his conviction should be reversed. The Supreme Court declined to prohibit police reliance on photographs of suspects despite the risk of misidentification. The Court reasoned that photos can assist in "apprehending offenders and sparing innocent suspects . . . arrest by allowing eyewitnesses to exonerate them through scrutiny of photographs." The majority of the Court recognized the possibility that an eyewitness may make an error and select a photo of an individual who closely resembles the person who actually committed the crime or that a photograph may be displayed in suggestive fashion that draws the eyewitness's attention to a particular suspect. The Court majority conceded that in such cases, the photographic image is likely to remain fixed in the mind of the eyewitness when identifying the perpetrator at a lineup or when making an in-court identification. The Court nevertheless ruled that "each case must be considered on its own facts" and that "convictions based on eyewitness identification at trial following a pretrial identification by photograph will be set aside . . . only if the photographic identification procedure was so impermissibly suggestive as to give rise to a very substantial likelihood of irreparable misidentification."

In this instance, the Supreme Court stressed that the FBI had to act quickly. The suspects remained at large, and it was essential to determine whether the FBI was "on the right track, so that they could properly deploy their forces in Chicago and, if necessary, alert officials in other cities." There was also little likelihood of misidentification. The Court observed that the employees viewed the robbers, who did not wear masks, for five minutes in a well-lighted bank. The photo identification took place the following day when the employees' memories were fresh. The witnesses viewed the photos alone, and there is no indication that they were coached by the FBI.

The five eyewitnesses who identified Simmons in the photographic display again identified Simmons in the courtroom. They all affirmed their courtroom identifications under cross-examination. None identified Andrews, who was not as clearly presented in the photos. The Supreme Court concluded that "[t]aken together, these circumstances leave little room for doubt that the identification of Simmons was correct, even though the identification procedure employed may have in some respects fallen short of the ideal. [T]he identification procedure . . . was not such as to deny Simmons due process of law." See *Simmons v. United States* (390 U.S. 377 [1968]).

Courts typically evaluate four areas in examining the suggestiveness of photographic identifications:

- *Display.* Whether the display of the photographs singled out a particular individual.
- *Police.* Whether the words, gestures, or actions of the police pointed to a particular photograph.
- *Photo.* Whether a particular photograph was sufficiently different in size, color, and the suspect's appearance to influence the selection of the eyewitness.
- *Instructions.* Whether the police indicated that the photograph of the offender may not be included in the photos.

17.1 YOU DECIDE

An armed robber entered a food store in Brewer, Maine. Witnesses reported to the police that a man was carrying a shotgun and demanded money that he stuffed into a paper bag, and fled. Sixteen-year-old Thomas was walking on a nearby street in the evening and spotted a man roughly sixty feet from him with "bushy hair" and a beard, wearing dark clothes, and carrying a paper bag and a "long object." Thomas was unaware that a robbery just had been committed. He watched as the man drove away in a "good looking" truck with mag wheels. The area was illuminated by a single streetlight.

Thomas, when questioned by the police, provided a description of the robber and immediately was taken to Robert Commeau's home. He identified the truck in the driveway as being the truck that he had seen earlier at the scene of the robbery. Two uniformed officers escorted the handcuffed Commeau out of the house. Commeau had bushy hair and a beard, and after a minute, Thomas, who was sitting in a squad car with a police officer sixty feet from where Commeau was standing, and despite the fact that it was "after dark," identified Commeau as the perpetrator.

A search of Commeau's house failed to result in the seizure of incriminating material. Two individuals who had been in the store were unable to identify Commeau. Thomas earlier had told a schoolmate that he could not be sure of the identity of the person whom he had seen leaving the store. As a judge would you permit Thomas to testify that he identified Commeau following the alleged robbery? See *State v. Commeau* (409 A.2d 247 [ME. 1979]).

You can learn what the court decided by referring to the study site, **http://study.sagepub.com/lippmance.**

17.2 YOU DECIDE

In December 2000, Theodore Rogers, a crack-cocaine addict living in Kentucky, accompanied his supplier, James Moorman, to Merrillville, Indiana. In return, Moorman gave Rogers some cocaine. The two left Kentucky in the morning and arrived at their destination in the afternoon. Rogers exited the vehicle, and Moorman drove off with an African American male who was waiting in the parking lot. Rogers returned after roughly twenty-five minutes, and Rogers took the wheel for the trip home. Rogers was pulled over for reckless driving, and the police uncovered a brick of cocaine in the glove compartment and $2,000 in cash hidden in the spare tire in the trunk. In September or October 2001, Rogers pled guilty. Shortly thereafter, Rogers agreed to assist the police but indicated that he did not believe that any of the photographs that he was shown pictured the African American male he had seen in the parking lot ten months earlier (it seems that the suspect's photo was in the array). Rogers did provide the police with a description of the man, which was not available to the Seventh Circuit Court of Appeals in its consideration of the case.

The police later arrested Winfred Owens, an African American male who the police believed had met with Moorman.

Rogers testified that he immediately recognized Owens when the two briefly were cellmates in a lockup in a federal courthouse in late October 2001. Owens had just been arrested and was inexplicably placed in the same cell as Rogers, who was returning from a hearing before the federal district court, which was considering whether to accept his guilty plea. At trial, Rogers testified against Owens and identified him in court as the man he had seen in December 2000. Rogers admitted on cross-examination that he remembered Owens "better because he had spent time with him in the same cell." Asked to describe the man he had first seen in December 2000, Rogers, who is an African American, replied that the man "was a black guy" and that, to him, "most black guys look alike." Rogers pled guilty pursuant to a plea agreement to one count of possession with the intent to distribute cocaine and was sentenced to fifty-one months in prison. Owens was convicted and sentenced to ninety-seven months' imprisonment. Owens appealed on the grounds that his identification had been unduly suggestive. Was Owens's identification "unnecessarily suggestive and conducive to irreparable mistaken identification"? See *United States v. Rogers* (387 F.3d 925 [7th Cir. 2004]).

You can learn what the court decided by referring to the study site, **http://study.sagepub.com/lippmance.**

CRIMINAL EVIDENCE AND PUBLIC POLICY

Consider the experience of Jennifer Thompson. On June 18, 2006, Thompson wrote an article in the *New York Times* recounting her devastating ordeal in 1984 when a male assailant broke into her locked apartment while she was asleep and raped her. Thompson was determined not to be a passive victim and told herself that she would ensure that her attacker was brought to justice. Her strategy was to

(Continued)

(Continued)

maneuver the rapist into the dimly lighted areas of her otherwise dark apartment in order to observe his distinguishing features: height, weight, hair, clothing, scars, and tattoos.

Thompson later provided the police with a detailed description of the crime and a composite sketch of her attacker. A few days later, Thompson, who is Caucasian, identified her African American attacker from a catalog of photographs and subsequently identified him in a lineup. She explained in an interview that her memory was relatively fresh and that Ronald Cotton looked exactly like the man who raped her. She was even more confident in this conclusion after listening to her assailant's voice and observing his height and weight. It also turned out that Cotton's alibi was fabricated and that his family's explanation that he was asleep on the couch on the evening of the rape was contradicted by testimony that he was seen riding his bike late at night. The police subsequently searched Cotton's bedroom and seized a flashlight under his bed that was similar to the one used by the rapist. Tests indicated that the rubber on Cotton's shoes was consistent with rubber found at the crime scene. Cotton was the only suspect included in the identification parade: the other six individuals were government employees. Thompson was confident that Cotton was her assailant and later recounted that, following the lineup, the police told her that they had already identified Cotton as the chief suspect based on his prior conviction for a similar offense. Another woman was raped on the same evening in Thompson's neighborhood by an assailant who followed the same pattern as the man who raped Thompson. The second victim observed a lineup, passed over Cotton, and identified a different individual as her attacker.

In 1986, Thompson took the stand at trial and identified Cotton as the rapist. The jury convicted Cotton, and he was sentenced to life imprisonment. The conviction was overturned on appeal. In 1987, Cotton once again was brought to trial. This time, the second victim explained that she was too scared to have come forward during the first trial and now felt confident in identifying Cotton as her attacker. Cotton's lawyers alleged that their client was innocent and that another inmate, Bobby Poole, had bragged that he was responsible. Thompson, however, strongly and confidently insisted that she had never encountered Poole in her life. Cotton was convicted of two acts of burglary and of two acts of rape and was sentenced to two life sentences plus fifty-four years. Thompson recounted that she was relieved that Cotton would never hurt or rape another woman.

In 1995, Thompson learned that DNA results indicated that her rapist indeed was Poole. Cotton was completely innocent and was released from prison. Poole had been arrested and convicted for two attempted sexual assaults that took place the same night that Cotton was arrested and now pled guilty to raping Thompson. In July 1995, the governor of North Carolina pardoned Cotton, resulting in his eligibility for $5,000 in compensation from the state. Thompson admits that even today, when she thinks of her rapist, she sees the image of Cotton, despite the fact that she knows he is innocent. How can this type of misidentification occur?

The federal government and each state and locality typically adopt their own procedures for identifications. The U.S. Justice Department and American Bar Association have suggested various modifications in the identification process to ensure greater accuracy. Several states have adopted some or all of these procedures, including New Jersey, North Carolina, Virginia, and Wisconsin as well as cities such as Seattle and Boston. These procedures have three goals:

- *Police influence.* To eliminate the possibility that the police officer conducting the identification will intentionally or unintentionally influence the eyewitness.
- *Pressure.* To limit the pressure on the victim or eyewitness to select one of the individuals in the lineup or photo array.
- *Accuracy.* To increase the accuracy of identifications.

Consider whether these innovations would have prevented Thompson from identifying Cotton as the man who raped her:

Blind administration. The individual administering the identification should not be informed which individual in the lineup is the suspect. This prevents the administrator from unintentionally or intentionally influencing the selection.

Double-blind. This means that neither the administrator of the identification process nor the eyewitness is aware of the identity of the suspect.

Instructions. The administrator instructs the eyewitness that the administrator does not know the identity of the suspect and that the suspect may not be in the lineup. This eliminates the possibility that the eyewitness will look to the administrator to guide his or her selection or will feel compelled to single out an individual as the perpetrator. Following the identification, the police should not indicate that the witness has selected the "right" person. These suggestive comments may unduly influence the suspect's future identifications.

Single eyewitness. One individual at a time should view the lineup, showup, or photo array, and eyewitnesses should not be permitted to confer with one another. This prevents witnesses from influencing one another. A witness also should not be told who was identified by other individuals. Witnesses, where possible, also should not be shown photographs of the suspect or permitted to view the suspect prior to the lineup.

Sequential presentation. The participants in the lineup or pictures in a photo array are presented to the victim or eyewitness one at a time. In this **sequential presentation**, the witness is asked to make a decision about each person immediately following the confrontation. The witness also is asked to rank his or her degree of confidence in the decision. This differs from the typical simultaneous lineup in which all the lineup members are shown to the witness at the same time. The theory behind the sequential lineup is that the eyewitness will examine each suspect separately and determine whether he or she is the offender. This is thought to eliminate pressure on an eyewitness to select the person who most closely resembles the perpetrator. The vast majority of police departments continue to use simultaneous lineups.

In 2003, the National Institute of Justice published a manual for training in identifications for law enforcement officers. The manual discusses one of the most difficult issues: the composition of a lineup or photographic display.

Balance. Participants in the lineup should be similar in age, height, weight, and race and should be dressed in a similar fashion. There must be a balance. On the one hand, the suspect should not clearly stand out from the other participants. On the other hand, a close resemblance between all the individuals will make the identification difficult and may lead to misidentifications. Selection should be based on information provided to the police by the victim following the crime rather than the actual physical appearance of the individual who the police believe committed the crime. Copies of the victim's initial description of the offender should be made available to the defense attorney.

Distinctive features. Fillers in the lineup should possess the offender's distinctive features mentioned by the victim or by an eyewitness to the police during the pre-lineup investigation. Courts have upheld the right of the police to order participants to shave or cut their hair or to alter their physical appearance. Individuals also may be required to speak or to make physical gestures.

Number. At a minimum, five fillers in photo arrays and four fillers in lineups are to be included to reduce the risk that an individual is selected as a result of a "guess" by a victim or by an eyewitness.

Preservation. Following a lineup or showup, the results should be recorded by the police on a standard form. This typically involves recording the number of the lineup member who was selected, the name of the eyewitness, the date, the investigator, and, ideally, a statement describing the identification. The lineup or showup should be photographed or videotaped. Photograph lineups also should be preserved to defend against legal challenges. Each eyewitness should complete a form indicating the assigned number of the individual whom he or she selected. Eyewitnesses also may make comments on the form explaining the basis for their choice. The police officer conducting the lineup should compile his or her notes and the forms and photographs into a final report that should be made available to the prosecution and defense attorneys.

Photographs. The photographs in photo arrays should be uniform and neutral in appearance to avoid influencing the selection. The photos should not mingle color photographs with "black-and-white pictures," and there should be no visible identifying marks, such as writing on the back of a photo indicating that an individual has been indicted or imprisoned.

In addition to these suggested procedures, some judges have taken steps at trial to help jurors evaluate courtroom identifications. This is intended to assist jurors in understanding that courtroom identifications by witnesses on some occasions may be mistaken.

Jury instructions. Jurors are instructed to evaluate whether the witness who made a courtroom identification possessed the opportunity and ability to observe the offender at the crime scene and whether his or her identification was influenced by outside influences. Jurors also typically are instructed to consider the length of time between the crime and the identification as well as any past failures by the eyewitness or victim to identify the suspect (see *United States v. Telfaire,* 469 F.2d 552 [D.C. Cir. 1972]).

Expert witness. Judges have permitted the defense to present expert testimony educating jurors on the psychological barriers to eyewitness identification. In *United States v. Brownlee,* the Third Circuit Court of Appeals reversed the district court's refusal to permit expert testimony, ruling that the expert witness would have proven helpful to the jury in evaluating the reliability of the courtroom identification (*United States v. Brownlee,* 454 F.3d 131 [3d Cir. 2006]).

■ THE REQUIREMENT OF POLICE INVOLVEMENT

In 2011, in *Perry v. New Hampshire,* the U.S. Supreme Court addressed the issue of eyewitness identification for the first time in over thirty-five years.

Nubia Blandon looked out her kitchen window around 2:30 a.m. and saw a tall African American man walking around the parking lot peering into the interior of automobiles. She watched as the man opened the trunk of her neighbor's auto and removed a large box. Officer Nicole Clay responded to a call and apprehended Barion Perry in the parking lot. Clay left Perry under the control of her fellow officer and went to talk to Blandon in her fourth-floor apartment. Officer Clayton asked Blandon for a more specific description of the suspect. Blandon responded by looking out her kitchen window and pointing at a man in handcuffs next to a police officer in the parking lot. A month later, Blandon viewed a photographic array that included a photo of Perry and was unable to identify the man who had broken into her neighbor's automobile. Blandon at the trial identified Perry as the individual who removed the stereo and amplifier from her neighbor's car. Perry was convicted of theft.

Perry claimed that he had been subjected to an unnecessarily suggestive identification in violation of due process that ran the risk of irreparable misidentification. He argued that his conviction should be overturned because the trial court judge was required to "screen" Blandon's identification testimony for reliability before allowing the jury to hear her testimony.

Justice Ruth Bader Ginsburg writing for the majority affirmed Perry's conviction and held that the "primary aim" of excluding identification evidence obtained through "unnecessarily suggestive circumstances . . . is to deter law enforcement use of improper lineups, showups, and photo arrays." Absent unnecessarily suggestive identification procedures created by the police, the Court held that due process does not require a trial court to "screen such evidence for reliability before allowing the jury to assess its creditworthiness." In contrast to previous identification cases, "law enforcement officials [in *Perry*] did not arrange for the suggestive circumstances surrounding Blandon's identification."

The Court stressed that the jury is the ultimate umpire of the reliability of witnesses and of a defendant's guilt and innocence. Jurors were given the opportunity to decide for themselves how much weight should be accorded to Blandon's courtroom identification of Perry. Perry's attorney was able to rely on cross-examination of Blandon to raise questions concerning the reliability of Blandon's identification. The attorney pointed out the distance between Blandon's window and the parking lot, noted that a van obstructed Blandon's view, and highlighted that Blandon was nervous and frightened and that she did not pay attention to what Blandon was wearing and could not describe his facial features. The defense lawyer stressed that Blandon was unable to pick Perry out of a photo array and that Blandon was standing next to a police officer at the time that she made the identification. He reminded the jury of all the issues surrounding the reliability of Blandon's eyewitness identification during the closing argument.

The Supreme Court further noted that judges may allow defendants to counter eyewitness testimony by presenting expert witnesses to testify on the dangers and shortcomings of eyewitness identification, and judges also have the discretion to give instructions to jurors cautioning them on placing undue weight on eyewitness testimony. In *Perry*, the trial court read the jury an instruction on the factors that the jury should consider in evaluating the reliability of eyewitness identification testimony and reminded jurors that the defendant's guilt must be proved beyond a reasonable doubt and cautioned that "one of the things the State must prove [beyond a reasonable doubt] is the identification of the defendant as the person who committed the offense."

Justice Sonia Sotomayor, in her dissenting opinion, noted that the Court and academic studies have recognized that eyewitness identification despite its unreliability has a powerful impact on the jury. She contended that a defendant's due process rights are violated whenever he or she is subjected to suggestive identification procedures involving the police that create a risk of misidentification whether the police have "intentionally or inadvertently created the suggestive circumstances." Do you agree with Justice Sotomayor? Would the Court have ruled differently if Officer Clay had directed Blandon to look out the window and to determine whether Perry was the individual that she had seen looking in cars in the parking lot?

A number of state supreme courts and several federal circuit courts of appeal have permitted the defense to present qualified expert testimony on the factors that may interfere with accurate eyewitness identification. The experts help jurors to focus on the factors that should be considered in evaluating the reliability of an identification such as the passage of time, tendency to focus on a firearm rather than on the perpetrator's facial features, and the race of the perpetrator and of the eyewitness. These courts have expressed skepticism over the ability of cross-examination and cautionary instructions to overcome the tendency of jurors to give extraordinary weight to courtroom identifications (*State v. Clopten*, 323 P.3d 1103 [Utah 2008]).

New Jersey has taken far-reaching steps to ensure the reliability of eyewitness identification. In *State v. Henderson*, the New Jersey Supreme Court adopted far-reaching reforms to ensure the reliability of eyewitness identification. The trial court judge is required to conduct a hearing concerning the accuracy of eyewitness identification when the defendant is able to present some evidence of suggestive identification. The trial court judge then is to use a checklist of factors to determine whether the identification is accurate. These factors include both "system variables" (e.g., how the police conducted the lineup) and "estimator variables" (e.g., race, distance, time of day) to determine whether the defendant shows a very substantial likelihood of irreparable identification. The law requires the police to conduct lineups in accordance with the most current scientific evidence and, for example, employ double-blind lineups and warn eyewitnesses that the perpetrator may not be in the lineup (*State v. Henderson*, 2011 N.J. Lexis 927).

17.3 YOU DECIDE

Theresa Ellen Barthel was in bed at about 10:00 P.M. on July 16, 1981, when she awoke to find a man standing next to her bed. The lights were on in the room, and she was able to see the intruder, who, after a brief struggle, began to rape her. During the rape, he placed a pillow over her face. Following the rape, she was able to see her assailant grab his clothes and run out of the apartment. She called her husband and reported that the rapist was five feet, eight inches to five feet, nine inches in height and weighed between 160 and 170 pounds with brown wavy or curly hair. Barthel stated that she did not know whether the assailant had tattoos on his body. Rosario Dispensa, who had recently moved into the apartment complex, was seen wearing only his pants at 3:00 A.M. heading toward his apartment. Dispensa explained that he typically returned from work as a restaurant manager at 2:00 A.M. and then frequently relaxed by taking a swim in the complex pool. His fingerprints were not found in Barthel's apartment, and a cigarette butt in the apartment was not the brand that Dispensa smoked. Although Dispensa has a great deal of body hair, only two hairs were on the sheets. A toxicologist testified that these were pubic hairs; one of the hairs possessed microscopic characteristics similar to the hair furnished by Dispensa. An alibi witness testified that Dispensa was asleep with her between 3:00 A.M. and 5:00 A.M. Dispensa was roughly six feet tall, weighed 180 to 185 pounds, wore glasses, and had straight hair, his body was marked by prominent tattoos on his arms and shoulders as well as by visible cuts and scabs, and he had a prominent moustache. His female alibi witness stated that his sexual organ was deformed.

Two Houston police detectives took Barthel to the restaurant where Dispensa worked. They reportedly did not disclose their purpose. Following lunch, one of the officers approached Dispensa in his office and told him that he was a suspect in a sex crime and directed him to walk through the restaurant so that the victim could observe him. Dispensa was warned that a refusal would result in his arrest and inclusion in a lineup. The first time Dispensa walked through the restaurant Barthel did not respond. He then was directed by Detective Ralph Yarborough, who was standing next to the cashier, to walk through the restaurant once again, and as he directly passed by Barthel, she identified him as the rapist, burst into tears, and fled the restaurant. Barthel testified that when Dispensa walked by, Detective L. W. Henning told her to "look." The first time that Dispensa passed, she did not see his face and identified him only the second time when he walked directly by the table. Barthel also testified that she did not see Detective Yarborough talking to Dispensa at the cash register between the first and the second times that Dispensa walked through the restaurant. Dispensa claimed that he was identified only on his third walk through the restaurant and that, during this walk, he was accompanied by Detective Yarborough. Barthel testified regarding her identification of Dispensa at trial and made an in-court identification. Was the evidence of Barthel's identification in the restaurant properly admitted into evidence? See *Dispensa v. Lynaugh* (847 F.2d 211 [5th Cir. 1988]).

You can learn what the court decided by referring to the study site, **http://study.sagepub.com/lippmance.**

17.4 YOU DECIDE

Defendant Joseph Arthur Emanuele was convicted of robbing both the Millvale Bank and the Waterworks Bank. Martha Hottel, a teller, observed the man who robbed the Millvale Bank before he approached her window. Five weeks later, she was shown a six-photo array and selected a photograph of the defendant but stated that she "wasn't one hundred percent sure." Several weeks later, Hottel was shown a second array and selected someone other than the defendant. The robber's image was not captured by the bank's security cameras, and the defendant's fingerprints were not detected in the bank. At the Waterworks Bank, a robber also demanded money from teller Lorraine Woessner. She first observed the man at close range for several minutes in the bank lobby. Woessner was unable to identify the robber's photograph from a six-photo array. His image was captured by the security camera in the bank.

The two tellers were waiting to testify when they saw defendant Emanuele escorted by two U.S. marshals being led from the courtroom in shackles. The two tellers talked to one another, remarking that "it has to be him." Woessner allegedly stated that "when she saw him she knew exactly that's who it was." The trial court permitted both witnesses to make courtroom identifications. The Third Circuit Court of Appeals held that the issue was whether this impermissibly suggestive confrontation created a substantial likelihood of misidentification in light of the totality of the circumstances. Was it an "abuse of discretion" for the trial court to permit Woessner to make a courtroom identification? What about Hottel? See *United States v. Emanuele* (51 F.3d 1123 [3d Cir. 1993]). See also *State v. Armijo* (549 P.2d 616 [Ariz. App. 1976]).

You can learn what the court decided by referring to the study site, **http://study.sagepub.com/lippmance.**

CRIMINAL EVIDENCE IN THE NEWS

Alaska, Florida, New York, and Texas are among the states that rely on dog scent lineups. Dog scent lineups involve using trained dogs to sniff items from a crime scene. The dog is walked past a series of containers in which are deposited samples swabbed from a suspect and from other individuals. The dog then barks or stiffens his or her posture when there is a match between the scent from the crime scene and the scent in the container. The dog scent then is relied on as evidence of guilt at trial.

The use of dog scents became controversial when a dog in 2007 indicated that Curvis Bickham and an alleged confederate were involved in a triple homicide in Texas and after eight months in jail the partially blind and physically limited Bickham was released when he was exonerated by DNA. Another Houston resident, Calvin Miller, filed a civil suit after being wrongly identified by a dog as responsible for a rape.

In Texas, the use of dog scent evidence was pioneered by sheriff's deputy Keith A. Pikett and was relied on in hundreds of cases. Pikett trained a group of bloodhounds that he claimed were able accurately to detect perpetrators in scent lineups. Pikett claimed that his dog Quincy, for example, only was wrong two times out of 2,931 lineups and that his two other dogs were equally as accurate. One of these dogs was honored by Texas veterinarians, and a Houston police group later named Pikett as officer of the year.

There is growing skepticism about dog scent evidence, particularly when relied on as primary evidence of guilt. Michael Buchanek, a retired sheriff's deputy, was arrested based on a dog scent lineup. Buchanek's claims of innocence were rejected by officials who insisted that "dogs don't lie—we know you did it." He later was released when DNA implicated another man who confessed to the crime.

In East Texas, Megan Winfrey, 16, her 17-year-old brother, and her father were indicted for murder primarily based on scent lineup evidence. Megan was convicted although the jury in her brother's case acquitted him and rejected the reliability of dog scent evidence. Her father's conviction was overturned in 2010 when the Texas Court of Criminal Appeals found that "scent-discrimination lineups, when used alone or as primary evidence, are legally insufficient to support a conviction."

Steven Nicely, a professional dog trainer and police dog consultant, described the now-retired Pikett in an affidavit as "an unprofessional charlatan." Robert Coote, head of the British canine police unit, stated that Pikett's scent identifications are the "most primitive police procedure I have witnessed. . . . If it was not for the fact that this is a serious matter, I could have been watching a comedy." Other experts warned of the possibility that the dogs had been picking up cues from Pikett and were being directed to respond to the scents of individuals whom the police suspected of involvement in the crime.

The FBI, though confident in the ability of dogs, limits the use of dogs to follow a trail or to indicate that an individual has been in a particular location.

Law enforcement officials who defend the use of dogs contend that there is nothing sinister about relying on scent evidence because the dogs merely match the scent in a container to the scent at the crime scene. Other criminal justice professionals believe that dog scents are a helpful investigative tool so long as they are not relied on as the sole evidence of a suspect's guilt. In the last analysis, the decision whether to arrest and to prosecute an individual is within the discretion of the police and prosecutors. What is your view?

■ CASE ANALYSIS

In *Foster v. California,* the U.S. Supreme Court decided whether Foster had been convicted based in part on an identification that was the product of a suggestive lineup.

Was the defendant subjected to a suggestive lineup?

Foster v. California, 394 U.S. 440 (1968), Fortas, J.

Petitioner was charged . . . with the armed robbery of a Western Union office in violation of California Penal Code 211a. The day after the robbery one of the robbers, Clay, surrendered to the police and implicated Foster and Grice. Allegedly, Foster and Clay had entered the office while Grice waited in a car. Foster and Grice were tried together. Grice was acquitted. Foster was convicted. The California District Court of Appeal affirmed the conviction; the State Supreme Court denied review. We granted certiorari, limited

to the question whether the conduct of the police lineup resulted in a violation of petitioner's constitutional rights.

Except for the robbers themselves, the only witness to the crime was Joseph David, the late-night manager of the Western Union office. After Foster had been arrested, David was called to the police station to view a lineup. There were three men in the lineup. One was petitioner. He is a tall man—close to six feet in height. The other two men were short—five feet, five or six inches. Petitioner wore a leather jacket which David said was similar to the one he had seen underneath the coveralls worn by the robber. After seeing this lineup, David could not positively identify petitioner as the robber. He "thought" he was the man, but he was not sure. David then asked to speak to petitioner, and petitioner was brought into an office and sat across from David at a table. Except for prosecuting officials there was no one else in the room. Even after this one-to-one confrontation David still was uncertain whether petitioner was one of the robbers: "truthfully—I was not sure," he testified at trial. A week or 10 days later, the police arranged for David to view a second lineup. There were five men in that lineup. Petitioner was the only person in the second lineup who had appeared in the first lineup. This time David was "convinced" petitioner was the man.

At trial, David testified to his identification of petitioner in the lineups, as summarized above. He also repeated his identification of petitioner in the courtroom. The only other evidence against petitioner which concerned the particular robbery with which he was charged was the testimony of the alleged accomplice Clay.

In *United States v. Wade*, 388 U.S. 218 (1967), and *Gilbert v. California*, 388 U.S. 263 (1967), this Court held that because of the possibility of unfairness to the accused in the way a lineup is conducted, a lineup is a "critical stage" in the prosecution, at which the accused must be given the opportunity to be represented by counsel. That holding does not, however, apply to petitioner's case, for the lineups in which he appeared occurred before June 12, 1967. *Stovall v. Denno*, 388 U.S. 293 (1967). But in declaring the rule of *Wade* and *Gilbert* to be applicable only to lineups conducted after those cases were decided, we recognized that, judged by the "totality of the circumstances," the conduct of identification procedures may be "so unnecessarily suggestive and conducive to irreparable mistaken identification" as to be a denial of due process of law.

Judged by that standard, this case presents a compelling example of unfair lineup procedures. In the first lineup arranged by the police, petitioner stood out from the other two men by the contrast of his height and by the fact that he was wearing a leather jacket similar to that worn by the robber. When this did not lead to positive identification, the police permitted a one-to-one confrontation between petitioner and the witness. This Court pointed out in Stovall that "[t]he practice of showing suspects singly to persons for the purpose of identification, and not as part of a lineup, has been widely condemned." Even after this the witness' identification of petitioner was tentative. So some days later another lineup was arranged. Petitioner was the only person in this lineup who had also participated in the first lineup. This finally produced a definite identification.

The suggestive elements in this identification procedure made it all but inevitable that David would identify petitioner whether or not he was in fact "the man." In effect, the police repeatedly said to the witness, "This is the man." This procedure so undermined the reliability of the eyewitness identification as to violate due process.

In a decision handed down since the Supreme Court of California declined to consider petitioner's case, it reversed a conviction because of the unfair makeup of a lineup. In that case, the California court said: "[W]e do no more than recognize . . . that unfairly constituted lineups have in the past too often brought about the conviction of the innocent." In the present case the pretrial confrontations clearly were so arranged as to make the resulting identifications virtually inevitable.

The respondent invites us to hold that any error was harmless. We decline to rule upon this question in the first instance. Accordingly, the judgment is reversed and the case remanded for further proceedings not inconsistent with this opinion. Reversed and remanded.

Black, J. dissenting.

My objection is to the Court's basic holding that evidence can be ruled constitutionally inadmissible whenever it results from identification procedures that the Court considers to be "'unnecessarily suggestive and conducive to irreparable mistaken identification.'" One of the proudest achievements of this country's Founders was that they had eternally guaranteed a trial by jury in criminal cases, at least until the Constitution they wrote had been amended in the manner they prescribed. . . . Of course it is an incontestable fact in our judicial history that the jury is the sole tribunal to weigh and determine facts. That means that the jury must, if we keep faith with the Constitution, be allowed to hear eyewitnesses and decide for itself whether it can recognize the truth and whether they are telling the truth. It means that the jury must be allowed to decide for itself whether the darkness of the night, the weakness of a witness' eyesight, or any other factor impaired the witness' ability to make an accurate identification. To take that power away from the jury is to rob it of the responsibility to perform the precise functions the Founders most wanted it to perform. And certainly a Constitution written to preserve this indispensable, unerodible core of our system for trying criminal cases would not have included, hidden among its provisions, a slumbering sleeper granting the judges license to destroy trial by jury in whole or in part.

The Court looks to the "totality of circumstances" to show "unfair lineup procedures." This means "unfair" according to the Court's view of what is unfair. The Constitution, however, does not anywhere prohibit conduct deemed unfair by the courts.

CHAPTER SUMMARY

Identifications by eyewitnesses and victims are one of the primary investigative tools in the arsenal of law enforcement. A positive identification narrows an investigation and may lead to a formal criminal charge and to criminal prosecution. In other instances, law enforcement authorities may conduct identifications of individuals against whom criminal charges already have been filed in order to build or to strengthen their case. Following these pretrial identifications, the victims or eyewitnesses typically are asked to repeat their identifications at trial. Prosecutors have learned that jurors view these courtroom identifications as powerful and persuasive evidence of a defendant's guilt.

There are three primary forms of eyewitness identification: lineup, showup, and photographic identification. These typically are used in combination with one another and with scientific identifications.

Two constitutional provisions regulate eyewitness identifications. The Sixth Amendment guarantees the right to an attorney at lineups and showups following the initiation of proceedings against a defendant. Pre-indictment identifications and photographic identifications are regulated by the Fifth and Fourteenth Amendments' Due Process Clauses. Post-indictment lineups also are subject to challenge on due process grounds.

Identifications are inherently subject to error and are the leading cause of false convictions. The question remains whether we can safeguard these procedures against the errors that inevitably occur in the process of perception, memory, and identification. Double-blind, sequential lineup procedures and other steps have been proposed to augment the constitutional protections surrounding identifications.

The Sixth Amendment right to counsel applies to all critical stages of the criminal process. Critical stages are those procedures following a formal charge at which representation by a lawyer is essential to a fair trial. The U.S. Supreme Court recognized in *Wade* and *Gilbert* that a lineup or showup is a critical stage because individuals who are unrepresented are at risk of being falsely identified. A defense attorney who observes a suggestive lineup is in a position to cross-examine the police who conducted the lineup or showup in order to call the identification into question in the minds of the jury.

The failure to permit a defendant to have access to a lawyer or to waive his or her right to a lawyer results in the exclusion from trial of the results of the identification. The prosecutor nevertheless may ask a witness for an in-court identification in those instances in which the prosecution is able to establish by clear and convincing evidence that the in-court identification is not the product of the tainted identification procedure.

In *Kirby v. Illinois*, the U.S. Supreme Court concluded that a showup after arrest but before "the initiation of any adversary criminal proceedings (whether by way of formal charge, preliminary hearing, indictment, information, or arraignment) is not a critical stage of criminal prosecution at which the accused is entitled to counsel."

In 1973, in *United States v. Ash*, the U.S. Supreme Court held that the Sixth Amendment does not entitle the accused to the presence of a lawyer at a post-indictment photographic display. The Court reasoned that post-indictment confrontations are considered critical only when the presence of a lawyer is essential to the protection of the defendant's ability to receive a fair trial. Photo arrays are easily re-created, and for this reason, there is no right for either the lawyer or the defendant to observe the identification.

In *Stovall v. Denno*, the U.S. Supreme Court held that all identification procedures, showups, and photo arrays are required to satisfy the standards of the Fifth and Fourteenth Amendments' Due Process Clauses. The due process test was fully elaborated in *Manson v. Brathwaite*. Identifications violate the Due Process Clause when they are unnecessarily suggestive and "conducive to irreparable mistaken identification." This is to be evaluated based on the totality of the circumstances.

In *Perry v. New Hampshire*, the most recent Supreme Court case on eyewitness identifications, the Court held that, absent unnecessarily suggestive identification procedures created by the police, due process does not require a trial court to "screen such evidence for reliability" before allowing the jury to assess its reliability.

CHAPTER REVIEW QUESTIONS

1. Distinguish lineups, showups, and photographic identifications.

2. Why do perception, memory, and identification create a risk of misidentification?

3. Discuss the procedures that have been proposed to ensure more accurate identifications.

4. Why are lineups, showups, and photographic identifications not considered a violation of the Fifth Amendment right against self-incrimination?

5. Why are lineups and showups a critical stage of a criminal proceeding?

6. Summarize the Sixth Amendment *Wade-Gilbert* rule.

7. What is the role of defense counsel at lineups under the *Wade-Gilbert* rule?

8. Why did the Supreme Court not follow the *Wade-Gilbert* rule in *Kirby v. Illinois*?

9. What is the holding in *United States v. Ash*? Why did the Supreme Court not follow the *Wade-Gilbert* rule in *Ash*?

10. Discuss the Fifth and Fourteenth Amendments' standard established in *Manson v. Brathwaite* for determining whether a witness may testify concerning the results of a suggestive identification procedure.

LEGAL TERMINOLOGY

confrontation

corporeal identification

critical stages of a criminal proceeding

distractors

eyewitness identification

fillers

foils

in-court identification

non-corporeal identification

photographic displays

sequential presentation

showup

simultaneous lineup

suggestive procedures

Wade-Gilbert rule

REFERENCES

Borchard, Edwin M. 1932. *Convicting the Innocent: Sixty-Five Actual Errors of Criminal Justice*. New York: Garden City Publishing.

Visit the Student Study Site at **http://study.sagepub.com/lippmance** to access additional study tools, including mobile-friendly eFlashcards and Web quizzes as well as links to SAGE journal articles and hyperlinks for *Criminal Evidence* on the Web.

■■GLOSSARY

abandoned property Property intentionally discarded by the owner.

administrative inspections Government agencies conduct searches to determine whether businesses, factories, apartments, and homes are conforming to a broad range of regulations.

admission An individual admits a fact that tends to establish guilt, such as his or her presence at the crime scene. An admission, when combined with other facts, may lead to a criminal conviction.

admission by party-opponent A defendant's confession and other admissions may be admitted into evidence as an admission by party-opponent. An admission is not required to be a statement of guilt. A damaging statement that undercuts the defendant's case also qualifies as an admission.

adoptive admission Occurs when a person reacts to a statement made by another person that may reasonably be interpreted as an affirmation that the statement is true.

affiant An individual who swears to a warrant.

affidavit A sworn statement setting forth facts constituting probable cause that an individual has committed a criminal offense.

***Aguilar-Spinelli* test** An affidavit must detail the informant's credibility and basis of knowledge.

ancient documents rule A document at least twenty years old is presumed to be authentic and is "fair on its face."

anonymous tip Information from an unidentified informant.

appellant The party appealing a lower court judgment.

appellee The party against whom an appeal is filed.

argumentative question A question that challenges a witness in a rude or hostile manner.

arraignment The defendant is informed of the charges against him or her and is required to enter a plea.

arrest Police custody of an individual based on probable cause that he or she committed a crime.

arrest warrant A judicial finding that there is probable cause to arrest an individual.

articulable suspicion A police officer in justifying an intrusion must present specific and articulable facts that together with rational inferences drawn from those facts reasonably suggest that an individual has committed a crime or is about to commit a crime.

attenuated A term used to describe a weak link between an unreasonable search and the resulting seizure of evidence; the exclusionary rule does not apply where evidence is attenuated.

attorney-client privilege A client can prevent his or her attorney from testifying about information revealed by the client in confidence.

authentication The party that wants to admit a document or object at trial has the burden of establishing the document or object is genuine, meaning the document or object is what the moving party claims it to be

automatic reversal rule The requirement that a violation of a fundamental constitutional right during trial results in the reversal of a conviction on appeal.

automobile exception The exception to the requirement that police obtain a warrant before conducting a search; a warrant is not required for an automobile.

ballistics Analysis of firearms and ammunition.

bench trial A trial in which a judge sits without trial.

best evidence rule Requires that "to prove the content of writing, recording, or photograph, the original writing, recording, or photograph is required" unless an exception applies.

beyond a reasonable doubt The standard for conviction in a criminal case.

binding authority A decision that establishes a precedent.

blood alcohol testing A test to determine blood alcohol content.

blood typing Analysis of blood type.

booking An administrative procedure in which the suspect's name, arrest time, offense charged, fingerprinting, and photographs are recorded.

***Brady* rule** The prosecution is required to turn over exculpatory information to the accused.

break in the custody rule An individual who invokes right to counsel may be interrogated after fourteen days.

brief A written legal argument that is submitted to a court.

bright-line rule A clear and unambiguous rule established by judicial precedent.

burden of persuasion The prosecution must prove every element of a criminal charge beyond a reasonable doubt.

burden of production Responsibility to produce sufficient evidence for the fact finder to consider the merits of the claim.

burden of proof The prosecution must prove every element of a criminal charge beyond a reasonable doubt.

business records A record kept in the course of a regularly conducted activity of a business or organization is admissible in evidence.

case-by-case determination The facts of each situation are evaluated to determine whether a police officer's conduct meets the applicable legal standard. An example is the standard for a reasonable suspicion stop in accordance with *Terry v. Ohio.*

case-in-chief The presentation of the prosecution's evidence at trial.

certiorari A decision to hear an appeal.

chain of custody Accounts for possession of real evidence from time seized by the police until introduced into evidence.

challenge for cause A juror may be excluded from the jury based on an actual or presumed inability to impartially evaluate the evidence.

character General tendencies such as honesty, violence, trustworthiness, and peacefulness.

circumstantial evidence Indirectly proves a fact and requires the fact finder to use an inference or presumption.

citation Notice to an individual to appear for trial at a later date.

clemency A reduction in a criminal punishment.

clergy-penitent privilege Penitent may prevent clergy from testifying about information revealed by penitent in confidence.

closely regulated business Subject to a number of regulations that are subject to warrantless searches without probable cause.

closing argument A summary of the evidence by the prosecution and defense.

collateral attack A constitutional challenge by an individual who has been convicted and incarcerated and has exhausted his or her state appeals.

collateral proceedings Permits the use of unlawfully seized evidence in proceedings that are not part of a formal trial.

collateral remedies Remedies that are available following the exhaustion of direct appeals.

competency to testify An individual is competent to testify as a witness who understands the duty to testify truthfully, possesses personal knowledge, and is able to recollect and to describe events.

competent evidence Relevant and material evidence admissible in court.

complaint A legal document that lists the charges, the legal elements of the crime, and the supporting facts against the individual and possible penalties.

conclusive presumption The jury is required to reach a conclusion from fact established at trial.

concurring opinion An opinion by a judge supporting a majority or dissenting opinion, typically based on other grounds.

confession An individual admits the commission of a crime in response to police questions.

confidential informant privilege The prosecution is not required to reveal the identity of an informant.

confrontation Physical presentation of a suspect to a witness or victim.

Confrontation Clause The Confrontation Clause of the Sixth Amendment provides that "in all criminal prosecutions, the accused shall enjoy the right . . . to be confronted with the witnesses against him."

consent search A search based on an individual's waiver of his or her Fourth Amendment rights.

constitutionalization of the Bill of Rights Extension of the rights and freedoms in the Bill of Rights to the fifty states.

contemporaneous A search incident to an arrest must take place immediately before, at the same time as, or immediately after the arrest.

contemporaneous objection rule With respect to searches, a requirement that the search must be undertaken immediately before the arrest, at the same time as the arrest, or immediately after the arrest; allows the judge to decide whether a question is permissible before the jury hears the witness's answer.

corporeal identification Identification of an individual who is physically present.

corroboration Evidence that supports without repeating the testimony of a prior witness.

corroborative evidence Evidence that adds new information that confirms prior testimony.

courts of general jurisdiction Courts that hear more serious criminal and civil cases.

courts of limited jurisdiction Courts with jurisdiction over a narrow range of cases.

courts of original jurisdiction Courts with jurisdiction over a broad range of cases.

credibility A witness whose testimony is worthy of belief.

crime-fraud exception The attorney-client privilege does not require a lawyer to maintain information about a future crime or fraud confidential.

critical stages of a criminal proceeding Procedures between arraignment and trial at which a failure to provide the defendant a lawyer may prevent the defendant from obtaining a fair trial.

cross-examination Questions regarding the direct testimony of a witness.

cumulative evidence Evidence that repeats evidence already admitted at trial.

curtilage The area immediately surrounding the home, considered part of the home.

custodial interrogation Questioning initiated by law enforcement officers after a person has been taken into custody or otherwise deprived of his or her freedom of action in a significant way.

dangerous patient exception A psychotherapist is obligated to reveal reasonable grounds to believe a patient poses a danger to others.

declaration against interest The statement when made must be against an important interest of an absent declarant. A reasonable person in the same position would not have made a statement unless he or she believed it to be true.

demeanor Appearance of victim.

demonstrative evidence Graphs, maps, charts, or models designed to assist the jury to visualize the facts of the case, such as a crime scene.

derivative evidence Evidence that is discovered as a result of an unlawful seizure.

direct evidence Evidence based on personal knowledge or observation of a witness and conclusively establishes fact or facts.

direct examination The questioning of a witness by the party who called the witness to testify.

directed verdict A motion made by a defense attorney at the conclusion of the prosecution's case-in-chief to dismiss the case based on the prosecution's failure to prove one or more of the elements of the criminal charge.

discovery The right for each side to have warning of the evidence that the other side will present at trial.

dissenting opinion An opinion by a judge disagreeing with the majority of judges.

distractors Individuals in a lineup who are not suspects.

DNA Deoxyribonucleic acid is a molecule that stores an individual's genetic code. Every individual other than a genetic twin has a distinct genetic code.

documentary evidence Documents and writings as well as photographs, medical images, and videos.

double jeopardy Prosecuting a defendant in the same jurisdiction on two occasions for the same crime.

drug courier profile A profile developed based on experience that isolates characteristics of a drug trafficker.

Due Process Clause The Fifth and Fourteenth Amendments to the U.S. Constitution guarantee individuals due process of law. The Fourteenth Amendment Due Process Clause incorporates most of the protections of the Bill of Rights.

dynamite charge The judge instructs the jurors who are in the minority to reconsider the reasonableness of their views.

emergency-aid doctrine Warrantless entry by the police into the home to provide assistance to the individual.

en banc The entire court.

encounters Informal police stops of individuals.

evidence Testimony, writings, material objects, or other things presented to the senses that are offered to prove the existence or nonexistence of fact.

excited utterance A statement relating to a startling event or condition while the declarant was under the stress of excitement caused by the event or condition.

exclusionary rule A rule that evidence that is obtained as a result of a violation of the Fourth Amendment prohibition on unreasonable searches and seizures is inadmissible in a criminal prosecution to establish a defendant's guilt.

executive privilege The president has the right to refuse to reveal the confidential decision-making process.

exigent circumstances Emergency circumstances justifying warrantless entry into the home.

expectation of privacy Protection from government intrusion; areas with a high expectation of privacy may generally not be searched without a warrant founded on probable cause.

experiment Simulation of conditions to determine reliability of trial testimony.

expert testimony A witness who is qualified as an expert by knowledge, skill, experience, training, or education may testify in the form of an opinion.

expert witness A witness qualified by knowledge, skill, experience, training, or education to provide expert opinion about evidence that is beyond the understanding of the average juror.

express questioning A direct question.

express waiver An affirmative relinquishment of a right.

eyewitness identification Identification of a suspect by a victim or witness.

false confession An innocent individual confesses to a crime that he or she did not commit.

Federal Rules of Evidence Rules on the admission of evidence in civil and criminal cases in the U.S. federal court system.

fillers Individuals in a lineup who are not suspects.

final judgment rule The rule that an appeal may be taken only following a verdict.

fingerprint evidence Evidence of ridge characteristics of fingers used to connect an individual to a crime.

first appearance Following an arrest, a suspect's initial appearance before a judge for the determination of probable cause, to be informed of his or her rights, for decisions to be made on pretrial release and bail, and the appointment of an attorney for the indigent.

fleeing-felon rule Common law doctrine that police may use deadly force to apprehend a suspected felon who is fleeing the police.

flight A defendant's leaving the crime scene immediately following the crime or leaving the jurisdiction after being identified as a suspect in a crime.

foils Individuals in a lineup who are not suspects.

forfeiture by wrongdoing A hearsay statement otherwise inadmissible may be admitted against a party who intentionally makes the declarant unavailable to testify.

former testimony Transcripts of a witness's testimony at an earlier deposition or proceeding in the same case or in another case admissible when declarant is absent.

Fourteenth Amendment An amendment to the U.S. Constitution passed in 1868 in order to provide equal rights and opportunity to newly free African American slaves.

Fourteenth Amendment due process voluntariness test Confessions may not be obtained through psychological or physical coercion that overcomes the will of the individual to resist.

frisk A police officer may pat down a suspect's outer clothing.

fruit of the poisonous tree Evidence derived from unlawfully seized evidence.

functional equivalent of express questioning Words or actions on the part of the police that the police should know are reasonably likely to lead a defendant to incriminate himself or herself.

fundamental fairness The Fourteenth Amendment Due Process Clause prohibits states from criminal procedures that are fundamentally unfair. States are otherwise free to structure their criminal justice systems.

general warrants Warrants allowing colonial authorities to search anytime and anywhere.

good faith exception An exception to the exclusion of illegally seized evidence in situations where an officer has acted in the good faith belief that his or her conduct complies with the Fourth Amendment.

grab area The area within a suspect's immediate control that may be searched incident to an arrest.

grand jury A jury that determines whether the prosecutor has sufficient evidence to proceed to trial.

grand jury confidentiality Grand jury proceedings are required to remain secret.

guilt beyond a reasonable doubt There is no "reasonable doubt" in the mind of a reasonable person that the defendant is guilty.

habeas corpus Latin for "you have the body"; a writ of *habeas corpus* is an order issued by a judge to a government official (usually the warden of a correctional institution) to bring an imprisoned individual to court and explain why the individual is in detention.

habit Regular response to a repeated specific situation, such as eating the same food for lunch at the same time each and every day, or parking in the same parking space.

harmless error An error made in admission of evidence that does not contribute to the conviction obtained. An appellate court must be convinced beyond a reasonable doubt that the error is harmless.

hearsay A statement other than one made by the declarant while testifying at the trial or hearing offered to prove the truth of the matter asserted.

hearsay within hearsay Not excluded by the rule against hearsay if each part of the "combined statements conforms with an exception to the rule."

hung jury A jury unable to reach a verdict.

husband-wife privilege The marital communication privilege allows either spouse to prevent the other from testifying about confidential communications during marriage. The marital testimony privilege provides that either spouse may refuse to testify against the other and either spouse may prevent the other from testifying against the other.

identifications A witness's identification of a "person made after perceiving the person" is admissible as an exemption to the hearsay rule.

impeachment Cross-examination of a witness's inconsistent statements, motive to fabricate evidence, specific acts, or reputation for untruthfulness, felony convictions, and criminal convictions for crimes of dishonesty or false statement.

implied waiver The waiver of a right as indicated by an individual's words and actions and the totality of the circumstances.

incommunicado interrogation Law enforcement questioning of individuals in the isolation of a police station.

in-court exhibitions Exhibition of physical characteristics in court.

in-court identification A witness identifies the perpetrator of a criminal act in court.

independent source doctrine The principle that provides that evidence unlawfully seized nevertheless is admissible where the police are able to demonstrate that the same evidence was also obtained through independent and lawful means.

indictment An accusation of criminal activity returned by a grand jury.

indictment states Eighteen indictment states, the District of Columbia, and the federal government provide that following the preliminary hearing a felony charge is to be brought before a grand jury. A prosecutor may "bypass" the preliminary hearing by immediately taking a charge before a grand jury.

inevitable discovery rule A rule providing that evidence seized as the result of an unconstitutional search is admissible where the government can prove that it would inevitably have been discovered in a lawful fashion.

inference Logical deduction of one fact from another fact.

informant An individual who provides information about criminal authority to law enforcement.

informant privilege An informant may not be required to testify.

information A document signed by a prosecutor charging an individual with a crime.

information states Prosecutors in twenty-eight states may bring a felony charge based on a "sworn information" and then may bring a charge either before a preliminary hearing or before a grand jury.

initiation The test for waiving a prior invocation of counsel under *Miranda*.

interlocutory appeal An appeal taken prior to the final verdict.

intermediate appellate courts Courts between municipal courts and the state supreme court.

interrogation Words or actions on the part of the police that are likely to lead a suspect to incriminate himself or herself.

inventory An administrative procedure recording the possessions of an arrestee and the content of impounded automobiles.

invited response A prosecutor's closing statement that responds to a statement by the defense attorney.

involuntary confessions Confessions that result from coercion, drugs, or a mental disability rather than free will.

irrebuttable presumption The jury is required to reach a conclusion from a fact established at trial.

journalist shield law A law allowing journalists to refuse to reveal their sources.

judicial notice A judge accepts fact as true without following the normal rules of evidence.

judicial review The U.S. Supreme Court reviews the decisions of the legislative and executive branches of government to determine whether they are consistent with the U.S. Constitution. The Court is the "final arbiter" of the meaning of the Constitution.

jury instructions Instructions issued to the jury by the judge.

jury nullification A jury disregards the law and acquits a defendant.

jury poll A questioning of individual jurors regarding whether they support the jury verdict.

knock and announce Refers to a requirement that police knock and announce their presence when serving a search warrant.

knock and talk searches Most courts approve of these searches on the grounds that the police by knocking on an individual's door are doing no more than any citizen might do and are not violating a resident's expectation of privacy.

lay witness A witness with knowledge that may be possessed by the average juror that does not depend on particular skill, training, or experience.

laying the foundation Establish preliminary facts before evidence may be admitted. Item of evidence must be what it claims to be.

leading question A question by a lawyer to a witness that suggests the desired answer.

legislative facts Facts relating to the larger social context of a case.

limiting instruction Judicial instruction restricting the purposes that evidence may be considered by the jury.

majority opinion The decision of a majority of judges on a court.

material fact Relevant to a fact at issue in the case.

medical treatment-diagnosis The hearsay exception allows for "[s]tatements made for . . . medical diagnosis or treatment and describing medical history, or past or present symptoms, pain, or sensations." The rule also states that the cause or source of the declarant's medical condition is admissible "insofar as reasonably pertinent to diagnosis or treatment."

***Miranda* warnings** The police are required to inform individuals of the right to remain silent, that anything they say may be used against them, and of the right to an attorney, retained or appointed.

misdemeanant An individual arrested for a misdemeanor.

modified indictment states Four states require indictments for felonies punishable by capital punishment and life imprisonment.

motion in limine "At the outset or at the threshold"; a motion to exclude evidence from trial or to obtain permission to introduce evidence at trial.

motion to suppress A motion to exclude unlawfully obtained evidence from trial.

narrative question An open-ended question to a witness that allows the witness to testify without interruption about the events that are the subject of the prosecution.

near-miss issue A statement that narrowly misses under an existing hearsay exception.

negative hearsay A hearsay exception for the absence of a business record or public record.

news media privilege A journalist is not required to reveal the identity of his or her sources or provide information gathered as a journalist.

no bill The grand jury refuses to indict an individual.

nolo contendere The defendant pleads "no contest"; a plea that has the legal effect of a plea of guilty but does not constitute an admission of guilt in proceedings outside of the immediate trial.

non-corporeal identification Identification of the perpetrator of a crime, who is not present, by viewing photographs.

nontestimonial evidence Evidence that is non-communicative in character.

oath or affirmation Every witness is required to swear an oath to affirm he or she will "testify truthfully."

official information privilege Information regarding criminal investigation, military plans and diplomacy, and other matters.

open fields Areas distant from the home that lack an expectation of privacy.

opening statement The prosecutor and defense attorney each indicate at the beginning of the trial the evidence that they plan to introduce at trial.

opinion rule A lay witness may not give an opinion.

ordeal Evidentiary proof based on an appeal to God or on various physical tests.

original jurisdiction The first court to hear a case.

other acts evidence Federal Rule of Evidence 404(b) provides that the prior acts of a defendant may be admissible by the prosecution to establish "motive, opportunity, intent, preparation, plan, knowledge, identity, absence of mistake, or lack of accident." Other acts evidence, however, "is not admissible to prove the character of a person in order to show action in conformity therewith."

pardon A release from additional criminal punishment.

past recollection recorded A document may be admitted into evidence presenting facts when a witness cannot fully and accurately recall events.

pattern jury instructions Standard jury instructions in a jurisdiction.

per curiam An opinion of an entire court without any single judge being identified as the author.

peremptory challenge Removal of jurors without an obligation to state a reason.

permissive presumption The jury may reach a conclusion from a fact established at trial.

persuasive authority A decision that does not constitute a binding authority but that a court may consult to assist in making a judgment.

petitioner An individual filing a collateral attack on a verdict following the exhaustion of direct appeals.

photographic displays Witness identification of the perpetrator of a crime through the use of photographs.

physical seizure An act in which a law enforcement officer takes hold of a suspect with the intent to prevent the individual from leaving.

physician-patient privilege A patient may prevent a doctor from revealing confidential information communicated during an examination for diagnosis or treatment.

plain exception An exception that permits an appellate court to review an error that was not raised in the trial court.

plain-feel doctrine An exception to the Fourth Amendment warrant requirement that allows a police officer to seize an item without a search warrant when (1) the officer is lawfully positioned and (2) there is probable cause to seize the objects.

plain view An exception to the Fourth Amendment warrant requirement that allows a police officer to seize an item without a search warrant when (1) the officer is lawfully positioned and (2) there is probable cause to seize the object.

plea bargain An agreement to plead guilty in return for a reduction in charges or other considerations.

plurality opinion A judicial opinion that represents the views of the largest number of judges on a court, although short of a majority.

polygraph Lie detector test.

prejudicial evidence Evidence whose probative value substantially outweighed by danger will impact objective evaluation of evidence by the jury.

preliminary hearing Determination whether a defendant should be bound over for trial.

present recollection refreshed A document, an object, or any item may be used to enable a witness to recall and to testify about events.

present sense impression A "statement describing or explaining an event or condition made while or immediately after the declarant perceived it." The statement must describe or explain rather than analyze the event and must be made immediately or within a brief period following the event.

presentence report A report prepared for a judge following a defendant's conviction presenting the factors that may be considered in sentencing the defendant and the sentencing options available to a judge.

presentment A report filed by a grand jury with the court on criminal activity.

pretext arrest An arrest that is motivated by the intent to investigate law violations for which no probable cause or event articulable suspicion exists.

pretrial motions Motions filed before the beginning of a criminal trial; the defense case at trial.

prior consistent statements Admissible to rehabilitate a witness but may not be introduced for truth of the matter asserted. Prior consistent statements thus are introduced to show that the statement was true rather than that the statement was made. Prior consistent statements are introduced on redirect examination after the witness has been impeached by a prior inconsistent statement or by allegations that testimony recently was fabricated or is based on a motive such as friendship or a bribe.

prior inconsistent statement Federal Rule 801(d)(1)(A) categorizes prior inconsistent statements as exempt nonhearsay although a number of states categorize prior inconstant statements to be an exception to hearsay. Inconsistent statements are statements made outside of court before the witness testifies that are inconsistent with the witness's direct testimony.

probable cause Facts and circumstances within officers' knowledge, and of which they have reasonable trustworthy information, that would warrant a person of reasonable caution to believe that an offense has been or is being committed.

probative value An item of evidence that tends to prove or disprove a fact at issue in the case.

property rights approach An approach to Fourth Amendment protection that assumes such protection is limited to physical intrusions of the home, comparable to trespassory approach.

psychotherapist-patient privilege A patient may prevent a psychotherapist from revealing information conveyed during treatment.

public record The public records of agencies include the courts, police, correctional institutions, and every other part of the government.

public safety exception Police may ask questions reasonably prompted by a reasonable concern with public safety without first advising a suspect of his or her *Miranda* rights.

purging the taint The effect of an attenuated connection between an illegal search and evidence seized in such a search; if the connection is attenuate, it is said to purge the taint of the illegal search.

question first and warn later Police may question an individual without reading Miranda, obtain a confession, and then read the *Miranda* rights and reinterrogate the suspect. The confession is admissible so long as the Miranda warnings function effectively to advise suspects of their rights.

racial profiling Stopping or arresting individuals because of their race, ethnicity, religion, or other characteristic rather than because of their activity.

rape shield laws Statutes limiting cross-examination of victims and prohibiting evidence of their reputation for virtuosity.

rape trauma syndrome A psychological pattern exhibited by rape victims.

real evidence Physical evidence other than testimonial evidence introduced to prove a fact at issue.

reasonable suspicion A police officer may undertake an investigative stop of a suspect where he or she has an objective, factual basis to suspect that "crime is afoot"; the suspect has engaged in criminal activity. This determination is based on the totality of the circumstances, and no single fact may be determinative. Factors to consider include the suspect's actions, nervousness, and evasiveness; frequency and type of criminal activity in the area; time of day; and the officer's prior knowledge of the suspect.

rebuttable presumption The jury may reach a conclusion from a fact established at trial.

rebuttal The defense case at trial.

redirect examination The lawyer who examined a witness on direct examination may ask the witness additional questions following the witness's cross-examination.

rehabilitation Repairing the witness's credibility.

relevant evidence Federal Rule of Evidence 402 provides that "[a]ll relevant evidence is admissible. . . . Evidence which is not relevant is not admissible."

respondent An individual against whom a collateral attack is directed.

retroactivity of judicial decisions The principle that a U.S. Supreme Court judgment should be retroactively applied to all cases that are yet to be filed and cases that already have been filed.

right of allocution The right of a defendant to make a statement to the judge prior to sentencing.

rule of four Four Supreme Court judges are required to vote to hear a case.

scientific evidence Forensic evidence and evidence involving application of scientific analysis.

scrupulously honor Police may question an individual who has invoked his or her right to silence about a crime different in time, nature, and place after waiting a significant period of time and giving a fresh set of *Miranda* warnings.

search Governmental intrusion on an individual's expectation of privacy.

search incident to an arrest A search that is authorized by the fact of an arrest; it includes a search of the person arrested and the area within his or her immediate control.

search warrant Authorization from a magistrate to search and seize specified objects.

secondary evidence Evidence other than the original that may be relied on to prove the content of an original document.

seizure A reasonable person would not believe himself or herself to be free to leave or to otherwise terminate the encounter.

selective incorporation The Fourteenth Amendment Due Process Clause incorporates only selected portions of the Bill of Rights.

selective incorporation plus The Fourteenth Amendment Due Process Clause incorporates selected portions of the Bill of Rights along with other rights.

self-authenticating documents Documents that require no independent proof of their authenticity.

sentencing guidelines A formula incorporating various factors that is employed to provide uniform, proportionate, and predictable sentences for criminal offenders.

sentencing hearing A hearing conducted following a defendant's conviction in which the prosecution and defense present their arguments to a judge on the appropriate sentence for the defendant.

sequential presentation Presentation of individuals in a lineup one after another.

show of authority seizure Demonstration of authority by law enforcement officers in which they direct a suspect to halt and/or display his or her weapons, block the suspect's movement, or otherwise conduct themselves in a manner that would result in a reasonable person not feeling free to leave or otherwise terminate the encounter. The suspect must actually submit to the demonstration of authority.

showup A victim or eyewitness is confronted with a single suspect.

silver platter doctrine A practice ruled unconstitutional in 1960, in which federal officials relied on evidence in federal prosecutions that had been seized by state officials in violation of the Eighth Amendment.

simultaneous lineup A victim or eyewitness confronts all the participants in the lineup at the same time.

Sixth Amendment protection against the deliberate eliciting of a confession A defendant may not be interrogated by the police following an indictment absent the presence of counsel unless the suspect waives his or her right to representation.

special-needs searches Searches that do not serve the normal needs of law enforcement.

speedy trial Sixth Amendment right to a trial without unreasonable delay.

spousal competence An individual may testify against his or her spouse.

standing A defendant's eligibility to contest the legality of a search.

Star Chamber A special court that was established by the English king in the fifteenth century and that was charged with prosecuting and punishing political and religious dissidents.

stare decisis The practice of following the precedent established by previous court decisions.

state secrets privilege The government may refuse to give evidence and to prevent any person from giving evidence upon a showing of a reasonable likelihood of danger that the evidence will disclose a state secret or official information.

statement An oral or written declaration to the police that may constitute an assertion of innocence.

statement of personal or family history When family relationships are at issue, a party may rely on hearsay to establish births, deaths, marriages, and adoption and other facts of personal and family history.

statement under belief of impending death A statement made by an unavailable declarant while believing that the declarant's death was imminent concerning the cause or circumstances of what the declarant believed to be impending death.

stipulations Agreement between the parties that a fact or facts exist.

stop and frisk The police may stop an individual in those instances in which they have a reasonable basis to believe that crime may be afoot. The police may conduct a frisk for weapons where the individual fails to dispel the officer's fear that the individual is armed and presently dangerous.

stop-and-identify statutes State laws that authorize the police to require a citizen subjected to a stop and frisk to prevent identification.

subpoena ad testificandum A court order to produce a tangible object.

subpoena duces tecum A court order to produce documents.

suggestive procedures Identifications that influence the result by highlighting one of the participants.

supervisory authority The Supreme Court has the authority to direct lower courts to follow rules that are not based on the U.S. Constitution.

Supremacy Clause Article VI, Section 2 of the U.S. Constitution provides that the Constitution, the laws of the United States, and treaties shall be the "supreme law of the land." This gives the federal government priority over the state government when there is a conflict between federal and state laws.

surrebuttal Witnesses presented by the defense attorney to attack the evidence presented by the prosecutor on rebuttal.

testimonial evidence Statements from a witness under oath or affirmation in a court proceeding.

testimonial privilege Individuals in various confidential relationships may not testify about information communicated during the relationship.

then-existing mental, emotional, or physical condition A declarant's internal (personal) view of his or her state of mind, emotional, sensory or physical condition. The statement is admissible to establish what the declarant truthfully believes about his or her condition.

third-party consent Consent to a search provided by an individual with common authority who exercises mutual use of property and has joint access or control for most purposes.

total incorporation The entire Bill of Rights is incorporated into the Fourteenth Amendment Due Process Clause.

total incorporation plus The entire Bill of Rights, along with other rights not contained in the Bill of Rights, is incorporated into the Fourteenth Amendment Due Process Clause.

trespassory approach An approach to Fourth Amendment protection that assumes such protection is limited to physical intrusions of the home, comparable to property rights approach.

trial de novo A new trial before a different court.

true bill A written statement by a grand jury that there is sufficient evidence to indict the defendant.

Uniform Rules of Evidence The National Conference of Commissioners on Uniform State Laws in an effort to standardize state laws of evidence drafted new Uniform Rules of Evidence.

venire A group of individuals from which a jury is selected.

vital statistics Birth, death, and marriage records are admissible.

voir dire Examination of potential jurors.

voluntary, knowing, and intelligent waiver
The standard that the prosecution must satisfy to demonstrate that a suspect waived his or her Miranda rights in an informed and free fashion.

Wade-Gilbert rule The suspect has a constitutional right to a lawyer at all post-indictment lineups and confrontations. Absent the presence or waiver of a lawyer, the results may not be introduced by the prosecutor at trial. A prosecutor may not ask a witness for an in-court identification unless the prosecution establishes by clear and convincing evidence that the in-court identification is not the product of a tainted identification procedure.

weight Importance attached to evidence by a fact finder.

writs of assistance Documents used by eighteenth-century American colonial authorities to compel individuals to assist in carrying out a search.

Abandoned property, 268, 275, 280–281, 280 (photo)
Abel, John, 120
Abel v. United States (1960), 280
Abney v. United States (1977), 49
ABO blood typing, 161
Absence of a public record, 210
Absence of business records, 208–209
Absten, Ronald, 294
Accusatorial system, 377
Acevedo, Charles Steven, 366
Acknowledged documents, 178
Actual-prejudice standard, 70
Adams v. Williams (1972), 295–296, 310
Adamson v. California (1947), 19, 20
Adjudicative facts, 72
Administrative inspections, 368–369
Admissions:
    by agent, 197, 197 (table)
    by co-conspirator, 197, 197 (table)
    defined, 378
    as hearsay exception, 195–198, 197 (table), 217 (table)
    by party-opponent, 196, 197 (table), 198, 217 (table)
    See also Confessions
Admissions doctrine, 182
Adoptive admission, 196–197, 197 (table)
Adversarial system, 381
Advisory Committee on Rules of Evidence. *See* Federal
    Rules of Evidence
Aerial surveillance, 276–277, 285–286
Affiants, 325
Affidavits, 321–322, 325, 344 (table)
Affirmation, 68, 105–106
Affirmative defenses, 3
African Americans:
    Ferguson, Missouri, 335–336
    Fourteenth Amendment, 16, 18–19
    jury selection, 38–39
    race and reasonable suspicion, 300, 301, 302
    racial profiling, 355–356
Agent, admission by, 197, 197 (table)
Aguilar, Nick Alford, 321
Aguilar v. Texas (1964), 321, 324
Aguilar-Spinelli test, 316, 321–323
Ahmed, Hussein Osman, 219
Ahrens, Dale, 389
Ahrens, Richard, 389
Airport screening of passengers, 370
Ake, Glen Burton, 158

Ake v. Oklahoma (1985), 158
Alabama:
    child testimony, 110
    DNA evidence, 163
    husband-wife privilege, 236
Alabama v. White (1990), 292, 296
Alaska:
    DNA evidence, 163
    eyewitness identifications, 420
Alcala, Joe, 361
Aldahi, Richard, 272
Alderman, Willie, 251
Alderman v. United States (1969), 251
Alford, Henry, 35
Alito, Samuel, 259, 278
Allen v. United States (1896), 44
Alvarado, Michael, 388–389
American Bar Association, 34, 386, 428
American Civil Liberties Union, 355–356
American Law Institute, 22, 283, 304
"American Skin" (song), 308–309
Ancient documents rule, 176
Anderson, Mark, 265, 266
Anderson, Patrick, 375, 380
Anderson, Stephen, 264
Andrews v. State (2002), 183
Anglo-American common law system, 4–6
Annulment, 123
Anonymous tips, 296
Anthony, Casey, 69, 70, 159
Anthony, Caylee, 159
Anthrax, 174 (photo)
Anticipatory warrants, 344 (table)
Antiterrorism and Effective Death Penalty
    Act (1996), 51, 52
Apodaca v. Oregon (1972), 44
Apparent authority third-party consent, 361–362, 364
Appeals, criminal, 48–50
Appellants, 9
Appellate courts:
    federal, 10, 11 (figure), 12 (map)
    state, 12, 13, 14 (figure), 15
    See also U.S. Supreme Court
Appellees, 9
Apprendi v. New Jersey (2000), 47
Arbeeny, Jason, 264
Arch City Defenders, 335
Argumentative question, 40

Arias, Jodi, 70
Arizona v. Evans (1995), 257, 258, 265, 266
Arizona v. Fulminante (1991), 380
Arizona v. Gant (2009), 259, 352–353
Arizona v. Hicks (1987), 274, 366
Arizona v. Johnson (2009), 307, 310
Arizona v. Roberson (1988), 400
Arkansas:
    knock and talk searches, 359
    school desegregation, 7
Arnold, Diana, 236
Arnold, James, 236
Arnold v. State (1977), 236
Arraignment, 31–32
Arrest warrants, 28, 264–266, 324–330
Arrests:
    about, 317, 318–319, 318 (photo)
    Aguilar-Spinelli test, 316, 321–323
    case analysis, 336–338
    deadly force and, 330–331, 336–338
    direct observations, 319–320
    exigent circumstances, 327–330
    hearsay, 316, 320–324
    in the home, 326–327
    misdemeanor, 334–335, 336
    non-deadly force and, 331–332
    probable cause and, 317–324
    reasonableness and, 324–336
    totality-of-the-circumstances approach, 322–323
    warrants and, 324–330
    See also Searches incident to an arrest
Articulable suspicion, 292
Aryan Brotherhood prison gang, 120
Ash, Charles, 421
Assertive statements, 191
Attenuation, 254–256, 264
Attorney-client privilege, 226–230, 226 (table)
Attorneys, defense, 49, 418
    See also Counsel, right to
Atwater, Gail, 334–335, 353
Atwater v. City of Lago Vista (2001), 326, 334–335, 353
Australia, 96
Authentication:
    of crime scene evidence, 154, 155–157
    of documents, 172, 173–176, 184–187
    of medical images, 179
    of objects, 179
    of photographs and videos, 178–179
    of real evidence, 69
    of visual images, 178–179
    of voice communication, 179–180
Authorized admissions, 197, 197 (table)
Automatic reversal rule, 50
Automobile exception, 364–366
Automobiles:
    checkpoints for, 370
    inventory of, 368
    passengers of, 251, 310
    probable cause searches of, 364–366
    search of, 259 (photo)
    searches incident to an arrest and, 352–353
    speed detection of, 165
    surveillance of, 284
    Terry searches of, 310–311
    Terry stops and, 307–308

Bad logic prejudice, 63
Bail, 49
Bailey, John, 421
Balancing test, 291–292
Baldwin, Lashon, 168
Balko, Radley, 349
Ballew v. Georgia (1978), 44
Ballistics, 164
Banks, Lashawn, 347
Barajas, Ronald, 157
Barber, Jessica, 172
Barker v. Wingo (1972), 33
Barnes v. United States (1973), 86
Barney, Phil, 254
Barrett, Arthur, 83
Barrett, William, 396
Barron v. Mayor & City Council of Baltimore (1833), 15–16
Barthel, Theresa Ellen, 431
Basic fact, 74, 75–76
Basis-of-knowledge prong, in *Aguilar-Spinelli* test,
    316, 321–322
Bates, Ruby, 18
Batson v. Kentucky (1986), 38
Battered child syndrome, 87, 147–148
Battered spouse syndrome, 87, 147–148
Battered woman syndrome, 149–150
Bean, Ralph, 419
Beard, Vance, 360
Beck, William, 319–320
Beck v. Ohio (1964), 319–320
Beckwith v. United States (1976), 386
Behrendt, Mrs., 424–425
Bell v. State (2003), 203–204
Belton, Roger, 352
Beltway snipers, 416
Benally, Kerry Dean, 115
Bench trial, 13
Benedetto, Carl, 126
Bennett, Vincent, 183
Bentham, Jeremy, 241
Benton v. Maryland (1969), 22 (table)
Berger v. United States (1935), 42
Berghuis v. Thompkins (2010), 394, 396–397, 401
Berkeley Premium Nutraceuticals, 272
Berkemer v. McCarty (1984), 388
Berry, William, 332
Bertine, Steven Lee, 368
Best evidence rule, 180–183

Bevis, Walter, 133
Beyond a reasonable doubt, 2
Bias:
    impeachment and, 119, 120, 130 (table)
    police, 386
    relevant evidence and, 58
Bickham, Curvis, 432
Biggers, Archie, 424
Bill of Rights (England), 6
Bill of Rights (U.S.):
    constitutionalization of, 15–17
    criminal procedure provisions, 8 (table)
    Fourteenth Amendment and, 21, 22 (table)
    history of, 7
    state and local governments, 15–17
    See also specific amendments
Binding authority, 15
Bite marks, 144 (photo)
Bivens v. Six Unknown Named Agents (1971), 249, 252
Bjork, Robert A., 146
Black, Hugo, 20, 21, 271, 322, 433
Black, Roy, 98–99
Black Souls street gang, 134–136
Blackmon, Thomas W., 229–230
Blackmon v. State (1982), 229–230
Blackmun, Harry, 45, 252
Blacksmith, Larry, 57
Blackstone, William, 6, 51
Blair, Todd, 349
Blake, Leeander Jerome, 404
Blakely, Ralph Howard, 47
Blakely v. Washington (2004), 47
Bland, Michael, 350–351
Blandon, Nubia, 429, 430
Blind administration, 428
Blood alcohol testing, 160–161, 164
Blood typing, 161
"Bloods" street gang, 350, 370–371
Bloomberg, Michael, 301
Blue v. State (1977), 420
Booker, Freddie, 47–48
Booking, 30
Boone, Judy Melinda, 254
Borchard, Edwin, 415
Bordenkircher v. Hayes (1978), 35–36
Border searches, 370
Boss, Kenneth, 308–309
Bostick, Terrance, 284
Bowles, Charles, 138
Boyd v. United States (1886), 271
Boyden, James, Jr., 205
Boykin v. United States (1979), 35
Bradshaw, James Edward, 401
Bradley v. State (2003), 181
Brady rule, 33
Brady v. Maryland (2012), 33
Brady v. United States (1970), 35

Brandeis, Louis, 248–249, 271
Branzburg v. Hayes (1972), 238, 239
Brathwaite, Nowell, 422–424
Bratton, Rosemary, 149
Break in custody rule, 401
Breathalyzer, 164
Breland, Kayla, 221
Brennan, William:
    eyewitness identifications, 419, 421
    good faith exception, 258
    habeas corpus, 51
    impeachment exception to exclusionary rule, 263
    inevitable discovery rule, 261
    selective incorporation, 20–21
    self-incrimination, right against, 380–381, 382
    state supreme courts, 12
    stop and frisk, 296
    totality-of-the-circumstances approach, 323
Brewer v. Williams (1977), 378, 405
Breyer, Stephen, 48, 352, 388–389, 392
Briefs, 9
Brigham City v. Stuart (2006), 329
Bright-line rule, 354
Brinegar v. United States (1949), 319
Brison, Dale, 416
Broday, Idelle, 108
Brown, Charles, 220–221
Brown, Henry Alton, 422
Brown, James, 354–355
Brown, Jerry, 129
Brown, Robert L., 384
Brown v. Allen (1953), 8
Brown v. City of Oneonta (1999), 300
Brown v. Heyd (1967), 384
Brown v. Illinois (1975), 254, 255
Brown v. Mississippi (1936), 19
Brown v. Texas (1979), 294
Browning, Richard, 221
Bryant, Richard, 194
Buchanek, Michael, 432
Buie, Jerome Edward, 311
Bullcoming v. New Mexico (2011), 158, 194
Bumper v. North Carolina (1968), 358
Bunch v. Commonwealth (2008), 274
Burbine, Brian, 392–393, 407, 408
Burch v. Louisiana (1979), 45
Burden of persuasion, 2, 3
Burden of production, 2, 3
Burden of proof, 2–3
Burge, Jon, 230, 402, 403
Burger, Joseph, 369
Burger, Warren:
    deadly force, 338
    exclusionary rule, 249, 252
    executive privilege, 236
    habeas corpus, 51
    interrogations, 406

Burglary prosecution, relevant evidence in, 62 (table)
Burr, Murray Wayne, 150–151, 167
Burton, David, 138
Bus sweeps, 284
Bush, George W., 356
Bushel, Edward, 5, 51
Bushel's Case (1677), 51
Business records, 207–209
Businesses, private, 275, 279
Butler, William Thomas, 396
Byndom v. State (2001), 108
Byrd, William, 203

California:
　constitution, 420
　court system, 14 (figure), 15
　exclusionary rule, 253
　eyewitness identifications, 420
California Evidence Code, 2, 58
California v. Acevedo (1991), 366
California v. Carney (1985), 364–365
California v. Ciraolo (1986), 276, 286
California v. Funston (2002), 161
California v. Greenwood (1988), 268, 280
California v. Hodari (1999), 284, 285
California v. Prysock (1981), 391, 392
Camara v. Municipal Court (1967), 368, 369
Campbell, Jacquelyn C., 150
Canarsky, Paul, 229–230
Capacity/incapacity:
　mental, 84–85, 107–108, 118, 358
　physical and psychological, 119, 129, 130 (table)
Cardozo, Benjamin, 247
Carella, Eugene John, 76
Carella v. California (1989), 76
Carrillo, Richard, 390
Carroll, George, 364
Carroll, Sean, 308–309
Carroll v. United States (1957), 50
Carroll v. United States (1959), 318
Carter, Benjamin, 281
Carter, Mark, 120
Carter, Wayne Thomas, 252
Case-by-case determination, 292, 387
Case-in-chief:
　defense's, 41–42
　prosecution's, 40–41
Casparian, Richard, 407
Catron, Sam, 138
CB radio transmissions, 203
Cell phones, 350, 370–373
Center on Wrongful Convictions at Northwestern University
　School of Law, 113
Central Park jogger case, 385–386
Centrella, John, 350–351
Certificate of rehabilitation, 123

Certiorari, 9
Chain of custody, 156–157
Chain of evidence, 40–41
Challenge for cause, 36–38
Chambers v. Maroney (1970), 364
Change of venue, 33
Chapman v. California (1967), 50, 251
Character:
　as crime element, 89
　example from news, 90–91
　habit and, 91–92
　public policy and, 87–88
　for truthfulness, 41, 119, 124–127, 130, 130 (table)
　of victim in a criminal case, 89
　of victim in a homicide case, 90
Character witnesses, 68, 88
Charges, 34, 35, 404
Charts, 183
Chatfield, Hazel, 206
Chavez, Ben, 381
Chavez, Pete Agapito, 353
Chavez v. Martinez (2003), 381
Chemerinsky, Erwin, 16
Chesternut, Michael, 284
Chicago Police Department, 312–313, 402–403
Child abuse cases, and medical treatment-diagnosis, 206
Child sexual abuse accommodation syndrome, 87, 147–148
Child testimony, 109–113
Chilton, Richard, 292
Chimel, Ted, 349
Chimel v. California (1969), 349–350
Christo, Christina, 141
Chunn, Jimmy S. "Bo," 164
Cicero, "Dickie Boy," 422
Ciraolo, Dante Carlo, 276
Circumstantial evidence:
　of ability to commit the crime, 83–85
　about, 66, 67, 67 (table), 82
　of identity, 93–94
　of inference of consciousness of guilt and of guilt, 85–86
　of intent, 94–97, 100–101
　of rape, 87
　See also specific types
Cirrito, Joseph, 363
Citations, 334–335
Citizen-informants, 320
City of St. Paul v. Uber (1990), 301
Civil law system derived from Roman law, 4
Civil tort suits, 250
Civilian review boards, 250
Clark, Kelly, 363
Clark, Lloyd, 78
Clark, Tom, 248
Clay, Nicole, 429
Clemency, 46
Clergy-penitent privilege, 230–232

Cline, Stephen, 230
Clinton, Bill, 356
Closely regulated business, 369
Closing arguments, 42–43
Cloud computing, 372
Cobham, Lord, 191
Co-conspirator, admission by, 197, 197 (table)
Code of Conduct for United States Judges, 113
Coercion:
    confessions and, 379
    public safety exception and, 390
    rape and, 98
    self-incrimination, right against, and, 381
    voluntariness in consent searches and, 357, 358–359
Cohen v. Beneficial Industrial Loan Corporation (1949), 49
Cohens v. Virginia (1821), 7
Coke, Lord, 240
Collateral attack, 9
Collateral proceedings, 253–254, 264
Collateral remedies, 50
    See also Habeas corpus
College of DuPage, 389
Collins, John, 262
Colorado v. Bertine (1987), 368
Colorado v. Connelly (1986), 380, 394, 395
Colorado v. Spring (1987), 392, 396
Colson, Jesse, 405
Command hallucinations, 375, 380
Commeau, Robert, 426
Commentaries on the Laws of England (Blackstone), 6
Commercial property, 275, 279
Commercial transactions, 252
Common authority third-party consent, 361, 364
Common knowledge facts, 72–73
Common law system, 4–6
Commonwealth v. Carey (1990), 320
Commonwealth v. Ferguson (1984), 421
Commonwealth v. Galvin (1989), 133
Commonwealth v. Gonzalves (1999), 307
Commonwealth v. Holden (1957), 61
Commonwealth v. Johnson (2006), 85
Commonwealth v. Lopez (2001), 87
Commonwealth v. McGrath (1974), 358
Commonwealth v. Puleio (1985), 204
Commonwealth v. Robertson (2013), 282
Commonwealth v. Stephenson (2006), 294
Communications Assistance for Law Enforcement
    Act (1994), 346 (table)
Commutation, 46
Competency hearing, 108
Competency to testify, 104–108, 109, 110–111, 119
Competent evidence, 61–62
Complaint, 28
Compliant false confessors, 386
Comstock, Cheryl, 388
Concealing evidence, 85–86

Conclusive presumptions, 74, 75–76, 77
Concurrent sentences, 46
Concurring opinion, 9
Confessions:
    defined, 378
    due process and, 378–380
    habeas corpus and, 52
    as hearsay exception, 195–198,
        197 (table), 217 (table)
    interrogations and, 376–377
    Sixth Amendment protection against deliberate
        eliciting of, 405
    taping of, 386
    See also Admissions; Interrogations
Confidential informant privilege, 237–238
Confidentiality, 225, 227, 231, 238
Confrontation, 413
Confrontation Clause, 41, 192, 193–194, 220–221
Confusing evidence, 65
Congressional Research Service, 52
Connecticut, child testimony in, 110
Connelly, Francis, 380
Connelly v. Georgia (1977), 325
Connolly, John, 295–296, 310
Connors, Marie Boyden, 205
Consecutive sentences, 46
Consent searches:
    about, 356–359
    scope of, 359–360
    third-party consent, 361–363, 362 (table), 364
    withdrawal of consent, 360–361
Constitutional interest test for attenuation, 255
Constitutionalization of the Bill of Rights, 15–17
    See also Due Process Clause
Constitutions, state, 10, 12, 13, 420
Containers, inventory of, 368
Contemporaneous objection rule, 40
Contemporaneous requirement, 351–352
Content witnesses, 124
Contraband, 269, 357
Convictions, prior, 118, 120–124, 122 (table),
    130 (table)
Co-occupants, 362–363, 362 (table), 364
Cooke, Luther, 304
Coolidge v. New Hampshire (1971), 325, 344 (table)
Cooper v. Aaron (1958), 7
Coote, Robert, 432
Corey, Angela, 91
Corporeal identification, 421
Corroboration, 98, 130–131, 202, 323
Corroborative evidence, 66
Cost, Darrio L., 312
Cost v. Commonwealth (2008), 312
Co-tenants, 362–363, 362 (table), 364
Cotton, Charles, 185, 186
Cotton, Ronald, 428

Counsel, right to:
    critical stages of a criminal proceeding, 417–419
    defense attorney, role of, 418
    eyewitness identifications, 413, 416–422,
        425–426, 432–433
    identifications and, 416, 417
    interrogations, 378, 404–406
    Miranda rights and, 383–384
    photographic displays, 421–422, 425–426
    prearrangement identifications, 419–420
    suggestive procedures, 417–418, 432–433
    tainted lineups and courtroom identifications, 418
County Court of Ulster County v. Allen (1979), 75–76
County of Riverside v. McLaughlin (1991), 30, 325
Court of Common Pleas, 4
Courts of appeal:
    federal, 10, 11 (figure), 12 (map)
    state, 12, 13, 14 (figure), 15
    See also U.S. Supreme Court
Courts of general jurisdiction, 13
Courts of limited jurisdiction, 13
Courts of original jurisdiction, 13
Coventry, Dale, 230
Covington, Anthony, 194
Cox, Terry C., 145
Cox, Vanessa, 251–252
Crandall, Keith, 168
Crawford v. Washington (2004), 193–194
Credibility, 71, 83, 262
Crehore, Charles, 328
Crime laboratories, 166, 194
Crime scene evidence, 155–156, 155 (photo)
    See also specific types
Crime-fraud exception, 228
Criminal appeals, 48–50
Criminal cases, victim's character in, 89
Criminal justice process, 28, 29 (figure)
    See also specific activities
Critical stages of a criminal proceeding,
    417–419, 432–433
Crockett, David, 272
Cross-examination, 41, 169, 190, 192, 263
Cruel trilemma, 381
Crump, Benjamin, 66
Cruz, Juan, 198
Cumulative evidence, 65–66
Cupp v. Murphy (1973), 367
Curd, Shirley, 352
Curd v. City Court of Judsonia (1998), 352
Curtilage, 275–277, 285–286
Custodial interrogation, 386–389
Custodian of business records, 207–208
Cutchall, Rex Dewayne, 64

Dahlin, Randall, 89
Dale County, Alabama, 265, 266

Dangerous patient exception, 233–234
Darden v. Wainwright (1986), 43
Daubert test, 158
Daubert v. Merrell Dow Pharmaceuticals (1993), 142–143
David, Joseph, 425, 432–433
Davies, Thomas, 252–253
Davis, B. C., 312
Davis, B. H., 296
Davis, Jordan, 90, 91
Davis, Willie, 259
Davis v. Mississippi (1969), 305
Davis v. United States (1994), 393, 401
Davis v. United States (2011), 259
Davis v. Washington (2006), 194
Dawson v. Delaware (1992), 184
Day, William R., 246
Deadly force, 330–331, 336–338
Dean, Brian, 180
Dean, John Wayne, 391
Death penalty, 5, 37, 38
Debate Clause, 49
DeCicco, Gary, 96–97
Declarant, unavailability of, 211–218
Declaration against interest, 216–217, 217 (table)
Defense attorneys, 49, 418
    See also Counsel, right to
Defense experts, right to, 158
Defense's case-in-chief, 41–42
Delaware, child testimony in, 110
Demeanor, 83
Demonstrative evidence, 69
Denver Police Department, 348
Deposition, 68
Derivative evidence, 246
Desegregation, school, 7
Desimone, Anthony, 353
Destruction of evidence, 328, 345
Diagrams, 183
Diallo, Amadou, 308–309
Dichiarinte, Anthony, 360
Dickerson v. United States (2000), 385
Dimas-Martinez v. State (2011), 70
Dioguardi, John, 116
Direct appeals, 50
Direct evidence, 66–67, 67 (table), 82
Direct examination, 40
Directed verdict, 41
Discovery, 33–34
Discretionary appeals, 13
Dishonest acts, 122–124
Dismissal of charges, motion for, 32
Dispensa, Rosario, 431
Dispensa v. Lynaugh (1988), 431
Dissenting opinion, 9
Distractors, 413
District Attorney's Office v. Osborne (2009), 162–163

District courts, federal, 10, 11 (figure)
District of Columbia v. Armes (1882), 118
Ditullio, John, 184
DNA, 161–163, 162 (photo)
Documentary evidence, 69
Documents, 69, 172, 173–178, 184–187
Dodson, Esker, 109
Doe v. United States (1988), 381–382
Dog scent lineups, 432
Dog sniffs, 278–279, 281
Dog-scent evidence, 150–151, 167
Dolls, 183
Donnelly v. DeChristoforo (1974), 43
D'Onofrio, Officer, 412, 422–423
Dookhan, "Little Annie," 166
Doorways, 327
Double hearsay, 220
Double jeopardy, 32, 48, 49, 50
Double-blind administration, 428
Douglas, William O.:
    eyewitness identifications, 419, 421
    jury unanimity, 45
    selective incorporation, 21
    stop and frisk, 290
    total incorporation plus, 20
Dow Chemical Company v. United States (1986), 276–277
Doyle v. Ohio (1976), 85, 127, 196
Draper, James Alonso, 321
Draper v. United States (1959), 316, 321
Dred Scott v. Sandford (1857), 16
"Drew's Law" (2008), 215–216
Driving under the influence (DUI), 160
Driving while black/brown, 355–356
Driving while intoxicated (DWI), 160
Driving with an unlawful blood alcohol level (DUBAL),
    160–161
Drizen, Steve, 386
Drug courier profiles, 289, 298–299
Drug Enforcement Administration, 298–299
Drug testing, 370
DUBAL. *See* Driving with an unlawful blood alcohol level
Duckworth v. Egan (1989), 392
Due process:
    confidential informant privilege and, 238
    eyewitness identifications and, 412, 413–414, 422–427
    freestanding, 17
    interrogations and confessions, 378–380
    voluntariness test, 378–380
    See also Due Process Clause
Due Process Clause:
    about, 15, 16–17
    Bill of Rights criminal procedure provisions incorporated
        into, 21, 22 (table)
    discovery, 33
    DNA testing, 162–163
    exclusionary rule and, 247

    fundamental fairness, 16, 17–19
    interrogations, 377
    jury size, 44
    selective incorporation and selective incorporation plus,
        16, 17, 20–21
    speedy trial, 33
    total incorporation and total incorporation plus, 16–17, 20
Duggan, Joseph, 77–78
DUI. *See* Driving under the influence
Dunaway v. New York (1979), 303
Duncan v. Louisiana (1968), 21, 22 (table)
Dunlop v. United States (1897), 43
Dunn, Kimberly, 330
Dunn, Michael, 90–91
Dunn, Ronald, 276
Dunne, Jeanne, 146
Duplicates, 181
Duty to warn, 233–234
DWI. *See* Driving while intoxicated
Dying declaration. *See* Statement under belief of impending
    death
Dynamite charge, 44

Eagan, Gary, 392
Eaton, Bonnie, 204
Eavesdropping, electronic, 273–274
Edwards, Eugene, 352
Edwards, Robert, 400
Edwards rule, 400–401
Edwards v. Arizona (1981), 400, 401
Edwards-Roberson rule, 400
Egolf, Ronald, 400
Ehle, Kurt, 120
Eighth Amendment, 8 (table), 21, 22 (table)
    See also Bill of Rights (U.S.)
El Monte Flores (group), 57
Electronic Communications Privacy Act (1986), 346 (table)
Electronic surveillance, 273–274, 346–347 (table)
Elkins v. United States (1960), 247, 248
Ellos, Tesfalem, 180
Elstad, Michael James, 397
E-mail, 272
Emanuele, Joseph Arthur, 431
Emergency-aid doctrine, 329
Emotion, 23
Employer-employee relationship, 362 (table)
En banc, 10
Encounters, 282–283
England, 4–6, 44, 377, 378, 381
Engle v. Isaac (1982), 52
Environmental Protection Agency, 276–277
Equal Protection Clause of the Fourteenth Amendment,
    37, 38, 301, 302
Equality, 23
Escobedo v. Illinois (1964), 377
Estelle v. McGuire (1991), 87

Estelle v. Williams (1976), 184
Ethnicity, 299, 300, 301, 302
Evans, Isaac, 258
Evidence:
    chain of, 40–41
    character, 87–92
    competent, 61–62
    concealing, 85–86
    confusing, 65
    corroborative, 66
    crime scene, 155–156, 155 (photo)
    cumulative, 65–66
    defined, 2, 58
    demonstrative, 69
    derivative, 246
    destruction of, 328, 345
    direct, 66–67, 67 (table), 82
    documentary, 69
    dog-scent, 150–151, 167
    extrinsic, 119
    fingerprint, 147 (photo), 159–160
    habit, 91–92
    intrinsic, 119
    marking, 154
    misleading, 65
    nontestimonial, 382
    physical, 69
    prejudicial, 63–64, 78–79
    propensity, 88
    real, 69, 69 (table)
    real-testimonial, 69
    relevant, 58–66, 62 (table)
    scientific, 157–158
    secondary, 182
    state rules of, 23
    substitutes for, 71–78
    syndrome, 149–150
    testimonial, 68, 414
    See also Circumstantial evidence; Other acts evidence;
        specific topics
Evidentiary alternative, 65
Ex parte Milligan (1866), 51
Excited utterance, 189, 203–204
Exclusionary rule:
    about, 244–246
    alternative remedies to, 250
    arguments against, 249–250
    case analysis, 264–266
    effect of, 252–253
    federal courts and, 246
    invoking, 250–252
    justification for, 248–249
    state courts and, 246–248
    See also Exclusionary rule exceptions
Exclusionary rule exceptions:
    attenuation, 254–256, 264
    collateral proceedings, 253–254, 264

    good faith exception, 256–260, 264–266
    impeachment, 262–263, 264
    independent source doctrine, 260, 261, 264
    inevitable discovery rule, 261–262, 261 (photo), 264
    See also Exclusionary rule
Executive privilege, 236
Exemplar fingerprints, 160
Exigent circumstances, 327–330, 366–367
Expectation of privacy, 271–273, 274–275, 281 (table)
    See also Searches and seizures
Experiments, 166
Expert testimony, 142–144, 144 (photo), 146–148, 147 (photo)
    See also Expert witnesses
Expert witnesses:
    about, 68
    court-appointed, 149
    defense's right to, 158
    example of, 148
    eyewitness identifications and, 429
    on eyewitness testimony, 167–170
    qualifying, 144–145
    role of, 139
    ultimate issues, testimony on, 145–146
    See also Expert testimony
Express questioning, 403, 404
Express waiver, 396
Extrinsic evidence, 119
Eyewitness identifications:
    about, 413–415
    case analysis, 432–433
    critical stages of a criminal proceeding, 417–419
    defense attorney, role of, 418
    due process, 413–414
    due process test, 422–427
    photographic displays, 421–422, 425–426
    police involvement, requirement of, 429–431
    prearrangement identifications, 419–420
    psychology of, 414, 415–417
    right to counsel and, 413, 416–422
    suggestive procedures, 417–418, 432–433
    suggestiveness, reliability, and totality of the circumstances,
        412, 422–427
    tainted lineups and courtroom identifications, 418
Eyewitness testimony, 167–170

Fact finder role, 3, 4
Fact witnesses, 68, 124
Factory sweeps, 284
Facts:
    adjudicative, 72
    basic, 74, 75–76
    common knowledge, 72–73
    indisputable, 72
    legislative, 73–74
    material, 59–60
    presumed, 74, 75–76
Fairness, 16, 17–19, 23, 75–76

False claims, 96, 358, 367
False confessions, 377, 385–386
False friend cases, 273
False statements, 122–124
Fare v. Michael (1979), 393–394, 395
Fay v. Noia (1963), 51
Federal Bureau of Investigation (FBI):
    Aguilar-Spinelli test, 321–322
    dog scent evidence, 432
    eyewitness identifications, 425–426
    fingerprints, 159
    knock and announce, 348
    Miranda warnings, 392
Federal courts of appeal, 10, 11 (figure), 12 (map)
Federal district courts, 10, 11 (figure)
Federal judicial system, 10, 11 (figure)
Federal Rules of Criminal Procedure:
    arrest warrants, 325
    discovery, 33
    first appearance, 30
    jury selection, 37, 38
    jury unanimity, 44
    plain error exception, 50
    plea bargaining, 34, 35
    search warrants, 344 (table), 345 (table)
    venue, change of, 69
Federal Rules of Evidence (FRE):
    about, 22–23
    ancient documents rule, 176
    authentication, 154, 156
    authentication of evidence, 173–175, 185, 186, 187
    authentication of photographs and videos, 179
    authentication of voice communication, 179
    best evidence rule, 180–182
    bias, 120
    business records, 207–209
    character evidence, 87, 88, 89, 90, 92
    character for truthfulness, 124–126, 130
    competency to testify, 104–105, 107, 110, 111, 118
    competent evidence, 61–62
    convictions, prior, 121–123, 122 (table)
    declarant, unavailability of, 211–212
    declaration against interest, 216–217
    documentary evidence, 173
    exclusion of evidence, 62–66, 78–79, 121, 122 (table)
    expert testimony, 143–144
    expert witnesses, 139, 143, 149
    forfeiture by wrongdoing, 218
    former testimony, 212
    habit evidence, 91
    hearsay, 190, 191–192
    hearsay exceptions, 195, 196, 201
    hearsay within hearsay, 220
    identifications, 200
    impeachment, 119
    judges as witnesses, 113–114
    judicial notice of adjudicative facts, 72, 73
    jurors as witnesses, 114–116
    knowledge, personal, 106–107
    lay witnesses, 140–142
    medical treatment-diagnosis, 206
    oath or affirmation, 105–106
    other acts evidence, 93, 97, 100–101, 121
    prejudicial evidence, 143
    present sense impression, 201–202
    prior consistent statements, 200
    prior inconsistent statements, 127, 128, 199
    privileges, 225, 227, 228, 231, 236–237
    public records, 209–210
    rape shield law, 98
    recorded recollection, 132–134
    relevant evidence, 59
    religious belief of witnesses, 117
    residual exception, 219–220
    self-authenticating documents, 177–178
    sexual offenses, 99
    statement of personal or family history, 217
    statement under belief of impending death, 214
    then-existing mental, emotional, or physical condition, 204–205
    ultimate issues, opinion on, 145–146
Federal Sentencing Guidelines, 47–48
Federalist Papers (Hamilton), 7
Feeley, Malcolm, 334
Fells, Korey, 99
Fells v. State (2005), 99
Felony convictions, prior, 118, 120–121, 122 (table), 130 (table)
Feltus, Henry, 215
Ferguson, Betty Ann, 105
Ferguson, Missouri, 335–336
Ferguson v. Commissioner (1991), 105
Fernandez, Walter, 363
Fernandez v. California (2014), 363
Ferranti, Detective, 407
Fields, Randall Lee, 388
Fifth Amendment:
    criminal procedure provisions, 8 (table), 22 (table)
    due process, 413–414
    exclusionary rule, 245
    eyewitness identifications, 413–414
    Fourteenth Amendment and, 21, 22 (table)
    grand jury, 31, 238
    indictment, 17
    racial profiling, 299
    See also Bill of Rights (U.S.); Self-incrimination, right against
Fillers, 413, 429
Final judgment rule, 49
Fingerprint evidence, 147 (photo), 159–160
First Amendment:
    Fourteenth Amendment and, 22 (table)
    freedom of religion, 105, 117

journalists, 225
  news media privilege, 238, 239–240
  See also Bill of Rights (U.S.)
First appearance, 30
First impression, 15
First Judiciary Act (1789), 51
Fischer, Gail, 258–259, 361–362
Fiske v. Kansas (1927), 22 (table)
Fitzgerald, Patrick, 403
Fleeing-felon rule, 331
Fletcher v. Weir (1982), 127
Flight, 85, 328, 336–338
Florida Highway Patrol, 368
Florida v. Bostick (1991), 284
Florida v. Harris (2013), 279
Florida v. J. L. (2000), 297
Florida v. Jardines (2013), 279
Florida v. Jimeno (1990), 359–360
Florida v. Powell (2010), 392
Florida v. Riley (1989), 271, 276, 285–286
Florida v. Royer (1983), 299, 303, 304–305
Florida v. Wells (1990), 368
Flowers, Demetrius, 389
Foils, 413
Footprints, 147 (photo), 153
Ford, Lamardus D., 312
Foreign government records, 177
Forensic document examiners, 175, 176 (photo)
Forfeiture by wrongdoing, 218
Former testimony, 212–213
Forrest, John, 67
Fortas, Abe, 425
Fortson v. State (2010), 86
Foster, John, 201
Foster v. California (1969), 425, 432–433
Foster-Brown, Kenneth, 284–285
"Fourteen Points" (Wilson), 18
Fourteenth Amendment:
  administrative inspections, 368
  Bill of Rights and, 21, 22 (table)
  criminal appeals, 49
  due process voluntariness test, 378–380
  Equal Protection Clause, 37, 38, 301, 302
  exclusionary rule, 245, 246–247, 248
  eyewitness identifications, 413–414
  racial profiling, 299
  text of, 16
  See also Due Process Clause
Fourth Amendment:
  administrative inspections, 368
  competent evidence, 62
  criminal procedure provisions, 8 (table), 22 (table)
  Fourteenth Amendment and, 22 (table)
  good faith exception, 257–258
  habeas corpus, 52
  historical background of, 270

text of, 269
  See also Bill of Rights (U.S.); Exclusionary rule;
    Probable cause; Searches and seizures;
    Stop and frisk
Fowler, E. L., 105
Frankfurter, Felix, 19, 246, 247
Franks v. Delaware (1978), 325
Frazier, Martin, 361
Frazier v. Cupp (1969), 361
FRE. *See* Federal Rules of Evidence (FRE)
Freedom of religion, 105, 117
Freeman, Joseph, 240
Freestanding due process, 17
Friedman, Stephen, 229
Friend, Travis, 199
Frisbie v. Butler (1787), 270
Frisks, 261 (photo), 262, 309–312, 366
  See also Stop and frisk
Fruit of the poisonous tree, 246
Frye, James Alphonso, 142
Frye test, 142, 158
Frye v. United States (1923), 142, 165
Fuentes, Juan Carlos, 360–361
Fulghum, Thomas A., 115
Fulghum v. Ford (1988), 115
Fulminante, Oreste, 380
Functional equivalent of custodial arrest, 387–389
Functional equivalent of express questioning, 403, 404
Fundamental fairness, 16, 17–19, 75–76
Funk v. United States (1933), 116, 241
Fyfe, James, 308

Gallegos, Francisco, 305
Gallegos v. City of Los Angeles (2002), 305
Gangs, 57, 120, 134–136, 350, 370–371
Gangsta rap lyrics, 180
Garage manager-customer relationship, 362 (table)
Garbage, 184–187, 268, 280–281
Garcia, Roy, 129
Gardner v. Florida (1977), 46
Garner, Edward, 337–338
Garner, Eric, 302
Garrison, Harold, 260
Gas chromatography/mass spectrometry, 163
Gates, Lance, 322–323
Gates, Sue, 322–323
Gender, 38, 299, 301
General warrants, 270
Gentile v. State Bar of Nevada (1991), 70
Georgia v. Randolph (2006), 362–363
Gerstein v. Pugh (1975), 325
Gianelli, Paul C., 60, 66
Gideon v. Wainwright (1963), 22 (table)
Gilbert v. California (1967), 417, 418, 420, 433
Ginsburg, Ruth Bader, 48, 256, 352, 430
Glasser v. United States (1942), 37

Global positioning system (GPS)
tracking device, 278
Glorious Revolution, 6
Glover, Jimmy D., 412, 422–424
Goldberg, Arthur, 321, 377, 381
Goldman, Ron, 155 (photo)
Goldman v. United States (1942), 271
Gomez, Jackie, 168
Gomez, Norman, 185
Gonzales, Edilberto, 358
Gonzalez-Lauzan, Luis, Jr., 398–399
Gonzalez-Lauzan, Luis, Sr., 398
Good faith exception, 256–260, 264–266
Goode, Clarence, 218
Gotti, Twain, 180
Government documents, 177–178
Government privileges, 236–238
GPS. *See* Global positioning system
tracking device
Grab area, 350
Graff, Gayle, 362
Graham, Delthorne, 332
Graham v. Connor (1989), 331–332
Graham v. State (1970), 157
Grand jury, 28, 31
Grand Jury Clause, 31
Grand jury confidentiality, 238
Granite State Baptist Church, 100–101
Grassi, Dante Angelo, 71
Gray, Robert, 218
Gray, Wilma, 218
Green, Aston, 78–79
Green, Thomas, 5
Greenfield, Gerard Anthony, 254
Greenwood, Billy, 268, 280
Gregg, Deborah, 129
Gregory, Roger, 239–240
Gregory, Tim, 148
Grendel v. State (2013), 220–221
Griffin, Staughan Lee, 404
Griffin v. Illinois (1956), 49
Griffin v. State (2010), 172
Griffith v. Kentucky (1987), 50
Grigson, James, 148
Grindle, Brandon, 220–221
Groh v. Ramirez (2004), 345 (table)
Grubbs, Jeffrey, 344 (table)
Guest, Darvell, 172
Guests, overnight, 251
Guilbert, Brady, 167–168
Guilt, inference of consciousness of, 85–86
Guilt beyond a reasonable doubt, 2
Guilty plea, 31, 32, 59
Gustafson, James, 354
Gustafson v. Florida (1973), 334, 354
Guzman, Harry, 198

Habeas corpus, 50–53, 251
Habeas Corpus Act (1867), 51
Habit, 91–92
Hair analysis, 165
Hairston v. United States (2006), 399
Haley v. State (2000), 73
Hallways, common, 327
Hamdi v. Rumsfeld (2004), 51
Hamilton, Alexander, 7
Hand, Learned, 372
Handwriting, 174, 175, 176 (photo), 178
Hanrahan, Richard, 398
Harlan, John M., 21, 271–272, 274
Harmless error, 50, 251
Harris, Joseph A. Moses, 297
Harris, Victor, 332–333
Harris v. New York (1971), 64, 263
Harris v. United States (1947), 342
Hart, Claude, 300
Hart v. A.G. (2003), 393
Hartford Police Department, 412, 422–424
Hasiak, Paul, 295
Hatley, Ralph, 358–359
Hauser, Melvin, 185, 186
Hawkins, Alfred E., 18, 19
Hawkins, Louise, 202
Hawkins v. United States (1958), 116, 241
Hayat, Akram, 117
Hayden, Bennie Joe, 327
Hayes, Paul Lewis, 35–36
Hayes v. Florida (1985), 306
Haynes v. Washington (1963), 379
Hearings:
competency, 108
preliminary, 28, 30–31
sentencing, 46
suppression, 32
Hearsay:
case analysis, 220–221
definition of, 191–192
objections, 193
probable cause and arrests, 316, 320–324
rule, development of, 191
rule, reasons for, 192
stop and frisk, 292, 295–298
See also Hearsay exceptions
Hearsay exceptions:
about, 195
admissions and confessions, 195–198,
197 (table), 217 (table)
business records, 207–209
declarant, unavailability of, 211–218
declaration against interest, 216–217, 217 (table)
excited utterance, 189, 203–204
forfeiture by wrongdoing, 218
former testimony, 212–213

medical treatment-diagnosis, 206–207
present sense impression, 201–203
prior statements, 199–201
public records, 209–210
residual exception, 219–220
statement of personal or family history, 217
statement under belief of impending death, 214–215,
220–221
then-existing mental, emotional, or physical condition,
204–205
vital statistics, 211
See also Hearsay
Hearsay within hearsay, 220
Hedgepeth, Ansche, 336
Hedgepeth v. Metropolitan Area Transit Authority (2004), 336
Helgert, Christopher, 396–397
Helstoski v. Meanor (1979), 49
Henderson, Jeff, 134–136
Henderson, Kevin, 363
Henderson, Patricia, 363
Henderson v. Morgan (1976), 35
Henning, L. W., 431
Henry, John Patrick, 323–324
Henry v. United States (1959), 290, 323–324
Henson v. State (1989), 87
Herd, William "Billy," 205
Hereford, James A., 316, 321
Herring, Bennie Dean, 264–266
Herring v. New York (1975), 42
Herring v. United States (2009), 258, 264–266
Hester, Charlie, 280
Hester v. United States (1924), 280
Hickey, Mary Jo, 407
Hicks, Anthony, 124
Hicks, Carl, 289, 300
Hiibel, Larry Dudley, 306
Hiibel v. Sixth Judicial District (2004), 306, 381
Hines, Johannes, 146
Hinton v. Uchtman (2005), 403
Hispanics, 300, 301, 302, 355–356
Hoffa, Jimmy, 273
Hoffa v. United States (1996), 273
Hoffman v. United States (1951), 381
Holden, Charles, 61
Holderead, Jennifer, 295
Holmes, James, 239
Home:
arrests in the, 326–327
custodial interrogation and, 387
expectation of privacy and, 275
searches and seizures of, 269, 277–278
Homicide cases, 62 (table), 90
Hooks, Willie, 202–203
Hoover, Paul, 401
Hope, Edgar, 230
Horizontal gaze nystagmus, 165

Horton, Christopher, 180
Hostile witnesses, 40
Hot pursuit, 327–328, 332–333
Hotels, 327, 362 (table)
Hottel, Martha, 431
Houghton, Sandra, 366
House, Paul Gregory, 162
House v. Bell (2006), 162
Howell, Lester Dale, 157
Huang v. McEwen (2012), 95
Huddleston, Isaac S., 141
Huddleston v. United States (1988), 93
Hudson v. Michigan (2006), 255
Huff, Vincent, 329
Hung jury, 44
Hurst, Gerald, 148
Hurtado, Jose, 17
Hurtado v. California (1884), 17, 19
Husband-wife privilege, 224, 234–236, 235 (table), 240–241
Hygh, William C., 145
Hygh v. Jacobs (1992), 145
Hymon, Elton, 336–338
Hypnosis, 103, 109

ICE. *See* Immigration and Customs Enforcement
Idaho v. Wright (1990), 219
Identifications:
exclusionary rule and, 245
eyewitness identifications and, 413
as hearsay exception, 200–201
inventories and, 367
race and reasonable suspicion and, 300
Identity, circumstantial evidence of, 93–94
Illinois American Civil Liberties Union, 355–356
Illinois Department of Transportation, 355–356
Illinois v. Caballes (2005), 151, 278–279
Illinois v. Gates (1983), 321, 322–323
Illinois v. Krull (1987), 257, 258, 259, 265
Illinois v. Lafayette (1983), 367
Illinois v. Perkins (1990), 389, 406
Illinois v. Rodriguez (1990), 257, 258–259, 361–362
Illinois v. Wardlaw (2000), 293, 294, 312–313
Illinois v. White (1968), 108
Immigration and Customs Enforcement (ICE), 389
Immigration and Naturalization Service, 284
Immoral acts, 125–126
Immunity, 31
Impeaching witnesses, 124
Impeachment:
about, 119–120
bias, 119, 120, 130 (table)
case analysis, 134–136
character for truthfulness, 41, 119, 124–127,
130, 130 (table)
convictions, prior, 122–124
cross-examination and, 41

as exclusionary rule exception, 262–263, 264
   felony convictions, prior, 120–121, 122 (table),
      130 (table)
   incapacity, physical and psychological, 119, 129, 130 (table)
   jury decision-making and, 83
   prior inconsistent statements, 41, 119, 127–128, 130 (table)
   specific contradiction, 119, 128
   uncharged crimes and immoral acts, 125–126
Implied waiver, 396–397
In re Grand Jury Investigation (1990), 231
In re Grand Jury Subpoena (2005), 238
In re Oliver (1948), 22 (table)
In re Verplank (1971), 232
Inbau, Fred, 376
Incapacity. *See* Capacity/incapacity
Incommunicado interrogation, 378
Inconsistent statements, 263
In-court exhibitions, 184
In-court identification, 413, 417
Incriminating statements, 269
Independent source doctrine, 260, 261, 264
Indictment, 31
Indictment states, 31
Indisputable facts, 72
Inevitable discovery rule, 261–262, 261 (photo), 264
Inference of consciousness of guilt and of guilt, 85–86
Informant privilege, 320
Informants:
   citizen-informants, 320
   hearsay and, 292, 295–298, 320–324
   interrogation by, 405–406
   jailhouse, 129, 198–199
   probable cause and, 320–324
   searches and seizures, 273–274
   stop and frisk and, 292, 295–298
Information, 17, 143
Information states, 31
Initial appearance, 30
Initiation, 400–401
Innis, Thomas J., 404
Innocence, presumption of, 76–77
Innocence Project, 198, 416
Innocent defendants, 35
Inns of Court, 4
Inquisitorial system, 377
Intent, circumstantial evidence of, 94–97, 100–101
Interlocutory appeal, 49
Intermediate appellate courts, 13
Internal Revenue Service (IRS), 281, 386
Internalized false confessors, 386
Internet service provider (ISP), 272
Interrogations:
   case analysis, 406–408
   confessions and, 376–377
   constitutional limitations on, 377–378
   due process and, 378–380

exclusionary rule and, 245
   by informants, 405–406
   lengthy, 386
   Sixth Amendment right to counsel and, 404–406
   taping of, 386
   techniques, 395
   See also Miranda v. Arizona (1966)
Intoxication, 85, 160
Intrinsic evidence, 119
Inventories, 367–368
Invited response, 43
Involuntary confessions, 377, 378–380
Irigoyen, Julian, 297–298
Irrebuttable presumptions, 74, 75–76, 77
IRS. *See* Internal Revenue Service
Irvin v. Dowd (1961), 70
Irvine v. California (1954), 249
ISP. *See* Internet service provider
Israel, Jerald H., 43
Ivy, James, 359

Jackson, Charles, 320
Jackson, John H., 198
Jackson, Robert, 8
Jackson v. Virginia (1979), 52
Jacobs, William, 145
Jacquez, Adam Orlando, 295
Jaffe v. Redmond (1996), 233
Jailhouse informants, 129, 198–199
James, Audry, 60–61
James, Jaylene, 60–61
James I (King of England), 191
James v. Illinois (1990), 263
J.D.B. v. North Carolina (2011), 389
J.E.B. v. Alabama ex rel. (1994), 38
Jencks, Richard, 353–354
Jenkins v. Anderson (1980), 127
Jensen, Annie, 76
Jewett v. United States (1926), 132
Jimeno, Enio, 359–360
Johns, Melvin, 252
Johns, William, 404
Johnson, Jamar, 85
Johnson, Lee Erwin, 262
Johnson, Lemon Montrea, 307, 310
Johnson v. Louisiana (1972), 45
Johnson v. United States (1948), 342
Johnson v. United States (1997), 50
Johnston, Kathyrn, 349
Jones, Antoine, 278
Jones, Antonio, 106
Jones, Fonta M., 295
Jones, Jeffrey, 202–203
Jones, Ralph, 61
Jones, Tina, 359
Jones v. Barnes (1983), 48

Jones v. State (1984), 93–94
Jones v. United States (1959), 320
Journalist shield law, 238–240
Judges, 3, 13, 113–114
Judicial discretion, 3
Judicial integrity, 248–249
Judicial notice, 72–73, 73 (table), 77
Judicial review, 7–9
Judicial sentencing process, 45–46
Judicial systems:
    federal, 10, 11 (figure)
    state, 12–13, 14 (figure)
Junta, Mary Ann, 380
Jurors, 114–116
Jury:
    decision-making by, 75, 83
    deliberations of, 44
    origin of, 4–6
    presumptions and, 75
    role of, 3, 4
    sentencing, role in, and 47–48
    size of, 44
    unanimity, 44–45
Jury instructions:
    criminal appeals and, 49
    eyewitness identifications and, 169–170, 429
    habeas corpus and, 52
    presumptions and, 76
    rape and, 98
    trials and, 43–44
Jury nullification, 45
Jury poll, 45
Jury selection, 36–39, 48
Jury Selection and Service Act (1968), 36, 37
Juveniles, presumption of criminal intent of, 77

Kalaydjian, Bedros, 117
Kallick, Mickey, 108
Kansas v. Ventris (2009), 263
Kassin, Saul, 146
Katz, Carl, 292
Katz, Charles, 271
Katz v. United States (1967), 271, 273
Kaupp, Robert, 254, 303
Kaupp v. Texas (2003), 254, 303
Keiser, Ronald, 90
Kennedy, Anthony, 163, 400
Kennedy, John F., 166
Keogh v. Commissioner (1983), 208
Ker v. California (1963), 328
Key-man system, 36
Kimbrough v. United States (2007), 48
King, Henry J., 43
Kirby, Thomas, 419, 420
Kirby v. Illinois (1972), 419, 420
Kirkwood, Quinton, 134–135

Kiro, John, 364
Klopfer v. North Carolina (1967), 22 (table), 33
Knapp v. State (1907), 61
Knock and announce, 341, 343, 345, 347–349
Knock and talk searches, 359
Knowledge, personal, 106–107, 214
Knowledge of the law, presumption of, 77
Knowles, Patrick, 354
Knowles v. Iowa (1986), 354
Kozlowski, Dennis, 65
Kruger, Daniel, 85
Kuhlmann v. Wilson (1986), 406
Kulkovit, Vira, 185, 186
Kumho Tire Company Ltd. v. Carmichael (1999), 143
Kunz, W. Jamie, 230
Kyles v. Whitley (1995), 52
Kyllo, Danny Lee, 278
Kyllo v. United States (2001), 277, 278, 287

LaFave, Wayne, 43
Lafayette, Ralph, 367
Lafler v. Cooper (2012), 36
Lamberth, John, 355
LaMothe, Jacqueline, 204
Landlord-tenant relationship, 362 (table)
Landry, Margery, 229
Lang, Scott, 168
Larichere, Pierre, 77
Lasky, Samuel, 319
Latent fingerprints, 160
Law giver role, 3
Lawless, Mark, 157
Lay witnesses, 139, 140–142
Laying the foundation, 40–41, 154, 158
Leading question, 3, 40
Leaming, Cletus, 261, 405
Leary, Timothy, 76
Leary v. United States (1969), 76
Leath, Hattie, 358
Lee, Henry, 166
Lee, Robert, 133
Lee v. Martinez (2004), 165
Legislative facts, 73–74
Lego v. Twomey (1972), 379
Leo, Richard, 386
Levine, Mike, 239
Libby, Lewis "Scooter," 146
Lie detector test, 165
Lilburne, John, 377
Lilly, Graham C., 195
Limiting instruction, 64
Limon, Javier, 113
Lincoln, Abraham, 51
Lineups, 417, 418, 425, 428–429, 432
    See also Eyewitness identifications
Littledale, Cynthia, 389

Littledale, Daniel, 389
Lofton, Ronald, Sr., 224
Logan, Alton, 230
Long, David, 310–311
Lopez, Abel, 363
Lopez, Jose, 353
Lopez, Mayra, 86
Louisiana, jury unanimity in, 45
Lowden, Trooper, 229–230
Lynch, Patrick, 308–309
Lyons, Judah, 350–351
Lyrics, 180

MacDonald, Heather, 356
Magee, Henry, 349
Magna Carta, 6, 33
Majority opinion, 9
Makin, John, 96
Makin, Sarah, 96
Makin v. Attorney General of New South Wales (1893), 96
Mallory, Eugene, 349
Mallory v. United States (1957), 30
Malloy v. Hogan (1964), 20–21, 22 (table), 380–381
Mandatory presumptions, 75–76, 77–78
Manson v. Braithwaite (1977), 412, 422–424
Maplewood, Missouri, 335
Mapp v. Ohio (1961), 22 (table), 244, 245, 248, 252, 253, 266
Maps, 183
Marbury v. Madison (1803), 7
Marital communications privilege, 234–235, 235 (table)
Marital testimony privilege, 235, 235 (table)
Marking evidence, 154
Markonni, Paul J., 298
Markonni drug courier profile, 298
Marks v. State (2008), 106
Marron v. United States (1927), 344–345 (table)
Marsh, John W., 321
Marshall, John:
    constitutionalization of the Bill of Rights, 15–16
    eyewitness identifications, 419, 421
    good faith exception, 258
    hearsay, 191
    impeachment exception to exclusionary rule, 263
    inevitable discovery rule, 261
    judicial review, 7
    Miranda warnings, 392
    pretext arrests, 354
    stop and frisk, 296
    totality-of-the-circumstances approach, 323
Marshall Project, 198
Martin, Trayvon, 66, 179
Martin v. Hunter's Lessee (1816), 7
Martinez, Jose, 353
Martinez, Oliverio, 381
Mary II (Queen of England), 6
Maryland, statement of charges in, 404

Maryland State Police, 355
Maryland v. Buie (1990), 311
Maryland v. Craig (1990), 111
Maryland v. Garrison (1987), 260, 344 (table)
Maryland v. King (2014), 163
Maryland v. Macon (1985), 279
Maryland v. Shatzer (2010), 400–401
Maryland v. Wilson (1977), 307
Mass spectrometry, 163
Massachusetts:
    attorney-client privilege, 230
    DNA evidence, 163
    "Peeping Tom" law, 281–282
    stop-and-identify statutes, 307
Massachusetts v. Sheppard (1984), 257–258, 259, 265
Massiah, Winston, 405
Massiah v. United States (1964), 405
Material fact, 59–60
Mathiason, Carl, 387–388
Mathison, David, 301
Matlock, William Earl, 362
Matoesian, Greg, 98–99
Matter of Rosaly S. v. Ivelisse T. (2010), 84
Mayhugh, Kristie, 112–113
McCarthy v. United States (1969), 35
McClain, Wiley, 348
McCrary-El, Jerry, 106
McCray, George, 320
McCray v. Illinois (1967), 320, 321
McCray-El v. Shaw (1993), 106
McDermott, Michael, 403
McDonald, Cornelio, 302
McDonald v. Chicago (2010), 22 (table)
McFadden, Martin, 292
McGlory, Reginald D., 185–187
McKinney, Amy, 138
McKinney, Brian, 138
McKinney, Shirley Bowles, 138
McKinney v. Commonwealth (2001), 138
McMellon, Edward, 308–309
McMorran, Ruth Anne, 358
McMorran v. Nevada (2002), 358
McNabb v. United States (1943), 9, 30
McNary v. State (1984), 153
McRae, Nancy, 64
McRae, Stephen, 64
McWebb, Lawrence, 260
McWilliam, Ted, 186
Mead, William, 5, 51
Medhin, Robel, 180
Medical images, authentication of, 179
Medical treatment-diagnosis, 206–207
Melendez-Diaz v. Massachusetts (2009), 158, 194
Memory, 190, 211, 414, 416
Mempa v. Rhay (1967), 46
Mendenhall, Sylvia, 283

Mental capacity/incapacity, 84–85, 107–108, 118, 358
Mercy rule, 88
Merrick, Sydney Ann, 103
Merritt, Deborah Jones, 68
Metzner, Jeffrey, 375
Michelson v. United States (1948), 88
Michigan, religious opinions of witnesses in, 117
Michigan v. Bryant (2011), 194
Michigan v. Chesternut (1988), 284
Michigan v. Fisher (2009), 329
Michigan v. Long (1983), 310–311
Michigan v. Mosley (1975), 399–400, 401
Michigan v. Thomas (1958), 364
Michigan v. Tyler (1978), 328
Microcrystalline test, 163
Military Rule of Evidence 707, 165
Miller, Calvin, 432
Miller, Judith, 238, 239
Miller, Marc, 230
Miller, Samuel Freeman, 16
Miller-El v. Dretke (2005), 38–39
Mills, Robert, 120
Mima Queen and Child v. Hepburn (1813), 191
Mincey, Rufus, 379
Mincey v. Arizona (1978), 327, 379
Minnesota, sentencing guidelines in, 47
Minnesota v. Carter (1998), 252
Minnesota v. Dickerson (1993), 309, 311
Minnesota v. Martinez (2008), 126
Minnesota v. Murphy (1984), 387
Minnesota v. Olson (1990), 251, 328
Minnick v. Mississippi (1990), 376, 401
Miranda, Ernest, 383 (photo)
Miranda rights:
    admission by party-opponent and, 196
    attenuation and, 255, 256
    exclusionary rule and, 245
    impeachment exception to exclusionary rule, 263
    interrogation and, 378
    invoking, 393–394
    prior inconsistent statements and, 127
    waiver following invocation of, 399–402
    See also Miranda v. Arizona (1966)
Miranda v. Arizona (1966):
    about, 383–384, 383 (photo)
    case analysis, 406–408
    Constitution and, 385
    custodial interrogation, 386–389
    express and implied waiver, 396–397
    interrogation, 403–404
    Miranda rights, invoking, 393–394
    Miranda rights, waiver following invocation of, 399–402
    Miranda warnings, 391–393
    public safety exception, 390–392
    question first and warn later, 397–399
    voluntary, knowing, and intelligent waiver, 394–396
    waiver, 394–402
    See also Counsel, right to; *Miranda* rights; *Miranda* warnings
Miranda warnings, 357, 391–393
    See also Miranda v. Arizona (1966)
Misdemeanants, 330–331
Misdemeanors, 326, 334–335, 336, 353–354
Misleading evidence, 65
Mississippi, open fields doctrine in, 276
Missouri Plan, 13
Missouri v. Frye (2012), 36
Missouri v. McNeely (2013), 161, 328
Missouri v. Siebert (2004), 397–398
Mitchell, Tyrone, 97
Mitchell v. United States (1999), 46
Model Code of Pre-Arraignment Procedure (American Law Institute), 283, 304
Model Penal Code, 131
Models, 183
Modified indictment states, 31
Modus operandi, 93–94
Moen, Judith, 206
Moen, Ronald Howard, 206
Mohamed v. Jeppesen Data Plan Inc. (1983), 237
Moler v. State (2003), 84
Montana, open fields doctrine in, 276
Montana v. Bauer (2001), 335
Montgomery, Wayne, 402
Montoya de Hernandez, Rosa Elvira, 304
Moody, Milo, 18
Moore, Eileen, 189
Moore, James R., 419–420
Moore v. Dempsey (1923), 18
Moore v. Illinois (1977), 419–420
Moorman, James, 427
Moot cases, 49
Morales v. Portundo (2001), 231
Moran v. Burbine (1986), 392–393, 394, 396, 405, 406–408
Morgan, Charles A., III, 168
Morgan, Leo, 57
Morgan, Sharon, 265, 266
Morris, Timothy, 389
Mosley, Richard Bert, 399–400
Mosley test, 399–400
Motels, 327, 362 (table)
Motion for dismissal of charges, 32
Motion for severance, 33
Motion in limine, 32
Motion to suppress, 32, 48
Motor vehicles. *See* Automobiles
Mulkey, Daniel Davis, 206
Muniz, Inocencio, 382
Munson, Allegra, 407, 408
Murder cases, 62 (table), 90
Murphy, Frank, 20, 247

Murphy, Marshall, 387
Murphy, Richard, 308–309
Murphy v. Waterfront Commission (1964), 380–381
Murray v. United States (1988), 260
MySpace profiles, 172

Narcotics, 163, 311
Nardone v. United States (1939), 254
Nardulli, Peter, 253
Narration, 108, 190
Narrative question, 40
National Academy of Sciences, 165, 166
National Bank of Andover, 113–114
National Conference of Commissioners on Uniform State
    Laws, 23
National Institute of Justice, 415, 416, 429
National Prohibition Act, 364
National Registry of Exonerations, 113
Nationalization, 15–17
Naturalization Service v. Delgado (1984), 284
Naval Criminal Investigative Service, 393
Nazzaro, Richard, 89
Neal v. Delaware (1881), 37
Near-miss issue, 219
Neder v. United States (1999), 50
Negative hearsay, 209
Neil v. Biggers (1967), 424, 425
Nelson v. United States (2009), 48
New, Donovan, 94
New Hampshire Division of Child Support Services, 94
New Jersey, eyewitness identifications in, 430
New judicial federalism, 13
New South Wales Ombudsman, 279
New York City:
    crime laboratory, 166
    race and reasonable suspicion, 301–302
    stop and frisk, 301–302, 308–309
New York Police Department, 264
New York State:
    child testimony, 110
    open fields, 276
    state court system, 13
    stop and frisk, 290
New York v. Belton (1981), 259, 352–353, 365
New York v. Burger (1987), 369
New York v. Harris (1990), 127
New York v. Quarles (1984), 390
Newman, Elsa, 229
Newman v. State (2004), 229
News media privilege, 238–240
Newsome, Roger, 357
Nicely, Steven, 432
Nichols, Deion, 352
Nichols, Ron G., 164
Nickerson, Glen "Buddy," 129
Nickl, Marc, 113–114

Nicot, Douglas, 352
Nix v. Williams (1984), 260, 261
Nixon, Richard, 236
No bill, 31
Nolo contendere, 31, 32
Non-corporeal identification, 421
Non-deadly force, 331–332
Nonparty witnesses, 121
Nontestimonial evidence, 382
Norman Conquest, 4
North Carolina crime laboratory, 166
North Carolina v. Alford (1970), 35
North Carolina v. Butler (1979), 396
North Carolina v. Pearce (1969), 49
North Carolina v. Riley (2002), 204
Northwestern University School of Law, 113
Not guilty by reason of insanity plea, 31
Not guilty plea, 31, 32
Notarized documents, 177–178
NuVox Communications, 272

Oath or affirmation, 105–106, 199
Objections, hearsay, 193
Objects, authentication of, 179
Observations, direct, 319–320
Obus, Michael J., 65
O'Connor, Sandra Day, 335, 338
Official acts, presumption of regularity of, 77
Official information privilege, 237
Official publications, 178
Ogden, David, 60–61
Ohio, child testimony in, 110–111
Ohio v. Roberts (1980), 193
Ohio v. Robinette (1996), 357–358
Old Chief, Johnny Lynn, 65
Old Chief v. United States (1997), 65, 71
Oliver, Ray E., 275
Oliver v. United States (1984), 275
Olmstead, Roy, 271
Olmstead v. United States (1928), 248–249, 271
Olson, Robert, 251, 328
O'Malley, Peter, 258
O'Mara, Mark, 66
Omnibus Crime Control and Safe Streets Act (1968),
    346 (table), 384
Open fields, 275–276
Opening statements, 39–40
Opinion rule, 138, 140–142, 149
Ordeals, 4
Oregon, jury unanimity in, 44
Oregon v. Bradshaw (1983), 401
Oregon v. Elstad (1985), 395, 397, 398
Oregon v. Mathiason (1977), 387–388
Original jurisdiction, 9
Original writing rule. *See* Best evidence rule
Ornelas v. United States (1996), 293

Orozco v. Texas (1969), 387
Osborne, William G., 162–163
Other acts evidence:
  about, 93
  case analysis, 100–101
  circumstantial evidence of identity and, 93–94
  circumstantial evidence of intent and, 94–97, 100–101
Otis, James, 270
Owens, James, 201
Owens, Martha, 138
Owens, Stella, 259
Owens, Winfred, 427

Palko v. Connecticut (1937), 19
Palva, James Earl, 141
Papers, searches and seizures of, 269
Pardon, 46, 123
Pardue, Corey, 262
Parent-child relationship, 362 (table)
Parrilla, Luis, 77–78
Part v. Shiflett (2001), 306
Partin, Edward, 273
Party-opponent, admission by, 196, 197 (table),
  198, 217 (table)
Past recollection recorded, 132–133
Patane, Samuel Francis, 256
Patent fingerprints, 160
Pattern jury instructions, 44
Paulino, John August, 351
Paulino v. State (2007), 351
Payne v. Tennessee (1991), 46
Payner, Jack, 252
Payton v. New York (1980), 326–327
"Peeping Tom" laws, 281–282
Pendleton, James, 334
Penile plethysmograph test, 145
Penn, William, 5, 51
Pennsylvania:
  eyewitness identifications, 420, 421
  spousal competence, 117
Pennsylvania v. Mimms (1977), 307
Pennsylvania v. Muniz (1990), 382
People v. Alonzo (1978), 326
People v. Bledsoe (1984), 87
People v. Bustamonte (1981), 420
People v. Campa (1964), 323
People v. Cardenas (1982), 57
People v. Conley (1989), 82
People v. Cutchall (1993), 64
People v. Dean (1974), 391
People v. Defore (1926), 247
People v. Hall (1969), 84
People v. Jefferson (1973), 359
People v. Jimenez (2005), 183
People v. Madson (1981), 306
People v. McCauley (1994), 393
People v. Pendleton (1982), 334

People v. Prentiss (2008), 106
People v. Schreiner (1991), 109
People v. Thomas (2004), 134–136
People v. Triggs (1973), 272
People v. Urbano (2005), 228
People v. Vandiver (1984), 108
People v. Wells (2006), 297–298
People v. Yeoman (2003), 86
Per curiam, 9
Perception, 143, 190, 414, 415, 423
Peremptory challenge, 36, 37, 38
Perjury, 104, 105, 131
Permissive presumptions, 74
Perry, Barion, 429–430
Perry, Belvin, Jr., 69
Perry, Rick, 148, 198
Perry v. New Hampshire (2011), 429–430
Personal knowledge, 106–107, 214
Persons, searches of, 269, 282–285, 282 (table)
Persuasive authority, 15
Pertinent trait, 88
Pertoso, Jerry, 284
Peters, John, 319
Peters v. United States (1968), 319
Peterson, Connor, 68 (photo)
Peterson, Drew, 215–216
Peterson, Laci, 68 (photo)
Peterson, Scott, 68 (photo)
Peterson, Stacy, 216
Petitioner, 9
Peyton v. New York (1980), 326
Photographic displays, 421–422, 425–426
Photographs, authentication of, 178–179
Physical and psychological incapacity, 119, 129, 130 (table)
Physical evidence, 69
Physical seizures, 283
Physician-patient privilege, 232–233
Picard, William, 107
Pierotti, Albert Rudolph, 323–324
Pikett, Keith, 151, 167, 432
Place, Raymond, 278, 304
Plain error exception, 50
Plain view, 274, 277, 366
Plain-feel doctrine, 311
Plame, Valerie, 238, 239
Plastic fingerprints, 160
Plea bargaining, 34–36
Pless, Christopher, 208
Pless v. State (2006), 208
Plumhoff v. Rickard (2014), 333
Plurality opinion, 9
Pointer v. Texas (1965), 22 (table), 193
Police:
  administrative procedures, 250
  arrest warrants, 28
  bias, 386
  coercive procedures, 357

eyewitness identifications and, 428, 429–431
hearsay and, 320
informants and, 297
personnel records, 33
photographic identifications and, 426
professionalism, 249
testimony, 110 (photo)
torture by, 402–403
Polygraph, 165
Pomodore, Debra, 150
Poole, Bobby, 428
Pope, Sandy, 265, 266
Post-traumatic stress disorders, 147–148
Potts, George, 168
Powell, Kevin, 392
Powell, Lewis, Jr., 52, 298, 334
Powell v. Alabama (1932), 18–19
Powers, Grady William, 145
Powers, Pamela, 261
Prearrangement identifications, 419–420
Precedent, 13, 15
Prejudicial evidence, 63–64, 78–79
Preliminary hearing, 28, 30–31
Premotive rule, 200
Present recollection refreshed, 131–132
Present sense impression, 201–203
Presentence report, 45–46
Presentment, 31
Preston v. United States (1964), 351
Presumed fact, 74, 75–76
Presumptions, 74–78
Pretext arrests, 354–355
Pretrial motions, 28, 32–33
Pretrial publicity, 69–70
Price, Victoria, 18
Prilla, John, 294
Prima facie, 31
Prior consistent statements, 200, 201
Prior inconsistent statements:
    as hearsay exception, 199–200, 201
    impeachment, 41, 119, 127–128, 130 (table)
Prison escape, 345
Privacy:
    bright-line rule and, 354
    expectation of, 271–273, 274–275, 281 (table)
    knock and announce and, 345
    privileges and, 225
    self-incrimination, right against, and, 381
    See also Searches and seizures
Privileges:
    about, 225–226
    attorney-client, 226–230, 226 (table)
    clergy-penitent, 230–232
    confidential informant, 237–238
    executive, 236
    government, 236–238
    husband-wife, 224, 234–236, 235 (table), 240–241

marital communications, 234–235, 235 (table)
    marital testimony, 235, 235 (table)
    news media, 238–240
    official information, 237
    physician-patient, 232–233
    psychotherapist-patient, 233–234
    state secrets, 236–237
    testimonial, 225
Probable cause:
    about, 317, 318–319, 318 (photo)
    Aguilar-Spinelli test, 316, 321–323
    arrests and, 317–324
    case analysis, 336–338
    direct observations and, 319–320
    hearsay and, 320–324
    inventories and, 367
    motor vehicles, searches of, 364–366
    plain view and, 274
    preliminary hearing and, 30
    reasonable suspicion and, 293
    search warrants and, 344 (table)
    searches and seizures and, 270, 364–366
    totality-of-the-circumstances approach,
        322–323
Probative value, 59, 60, 63
Process Is the Punishment, The (Feeley), 334
Propensity evidence, 88
Property:
    abandoned, 268, 275, 280–281, 280 (photo)
    commercial, 275, 279
    public, 275, 279
    See also Searches and seizures
Property rights approach, 271
Prosecutors and prosecution:
    case-in-chief, 40–41
    criminal appeals and, 49
    misconduct by, 52
    prearraignment identifications and, 419
    presumptions and, 75
    rebuttal, 42
Pruitt, Norma, 186
Prysock, Randall, 391
Psychological abuse and manipulation, 379
Psychological and physical incapacity,
        119, 129, 130 (table)
Psychotherapist-patient privilege, 233–234
Public policy and character, 87–88
Public property, 275, 279
Public record, 176, 209–210
Public safety exception, 390–392
Publicity, pretrial/trial, 69–70
Puleio, Joe, 204
Punishing/rewarding prejudice, 63
Purging the taint, 254

Question first and warn later, 397–399
Quintana-Garcia, Guadalupe, 294

Race, 38–39, 299–302
Racial profiling, 299, 355–356
"Raise or waive" rule, 49–50
Rakas v. Illinois (1978), 251
Raleigh, Walter, 191
Ramirez, Elizabeth, 112–113
Ramsey, Jon Benet, 176 (photo)
Randolph, Janet, 362–363
Randolph, Scott, 362–363
Ranieri, Eric, 106–107
Ransom notes, 176 (photo)
Rap lyrics, 180
Rape, 97–99
Rape shield laws, 81, 98–99
Rape trauma syndrome, 87, 147–148
Rape victims, 87
Ratliff, Phillip, 262
Rawlings, David, 251–252
Rawlings v. Kentucky (1980), 251–252, 351
Rawls, Jerry Lee, 361
Real evidence, 69, 69 (table)
    See also specific types
Real-testimonial evidence, 69
Reasonable suspicion:
    balancing test, 291–292
    determination of, 292–293
    drug courier profiles and, 299
    facts constituting, 293–294
    race and, 299–302
    stop and frisk and, 290, 291–295, 299–302
Reasonableness and arrests:
    about, 324
    arrests in the home, 326–327
    deadly force, 330–331, 336–338
    exigent circumstances, 327–330
    misdemeanor arrests and citations, 334–335, 336
    non-deadly force, 331–332
    probable cause, warrants, and the courts, 324–325
Rebuttable presumptions, 74, 75, 76–77
Rebuttal, 42
Recorded recollection, 131–134, 134 (table)
Re-cross examination, 41
Rector, Donald, 397–398
Redirect examination, 41
Reed, Dwayne, 213
Reese, Curtis, 404
Rehabilitation, 41
Rehabilitation of witnesses, 129–130, 130 (table)
Rehnquist, William, 51, 338, 385
Reichbach, Gustin L., 264
Reid v. Georgia (1980), 298–299
Rejoinder, 42
Relevant evidence:
    about, 58–61, 62 (table)
    exclusion of, 62–66
Religion, 105, 117

Reply letter doctrine, 176
Reputation, 88, 92
Residual exception, 219–220
Respondent, 9
Retroactivity of judicial decisions, 50
Rex v. Warickshall (1783), 378
Reyes, Matias, 385
Reyes, Ramon, 390
Reyna, Rogelio Trevino, 183
Reyna v. State (1990), 183
Reynolds, P. A., 296
Rhode Island v. Innis (1980), 403–404
Richards, Steiney, 341, 347
Richards v. Wisconsin (1997), 341, 347
Rickard, Donald, 333
Rideau v. Louisiana (1963), 70
Right of allocution, 46
Riley, David, 350, 370–371
Riley, Michael A., 276, 285–286
Riley v. California (2014), 350, 370–373
Riley v. Connelly (1986), 375
Risen, James, 239–240
Rivera, Cassandra, 112–113
Roberts, Edwin Lee, 240
Roberts, John G., 163, 297, 350
Robertson, Michael, 281–282
Robinette, Robert D., 357–358
Robinson, Gerald, 157
Robinson, Scott, 330
Robinson, William, 167–168
Robinson, Willie, 353–354
Robinson v. California (1962), 22 (table)
Rochin, Richard Antonio, 247
Rochin v. California (1952), 247
Rock v. Arkansas (1987), 109
Roddy, Stephen R., 18
Rodney, Dylan, 360
Rodriguez, Edward, 258, 361
Rodriguez, Javier, 198
Rodriguez v. Commonwealth (2003), 85
Rodriguez-Minozo, Jose, 358
Roettger, Norman, 78–79
Rogers, Theodore, 427
Rojas, Roxanne, 363
Roman law, 4
Romero, Victor, 90
Roommates, 362–363, 362 (table), 364
Rose v. Mitchell (1979), 52
Rosen v. United States (1918), 104, 118
Ross, Terry, 167, 168
Ross v. Moffitt (1974), 48
Rothgery v. Gillespie County (2008), 405
Rouer, Rhonda, 90–91
Roviaro v. United States (1957), 237
Royer, Mark, 299, 303
Rozier, Robert, 78

Rule of four, 9
Rules of evidence:
  about, 21
  Federal Rules of Evidence, 22–23
  need for, 23–24
  state rules of evidence, 23
  Uniform Rules of Evidence, 23
  See also Federal Rules of Evidence
Rush, Genena, 116
Rutledge, Wiley, 20
Ryan, George, 46, 403
Ryan, James, 229
Ryan, Keri, 149
Ryan, Roy Dale, 149
Ryan v. State (1999), 149
Ryburn, Darin, 329
Ryburn v. Huff (2012), 329

Safety, 328, 349, 354, 367
Saint Louis County, Missouri, 335–336
Saint Paul, Minnesota, 166, 281, 301
Salas-Galaviz, Leandro, 86
Salinas, Genovevo, 394
Salinas v. Texas (2013), 394
Samet, Mordechai, 178
San Antonio Four, 112–113
Sanchez, Rudy, 294
Sanders, Carlos, 121
Sanders v. United States (1963), 51
Sandstrom, David, 76
Sandstrom v. Montana (1979), 76
Sanity, presumption of, 77
Santana, "Mom," 327–328
Santobello v. New York (1971), 35
Sargent, Bryan, 258
Sarivola, Anthony, 380
Savage, Donald Davis, 304
Savio, Kathleen, 215–216
Scalia, Antonin:
  confessions, 376
  death penalty, 198
  independent source doctrine, 260
  searches and seizures, 278, 352
  stop and frisk, 297
Scheindlin, Shira, 301–302
Schlup v. Delo (1995), 52
Schmerber, Armando, 382
Schmerber v. California (1966), 382
Schneckloth v. Bustamonte (1973), 356–357, 361
School desegregation, 7
School drug testing and searches, 370
Scientific evidence, 157–158
  See also specific types
Scientific tests, 159–165, 162 (photo)
Scott, Alan, 281
Scott, Cedric, 120

Scott, Timothy, 332–333
Scott v. Harris (2007), 332–333
Scott v. Sandford (1857), 16
Scottsboro Boys, 18–19
Scrivener, Louise, 229
Scruggs, James Wilbur, 199
Scrupulously honored test, 399–400, 401, 402, 403
Search warrants:
  about, 343, 343 (photo), 344–345 (table)
  electronic surveillance, 346–347 (table)
  good faith exception and, 257–258
  knock and announce, 341, 343, 345, 347–349
Searches and seizures:
  abandoned property, 268, 275, 280–281, 280 (photo)
  about, 269–270, 342
  administrative inspections, 368–369
  aerial surveillance, 276–277, 285–286
  case analysis, 285–286, 370–373
  consent searches, 356–364, 362 (table)
  curtilage, 275–277, 285–286
  dog sniffs, 278–279
  electronic surveillance, 346–347 (table)
  expectation of privacy, 271–273, 274–275, 281 (table)
  informants and electronic eavesdropping, 273–274
  inventories, 367–368
  knock and announce, 341, 343, 345, 347–349
  open fields, 275–276
  plain view, 274, 277
  probable cause searches of motor vehicles, 364–366
  public places and private businesses, 279
  racial profiling, 355–356
  search warrants, 341, 343, 344–345 (table), 345, 346–347 (table), 347–349
  searches of persons, 269, 282–285, 282 (table)
  searches of the area of immediate control and automobiles, 352–353
  special-needs searches, 369–370
  technology and, 277–278
  See also Searches incident to an arrest; Warrantless searches
Searches incident to an arrest:
  about, 349–351
  automobiles and, 352–353
  case analysis, 370–373
  contemporaneous requirement for, 351–352
  misdemeanors and, 353–354
  pretext arrests and, 354–355
Searcy, Kane, 358
Second Amendment, 22 (table)
  See also Bill of Rights (U.S.)
Secondary evidence, 182
See v. City of Seattle (1967), 369
Seibert, Jonathan, 397–398
Seibert, Patrice, 397–398
Seizures. *See* Searches and seizures
Selective incorporation, 16, 17, 20–21

Selective incorporation plus, 16, 17
Self-authenticating documents, 177–178
Self-defense, 59–60
Self-incrimination, right against:
    about, 380–381
    attenuation and, 256
    blood alcohol testing and, 160–161
    criminal appeals and, 48
    fingerprints and, 160
    fundamental fairness and, 17–18
    interrogations and confessions, 377–378, 380–382, 384
    selective incorporation and, 20–21
    tattoos and, 184
Sell v. United States (2003), 49
Semayne's Case (1603), 343
Semeina, Wendell, 77–78
Sentence recommendation, 34
Sentencing guidelines, 47–48
Sentencing hearing, 46
Sentencing process, 45–46
Sentencing Reform Act (1984), 47
Sepulveda, Alberto, 349
Sequential presentation, 428–429
Setliff, Jackie, 359
Seventh Amendment, 21
    See also Bill of Rights (U.S.)
Severance, motion for, 33
Sexual offenses, 97–101
Shadur, Milton, 403
Shard, Willie, 419
Sharpe, Norma, 200
Sharpe, William Harris, 304
Shatzer, Michael Blaine, 400–401
Shaw, Lemuel, 82
Sheehan, Barbara, 149–150
Shember v. California (1966), 184
Shepard, Charles A., 214
Shepard, Zenana, 214–215
Shepard v. United States (1933), 214–215
Sheppard, Osborne, 258
Sheppard, Sam, 69–70
Sheridan, Luke, 134
Shoe prints, 147 (photo), 153
Shoulder bags, inventory of, 367
Show of authority seizures, 283, 284
Showup, 419, 424–425
Sibron v. New York (1968), 310
Signature *modus operandi* rule, 93–94
Silver platter doctrine, 247
Silverthorne Lumber Company v. United States (1920), 260
Simmons, Frank, 213
Simmons, Ric, 68
Simmons v. State (1987), 87
Simmons v. United States (1968), 425–426
Simpson, Nicole Brown, 155 (photo)
Simpson, O. J., 155 (photo)

Simultaneous lineup, 428–429
Sixth Amendment:
    Confrontation Clause, 41, 192, 193–194, 220–221
    criminal procedure provisions, 8 (table), 22 (table)
    exclusionary rule, 245
    jury selection, 37
    jury size, 44
    jury trial, right to, 21
    jury unanimity, 44, 45
    protection against deliberate eliciting of confession, 405
    sentencing, 47
    sentencing hearing, 46
    speedy trial, 33
    witnesses, 104
    See also Bill of Rights (U.S.); Counsel, right to
Skinner, Angela, 262
Slade, Roland, 185
Slater, Ellen, 391
Slaughter-House Cases (1873), 16
Slobodow, Arlen, 229
Slobodow, Herbie, 229
Slobodow, Lars, 229
Small, Dean D., 180
Smart phones, 350, 370–373
Smell, 319
Smith, Cora, 61
Smith, William Kennedy, 98–99, 166
Smith v. Cain (2012), 33
Snow, Sharon Ann, 204
Social media, 70, 172
Soto, Paul, 388
Sotomayor, Sonia, 194, 430
Souter, David, 256, 279, 334–335, 393
South Dakota v. Neville (1983), 161, 381
South Dakota v. Opperman (1976), 368
Spano v. New York (1959), 379
Special-needs searches, 369–370
Spectrographic voice identification, 165
Speech or Debate Clause, 49
Speedy trial, 33
Spinelli, William, 321–322
Spinelli v. United States (1969), 321
Spitchenko, Alexander, 125–126
Spousal competence, 116–117
Spring, John Leroy, 392
Springsteen, Bruce, 308–309
Stack v. Boyle (1951), 49
Staggs, Lonnie Paul, 88
Stamps, Eurie, 349
Standing, 251–252
Standing mute, 32
Stansbury v. California (1994), 387
Star Chamber, 377, 381
Stare decisis, 13
State and local governments, 15–17
State constitutions, 10, 12, 13, 420

State court judges, 13
State courts, 12–13, 14 (figure), 15, 246–248
State judicial systems, 12–13, 14 (figure)
State of Maine v. Brandon Thongsavanh (2004), 63
State rules of evidence, 23
State secrets privilege, 236–237
State supreme courts, 12, 13, 14 (figure), 15
State v. Ahmed (2010), 219
State v. Allen (1995), 91–92
State v. Armijo (1976), 431
State v. Armstrong (2011), 110–111
State v. Ayer (2004), 97
State v. Barber (1992), 300
State v. Bayard (2003), 335
State v. Brewster (2002), 94
State v. Brown (2003), 335
State v. Bryant (2008), 277
State v. Carter (2005), 281
State v. Clopten (2008), 430
State v. Commeau (1979), 426–427
State v. De Jesus (2004), 81
State v. DeValle (2006), 294
State v. Dominguez (2010), 228
State v. Dukette (2000), 95
State v. Edwards (2001), 87
State v. Everett (2006), 89
State v. Ferrier (1998), 359
State v. Ford (1997), 312
State v. Forrest (1987), 67
State v. Gardner (1997), 92
State v. Gilbert (2012), 167–170
State v. Henderson (2011), 430
State v. Holland (2008), 112
State v. Jackson (1984), 323
State v. Jackson (1989), 74
State v. Jakobetz (1992), 162
State v. Joe (2014), 128
State v. Johnson (1986), 111
State v. Jones (1987), 203
State v. Kelly (1984), 150
State v. Kim (2006), 95
State v. Kirsch (1995), 100–101
State v. Krueger (2003), 85
State v. Mayo (1981), 73
State v. McGuire (1978), 73
State v. Minkner (1994), 184
State v. Moen (1990), 206
State v. Munson (1999), 305
State v. Ranieri (1991), 106–107
State v. Robinson (2009), 330
State v. Sawtell (2005), 95
State v. Shamblin (1988), 367
State v. Sladek (1999), 93
State v. Small (2007), 180
State v. Stephenson (1996), 96
State v. Stritch (2005), 73

State v. Swan (1990), 111
State v. Thomas (1981), 150
State v. Thompson (1961), 84
State v. Tuttle (1989), 103
State v. Tye (2003), 358
State v. Vorhees (2008), 94
State v. Woodall (1989), 162
Statement of personal or family history, 217
Statement under belief of impending death, 214–215, 220–221
Statements:
    assertive, 191
    defined, 378
    as direct observation, 319
    false, 122–124
    in hearsay definition, 191
    inconsistent, 263
    incriminating, 269
    opening, 39–40
    prior consistent, 200, 201
    See also Prior inconsistent statements
Steagald v. United States (1981), 327
Stein v. Bowman (1839), 116
Steinberg Nelson, Debra, 66
Stevens, John Paul:
    attenuation, 256
    exigent circumstances, 333
    knock and announce, 347
    Miranda warnings/rights, 392, 400
    searches, 352–353
    stop and frisk, 296
Stevens, Richard, 97
Steward, Paula, 113–114
Stewart, George, 348
Stewart, Potter, 42, 334, 352, 405
Stipulations, 71, 77
Stone v. Powell (1976), 52, 256–257
Stop and frisk:
    about, 290–291
    case analysis, 312–313
    drug courier profiles, 289, 298–299
    frisks, 309–312
    informants and hearsay, 292, 295–298
    race and reasonable suspicion, 299–302
    reasonable suspicion, 290, 291–295
    stop-and-identify statutes, 306–308
    Terry stops, scope and duration of, 302–306, 307
Stop-and-identify statutes, 306–308, 381
Stovall, Theodore, 424–425
Stovall v. Denno (1967), 422, 424–425, 433
Stracner, Jenny, 268
Strauder v. West Virginia (1879), 37
Subpoena ad testificandum, 31
Subpoena duces tecum, 31
Substitutes for evidence, 71–78
Suggestive procedures, 417–418, 432–433
Suicide, presumption against, 77

Sulimov (dog breed), 279
Sumpter, Richard, 328
Supeh, John, 295
Supervisory authority, 9
Suppress, motion to, 32, 48
Suppression hearing, 32
Supremacy Clause, 7
Supreme courts, state, 12, 13, 14 (figure), 15
  See also U.S. Supreme Court
Surrebuttal, 42
Surveillance:
  aerial, 276–277, 285–286
  electronic, 273–274, 346–347 (table)
  vehicle, 284
Sutherland, Arthur, 19
Swain, Robert, 38
Swain v. Alabama (1965), 38
Swindle, Swazine, 284, 285
Swindler & Berlin v. United States (1998), 227
Syndromes, 147–150

Tague v. Louisiana (1980), 395
Tainted testimony, 111
Talladega County, Alabama, 38
Tanner v. United States (1987), 45, 115
Taping of interrogations/confessions, 386
Tattoos, 184
Taylor v. Illinois (1988), 62
Technology, 277–278
Teeth, 144 (photo)
Tennessee:
  deadly force, 337–338
  open fields, 276
Tennessee v. Garner (1985), 331, 333, 336–338
Terry, John W., 292
Terry frisks, 262, 309–310
Terry searches, 310–311
Terry stops:
  automobiles and, 307–308
  intrusiveness and, 303, 304–306, 307
  length of detention and, 303–304, 307
  movement and, 303, 307
  scope and duration of, 302–306, 307
  stop-and-identify statutes, 307–308
Terry v. Ohio (1968), 262, 290–291, 291–292,
  291 (photo), 313, 366
  See also Stop and frisk
Testimonial evidence, 68, 414
Testimonial privilege, 225
  See also specific privileges.
Testimony:
  child, 109–113
  expert, 142–144, 144 (photo), 146–148, 147 (photo)
  eyewitness, 167–170
  former, 212–213
  police, 110 (photo)

prior inconsistent statements and, 199
  tainted, 111
Texas:
  dog scent evidence, 432
  racial profiling, 356
Texas v. Brown (1983), 277, 365
Texas v. White (1975), 364
Texidor, Alexander, 398–399
Thames, Linord, 134–135
Thauthong, Yongyos, 186
Thayer, J., 101
Then-existing mental, emotional, or physical condition,
  204–205
Thermal imaging, 277, 278
Thies v. State (1922), 30
Third Amendment, 21
  See also Bill of Rights (U.S.)
Third-party consent, 361–363, 362 (table), 364
Thomas, Antonio, 134–135
Thomas, Clarence, 256, 343
Thomas, Duel, 134–136
Thompkins, Van Chester, 394, 396–397
Thompson, Jennifer, 427–428
Thompson, Kimberly, 252
Thongsavanh, Brandon, 63
Thornton, Marcus, 352
Thornton, Patricia, 178
Thornton, Richard, 275
Thornton v. United States (2004), 352
Thrasher, Kenneth, 304
Threats, 95, 358, 390
Throckmorton, Nicholas, 5
Tolbert, Terrance, 404
Tome, Matthew Wayne, 200
Tome v. United States (1995), 130, 200
Torture by police, 402–403
Total incorporation, 16–17, 20
Total incorporation plus, 16, 20
Totality-of-the-circumstances approach, 322–323, 387–389,
  394, 395, 423–424
Totten v. United States (1875), 237
Toxicology tests, 164
Toy, James, 255–256
Trammel, Elizabeth Ann, 240
Trammel, Otis, 240
Trammel v. United States (1980), 116, 231, 240–241
Transactional immunity, 31
Trash, 184–187, 268, 280–281
Treason, 131
Trespassory approach, 271
Trevizo, Maria, 307, 310
Trial courts, California, 14 (figure)
Trial de novo, 13, 48
Trials:
  closing arguments, 42–43
  defendant's surrebuttal, 42

defense's case-in-chief, 41–42
    jury deliberations, 44
    jury instructions, 43–44
    jury unanimity, 44–45
    opening statements, 39–40
    prosecution's case-in-chief, 40–41
    prosecution's rebuttal, 42
    verdict, 45
Triggs, Leroy, 272
True bill, 31
Trujillo, Frank, 359–360
Trustworthiness, 208, 219
Truthfulness, character for, 41, 119, 124–127, 130, 130 (table)
Turek, Barton, 334–335
Tuttle, Wesley Allen, 103
Twining, Albert, 17–18
Twining v. New Jersey (1908), 17–18, 19
Tyco International, 65
Tye, Clarence, 358
Tyler, Willie, 400

Uber, Stephen D., 301
Ultimate issues, opinion on, 145–146
Ultraviolet spectrophotometry, 163
Unavailable witnesses, 139
Uncharged crimes, 125–126
Uniform Rules of Evidence, 23
United Nations Committee against Torture, 402
United States Army Criminal Investigation Division, 97
United States ex rel. Maxwell v. Gilmore (1999), 403
United States v. Able (1984), 120
United States v. Alaniz (2013), 86
United States v. Al-Azzawy (1985), 327
United States v. Alexander (1955), 124
United States v. Anglin (1999), 200
United States v. Angwin (2001), 91
United States v. Apodaca (1974), 235
United States v. Arvizu (2002), 293
United States v. Ash (1973), 421
United States v. Baker (1988), 187
United States v. Banks (2003), 347–348
United States v. Barrett (1976), 83
United States v. Bautista (1982), 300
United States v. Bay (1984), 184
United States v. Benally (2008), 115
United States v. Benedetto (1978), 126
United States v. Bennett (2004), 183
United States v. Berkowitz (1991), 327
United States v. Blake (1989), 360
United States v. Blake (2009), 404
United States v. Blakeney (1991), 345 (table)
United States v. Bloome (1991), 118
United States v. Booker (2005), 47–48
United States v. Boone (1995), 254, 255
United States v. Booty (1980), 120
United States v. Bourque (1976), 72

United States v. Brownlee (2006), 429
United States v. Calandra (1974), 248, 253
United States v. Call (1997), 65
United States v. Carrillo (1994), 390
United States v. Carter (1992), 120
United States v. Ceballos (2004), 274
United States v. Ceccolini (1978), 255
United States v. Cedeno (2007), 228–229
United States v. Chadwick (1977), 365
United States v. Chavez (2009), 353
United States v. Copeland (2003), 95
United States v. Cortez (1981), 293
United States v. Crowley (2003), 126–127
United States v. Dahlin (1984), 89
United States v. De Georgia (1969), 209
United States v. DeCicco (2004), 96–97
United States v. Delvi (2003), 204
United States v. Dichiarinte (1971), 360
United States v. Dioguardi (1974), 116
United States v. Dior (1982), 73
United States v. Drayton (2002), 284
United States v. Dunn (1987), 275–276
United States v. Edwards (1974), 352
United States v. Elmore (1979), 298
United States v. Emanuele (1993), 431
United States v. Felton (2005), 64
United States v. Foster (2004), 293
United States v. Fowler (1979), 105
United States v. Frady (1982), 52
United States v. Fuccillo (1987), 345 (table)
United States v. Fuentes (1997), 360–361
United States v. Gaddy (1990), 395–396
United States v. Gaitan-Acevedo (1998), 328
United States v. Garcia (2006), 310
United States v. Gonzalez-Basulto (1990), 357, 358
United States v. Gonzalez-Lauzan Jr. (2006), 398–399
United States v. Grassi (1979), 71
United States v. Gravely (1988), 127
United States v. Gray (2005), 218
United States v. Grayson (1978), 46
United States v. Green (1991), 400
United States v. Greer (2011), 184
United States v. Grubbs (2006), 344 (table)
United States v. Guzman (2010), 198
United States v. Hall (1978), 121
United States v. Hanson (2000), 86
United States v. Harris (1971), 321
United States v. Harris (1976), 109
United States v. Hatley (1993), 358–359
United States v. Havens (1980), 263
United States v. Hawkins (1995), 202
United States v. Hayes (2000), 233–234
United States v. Henderson (2008), 363
United States v. Henry (1980), 405–406
United States v. Hensley (1985), 297
United States v. Hines (1999), 146

United States v. Holland (1985), 327
United States v. Houlihan (1994), 205
United States v. Huddleston (1987), 141
United States v. Humphries (2004), 319
United States v. Irvin (1996), 184
United States v. Ivy (1998), 359
United States v. Jackson (1988), 96
United States v. James (1999), 61
United States v. Janis (1976), 252
United States v. Jaquez (2005), 295
United States v. Johnson (1994), 262
United States v. Jones (2001), 300, 355
United States v. Jones (2010), 295
United States v. Jones (2012), 278
United States v. Kalaydjian (1986), 117
United States v. Karo (1984), 277
United States v. Keiser (1995), 90
United States v. Kincade (2004), 163
United States v. Knotts (1983), 277
United States v. Koon (1994), 212
United States v. Ladd (1989), 157
United States v. Lattimore (1996), 360
United States v. Lawson (1981), 141
United States v. Lentz (2008), 228
United States v. Leon (1984), 257, 259, 265, 266
United States v. Lewis (1977), 200
United States v. Libby (2006), 146
United States v. Lightly (1982), 107
United States v. Littledale (2011), 389
United States v. Lizardo (2006), 141
United States v. Lofton (1992), 224
United States v. Looper (1969), 106
United States v. Lopez-Arias (2003), 305
United States v. Luciano (2005), 203
United States v. Luschen (1980), 187
United States v. Lyons (1983), 350–351
United States v. Mahecha-Onofree (1991), 156
United States v. Matlock (1974), 362
United States v. McGauley (1955), 125
United States v. McGlory (1992), 184–187
United States v. McRae (1979), 64
United States v. Mendenhall (1980), 283, 298
United States v. Modica (1981), 43
United States v. Monclavo-Cruze (1980), 368
United States v. Montgomery (1983), 402
United States v. Montoya de Hernandez (1985), 304
United States v. Morales (1984), 327
United States v. Napier (1975), 189
United States v. Nazzaro (1989), 89
United States v. New (2007), 94
United States v. Nickl (2005), 113–114
United States v. Nixon (1974), 236
United States v. Nosov (2002), 125–126
United States v. Oguns (1990), 193
United States v. Olano (1993), 50
United States v. Ortiz (1975), 318

United States v. Owen (1988), 201
United States v. Paiva (1989), 141
United States v. Pardue (2004), 262
United States v. Patane (2004), 256
United States v. Payner (1980), 252
United States v. Peyro (1986), 107
United States v. Phibbs (1993), 107–108
United States v. Place (1983), 278, 303, 304
United States v. Poland (1981), 213
United States v. Powers (1995), 145
United States v. Prout (1978), 344 (table)
United States v. Quintana-Garcia (2003), 294
United States v. Quinteros (1991), 184
United States v. Ramirez (1998), 347
United States v. Redmon (1998), 276
United States v. Reed (2000), 213
United States v. Reyes (1986), 186
United States v. Reyes (2003), 390
United States v. Reynolds (1953), 237
United States v. Riccardi (1949), 133
United States v. Richardson (1985), 118
United States v. Robinson (1973), 334, 353–354
United States v. Rodney (1992), 360
United States v. Rogers (2004), 427
United States v. Ross (1982), 345 (table)
United States v. Rubin (1973), 328
United States v. Salameh (1988), 200
United States v. Samet (2006), 178
United States v. Sanders (1992), 121
United States v. Sanges (1892), 50
United States v. Santana (1976), 327–328
United States v. Saunders (1991), 98
United States v. Scheffer (1998), 143, 165
United States v. Scott (1992), 281
United States v. Scruggs (2004), 199
United States v. Seeley (1987), 305
United States v. Sharpe (1984), 304
United States v. Snyder (1999), 111
United States v. Staggs (1977), 88
United States v. Stelmokas (1996), 176
United States v. Stevens (1991), 97
United States v. Stewart (1989), 348
United States v. Stewart (2005), 156
United States v. Swindle (2005), 284–285
United States v. Taylor (2009), 164
United States v. Telfaire (1972), 429
United States v. Thomas (2003), 184
United States v. Thomas (2005), 359
United States v. Thompson (1989), 360
United States v. Tolliver (2006), 195
United States v. Towns (1990), 183
United States v. Tyler (1998), 400
United States v. Ventresca (1965), 320
United States v. Verrusio (1985), 86
United States v. Wade (1967), 416–417, 418, 420, 421, 433
United States v. Ward (1993), 106

United States v. Waterman (2009), 285
United States v. Watson (1976), 325–326
United States v. Weaver (1992), 289, 300
United States v. White (1971), 273–274
United States v. Whitmore (2004), 126
United States v. Williams (2006), 118
United States v. Wilson (1976), 187
United States v. Wurie (2014), 350
United States v. Yahweh Ben Yahweh (1992), 78–79
United States v. Yazzie (2001), 140
United States v. Young (1985), 43, 50
United States v. Zinc (1980), 157
United States v. Zolin (1989), 236
Uniting and Strengthening America by Providing Appropriate
    Tools Required to Intercept and Obstruct Terrorism
    Act (2001), 346 (table)
University of Michigan Law School, 113
Upjohn Co. v. United States (1981), 226
"Upskirt" photos, 281–282
Urbano, Raymond Guadalupe, 228
Urine tests, 165
U.S. Constitution:
    competent evidence, 62
    corroboration, 131
    exclusionary rule and, 248, 249
    federal judicial system, 10
    habeas corpus, 51
    hearsay, 192
    history of, 6–7
    jury unanimity, 44
    Miranda v. Arizona (1966) and, 385
    pardons, 46
    plea bargaining, 35
    Speech or Debate Clause, 49
    Supremacy Clause, 7
    See also specific amendments
U.S. Justice Department, 428
U.S. Sentencing Commission, 47
U.S. Supreme Court:
    certiorari, 9
    constitutionalization of the Bill of Rights, 15–16
    in federal judicial system, 11 (figure)
    Federal Rules of Evidence and, 22–23
    fundamental fairness, 16, 17–19
    judicial review, 7–9
    opinion types, 9
    original jurisdiction, 9
    precedent, 15
    selective incorporation and selective incorporation
        plus, 16, 17, 20–21
    supervisory authority, 9
    tenure of justices, 10
    total incorporation and total incorporation plus, 16–17, 20
    See also specific cases and topics
USA PATRIOT Act (2001), 346 (table)
Use immunity, 31

Utah:
    child testimony, 110
    stop and frisk, 306
Utter, Robert, 12

VA. *See* Veterans Administration
Values, 23
Van Mierlo, Steve, 57
Vasquez, Anna, 112–113
Vasquez, Larry, 157
Vasquez v. State (2006), 106
Vass, Arpad, 159
Vaughan, John, 5
Vehicles. *See* Automobiles
Venire, 36
Venue, change of, 33, 69, 70
Veracity prong, in *Aguilar-Spinelli* test, 321–322
Verdict, 45, 49
Vermont, open fields doctrine in, 276
Verplank, Gordon, 232
Veterans Administration (VA), 96
Victim's character:
    in a criminal case, 89
    in a homicide case, 90
Video Voyeurism Prevention Act (2004), 282
Videos, authentication of, 178–179
Villalba, Timothy, 129
Virgin Islands v. Parrilla (1993), 77–78
Virginia v. Harris (2009), 297
Visual images, 69, 178–179
Vital statistics, 211
Voice communication, authentication of, 179–180
Voir dire:
    juries, 36, 37, 38, 115
    scientific evidence, laying foundation for, 158
    witnesses, 108, 110
Voluntariness in consent searches, 356–359
Voluntariness test, due process, 378–380
Voluntary, knowing, and intelligent waiver, 394–396
Voluntary false confessors, 386
Vorhees, Shane A., 94

Wade, Billy Joe, 417
Wade-Gilbert rule, 417, 433
Wagner v. State (1998), 179
Wainwright v. Torna (1982), 49
Wainwright v. Witt (1985), 37
Waiver:
    of clergy-penitent privilege, 232
    express, 396
    of husband-wife privilege, 234
    implied, 396–397
    of *Miranda* rights, 394–402
    of privileges, 225, 232, 234
    of right to counsel, 406
    voluntary, knowing, and intelligent, 394–396

Walder, Sam, 263
Walder v. United States (1954), 263
Ward, Wallace, 106
Warden v. Hayden (1967), 269, 327
Wardlow, William "Sam," 294, 312–313
Warn, duty to, 233–234
Warrantless searches:
    administrative inspections, 368–369
    automobiles, 352–353
    case analysis, 370–373
    consent searches, 356–364, 362 (table)
    contemporaneous requirement for, 351–352
    inventories, 367–368
    misdemeanors and, 353–354
    other, 366–367
    pretext arrests and, 354–355
    probable cause searches of motor vehicles, 364–366
    searches incident to an arrest, 349–355, 370–373
    special-needs searches, 369–370
Warrants:
    anticipatory, 344 (table)
    arrest, 28, 264–266, 324–330
    general, 270
    See also Search warrants
Warren, Earl, 51, 291, 292
Warshak, Steven, 272
Warshak v. United States (2007), 272
Washington State:
    child testimony, 111
    knock and talk searches, 359
    open fields, 276
Washington v. Lambert (1996), 355
Washington v. Texas (1967), 22 (table), 104
Waterman, Christopher, 285
Waters v. O'Connor (2004), 231
Watson, Henry Ogle, 325–326
Wealth, sudden, 86
Weaver, Arthur T., 289, 300
Webb, Johnny E., 198
Webb v. Paiva (1997), 142
Weeks, Fremont, 246
Weeks v. United States (1914), 245, 246, 247
Weight, 83
Wells, Susan, 298
Welsh, Edward G., 328–329
Welsh v. Wisconsin (1984), 328–329
Wetli, Charles, 78, 79
White, Anita, 108
White, Byron, 21, 44, 256, 257
White, Leslie, 129
White, Vanessa, 296
Whitty v. State (1967), 87
Whren, Michael, 354–355
Whren v. United States (1996), 354–355
Wife-husband relationship, 362–363, 362 (table)
Wigmore, John Henry, 4, 191

William III (King of England), 6
William the Conqueror, 4
Williams, Cedric, 167, 168
Williams, Robert, 261, 295–296, 405
Williams, Vernon, 185
Williams v. Florida (1970), 44
Williams v. New York (1949), 46
Williamson v. United States (1994), 192
Willingham, Amber, 198
Willingham, Cameron Todd, 148, 198
Willingham, Kameron, 198
Willingham, Karmon, 198
Wilson, Andrew, 230, 403
Wilson, Stan, 215
Wilson, Woodrow, 18
Wilson v. Arkansas (1995), 343, 345
Wilson v. City of Chicago (1993), 125
Wilson v. State (1970), 215
Wilson v. State (2005), 157
Winfrey, Megan, 432
Winfrey, Richard Lynn, 167
Winfrey v. State (2010), 150–151, 167
Winter, Jana, 239
Witherspoon v. Illinois (1968), 37
Withrow v. Williams (1993), 52
Witnesses:
    business records and, 207–208
    categories of, 68
    character, 68, 88
    child, 109–113
    competency to testify, 104–108, 109, 110–111
    content, 124
    fact, 68, 124
    felony convictions to impeach, 121, 122 (table)
    grand jury confidentiality and, 238
    hostile, 40
    hypnosis and, 103, 109
    impeaching, 124
    judges as, 113–114
    jurors as, 114–116
    lay, 139, 140–142
    mental capacity/incapacity of, 107–108, 118
    names and addresses of, 33
    nonparty, 121
    oath or affirmation, 105–106
    recorded recollection, 131–134, 134 (table)
    rehabilitation of, 129–130, 130 (table)
    religion and, 117
    spousal competence, 116–117
    unavailable, 139
    writing used to refresh, 132
    See also Expert witnesses; Impeachment
Woessner, Lorraine, 431
Wolf, Josh, 239
Wolf v. Colorado (1949), 22 (table), 246–247
Wong Sun, "Sea Dog," 255–256

Wong Sun v. United States (1963), 255–256
Woodside, Ricardo, 78
Work product, 229
Workplace drug testing, 370
Would, Diane, 403
Wright, Leslie, 336–338
Wright, Roy, 18–19
Writing used to refresh witnesses, 132
Writs of assistance, 270
Writs of Assistance case (1761), 270
Wurie, Brima, 350
Wyoming v. Houghton (1999), 366

Yarborough, Ralph, 431
Yarborough v. Alvarado (2004),
    388–389
Yazzie, Johnny, Jr., 140
Yee, Johnny, 255, 256
Young, Cathern, 64
Young, David, 366

Zepeda, Edmundo, 329
Zimmerman, George, 66, 179
Zink, Danny, 157
Zurcher v. Stanford Daily (1978), 238

■■ ABOUT THE AUTHOR

Matthew Lippman has taught criminal law and criminal procedure in the Department of Criminology, Law and Justice at the University of Illinois at Chicago (UIC) for more than twenty-five years. He has also taught courses on civil liberties, law and society, and terrorism and teaches international criminal law at John Marshall Law School in Chicago. He earned a doctorate in political science from Northwestern University, earned a master of laws from Harvard Law School, and is a member of the Pennsylvania Bar. He has been voted by the graduating seniors at UIC to receive the Silver Circle Award for outstanding teaching on six separate occasions and has also received the UIC Flame Award from the University of Illinois Alumni Association, as well as the Excellence in Teaching Award, Teaching Recognition (Portfolio) Award, and Honors College Fellow of the Year Award. The university chapter of Alpha Phi Sigma, the criminal justice honors society, named him "criminal justice professor of the year" on three occasions. In 2008, he was recognized as College of Liberal Arts and Sciences Master Teacher. He was honored by the College of Liberal Arts and Sciences, which named him Commencement Marshal at the May 2012 graduation. Professor Lippman is also recognized in Who's Who Among America's Teachers.

Professor Lippman is author of one hundred articles and author or co-author of six books. These publications focus on criminal law and criminal procedure, international human rights, and comparative law. He also is author of four other SAGE volumes: *Contemporary Criminal Law: Concepts, Cases, and Controversies,* 3rd ed., 2013); *Criminal Procedure* (2nd ed., 2014); *Essential Criminal Law* (2014); and *Law and Society* (2015). His work is cited in hundreds of academic publications and by domestic and international courts and organizations. He has also served on legal teams appearing before the International Court of Justice in The Hague, has testified as an expert witness on international law before numerous state and federal courts, and has consulted with both private organizations and branches of the U.S. government. Professor Lippman regularly appears as a radio and television commentator and is frequently quoted in leading newspapers. He has served in every major administrative position in the Department of Criminology, Law and Justice including Department Head and Director of Undergraduate Studies and Director of Graduate Studies.